DISCIPLINARY AND CONTENT LITERACY FOR TODAY'S ADOLESCENTS

D1568634

Disciplinary and Content Literacy for Today's Adolescents

SIXTH EDITION

Honoring Diversity and Building Competence

WILLIAM G. BROZO

THE GUILFORD PRESS
New York   London

Copyright © 2017 The Guilford Press
A Division of Guilford Publications, Inc.
370 Seventh Avenue, Suite 1200, New York, NY 10001
www.guilford.com

Printed in the United States of America

This book is printed on acid-free paper.

Last digit is print number: 9   8   7   6   5   4   3

Library of Congress Cataloging-in-Publication Data is available from the publisher.

ISBN 978-1-4625-3008-3 (paperback) — 978-1-4625-3009-0 (hardcover)

To Ursula,
whose unflagging support kept me inspired
throughout the many long months of writing and editing

And to Hannah,
in whom my pride is boundless

About the Author

William G. Brozo, PhD, is Professor of Literacy in the Graduate School of Education at George Mason University. A former secondary school teacher, he is the author of numerous articles and books on the literacy development of children and adolescents, and is a contributing author to *iLit*, a digital intervention program for struggling readers. Dr. Brozo has served on the editorial board of the *Journal of Adolescent and Adult Literacy* and authored the "Strategic Moves" column for the international journal *Thinking Classroom* and the "Content Literacy" column for *The Reading Teacher*. He is a past member of the Commission on Adolescent Literacy and the Adolescent Literacy Committee of the International Literacy Association (ILA), as well as past chair of the ILA's PISA/PIRLS Task Force.

Preface

In Alberto Manguel's now classic book *A History of Reading* (1996), he says in the introduction:

> In every case, it is the reader who reads the sense, it is the reader who grants or recognizes in an object, place, or event a certain possible readability; it is the reader who must attribute meaning to a system of signs, and then decipher it. We all read ourselves and the world around us in order to glimpse what and where we are. We read to understand, or to begin to understand. We cannot do but read. Reading, almost as much as breathing, is our essential function. (p. 7)

These words made me realize that I must be one of those who "cannot do but read" and that reading has been one of my most "essential functions." To be a reader, Manguel further enlightens us, is to be part of a culture of letters dating from the first Sumerian tablets of the fifth millennium B.C.E. to Greek scrolls, from the codices of St. Augustine to the quartos of Shakespeare, from graphic novels to e-readers and smartwatches. Every word, text, and image read is part of a history of language and sense filled with tales of anarchy, censorship, triumph, and passion. To read and write, then, is to become part of that history and, moreover, to learn from the voices of the past.

Just as the printing press and mass production of books, plays, and pamphlets revolutionized the concept of literacy in the Renaissance, today ever-evolving new digital technologies are changing the ways we think about what it means to be literate. At the same time, researchers are calling attention to social, cultural, and political dimensions of literacy, leading us to see that literacy should no longer be defined as mere reading and writing of print but something much more complex, fluid, and multifaceted.

As a compulsive reader and idea gatherer, when I got to the epilogue of Leonard Mlodinow's (2015) fascinating book *The Upright Thinkers*, I found this point to be especially worth remembering: "Powerful thinking," he says, "is a craft, and it is one worth doing well." Just consider this—powerful thinking is a "craft." In other words, it is not an ability conferred on us by virtue of our birth or a quality we might acquire through an injection. Instead, it is each of our responsibilities to develop and hone the craft of thinking and, as teachers, to support others in the development and refinement of theirs. And now consider that powerful thinking is made possible with language, and that reading and writing literacy are the conveyances of language.

Let's reflect on the contributions literacy makes to powerful thinking. Youth who develop this craft are able to engage with, integrate, and express complex ideas through reading, writing, speaking, and listening. In the service of this craft, they employ strategic processes to navigate difficult text. They call on this craft when they purposefully select appropriate media to communicate what they know and to share their unique conceptions about text and the world. And they use text and other related media to enlarge understandings of topics of interest. The more youth exercise literate processes, the more they take advantage of—while also increasing—their ability to think powerfully.

I invoke the ideas of Manguel from the book I read over 20 years ago, and Mlodinow from the book I just finished, to demonstrate how authors and experts from fields as diverse as journalism and physics can inspire those of us who are active readers. Drawing on inspiration from these authors and countless others I have encountered on my literate journey, I am pleased to introduce *Disciplinary and Content Literacy for Today's Adolescents: Honoring Diversity and Building Competence*. Those of you familiar with one of my previously coauthored books with a very similar title will find that this new edition reflects the most current thinking in the fields of adolescent, content-area, and disciplinary literacy. Though these changes are substantial, the core theme of the book has not changed. And like my other work, *Disciplinary and Content Literacy for Today's Adolescents* shows deference to the lifeworlds of middle and secondary school teachers while supporting their desire to make instruction more responsive to the literacy and academic needs of an increasingly diverse population.

THE GUIDING PHILOSOPHY

As the book's title suggests, I have chosen to foreground the seminal and most current research and practice that honor the academic and cultural diversity of today's youth. Numerous scenes of teaching and instructional approaches are described that demonstrate how youth can be taught to bridge their literate practices outside of school with the literacies required in academic settings. The evidence clearly shows that as youths' discourse flexibility and critical thinking skills expand, confidence in their ability to succeed in school, life, and the workplace expands as well.

Although many of today's adolescents continue to find entry points to literacy in traditional print texts and use them in school and at home, most now spend more time than ever reading, writing, and learning with digital media. This new reality has had and will continue to have profound implications for teaching and learning in middle and secondary schools. In order to take full advantage of the resources all youth bring to the classroom, teachers will need to employ innovative practices that value the literate activity today's youth engage in with these new media, while building their competence to perform academic literacy tasks. In this book, I take the position that guiding youth to be critical readers of new media and traditional print in addition to a range of alternative information sources can be complementary and mutually supportive.

Another vital message of this book is that teachers continue to inform me as much as I inform them, and their students are the ultimate curricular informants. The growth and improvement of adolescents' language processes and disciplinary knowledge will depend on the strength of the transactions between teachers in higher education and teachers in middle and secondary schools, as well as the strength of the relationships between students and their teachers.

Being an active reader can expand a young person's life and career options and enlarge his or her sense of self. This book is about widening life and career options for youth in the middle and upper grades through literacy. I am confident *Disciplinary and Content Literacy for Today's Adolescents* will be used as a resource by teachers in every discipline to create engaging and constructive learning environments where youth use literacy for personal pleasure, as a tool for academic achievement, to expand self-efficacy, and to envision new possible futures for themselves.

ORGANIZATION OF THE BOOK

This book is designed to help you teach secondary literacy disciplinary content more effectively and to develop independent learners who can think about information and ideas in competent and critical ways. This book is also designed to help you envision the possibilities for exciting teaching and learning in your classroom. To this end, I have filled *Disciplinary and Content Literacy for Today's Adolescents* with practical examples, teaching scenarios, and classroom dialogues. I want to stress that the strategies and practices in this book should always be regarded as suggestions rather than prescriptions, which in the hands of innovative and caring teachers can be adapted to meet the needs of every learner.

Chapters 1 and 2 provide important foundational and contextual information about adolescents, as well as content and disciplinary literacy. Chapter 1, "Adolescent Literacies and Identities Inside and Outside of School," paints in broad strokes the character and culture of today's adolescents. You will quickly come to learn that adolescence is multifaceted and that each individual youth brings to school a set of unique and valuable experiences. When viewed as a resource, adolescent experience with literacy and language provides a connection to academic literacy and disciplinary knowledge. Additionally, Chapter 1 explicates the relationship between approaches to content-area literacy and newer conceptions and practices related to disciplinary literacy. You will learn how content literacy offers secondary teachers a wide variety of instructional routines that, with adaptations, can be applied in virtually any classroom and with nearly any content. You will also learn that disciplinary literacy is concerned with those unique reading and writing processes emerging from the specific texts and tasks of history, science, math, English language arts, and all the other subject areas. Although I delineate important distinctions between content-area and disciplinary literacy, I also emphasize and demonstrate how secondary teachers can take advantage of practices derived from both traditions.

In Chapter 2, "Building Literacy Competence across the Disciplines for Diverse Learners," I present new and relevant theory, research, and practice related to youth who enrich our middle and high school classrooms with their varied cultural and linguistic backgrounds and experiences. In many settings, particularly in and near large urban school districts, students once labeled "minorities" are now the new majorities. You are reminded in this chapter to continue to expand culturally and linguistically relevant practices in order to engage diverse youth and increase their literacy competencies.

I strongly recommend you read these first two chapters before reading the others, because the chapters that follow build on the foundations established in Chapters 1 and 2.

Sequencing chapters for a book on content literacy is never easy. Regardless of the content you teach or plan to teach, each chapter can provide you with insights into effective classroom interactions and practical examples of teaching strategies. Chapters 3 through 7 are filled with strategies and ideas for classroom implementation. Chapter 3, "Practices for Expanding Text Comprehension," reflects the most current ideas about how to foster meaningful reading and critical thinking. Chapter 4, "Assessment for Literacy Growth and Disciplinary Learning," presents a range of useful assessment practices and strategies to inform teachers' instructional decisions and students' self-awareness as learners. Chapter 5, "Creating Motivating Contexts for Literacy and Learning," includes content-area and disciplinary-based strategies and practices for motivating youth to read and learn at any phase of instruction. Chapters 6, "Developing Academic Vocabulary Knowledge," and 7, "Writing to Learn in the Disciplines," discuss new and exciting practices for expanding youths' word knowledge as well as engaging adolescents in the use of writing as a tool for learning disciplinary content.

Chapter 8, "Reading and Learning from Multiple Sources," provides principles and practices related to an increasingly commonplace expectation in disciplinary classrooms—that students read and learn from a variety of sources in addition to or other than a core text. To maximize the benefits of using multiple sources, I describe numerous strategies and approaches using traditional print and a variety of popular and new media that have been found to be effective for increasing literacy abilities and content knowledge in disciplinary classrooms. Finally, Chapter 9, "Strategic Literacy and Learning Processes," focuses on ways of developing independent, strategic readers, writers, and thinkers. Throughout these nine chapters, I have infused new ways that content-area and disciplinary teachers are employing digital technology to increase student motivation, expand opportunities for language development, and make learning more accessible and memorable.

IMPORTANT FEATURES

Readers of this book will appreciate the following special features in both format and content that encourage interaction with information and ideas and increase the likelihood of application of the literacy strategies and practices.

- **Guiding questions.** Each chapter opens with a set of questions to guide readers to activate their prior knowledge and foreshadow the important concepts and information in each chapter. Readers are asked to reflect on these questions as they read and study each chapter. This approach can lead to helpful self-assessment of their learning. I strongly advocate the use of the questions to guide reading focus, and the prequestioning process represents an approach teachers can use with their own students.
- **Case studies**. All nine chapters include case studies. After each chapter's guiding questions and introduction, you will be asked to consider a particular problem or issue from an actual teaching scenario related to the content of the chapter. At the conclusion of the chapter, the case study is revisited, and you are invited to offer teaching or problem-solving suggestions. This process makes your reading and studying more interactive, and it is hoped you will become better able to envision the potential applications of the strategies in genuine classroom environments. I urge you to take full advantage of the case studies as you read and reflect on chapter content.
- **Many actual teaching vignettes**. I weave numerous scenes of teaching into the description of content and disciplinary literacy strategies and practices. With actual teaching situations and scenarios in the form of vignettes, readers find it easier to envision application of the strategies I present. The scenarios demonstrate the valuable lessons to be learned from content-area teachers struggling and succeeding as they implement stimulating reading, writing, and learning strategies. These vignettes and examples offer glimpses of teachers making content and disciplinary literacy work.
- **Common Core State Standards in perspective.** Much has been made of the Common Core State Standards, which, in spite of waning enthusiasm for them, have had considerable influence on the content and nature of teaching and learning across the United States. The Standards have helped us refocus

on the central role reading and writing play in learning in the content areas and disciplines. I believe this has been the most important contribution of the Standards, and throughout the book I link practices and strategies to those positive influences of the Common Core.

ASSUMPTIONS UNDERLYING THE LITERACY STRATEGIES AND PRACTICES IN THE BOOK

A major theme of this book is that teachers who employ practices based on sound and supportable theory and research are more likely to engender active learning and expand literacy for youth in the middle and upper grades. Throughout *Disciplinary and Content Literacy for Today's Adolescents,* I describe instructional approaches and scenes of teaching in which adolescents' beliefs, abilities, and backgrounds are exploited, leading to new, imaginative experiences for helping them to find reasons to learn. The strategies and practices explained and demonstrated provide literacy and disciplinary teachers the information and examples needed to support youths' efforts to become independent, active learners. Above all, the strategies and practices in this book are intended to make learning engaging and accessible for all.

My selection of strategies and practices for this book was guided by my belief that students can become engaged and purposeful learners when provided opportunities for sustained experiences in constructing meaning from and with text and when they are made to feel welcome as active participants in content and disciplinary classrooms. Youth are likely to become active members of a classroom community when teachers create learning experiences that are positive and authentic, when they make learning meaning centered, when they work with youth to shape the nature of learning, and when they give youth personally relevant reasons to learn.

The following assumptions form the foundation on which my ideas for teaching and learning rest.

1. **Teaching is more than dispensing information, because learning is more than receiving and remembering information.** Learning is the construction of meaning, an active process on the part of the individual learner through interaction in a community of learners. Teaching, therefore, is creating classroom contexts that support the knowledge construction process.
2. **A major goal of education should be the development of critical thinkers and active, independent learners.** Youth should be provided opportunities to play active roles in the meaning-making process. Students should be engaged in learning experiences that help them critically evaluate their worlds and participate in active problem solving of real-world concerns.
3. **To be literate is to use literacy as a tool for learning.** In supportive

learning environments, adolescents can learn to use literacy as a tool for meaningful and functional learning.

4. **Content and process should be taught simultaneously.** Youth should be led to see that *what* is learned is inextricably tied to *how* one learns. Furthermore, youth should come to see that learning content and learning the literacies of the disciplines are essentially one and the same.

5. **Content-area and disciplinary teachers need to develop students' will to learn.** Literacy and learning skills are of little help if youth are unmotivated to learn. Motivation results when teachers create interesting learning environments and help students develop their own personally relevant reasons for learning.

ACKNOWLEDGMENTS

This book would be incomplete without recognizing the supporting role of The Guilford Press's editorial and production staff. A very special thanks to Craig Thomas, my editor. Without his generosity of time and advice, as well as his faith in the power of my message about content-area and disciplinary literacy, this book would never have been transformed into a new and better resource for teachers. Thanks as well go out to Anna Brackett and Elaine Kehoe for their specific assistance in ensuring each word in this book was accessible to readers. And I would like to add a special word of gratitude to Jennifer Lindenauer for the many ways she supported the completion of this project.

I am, of course, extremely indebted to all the students, teachers, and colleagues whose experiences inspired me and continue to influence my work.

In physics they call it the "butterfly effect"—small influences that create dramatic effects—derived from the idea that the mere flap of an insect's wing in your backyard might ignite a chain of meteorological events leading to a hurricane on the other side of the globe. This book is dedicated to small influences that bring about big changes in the way adolescents and teachers in middle and secondary schools interact around literacy to enhance the quality of and ensure equity in youth learning.

Contents

Adolescent Literacies and Identities Inside and Outside of School

To understand just one life you have to swallow the world.
—SALMAN RUSHDIE

As you read Chapter 1, reflect on the following questions:

- How do popular stereotypes about today's adolescents influence your thinking about and instructional approaches with youth?

- In what ways does the "mediasphere" affect you and your students' attitudes toward and perceptions of literacy?

- What literacy challenges do youth from diverse backgrounds and their teachers face today?

- How have the Common Core State Standards changed the way literacy activities and assignments are structured for adolescent students?

- How can teachers of youth balance content and disciplinary literacy practices?

- What can be learned from international reading literacy assessments for making instructional literacy practices more responsive to the needs of youth?

- Which approaches to literacy instruction help foster healthy literate identities for adolescents?

Understanding today's youth requires an attitude of openness to their unique and diverse nature. As the opening quote to this chapter implies, it is perhaps only through an appreciation of the lifeworlds of adolescents, and how they shape and are shaped by their worlds, that we can ever really come to know them. Popular stereotypes about adolescents are conveniences that belie the multidimensionality and complexity of this stage in human development (Lewis, Enciso, & Moje, 2007; Moje & Luke, 2009; Vadeboncoeur & Stevens, 2005). As some would have it, adolescents, at best, are merely imperfect adults in transition (Serafini, Bean, & Readence, 2004); at worst, they are a bundle of raging hormones, callow and self-centered, and even menacing (Lesko, 2012).

Case Study

Bridging her students' culture and personal interests with the content of her high school business classes is the only way Marta knows how to teach. Some topics, however, have been more difficult to link to students' lifeworlds than others. One such topic, writing business contracts, created unique challenges for Marta because most of her students were from financially strapped homes and had parents who were employed part time. Few, if any, had ever seen an actual business contract before or had any experience at all with the work world.

To the reader: In this chapter we raise several important issues about adolescent literacies and identities. One overarching theme is that adolescents are more likely to remain engaged readers and learners if their everyday experiences and discourses are honored and made to enrich the classroom culture. As you read, consider how a teacher like Marta might capitalize on what her students bring to the business class as a link to understanding the topic of business contracts.

Stoking these stereotypes are media that sensationalize teen violence and sexual promiscuity (Rivers & Barnett, 2011), as well as myths about young adults' poor reading habits (Rideout, Foehr, & Roberts, 2010) and academic shortcomings. Males (2002) responds to these characterizations of teenagers by insisting that adults raise a mirror to themselves when passing harsh judgment on youth behavior:

> Adolescents behave like the adult society that raises them. They did not land on a meteorite. We raised them. They share our values. They act like us. . . . If teenagers behave like the adult society that raises them, their evil is the same as ours, and it is not curable by aiming increasingly absurd, cosmetic panaceas at the young. (p. 40)

A growing body of research into youth culture has expanded our understanding of what it means to be an adolescent while challenging our traditional constructions of adolescence (Alvermann, 2009; Gee, 2012; Moje, Overby, Tysvaer, & Morris, 2008). It is fruitful, then, for all of us to evaluate our own opinions about adolescents. Using the *Opinionnaire about American Teens* in Figure 1.1, decide where you stand relative to each statement about America's teens. Afterward, read the statements in the box "Facts about Adolescents" and compare them with your own opinions.

Directions: Consider carefully each of the following 10 statements and then write a sentence stating your own opinion about each statement. Afterward, look at the *Facts about Adolescents* in the box that follows and compare your opinions with the facts.

1. **Teenagers are uniquely violent and crime-prone.**

   Your opinion: _____

   _____

2. **The worst danger to youth is children killing children.**

   Your opinion: _____

   _____

3. **Youth violent crime is skyrocketing while adult violence is declining.**

   Your opinion: _____

   _____

4. **Teenagers are innately prone to reckless behavior and are stimulated to violence primarily by media images, impulsiveness, and gun availability.**

   Your opinion: _____

   _____

5. **Today's schools are cauldrons of violence.**

   Your opinion: _____

   _____

6. **Teenage birth rates are out of control.**

   Your opinion: _____

   _____

7. **Teenagers are the most at risk for AIDS.**

   Your opinion: _____

   _____

8. **Teenagers are at high risk for suicide.**

   Your opinion: _____

   _____

9. **Teenagers are the group most at risk of drug abuse.**

   Your opinion: _____

   _____

10. **Teenagers smoke because of immaturity, peer pressure, and tobacco ads.**

    Your opinion: _____

    _____

FIGURE 1.1. An opinionnaire about American teens.

FACTS ABOUT ADOLESCENTS

1. Youth and adults commit crimes at roughly equal rates.

2. The great majority of homicide victims 17 years and younger are killed by adults.

3. Violent crimes committed by youth and adults have increased at similar rates.

4. U.S. society as a whole has a violence problem. Senior citizens in the United States are more likely to kill someone than is a European teenager.

5. Risks of murder or being victim to other crimes of violence are extremely low in schools as compared with neighborhoods and homes.

6. Teenage birth rates are identical to those of the adults around them. Three-quarters of babies born to teenagers are fathered by adult men.

7. Teens rank third by age at which HIV infection was acquired. Nearly all HIV transmission is from adults.

8. Suicide rates for high-school-age youth are half those of adults.

9. Teens are the age group least likely to abuse drugs, whereas there have been record levels of drug abuse among middle-aged adults.

10. Youth from homes where parents smoke or who are from social groups with high proportions of adults who smoke are three times more likely to smoke than others.

I believe it is productive to deconstruct stereotypes about American teens by exposing the worst myths that have built up around them. The 10 statements in the opinionnaire come from prominent myths about adolescents identified by sociologist and youth advocate Mike Males (2002, 2010). This exercise highlights the need among those of us involved in the care and education of youth to reject the glib and largely groundless accusations about their behavior. Instead, we should recognize that teens are more likely than not to mimic the adults around them. Thus, as we come to appreciate how adult and teen behaviors are interconnected, the chances grow for improving dialogue, understanding, cooperation, and learning.

I suggest, therefore, that the search for tidy all-inclusive definitions of youth is doomed to failure, because of the complex nature of adolescent life. Due in large part to persistent stereotypes and rigid perceptions of adolescence, it is only relatively recently that youth culture has been the focus of scholarship. New perspectives on youth offer a more complete and nuanced view of the shared experiences and values of adolescents that can lead to insights for teaching and reaching adolescents (Tatum & Muhammad, 2012).

This chapter is devoted to discussing various facets of youth culture and the part literacy plays in adolescent identity formation. By opening the lens wide to view the ever-shifting and multifarious nature of adolescence, as well as current and enduring influences on this stage of development, I hope to make clear just how important it is to increase our understanding of the individuals for whom all the instructional attention contained in this book is intended. I believe that it is only with a disposition of openness toward newer conceptions of today's youth and the literacies they use and need can we become better teachers of subject matter, as well as more responsive teachers of students.

ADOLESCENT LITERACIES AND IDENTITIES

On a recent work trip to Germany, I found myself with an unexpected free day and decided to make an excursion to Mainz, which was only 30 minutes by train. There are certain highly revered places in the world that attract devotees for reasons of religious or historical significance, such as St. Peter's Basilica, Mecca, the pyramids of Giza, the Taj Mahal, and the Parthenon. For literacy scholars, however, none can be more important than the birthplace of Johannes Gutenberg. A short walk from the station, a monument to the vaunted inventor of movable type looms over the many beer- and coffee-drinking tourists in the large *platz* named in his honor. Further down through the old city is the remarkable Gutenberg museum, home of original and replica 15th-century presses that permitted the circulation of texts on a scale unimaginable previous to that time. And, of course, the numerous period books produced on these and future printing machines, including the Gutenberg Bible, are everywhere to peruse.

Later, sitting in a café next to the river, I ruminated, as only someone who has made reading and literacy his life's project could, on the significance of Gutenberg's invention for those of us living in the 21st century. The most salient impression I was left with was that printing made it possible for individual readers to have access to larger numbers of books, which changed the relationship they could have with text. When books were rare, expensive, and sacred in nature, the task of reading was principally one of preservation and memory. After mechanical printing, as books on an ever-expanding range of topics were made available, the reading process took on a greater degree of serious "intellectual labor" (Cavallo & Chartier, 1999, p. 24). This shift would seem to presage challenges in the field today, as teachers continue to seek ways of moving their students beyond the memorization phase of reading to thinking about text in more meaningful and critical ways.

Gutenberg's revolutionary invention evolved to become more technologically efficient over the intervening centuries, though the basic process of printing remained largely unchanged right up to just a few decades ago. Yet, within my lifetime, the printing industry experienced another revolution that has forever altered the way texts are produced and how we encounter and interact with text itself. We live in a digital age surrounded by electronic print and media. Books, newspapers, articles, and every imaginable text form are no longer "typeset" but are created and formatted digitally, including the paper version of *The Washington Post* that arrives at my door predawn and that I read every morning at breakfast. Virtually all print media are made available on the Internet and delivered directly to any variety of e-readers, smartphones, and even smartwatches.

Today's adolescents have only experienced life as so-called digital natives (Prensky, 2009). And a growing number of teachers, especially those new to the ranks, are steeped in digital and social media, as well (Boyd, 2014). Thus instructional methods are reflecting these new times. On a near daily basis, messages arrive in my email box touting the advantages of new technologies for teaching and learning. "Learn how to use video games as a tool for increasing reading skill and motivation," says one ad; "6 tactics for using e-mail to improve student writing," says another; and "Media literacy lesson plan guides for the Language Arts class," proclaims a third. Developing facility with these ever-evolving information and communication technology (ICT) tools and thinking about them in terms of curriculum, as well as understanding their value to today's adolescents, is becoming as important a part of the skill set of secondary teachers as possessing expert knowledge on the topic of instruction and interpersonal competencies (Burke & Hammett, 2009; Coiro, 2015).

YOUTH CULTURE: A MULTIPLE-LITERACIES PERSPECTIVE

Calls for secondary schools to honor the literacies and discourses of youth derive from the realization that we live in a "mediasphere" (O'Brien, 2001), "a world saturated by inescapable, ever-evolving, and competing media that both flow through us and are altered and created by us" (Brozo, 2005a, p. 534). O'Brien further describes this concept and what it means to youth in these terms:

> I use the adapted term mediasphere to refer to the mediacentric world of young people. Within youth culture, we have been concerned that this massive, continual media absorption would render our young people as passive consumers, manipulated by the bombardment. In fact, life in the mediasphere has turned our kids into keen interactors (rather than passive receptors) who understand media . . . [and have] become increasingly powerful and adept at using [media] to define themselves.

The ubiquitous nature of new media in the lives of today's youth was confirmed in a recent report suggesting that teens in America are spending nearly 9 hours a day using media such as online video and music (Common Sense Media, 2015). After undertaking multiyear case studies of adolescents and their digital media, Boyd (2014) discovered that to teens "these technologies—and the properties that go with them—are just an obvious part of life" (p. 42). She further maintains that adolescents "don't try to analyze how things are different because of technology; they simply try to relate to a public world in which technology is a given" (p. 41). Furthermore, Plester, Wood, and Bell's research (2008) suggests that concerns about whether texting and other abbreviated digital messaging adversely affect student writing may be unwarranted.

Fears that new media would bring with them moral and intellectual decline and would turn young people into passive consumers—an idea O'Brien rejected—echo similar cries of angst about the latest technologies and texts since at least the time of ancient Greece. Socrates, for example, warned that print would be the end of memory for his students. In *Phaedrus*, a Socratic dialogue by Plato (2007) from about 370 B.C.E., Socrates laments about print:

> For this invention will produce forgetfulness in the minds of those who learn to use it, because they will not practice their memory. Their trust in writing, produced by external characters which are no part of themselves, will discourage the use of their own memory within them . . . you offer your pupils the appearance of wisdom, not true wisdom, for they will read many things without instruction and will therefore seem to know many things, when they are for the most part ignorant and hard to get along with, since they are not wise, but only appear wise. (274c–275b)

In early colonial America, certain Puritanical rectors advocated the abolition of printing of all books other than the Bible, because secular texts were believed to contaminate the minds and souls of Christians, but especially of young Christians (Carden, 1983). More recently, dime novels and comic books were thought to surely turn youth into dull-witted wastrels (Springhall, 1999).

Regarding technology and memory, Sparrow and her colleagues (Sparrow, Liu, & Wegner, 2011) have learned through a series of experiments that transactive memory, or the process of social information sharing, is being rapidly replaced by computers and the Internet. The researchers assert that the:

> processes of human memory are adapting to the advent of new computing and communication technology. Just as we learn through transactive memory who knows what in our families and offices, we are learning what the computer "knows" and when we should attend to where we have stored information in our computer-based memories. We are becoming symbiotic with our computer tools, growing into interconnected systems that remember less by knowing information than by knowing where the information can be found. This gives us the advantage of access to a vast range of information. (p. 778)

From this perspective, instead of a hindrance to memory, ICT tools, such as Google and other search engines and electronic databases, are helping to transform memory processes by making them more efficient. A 21st-century cognitive skill, then, doesn't necessarily include the capacity to memorize a vast amount of information but the ability to remember where and how to access needed information stored in digital spaces. Nostalgia may impel some of us living in the mediasphere to wish we were less dependent on our computers, tablets, and smartphones, but we have come to rely on them in essentially the same way we have relied on any source of information and knowledge. Thus, we can argue whether it is good for youth to be constantly "plugged in," but they, like all of us, must stay connected to have efficient access to the vast memory banks available in cyberspace (Pew Internet & American Life Project, 2012).

An important caveat must be given here as regards computer use and online activity in school. At least for some reading tasks, such as those found on PISA (described below), for both traditionally and digitally formatted texts, an excessive amount of computer time in school may actually depress achievement (Organization for Economic Cooperation and Development [OECD], 2015a). Not too often and for deliberately chosen activities were found to be the conditions of optimal school use with computers. This does not imply that browsing the Internet for assignments is harmful, except that this kind of online activity, when performed daily without appropriate teacher guidance and not commensurate with challenging and higher-level reading and navigation tasks, may fail to benefit adolescent learners. At the same time, little or no school-based computer activity also appears to be related to lower reading performance.

It might be the case that 20th-century schools do not become 21st-century learning environments merely by retrofitting them with computers and Internet access. This hard lesson was learned in Los Angeles, where over 1 billion U.S. dollars were spent to put iPads in the hands of every student in the district. Instead of bringing about quick and significant achievement gains, the strategy has been deemed unworkable due to a general lack of digital infrastructure in the school district, the absence of an overall instructional technology strategic plan, and, perhaps more critically, an insurmountable shortage of teachers skilled in ICT pedagogy (*http://laschoolreport.com/wp-content/uploads/2015/01/Federal-Ipad-MiSiS-report.pdf*). This reminds us that availability of ICT tools and their indiscriminate use do not necessarily lead to improved student learning nor guarantee students will land decent-paying jobs after graduation (David & Cuban, 2010). Secondary school teachers must have support for and employ practices that use new ICTs responsively.

Despite potential overuse of computers in school settings, a notable consequence of the spread of ICTs in the general public, reading is massively shifting from print to digital texts. For example, computers have become the second source of news for American citizens, after TV and before radio and printed newspapers and magazines (American Press Institute, 2014). Similarly, British children and teenagers prefer to read digital texts over printed texts (Clark, 2014), and a recent UNESCO report showed that two-thirds of users of phone-based readers across five nations indicated that their interest in reading and time spent reading increased once it was possible to read on their phones (United Nations Educational, Scientific, and Cultural Organization [UNESCO], 2014). This shift has important consequences for the definition of reading as a skill.

Acquiring and expanding competence with the new literacies of the Internet and other ICTs will require youth to engage in practices that stretch beyond foundational literacies that may be sufficient for past forms of reading and writing (Hartman, Morsink, & Zheng, 2010; International Reading Association, 2009). Communicative competence in the 21st century involves negotiating and creating new forms of text found in evolving combinations of traditional offline environments with new online media within complex information networks (Dalton & Proctor, 2008; Wyatt-Smith & Elkins, 2008).

The realization that adolescents are the most active participants in the media-sphere means that these new forms of discourse they experience and create should be acknowledged and appreciated in school settings, as competency in these new forms of communication serve youth well in the ever-evolving global reach of the digital age (Alvermann, 2010; Squire, 2011). I believe the digital discourse worlds most teens inhabit, if validated in the public sphere of schools and classrooms, could narrow achievement gaps (Leu et al., 2015) and increase engagement in literacy and content learning (Walsh, 2010). Secondary school is the setting in which youths' multiple literacies—digital, graphic, aural—could find expression in the understanding, critical analysis, and reinterpretation of concepts and content (Leu, Kinzer, Coiro, Castek, & Henry, 2013; O'Brien & Scharber, 2008).

YOUTH CULTURE: A DEMOGRAPHIC PERSPECTIVE

So who are the individuals and groups that comprise youth culture in the United States? From the perspective of the most recent census data available (U.S. Census Bureau, n.d., 2013), the adolescent population today ages 10–19 totals nearly 42 million and is growing. This represents 14% of the total U.S. population and is more racially/ethnically diverse than the adult U.S. population. Recent data from the *Digest of Education Statistics* (*http://nces.ed.gov/programs/digest/d13/tables/dt13_203.50.asp*) show that the number of White students has been declining steadily over the past two decades, from 65% in 2001 to, at present and for the first time, just under 50% of the total share of public school enrollment. Meanwhile, Hispanic student enrollment has increased from 17 to 24% of the overall student population in pre-kindergarten through 12th grade. During this same period, Black students' share of public school enrollment has decreased from 17 to 16%, and the number of Asian/Pacific Islanders has increased by 1%, from 4 to 5%.

It is clear from demographic trends that this diversity among adolescents will only continue to increase over the coming years and decades (Colby & Ortman, 2015). In fact, before the end of this decade, children and adolescents of color, age 18 and under, will be the majority youth population and by 2060 are expected to comprise 64% of the overall youth population (Ortman, 2013). This growth among young, non-White populations is occurring largely in suburbs and small cities.

As of 2014, 24% of all children (ages 0–17) were first- or second-generation immigrants (defined as living in the United States with at least one foreign-born parent), and 22% of those between the ages of 5 and 17 in 2012 did not speak English at home (Federal Interagency Forum on Child and Family Statistics, 2015). Meanwhile, the percentage of English learners in the 2012–2013 school year had risen to 9.2%, as compared with 9.1% a year earlier (Kena et al., 2015).

The expected increase in the numbers of Hispanics, Asians, and other youth of color comes as a result of an unprecedented wave of immigration the United States is experiencing nationwide. The past two decades saw immigration population growth that has rivaled any period in the nation's history (Colby & Ortman, 2015). This unparalleled level of transnational migration has introduced into U.S. middle and secondary schools ever-growing numbers of students with limited English skills. The number of public school students in the United States who are English learners is approaching 5 million, an increase of nearly 1 million students since 2003 (National Center for Education Statistics [NCES], 2015b).

While the growing number of immigrants has enriched the racial, ethnic, cultural, and linguistic diversity within the United States, the increased diversity in population challenges long-held beliefs about what it means to be "American" (Suárez-Orozco, Suárez-Orozco, & Todorova, 2008). At the same time, data point to a shortage of teachers across the nation, especially general education and content-area teachers, who are qualified or trained to teach these new immigrant children, many of whom are English learners (Sampson & Collins, 2012). Furthermore, across the United States there is an overall lack of quality and consistency in the preparation of teachers to work with these students in their classes (Goldhaber, Lavery, & Theobald, 2015; Lucas, 2011).

Another adolescent demographic that demands our attention is the increasing numbers of youth coming from low-income families, up from 35% in 2007 to 41% in 2013 (Federal Interagency Forum on Child and Family Statistics, 2015). Nearly 20% of the 12- to 17-year-old age group lives below the poverty line (Jiang, Ekono, & Skinner, 2015). This equates to one in five school-age youth living in poverty, as compared with one in seven in 2000. Black and Hispanic youth, at 61%, comprise the largest share of those from low-income families, over twice as large as the percentage of their White counterparts from low-income backgrounds. Furthermore, over half (53%) of children of immigrant parents have low incomes (Annie E. Casey Foundation, 2014; Jiang, Ekono, & Skinner, 2015). Taken together, the challenges of meeting the language and learning needs of immigrant students and the growing number of those in poverty will require our most creative and responsive literacy practices.

One demographic trend that shows signs of improvement is the level of national school dropouts. Since 2000, when the overall rate of dropouts among 16- to 24-year-olds was at 12%, there has been a decline, to about 7% today. These numbers are staggering, nonetheless, when put into perspective. For instance, 7% represents 2,215,000 annual dropouts, or more than 6,000 students per day leaving our schools (U.S. Census Bureau; see *www.census.gov/hhes/school/data/cps/historical/index.html*).

Furthermore, economic background influences these rates. Lower-income students have always had lower high school graduation rates. In 2009, for example, students from families in low-income brackets ran a risk of dropping out that was five times higher than their high-income peers (NCES, 2015a). Poor academic performance and grade retention, more common among students from low-socioeconomic-status backgrounds, are strong predictors of early school leaving (Bowers, 2010; Jimerson & Ferguson, 2007; Stearns, Moller, Blau, & Potochnick, 2007).

About dropouts we can say very little, other than that these youth are not enrolled in school and do not have a high school credential. What is certain, however, is that dropping out of high school has long-term social and economic consequences. Without even a high school diploma, it is difficult to obtain many minimum-wage jobs and virtually impossible to enroll in postsecondary schools.

High school completion, therefore, is even more crucial today as we face the demands of rapidly changing and expanding global markets. Consider that from 1997 to 2012, the U.S. population of working-age citizens increased from 203 million to 243 million, while shedding close to 5 million manufacturing jobs. This equates to a decline of 33%; only the United Kingdom among industrialized nations had a greater loss as a percentage of the total workforce (Bureau of Labor Statistics, 2013b). With fewer and fewer well-paying manufacturing jobs available to them, youth who leave high school before graduating may find themselves competing for low-skilled and extremely low-paying jobs in the expanding service sector (Bureau of Labor Statistics, 2015).

With scant opportunities for advancement, high school dropouts are more likely to live in poverty as adults. As compared to those with higher educational attainment, they have a greater likelihood of committing criminal acts and of becoming dependent on welfare and government programs. They also exhibit higher levels of alcohol consumption, as well as poorer mental and physical health (Glennie, Bonneau, Vandellen, & Dodge, 2012).

YOUTH CULTURE: A COMMON CORE PERSPECTIVE

An interesting influence on youth and the ways they practice literacy in middle and high school is the Common Core State Standards Initiative (CCSSI; 2010) (see *www.corestandards.org*). Although questions remain about whether all states will adopt the standards or how long they will remain in force in states that have already adopted them, the Common Core has had a significant impact on how reading is taught in the middle and upper grades, and it appears inevitable that it will continue to do so in the coming years (Calkins, Ehrenworth, & Lehman, 2012; Rothman, 2011; Walker, 2013).

For me, what was unexpected about these new standards is that they situate literacy and language development squarely within the content areas. For three decades I have been a staunch advocate of literacy across the curriculum, so it was particularly gratifying to know the federal government was finally endorsing this approach to literacy. Citing the failure of traditional reading schemes to leaven achievement of children and youth in the United States—as evidenced by flat trend lines on the National Assessment of Educational Progress and a slipping in rank on international assessments—Common Core proponents assert that prevailing literacy curricula need to shift from a focus on developing reading skills and building fluency with simple narratives toward reading and writing to gain knowledge and express new understandings with a variety of texts.

Even the title of the Common Core English language arts standards for grades 6–12 makes clear this significant shift in emphasis: "Common Core State Standards for English Language Arts and Literacy in History/Social Studies, Science, and Technical Subjects" (CCSSI, 2010). This new focus on literacy in the service of content learning is defended on the grounds that building "a foundation of knowledge in these fields [will give students] the background to be better readers in all content areas" (CCSSI, 2010, p. 10). This is an extremely important assertion that might serve as one of the overarching themes of this book. The fact is that highly capable readers at the secondary level possess more than skills and strategies; they also possess knowledge. And, more critically, this knowledge derives primarily from reading. Thus a virtuous cycle develops for successful readers—the more they read, the more they know, and the more they know, the more efficient reading becomes for them (Brozo, 2010b; Mol & Bus, 2011; Pfost, Dörfler, & Artelt, 2013).

At least four decades of research in reading comprehension support the primacy of relevant prior knowledge (Duke & Carlisle, 2011). As the so-called fourth-grade slump (Brozo, 2005b) demonstrates, children who acquire good reading skills may not be able to transfer those abilities to comprehending content text if they lack relevant prior knowledge for that content. In other words, reading is domain specific (Chiesi, Spilich, & Voss, 1979; Kintsch & Kintsch, 2005; McNamara & Magliano, 2009).

The force of domain-specific knowledge on comprehension cannot be dismissed. This phenomenon became vivid for me once again when I was jarred from sleep by my alarm clock early one morning at a recent literacy convention in Chicago, Illinois. While I slowly sat up in bed, the local newscaster calmly uttered these words: "Live hogs found July unchanged." What an odd expression, I thought, as I hastily wrote the words out on the small hotel notepad. A few days later in a graduate practicum I was directing, I presented this sentence to one of our third-grade tutees. He was able to read it flawlessly and fluently but had no idea what it meant. Indeed, when I shared the sentence with my graduate tutors, only one, who had grown up on a farm with livestock, got the gist. The point is that to comprehend this expression, reading skill alone is not enough; one must also possess the needed background knowledge, in this case, of trading in commodities. As I was to discover, Chicago is the home of the Mercantile Exchange, where trades in live hog futures take place daily.

My episode in domain-specific reading comprehension should remind all of us that knowledge about life and all manner of things (even trading in commodities) is necessary to have successful meaning-making experiences with texts that inform. This knowledge can be gained by exploring content topics through reading. Secondary teachers skillful in content and disciplinary literacy practices can increase students' reading capacity, vocabulary, and knowledge with texts focused on real content.

After all, learning is inherent in every act of reading. Whether about the structure of language or the structure of a molecule, about what motivates a main character or what motivates a political leader, about places in the heart or places in Africa where French is spoken, all text encounters involve some type of learning. Children should be brought to see this as the purpose of reading right from the start. Approaching instruction around text in this way may hold a key to engaging curiosity, as well as expanding ideas and content knowledge (Brozo, 2010b). If texts are properly selected and appropriate instructional support is provided, students' innate curiosities about the world around them can be ignited through reading, helping them gain knowledge and build cognition even as they build vital reading and thinking skills (Duke, Caughlan, Juzwik, & Martin, 2012). The Common Core proponents argue that proficiency in reading and writing can only be achieved through a curriculum that is "coherently structured to develop rich content knowledge within and across grades" (CCSSI, 2010, p. 10).

One unintended consequence of the Common Core is that as standards increase, dropout rates increase as well, disproportionately affecting youth from the lower ends of the socioeconomic scale (Glennie et al., 2012). It is imperative, therefore, that teachers of adolescents possess the instructional expertise to ensure that students at all ability levels expand their literacy skills and continually use these expanding skills to grow their knowledge, too (Paris & Block, 2007).

YOUTH CULTURE: A CONTENT-AREA AND DISCIPLINARY LITERACY PERSPECTIVE

This is a book about content-area and disciplinary literacy. Both are advocated and exemplified. In the preface, I referred to the ways in which these approaches to literacy are similar and the ways in which they are unique. In brief, content literacy focuses on skills and strategies that are generalizable across disciplinary boundaries and subject-area domains, whereas disciplinary literacy is concerned with the unique language and communication processes of each subject area (Gillis, 2014). As calls increase to better prepare youth for the demands of learning in the 21st century, it is essential that we consider how these approaches affect adolescents' literacy and identity.

When I entered high school, I knew I was a good reader. Up to that time, for virtually any text, meaning seemed to leap into consciousness as my eyes tracked across the pages. English, history, science, and even math texts rarely posed any problems for me. My strong reading ability, along with an efficient memory, translated into high grades and overall academic success.

I came to assume that this pattern of success would continue, and it did, until I took chemistry in the 11th grade. I remember being staggered by the density of concepts, the new and specific vocabulary, the descriptions of chemical processes, and explanations about how to balance chemical equations that seemed written for those who already possessed an extensive background in the field. Furthermore, my struggles were cumulative, as I failed to absorb critical content early on and fell further and further behind with each new assigned textbook section and chapter. When I finally reached a point of utter despair, I made an appointment with the chemistry teacher and threw myself at his mercy. He was kind of a geeky scientist type, whose empathic side was underdeveloped; however, he said something to me then that only now, more than 40 years later, I realize was the key: "You gotta read like a chemist, Bill." In addition to this exhortation, he also showed me a few ways that he, who was trained as a chemist, approached the chapters in the textbook and, especially, how he read and analyzed problems related to balancing chemical equations. After a couple of more meetings with him, I was beginning to catch on, and what I realized was that there really was a kind of insider's way of reading, thinking about, and solving problems in chemistry.

I never became an aficionado of chemistry, but I did manage to eke out a B+ in the course, which I regarded as a major academic triumph. And the foundational knowledge I developed through that experience so many years ago continues to serve me, as I recently read a book called *The Upright Thinkers* (Mlodinow, 2015) that included a long section about 19th-century Russian chemist Dmitri Mendeleev, who discovered the periodic table, and I understood most of it. Moreover, what did stick with me was the idea that my generally effective reading skills may not always be enough when it comes to negotiating complex, domain-specific texts. In other words, to maximize understanding in chemistry or math or history, readers need not only general content-area skills and strategies but also specialized ones tailored to the literacy demands unique to each.

My experience might be thought of as a kind of case of one challenging a generally accepted premise that basic literacy skills learned in the primary grades provide the essential foundation for reading and writing more complex texts as students advance through school. Although foundational skills are important, I discovered firsthand what a long-standing and growing body of evidence attests (Sturtevant et al., 2006; Conley, Freidhoff, Gritter, & Vriend Van Duinen, 2008; Heller & Greenleaf, 2007): When youth move into the intermediate grades, middle school, and beyond, they need to develop advanced and, even more, specialized literacy skills and strategies necessary to negotiate and compose increasingly complex text in the disciplines (Langer, 2011; Lee & Spratley, 2010).

Despite these accepted understandings, questions continue to be raised about the most efficacious literacy skills and strategies youth should possess. Some, for example, suggest that generic content literacy strategies fade in importance as students progress through the grades, arguing instead that students need to engage in sophisticated discipline-specific literacy practices (Shanahan, Shanahan, & Misischia 2011; Moje, 2008; Draper, 2008). Proponents of disciplinary literacy approaches assert that each discipline requires a specialized set of heuristics and mental dispositions (Greenleaf, Cribb, Howlett, & Moore, 2010). Thus, in history, youth need deep knowledge to be able to challenge texts with critical questions, such as, Who wrote this text? What is the writer's background? What are the writer's positions and perspectives? and Whose knowledge is being privileged? (Nokes, 2010; Reisman, 2012; Schleppegrell, Greer, & Taylor, 2008). Similarly, other disciplines have their own unique discursive practices (Brock, Goatley, Raphael, Trost-Shahata, & Weber, 2014; Siebert & Draper, 2008; Fang, 2012; Pearson, Moje, & Greenleaf, 2010).

In math, disciplinary literacy is highly specialized, requiring forms of reading and writing not routinely found in word-rich text environments. For this reason, typical content-area literacy strategies are generally not applicable to the actual problem-solving processes inherent in genuine math-related tasks. For example, reading strategies such as KWL or SQ3R are composed of steps that may have little resemblance to the thinking needed to read, understand, model, and execute a problem-solving strategy in math. In fact, it may be true that generic strategies actually hinder effective problem solving by drawing students' attention away from the required mental operations needed for specific math tasks (Draper, 2008).

What all of this means for today's middle and high school teachers is that they need to know the content, practices, and discourse of their disciplines, as well as to have knowledge about the language, culture, cognition, motivation, and social/emotional realities of their students (Lee, 2007). This may be particularly critical for struggling adolescent readers, if one accepts Lee's contention that the achievement gap is attributable in large part to a limited knowledge base. What is being suggested here is that reading in the disciplines builds knowledge, and, as knowledge expands, reading and learning ability expand, also (Brozo, 2010b). While I make a strong case in this book for youth pursuing their interests by reading about who they are and who they aspire to become, when it comes to disciplinary literacy, youth are what they read.

YOUTH CULTURE: AN INTERNATIONAL LITERACY ASSESSMENT PERSPECTIVE

Another picture of American youth comes from results they have achieved on important literacy assessments. To capture this perspective, I focus this section on the performance of U.S. adolescents on the Program for International Student Assessment (PISA). I do so because the results of this assessment position American youth and their literacy abilities within a global context. Moreover, media-grabbing pronouncements from policy makers and others that the United States is losing the race for global economic competitiveness often highlight international assessment results (Gates, 2009; Obama, 2010). Some, to rally support for their initiatives, use these results to characterize American education as in a state of "crisis" (Ravitch, 2010). Meanwhile, broad economic indicators show that the U.S. economy, which remains by far the largest in the world, is not falling behind its competitors, including those with superior achievement levels on PISA, such as Russia and Japan (Reich, 2011). Furthermore, worker productivity in America has risen substantially since the 1990s (Chang, 2011), and the United States actually has a surplus of highly skilled workers (Bureau of Labor Statistics, 2013b).

PISA data are helpful in that they paint a highly complex picture of American adolescents' reading abilities, motivation, and schooling. For example, Asian American and White students in the United States have scores that rival the best in the world, but Black and Hispanic students score at levels that are comparable to those in some of the lowest-performing countries. With respect to gender, girls significantly outperform boys in reading literacy (OECD, 2015b). PISA findings also reinforce a vexing and persistent pattern of consistent underachievement by youth from low-income families and communities, leaving some to assert that where students live and go to school in the United States determines whether they receive a world-class education or one that is second rate (Carnoy & Rothstein, 2013; Berliner, 2009).

When analyzed critically, findings from international assessments such as PISA can provide a reflection on the context and quality of American schooling for its youth. First and foremost, because large numbers of U.S. 15-year-olds participate, key findings for American adolescents have relevance to literacy policy, curriculum, and instruction, especially when those findings are parsed by race, gender, socioeconomic status, and other key variables. Second, we hear much in the rhetoric of national leaders that raising reading achievement will ensure that youth possess needed 21st-century literacy skills to better prepare them for the new global economy (Resmovits, 2013). This assumption appears to be supported by the results of the other OECD-sponsored global assessment, the Program for International Assessment of Adult Competencies (PIAAC). Adults in the survey who were skilled in reading were more successful in their personal and professional lives as compared with their less skilled peers (OECD, 2013a). Thus it would be prudent to learn what we can from PISA about how to prepare youth for these new global challenges, which will surely require sophisticated and adaptive literacy abilities (Learning Metrics Task Force, 2013; OECD, 2010a).

What Is PISA?

Before exploring important trends and patterns in reading literacy achievement on PISA for American youth, here is a brief description of the assessment. The

Program for International Student Assessment is a study of the achievement of 15-year-olds in reading, math, and science literacy from participating countries around the world. PISA occurs in 3-year cycles, with one of the three domains of literacy emphasized. Under the auspices of the OECD, the first PISA cycle emphasizing reading literacy was launched in 2000; math literacy in 2003; scientific literacy in 2006; then reading was once again the focus in 2009 and math in 2012. When a particular domain is the focus in a PISA cycle, it is assessed with greater emphasis. Thus PISA 2009 has yielded very rich databases of reading literacy achievement, as well as of demographic, instructional, and attitudinal variables related to reading habits and practices.

PISA seeks to measure how well young adults approaching the end of compulsory schooling are prepared to meet the challenges of today's knowledge societies. The assessment targets youths' ability to use their knowledge and skills to meet real-life challenges, rather than sampling learnings they have mastered based on specific school curricula.

The PISA test of print reading comprises both continuous (articles, essays, etc.) and noncontinuous (graphs, data tables, etc.) texts. Questions are categorized as Access and Retrieve, Integrate and Interpret, and Reflect and Evaluate. Texts and questions are distributed over four reading situations—Personal, Public, Occupational, and Educational. The digital reading test also comprises continuous and noncontinuous texts, though most electronic texts are categorized as multiple texts, which are defined as discrete texts that are juxtaposed for a particular occasion or purpose (e.g., a job advertisement and a follow-up email). Similarly, digital texts include the three question types referred to above, as well as "complex" questions, which involve multiple demands (OECD, 2009).

I want to unpack the specific findings from PISA related to race, socioeconomic status, engagement, and skills and strategies. A closer look at these important variables offers a more nuanced perspective on the performance of U.S. adolescents and can suggest potential directions we might take to further explore these correlates to reading literacy competence, as well as programs and practices that might address particular areas of need.

Race

As was noted, classrooms in elementary and secondary schools in the United States are becoming increasingly diverse. With this diversity has come a pattern of starkly contrasting scores for Asian and White American students on the one hand and Hispanic and Black American youth on the other, as Table 1.1 reveals. Instantly noticeable is the full 100-point difference in favor of Asian students (541) as compared with Black students (441). This gap is equal to a span of 2–3 years of achievement. Furthermore, Asian and White students have average scores in the upper ranges of PISA proficiency level 3 on a 6-level reading literacy scale. Level 3 ability

TABLE 1.1. Average 2009 PISA Reading Literacy Scores of U.S. 15-Year-Old Students by Race/Ethnicity

Race/ethnicity	Score
Asian	541*
White	525*
Hispanic	466*
Black	441*
U.S. average	500
OECD average	493

*Significantly different from U.S. and OECD averages at the .05 level.

means that students are successful at "reading tasks of moderate complexity, such as locating multiple pieces of information, making links between different parts of a text, and relating it to familiar everyday knowledge" (OECD, 2010b, p. 51). Hispanic and Black students, on the other hand, have average scores at level 2, which is "considered a baseline level of proficiency" (OECD, 2010b, p. 52).

The contrast among these groups is brought into sharper focus when juxtaposing average scores by race with other countries. Asian American youth, for instance, have an average that rivals the top-performing jurisdiction in the world, Shanghai-China (556), and ranks them second among all 65 participating countries and jurisdictions in PISA 2009. American White 15-year-olds also fare exceptionally well in comparison with top-performing countries, ranking sixth, just 1 point below Singapore's average score of 526. At the same time, Hispanic youths' score (466) looks more like those of Lithuania (468) or Turkey (464), and Black students' score of 441 is similar to those of Serbia (442) and Chile (449).

Socioeconomic Status

Socioeconomic status (SES) is a metric that combines economic and sociological factors to gauge a person's social position in relation to others. For individuals and families, factors typically included in SES are household or combined income, education attainment, and occupation (Marmot, 2004). Individual and family economic well-being has been linked to a variety of benefits for children and youth, including overall academic achievement (Ladd, 2012), early word learning and language development (Farrant & Zubrick, 2012; Schiff & Lotem, 2011), reading achievement and growth (Aikens & Barbarin, 2008; Benson & Borman, 2010) and even physical and psychological health (Marmot, 2004).

Although state, district, and individual information related to SES is not available in the PISA databases, analysis of SES can be achieved using proxy variables.

For instance, reading scores can be correlated with free and reduced-price lunch rates, which represent students' family income. Table 1.2 confirms the linear relationship between these two variables. American students from the most privileged backgrounds, attending schools with a subsidized-meal rate of 10% or less, have an average PISA score (551) that is second in the world, just shy of the top performing jurisdiction, Shanghai-China (556). The score achieved by students who fall in the next category (attending schools with 10–29.9% of enrolled students qualifying for free and reduced-price lunch) would rank them fifth in the world, just ahead of Singapore (526) and a few score points below Hong Kong-China (533).

A very different outcome is evident for groups of students attending schools with high eligibility rates for free and reduced-price lunches. At 50–74.9%, a score of 471 is comparable to a rank of about 31st among the 34 OECD countries participating in the 2009 assessment. The lowest score, 446, associated with students who are enrolled in schools with at least 75% of the student body eligible for subsidized meals, ranks 33rd among the OECD countries, higher only than Mexico at 425.

We also learn from the PISA 2009 database that nearly a quarter of the U.S. students who completed the assessment were from single-parent families. This is representative of the population of youth as a whole. Additionally, households with a single parent, especially if the parent is the mother, are much more likely than two-parent families to have low incomes (Ladd, 2012). Students living with one parent achieved scores that averaged 45–50 points lower than those of their peers from families other than with a single parent. A further telling indicator of achievement related to SES is immigrant status. This variable often links closely to family income, as well as the level of academic support and preparation for school that students are provided at home. For instance, immigrant children in the United States are nearly twice as likely to be living in poverty (21%) as compared with their native peers (14%; Hernandez, 2004). As a consequence, low-income immigrant families lack resources to purchase material goods, services, and experiences that

TABLE 1.2. Relationship between Eligibility Categories for Free and Reduced-Price Lunch and 2009 PISA scores for U.S. Students

School-subsidized meal rate as percentage of eligible students	PISA score
Less than 10%	551*
10–29.9%	527*
25–49.9%	502
50–74.9%	471**
75% or more	446**

*Significantly higher than U.S. average of 500.
**Significantly lower than U.S. average of 500.

promote children's educational development (Mistry, Biesanz, Chien, Howes, & Benner, 2008). The point is that the greater socioeconomic risks experienced by children of immigrants undoubtedly exacerbate the linguistic challenges they face. Whereas about 16% of all U.S. students from nonimmigrant backgrounds scored below proficiency level 2, close to 20% of second-generation immigrants and nearly 25% of first-generation students scored below this level.

Engagement

Nobel Prize–winning economist James Heckman argues in favor of what he refers to as "soft skills"—those personality traits that may be even more essential than cognitive abilities to successful learning and achievement inside and outside the classroom (Heckman & Kautz, 2012). According to Heckman and his colleagues (Heckman, Stixrud, & Urzua, 2006), traits such as curiosity and perseverance might have greater predictive power for success in life than cognitive skills.

Engagement for learning, like perseverance, is one of the soft skills that has been shown to be a potent predictor of academic success (Pintrich & Schunk, 2002). Generally speaking, learning improves when students are inquisitive, interested, inspired, or otherwise "engaged." Engagement is the variable above all others that has the greatest shared variance with performance on PISA (OECD, 2013b).

Reading engagement is a multidimensional factor in PISA indexed to overall attitude toward reading, time spent reading, and breadth of reading preferences. To derive composite indices comparable to achievement and other variables, the reading literacy tasks of PISA 2009 were accompanied by a student questionnaire that gathered data on these three aspects of reading engagement.

The pattern for U.S. 15-year-olds is similar to the pattern for all students on PISA. Higher reading engagement, as indicated by reading enjoyment, extensive daily and weekly reading time, and reading a wide variety of fiction and nonfiction texts, is related to higher achievement (Brozo, Sulkunen, et al., 2014). American students who read 1, 2, or more hours per day had scores from 541–544, whereas those who do not read for enjoyment at all had a score of 467. Similarly, students who strongly agree with the statement "I read only if I have to" had a score of 459, while those who strongly disagree had a score of 552. Students who view reading as a favorite hobby scored 562 on average, whereas those who do not had an average score of 466. The difference in performance in each of these cases ranges from near 80 to 100 score points, or the equivalent of nearly 2 years of schooling between highly engaged and unengaged readers.

As might be expected, given their overall superior performance on PISA, girls from the United States had significantly higher indices of reading engagement as compared with boys. Girls enjoyed reading more, spent a greater amount of time reading, and had a wider range of reading preferences as compared with their male peers (Brozo, Sulkunen, et al., 2014).

Skills and Strategies

All demanding cognitive processes require sophisticated skills and strategies. We know that proficient readers enhance comprehension and elaborate understandings by using their prior knowledge as they interact with text (Best, Rowe, Ozuru, & McNamara, 2005). Good readers also construct meaningful summaries of text (Pressley & Hilden, 2004), actively monitor comprehension (Kintsch & Kintsch, 2005), and employ a host of other possible actions to ensure retention and recall of important information (Caccamise & Snyder, 2005).

Fifteen-year-olds in the United States who reported using reading strategies and processes regarded as effective ways of aiding comprehension had higher scores on PISA 2009 than those who did not. Executive control strategies such as monitoring comprehension, determining importance, connecting new information with prior knowledge, summarizing, and questioning were all associated with higher achievement.

A closer analysis of the PISA results related to skills and strategies for U.S. students (see Table 1.3) reveals that those who almost always check their understanding after reading had a significantly higher score (521) than those who almost never do this (465). Similarly, those who almost always try to identify the important points while reading had a score nearly 100 points higher (532) than those who almost never do (436). This same pattern is evident for students who relate new information to what they've already learned (526) versus those who almost never do this (480); for students who summarize what they read (519) compared to those who rarely do this (460); and for students who always ask their own questions while reading (519) compared with those who almost never do this (445).

Since PISA is intended for adolescents who are approaching the end of compulsory education, it offers one way to gauge the impact of schooling by considering its cumulative effects on American youth. What we learned is that, overall, the American educational system has proven that it can endow many of its future citizens with the critical 21st-century skills necessary to compete in the global economy and to actively participate as citizens of the world. And yet, this same system

TABLE 1.3. Comparison of 2009 PISA Scores between U.S. Students Who Use Reading Comprehension Strategies and Those Who Do Not

Reading comprehension strategy	Frequently/always	Rarely/never
Check understanding after reading	521	465
Identify important points while reading	532	436
Relate new information to prior knowledge	526	480
Summarize what has been read	519	460
Ask questions while reading	519	445

has also revealed its limitations in addressing through education the needs of a large segment of youth. As was pointed out, any system that elevates the reading literacy achievement of its students on such measures as PISA stands to reap economic and societal benefits for decades to come. And the United States may be one of the biggest beneficiaries of that kind of systemic effort, due in large part to its particularly large divide between the economic haves and have-nots, but also because of the economic potential to be realized through higher achievement in the unquestionably richest of all OECD countries. Thus those students coming from the lower rungs of the economic ladder are likely to advance the highest and claim a larger share of the nation's vast wealth as their cognitive abilities expand.

Some, such as Rueben and Murray (2008), argue that the United States runs separate and unequal schools and neighborhoods. The conditions of the schools and neighborhoods for poor, African American, and Hispanic youth, they assert, are not designed to develop high levels of literacy. Furthermore, they contend that if poverty, violence, drugs, unequal school funding, uncertified teachers, and de facto segregation are allowed to exist in the schools that serve these children and in the neighborhoods in which they live, then the United States will continue to fall short in international comparisons when the scores of ill-educated youth are combined with those of youth who enjoy better resources.

However, this gap in educational achievement between advantaged and disadvantaged students is more than an issue of social justice; it may also carry significance for the economic well-being of the nation. Raising PISA scores of Black and Hispanic youth could have a positive impact on the U.S. economy, according to Lynch and Oakford (2014). They found that if this racial achievement gap were closed, the United States could see a cumulative increase in gross domestic product (GDP) of $20.4 trillion by the year 2050.

Eliminating racial achievement disparities and bringing all students, regardless of color, up to the level of the highest-performing racial groups, then, may be one of the most pressing social and economic goals of 21st-century American schooling, especially because, in the coming decades, expansion of the nation's population of color is expected to continue.

YOUTH CULTURE: AN IDENTITY PERSPECTIVE

If there is one safe assertion we might make about this period of development, it's that adolescence is marked by an active and self-conscious process of identity construction. Indeed, shaping one's sense of self is considered by many to be the primary developmental task for adolescents (Erikson, 1980; Gee, 2008; Steinberg, 2008). Most adolescents tie their identities to their interests and desires, such as athletics, music, hobbies, nonconformity, and pop culture. And any of these and more might be facets of a single youth's sense of herself. Teen and preteen youth struggle with concerns and questions about how they're perceived by others, how they define themselves, and what they are to become. At the same time, adolescents develop a growing awareness of their membership in various discourse communities, both in face-to-face and virtual spaces, which they help define and which serve as funds of knowledge in their burgeoning awareness of the world and of themselves (Moje et al., 2004; Thomas, 2007). Family, friends, school, work, and virtual worlds contribute to a multifaceted self that defies stereotypes and simple categories. My own daughter, Hannah, when she was a 15-year-old 10th grader, offered these insights into the complex nature of adolescent identity during this crucial period in her life:

> It's difficult fitting-in. It's difficult to be your own person and be accepted. There's a lot of pressure to conform and become someone you may not be or do something you don't normally do or feel. It's like personalities going everywhere. . . . (Brozo, 2003, p. 7)

Identities structure the way adolescents understand themselves and their world. In the course of young people's biological and social development, their identities will change according to circumstance and preference, resulting in complex, often contradictory understanding of the nature of themselves and others, as 10th-grader Hannah observed. In this way, identity negotiation is a dynamic process.

Culturally specific assumptions related to a diverse range of interrelated practices, such as language, gender, and ethnicity, mean that a youth's identity is always a multidimensional composite of many identities (Tong & Cheung, 2011). Cultural diversity further compounds the complexity of identity insofar as it opens up gaps and discontinuities between the way in which a particular youth might perceive herself and the way she is perceived by others (Hermann & Lucas, 2008).

Language is an especially powerful identity marker and tool for identity construction (Gee, 2008; Moje, 2007). In schools and communities across the United States, language functions as a social tool for helping individuals understand themselves, each other, and their world and plays an important role in how individuals develop their identities, accomplish social action, and become positioned inside and outside of school (Orellana, 2007). Through written and spoken language, individuals can send and receive messages, develop or end relationships, provide feedback, and attempt to influence each other (Johnston, 2004). As many studies in the United States have documented, language use serves as a way for people to learn what is or is not valued within a community, to establish social identities for themselves and others, to develop understandings about texts, and to gain access to tools that can facilitate their reading comprehension or production of written texts (Agha, 2007).

Who we are is inextricably tied to the ways we express ourselves. Dat, a senior in high school whose second language is English, explains how the full breadth of his personality goes unrecognized for those who only know his English persona: "Even though my English is pretty good, I don't feel like myself unless I'm speaking

Vietnamese." Indeed, Dat's awareness of the connection between language and identity must be shared by countless numbers of immigrant youth in schools and communities across the land struggling daily to meet the linguistic expectations of school and the dominant culture (Goldenberg, 2008; Smith & Kumi-Yeboah, 2015).

As you can see, for most language-minority students like Dat who are entering our secondary schools in larger and larger numbers, many issues of identity are at stake. Although most English-learner (EL) students acquire English language proficiency at varying levels, many of them have problems with adjustment and identity that may go unaddressed in school. It's critical to point out that immigration issues for people of color have been unfairly and inappropriately compared to those of previous waves of immigrants of European descent. Unlike earlier largely White immigration, immigrant youth of color are confronted by unfounded social stereotypes and generalizations about achievement and behavior that act as barriers to personal and academic advancement (Jiménez, Eley, Leander, & Smith, 2015). Some argue that that the vast majority of students of color who fail to live out the "American Dream" begin to fix blame for their failure on themselves, their parents, and their racial or cultural group (Hill & Torres, 2010; Hones, 2002). Our secondary schools could be sites of critical self-exploration for these students, where identity construction, language development, and academic success occur within supportive and caring learning environments.

Linked closely to the process of identity construction is what it means for young adults to be competent and literate learners in both academic and out-of-school contexts (Alvermann & Eakle, 2007; Skerrett, 2012). A body of evidence (Alvermann, 2009; Cook-Sather, 2010; Sturtevant et al., 2006; Tatum, 2006) makes clear that youth are more likely to succeed academically and go on to be successful in adulthood when their literate practices are valued and when they see themselves as able and authorized members of learning communities. Yet many adolescents who possess talent, energy, and intelligence find themselves in school settings in which these competencies may go untapped (Hinchman, Alvermann, Boyd, Brozo, & Vacca, 2003–2004; Stewart, 2013).

The results of failing to align school curricula with students' interests and outside-of-school competencies are not inconsequential. The reason is that the process of literacy learning itself leads to changes in identity that are either empowering and transformative or demotivating and, worse, demeaning (Moje, 2007). For example, how Dat's teachers engage him in literacy activities and make decisions about the ways he should read and write influences how Dat thinks about himself and how others regard him as a literate learner. Moreover, as Dat learns to read and write, these practices change not just what he knows but also who he is (Alvermann, 2010).

Thus we are reminded that youths' identities are social constructions that mediate and are mediated by the adults in their lives, such as parents, relatives, and teachers; the discourse communities to which they belong and transect, such as family, neighborhood, gamers, or rappers; and the texts they read, write, and talk about (Moje & Luke, 2009). Literate identity also goes to the heart of students' motivation and aspirations for what they want to be (Alvermann, 2010).

Even gender appears to be linked to adolescent literacy identities. Recall from the PISA findings presented in this chapter that boys were universally and significantly poorer achievers in reading and had lower levels of reading engagement than girls. Although these findings are based on overall averages, they suggest important patterns that merit scrutiny. Beyond the broad results of PISA and other large national and state assessments, there is ample evidence that too many boys in the United States do not possess positive literate identities (Brozo, 2010a). This is especially true of boys who come to school as struggling readers and of many boys from low-SES backgrounds (Tatum, 2009). Male youth, like all adolescents, increase their chances of developing the literate abilities and dispositions necessary for full participation as global citizens if they're exposed to and have meaningful and enjoyable literacy and learning experiences centered on texts of interest. In this book, I make repeated calls for schools to know and learn to value adolescents' interests and literate practices beyond the school walls. The texts and the literate practices boys already engage in outside of school can be honored in school to capture their unique imaginations, sustain their attention, and lead to more thoughtful reading and writing.

As young adolescents become more cognitively astute and self-aware, they seek contexts that support their growing sense of autonomy, desire for social networking, and identity development (Alvermann et al., 2012; Lesko, 2012). If they encounter traditional, teacher-centered instructional practices in middle and secondary schools, positive affect for learning diminishes, and a psychological distance from school-related activities increases (Guthrie, Klauda, & Ho, 2013; Legault, Green-Demers, & Pelletier, 2006; Serafini et al., 2004). On the other hand, when offered a curriculum that is responsive to the interests and abilities they bring to school and that pays attention to who they are as individuals, young people will sustain their engagement in learning (Guthrie & Klauda, 2014; Brozo, 2011; Heron, 2003).

Case Study Revisited

Remember Marta, the business teacher? She was trying to generate ways of linking classroom topics to the real-world interests and cultural values of her students. Now that you have read Chapter 1, write your suggestions for how Marta might accomplish this goal.

As Marta observed her business students enter the classroom one day, she became inspired by an obvious way the topic of writing business contracts could be linked to their real-world interests and desires. Many had Tejano music pulsing from their headsets, which led Marta to consider how her students' love of this Mexican American musical hybrid could form the basis of a fun and meaningful lesson.

She began by inviting students to play their favorite Tejano music CDs for the class. With the music playing quietly in the background, Marta initiated a discussion about Tejano music artists and their recording companies. She asked questions about the agreements and contracts that need to be signed and formalized in order that the musicians get paid for the sale of their CDs. She described the familiar life story of the late Selena and what business contracts meant to her short but illustrious career. Marta then went on to inform the class that the topic for the day was business contracts and that by studying recording agreements and then negotiating and writing their own agreements, the class would have a much better appreciation for the importance of these business instruments.

With her students' interest piqued, Marta asked them to form pairs so that one could represent a recording artist and another a record company. She then handed each group a set of directions to complete their in-class assignment. First, they had to write out on a formatted sheet a fictitious name for both the company and the artist. Next, groups were asked to access helpful Internet sites from a list provided to obtain background on the language and format of contracts in the music recording business. Sylvia, representing a recording artist she called "Baby Sister," and Juan, representing a recording company he called "Sanchez Records," went to the computer lab and acquired information on music industry contracts from websites such as Mo's Music Management Recording Agreement (*www.planmagic.com/mmm/recdeal.htm*), Record Contract Basics (*www.music-law/contractbasics.html*), and Recording Agreements (*www.musicianunion.org.uk/files/recording.html*). Sylvia and Juan took notes on relevant pages printed from the sites as they answered key questions given each group: What are the most important issues addressed in a music recording contract? and How can the rights of both the record company and the recording artist be protected in a contract?

When students returned to the classroom after completing the Internet research, Marta engaged them in a discussion over the answers to the key questions. As comments were made, Marta wrote important points on the board. She then posed a couple of typical problems in contract disputes: (1) a band is wrongfully denied payment for services and (2) a band is in breach of contract. Groups were asked to explore these issues in a short passage Marta gave them entitled "When Someone Refuses to Pay the Band" (*www.music-law.com/payrefusal.html*). Lively discussion emerged out of this exercise, particularly between students representing the two parties in such an agreement.

Juan wondered whether his partner's Tejano singer, "Baby Sister," could claim "lack of creativity" as a legitimate reason for failing to record a certain number of original songs for an upcoming CD. Marta explained that such an excuse could be acceptable if provided for in the record contract and that these provisions are not uncommon.

Johnny, who represented a Tejano band, suggested that a "sickness and injury clause" be included in a contract to protect his musicians from ill-timed health problems or accidents that might occur just before a recording date. This comment led to a variety of exaggerations and jokes from both sides. Marta allowed the class its fun because she knew they were beginning to develop critical understandings of contract law by connecting it to their interest in music and by role-playing the principal parties in a Tejano music recording agreement.

In the last phase of the lesson, Marta asked her student pairs to reflect on the important points that emerged from their research and class discussion and, based on these points, to write an actual recording contract. To guide their negotiations, the groups used standard clauses from authentic music industry contracts (*http://banradio.com/law/samples.html*). So others could observe the role plays, Marta employed a fishbowl discussion strategy (see Chapter 3). While one pair of students hammered out a contract, other pairs of students looked on; then the roles were switched. At regular intervals, student observers were given the opportunity to share reactions to and ask questions of the pair of negotiators they were observing.

When Sylvia and Juan finally hashed out the fine points of an agreement, they signed their contract and shook hands. Marta then urged comments and questions from the observers. Manolo asked Sylvia why she didn't include a clause that would protect "Baby Sister" from liability if she was irresponsible and missed a recording deadline. While some snickered, Marta assured the class that if such a provision could be agreed upon by both parties, it and numerous other "wild" protections could be written into a record contract.

Marta requested that when students finished they place the final drafts of their contracts on the class website, which was linked to the school site. In this way, other students could refer to them as examples for help in completing a similar assignment.

Her students accumulated many such products at the site as source material to select from when compiling a professional portfolio.

LOOKING BACK, LOOKING FORWARD

The goal of this chapter has been to dispel myths and deconstruct stereotypes of adolescents while stressing the need for middle and secondary school teachers to embrace youth in all their dimensions as a valued resource in content-area learning and literacy. When youth are taken up by popular cultural media and education systems as "irresponsible" and "out of control" because of hormones or some other nonspecific developmental etiology, attention is drawn away from the role of instruction and texts in promoting and sustaining engaged learning and community. Like the adults who influence them, adolescents are never one way, either in behavior or discourse. Instead, as youth studies have revealed, they are individuals in search of agency and autonomy with multiple identities formed within the various worlds they inhabit, as well as by the different texts they encounter and create, both in and beyond school. To throw off rigid constructions of adolescence is to see youths as constantly creating and recreating new selves that are hybrids drawn from all the text experiences and funds of knowledge in their daily lives.

As you progress through this book, I hope you will come to appreciate the exciting possibilities for crafting and supporting responsive literacy experiences for youth. In the next chapter, I describe the ever-expanding population of diverse learners in our middle and high schools. I argue, as I do in this first chapter, for attitudes and practices that position these culturally and linguistically diverse youth as assets who will grow as literacy and language learners even while they enrich the cultural competencies of their peers and teachers. By honoring adolescents' identities, engaging them as learners, and expanding their range of literate competencies, the potential and resourcefulness of all youth are given expression in the classroom.

Building Literacy Competence across the Disciplines for Diverse Learners

As you read Chapter 2, reflect on the following questions:

- What are the unique characteristics of today's culturally and linguistically diverse youth?
- What instructional approaches and teacher support do diverse youth deserve?
- How can academic language across the disciplines be developed and expanded for diverse youth?
- In what ways can adolescents' everyday literacies be tied to academic literacy and learning?
- How can diverse youth who are striving readers be supported in their literacy development by student tutors and reading buddies?

As I was writing this chapter, presidential candidates in the United States were making dramatic pronouncements about immigrants already in and those trying to reach America. For some, "otherness" is to be feared, and they insist that only a massive wall erected at the border would control the flow. Those holding another point of view say in a country where perhaps only Native Americans are the true nonimmigrants, embracing otherness defines us as a nation and as a people. During this same time, an endless stream of asylum seekers and refugees were fleeing war-torn countries in the Middle East and Africa on an often perilous and sometimes deadly journey to Europe, where contrasting sentiments such as those in the United

States were being boldly expressed and acted upon. These developments served as fitting backdrop for the topic and themes I had taken up around diversity and the roles secondary teachers and schools must play to ensure that all youth receive a responsive and, indeed, a transformative literacy education.

There were moments when these political and global events would cause me to drift into reverie about my own childhood, steeped in the American melting-pot experience. Growing up in Detroit, Michigan, the epicenter of the all-powerful automobile industry, in the 1950s and 1960s, in our working-class neighborhood like countless others throughout that blue-collar city, I was the son of ancestry that had a mere two generations prior arrived from Canada as Irish and French newcomers and from Lebanon as truly "foreigners." But we were all like this. My best friend's grandparents were from Sicily on his father's side and Poland on his mother's. I walked to school with Larry Trevino, whose Mexican dad's and German mom's immigrant parents resided with them. And the Moores down the street, an African American family from Virginia, lived next door to the Hutchinsons from Tennessee, the fathers of both families having left their own ancestral communities and homes for the lucrative and abundant factory jobs in the Motor City.

Like virtually all working-class families, those in my neighborhood desired nothing more than that their children receive a "good" education so they might take advantage of the enormous opportunity the United States made available to most of its citizens. And many did just that. The sons and daughters of men and women who stood at assembly lines all day became doctors, lawyers, engineers, business owners, and, like me, professors.

However, as multiethnic as my neighborhood and city were then, it pales in comparison to the diversity that characterizes the United States today. People from every corner of the globe now call America home. And with this new and ever-expanding population have come challenges and possibilities for schools and society. One ongoing educational challenge for all of us concerned with the literacy and language development of youth is finding the most effective practices for supporting English learners (ELs).

In this chapter I assert that our work with culturally and linguistically diverse adolescent learners should be guided by all that we know about effective reading and learning and that it requires the collective energies and creativity of every teacher who comes into contact with these youth. Consequently, disciplinary practices will make a difference if they connect diverse readers' outside-of-school literacies with academic literacies; help them learn to self-assess; keep them engaged in reading, writing, and learning; move them to deeper and more critical levels of understanding of disciplinary content; endow them with the skills to gather and organize multiple sources; and teach them to use ICT as a tool for learning. Above all, diverse learners will grow as readers and writers if they are viewed as an asset and given frequent opportunities to enrich classroom and school life. This is more likely to occur when teachers form meaningful relationships with them and design responsive instruction based on their authentic needs and desires as readers and learners.

Case Study

Rene is the biracial daughter of an Asian mother and Hispanic father. She is in the 11th grade at a high school in a major urban center in the Midwest. Her school is situated in a community of ethnic and socioeconomic diversity. The school is a large, decaying, fortress-looking building with few windows. Its grounds are littered and unattended. Rene has been in special education classes since the third grade. She recalls with bitterness the experience that seemed to mark her for special services:

> "It was the first or second day of school. My mom was real sick, she was having a miscarriage I think. I was really scared. I thought she was going to die. Anyway, the teacher would write a word on the board, erase it, then go around the room and call on someone to say the word and spell it. Well, she finally called on me, but I wasn't paying attention because I was so upset about my mom. I had to stand up. . . . I just couldn't remember the word. The kids started laughing, and the teacher told me to sit down and for not paying attention I had to write the word 50 times. It seems like from that time on I started having a lot of trouble reading, and they put me in special ed."

As an 11th grader, Rene was still in a special reading class. The class included 23 students; all but two were youth of color. The classroom was small, cramped, and cluttered. During the winter, the radiators generated stifling heat and clanged uncontrollably. According to the teacher of this special reading class—a former driver's education teacher with 4 graduate hours of reading coursework from a nearby university—students were supposed to be working on their own with self-paced workbooks and programmed materials. Reading kits with 25-year-old copyright dates and some spelling and phonics books were stacked irregularly on the one small bookcase next to the teacher's desk. Very few of these materials were being used, however. Most of the students either slept, listened to music, or talked quietly. The teacher felt that as long as they weren't disruptive they could do what they wanted. "I'll help the ones who want to help themselves," he commented.

Rene used the time to visit with the only other girl in the class. She commented on her experiences in remedial reading:

> "It's a joke. I'm wasting my time in there. Nobody works. We just catch up on what's going on, you know, who's going with who and stuff like that. Mr. Willis hates it, too, so he just says, 'Don't bother me and I won't bother you.' That's cool, but my reading is still bad and I still have to take a test in May like everyone else."

Rene commented on how she gets by in her history, science, and math classes, where reading assignments are given frequently.

"Math's no problem for me. I've always been good in math. History is harder. I sit next to my girlfriend, Stella. She's real smart, she tells me what to do. I don't like that teacher . . . I never look at him, and he never calls on me."

To the reader: When reflecting on this challenging scene of dysfunctional teaching and learning, consider ways in which Mr. Willis's class could become a place for meaningful literacy opportunities. How could Rene be reached? How could her reading class be restructured so that it is no longer a waste of time for students like her? Be prepared to write down your ideas and recommendations after reading this chapter.

WHO ARE CULTURALLY AND LINGUISTICALLY DIVERSE LEARNERS?

When attempting to describe and identify culturally and linguistically diverse learners, it is critical to ask the question, "Diverse learners relative to what standard?" We most often think of diversity relative to a standard way of speaking, a standard way of behaving, and other standardized cultural norms. The United States, in spite of its history and legacy as a nation of immigrants, is also a nation some have called "obsessed" with educational and testing standards (Kamenetz, 2015). It's important to remember that in spite of the diversity of my childhood neighborhood, we were all "pressured" to conform to the standards of behaving in blue-collar America and to the univocal ways of speaking, reading, and writing in our public and parochial schools of the time.

The point is, when we refer to diversity, it always implies that some are "more" diverse than others, depending on the context. After all, as I noted in the first chapter, the United States already has a majority minority population of schoolchildren. According to the National Center for Education Statistics (2015b), less than 50% of students enrolled in American schools are White, a group that has been in decline. In contrast, there has been dramatic growth in the Latino/a population and a steady rise in the number of Asian Americans. Meanwhile, African American growth has been mostly flat.

This means that as a White American, I add an element of diversity to one of the schools in a part of Washington, DC, where I have been a literacy consultant for some years, because the student body as well as the teachers and administrative staff are either Hispanic American, African American, or Asian American. In a similar vein, I want to stress that challenges of identity arising out of linguistic differences between students and school are not restricted to immigrant or so-called minority populations (LeMoine & Hollie, 2007; Tatum, 2009). Speakers of any dialect at variance from that of the school and dominant culture are often made to feel incompetent and must cope with stereotypes others have of them based on their language difference (Short & Fitzsimmons, 2007; Willis, Garcia, Barrera, & Harris, 2003). This idea shouldn't be that difficult to understand for any of us who travel abroad or spend time as a dialect-different speaker in monolingual cultures here at home. And because our identities matter a great deal to us, so too must our language. Consequently, ignoring, denying, or demeaning the language of identity of a young person is in a very real sense devaluing the individual him- or herself.

Few teachers are guilty of intentionally demeaning the language identities of students, yet a dispiriting message is received daily by many youth who bring to school literacy and language tools different from those expected in academic contexts (Labov, 2003; Roy-Campbell, 2012). Morrell (2008) posits that one of the biggest challenges facing literacy educators in the United States today is finding effective ways to teach an increasingly diverse student population. At the heart of the challenge is the struggle to develop academic literacies through curricula and strategies that are inclusive and affirm the cultural values and individual identities of every adolescent (Freeman & Freeman, 2009; Janzen, 2008).

ELs are one of the fastest growing student populations in the United States (National Clearinghouse for English Language Acquisition [NCELA], 2010). In the 2012–2013 school year, more than 4.85 million students were designated as ELs in K–12 U.S. public schools, making up almost 10% of the entire student population (U.S. Department of Education National Center for Education Statistics [NCES], 2014). Although the mother tongues of ELs may literally number in the hundreds (Ryan, 2013), the dominant language by far is Spanish, with 38 million people indicating that they speak it in the home; a dramatic increase of 27 million since 1980, making the United States the fifth largest Spanish-speaking country in the world (Ryan, 2013).

Although some states, such as California and Texas, have seen continuous growth in their EL population in the past 10 years, many other states, such as Nevada, Virginia, and North Carolina, have only recently seen a spike in this population (U.S. Department of Education NCES, 2014). According to the Migration Policy Institute (2015), from 1990 to 2010, California's EL population grew by 56%, and Texas's EL population grew by 96%. During the same time frame, the EL population in Nevada grew by 398% and in North Carolina by 395% (Migration Policy Institute, 2015).

Generally speaking, *EL* refers to a subgroup of students who are not "proficient" in English based on annual assessments given to determine their proficiency levels. Many of these assessments require demonstrations of reading, writing, listening, and speaking and measure students' social and academic language proficiencies within these language systems (Crawford, 2004). An English learner might also be referred to as an *English as a second language* (ESL) *student,* an *English language learner* (ELL), or a *language-minority student*, although this latter label refers to someone who may already be a proficient English speaker but whose parents indicated that a language other than English is spoken in the home. An additional label is *limited English proficient* (LEP), a federal designation for a student who is learning English. In this chapter and throughout this book, I will be using the term *English learners*, or *ELs*.

Within the EL subgroup of students, long-term ELs (LTELs) make up the majority in the United States (Calderon & Minaya-Rowe, 2011). LTELs are typically students who are born and raised in the United States and have primarily attended U.S. schools, yet they continue to show consistent gaps in their education, primarily in areas of academic literacy (Olsen, 2010; 2012). Federally mandated standards-based testing and accountability measures have made states and school districts responsible for providing quantitative evidence of the achievement of all students, including ELs (Uro & Barrio, 2013). Corresponding to this continuing growth of EL populations, educators, policy makers, and educational stakeholders have been focusing on the academic needs of these students to find ways to help them be successful in U.S. public schools. It's clear that in order to address the needs of LTELs, secondary schools will need to redouble their efforts to gain a deeper understanding of why these students continue to struggle, as well as to explore innovative and responsive programs to close the academic achievement gaps for these students.

THE LITERACY INSTRUCTION THAT DIVERSE LEARNERS DESERVE: CONFRONTING THE CHALLENGES

Diverse Learners Deserve Effective Teachers Who Have the Knowledge and Practices to Address Their Needs

If it is difficult to bring secondary teachers to an understanding that language and communication skills are equally important to teach as the substance of their disciplines, it becomes doubly hard to convince them that they are responsible for the literacy development of all their students, not just the ones who "get it."

The influx of students from diverse backgrounds has in some cases been so rapid and of such volume that some schools and districts have found it difficult to keep up. I recall the middle school my daughter was attending in east Tennessee. Scores of Mexican American families moved into the area to take advantage of employment opportunities at a booming local mushroom factory. Overnight, this monocultural and monolingual community was transformed. Just as rapidly, numerous Spanish-speaking students entered the middle school, in which the one minimally trained ESOL (English for speakers of other languages) teacher on staff at the time, whose first language was Arabic, was woefully unsuited to handle their literacy and learning needs. And similar stories are being played out in hundreds of cities, towns, and suburbs across the country.

Arguably, it is unacceptable for districts and schools to employ so-called specialized staff who possess limited skills to work with linguistically and culturally diverse students, but the situation for these learners is compounded when general education teachers also lack knowledge and practices for meeting their academic needs (Lucas, 2011). According to Samson and Collins (2012), "To date, there has been relatively little attention paid to the essential standards, knowledge, and skills that general education teachers ought to possess in order to provide effective instruction to ELLs placed in their classroom" (p. 2).

In schools that have high populations of diverse learners, there appear to be even fewer qualified teachers to serve their needs. Teachers with lower qualifications typically have less than 3 years of experience, hold only a bachelor's degree, and carry few if any additional certifications or endorsements (Haycock & Crawford, 2008; Stronge, 2010). Furthermore, low-qualified teachers tend to come from less prominent teacher preparation institutions and are more likely to teach in schools with higher proportions of minority, poor, and low-performing students (Goldhaber et al., 2015). What we also know about low-qualified teachers is that they have been linked to poor student performance among minority groups and ELs (Aaronson, Barrow, & Sander, 2007; Clotfelter, Ladd, & Vigdor, 2005). According to Barton (2004), minority and low-income students are more likely to be taught by teachers with fewer than 3 years of experience and minority students to be taught by substitutes at more than double the rate of White students.

It is certainly true that not all ELs receive instruction from low-qualified teachers; however, many are taught by teachers who have not previously been exposed to teaching students whose first language is not English (Samson & Collins, 2012; Short & Fitzsimmons, 2007). Gandara and Contreras (2010) claim that even in the contexts in which ELs might be exposed to high-quality teachers, the teachers are often not sufficiently trained in teaching students about language and its use across genres and multiple disciplines. High-quality teachers understand the kinds of responsive and supportable instructional practices students from diverse backgrounds should receive in order to help them achieve at levels comparable to their peers who are accustomed to quality instruction (Desimone & Long, 2010). Effective teachers afford diverse students more quality instructional time than less effective teachers, and these same low-qualified teachers are more likely to have higher numbers of diverse students in their classrooms (Kalogrides, Loeb, & Beteille, 2013).

Another characteristic of a skillful and effective teacher of diverse learners is the ability to set high and achievable academic expectations (Yatvin, 2009). Teachers of diverse learners should hold these students to high academic expectations and encourage rigorous efforts to achieve literacy and learning goals. It is clear that, whether through teacher credentials, time on instruction, or attitudes about the abilities of their students, teachers play a significant role in the achievement of culturally and linguistically diverse students (Brown, Anfara, & Roney, 2004; Huang & Moon, 2009; Stronge, Ward, Tucker, & Hindman, 2008).

Diverse Learners Deserve the Best Instruction from All Teachers

We know that students who bring language and learning challenges to our secondary schools need more than compensatory classes and tutoring from any single teacher or specialist. For many years, we have been fond of saying, in the field of content literacy, that every teacher should be a teacher of reading. Although this mantra has lost some of its punch over the decades with the rise of disciplinary literacy, which has redefined what it means to be literate in academic settings, the idea that every teacher who interacts with diverse learners should put a common shoulder to the wheel to ensure that these students succeed is as viable as ever.

As an experienced university professor in teacher preparation and education programs, I know firsthand the minimal training teachers receive that focuses on practices for youth who are linguistically and culturally diverse. So I could begin with a self-indictment of sorts of the failure of higher education to meet the needs of teachers who must work with these students. Others have recognized a gap between what secondary teachers learn in their preparation programs in the university and the knowledge and instructional practices they are expected to possess for meeting the needs of the ever-increasing numbers of diverse learners in their classrooms (Harper & de Jong, 2009). Nevertheless, while reforms are desperately needed in teacher training programs, the issues diverse adolescent readers bring to the classroom continue to mount. Any teacher may be technically correct to say that she or he did not receive adequate training in this area, yet a refusal, benign or otherwise, to try to address the literacy and learning needs of these students would be unacceptable regardless of the self-justifications.

The challenge, however, as I have just described it is that many secondary teachers, especially those in the academic disciplines, such as history, science, and math, have had little university training or professional development for teaching literacy to adolescents, let alone to adolescent ELs and other diverse learners. This lack of adequate teacher development conflicts with the fact that the relationship between literacy proficiency and academic achievement grows stronger as students move through the grades (Heller & Greenleaf, 2007; Reardon, Valentino, & Shores, 2012). Therefore, linguistically and culturally diverse adolescent learners need skillful teachers across the disciplines so they can develop content and disciplinary literacy skills by acquiring and expanding academic language and domain-specific vocabulary. For ELs, as academic and disciplinary language develops, they will simultaneously learn, comprehend, and apply content-area concepts through use of their burgeoning second language (Klingner, Morrison, & Eppolito, 2012; Rubinstein-Ávila & Leckie, 2014). It has been shown that when disciplinary teachers focus on the academic welfare of striving ELs, creative practices emerge that integrate language and content (Dong, 2002).

As the number of adolescent ELs grows throughout the United States, it is becoming increasingly important for middle and high school teachers in all areas of instruction to develop effective second-language literacy practices and an understanding of the second-language acquisition process. In the International Literacy Association's 2015 report on teacher preparation for literacy instruction, based on an examination of program and course requirements at colleges and universities across the United States, an obvious shortcoming uncovered was the lack of coursework and experiences in working with diverse learners. The report recommends that "preservice teachers should be better prepared to address the needs of learners with diverse cultural and linguistic backgrounds across all grades and in all disciplines" (p. 8). This does not mean that all teachers and administrators must receive the same levels of training in working with ELs, but in districts and schools with moderate to large EL enrollments, intensive professional development for teachers, coaches, and administrators is needed (Samson & Collins, 2012). The outcome of this professional development should be that all teachers assume responsibility for helping their students learn academic English and acquire literacy competencies specific to their subject-area disciplines.

Given the sluggishness that teacher preparation programs appear to be exhibiting with respect to adequately training teachers for the new and growing diversity they will find in their schools and classrooms, what secondary teachers in the field need now is well-structured and ongoing professional development devoted to culturally and linguistically responsive pedagogy (Li & Protacio, 2010; Trumbull & Pacheco, 2005). Administrators, curriculum specialists, ESOL directors, and reading coaches should be the instigators and supporters of such professional development (Sturtevant et al., 2006). They should also provide teachers with numerous opportunities to collaborate on ways of meeting the literacy needs of diverse learners, to reflect on and analyze practices with these students, and to modify instruction as appropriate. To tell teachers to increase achievement for diverse learners without providing appropriate support is no different from telling students to read better without showing them how. Both need scaffolding for their respective challenges with teaching and texts (Calderon & Minaya-Rowe, 2011; García & Kleifgen, 2010; Mariage & Englert, 2010).

Although effective teaching for diverse learners cannot be distilled, bottled, and taken as an elixir, we know that middle and secondary teachers who are accomplished at meeting the needs of these students exhibit certain general characteristics that can serve as guidelines for helping you become a better teacher.

- *Effective teachers of linguistically and culturally diverse learners possess knowledge of language and language development.* These teachers are models of language proficiency in the languages in which they are expected to teach. They draw on their knowledge of language and language development to understand the learning process and to make necessary curricular modifications (Short & Fitzsimmons, 2007).

• *Effective teachers of linguistically and culturally diverse learners possess knowledge of culture.* These teachers are knowledgeable about and sensitive to the dynamics of culture in general and their students' cultures in particular, which enables them to understand their students and to structure a successful academic experience for them (Ladson-Billings, 2005, 2009).

• *Effective teachers of linguistically and culturally diverse learners possess knowledge of subject matter.* These teachers draw on a comprehensive command of subject matter, language of instruction, and their relationship to each other to establish goals, design curricula and instruction, and facilitate student learning. They do so in a manner that builds on students' linguistic and cultural diversity (Allison & Harklau, 2010).

• *Effective teachers of linguistically and culturally diverse learners promote meaningful learning.* These teachers use a variety of approaches that allow students to confront, explore, and understand important and challenging concepts, topics, and issues in meaningful ways (Rubinstein-Ávila & Leckie, 2014; Walker & Stone, 2011).

• *Effective teachers of linguistically and culturally diverse learners create multiple paths of knowledge.* These teachers provide multiple paths to help students develop language proficiency, learn the central concepts in each pertinent discipline, build knowledge, and strengthen understanding of the disciplines. They effectively use ICT to enhance language development, literacy, and subject matter learning (Echevarría, Vogt, & Short, 2010).

• *Effective teachers of linguistically and culturally diverse learners create positive learning environments.* These teachers establish a caring, inclusive, safe, and linguistically and culturally rich community of learning in which students take intellectual risks and work both independently and collaboratively (Goldenberg & Coleman, 2010).

• *Effective teachers of linguistically and culturally diverse learners collaborate with students, teachers, parents, second-language specialists, and administrators.* Many people share an interest in diverse students' reading, writing, and learning development, including, as I demonstrate in subsequent sections, the students themselves. The prospects of students becoming active learners and developing lifelong reading habits greatly increase when all persons concerned about the academic and personal welfare of these students work collaboratively to honor their diversity and build their literacy competence. With these collaborative efforts, your teaching effectiveness is sure to increase as well. Following are suggestions for developing collaborative relationships with teachers, parents, administrators, second-language specialists, and students.

o *Let all interested groups know your expectations for reading, writing, and learning.* To work collaboratively, it isn't necessary to convert others to your approach to teaching, but it is important that they be made aware of the nature of your curriculum and the rationale behind it. Otherwise, suspicion, distrust, and confusion may develop. Before others make judgments about you based on piecemeal or incorrect information, share with them as honestly and as accurately as possible your teaching philosophy and classroom strategies for diverse learners.

o *Make sure students understand your expectations for them as readers, writers, and learners.* Diverse learners must "revalue" reading and writing as meaningful, functional processes that can be used as vehicles for learning and expanding subject matter knowledge. All the strategies discussed in this book are intended to help you incorporate into your content curriculum learning experiences that demonstrate this revaluing of literacy.

o *Develop collaborative relationships with students.* It has been said that teachers can teach, but they cannot force students to learn; learning is each student's prerogative (Rhodes & Dudley-Marling, 1996). Diverse learners in the middle and upper grades are more likely to choose to learn when they are respected as curricular informants and allowed a hand in determining course topics, materials, learning experiences, projects, and evaluation (Cook-Sather, Bovill, & Felten, 2014). Involving students in course decisions will encourage commitment to and cooperation and investment in the learning process. Without students' active complicity in their own education, the chances of expanding their content knowledge, as well as their literacy skills, are greatly diminished (Brozo, 2006).

o *Develop collaborative relationships with parents.* Parents play a vital role in the literacy development and motivation of students, especially diverse learners (Bean & Valerio, 1997; Brozo, Valerio, & Salazar, 1996; García & Guerra, 2004). Teachers and parents can work together to facilitate students' literacy at home (Haneda, 2006). Most of the suggestions that teachers make to parents should be reminders of how parents have been supporting literacy at home for generations. When support for literacy at school is provided at home, diverse learners discover the importance of reading and writing and become more engaged academically (Calderon, Slavin, & Sanchez, 2011; Jeynes, 2007; Suárez-Orozco, Onaga, & de Lardemelle, 2010). Parents, in turn, can be useful informants about their children's attitudes, interests, hobbies, and other behavioral and personality insights that the teacher can use when selecting texts and planning projects.

One of the biggest challenges for teachers of diverse students is finding ways to engage and involve parents in the academic development of their adolescents. This has become even more difficult as culturally and linguistically diverse students increasingly live in communities and schools segregated by language, ethnicity, and SES. For example, Lee (2006) documented decreasing Black and Latino/a exposure to White students. For Latino/a ELs, Lee found that on average they attend schools in which over three-fifths of the student population is Latino. Furthermore, two out of three secondary EL students live in households in which no English is spoken (Arias & Morillo-Campbell, 2008).

Schools with a high population of ELs face the challenge of communicating with parents, many of whom have comparatively low levels of literacy in their native language, in addition to not speaking or reading English. Many EL parents have not completed a high school education and have little formal education compared with native-born parents (Capps, Fix, Murray, Ost, Passel, & Herwantoro, 2005). In spite of their language differences and education backgrounds, there is plenty of evidence that parents of linguistically and culturally diverse youth share a deep concern about the education of their children (Hutchins, Greenfeld, Epstein, Sanders, & Galindo, 2012; Jeynes, 2012).

There are many steps that teachers and schools can take to address the barriers to parental involvement and to thereby increase participation (Quezada, Alexandrowicz, & Molina, 2013). In Figure 2.1, I present a list of approaches to promoting stronger ties between teachers and schools and parents of culturally and linguistically diverse students.

One of the best ways parents and caregivers can be involved in their adolescent son's or daughter's literacy development is by encouraging and modeling personally meaningful reading in any language. Even parents with limited proficiency in their first language can demonstrate the value of reading. This is what I stress to them when we meet. Often, what I discover from parents themselves or their adolescent providing translation is that the adults at home are reading—whether it's the sports page in a Korean newspaper, a Spanish magazine on movie stars and music artists, an Internet article in Persian about new styles of chadors, or a Cajun-style recipe book.

I encourage all parents, but especially those from diverse backgrounds, to make sure they let their sons and daughters observe them reading, whether from print or digital sources. Instead of ordering them and demanding that they read, parents should set an example for their adolescents of the importance and joy of literacy by keeping print books in the home, reading themselves, and setting aside time daily for their children to read (Rideout, 2014). There is a strong relationship between these parental actions and the frequency with which youth read. For example, among youth who are frequent readers, 57% of parents set aside time each day for their child to read, compared to 16% of parents of children who are infrequent readers (Rideout, 2014).

For nearly four decades, I have been coordinating reading centers and literacy assessment and tutorial practicums in my role as a university professor. Most of those who have received services are culturally and linguistically diverse youth. Since parental and home involvement has been critical to the effectiveness of the services my staff and university students provide, I have had to address the challenges of engaging lower-SES parents, those who are not accustomed to participating in school-based activities, and those who have limited English proficiency. The following represent an array of strategies that in combination can promote parent–student collaboration.

Lack of English language proficiency

- Provide home–school coordinator or liaison.
- Initiate home visits by teachers.
- Send out bilingual newsletters.
- Provide a multilingual telephone homework line.

Disjunctures between school culture and home culture

- Create an environment that is warm, caring, inviting, and receptive to parents.
- Acknowledge parents' cultural values.
- Incorporate community into curriculum.
- Invite extended family members to classroom and school activities.

Logistics

- Modify meetings to accommodate parents' work schedules.
- Allow parents to bring other children to meetings, classrooms, and school functions
- to facilitate their attendance.
- Arrange transportation to facilitate student involvement in school activities.
- Schedule monthly meetings at a local community center.

FIGURE 2.1. Promoting parent–school collaboration for youth from diverse backgrounds.

MEETING THE LITERACY AND LEARNING NEEDS OF CULTURALLY AND LINGUISTICALLY DIVERSE YOUTH

It is important to emphasize that being associated in some way with the label "diverse learners" does not axiomatically mean that these learners are struggling academically in school. Of course, many so-called diverse learners achieve at very high levels, surmounting the cultural and linguistic challenges of "otherness" and going on to experience success in their careers and in their personal and family lives. Because I want all diverse learners to reach their highest potential, as I do with every young person, secondary programs and practices must be able to enrich diverse learners' academic and literate identities and help them maximize their potential.

One way secondary teachers can make a difference in the lives of these youth is to avoid the proclivity to assume that cultural and linguistic diversity means that these students are destined to struggle or are somehow *at risk*. Like all terms and labels, once embedded in the professional vernacular, they have a way of reifying expectations and practices for students. Throughout my career I have avoided using this label because I believe it inappropriately stigmatizes youth (Brozo, 1995; Polakow & Brozo, 1994). The expression *at risk* must always be followed by the question *At risk of what?* A seventh grader of color from a single-parent household in poverty who is a recent immigrant may possess, according to a school district's definition, all of the risk factors for failure; yet we might also ask whether the seventh grader is at risk of unresponsive instruction because the school he attends employs teachers ill prepared to deal with his needs (Brozo & Brozo, 1994; Cramer, 2015). Flipped completely on its head, *at risk* might become *at promise* when schools and teachers see youth from diverse backgrounds as resources and assets with multilingual and multicultural flexibility and the potential to make great strides given quality instruction (Sylvan, 2013).

Even though I believe we need to erase from our thinking any automatic connection between diversity and deficit or deficiency, I want to stress that the reason is not that I fail to appreciate the challenges posed by many youth from diverse backgrounds who are in need of further development in literacy. Nevertheless, I want to urge a different set of expectations and practices based on valuing the strengths these youth possess that expands their effort and potential.

Although many strategies for supporting literacy for all youth are applicable to adolescents who are culturally and linguistically diverse, there are differences in the ways that successful literacy practices and interventions for these students should be designed and implemented. Moreover, because diverse learners are themselves diverse in terms of their educational backgrounds, native language literacy, cultural heritage, SES, and more, any approach to expanding their literacy and learning in middle and high school may require modifications and shifts in emphasis depending on particular needs.

Concerning diverse learners who are ELs, it should be remembered that these students are still developing their proficiency in academic English. Thus, unlike their native English-speaking peers, they are learning English at the same time that they are studying core content areas through English. In the next section, I describe and exemplify instructional practices designed to broaden understanding of and facility with academic language for ELs and other diverse youth for whom disciplinary discourse is difficult to access.

Academic Language and Vocabulary

Many students, not only culturally and linguistically diverse learners, experience difficulties learning the large number of academic English words they see and hear daily in U.S. secondary schools. Academic language is primarily accessed through texts, not conversation, and some youth are well positioned to gain access to this language whereas others are not. Few ELs, for example, will read the same amount of academic language text in English as their native-speaking counterparts (Lightbrown & Spada, 2006).

Because academic language is different from everyday language, many students who are highly successful in communicating in informal contexts may struggle at school (Pilgreen, 2007; Snow & Uccelli, 2009). Learning language forms valued in school is a challenge for all students, but it is especially challenging for those with minimal exposure to and use of such language outside of school (Schleppegrell, 2004). Thus, for many adolescents who do not have regular opportunities outside the classroom to use academic words, in English or any other language, learning these words becomes an enormously challenging undertaking (Craig, Zhang, Hensel, & Quinn, 2009; DeCapua & Marshall, 2010; LeMoine & Hollie, 2007).

Academic vocabulary words are found in school-based texts and professional books and include specific linguistic features related to one or more academic disciplines (Flanigan, Templeton, & Hayes, 2010). Understanding of and facility with academic language is required for success in challenging literacy tasks, such as reading textbooks or writing school-based texts across content areas (Snow & Uccelli, 2009).

Fortunately, the same generally effective approaches to expanding word knowledge can be successfully adapted for culturally and linguistically diverse students (Shanahan & Beck, 2006; Townsend, 2009). These approaches to building academic vocabularies for ELs and other diverse learners should ensure that these students receive (1) multiple exposures to words in multiple contexts, (2) opportunities to process words over time, (3) opportunities to personalize newly learned words, and (4) visual support and extra practice time whenever possible. In addition to the following ideas and strategies to support diverse learners' word growth, you will find many other complementary and new strategies in Chapter 4, which focuses solely on vocabulary.

Sustained Encounters with Diverse Texts

Nothing beats wide reading for enlarging meaningful vocabularies, especially academic language vocabularies (Lapp, Fisher, & Jacobson, 2008). This makes sense, because there is a limit to the kinds of language and types of words we hear and see in our homes and communities. Think about it: For most of us, once we understand the words encountered in everyday language contexts—conversation with friends and family, watching TV programs, reading magazines and newspapers— what other sources are there for encountering new words? Most people do not speak using formal language forms, and popular TV and print necessarily keep the vocabulary complexity low in order to make the language accessible to large numbers of viewers and readers.

Like native-speaking students, ELs can increase vocabulary knowledge through wide reading (Folse, 2004; Ivey & Broaddus, 2007). Along with increasing word knowledge, many other benefits accrue as a result of frequent engagement with a variety of texts; most significant among them is long-lasting impact on academic success (Mol & Bus, 2011).

Although the surest road to a richer vocabulary and expanded literacy is wide and sustained reading (Allington, 2012; Sullivan & Brown, 2013; Worthy & Roser, 2010), many ELs and other diverse learners who are striving readers do not travel down this road, even though we have known for some time that book reading contributes in significant and positive ways to second-language acquisition (Elley, 1991; Pichette, 2005). Like any of us who experience failure, these students tend to avoid activities they find difficult and thus erode their self-efficacy. Avoiding reading may bring serious consequences, which limit life and career options.

It is critical, therefore, that ELs and others who may be striving readers be given frequent opportunities for sustained encounters with diverse texts in a variety of genres and that offer multiple perspectives on real-life experiences (Freeman & Freeman, 2011; Jiménez, 2014). It has been found that when students are provided with easy access to a wide range of interesting texts within classrooms, the effects on comprehension and motivation to read are enormous (Allington, 2012).

Through extensive reading of a variety of texts, supported by strategy lessons and discussions, readers become familiar with written language structures and text features, develop their vocabularies, and read for meaning more efficiently and effectively (Atay & Ozbulgan, 2007). Conversations about their reading that focus on the strategies they use and their language knowledge help adolescents from diverse backgrounds build confidence in their reading and become better readers (Zwiers & Crawford, 2011). Furthermore, it is important to remember that, even when innovative teachers expose students to many different texts in their curricula, some should be self-selected and of high interest to diverse youth. And, as I stress throughout this book, *text* should be broadly viewed to include print, electronic, and visual media.

History

Hector, an ESL teacher, team teaches a section of 11th-grade American history in the general curriculum with Maria. Nine of his ELs are in her class. They come from Brazil, El Salvador, Haiti, Liberia, Myanmar (Burma), Pakistan, South Korea, Syria, and Thailand. Hector has made Maria aware that some of these students have recently escaped war and violence in their home countries and missed years of schooling. The female students came to the United States from countries where it was very difficult for girls to receive an education. And the other ELs had to leave school in their home countries in order to work and help support their families. Interrupted education plagues many ELs, so it is especially important for those providing educational and other services for these students to keep them engaged in school and literacy learning.

Maria is a passionate and knowledgeable historian who has relied over the past several years on instructional practices restricted to lecture and textbook reading. As the number of students from diverse backgrounds has increased, however, Maria has come to recognize that her teaching approach needs to be modified to ensure that the content is accessible and interesting to the increasing number of ELs and other striving readers entering her classes each year. Though a newer teacher than Maria, Hector has developed a repertoire of engaging and responsive strategies in order to meet the reading and learning needs of his ELs. Together, they worked to craft a curriculum that included strategies to increase reading engagement and time spent with a variety of texts. This was done primarily to help Hector's students improve their vocabulary, comprehension, and thinking skills by creating more time in the history block for reading. Much to Maria's delight, these practices helped increase the level of enthusiasm and participation of the striving native English speakers, as well as her more capable readers.

The upcoming unit on immigration to America presented an ideal opportunity to integrate high-interest accessible texts into the study of a topic very close to the lived experiences of these young people. Through Hector's efforts, several texts were made available, and time was built in for whole-class read-alouds, small-group sharing, and independent reading. Instruction and independent reading opportunities were planned around the following books:

- Rene Colato Lainez and Fabricio Vanden Broeck's picture book, *My Shoes and I*, follows a young boy as he leaves El Salvador with his father to reunite with his mother in the United States. He wears the new shoes his mother sent, but they become dirty and tattered as he crosses mountains, deserts and rivers. The shoes are a metaphor for the bright hopes that remain, even through the wear and tear of a long journey.

- Gene Luen Yang and Lark Pien's *American Born Chinese* is a young adult graphic novel that chronicles a story of Chinese American boyhood and how the dominant culture impacts minorities. Written in comic book style, with sophisticated plots and themes, this book explores themes of stereotypes, racism, friendship, and forgiveness.

- Shaun Tan's *The Arrival* is a wordless black-and-white illustrated graphic novel. The main character, a young man, arrives in the new country, where he relies on the kindness of strangers to find lodging, learn the language, and obtain a job. Despite his obstacles and setbacks in a new culture and land, he eventually earns enough money to pay for his family to join him in this new country. The author, Tan, of immigrant parents himself, based his illustrations on museum and archival photographs of Ellis Island at the turn of the 20th century.

 • Sonia Nazario's *Enrique's Journey* tells the story of a 17-year-old boy's harrowing pilgrimage from Honduras to Texas in search of his mother. Traveling on top of trains, hitchhiking, taking buses, experiencing harassment, abuse, and constantly facing deportation, Enrique finally reunites with his mother.

 • Bernard Wolf's *Coming to America: A Muslim Family's Story* describes in photographs and text the Mahmouds, an Egyptian family living in Queens, New York. The transition to American life has not been easy for the Mahmouds, but devotion to family and religion keep them strong. While the Mahmouds live in a way that preserves their culture and religious identity, they are also seen spending time with non-Muslim friends and celebrating a birthday American style. The book brings readers to view the Mahmouds, and immigrant families like them, more like neighbors, rather than strangers.

The gripping modern-day Odyssey *Enrique's Journey* was assigned as independent reading for Maria's more capable readers while delivered as a read-aloud by Hector to his EL students whose skill level was not commensurate with the readability level of the book. Haunting and hard-hitting, *Enrique* stimulated extensive discussion and reaction from all students in the class, providing the ELs opportunities to converse with their higher-ability classmates about the book's events and themes. The tone and content captured the attention of the entire class, not just Hector's EL students.

In each 90-minute class block, 20 minutes were set aside for independent silent reading. All students were allowed to self-select materials. Some went to the Internet for interesting things to read, others used the time to read the textbook. Hector's students were encouraged to take advantage of the young adult books he and Maria brought into the classroom for the unit. With guidance, Hector's students found books they could read on their own, taking advantage of the illustrations to support word identification and comprehension with selections such as *My Shoes and I* or *American Born Chinese*. For his students with the least developed English reading skills, Hector encouraged them to generate their own text for *The Arrival*, the wordless graphic novel, by writing descriptive and reactive comments on sticky notes and putting them on the appropriate pages. Because these alternative texts were written at an accessible level for the culturally and linguistically diverse students in Maria's and Hector's class, the students benefitted from print exposure with engaging books while gaining greater understanding of the topic.

Science

Allington (2012) summed up the need to make available to youth modified texts that match their ability levels by saying "you can't learn much from books you can't read" (p. 16). As I have pointed out, linguistically and culturally diverse adolescents who are striving readers often lack the skills and background knowledge to handle the demands of the complex texts they encounter in middle and high school (Klingner, Boardman, Eppolito, & Schonewise, 2012; Short & Fitzsimmons, 2007). And as we have seen, growing numbers of these youth are entering secondary content classrooms with reading ability levels that do not come close to matching the level of difficulty of the required texts. For students with large ability gaps, who are reading two, three, or more grade levels below their grade placement, engagement with the texts they encounter in their subject-area classes is unrealistic if not impossible. To address this need, it may be necessary to make available modified texts that are accessible and content focused.

Thandi, a ninth-grade general science teacher, was witnessing for herself how the increasing number of students from diverse backgrounds entering classrooms with ability levels far below expectation posed special challenges to most secondary-level teachers. She realized most of these students were expected to read content text without sufficient knowledge of academic terms or oral reading facility with discipline-specific language. To overcome this challenge, Thandi knew that her linguistically and culturally diverse students who were striving readers needed access to topically related texts that they could read. However, like most teachers, she did not have at her immediate disposal texts at a range of difficulty levels on the same topics of the curriculum. Thandi handled this issue by locating and formatting short readings on the various topics she covered in her science class and making them available to her ELs and other striving readers as alternatives to the textbook.

Thandi was quick to realize there was a problem when, early in the school year, three of her EL students began feigning sleep during independent study and research time. Her efforts to rouse them produced limited involvement at best and complaints that the work was "too hard." After further consultation with the literacy coach and ESL coordinator, Thandi learned that the students' reading levels were in the fifth-grade range, nearly 4 years below the reported readability level of the class textbook. To discuss their reading and learning concerns and how she might best assist them, Thandi held individual conferences with the three students. To her question about how she could help them, Thandi received the same response from all three: "Give us something easier and fun to read."

Soon into her search for science materials appropriately leveled for her EL striving readers, Thandi discovered that commercially available products were sparse and did not cover topics relevant to her curriculum. Furthermore, there wasn't any money in the school budget for teachers to purchase supplemental materials. This brought Thandi back to the school literacy coach and ESL coordinator, both of whom encouraged her to look for sources on the Internet. Within a few hours of searching the Web, Thandi found that it offered access to vast amounts of reproducible material on virtually any school-related topic.

For an upcoming unit introducing her ninth graders to basic chemistry, Thandi was able to locate websites, such as *www.chem4kids.com*, with easy readings on carbon bonding, the periodic table, and balancing equations. She copied and pasted the readings into a Word document, then used the readability feature on the Tools tab to calculate a Flesch–Kincaid difficulty level. To her surprise, even these easy readings required further simplification to ensure that the neediest of her striving readers could access the content. With help from the literacy coach and ESL coordinator, Thandi was able to modify the readings in such a way as to reduce their difficulty while preserving the essential scientific information. She added pronunciation guides for the technical terminology and supported students' understanding of those terms through PowerPoint presentations of the content and other class activities.

During the 90-minute instructional block, when students were expected to consult their textbooks for information to solve problems or read and study independently, Thandi allowed her ELs and other less skillful readers to use the alternative texts as their information source. Thanks to students in her colleague's keyboarding class, these simplified texts were reformatted and given inviting "cool" covers to avoid stigmatizing the less able readers. These texts made it possible for Thandi's EL striving readers to have vitally important print experiences in her classroom while acquiring relevant information about specific science topics. Once her formerly reluctant students knew they had something they could successfully read in Thandi's classroom, they rarely put their heads on the desk when it was time for independent work.

By providing their linguistically and culturally diverse students who are striving readers with alternative texts, history and EL teachers Maria and Hector and science teacher Thandi increased sorely needed print experiences for these students. It is significant to remind ourselves that the ability to understand and use correct grammar and vocabulary in a second language comes largely from reading and listening. When text is accessible, engaging, and relevant to their lives, and when texts offer readers a realistic and authentic mirror of their own lives and experiences, ELs are far more likely to understand and pay attention to this linguistic input (Crawford & Krashen, 2007; Lehman, Freeman, & Scharer, 2010).

Morphological Analysis

When my daughter Hannah was about 2 years old, she, like many children going through that explosive period of language growth, invented unique word forms based on her burgeoning knowledge of grammar and everyday expressions. One of her more interesting inventions was to say "in a couple whiles" instead of "in a little while." Notice that even though this is a highly irregular variation of a common English phrase, it is understandable. To think of the word *while* in this context as a singular word that can be pluralized with the suffix *-s* is not really that farfetched and demonstrates how easy it is for most skilled adult readers to understand the statement "in a couple whiles," despite never having encountered such an expression before. This embodies the power of morphology.

Morphology is the study of word structure. It can signal grammatical relationships, such as with inflectional endings (e.g., *think > thinks, thinking*), and allows the building up of complex new words from simple roots (*run > runner > forerunner*). Because morphology allows readers to analyze how combinations of word parts, such as roots, suffixes, and prefixes, create new words, it can be a powerful tool to accelerate ELs' and other striving readers' word learning of academic vocabulary. As Fang (2008) points out, the task of understanding the many new words necessary for successful reading of secondary-level texts in English language arts, social studies, math, and science is made easier when ELs and other striving readers can break apart complex words. Furthermore, understanding word structure can help adolescent diverse learners unlock meanings of new and unknown words they encounter while reading on their own (Kieffer & Lesaux, 2010).

To develop expertise with a morphological analysis strategy, students need explicit instruction in the following four steps:

1. Recognizing that a word is unknown or inadequately understood.
2. Analyzing the word for recognizable roots, prefixes, suffixes.
3. Making a best guess of the meaning of a word based on the word parts.
4. Checking the guess against the context.

These four steps will need to be modeled frequently with meaningful examples, and students should be given ample time and guidance to practice them. It is critical in this instruction to help students avoid the proclivity to "overanalyze" a word without checking the meaning of the parts against the meaning of the overall sentence, paragraph, and passage. For example, if taught that the prefix *in-* often means "without" or "lacking," as in the words *insane* and *insufficient*, students may find themselves puzzling over the meaning of such words as *input* or *invest*. This is because *in-* can also mean "into." Therefore, students need to be taught how to progress from an analysis of the word parts to an analysis of word meanings in context.

Additional instructional information and ideas related to word morphology are taken up in Chapter 4 of this book.

Social Studies

Arleta's approach to teaching morphological analysis to her ELs and other students with reading challenges in her social studies class emphasizes the parts-to-whole process. Using the document camera, she projected the following passage from their textbook on the whiteboard. With this text she engaged students in an instructional dialogue as they worked through the four steps described above, allowing her students to benefit from her explanations, modeling while constantly eliciting similar word part analysis behaviors from them.

> Although the war had begun, the American colonists still debated whether to *remain connected* to Great Britain. A growing number, however, favored *independence*. They heard the *persuasive arguments* of colonial leaders such as Patrick Henry, John Adams, and Benjamin Franklin. These leaders used Enlightenment ideas to *justify* independence. The colonists said they had asked for the same political rights as people in Britain, but the king had stubbornly refused. Therefore, the colonists were justified in *rebelling* against a tyrant who had broken the social *contract*.

Arleta began her instructional dialogue by highlighting particular words that could pose problems for her students and were amenable to word part analysis. She wrote these words out in a chart (see Figure 2.2) with their identifiable word parts and related definitions on the board.

connected	co-	with, together
	nect	
	ed	past tense
contract	con	with, together
	tract	drag, draw, pull
remain	re-	again
	main	
rebelling	re-	again
	ing	present participle
	rebel	root
independence	in-	in; not
	ence	noun: action, state, quality or process
	depend	root
persuasive	per	through, intensive
	persuade	
arguments	ments	noun: condition or result
	argue	root
justify	ify	verb: cause
	just	root

FIGURE 2.2. Chart of highlighted words for word part analysis.

ARLETA: I'm going to show you how to figure out the meanings of words by breaking them into parts. But first, I want you to become familiar with four steps to the process. (*Goes over each step and explains the purpose, emphasizing the interaction between the meaning of the smallest word part, the meaning of the word, and the overall meaning of the sentence, paragraph, and passage.*) I'll begin reading the passage from our social studies book and go through each step with the words on the board. (*Reads the first sentence, and then goes back to the words "remain connected."*) When I see the words *remain* and *connected*, the first thing I have to ask myself is whether I know what these words mean. If I already know them or can figure them out through context, then I keep reading. But if I don't know what they mean, I can begin word part analysis. This is step one of the process I'm showing you today. Okay, I see that with the word *remain*, I can break it into *re-* and *main*. I'm not sure what *main* means, but I have seen *re-* in many words, like *remind, repeat* . . . what else?

STUDENTS: *Return, rerun, redo* . . .

ARLETA: Good. Thinking about all the words with *re-* I see a pattern, do you? Words that begin with *re-* tell us that something is happening over again or continuing. So, *remain* must refer to doing something again, and we get the clue as to what that is in the next word, *connected*. What smaller parts do you see in the word *connected*? I see *con-* and *-ed* and possibly *nect*. Can you think of other words that begin with *con-*?

STUDENTS: *Control, consist, contest, convict* . . .

ARLETA: All great *con* words. This is the second step in the process; trying to find smaller parts of the word that look familiar. Is there a pattern in words that begin with *con*? The commonality among these words is the idea of bringing something together or joining one thing with another. If we consider our two words again, *remain connected*, it might be possible to figure out the meaning by considering that *re-* in *remain* refers to again, and *con-* in *connected* refers to together. Could we then say "together again" as one possible meaning for these two words? This is the third step in the process; using the word parts to make a guess about what a word means. Before we can be certain that our guess as to the meaning of these two words is correct, let's go through the fourth and final step. Let's reread the sentence and even continue reading the next sentence to make sure our guess fits with the other words and sentences. (*Rereads the first sentence and inserts "together again" for the words "remain connected."*) My guess seems to work pretty well, when I think that one of the biggest issues of the American Revolution was whether to stay together or break apart from England. And when I read the next sentence that many colonists wanted independence, then I think the meaning I gave for those two words fits.

Arleta continued to read through the passage and talk out loud about the next couple of highlighted words, using the same four-step process. For the final two words, *justify* and *rebelling*, she had students work in pairs to talk through and take notes on each step, documenting how they identified word parts, guessed meanings, and then checked the context. When students shared their work, Arleta was able to clarify, reteach, and correctly model the morphological analysis strategy.

As a follow-up to her instructional dialogue, Arleta gave each student a comprehensive list of common prefixes, suffixes, and roots that they could consult on their own when encountering unfamiliar words. Arleta also reinforced students' developing skills with morphological analysis by repeatedly demonstrating for them how to look for smaller units of meaning within larger unknown words and engaging them in instructional dialogue about their own attempts to do so. By giving her EL students and other striving readers in her social studies class multiple exposures to a variety of common and less common word parts and their definitions, their ability to determine meanings of new words independently became more efficient.

English

Sharmayn embeds morphological analysis skill development within a broader instructional approach to expanding strategic reading and metacognitive thinking for her ELs. This approach stemmed from her dissatisfaction with not finding answers to her questions about how to address the serious needs of her culturally and linguistically diverse students who were striving readers. Her fellow eighth-grade English colleagues said intensive phonics was the only way two of her students, who scored at the third-grade level on an informal reading inventory, could ever hope to improve their reading skills. But Sharmayn was dubious. She had become well acquainted with her striving middle graders and their disaffection for reading the stories, poems, and essays in the class anthology. She wisely reasoned that an approach based exclusively on skill and drill could alienate them further from books and print. But what was the alternative? The evidence was clear; the students' demonstrated a significant need for word attack skills and vocabulary development on the reading inventory. And these issues appeared to be the primary reasons for their limited overall comprehension of the inventory passages, as well as the class readings.

At a professional development workshop, Sharmayn had a chance to explain her concerns to the district literacy specialist, who suggested an alternative to programmed and systematic phonics instruction. The specialist agreed with Sharmayn that her eighth-graders were not likely to enjoy or stick with an approach that forced them to review basic letter–sound relationships. Instead, she recommended that the skills these students needed be embedded within meaningful and authentic literacy practices. With interesting and accessible texts, Sharmayn's striving readers might come to recognize the value and rewards of learning word attack skills. Following up through email, Sharmayn wrote to and acquired further specific ideas from the specialist. Soon, she had a coherent set of activities for building word attack skills ready to try out with her diverse and striving readers.

The most important realization for Sharmayn was that her two seriously striving readers were not going to be able to make much, if any, meaning from the stories, poems, and plays in the literature anthology unless she provided major scaffolding. The students had developed excellent listening skills to compensate for their inability to read most course material, which was a strength on which Sharmayn thought she could build. They also had a rich background of experiences. Carlos was born in Central America, Masood in Sudan. Both had journeyed with their parents as young children to the United States. Both were proud of their culture and, with their families, continued to celebrate native holidays and traditions.

When the rest of the class was involved in independent reading, Sharmayn used the time to work with Carlos and Masood on building vocabulary and fluency through an apprenticeship approach. Sharmayn, as a knowledgeable and sophisticated role model, provided explicit instruction and created productive opportunities for Carlos and Masood to develop familiarity with and control of critical word-level skills. She worked reciprocally (Alfassi, 2004) by modeling strategies and reading behaviors and then eliciting those same strategies and behaviors from the boys.

Many of the readings in the class literature anthology were too difficult for Carlos and Masood, but some were within their instructional range. To determine this, Sharmayn used a procedure for matching a reader with a text that she learned from the literacy specialist. (See Figure 2.3 for a complete description of the procedure.) She found, for example, that the Robert Frost poem "The Road Not Taken" contained only a few words that were difficult for the boys, making it ideal for the focus of her apprenticeship teaching approach. The ensuing discussion illustrates the productive modeling and eliciting practices Sharmayn employed for developing the boys' word attack and word-learning strategies.

> SHARMAYN: Okay, I'll read the entire poem first, like we've done before, then we'll go through it together more slowly. (*Reads "The Road Not Taken" aloud*.) Now, who wants to read from the beginning? Masood?
>
> MASOOD: Two roads di . . .
>
> SHARMAYN: Let's skip that word for now and go back to it after this line and the next one.
>
> MASOOD: Okay, Two roads . . . blank . . . in a yellow wood, and sorry I could not travel both. . . .
>
> SHARMAYN: Great, okay, let's stop for a minute. Have you ever taken a walk in the woods? You know there are footpaths and sometimes you go down one and then another one might go off from it, too.

Without testing students using standardized and formal procedures to establish their reading levels, you can determine whether a text is readable or not by following these steps:

1. Determine the readability of a text you plan to use with a student. The simplest way to do this is to use the Flesch–Kincaid readability estimator from the Tools tab in MSWord.
2. Make the best guess you can about for whom the text is most appropriate.
3. Give the text to the student and have him or her read a section without assistance. Obviously, if the student struggles with most of the words, discontinue the use of this text, because it is at his or her Frustration level.
4. While the student is reading, record miscues.
5. When finished, check the miscues to determine how many were related to a failure to decode the cued word. Do not pay attention to repetitions or self-corrections.
6. Tally the total number of words the student was unable to decode or recognize. Divide that number by the total number of words read. Do not count the same word twice. Do not count proper nouns. The percentage you get can be converted to an overall percentage of accurately decoded/recognized words. Use the chart below to determine the reading level of material for a particular student.

Level	% of word recognition miscues	% of decoded/recognized words
Independent	0–2%	100–98%
Instructional	3–5%	97–95%
Frustration	6% and above	94% and below

Definitions of Reading Levels

Independent—The level at which a reader can make maximum progress without teacher assistance.

Instructional—The level at which a reader can make maximum progress with teacher assistance.

Frustration—The level at which a reader cannot make progress even with teacher assistance.

FIGURE 2.3. Steps for matching readers with texts.

CARLOS: Yeah, I go walking with my cousin near his house and there's a field with all these trails going through it where you can walk one way or another.

SHARMAYN: Good, see how you can think about what you already know or the things you do that are like what you're reading about? So where is the poet, I mean the person in the poem? What's he doing?

CARLOS: He's in the woods.

MASOOD: And there are two roads.

SHARMAYN: Is he going to walk down both roads?

MASOOD: No . . . he says he's sorry he can't take both.

SHARMAYN: Yes, so he's in a yellow wood. . . . Why does he say yellow? (*The boys are unsure and shrug their shoulders.*) Well, forests and woods can be different colors depending on the season, right? Like in the summer, the woods are usually what color?

CARLOS: Green. Oh, I think I know, it's fall and the leaves have turned yellow.

SHARMAYN: Do you see that, Masood? Here, look at this picture. (*They turn the page in their literature books to look at a picture of a forest of bright yellow leaves with a road covered in leaves running down the center.*) Now, let's take another look at the word in the first line that begins with the letter *d*. The first thing I would do to figure it out is look for little parts. I see *di*. You know the word from math, *divide*. What does that mean? What happens when you divide something?

MASOOD: To break into two pieces . . .

SHARMAYN: Yes. So this word also has "ver". . . .

CARLOS: That's ver.

SHARMAYN: And the *ged* gets a soft /j'd/ sound like aged or large. So let's see if we can say the word now. . . . (*Masood and Carlos say "diverged" along with their teacher, Sharmayn.*) Great! Now, if two roads diverge in the woods, what kind of word is *diverge* . . . I mean by where it is in the line is it another noun, a verb? As I look at it, it's telling me the roads are doing something, so what kind of words do that?

MASOOD: Verbs?

SHARMAYN: Right. *Diverge* is a verb . . . and knowing that can help you figure out what it could mean. Try to do that when you get stumped by a word; see if you can't figure out how it's used in the sentence. Okay, so now where do you think the narrator of the poem is? Let's look at the first two lines of poem for hints again.

CARLOS: He's right there where the two roads come together and you can't go down both at the same time.

SHARMAYN: Excellent. Do you see that, Masood? So what do you think diverge means? Is it where two things come together or . . .

MASOOD: Where two things divide or go different ways.

SHARMAYN: Perfect!

Sharmayn went on to review strategies for attacking pronunciations and meanings of unfamiliar words. (See Figure 2.4 for helpful independent word-learning prompts and strategies.) She reminded Carlos and Masood of the steps they went

When striving readers come to an unfamiliar word, have them ask and try to answer the following questions:

1. What is the purpose of the word? Does it name something? Show action? Describe something?
2. What clues are in the sentence? Is there a common expression, a synonym, a definition, extra description?
3. Are there any clues in the sentences before and after the sentence containing the word?
4. What things in my life can I connect with the text and the word?
5. Can I pronounce the word? Does the pronunciation give me any clues about what the word might mean?
6. Does the word have smaller parts? Do they tell me something about the word?
7. Is this word so important I need to use the dictionary to look it up?
8. If I look up the word in the dictionary, can I say the meaning in a way that makes sense in the text?

FIGURE 2.4. Independent word-learning prompts and strategies.

through to figure out the pronunciation and meaning of *diverged*. Notice how Sharmayn focused the boys' attention on the various cuing systems for word learning. She modeled the use of graphophonic cues by drawing their attention to the sounds of individual letters and syllables. She demonstrated the utility of syntactic cues by helping the boys figure out the way *diverge* was used in the sentence of the poem, or its part of speech. And she invoked the semantic cuing system by tapping the boys' prior knowledge about seasons and forests, relating the prefix *di-* to a related word from math and rereading the couple of lines of the poem to put the word *diverge* in context. As Sharmayn continued the model/elicit process, she had the boys demonstrate these same word-learning strategies with new unfamiliar vocabulary they came upon in the poem. She made sure they applied the practices she modeled for them and talked out loud about what they did, so as to reinforce their strategic and metacognitive thinking.

To build fluency, Sharmayn ensured that Masood and Carlos had multiple opportunities to read and reread familiar text. For instance, after working reciprocally through the entire Robert Frost poem, "The Road Not Taken," she had the boys practice reading it silently, then orally several times until they could get through it without any interruptions or miscues and with appropriate expression. To guide them through oral reading, Sharmayn took the lead while the boys echoed her words. As fluency further developed, the three read the poem together in choral fashion. Finally, the boys read the poem aloud on their own. Once Carlos and Masood felt totally comfortable with the poem, she invited them to give their oral rendition for the entire class. They particularly enjoyed demonstrating their competence with a reading from the class anthology because it was the same text all of their classmates had to read, too.

Word Generation

Perhaps *the* overarching principle of effective vocabulary development is to give students multiple exposures to words in multiple contexts (Stahl & Nagy, 2006). (See Chapter 4 for a full explanation of this principle.) With culturally and linguistically diverse adolescents who are learning English or struggling to comprehend the complex discourse forms in school, instruction inspired by this principle is imperative (August & Shanahan, 2008; Dixon et al., 2012). An instructional approach that capitalizes on the principle of multiple exposures in multiple contexts for expanding word knowledge in the academic disciplines is word generation (Lawrence et al., 2012; Lawrence, White, & Snow, 2010).

Word generation is an approach to teaching academic language for diverse middle-grade students through a collaboration of teams of teachers in English language arts (ELA), math, science, and social studies. The approach has been shown to significantly improve urban students' acquisition of academic vocabulary (Snow & Lawrence, 2011). This multidisciplinary approach begins with the ELA teacher introducing a passage on a controversial topic. Students read the passage and complete a word chart with focus words from the passage. In math the next day, students solve a math problem that is related to the passage and that features the focus words. In science, students read about a science experiment that contains the focus words and engage in a scientific discussion about the experiment. In the social studies classroom, students debate the issue raised in the passage on the first day, take a position on the topic, and write about their position using the targeted vocabulary words.

In the word generation approach, word learning is reinforced across disciplines as students are provided multiple exposures to the targeted words within multiple linguistic contexts. Moreover, by introducing an element of controversy into the study of cross-disciplinary content, students' reading and learning engagement increases (Snow & Lawrence, 2011). Successful variations on this instructional pattern involving most of the targeted academic language instruction occurring in the ELA classroom have been observed in major urban areas across the country (Lawrence et al., 2012).

Multiple Disciplines

When genuinely concerned teachers in a large, suburban multicultural middle school in the mid-Atlantic region of the United States decided to collaborate on developing the academic language of their culturally and linguistically diverse students, they fashioned an approach based on word generation. With support from the literacy coach, ESL teacher, and principal, a team of seventh-grade teachers from ELA, social studies, science, and math working with the same group of diverse students met regularly during the summer to plan cross-disciplinary academic language lessons. They made an extensive study of the word generation model, reading numerous articles and reports, contacting schools in which word generation had been employed successfully and talking with teachers and administrators, and attending conference sessions on the topic. By September they were prepared to launch the approach, study its effectiveness, and make any needed modifications to improve future word generation–inspired lessons.

Louisa, the ELA teacher; Kate, the social studies teacher; Reva, the science teacher; and Melvin, the math teacher, were responsible for a cohort of EL students. A cohort model had been introduced a few years earlier to encourage cooperation among teachers working with the large number of culturally and linguistically diverse students at the middle school. It was designed to reinforce learning for ELs and to ensure that they received consistent personal attention to their literacy and learning needs.

Louisa began the multidisciplinary unit by introducing students to a controversial issue described in a short reading. The issue of violence in video games was chosen because these games have tremendous appeal to youth and because major acts of school-related gun violence had recently been in the news. Within the reading, several words were highlighted. These target words became the focus of a weeklong study in all four content classrooms, with each teacher finding a way to link the topic and academic language work to ELA, social studies, science, and math.

SHOULD VIOLENT VIDEO GAMES BE BANNED?

As many as 97% of U.S. kids ages 12–17 play video games, **contributing** to the $21.53 billion domestic video game industry. More than half of the 50 top-selling video games contain violence.

Violent video games have been blamed for school shootings, increases in bullying, and violence toward women. Critics argue that these games **desensitize** players to violence, reward players for simulating violence, and teach children that violence is an acceptable way to **resolve** conflicts.

Video game **advocates** contend that a majority of the research on the topic is deeply flawed and that no **causal relationship** has been found between video games and social violence. They argue that violent video games may provide a safe outlet for aggressive and angry feelings and may reduce crime.

Louisa first read aloud to her class the short passage about video games and violence, giving particular emphasis to the target words. She then held a general discussion about the topic and issues described in the reading, encouraging students to talk about their ideas, connections, and feelings. With the overall meaning of the reading as a backdrop, she shifted the focus to the target words.

Each word, along with its base or root, was provided for further analysis, and the words were written into new sentences. Louisa did not give away the definitions of the target words at this point; instead, to catalyze students' language production as they used word part analysis and context to suggest meanings, she asked them to turn to a partner and talk. For example, the words *causal* and *relationship* were presented as follows:

Word	Base/Root	Sentence
causal	*cause*	• It is not necessarily **causal** that watching violent video games makes teens violent. • Do you think skipping school is the **cause** of bad grades?
relationship	*relate*	• The **relationship** between violent video games and teen violence is not clear. • Can you see how skipping school might **relate** to bad grades?

In science, Reva reinforced the targeted academic words by allowing the students to apply their growing understanding of them within a scientific context. She told the class that the controversy surrounding violent video games could be explored using the scientific method. Based on the steps involved in the scientific method, Reva set up the conditions for students to design their own investigations to explore answers to questions about video game violence. The set-up in the next box included the targeted words, offering students additional experiences reading, speaking, writing, and thinking about these cross-disciplinary terms.

After reviewing the steps of the scientific method and giving special attention to the target vocabulary in the description of the steps, Reva then formed teams of three students and tasked them with generating a proposal for studying the relationship between playing violent video games and teen violence. She told them to think of a "pilot" study that could be conducted right at their own middle school. She asked the teams to consider how they would find participants for the study, what would the participants be asked to do, and what approach they would use to relate violent video games to teen violence. Students were to write these ideas out in their science notebooks and were urged to include all pertinent target words in their explanations.

When the students took their ideas about how to structure an experiment to look at the issue of violent video game playing and youth violence into Melvin's math class, he had anticipated their arrival. Based on previous and ongoing planning with his colleagues, Melvin had also prepared activities around the target words as they relate to mathematics.

THE SCIENTIFIC METHOD AND VIOLENT VIDEO GAMES

The scientific method is a way to ask and answer scientific questions by making observations and doing experiments. The steps of the scientific method are to:

- *Ask a question.* The first step in the scientific method is to ask a question that interests you. On the topic of violent video games, a good question would ask if watching violent video games is **contributing** to an increase in violent behavior.

- *Do background research.* The next step is to gather additional information about the issue. Among the actual evidence, you are likely to find opinions, too. For instance, you are likely to learn that **advocates** of video games do not think they **desensitize** youth to violence, whereas others disagree.

- *Construct a hypothesis.* The third step in the scientific method is to form a hypothesis, or an informed guess about the **relationship** between one thing and another. In this case, you should hypothesize whether the **relationship** between playing violent video games and teen violence is causal.

- *Test your hypothesis by doing an experiment.* In this step, you are conducting a study to determine whether your hypothesis is correct or not. In this case, you would design an experiment to **resolve** whether there is a relationship between playing violent video games and teen violence.

- *Analyze your data and draw a conclusion.* In this step, you will gather and organize all of the information you found in your experiment and determine whether it proves, partially proves, or disproves your hypothesis about the **relationship** between violent video games and teen violence.

- *Communicate your results.* In the final step of the scientific method, you share the results of your experiment and what the results mean with others who are also concerned about the issue of violent video games and teen violence.

The biggest challenge with their proposed experiments was figuring out how to relate the two primary variables, playing violent video games and teen violence. One team, for example, had the clever idea of giving as many students as possible a survey with questions about how often they play or have played certain violent video games and other questions about their attitudes toward youth violence. Another team wanted to find out which students had the highest incidence of fighting and other similar infractions and then interview them about whether they played video games and how often. In both cases, neither team was sure what to do with the results.

Before assisting them with the math needed to help with their scientific proposals, Melvin first, like his colleagues before him, extended the students' understanding of the targeted vocabulary words by relating them to math, as in the example in the next box.

MATH LEARNING SHOULD BE FUN AND USEFUL

Many students like you have asked the question: How is learning math **contributing** to my future? If you do not see a **relationship** between your daily life or what you want to be when you grow up and learning the four functions (adding, subtracting, multiplying, and dividing), solving algebra problems, and measuring an isosceles triangle, well, you are not alone. Those of us math teachers who are **advocates** for making math more useful and interesting to students think cell phones and other handheld devices **desensitize** youth to the importance of math. In your everyday worlds today, we **resolve** math-related problems so quickly and easily by hitting some number keys on our built-in calculators on our smartphones, or we go to a website that does calculations for us. In this way, we do not realize how math plays a part in our daily lives, from figuring out the price of a Nike T-shirt discounted 25% to consulting player statistics for fantasy football. We know from research that students who are interested and engaged in learning math have higher math achievement than students who are bored by math. Since this relationship is **causal**, I am going to do everything I can to make math fun and useful to you.

After reading through the passage with his students, Melvin made certain they focused on the highlighted words and reminded them that these were the target words for the week that they had seen in their English and science classes. He invited students to turn to a partner and discuss their understanding of the words so far and what sense they made in the passage about math. Afterward, when students shared their ideas, Melvin realized that most had already developed a working understanding of the target academic vocabulary.

In an effort to reinforce students' word knowledge, as well as to facilitate their proposals for exploring a relationship between playing violent video games and youth violence, Melvin consulted with each team individually. He reviewed their ideas for a study, offered suggestions for strengthening their research plans, and then followed up the individual team conferences with a whole-class lesson on math functions and statistical correlation, as well as the difference between correlation and causation.

Melvin began by using a simple function that everyone could understand, the relationship between height and weight. Students provided these statistics anonymously, making a best guess about their own height and weight in feet, inches, and pounds. On the board, he wrote each height in one column and each corresponding weight in another column, with the tallest first and the shortest last. Melvin then asked students to turn to a partner and talk about the patterns they saw in the numbers. What became readily noticeable for most students was that the taller the height, the higher the weight, and vice versa. Melvin labeled this pattern a *relationship*, but then asked students whether height *contributed* to or *caused* more weight or the other way around, being purposeful about repeating relevant words from the target list. His students had much more difficulty answering this question, with some arguing for one causal direction and another arguing for the opposite direction.

Melvin then transitioned to the students' proposed experiments from science class. Using the idea for a study by the team that wanted to survey students about how often they played violent video games and their attitudes about youth violence, he explained that when gathering data in this study, two sets of numbers would be obtained and that these were similar to the two sets of numbers for height and weight. Melvin then posed this question to the class: Assuming there is a *relationship* between these two sets of numbers, is it possible to know whether the relationship is *causal*? He asked students to discuss their thinking with a partner first before writing out an explanation in their own words in their math notebooks, while he encouraged them to incorporate as many of the relevant target words as possible.

By the time the students entered their social studies class for the final word generation cycle, they had had numerous opportunities to (1) hear the target words read to them in meaningful contexts, (2) read the words themselves, (3) talk about the words in connection with the controversial topic of video game violence and with math and science thinking, and (4) write using the words in those two disciplines. As the social studies teacher, Kate's role in reinforcing the academic vocabulary was to create an additional context for working with the words.

Kate, like her predecessors, invited students to consider how the target words could be found across the disciplines. She had gone through the class e-textbook, located sentences in which each of the six target words was found, and projected them on the whiteboard, asking students to talk with a neighbor about the contextual definitions of the words:

- **Contributing** to the low standard of living for many during the Middle Ages was the fact that few people could read or write.
- Researchers say constant exposure to cigarette smoke can **desensitize** us to its harmful effects.
- The reduction of coal-burning factories and coal furnaces is seen as a major way to **resolve** problems of global warming.
- **Advocates** of reason and scientific thinking, such as John Locke and Rene Descartes, were at the forefront of the age of Enlightenment.
- Scientists believe there is a strong **causal relationship** between air pollution and cancer.

After eliciting definitions from the class and modeling contextual reading, Kate shifted everyone's attention back to the initial controversy surrounding violent video games that framed the word generation activities for the week. She reviewed the original short reading on the topic, explaining that issues like that one are what concerns modern social scientists. Kate told them the social sciences involve the study of how groups of people behave and how they might behave in the future. She went on to make sure that students appreciated the breadth of the social sciences, which include economics, anthropology, sociology, political science, and aspects of psychology and history. Therefore, Kate stressed, studying whether playing violent video games contributes to violent youth behavior fits naturally within the social sciences.

Kate now invited students to take a stand on the issue. She told them to reflect on how they experienced the topic in their various subject-area classes and then provide a written answer to the question: Should video games that are violent be banned? She emphasized that they were to support their position with clear reasons and specific examples. She also urged them to use as many relevant words from the target list in their responses as they could. The process and mechanics of writing these position statements allowed Kate and Louisa the chance to confer with students and embed lessons on composing strong arguments, help fill in gaps in prior knowledge, and review spelling and punctuation patterns and rules.

In the final phase of word generation designed by the seventh-grade teachers, students who had written in favor of banning violent video games were asked to debate classmates who had argued against banning the games. All four teachers participated in organizing and facilitating the debate, and other teachers and school administrative staff were invited to join.

In the end, the seventh-grade teachers decided the word generation–inspired approach to developing academic vocabulary proved highly valuable to their culturally and linguistically diverse middle graders. The cross-content nature of the vocabulary instruction offered these students numerous rich word-learning opportunities, as well as multiple contexts for reading, speaking, writing with, and listening to the words. In this way, word learning of academic language was more permanent and contributed to an increase in important background knowledge, more fluent reading, and improved comprehension.

Bridging Students' Other Literacies with Academic Literacy

The idea of linking youths' out-of-school literacies with academic literacy is an overarching theme of this book. In virtually every chapter I have asserted the importance of practices that honor who adolescents are in all their diversity and that demonstrate the value we place on their lifeworlds beyond the classroom walls (Jiménez, 2014; Moje, 2007). This is so because of the growing realization that strong teacher–student relationships and respect for individual and cultural identities have a positive effect on learning engagement and achievement (Sturtevant et al., 2006). We have also learned the importance of creating spaces in secondary schools for diverse youth's everyday literacies so they can showcase and build on their strengths with the print and digital media they use on their own (Alvermann, 2010; Alvermann & Eakle, 2007; Morrell, 2008).

Self-Contained English

The use of flash cards and workbooks as the basis for word study was yielding complaints and despondency from Nathan's eighth-grade self-contained English students. This year was the worst of all. His suburban school district had been going through a major demographic shift away from virtually all-White, European American students to a rapidly growing percentage of African American, Latino/a American, and Asian American students. Many were new or recent immigrants with strong ties to their native cultures. Nathan's methods, which had served him well for several years, were no longer viable for the new population of youth being placed in his classes. In a word, his pedagogy needed to become more culturally responsive.

An aficionado of popular music himself, Nathan came up with a new idea for doing word studies after talking with his students before class about what they had programmed on their smartphones. Most were listening to rap, Tejano, or country. He wondered if the lyrics from the songs and raps themselves might serve as the text for learning word families. After getting a few of the most popular titles of tunes from his students, he tracked down the lyrics on the Internet and found that they contained a variety of words that could be studied as families. These words could then be used as models for other, similar words in school texts and in their own writing.

The excerpt below highlights how Nathan and his students worked with rap lyrics to engage in word study practices. You'll see how they created and studied a particular word family, then expanded on the words from the family to generate new words for their individual vocabulary notebooks. Nathan and his class of seven students were sitting at their desks arranged in a circle.

"All of you should have the sheet with the Snoop Dogg rap lyrics. This rap is called 'I Love to Give You Light,' compliments of Derek. How many of you know this song? Let's first listen to it and then we'll read the lyrics. [Nathan had downloaded the song from the Internet, and he played it for the class on his computer.] Okay, now I want you to turn to someone next to you and look at the lyrics for words that have similar sounds or spellings. We're going to try to find some word families in here."

Nathan moved around the interior of the circle to monitor and assist his class. After a few minutes, he invited students to share the words they found that might form word families.

TORI: What about the word *I*? It says that a lot.

JAMES: There are a lot of words that start with /d/, like *Dogg* and *don't*.

NATHAN: That's possible . . . good. What else?

HUGO: Me and Casey saw all these words like *block* and *black*. . . . I don't know what you call them. They have the letters *c* and *k* in them.

NATHAN: Those are really good. I was looking at those words, too. And did anyone find the words with *ch*? There are quite a few of those, too. Let's see what we can do with those words, the ones with *ck* and the ones with *ch*.

Nathan directed the students to get out their vocabulary notebooks. Each notebook has a personalized cover. Some are collages of magazine images and words. Others have freehand illustrations of symbols. And others are decorated with graffiti. He drew a T-chart on the board and asked students to copy it in their notebooks. At the top of the left column he wrote "ck" and on the right side "ch."

"Let's read through the rap now together and look for all the words that have either a *ck* or a *ch*. Make sure you stop whoever's reading when we find one. I'll start, okay?"

Nathan read aloud a few lines and stopped to point out a couple of words that fit in the two-word family categories. He was also stopped after reading another word in the *ch* family. These words were written in the T-chart. He then asked for volunteers to read aloud, going through the same process until he and his students completed the entire rap and gathered all the words they could find that fit in the two columns. This is what the T-chart looked like when finished:

ch	ck
choir	background
such	jackers
alchemist	glock
preach	block
church	locked
teachin	black
watchin	
each	
preachin	
reach	
purchase	
beach	
child	

With the /ch/ words, Nathan and his students identified all of them that had the same sound, as in *such, preach, church,* and so forth. Only two of the words in this column had dissimilar sounds, *choir* with a /kw/ sound and *alchemist* with a /k/ sound. These were put into a separate group. They repeated saying the words aloud, emphasizing the /ch/ sound, and looked at how each word was used in the rap. The same pattern of analysis was used with the /ck/ words. The pronunciation of the /ck/ sound was consistent for words in this column.

Nathan then asked students to work with a partner again and think of new words with the /ch/ and /ck/ sounds. Again, as students worked in pairs, Nathan moved around the circle to facilitate and answer questions. When finished, he called on students to go to the T-chart and add their new words. They also wrote them in their notebooks. In the left column, words such as *catch, match, reach,* and *bunch* were added. In the right column, new words included *socks, locker, backpack, kick,* and *duck.*

Finally, Nathan asked student pairs to work together on writing their own rap lyrics that would contain all or some of the new words from the T-chart. Casey read the rap she and Hugo wrote while Hugo kept rhythm on his desktop. It went like this:

> I put my *socks* in my *backpack* when I go to school.
> I put my backpack in my *locker* or I look like a fool.
> I get my *socks* from my backpack when I go to gym.
> I gotta *catch* a ball then I *kick* it to him.

Nathan's students never had such fun doing word study work as when they used song lyrics for analyzing related vocabulary. His students' enthusiasm translated into genuine learning as he noticed their ability to recognize many of the same words in other texts. By eliminating barriers between outside-of-school interests and literacies and classroom practices, Nathan was able to increase engagement in learning and build language competencies for his striving readers.

Cross-Age Tutoring

Research evidence has been growing for the benefits of peer-mediated instruction in literacy (Jun, Ramirez, & Cumming, 2010). Structuring classroom interaction so that youth have opportunities to learn from and with one another has contributed to higher student engagement and self-esteem (Miller, Topping, & Thurston, 2010). Small groups and pairs seem to be particularly beneficial arrangements for striving readers, who find it more difficult to learn in whole-class instructional contexts (LaGue & Wilson, 2010). One such promising context for accelerating ELs and striving readers' literacy development is cross-age tutoring (Jacobson et al., 2001; Richards & Lassonde, 2009). This approach has been found to be a viable alternative to pull-out programs and remedial reading (Dufrene et al., 2010; Fisher, 2001; Paterson & Elliot, 2006). In the example that follows, two diverse learners, one older and one younger, were both beneficiaries of a buddy reading program.

Buddy Reading: A Special Program for Striving Readers

Dimitrius started the tenth grade fully expecting to drop out. Both of his older brothers had left school early, and his sister, who had recently had a baby, was receiving homebound instruction. Rohama, the literacy coach working in Dimitrius's school, looked through his file and saw that he was an ideal candidate for the buddy reading program she was launching. While Dimitrius's reading scores were 3–4 years below where they should have been for a 16-year-old, he was described by his teachers as "friendly" and even "caring." A repeated theme, however, was that he lacked motivation. Rohama saw another possible future for this young teen and recruited him for the cross-age tutoring program as part of an overall plan to improve reading skills for striving youth and keep them in school.

The program Rohama put together targeted young men and women like Dimitrius, students at risk of dropping out due to poor academic performance, low ability levels, or difficult home circumstances. She had made arrangements with the elementary school, which was only a short walk across the track field, to host tutorial sessions twice weekly involving second and third graders and high school reading buddies.

After speaking with Dimitrius and several other students individually about participating in the program and getting commitments from six of them, Rohama prepared them for their roles. Dimitrius and the others were in the same third-block study hall, which was an ideal time to run the program. Before meeting their elementary buddies, the high school tutors learned techniques for finding out the children's interests. They were taught simple read-aloud and vocabulary strategies. They learned how to facilitate writing in response to reading and how to make books. Throughout the training in preparation for tutoring, Rohama stressed the need to be encouraging of their younger buddies and help them see that reading and writing can be enjoyable. Above all, Rohama hoped that by developing literacy strategies for helping younger, less able readers than themselves, these adolescents would, in fact, expand their own reading and writing skills.

Dimitrius's reading buddy was a second grader by the name of Barry, who was already experiencing difficulties with grade-appropriate reading materials. Dimitrius learned in their first meeting that Barry was almost a neighbor of his. The young boy lived in a housing project just a couple of streets away from Dimitrius's building. Right from the start, Barry told Dimitrius about how much he "loved" football. He said his father lived in Chicago, and that was the team he wanted to play for when he grew up. Barry also told Dimitrius what he always wanted, his own computer so he could play "cool games."

After spending most of the first tutoring session getting to know one another, Dimitrius read some pages he had practiced from a short biography about Michael Jordan. Before reading, he talked about how much he liked "roundball." As Dimitrius was gathering his materials to leave, Barry asked him if he was coming back, and Dimitrius reassured him he would return in a couple of days. It was a humble start to what was to become an important experience for the two of them.

Whereas some tutors dropped out over the next couple of months, Dimitrius stuck it out and came to enjoy his newfound status as a role model and "expert" reader for his young buddy, Barry. Much of what the two of them read and wrote about had to do with football. Rohama found appropriately difficult high-interest books for them to enjoy together, such as biographies of great Bears players from the past, such as Dick Butkus, Walter Payton, Jim McMahon, and "The Fridge" Perry. They kept a scrapbook of the Bears' performance that season, reading newspaper stories and cutting out pictures of their favorite players. Along with these, they wrote captions, statistics, and bits of trivia from players' records.

While cutting out a magazine photo of the Bears' premier running back, Anthony Thomas, better known as the "A-Train," Barry commented about his powerful physique, wondering out loud how he got so big. Dimitrius thought they could find information on that topic using the Internet. Since the cross-age tutoring sessions were held in the elementary school's media center, computers were available throughout the large open room. Rohama helped get their search started using descriptors such as "football players training," and they found pages of sites concerned with bodybuilding and fitness. What caught Dimitrius's eye, however, were references to performance-enhancing drugs. Rohama helped them locate sites with straightforward, objective information about these supplements, which they printed for reading later.

Rohama talked with Dimitrius about how he might share this information with Barry, cautioning him not to present it in a way that might inadvertently glorify drug use. Dimitrius assured her he was going to "set him straight about that junk." Under Rohama's watchful eye, Dimitrius planned ways he would read, write, and talk about performance-enhancing drugs in the next few sessions. She helped Dimitrius develop strategies for sharing selected content from the book that would help Barry begin to appreciate the drug-free ways of building muscle and stamina for athletic competition.

It was Dimitrius, however, who came up with the idea of a digital activity related to the topic. Aware of Barry's keen interest in computers, he developed a plan for taking a closer look at the characters from popular computer games. His plan was inspired by reading that one of the most common pastimes among many American football players when on the road or during the off season was playing such games as True Crime: Streets of LA (Activision) and WWF Wrestlemania (THQ). Typically, the heroes and villains in these games are exaggeratedly muscled in ways that football players and bodybuilders must envy and, perhaps, strive to resemble. Demonstrating once again for Rohama his ability to reason critically, Dimitrius saw how these images might influence certain athletes to do whatever it takes, including using drugs, to achieve unusual physiques.

With Rohama's help and assistance from the elementary school media specialist, Dimitrius and Barry used the Internet to find pictures of popular computer game figures from Take No Prisoners (Red Orb), The Hulk (Vivendi-Universal), Army Men: Mobile Ops (3DO), and X-Men: Next Dimension (Activision). These pictures were then downloaded into Adobe Photoshop so they could be altered. The reading buddies learned how to rework the main characters' physiques, reshaping them in ways that were more proportional to normal muscle development. They displayed their work in a PowerPoint presentation with "before" slides, accompanied by captions warning of the dangers of steroids and other illegal substances for building muscle, and "after" slides, with statements about good health, diet, and fitness. Proud of the brief PowerPoint show they had created, Dimitrius and Barry were given special opportunities to share the slides with other students in the cross-age tutoring program. The elementary school's principal was so impressed she made sure the slides were shown to the children during drug awareness events that year.

Rohama's buddy reading program offered Dimitrius and Barry the opportunity to establish a positive relationship, increase time spent reading, and develop critical thinking skills. This approach to cross-age tutoring offers striving adolescent readers a context for expanding their skills and motivation while enlarging their self-efficacy through positive role modeling.

Case Study Revisited

I hope by now you have had a chance to give some thought to Rene's situation. We're sure it became obvious as you read this chapter that a variety of effective practices are possible with striving readers. The fact that Mr. Willis has provided very few meaningful literacy experiences for Rene and her classmates is largely inexcusable, we believe, in spite of the less than ideal condition of the school and classroom. Here is your chance to suggest ways of transforming Rene's special reading class to make it a more culturally and intellectually responsive environment. Take a moment to write your suggestions now.

I next offer my suggestions for transforming Mr. Willis's classroom. To do so, I describe the outstanding work of a remedial reading teacher who I believe embodies what it means to engage striving adolescent readers in meaningful and personally relevant print experiences.

Liliana teaches remedial reading in a large suburban high school just outside the boundary of a sprawling city in the mid-Atlantic region. Many of her students are ELs, and all have a history of poor academic achievement. In her classroom, she has created a learning environment that supports authentic uses of print. She also regularly demonstrates for students her own comprehension processes, thereby allowing them to observe effective reading and writing strategies. Liliana believes that development in reading and writing can take place only in contexts in which students have frequent opportunities to read and write as meaningful communication.

Youth who enter her classroom are immersed in a language-rich environment characterized by:

- A reading center—a comfortable corner of the classroom crammed with fiction and nonfiction books, magazines, graphic novels and comic books, newspapers, pamphlets, taped stories, high-interest/easy-reading books, two Internet-ready computers, and other print material.
- Displays of students' work, including stories, poems, song lyrics, essays, and artwork.
- Functional reading and writing spaces, including a message board for exchanging notes and information among students and between Liliana and her students, lunch menus, part-time job notices, classified ads, and more.

Liliana demonstrates how reading and writing can be functional and enjoyable. For 15 minutes of every class she reads aloud from a young adult book. Students have enjoyed the experience of hearing and discussing books such as *The Misadventures of Awkward Black Girl* (Rae, 2015), *Written in the Stars* (Saeed, 2015), *Dark Dude* (Hijuelos, 2009), and *Spare Parts: Four Undocumented Teenagers, One Ugly Robot, and the Battle for the American Dream* (Davis, 2014).

LOOKING BACK, LOOKING FORWARD

Helping striving adolescent readers develop levels of reading and writing competence necessary for content-area learning is a demanding task. To be successful, a total commitment is required of all teachers with whom striving youth interact during the course of a school day. Growth may not always be as rapid as would be hoped, but it is far more likely to occur when secondary teachers, administrators, and support staff dedicate themselves to responsive and culturally sensitive practices for striving readers.

As you reflect on the ideas and practices discussed in this chapter and throughout this book, consider the approaches you might use to meet the needs of striving readers. As you do, remember that these students will need the best of what we know about literacy and youth culture. They will need engaging and meaningful strategies that expand interest, build competence, and promote a sense of agency and independence. They will need highly knowledgeable and skillful teachers, as well as comprehensive literacy programs that offer opportunities for encounters with multiple texts and forms of representation throughout the school day. And, perhaps most critically, striving readers will need teachers and school personnel interested in forming close and supportive relationships with them as a context for literacy and learning growth.

CHAPTER 3 ▮▮▮▮▮▮▮▮▮▮▮▮▮▮▮▮▮▮▮▮▮▮▮▮▮▮

Practices for Expanding Text Comprehension

As you read Chapter 3, reflect on the following questions:

- How can youths' comprehension abilities be increased while honoring their outside-of-school literacies, interests, and competencies?
- How can the four dimensions of text comprehension guide practices for learning in the disciplines?
- What are the roles of the personal and social dimensions for promoting text comprehension?
- How can youth be taught to think in deeper and more complex ways about text?
- What instructional practices challenge students to be responsible for their own text processing and comprehension?
- What are the implications of the Common Core State Standards for teaching reading comprehension?

When 15-year-old Aurora reads aloud to her father an article from a Spanish-language newspaper online about their favorite soccer team in Mexico, then discusses the implications for postseason play, she is demonstrating her ability to comprehend. When Hillary texts her friend Maya with a terse description of a movie she saw over the weekend and her personal reactions to it, she is demonstrating her ability to comprehend. When Fareed downloads a "cheat sheet" of shortcuts and consults it for strategies for a popular computer game, World of Warcraft, he is demonstrating his ability to comprehend. And when Tony uses an owner's manual to adjust the idle speed on his motorcycle, he, too, is demonstrating his ability to comprehend.

These examples of everyday acts of meaning making from and with text that adolescents like Aurora, Hillary, Fareed, and Tony engage in for authentic purposes speak to the resources youth take with them into disciplinary classrooms. Although the demands of academic literacy and learning are considerable, teachers have adolescents' experiences with communication, problem solving, and critical thinking to build upon (Goldman, 2012; Moje et al., 2008).

I asserted in Chapter 1, and again in relation to the discussion of diverse literacy and language learners in Chapter 2, that secondary teachers should be ever mindful of ways to capitalize on youths' outside-of-school literacies as bridges to academic, disciplinary text reading and learning. This is especially important for today's youth, who live in a world saturated by attention-competing media where conceptions of what counts as text, are continually evolving (Alvermann, 2010; Coiro, Knobel, Lankshear, & Leu, 2008; Leu et al., 2013). In this new world, we are being asked to think of text not as a mere sequence of alphabetic characters on a piece of paper or screen (Lankshear & Knobel, 2013; Perry, 2012; Street, 2009), but as "any configuration of signs that provides a potential for meaning" (Smagorinsky, 2001, p. 135). According to this definition, many things can be "read" as text, such as clothing, graffiti, architecture, sports, and new technologies (Gee, 2012). A preservice teacher put it this way: "If you are deriving a message from it, you are reading it" (Alvermann, 2002, p. 73). It's easy to see, then, how youth are routinely reading the signs in their worlds (Friere, 1987; Lankshear & Knobel, 2011).

Exploring ways of apprenticing and scaffolding youths' acts of meaning making with print and digital and other texts so as to increase academic literacy in school is the focus of this chapter. I believe it is the teacher's role to recognize how thinking, reading, and communicating are inseparable from the content of the disciplines and, therefore, must become part of the instructional practices in science, history, math, and all the other subjects (Gillis, 2014). Here is why I believe this notion is so important. A seventh grader who is knowledgeable in science also possesses excellent science literacy skills enabling him or her to read, comprehend, critically consider, write and talk about science information and concepts (Cervetti & Pearson, 2012). Even if the seventh grader developed these literacy skills on his or her own, that does not diminish the need for them to be taught in systematic and routine ways in order to make it possible for all students to become highly competent in science. It is helpful at this point to restate an assertion I made in the previous chapter: I believe *literacy* and *learning* in the content areas and disciplines are one and the same. Thus effective teachers of the disciplines cannot help but be effective teachers of processes for reading and communicating about the disciplines.

This chapter is dedicated to practices for expanding comprehension in the content areas. The practices I share emerge from my understanding of youth, as well as the principles that guide effective literacy teaching and learning. I begin with a discussion of four dimensions of text comprehension as a practice for learning in the disciplines. This is followed by descriptions and examples of several principle-based strategies that account for the multidimensional nature of text processing and promote purposeful, thoughtful, and skillful reading.

Case Study

Charles teaches 10th-grade general biology in a large consolidated high school in the Midwest. After 3 years of teaching, he has noticed that many of his students (1) generally have a difficult time understanding the textbook, (2) do not complete homework reading assignments, and (3) seem to be trying to memorize information while failing to learn to observe and think about scientific phenomena. Charles is highly interested in discovering ways to help his students become more enthusiastic about science learning and better able to deal with and benefit from textbook reading.

Midway through the first semester of the new school year, Charles has begun a 2-week unit on genetics. Within the unit, he wants to emphasize students' understanding of genetic engineering and the implications of this technology for their personal lives. In the preceding 2 months, his students studied the scientific method, the cell, and the classification of living things, including the life cycle and basic requirements of life.

To the reader: As you read and work through this chapter on comprehension strategies, think about and be prepared to generate some strategies that could help Charles accomplish his goals. Consider how the strategies described in this chapter and those generated from your own experience and imagination could be adapted to the teaching and learning of science material.

THE DIMENSIONS OF COMPREHENSION

Like most serious readers, virtually everything I choose to read, either for work or pleasure, is either readily or eventually understood. With some texts, meaning making is effortless. Others, for which I may have less developed background knowledge, require more stamina, though even with more complex text, sense making is all but guaranteed. Because comprehension is the expected outcome of reading by those of us who are experienced, active readers, we desire the same for those less skillful so that they may experience the joys and benefits of a reading life.

I recall early in my career as a literacy specialist, while serving as a clinician in a university reading center, encountering unexpected cases from time to time of individuals who had never bathed in the energies of a book, as Sven Birkerts in *The Gutenberg Elegies* (2006) terms it. For instance, one day an impeccably dressed 30-something guy knocked on my office door and said he needed advice. I'll call him Gil. When Gil began by explaining that he was the state assistant superintendent of public instruction, I immediately thought he was planning to consult me on the revision of the state's reading curriculum or its goal for improving teacher training and professional development in reading. What came next nearly propelled me out of my chair. Gil said that because of the very important position he had just been appointed to, the time had finally come to address the fact that he could not read! He went on to tell about the elaborate measures he undertook to bluff his way through college and how he relied on the writing and editing skills, as well as the confidentiality, of his secretary to survive in his current position.

And it was true; he couldn't read. On one diagnostic test, Gil failed to correctly identify all the letters of the alphabet. Nonetheless, we both rolled up our sleeves and over the next several months got to work developing his basic reading and comprehension skills. From there his rapid rate of progress hardly surprised me, given his drive, intelligence, and life knowledge. I can still see the pride and joy written on Gil's face when he read his first book from cover to cover.

I had the professional latitude at this reading center to use any approach I deemed appropriate to the needs of the students and others who came in for assistance. With Gil, I emphasized meaning making as the purpose of reading right from the start. Even as we began instruction around very basic words with familiar letter patterns, the goal was never just to decode but also to comprehend. This is because, for me, reading *is* comprehending.

And what is reading comprehension? Research and theorizing tells us that it is a complex, developmental, contextual process (Afflerbach, 2015). It is developmental in that one's ability to understand text continues to increase throughout life (Reardon et al., 2012). It is contextual in that meaning making is bounded by place, history, social interaction, and function (Gee, 2012). On the developmental side, the ever-expanding skills of reading might be thought of as an independent or autonomous set of abilities, such as the ability to decode words and to comprehend sentences and paragraphs (Vaughn et al., 2013). On the contextual side, according to Gee (1996), language "always comes fully attached to 'other stuff': to social relations, cultural models, power and politics, perspectives on experience, values and attitudes, as well as things and places in the world" (p. vii). In other words, every act of reading comprehension, as autonomous as it may seem, is "ideologically embedded," says Alvermann (2009). She goes on to capture the essence of this involved interplay between the act and ideology of reading when she says:

> Viewing literacy as ideologically embedded does not require giving up on the cognitive aspects of reading and writing, nor on the technical skills associated with the autonomous model. Rather . . . the ideological model subsumes the autonomous model and simultaneously incorporates an array of social and cultural ways of knowing that can account for seemingly absent but always present power structures. (p. 16)

In light of this complexity, it can never be assumed that once students are taught to read in elementary school, they are set for life. It is well recognized that mastering foundational skills in the early grades may be an important first step (National Institute of Child Health and Human Development, 2000; Reardon et al., 2012; Shanahan & Shanahan, 2012) but not nearly enough for a lifetime of successful comprehension. There is plenty of evidence that skills and abilities for text comprehension developed in the elementary years are not adequate for the challenges of increasingly complex text students find in middle school and beyond (Heller & Greenleaf, 2007; Kamil et al., 2008). Every new text and reading situation requires a refined application of literacy skills and abilities. This is especially true of content-area and disciplinary literacy. Findings from the NAEP (National Center for Education Statistics, 2013) reveal a very close relationship between adolescents' overall reading achievement on the NAEP reading assessment and academic achievement in school. In other words, youth who can comprehend complex prose are better students in all the subject areas as compared with their peers who struggle to understand what they read.

The ability to read increasingly complex text is considered an essential foundation for college and career readiness, according to the Common Core State Standards (CCSS). Indeed, the reading standards require deep and meaningful comprehension of fiction and nonfiction, emphasizing abilities such as (1) close, attentive reading, (2) reasoning and use of evidence, and (3) evaluating and synthesizing (Coleman & Pimentel, 2012). Reading comprehension from a CCSS perspective, then, is to emphasize analysis of text and author meaning (Calkins et al., 2012).

It should be evident by now that reading comprehension involves several overlapping dimensions, from intense analysis of language and structure to determine authors' meanings to relating prior knowledge to and personalizing interpretations to creating and deconstructing social and political intentions of text. Thus comprehension's complexity makes it difficult to define in simple terms. Nonetheless, here is my attempt to capture the multifarious nature of reading comprehension that builds on the various perspectives and theories just described:

> Comprehension of print and other forms of text is a *meaning-making* and *meaning-using* process. Meaning is constructed through the interaction of the learner (in all of her or his complexities) and the text (in all of its complexity and in all of its various forms of representation) within sociocultural contexts. Meaning is used in direct relation to the level of interest in the learner and the level of functionality of the learning. The degree of interaction and use varies depending upon factors such as (1) the learner's culture, funds of knowledge, strategies, engagement, interests, identity, and agency; (2) the considerateness and type of text; and (3) the classroom environment, instructional strategies, and meaningfulness of the comprehension experiences.

Notice in this definition that our overall goal as comprehenders is to use literate practices to make sense of and to act on our worlds. Like all good thinkers, your ability to make meaningful interpretations of this book and use what you learn from it is directly related to:

- How much you already know about the topic of content and disciplinary literacy for adolescents.
- How much experience you have with the organization and discourse of text-book prose.
- How interested and engaged you are in reading this book.
- What strategies you employ for studying and retaining the ideas and information.
- The extent to which comprehension of the ideas and information reinforce a positive literate and professional identity.
- The extent to which comprehension of the ideas and information lead to a greater sense of agency.
- How the instructor uses the book, structures the literacy context, and provides classroom experiences for learning the concepts and strategies in the book.
- How well I as the author have been considerate of you, the reader, in structuring and communicating my message.

The various factors inherent in acts of meaning making and meaning using can be framed around what I consider to be four critical, interrelated dimensions: *cognitive, textual, personal,* and *social.*

The Cognitive Dimension

Comprehension as a cognitive process is concerned with the skills, strategies, and background knowledge of the reader. All of a youth's cognitive abilities must come into play when he or she is trying to understand such varied texts as a chapter on the bicameral nature of the U.S. legislature in a government textbook, an informational book in biology about prey–predator relationships, or an explanation of a balance sheet on a small-business website.

We have known for some time that active readers and learners use their prior knowledge as they interact with text to enhance comprehension (Afflerbach, 1986; Chiesi et al., 1979). Youth who have been the beneficiaries of rich and varied funds of knowledge are likely to possess well-developed knowledge structures or schemas that allow them to comprehend texts at deep levels (Kintsch, 1998; Ozuru, Dempsey, & McNamara, 2009; Tarchi, 2010).

To demonstrate the potency of relevant prior knowledge for successful reading comprehension, complete the reading activity in Figure 3.1.

We also know that in order to construct and use meaning, students must possess a repertoire of strategies (Lei, Rhinehart, Howard, & Cho, 2010; O'Reilly &

McNamara, 2007; Ruddell & Unrau, 2004). Good comprehenders summarize and organize as they interact with text (Duke & Pearson, 2008–2009), think critically and generate new understandings (McNamara, 2004; Anderman, 2010), and are metacognitively aware (Palincsar & Brown, 1984; Klingner et al., 2011). They set purposes for reading and learning and actively monitor whether they meet them (Cera, Mancini, & Antonietti, 2013; Kintsch & Kintsch, 2005). During the meaning-making process, good comprehenders notice when something does not fit with what they already know or is unclear, then engage in appropriate strategies to clarify understanding, which might include rereading, seeking help from an expert, creating a visual aid, asking questions and searching for answers, or a host of other possible actions (Best et al., 2005; Caccamise & Snyder, 2005).

Read the following passage and be prepared to discuss the main points, the supporting details, and the relationships between the themes in the passage and other related passages you have read.

> It is highly unsettling for some to come into close contact with them. Far worse to gain control over them and to deliberately inflict pain on them. The revulsion caused by this punishment is so strong that many will not take part in it at all. Thus there exists a group of people who seem to revel in the contact and the punishment as well as the rewards associated with both. Then there is another group of people who shun the whole enterprise: contact, punishment, and rewards alike.
>
> Members of the first group share modes of talk, dress, and deportment. Members of the second group, however, are as varied as all humanity.
>
> Then there is a group of others, not previously mentioned, for the sake of whose attention all this activity is undertaken. They too harm the victims, though they do it without intention of cruelty. They simply follow their own necessities. And though they may inflict the cruelest punishment of all, sometimes—but not always—they themselves suffer as a result. (Gillet & Temple, 1986, p. 4)

Do you have any idea what this passage is about? Every time we ask our students to read it, they first try desperately to impose a sensible interpretation on the words, offer possibilities that leave them uncomfortable, and finally give up, resorting to protests that sound all too familiar to any classroom teacher: "This is too hard." Most complain that this reading exercise is unfair because the passage has too many unclear referents or is without a title, which makes it impossible to understand with any certainty. The typical guesses we get vary widely from *parents and children, concentration camps, corporal punishment,* and *teachers and students.*

This passage helps us simulate for you the essential nature of schema or relevant prior knowledge for understanding text. By the way, the title is "Fishing Worms." Does that help? Go back and reread it now, and notice as you read how all the ideas seem to fit together, how meaning jumps automatically into consciousness. The title acts as an organizer, a unifying theme, and brings to mind your schema, or prior experiences, memories, and knowledge, related to fishing and worms.

FIGURE 3.1. Prior knowledge activity.

Cognition is thinking, and the CCSS and new scholarship related to disciplinary literacy foreground the goal of helping students think like scientists when they read science texts, think like historians when they read history texts, think like mathematicians when they read math texts, and so on with all the disciplines (Brozo, Moorman, Meyer, & Stewart, 2013; Goldman, 2012; Lee & Spratley, 2010).

Insiders within the disciplines have documented the cognitive input required for thinking and reasoning about disciplinary texts. For example, it has been shown that mathematical reading and thinking involves processes such as asking contextually relevant questions, developing a framework for the details, paying attention to the precise use of words and sentences, reading actively by organizing details and asking questions (e.g., Why is this result true? Can I accept this point without understanding the details of why it is true? Will my understanding of the whole suffer from not understanding why the point is true?), reading word and numerical explanations deliberately and repetitively, and taking notes to paraphrase ideas and explanations (Bass, 2006; Silverman & Thompson, 2008). Scientists read by using representations and models to analyze situations and solve problems, determining important information in multiple forms of text, and expressing key relationships among quantified variables (Fang & Wei, 2010). Historians, on the other hand, need to organize information from multiple sources, to determine the veracity of sources and assertions, to contextualize events under consideration in the economic, cultural, technological, and political circumstances of the time, and to evaluate alternative accounts of historical events (Schleppegrell et al., 2008).

Finally, I want to emphasize once more that cognition for reading, as with all dimensions of comprehension, does not occur in a vacuum (McCrudden & Schraw, 2007; Rouet & Britt, 2011). The reading most of us do in our daily lives is purposeful and goal based (White, Chen & Forsyth, 2010). Thus reading as a cognitive skill involves a specific set of processes that competent readers make use of when engaging with texts for particular purposes and to achieve their goals. Purposes and goals drive readers' decisions to engage with texts and to compare and integrate information across multiple texts (Britt & Rouet, 2012).

The implications from current research for developing cognition for comprehension are many. Not only should teachers have a thorough understanding of their discipline and be capable of deep and meaningful thinking about text, but they should also possess the skills to make the processes involved in maximizing meaning making and meaning using obvious for students (Coiro, 2011; Lapp, Fisher, & Grant, 2008; Topping & Ferguson, 2005). Later in this chapter, I describe and exemplify comprehension strategies that foster these thinking skills.

The Textual Dimension

The textual dimension of comprehension requires us to consider how the structure and properties of prose and other texts interact with and stimulate a reader's

capacity for constructing and using meaning. As noted, textual aspects of comprehension, as well as the other dimensions, are linked together and cannot be analyzed in isolation from one another. This is particularly true of textual dimensions,
because a text, it is theorized, has little inherent meaning but is given meaning
by a reader, listener, or interpreter (Smagorinsky, 2001). In other words, a person's
cognition and motivation, as well as contextual and relational factors, influence
the degree to which a text is comprehensible. Stated another way, a text is not difficult or easy but rather difficult or easy relative to a person's abilities, enthusiasm,
perseverance, level of scaffolding from an expert, and mediation from a teacher
(Moje, 2011).

At the same time, a text is not a featureless collection of letters, words, and
punctuation. The way it is written, as well as other lexical and formatting characteristics, can have a significant effect on comprehension (Crossley, McCarthy, Louwerse, & McNamara, 2007; Graesser, McNamara, & Kulikowich, 2011), especially
for those readers who have underdeveloped relevant prior knowledge (Barth, Tolar,
Fletcher, & Francis, 2014; Best et al., 2005). For example, an eighth grader may
have limited knowledge of science facts and concepts but may achieve a moderate degree of success with the class textbook if the author included structures and
features designed to support novice readers of science. These might include helpful
microstructure features that signal the relationships between and among information and ideas, such as connectives, conjunctions, pronouns, and overlapping sentences (Graesser, McNamara, Louwerse, & Cai, 2004; Puranik, Lombardino, &
Altmann, 2008), as well as *macrostructure* features that tie the overall text together,
such as titles and subheadings, advance organizers, outlines, summaries, and logical patterns of organization (Heuboeck, 2009; Louwerse & Graesser, 2006; van
Dijk, 2007). Figure 3.2 provides a list of additional textual characteristics that are
"considerate" of intended audiences and that, consequently, make for more readable
prose.

Although teachers can't be expected to rewrite all the texts students are
expected to read, they can familiarize adolescent readers with texts' organizational
structures and other features that can be used to improve comprehension (Akhondi,
Malayeri, & Samad, 2011; Kendeou & van den Broek, 2007). Middle and high
school students can also be shown how to make logical connections through inferencing when navigating text that lacks cohesion or a well-organized format. Ways
of helping students to capitalize on these text features and to make inferences are
presented later in this chapter.

Adding to the challenges posed by complex and inconsiderate text is the need
for adolescents to be sensitized to disciplinary text genres (Moje, 2011). Text in
the social sciences, science, and math present readers with unique structures and
conventions (Moje & Speyer, 2008; Wallace & Clark, 2005). These features can
be made explicit for students in disciplinary classrooms in order to improve reading
ability and expand content knowledge (Lee & Spratley, 2010). Figure 3.3 describes

the general characteristics of common text genres found in social studies and science.

Too many students read and think about text in just one way. For instance, it would be silly to read fiction and ask oneself what is the author's source for choosing a hero who is named Kurt. On the other hand, it would be wrong to read nonfiction and not ask questions about the author's assertions and ideas. Making students aware of the characteristics, genres, and style of disciplinary text will help them read more like a disciplinary insider and thus develop practices for comprehension appropriate to language and literature, science, social studies, math, and the other content domains.

We have a good understanding of the features that make a text complex and relatively *inconsiderate* (Fang & Pace, 2013):

- High frequency of discipline-specific vocabulary.
- Lack of cohesive elements at the micro and macro levels.
- Frequent use of figurative language.
- Packing many disciplinary vocabulary terms into clauses, sentences, and paragraphs.
- Inclusion of many long sentences strung together with multiple clauses.

We also know that **considerate** text is written and formatted in ways to help intended readers follow the ideas easily (Kumpf, 2000). Considerate text is achieved when authors (Alexander & Jetton, 2000):

- Effectively communicate their purpose or aim.
- Consider the audience for their text and provide sufficient background information, a judicious use of well-defined (in context and with glossaries) technical words, and referents for any figurative or literary allusions (e.g., myths).
- Have a focus and share that focus with the readers via an overall organization or macrostructure (e.g., headings, subheadings, main ideas that are linked to each other, etc.).
- Have a focus and share that with the readers through a microstructure that provides development via examples, anecdotes, supporting details, explanations, and quotations from primary sources.
- Employ clear use of graphic elements such as tables, charts, and graphic organizers.
- Use a style of writing that is clear and explicit.

If authors and editors of school-based texts fail to produce text that is considerate of the reader, then teachers and curriculum directors need to choose texts and supporting readings that are appropriately considerate of the target readers. For complex text, teachers need to learn to recognize those elements that make the text complex and plan activities to help students deal with the complexity, such as preteaching vocabulary, paraphrasing figurative language, and analyzing intricate sentences to get at the meaning.

FIGURE 3.2. Characteristics of considerate text.

Social Sciences

Characteristics

- Knowledge making begins with questions that build on previous research. Evidence comes from observation.
- Use of methods and instruments to observe.
- Validity achieved by adequate evidence and sound reasoning about the evidence.

Common Genres

- Reports of original research (using research report format used in sciences).
- Literature reviews.
- Summaries.
- Case studies.
- Proposals.
- Position papers.
- Critiques.

Styles

- The detached persona: "This study investigates" rather than "In this study I will investigate."
- Use of passive voice.
- Prevalent use of jargon.
- Use of acronyms and initialisms.
- Unbiased and inclusive language: gender-neutral references, for example.

Sciences

Characteristics

- Knowledge making begins with questions that, once answered, can be answered similarly by future studies using the same methods.
- Hypotheses are based on outside sources.
- Hypotheses are tested following the scientific method.
- Evidence comes from observation that is repeatable.
- Validity is achieved by adequate repeatable evidence and sound reasoning about the evidence.

Common Genres

- Reports of original research (using sections such as abstract, introduction, experimental materials and methods, results, discussion).
- Summaries.
- Proposals.
- Position papers.
- Journal article critiques.

Style

- The detached persona: "This study investigates" rather than "In this study I will investigate."
- Use of passive voice.
- Prevalent use of jargon.
- Use of acronyms and initialisms.
- Unbiased and inclusive language: gender-neutral references, for example.

FIGURE 3.3. Common disciplinary text features.

Humanities

Characteristics

- Knowledge can come from the self and the work or from what others have written or said.
- Evidence for an assertion or thesis comes from the work or text.
- Validity or proof comes from the persuasive power of the examples or textual evidence.

Common Genres

- Interpretation of a work.
- Development of a new theory for interpretation.
- Application of a theory to a new work.
- Critical analysis of an article.
- Research paper.
- Proposals.
- Position paper.

Style

- Use of "I."
- Use of active voice.
- Use of jargon or specialized language in academic work.
- Use of informal vocabulary if appropriate for rhetorical situation.
- Use of colorful vocabulary.

Mathematics

Characteristics

- Arguments flow in a linear order from beginning to end.
- Blocks of explicitly typeset mathematics separate from the surrounding text.
- Inclusion of numerous variables and assumptions.
- Numerous definitions, theorems, and proofs.
- Combinations of words, formulas, and equations.
- Symbolic grammar.

Common Genres

- Research papers.
- Expository or survey articles.
- Book and paper reviews.
- Laboratory reports.
- Personal journals.
- Solutions to problems.

Style

- The detached persona: "This study investigates" rather than "In this study I will investigate."
- Use of active voice.
- Prevalent use of jargon.
- Use of acronyms and initialisms.
- Unbiased and inclusive language: gender-neutral references, for example.

FIGURE 3.3. *(continued)*

Personal Dimension

Issues of engagement, identity, agency, and goals constitute the personal dimension of comprehension. As you learned in reading Chapters 1 and 2, these aspects of literacy are highly complex, which might explain why they are so often overlooked in the instructional planning of many teachers of youth. Ignoring the personal dimension when setting expectations for reading with adolescent learners often leads to disappointment and frustration for both teacher and students. This is because individual personal attitudes play a vital role in the reading, learning, and remembering process, as researchers have confirmed (Anderman & Wolters, 2006; Petscher, 2010).

Consider the case of Keshawn, an African American ninth grader and member of Mary Kay's history class. Bright and energetic, he possessed adequate reading skill to comprehend the information and concepts in the textbook but lacked the will or desire to read it. Mary Kay was unsure how to work with Keshawn and tended to blame his low test grades on laziness. After observing the class and discussing her concern with Mary Kay, we helped her develop motivational readiness activities for upcoming chapters, demonstrated how alternative texts by and about African American historical figures could be incorporated into lessons, and explored ways of expanding Keshawn's choices for reading and responding to the content. These strategies, along with Mary Kay's efforts to create closer ties with Keshawn to help her better understand his personal and career goals, brought about a significant improvement in his performance.

Students like Keshawn need experiences in content classrooms that turn interest into engagement (Taboada, Tonks, Wigfield, & Guthrie, 2009) and cultivate their desires for autonomy and control (Behrman, 2003; Van Ryzin, Gravely, & Roseth, 2009). Offering students choices of texts and options for responding to them encourages investment in their own learning, which has been shown to improve comprehension (Ainley, Hidi, & Berndorff, 2002; Cervetti, Bravo, Hiebert, Pearson, & Jaynes, 2009). Improving comprehension of text can, in turn, serve as a conduit for increasing students' agency. In learning environments in which youths' cognitive and personal learning needs are supported, they are more likely to persevere with academic texts and expend the energy to understand them (Brozo, 2009; Greenleaf & Hinchman, 2009).

In addition to helping students increase their independence and control over the meaning-making process, teachers mindful of the importance of the personal dimension will also find ways of building youths' literate identities (International Reading Association, 2012). I made clear in Chapter 1 that adolescents' sense of themselves as readers is bound up in their identities in and out of school. The more that content teachers do to make text engaging and comprehension possible for students, the more confident they become in their identities as capable readers and meaning makers (Alvermann, 2010; Guthrie, 2008). This confidence then translates into greater effort to understand text and apply new knowledge in meaningful ways.

The Social Dimension

This dimension takes into account the fact that making, extracting, and using meaning is a social process. Social processes fashion social languages, according to Gee (2001), that are "used to enact, recognize, and negotiate different socially situated identities and to carry out different socially situated activities" (p. 413). From this point of view, an individual's meaning making is understandable only when it is viewed in relation to others (Knoester, 2010). For instance, when Monica, a tenth grader, confides in her English journal that her boyfriend has been unfaithful, she might write: "I'm feeling really angry today because Jack, my boyfriend, or should I say my ex-boyfriend, is seeing someone else." After school, on the walk home with her best friend, Tara, Monica tells her: "I found out today that Jack's goin' out with Kristi. That scumbag is dead!" For her English teacher, Monica uses socially agreed-upon discourse conventions; while talking with her friend away from school space, she uses another culturally distinctive language form that defines herself and her friend as socially intimate partners.

To be a meaning maker, then, is to be part of a social context. Even when you curl up with a book in the "private" act of reading, you are not alone—you are interacting with an author who holds other ideas, points of view, styles of expression. In this way, writers are literally "speaking" to you through the words and pictures of a text that provides a potential for shared and unique meanings to be realized by you and other readers (Connell, 2008; Smagorinksy, 2001). Adolescent learners' construction and use of meaning for any given text depends on other meanings acquired through interaction in the various discourse communities they transect and the funds of knowledge upon which they can draw (Martínez-Roldán & Fránquiz, 2009). It has been demonstrated that acts of meaning making and meaning using increase when teachers exploit the social world of the classroom and socially derived texts from their students (Alvermann & Moje, 2013).

The instructional implications of the social nature of text comprehension are many and varied. On a general level, youth in disciplinary classrooms should be encouraged to build shared meanings of information and concepts through numerous formal and informal interactions with peers and teachers. The meanings of texts can be analyzed through various cultural lenses for their universality, bias, and relevance. Within a community of learners, teachers can apprentice youth in the practices of content literacy through modeling, reciprocal teaching, and a host of other collaborative experiences. On a practical level, the classroom itself should be arranged to encourage social interaction among the teacher and student meaning makers. Instead of organizing desks in rows, for instance, with the lines of communication moving from the teacher to individual students, we recommend a more flexible seating arrangement and flexible grouping patterns that encourage student–student dialoguing and problem solving. In the next section, I offer more detailed suggestions for promoting meaningful comprehension of classroom texts within dynamic social contexts.

MULTIDIMENSIONAL APPROACHES TO DEVELOPING TEXT COMPREHENSION

Teachers who are mindful of the complex and overlapping network of obvious and sometimes not so obvious factors at play in the meaning-making process are better able to support their students' comprehension of content texts (Braunger, Donahue, Evans, & Galguera, 2005). Although the strategies shared here have been aligned with one particular dimension of comprehension, in the hands of the knowledge-able and responsive teachers spotlighted in the vignettes, you will see how they can be expanded to account for the multidimensional nature of text comprehension in order to meet the needs of all learners.

Cognitive Dimension Strategies

Developing a Language of Process about Text

Disciplinary teachers need to create multiple opportunities for students to eavesdrop on their thinking while negotiating text, so they can model the process of constructing and extracting meaning. Too often classroom text talk remains focused on the content, while rarely including conversation about the processes involved in understanding the content. For example, a teacher might state a main idea for a paragraph or passage but not take that next step and explain to her or his students how she or he determined the main idea. Failure to apprentice youth in the ways of thinking about text that lead to comprehension leaves them without the cognitive tools to construct and apply meaning independently. On the other hand, by ensuring that classroom discussion about text always includes process comments, in addition to content statements, teachers will be providing students a language for describing *how* they're thinking (Kymes, 2004; Wilhelm, 2001) to go along with the language they use to describe *what* they're thinking. In this way, students not only increase their knowledge of disciplinary content but also increase their abilities to learn from text. See Figure 3.4 for a description and examples of common content statements and process comments.

Manolo scaffolds his sixth-grade science students' thinking about text by teaching them to divide their mental focus into both processing activities and comprehension-monitoring activities. He does this through a model–elicit teaching approach.

A *language of process* refers to the labels we use to describe thinking processes while constructing meaning from text. Content statements, on the other hand, are those that are made about specific information and ideas in a text. To illustrate, look at the examples below of process comments and content statements. You will notice that content statements derive directly from the words and ideas in the text, whereas process statements are a reflection of metacognitive thinking about these words and ideas.

Making and Checking Predictions

Content Statement

"Okay, it says here 'Where Have All the Nurses Gone?' so I think the author is going to explain in this next section why the number of nurses is declining."

Process Comments

"What I'm doing now is **predicting** what the text is going to be about based on the title and subheading. As I read further, I can check to see if my predictions are correct or need to be changed. This will help me concentrate more closely on the information."

Using Contextual Strategies for Word Learning

Content Statement

"It says here that the Romans had *agrarian* laws giving all citizens equal shares of land . . . so *agrarian* probably refers to land or agriculture."

Process Comments

"See how I'm using the **context clues** right within this sentence . . . the words before and after *agrarian* . . . to figure out what *agrarian* means. When you're trying to figure out the meaning of a word, you can do the same thing."

Imaging

Content Statement

"I can just picture this guy, Ian, trapped in a mine shaft, with no light, and not knowing which way to turn."

Process Comments

"By creating an **image** in my mind of the events of the story, I can almost see them happening, and the story becomes more understandable. Do this when you read; try to create a little movie scene in your mind of the characters and scenes and action."

Linking Prior Knowledge to Text

Content Statement

"They're really in trouble now, aren't they? See, their truck broke down on the way to California. That reminds me of the time I was driving to Michigan in the middle of the winter and my car overheated on this back road in the middle of nowhere . . ."

(continued)

FIGURE 3.4. A language of process.

Process Comments

"I'm thinking about my **prior knowledge,** something from my past, an experience that I can relate to the text so I can understand it better. As you try to make sense of text, see if you can't think about what you already know because you've read about it, seen it, or actually had a similar experience. When you do this, text doesn't seem so separate from your own life, and you'll find it easier to comprehend."

Summarizing and Paraphrasing

Content Statement

"What the author is getting at on this page is that Native Americans made many positive contributions in the United States' effort to defeat the Germans in World War II."

Process Comments

"Do you see how I've **created a summary**? I've taken all of these positive words the author used in reference to Native Americans, like *helped* in the first paragraph, *served honorably and bravely* in the next one, and *valuable asset* in the last paragraph and grouped them together around "important roles." That's how I **make a summary,** I look for things that are emphasized with bold print or italics, or ideas that are repeated. In this case these positive terms are repeated. Then I come up with a straightforward, general statement without including all the details and examples."

Verbalizing Points of Confusion and Demonstrating Fix-Up Strategies

Content Statement

"The text says that the sun is actually slightly closer to the earth during the winter than it is during the summer. So when the sun is closer to the earth it's colder, and when it's farther away, it's warmer on earth."

Process Comments

"This is very confusing to me . . . is it confusing to you, too? Doesn't it make more sense to think about it just the opposite way? What I'm doing now is **talking about the stuff that's confusing,** or if I were reading this alone I'd be **thinking about how this makes me confused**. When I do this, I can either work through the confusion or do something else to **fix the problem I'm having with comprehension**. One thing I can do is reread this section, or I can read further to get more explanation. I might also look at the illustrations more closely or even ask a friend or look through another book for clarification."

FIGURE 3.4. *(continued)*

First, he models a way of thinking about text; then he elicits the same thinking behaviors from his students. By repeatedly demonstrating and gathering demonstrations of certain comprehension processes, Manolo is able to foster understanding of science material while elevating his class to higher levels of metacognitive awareness.

In the following excerpt, Manolo and his students are engaged in a discussion about lightning from a chapter in the class textbook. He and his students are taking turns commenting about the information in the chapter *and* using a language of process to label how they are monitoring their understanding of the material. Students are sitting in clusters of four around small tables with their books open to the chapter on lightning. In a scaffolded think-aloud instructional context (Pol, Volman, & Beishuizen, 2010), Manolo makes both a content statement and a process comment after reading the first short paragraph.

Content Statement

"Okay, this chapter starts out by saying that up until very recently we haven't known much about lightning, but now things are changing. I'd guess that we'll probably read about the technology we're using to figure out how lightning occurs."

Process Comment

"You see how I'm using the information to make a prediction about what the author will say next about lightning. I may be wrong, but by making a prediction and then checking to see if I'm right, I'll pay closer attention to the information and ideas. Do you see what I mean? Okay, at your tables talk about how you can make and check a prediction for the next couple of paragraphs, and I'll call on someone to talk us through how you did it."

Later in the chapter, Manolo modeled another important comprehension-monitoring strategy, gave it a process label, and elicited similar verbalizing of cognitive behavior from his students.

Content Statement

" . . . this bit about how it's a folkway to seek shelter under trees during a thunderstorm is something I found out when I was playing golf last summer. I was with a couple of buddies and when it started to rain we ran for cover in this stand of tall oak trees. We were all huddled around a tree when all of a sudden there was a really loud boom, and just 50 feet away or so lightning had struck a tree and a giant branch crashed to the ground."

Process Comment

"By linking textual information to prior experiences I've had, I'm able to make more sense of this . . . because I see how it fits with real life. You can do the same thing when you read, even if your experiences aren't exactly the same as what the author is describing. After you read the next short section on page 103, see if anyone in your group can come up with a way of relating it to prior experience or something you already know about the topic."

Nicola volunteered to share content statements and process comments related to prior knowledge she and her group generated for the next section in their chapter.

Content Statement

"It says here that lightning strikes between positive and negative particles in cumulonimbus clouds."

Process Comment

"We related this to something we learned last year about magnets. Opposite charges attract, just like how lightning bolts go from one charged particle to the opposite charged particle. It made it easier for us to see how lightning happens when we think about it this way."

When the class finished the entire section on lightning, Manolo modeled a third important cognitive process, summarizing.

Content Statement

"Overall, it's talking about how technology is helping us to better understand lightning so that we can figure out how to protect ourselves from it."

Process Comment

"Okay, to summarize what we've just read, the first thing is, I'm going over it and skimming through the section again so I can remember where I saw the important things. The important information is highlighted for us in bold print and italics. Be sure to look for these signals from authors of what's important. If it isn't in italics or bold print, it might be repeated words or phrases or even using the words *important, critical, necessary,* and like that. Okay, so then I thought of how the important things fit together, and I came up with technology and safety because it's mentioning all these high-tech ways we're learning about lightning and it's also giving examples of poor and wise decisions when there's a lightning storm."

Manolo then asked his students to continue working with the groups at their tables and to find either an information book of their choosing from among those he had brought into the classroom or a website that addressed the topic of weather and lightning. With this material, students were to prepare a summary, and a spokesperson from the group was to share the summary with the class, along with an explanation of the thinking processes involved in generating it.

Notice how this approach to teaching comprehension of text brings into play virtually all the dimensions we discussed earlier. The cognitive dimension is accounted for by modeling and eliciting thinking processes and metacognition while making meaning of the material on lightning. The textual dimension is foregrounded by drawing students' attention to text features that signal important information in the development of their summaries. The personal dimension is taken into account when Manolo gives his students choices for identifying texts related to the topic of study for creating summaries. And, finally, the social dimension is embodied in the interactions Manolo has with his class during modeling and eliciting of meaning-making processes, as well as the student–student interaction in their groups.

Generating Understandings of Text

Modeling and eliciting comprehension processes, as we have stated, is a great way to help youth develop thinking strategies they can use on their own with virtually any text. Another way to promote independence is to encourage adolescents to become generative readers and learners. Too often students are in passive roles in secondary classrooms, responding only to the teacher's or the text's prompts. Yet we know that students learn best when they are actively engaged in meaning-constructing processes. Generative learning theory (Wittrock, 1990) holds that students learn best when they are taught how to create or generate their own learning prompts and demonstrations (Pressley, 2000; Nist & Simpson, 2000).

Disciplinary teachers can increase engagement and promote long-term recall of newly learned information and ideas by teaching students how to generate their own comprehension prompts and aids. Through scaffolding and guided practice, students can learn to transform any text- or teacher-provided prompt they normally receive into a generative learning aid (see Figure 3.5).

Snikta has taught her 11th-grade keyboarding students to become generative learners by insisting they not wait for questions and other prompts from her but create them on their own to challenge themselves and their peers. In Snikta's class, students learn keyboarding with word processing and other text formatting programs. She uses a textbook, additional supporting material and activities online, and her own questions and directives as examples of prompts, then guides her class in the development of their own prompts. For example, students encounter a series of requests online requiring the application of keyboarding and word processing techniques to fulfill, such as *Demonstrate as many ways as you can to frame or box text* and *Reproduce this paragraph, then edit it so that it matches the original.* Students are asked to create similar prompts and then post them with their names attached on the class blackboard site so that everyone can access them. As individual students complete the requested tasks, they check the site again for the suggested response

If the text or teacher provides . . .	Then the learner should be taught to . . .
Headings and subheadings	Compose headings and subheadings
Titles	Compose titles
Highlighted words or phrases	Highlight important words and phrases
Questions	Develop questions
Objectives	Write objectives
Summaries	Produce oral and/or written Summaries
Marginal gloss	Create marginal gloss
Analogies	Give analogies
Examples	Provide examples
Graphs and tables	Prepare graphs and tables
Maps	Draw maps
Problems to be solved	Create problems to be solved
Graphic overviews	Make graphic overviews

FIGURE 3.5. Generative text comprehension prompts and aids.

supplied by the author of the prompt. Where there are significant discrepancies, students send text messages to one another to reconcile them. In this way, Snikta is able to combine regular and meaningful keyboarding practice with generative thinking activities.

In another example, Snikta projects from the computer screen a new section from the textbook that has been scanned with the headings and subheadings deleted. She goes over the section as students follow along from their terminals. Next, working with a partner, students type in what they believe to be appropriate headings and subheadings. Snikta then supplies the author's headings and subheadings, and these are compared and contrasted with those generated by the class. A similar approach is used when generating summaries, graphic overviews, and other comprehension aids.

Not only do Snikta's teaching practices develop students' cognition for text comprehension, but they improve meaning-construction and extracting abilities by accounting for the other dimensions of comprehension as well. Her approach to generative learning includes students working together while focusing on and generating critical text features. These activities are accomplished within an engaging and supportive classroom context. It doesn't surprise me, therefore, that Snikta reports that, since she adopted these generative strategies, her students have become more effective independent comprehenders of text information and ideas. She has also heard from colleagues that her students are applying the generative thinking strategies learned in the keyboarding class to their other disciplinary subjects.

Processing Text at Different Levels of Understanding

One important way you can encourage your students to think deeply and meaningfully about disciplinary texts is through a strategy that sensitizes them to the fact that comprehension is more than understanding just the surface or verbatim message of the author. Text comprehension also involves inferencing, application, and other critical cognitive abilities that create meanings beyond the directly stated words.

Students can be shown that comprehension falls along a continuum that is text-based at one end and reader-based at the other (see Figure 3.6). Text-based processing is literal-level comprehension, or, in the kid-friendly parlance of cognitive researchers Raphael and Pearson (1985), *right-there* thinking. Right-there thinking means the information and ideas can be found nearly word-for-word in the text. As we progress along the continuum, we enter a realm of comprehension that relies increasingly on the inferencing abilities of the meaning maker. Raphael and Pearson refer to this type of text processing as *author and me*. In other words, the author's words are combined with the ideas of the person processing the text to create interpretations, generalizations, and other implied understandings. Finally, at the other end of the comprehension continuum is a form of thinking that is far removed from a dependency on individual printed or spoken words. This kind of processing, known as *on my own* thinking (Raphael & Pearson, 1985), requires that learners possess relevant prior knowledge for the topic sufficient to create sophisticated understandings based on minimal print cues.

To experience comprehension along this continuum, complete the activity in Figure 3.7.

The ultimate goal of teaching levels of understanding is to move adolescent learners further down the comprehension continuum beyond text-based processing by sensitizing them to the idea that there are various ways of thinking about a text. The classroom description that follows demonstrates how a science teacher was able to help her students recognize that effective comprehension occurs when they are able to move flexibly from text-based to reader-based processing.

Beth, an eighth-grade science teacher, exploits the social dimension of comprehension by allowing her students to work in cooperative groups throughout the school year with nearly every topic she and her class explore. Students in this class develop a deeper understanding of science content through interactions with their peers by speaking, listening, reading, and writing. All students are provided greater

FIGURE 3.6. Comprehension continuum.

To provide you with firsthand experience identifying the different levels of processing, read the following short passage, then read the questions and answers that follow it and write in the space next to each one the type of thinking required for each (*right there*, *author and me*, *on my own*). The experience will give you a much better grasp of the processing requirements placed on students in a typical text comprehension exercise.

The Story of Buck Billings

"Buck" Billings left Teddy's Rough Riders the very day peace was signed with the Spanish. There were wild stories about gold in the Klondike, and he couldn't wait to claim his stake. In the port of Havana he planned to pick up a boat to Tampa, then head north by train. After 3 days' trek through mosquito-infested swamps, he found that all the boats were packed with soldiers and civilians leaving for the States. He hopped aboard a ship bound for Venezuela. From there he found passage on a banana boat heading for South Carolina. The boat was turned back by a hurricane and forced to dock in Santiago Harbor. On a small sailing vessel he was finally able to reach the southern coast of Florida. He walked for 2 days to a train depot. After several weeks, he made it through the southern plains and eventually arrived in Denver, the town of his birth. Since it was already November, he moved back into his Aunt Dolly's boarding house, where he planned to stay for the next 4 months. During that winter, however, his yellow fever returned, and he succumbed to it on the first day of the new year.

Questions and Answers

1. Why was the boat forced to turn back? (Because of a hurricane) _____
2. Where is Aunt Dolly's boarding house? (Denver) _____
3. Where is the Klondike? (In Alaska) _____
4. Where was Buck's ship forced to dock after the hurricane? (In Santiago Harbor) _____
5. If Buck intended to head back to the States, why did he take a boat to Venezuela? (Because all the boats heading for the States were packed, and he thought he could get back to the States from Venezuela) _____
6. Where did Buck get yellow fever? (Cuba) _____
7. What was the boat carrying that was heading for South Carolina? (Bananas) _____
8. Did Buck make it to the coast of South Carolina? (No, the boat was forced back by a storm.) _____
9. Where was Buck the day peace was signed with the Spanish? (Cuba) _____
10. Who is Teddy? (Teddy Roosevelt) _____

Explanation

Think about how you categorized these questions and answers as you read our categorization and rationales. We placed questions 1 and 4 in the *right there* category because these questions cue the reader to the answers with words taken directly from the relevant sentence in the text.

Questions 2, 5, 7, and 8 we identified as *author and me* questions. Question 2 requires the reader to combine ideas from two sentences—the one stating that Buck arrived in Denver and the next one stating that Buck moved back with his aunt. The inference is that Buck is from Denver and has lived with his aunt before. To answer question 5 also requires some inferential reasoning. Buck was unable to go directly north to the States because all the ships were filled. By heading south first, he hoped to get

FIGURE 3.7. Comprehension continuum activity.

there from Venezuela by avoiding Cuba altogether. Unfortunately, he found himself back in Cuba anyway. Question 7 asks the reader to make a low-level inference that connects the words in the question "What was the boat carrying?" to the sentence in the text that refers to the boat heading for South Carolina as a "banana boat." To answer question 8, the reader must combine information from two sentences—one stating that Buck was on a boat bound for South Carolina and the next one stating that the boat was forced to dock in Santiago Harbor. To answer "no" to this question requires more inferencing than may initially meet the eye. Notice that the reader must realize that Santiago Harbor is not in South Carolina, and because no other mention of South Carolina is made in the passage, it can be assumed that Buck never arrived there.

We grouped questions 3, 6, 9, and 10 in the *on my own* category. Certainly, to answer question 3, the reader must already know the geographical location of the Klondike. The text provides no clue. If the reader also realizes that peace with the Spanish over Cuba was signed at around the turn of the century, this knowledge could reinforce the time frame for the Alaskan gold rush. To know that Buck probably contracted yellow fever in Cuba (question 6) means that the reader has prior knowledge that yellow fever is a tropical disease and that many soldiers suffered and died from it as a result of their experiences in the war with Spain over Cuba. To answer question 9, the reader must integrate several bits of textual information with a great deal of prior knowledge. The reader must possess knowledge about the Rough Riders and Teddy Roosevelt and know that they fought the Spanish in Cuba. Question 10 requires prior knowledge related to question 9; certainly, the reader must know that it was Teddy Roosevelt who commanded the Rough Riders.

FIGURE 3.7. (*continued*)

opportunities to articulate and reinterpret text concepts and vocabulary, raise questions, discuss answers, and become more active class members.

The topic the class was considering was "What Makes Ice Ages?" Beth first asked students to form into their study reading groups, three to a group. Her students were used to many different grouping arrangements that allowed them to move in and out of groups, interacting with different students, depending on the purpose of the group. For instance, two other common grouping patterns in Beth's classroom were interest groups and research groups. Beth briefly rehearsed the "Rules for Group Membership," which students had in their notes and which were also written in bold letters on the side wall bulletin board.

- Each member must be strongly committed to doing the work and carrying out his or her specific role within the group.
- Each member should understand and follow the directions for completing assigned work.
- Each member should respect other members' input.
- A member who disagrees with another member should defend his or her own point of view, giving specific reasons based on the text or on personal experience.

- No member should dominate or withdraw; every member should add something to the discussion.
- Each member should be positive and encourage other members.

Beth then introduced the idea of levels of processing text using PowerPoint slides to focus the discussion. She discussed with the students how becoming more sensitive to *right there, author and me,* and *on my own* thinking can improve their ability to get more out of their textbook reading. She explained each of the levels of thinking and provided a handout with the labels and explanations. Beth asked students to open their science textbooks to the beginning of the section on ice ages. Using the computer projector, she presented a series of questions, accompanied by answers, covering the first page of this section. In their groups, students discussed among themselves what level of processing was required to answer each question. Afterward, students shared their responses and rationales with the whole class. Beth allowed students to debate their answers, providing support, feedback, and demonstrations of her own processing-level designations for her answers.

In the next phase, she assigned responsibilities to each of the three group members. Beth asked each student in the groups to generate questions with answers for one of the three levels of thinking. The groups then went over their questions, helping each other focus on the appropriate question for the assigned level. Beth then asked groups to exchange questions, emphasizing that the questions not be labeled. The groups worked with their new questions, determining levels of thinking required and rationales. During this time, Beth sat in on each group's discussion, answering questions, providing necessary input, and reinforcing group efforts. Questions were given back to their authors with comments so students could rework them.

To get a better idea of the kinds of group discussions students had as they worked cooperatively on identifying levels of understanding, here is a short excerpt. This discussion took place between three students trying to determine whether a question required *author and me* or *on my own* processing.

STUDENT 1: The question is, "If the greenhouse effect is true, what kind of climate will Chicago have in 50 years?"

STUDENT 2: What's the answer?

STUDENT 1: It says "6 to 12 degrees warmer. Like Florida."

STUDENT 3: How are we supposed to know that?

STUDENT 1: We can figure it out. We have to look in the book first to make sure it doesn't tell us about Chicago.

STUDENT 3: I don't remember anything about Chicago.

STUDENT 2: It doesn't, I'm looking right now. I can't find anything about it.

STUDENT 1: It does say that if carbon dioxide keeps getting worse, the world temperature is going to go up. You see where I am, on page 128.

STUDENT 3: It's for sure not a *right there* or in-the-book question.

STUDENT 1: Does it say by how many degrees? I'm looking down here. Yeah, here it is. It says that "if carbon dioxide levels continue to increase at the present rate, in 40 to 50 years the greenhouse effect will cause temperatures worldwide to increase by about 6 to 12 degrees centigrade."

STUDENT 2: So, big deal, that doesn't sound like very much. How could that make us as warm as Florida?

(Students attend to the text.)

STUDENT 3: Look, I found this part up here that says that 100 million years ago the earth was a lot warmer even at the poles. So maybe if the poles were warm, we would be really warm too. What do you think?

STUDENT 1: I like it. This is a hard one.

STUDENT 2: So we're saying it's what, *on my own* or *author and me?*

(They ponder.)

STUDENT 3: I think it's sorta like both. You can find some of the information in the book, but you have to figure it out by yourself when it comes to the part about Chicago.

STUDENT 1: Don't we have to say one or the other?

STUDENT 3: I don't think so. She said they could be one or the other or anywhere in between.

(Student 1, designated as the recorder, writes down the group's rationale. They move on to the next question.)

Levels of understanding training promotes sensitivity to various ways of thinking about text while constructing and applying meaning. Levels of processing practices should be designed to refute the common misconception held by students that the text tells all. Reliance on the text as the sole source of information limits students' interactions with text and consequently their depth of understanding. If students are only required to process information at the *right there* level, they will likely form only a superficial understanding of text. On the other hand, if students are taught to extend their thinking along the comprehension continuum, they will come away from text encounters with more meaningful and critical understandings.

Using a question-and-answer-generating strategy was helpful to Beth and her students. Because Beth's approach integrates multiple dimensions of the meaning-making process, her students are able to think about text in a more elaborative fashion and move toward greater independence in comprehension.

Reading Closely and Accurately

The CCSS for English/language arts endorse a form of reading that begins with a close and accurate understanding of a text author's message. The emphasis, according to the standards, should be on instruction that ensures that students avoid the all-too-common propensity to "jump to conclusions" about a textual interpretation or fixate on a connection to their own lives that blocks thorough and evidentiary meaning making. To clarify, text-to-self connections are valuable for sustaining attention during reading, and the ability to draw conclusions is the hallmark of interpretive thinking. Therefore, we do not want to inhibit youths' efforts to process text in these ways. Nevertheless, we need to demonstrate for them how conclusions should be made based on all the important textual evidence and that relating an author's ideas to oneself is a helpful impulse but should not divert attention away from a full appreciation of an author's information and ideas. In sum, close reading is seen as the prerequisite for higher-level processing of text.

To foster text-dependent thinking, Min-jun begins instruction with her seventh-grade math students using short passages, such as the one in Figure 3.8.

"Okay my dear mathematicians, we're going to begin today's lesson by reading about how to become a millionaire. How many of you would like to be a millionaire? (*Hands shoot up.*) I want you to follow along as I read, because I will be showing you a way to read all your math stories and passages. When you read in math class, you have to read very carefully so that you have a clear understanding of what the author is saying. And when you finish reading, you should be able to use the information in the passage to formulate and solve problems or defend interpretations. We're going to call this *close reading*, because we will be sticking very close to the words of the passage."

When Min-jun finishes her read-aloud of the passage and modeling of the close reading process, she directs her students' attention to a framework for relating interpretations to textual evidence.

I learned that _____.

The evidence that supports my interpretation includes _____.

One new idea of mine that the author doesn't include is _____.

The reason I believe this is based on _____.

With the passage, Min-jun models important close reading processes, such as reading slowly, using a pencil or marker, rereading, and showing students that it's acceptable to struggle with meaning making. Min-jun also teaches her class how to use argumentation based on evidence.

How to Become a Millionaire

In class today, Ms. Jones revealed a secret to her students. All of them could become million-aires if they followed a few important rules. It might take 47 years, she told them, but if they followed her rules exactly, she guaranteed them that they would become millionaires. Martin and the other students thought Ms. Jones was joking . . . or crazy. If she knew the rules for becoming a millionaire, why wasn't she one already, instead of teaching seventh-grade math?

After school, Martin raced home to tell his mother, who studied math in college and used it in her job as a loan officer at a bank. Because she knew a lot about money and financial matters, she laughed and told Martin that Ms. Jones was correct.

The next day, Ms. Jones asked her class how many parents agreed with her guaranteed plan for becoming a millionaire. Out of 25 students in the class, 20 said their parents agreed with Ms. Jones. The other students said their parents were as doubtful as they were.

After much anticipation, Ms. Jones finally revealed to her math class the "secret" formula for becoming a millionaire. First, she said, students needed to save early and often. The next rule was to save as much as possible. The third rule was to invest in an account that yields compound interest. The fourth rule was to invest in an account that had the highest rate of return. And the fifth and final rule was to leave deposits and interest in the account as long as possible.

FIGURE 3.8. Sample passage for text-dependent thinking in math.

Process Guides

Process guides provide students with models and suggestions on how they should summarize and organize key content-area concepts. These guides, however, are written suggestions that "walk" students through the processes involved in reading like an expert in biology or an expert in history. The process guide is a particularly effective and efficient way to begin a new year or semester, because it provides students with the necessary assistance and scaffolding as they adjust their reading approaches to a particular content area.

You can provide a variety of suggestions in a process guide. Some of these suggestions might guide students in how to read their paper and e-text assignments (e.g., "skim," "slow down," "notice the graph," "select a particular button," "highlight a word for definition," "follow a hyperlink"), others remind students to employ strategic reading processes (e.g., "take notes," "organize into a visual aid," "ask questions"), and some suggestions might point out an important idea or relationship that students must understand. The following are examples taken from a variety of disciplines and from paper and electronic texts:

- "Page 93, paragraphs 3–6: Pay special attention to this section. Make sure you identify three reasons for Hunter's actions."
- "Page 145: Notice the three subtopics under the boldface heading titled 'Involvement in Vietnam.' These three subtopics represent three reasons for our involvement. What are those three reasons?"

- "Page 22: Study the graph. Be prepared to explain the processes represented in the graph. *Hint*: Read the graph from top to bottom."
- "Read the summary on page 223 *before* you begin to read. Why? The section's key ideas are highlighted for you."
- "Page 99: Skim the first three paragraphs. Then slow down and read very carefully about the two hormonal control systems. Make sure you can explain the two systems using your own words."
- "Page 11, paragraph 4: This paragraph explains why settlers chose this spot for their homes. There are three reasons why—the authors cue these reasons with words like *first* and *furthermore*. Make sure you know the three reasons."

As you can see, the process guide can accomplish a variety of goals. One marine biology teacher I know, Christina, described the process guide as being a "personal tutor for each of my students." Christina was concerned that a majority of her students were trying to memorize all the details when they were reading. Some of her students seemed to give up on their reading or chose not to read, hoping she would summarize the information for them. Christina wisely chose not to lecture on the information contained in each course text. Rather, she decided she would help her students learn the concepts in her course while modeling the processes involved in reading biology material. Her solution was to use process guides.

To prepare one particular process guide, Christina began by asking herself what she wanted her students to know when they finished reading a section in their electronic textbook about the sea floor. Like many e-textbooks, the book Christina and her students used had multimodal features, such as video, audio, and hyperlinks. It also offered readers the capability to interact with the text through highlighting passages, underlining, adding comments, attaching files, or recording audio comments. Functions for manipulating the page format, text size, and screen layout were also available. Search features allowed Christina and her students to locate specific words or phrases within the text or to access a particular page. This medium has been shown to increase engagement and foster reading comprehension (Larson, 2011).

Once she identified the major concepts and ideas, she then read the section carefully so she could identify potential problems her students might encounter with the content and format. As she read, she realized that many of them would skip the charts and graphs, some of which illustrated important information not contained in the written presentation. She also realized that they might follow hyperlinks that would take them to information that could draw their attention away from the essential content and ideas. She also wanted to reinforce application of newly learned study reading processes, such as summarizing and notetaking. Based on her review of the section about the sea floor in the class e-textbook, Christina wrote her suggestions, cued to certain pages and paragraphs. As illustrated in Figure 3.9, her guide offered specific reading suggestions and asked the students to jot down brief responses to her probes.

Directions: The purpose of this guide is to help you to "read like a scientist" as you read the section in your marine biology e-textbook entitled *The Sea Floor*, on pages 33 through 38. Remember that reading science in the textbook is very different from reading a newspaper or short story. You will need to read more slowly and carefully and focus on definitions, examples, characteristics, and processes.

1. Begin your reading by examining Figure 2.17 on page 33. Read the caption. Also, click on the link for "continental margins," and watch the short video clip. You should now know the three parts to a continental margin.
2. Now focus on the first major boldface heading, "Continental Margins and Oceanic Basins." After reading this short section, open a comment box and write a short description of a continental margin using key terms from the text and your own words.
3. The first subheading on page 34 is "The Continental Shelf." Read this section and then click on the notetaking link and organize information from this section into two-column notes.

Continental shelf	—the shallowest part of the continental margin
	—biologically very rich
Continental slope	—
	—
Continental rise	—
	—

Active margins
    How they are
    formed
	—
	
	—

Characteristics	—steep, rocky shorelines
	—
Examples	—
	—

4. Did your characteristics of the continental shelf include the following key terms: *submarine canyons* and *shelf breaks*? If you have not examined Figure 2.18, *do this now*! Remember that figures and graphs are very important in science and often present information *not* explained with words in the text. What do you learn from Figure 2.18? If you are struggling, click on the link at the bottom of the figure for additional explanation. (*Hint*: You will obtain an example of an important concept.)
5. The second subheading on page 35 is "The Continental Slope." As you read this section, continue to add information to your two-column notes about continental slope.
6. The third subhead on page 36 is "The Continental Rise." As you read this section, add information about continental rise to your two-column notes. Be sure to include *how* a continental rise is formed.

(continued)

FIGURE 3.9. Process guide for marine biology.

7. Read the italicized summary at the bottom of page 36. Does this information make sense to you? It should. If you still have questions, open a comment box and write them there.
8. On page 37 you will find another boldface heading—"Active and Passive Margins." Before reading this section, examine Figure 2.19. Read the caption. Again, an example is provided. What country is given as an example of active and passive margins? _____
9. Read the first two paragraphs of that section; they explain how continental margins and habitats are influenced by plate tectonic processes. Obviously, you will need to be able to explain an active and passive margin and how they are formed. Make sure you stop to read Figure 2.20 when the authors ask you to do so. Click on the link at the bottom of the figure and watch the short video clip about these two types of margins. Return to your two-column notes and add information you learned about active and passive margins.
10. Now, before you read the last paragraph for this section on page 38, ask yourself what you predict this paragraph will describe. _____
_____
What should you know when you finish this paragraph? (*Hint*: Look back at your two-column notes over this section on continental margins.) Write key ideas and questions in a comment box.
11. Look at the boxed information at the very end of the chapter. You are asked to follow the two links to read about different points of view concerning oil and gas drilling on the continental shelf. As you read, summarize the main points from each point of view *and* list words and phrases that indicate a bias.

Article	Summary of main points	Bias words
Offshore Drilling Too Risky		—too risky — —
Path to Wisdom: Open Up Continental Shelf to Gas Drilling		—create reliable electricity — — —

FIGURE 3.9. (*continued*)

Christina introduced the guide to her students with an explanation as to its purpose. After demonstrating how to answer the first two questions, she gave her students 15 minutes at the end of the period to begin their reading. As they read the electronic text and their process guide, she circulated the room, guiding and prompting. Before the bell rang, she assigned her students to finish their reading and hinted at the possibility of a pop quiz over the material. As she informed us, her announcement that students could use their completed process guide if there were a quiz motivated most of her students to do the reading.

Of course, Christina is not planning on writing process guides for all her chapters, because she is hoping that her students will soon "figure out" how to read her biology materials. To her critics in her department who suggest she is telling her students too much, she responds that she is merely guiding her students in how to read and think and encouraging many of them to open their books.

Endowing youth with cognitive strategies to improve their comprehension is the responsibility of all disciplinary teachers. As expert thinkers and readers, content-area teachers can model for students the ways in which they make, extract, and use meaning from text. Scaffolding can be provided as the students navigate the complexities of expository prose in order to promote text-based and reader-based processing. And youth should be nudged out of passive roles during the comprehension process and taught how to generate their own prompts and aids to understanding.

Textual Dimension Strategies

As you have been reading, you have been using the structure or organization of this chapter to help you identify and summarize important ideas. That is, you may have focused on boxed content and ideas marked by typographical features such as boldface headings, or you may have noted information that we cued using words such as *furthermore* or *in summary*. We know from the research that skilled readers use text organization to aid their understanding, especially when they find the material they are reading unfamiliar or somewhat challenging (Goldman & Rakestraw, 2000). More specifically, skilled readers use all of these signals to organize what they read:

- Previews or introductory statements
- Summary statements
- Typographic clues such as underlining, italics, and boldface print or headings
- Pointer words and phrases, such as *the most important reason why*
- Enumeration devices (e.g., *first, furthermore, finally*)
- Connectives (e.g., *because, the reasons why, however, the consequences*)

You might find it surprising that a majority of adolescents do not understand and capitalize on these signals that authors use to explain and organize their ideas (Chambliss, 1995). Among the many explanations for this situation is that secondary students have had far more experiences with the narrative or story format of writing than they have had with the expository or explanatory format of writing. In fact, we teach children to read with stories because they are already familiar with the structure of stories and their narrative styles most closely approximate oral language patterns (Dymock, 2007).

Stories or narrative texts have predictable structures or patterns, called *story grammars* (Mandler, 1987). For instance, stories have settings; they have characters;

the main character is usually en route to a goal; to reach his or her goal, the main character must confront obstacles, essentially conflict; and the conflict is resolved in some way. Apparently, as readers or listeners receive constant exposure to well-structured stories, they internalize these grammars in the form of a story schema, which assists them in understanding and writing stories.

Because most of us prefer the narrative structure, interest in stories rarely wanes throughout our lives. However, most textbooks and classroom presentations do not typically use a narrative structure. Rather, most learning situations in school are organized around an expository or explanatory structure that is more formal and demanding than our oral language. Try to recall the last time you relished the opportunity to crack open one of your textbooks before going to bed. Most of us rarely do, and the same is true of students.

We have observed students plowing through their assigned government and science reading, eager to finish so that they can put down the book. Students in middle and secondary school must learn to deal with the formal expository styles of writing and speaking if they are to be successful readers and learners. By helping them develop an understanding of how writers organize expository text, we can improve their comprehension (Goldman & Rakestraw, 2000). Thankfully, the research shows that almost any approach to teaching youth about the structure of disciplinary texts improves comprehension and recall of information and ideas (Duke, Pearson, Strachan, & Billman, 2011).

Bridging Text Ideas

I spoke earlier about the need to supply youth with considerate texts. One important feature of considerate text is cohesiveness (Caccamise & Snyder, 2005). Cohesive texts provide ample cues that help readers link information presented in different sentences. Authors of cohesive texts do this by continuously adding and integrating newly introduced information with previously cited information. They also achieve cohesion through the liberal use of logical connectors, such as conjunctions.

Unfortunately, many of the texts adolescents encounter in their disciplinary classes may lack appropriate cohesive ties. Consequently, students need to (1) recognize and take advantage of cohesive ties that appear in text and (2) learn how to use information stated previously to infer a logical connection with information that comes after when connectors aren't supplied. Using and inferring logical connectives is a microstructure strategy. Complete the bridging activity in Figure 3.10 to gain a greater appreciation for the importance of inferring logical connectives in expository text.

Rita teaches ninth- and 10th-grade history in a large suburban high school, where she has developed a method for helping her students use connectives in comprehending their history textbook. For a list of common connectives used to join ideas, see Figure 3.11.

Directions: Using the list of connecting words from Figure 3.11, insert one that makes logical sense in the spaces of this passage. Compare your entries with those of a classmate. Entries may vary, because multiple connectors have similar meanings.

An Odd Incident at Antietam Creek

America was well into the Civil War, (1) _____ many battles had been fought between North and South. (2) _____ no battle was bloodier nor more puzzling than the Battle of Antietam Creek. General George McClellan was chasing General Robert E. Lee's Confederate Army in Maryland, when on September 13th, an odd thing happened. McClellan's army was near Frederick, Maryland (3) _____ one of his soldiers found three cigars wrapped in a piece of paper lying in a field. The paper turned out to be an order signed by General Lee instructing his generals to split their army into four parts. Generals almost never split up their army in the face of the enemy (4) _____ each part is small and weak by itself. (5) _____ the order must have seemed unusual to McClellan, (6) _____ he chose to take it seriously and revised his battle plans accordingly.

Suggested Answers

1.

2.

3.

4.

5.

6.

FIGURE 3.10. Bridging activity.

In groups of three to four, students were asked to generate a couple of statements about the Civil War that reflected what they already knew about the topic. Afterward, the groups read their statements to the whole class. Rita copied the statements on the board. She studied the list for a moment, and then placed stars next to six of the sentences:

> The Civil War was fought for many reasons.
> The major reason for the Civil War was to free slaves.
> The Civil War was not with a foreign country.
> American fought American in the Civil War.
> Abraham Lincoln was president during the Civil War.
> Many soldiers from both sides died.

Besides laying the foundation for manipulating connectives, Rita provided students with a stimulus for prior knowledge activation with this activity. Plenty of interesting discussion ensued as groups of students offered their statements. For instance, when the statement "The major reason for the Civil War was to free

Time words
- then
- presently
- now
- thereupon
- somewhat later
- hereafter
- finally
- since
- as soon as
- when
- meanwhile
- at the same time
- at last
- eventually
- now

Illustration words
- for example
- for instance

Order of sequence words
- next
- secondly
- first
- finally
- to begin with
- in conclusion

Conclusion words
- hence
- therefore
- so
- thus
- it follows that
- for this reason
- since
- to sum up
- accordingly
- in conclusion
- in other words
- in general terms
- as a result
- because

Restatement words
- in fact
- that is to say
- indeed
- in other words
- briefly

Additional thought words
- an
- again
- next
- in the same way
- also
- besides
- furthermore
- similarly
- too
- moreover
- in addition
- further
- most of all
- in like manner

Contrast words
- but
- in spite of
- yet
- conversely
- rather
- even though
- instead
- nevertheless
- still
- however
- on the other hand
- notwithstanding
- on the contrary

FIGURE 3.11. A list of common connecting words and what they signal.

slaves" was read, another student quickly commented that she didn't think that was quite true, and a small debate commenced over the issue. The students finally agreed that the slave issue was one of the significant reasons for the war. During this discussion, Rita did all she could to facilitate by prodding and asking open-ended questions.

Rita then passed around a list of connecting words (see Figure 3.11). She provided information about the significance of the words and modeled how she would use them in her speaking and writing. She then asked students to remain in their small groups and write a paragraph using the connecting words to join together the statements the class generated about the Civil War. Afterward, a spokesperson from each group was invited to read while the rest of the class was asked to listen carefully for whether or not the connectives used signaled the correct relationships among the sentences. Here is the way one group connected the statements:

Although the Civil War was fought for many reasons, the major reason it was fought was to free slaves. The Civil War was not fought with a foreign country; **rather**, American fought American, **and** many soldiers from both sides died. **At that time**, Abraham Lincoln was president.

Rita takes some time within every unit to reinforce students' knowledge of how connectives and other bridging structures operate within the various class texts. For instance, she distributes passages with connectives removed and expects students to supply these missing links. When she reads aloud, the class is asked to listen closely for connectives and overlapping words and phrases, jot them down, and share what they heard during a pause at the end of a sentence or paragraph.

Rita regularly reminds the students to keep a watchful eye out for cohesive ties provided by the authors of the other texts they read, and she encourages them to use cohesive structures in their writing to help explain how their ideas are related. Rita has found that when students are sensitized to the role of connectives in text, they not only improve their comprehension by becoming better able to compensate for disconnected text, but they also compose better organized written work.

Text Mapping: Scaffolding Understanding of Textbook Features and Organization

If you are a student taking a class for which this textbook is required, or if you have purchased this book on your own to increase your knowledge and skills in content-area literacy, you have probably made numerous markings in the book already. Most of us highlight, underline, or write notes in the margin to aid our comprehension and recall of information and ideas we think are important or that we intend to use. We developed text markup strategies over time by trial and error, because few of us were fortunate enough to have been provided instruction in these important skills. Furthermore, a significant barrier to developing text marking skills in middle and high school is that students are forbidden to write in their books because they do not own them. Fortunately, the expanding availability of e-textbooks is slowly changing this situation. And with a growing array of technology tools at teachers' and students' fingertips in classrooms today, text markup skills to improve comprehension can be developed more vigorously.

Working with copies of selected pages from required texts, however, we can help youth learn to identify important organizational features that facilitate meaning making. One such strategy for sensitizing students to both micro- and macrostructures of expository and informational prose is *text mapping* (*www.textmapping. org/overview.html*).

When Matt teaches text mapping to his 10th-grade biology students, he follows these steps:

1. At the beginning of the year, he identifies pages from the class textbook that contain important organizational features, such as table of contents pages for the first chapter; introductory pages of the first chapter with title, headings, and subheadings; pages with highlighted terms; pages with graphs and charts; glossary and index pages.

2. With his iPhone or iPad, he takes a picture of the print textbook pages he intends to use to demonstrate markups of key text features.

3. Using Explain Everything, a screencasting whiteboard app, Matt organizes the pages, from table of contents through index pages, edge to edge and connects them together into a long scroll on the whiteboard. (See illustration in Figure 3.12.)

4. With the writing and marking tools in the app, as well as the stylus, he marks up the scrolled text. For instance, he draws a circle around the hierarchical diagram that serves as a graphic organizer at the opening of the first chapter and writes next to it "visual outline of the chapter." In another case, Matt highlights the words "first," "second," and "third" that appear over two pages and talks about how authors signal the organization of their exposition with enumerative words. He makes sure to highlight headings and subheadings, as well as other format and organizational features, drawing arrows to identify key terms and connecting words, and making notes in the margins to signal the value of author-provided questions, summaries, graphs, charts, and boxed material.

As Matt demonstrates text features on the whiteboard, he talks about the purpose of the activity. He explains to his students how the process of mapping the scrolled text will help them see more explicitly its structure and organization. He explains further the importance of recognizing and using textual cues and formatting features to guide reading comprehension.

FIGURE 3.12. A text mapping scroll.

5. Next, Matt projects new pages on the interactive whiteboard and invites students to come up and mark particular text features. He asks them to explain how the features can be used to guide comprehension or contribute to better understanding of chapter or book content. This is repeated until a page is fully mapped and discussed, and then a new page is projected and the process continues with new students invited to the board to map the text and analyze the features.

6. As a wrap-up to the instruction on text mapping, Matt distributes a photocopied page from the textbook to each of his students and asks them to use markers and pens to map the page. After they have done the work of mapping for nonfiction elements, he hands out a multiple-choice and matching worksheet. As students complete the worksheet, they are requested to go back to their mapped page to find answers and add additional text markings to facilitate correct responses. Matt takes advantage of this activity to reteach and elaborate on previous instruction on the process and value of text mapping.

The Explain Everything app allows Matt to save the text mapping work he and his students have done, so he can project it anytime students need reminders to be vigilant, while previewing and reading a chapter or article, in looking for important cues to organize their thinking of expository prose. Eventually, Matt's students demonstrate increasing competence with mentally mapping the organization of chapters.

Personal Dimension Strategies

For each of the strategies already described, the teachers using the strategies have accounted for the personal dimension of comprehension in some way. Those that follow are particularly designed to foreground critical personal variables in the meaning-making and meaning-using process. They create spaces for youth to engage in identity work. They exploit youths' desire to have choices and to feel a sense of agency about their reading and learning. And they are meant to involve youth in active learning experiences.

Opinionnaires

Every adolescent has an opinion on something, whether it's about a teacher, a class, a classmate, a team, parents, musical artists, social media sites, or current events. The opinionnaire strategy capitalizes on adolescents' propensity to form opinions by asking them to take a stand on declarative statements centered on critical concepts and issues related to the content. White and Johnson (2001) discovered that opinionniares are highly beneficial in promoting deep and meaningful understandings of content-area topics by activating and building relevant prior knowledge and building interest in and motivation to learn more about particular topics. Opinionnaires also promote self-examination, value youths' points of view, and provide a vehicle for them to influence others with their ideas.

Opinionnaires are developed by generating statements about a topic that force students to take positions and defend them. The emphasis is on students' points of view and not the "correctness" of their opinions. Virtually every disciplinary topic lends itself to opinionating, even topics traditionally regarded as fact-based and objective. For example, Olga, a health teacher, used an opinionnaire (see Figure 3.13) to elicit attitudes and feelings from her students about the nature of health and the role of personal responsibility in maintaining good health. Although there

---

What Are Your Opinions about Health?

Directions: After each statement, write SA (strongly agree), A (agree), D (disagree), or SD (strongly disagree). Be prepared to explain your opinions.

1. Only doctors can heal you when you are unhealthy. _____

2. I can help a friend get healthy by just being supportive. _____

3. Each of us should take care of our own health needs. _____

4. It is important to know how to make yourself healthy. _____

5. If I had a serious disease like cancer, I could only get healthy with medical treatment. _____

6. When each of us takes care of our health, our whole society is healthier. _____

7. Being healthy means more than being physically fit. _____

8. Health is a state of mind. _____

9. Drugs and medicine are necessary to maintain health. _____

10. Home remedies are not as effective as treatment from doctors. _____

FIGURE 3.13. Opinionnaire on attitudes about health.

is a science of health and medicine, there is also room for challenging traditionally held views about health. Olga purposely did not include a "maybe" or "not sure" option because she had found many of her students chose it as an easy way out of the discussion.

Olga's students eagerly dug into her opinionnaire statements, questioning many of the assumptions about what it means to be healthy and maintain good health. To take full advantage of the strategy, Olga separated supporters from nonsupporters of each statement and facilitated brief but sometimes charged exchanges among her students. By taking a stand on health issues and engaging in critical discussion about those issues, Olga's students not only heightened their expectation of the content to follow but also made many new connections from their opinions and ideas to those of their classmates.

In another case, Julian employed the opinionnaire strategy to instigate critical thinking about personally held beliefs about his students' place in the natural world as an introduction to the study of ecosystems in science. For the particular topic of rain forests, Julian asked his students to locate themselves relative to statements in Figure 3.14. He constructed statements that students could relate to their own experiences with people and animals. The discussion the statements inspired then

---

Where Do You Fit into the World around You?

Directions: Read each statement carefully and decide whether it "Describes Me," "Sort of Describes Me," or "Doesn't Describe Me," Write your responses in the spaces provided. Be ready to defend your position.

1. No one else is affected by what I do. _____

2. I don't care if forests are cut down if it's to make room to build houses for people. _____

3. My needs as a human being are more important than those of other living things. _____

4. I believe it's important to live and let live. _____

5. There is a lot we can learn from nature that can help improve our lives. _____

6. Variety in people, animals, and plants makes for a better world. _____

7. Everybody and everything is connected in some way. _____

8. There is a lot I can do to help improve the natural world. _____

9. Things like droughts and famine are beyond our control. _____

10. The natural world should be used to make the lives of humans easier. _____

FIGURE 3.14. Opinionnaire on beliefs about the natural world.

served as a bridge to information and ideas in the science textbook and other class readings.

Opinionnaires, as we have seen, privilege students' personal insights, feelings, and ideas while catalyzing them to think deeply and critically about content-area topics. Tapping the personal dimension in comprehension teaching and learning is necessary in order to ensure that students are engaged, find relevance, and feel valued as members of the classroom culture.

Alternative Texts in the Content Classroom

Engaging youth in disciplinary text reading is not the easiest of tasks, especially for reluctant and struggling readers. Yet, we know that in order to improve comprehension abilities, adolescents need to have frequent, sustained print encounters. In the disciplines, these print encounters should be with texts that are thematically or topically related to the content under study. Making a variety of accessible, content-focused texts available in the classroom, giving self-selection of reading choices, and linking the texts to instructional activities will help students find personal connections to disciplinary topics. The following are recommendations derived from the work of secondary teachers we have observed who use a variety of texts to engage students in reading and learning about the subject matter.

• *Use information books and graphic novels to research class topics.* When Terri teaches about the world wars of the 20th century in American history, she fills the classroom with related books and graphic novels to encourage further reading and promote research skills. Students are given time out of every 90-minute class block to work on individual research assignments that offer wide latitude with respect to particular topics to research and modes of expression. For example, Gino investigated World War I fighter pilots and used the graphic novel *Enemy Ace: War Idyll* (Pratt, 1992) and *The Red Baron: The Graphic History of Richthofen's Flying Circus and the Air War in WWI* (Vansant, 2014) as two of his sources. Gino was transfixed by these books that provide a remarkably vivid and emotive pictorial and written account of the horrors of World War I from the perspective of flying aces.

• *Make available less difficult/modified texts.* Evidence can be found in the literature that clearly supports the approach of matching adolescents with content-based texts that are commensurate with students' ability levels (Brozo & Hargis, 2003a, 2003b). Youths' identities as readers and learners get a boost when they find themselves able to access comprehensible text in science, social studies, math, and other disciplines. Furthermore, these kinds of texts provide sorely needed reading practice for reluctant readers and can build their schemas of disciplinary topics at the same time. Garrison's science students benefit from his dynamic, activity-based lessons, but they also benefit from the readings he makes available to them that are easier to comprehend than the textbook. Garrison has discovered several useful websites with explanations and passages covering many different science topics. One of his favorite sites, *chem4kids,* has material that even his lowest performing readers can use profitably. Garrison has compiled an organized guide to the readings from the site around the topics he covers in class.

After learning about the physical structure of atoms, his students were told they could explore the various print resources in the classroom to answer questions about atoms. Erin, a special education inclusion student, made her way to one of three computers and went directly to the *chem4kids* website. After consulting Garrison's guide to the site, she found several short, colorful readings with easy-to-follow diagrams and illustrations detailing the makeup and function of atomic particles. Erin proudly offered information she gleaned from the site to help answer the questions about atoms Garrison had posed to the class.

- *Read articles from popular magazines and newspapers.* Helping youth personalize understandings of text topics is an achievable goal if students are allowed to find links from the everyday texts in their environments to the ideas and information under study in the content classroom. For Leyla's geometry class, students are asked to find anything in the magazines and newspapers they read or that are around the house that relates to geometry and share it with their classmates. Joey brings in a PowerPoint slide show of his favorite e-zine on skateboarding. He displays photos of stunts by professionals from the website courtesy of *Thrasher,* a print skateboard magazine, and talks about angles, parabolas, and trajectories.

Accounting for the personal dimension of comprehension is vital to keeping youth engaged in meaning-making and meaning-using processes. This concern for the personal side of readers reminds me of a self-styled maxim from a high-school teacher friend of mine who would say "You can lead a kid to a book, but you can't make him take a look." To ensure that students are looking at and thinking about the information and ideas in a book and other texts, we need to engage their imaginations, find ways of linking the meaning-making process to their identity construction, and help them discover applications of new understandings to their daily lives.

- *Build comprehension with popular movies.* Many of Lee's students in her ninth-grade English class are recent immigrants. She employs unique practices to help them build their English vocabularies and develop comprehension abilities. One such practice is the use of movies. Movies provide visual context for learning new words, and scenes can be viewed many times over for in-depth analysis and to gain deeper understanding (Holmes, 2005).

A popular movie with Lee's class is *Crouching Tiger, Hidden Dragon II: The Green Legend* (Weinstein, 2016), which is the long-awaited sequel to *Crouching*

Tiger, Hidden Dragon. Set in 19th-century China in and around Peking during the latter part of the Ch'ing Dynasty, this action fantasy chronicles the stories of martial arts warriors who possess superhuman qualities, including the ability to defy gravity. Her students can't get enough of the remarkable special effects and nonstop action, but they also come to appreciate the film's symbolism, character motivation, and themes. It's also a movie that has strong appeal to both her boys and girls, since the four main characters include two men and two women with equal fighting prowess.

Before the movie, Lee provides her class with a list of the characters and goes over the spellings and pronunciation of their Chinese names. Lee's three students from Taiwan, whose mother tongue is Mandarin, are especially helpful to the rest of the class in pronouncing the character's names correctly, as their language is the same as the language of the film. Lee also encourages the students to make connections to the main plotline of the film by reflecting on their own experiences. She asks them to think of a time when someone close to them might have been *revengeful.* This word, along with several others that appear in the subtitles, such as *manipulative, invincible, defeated foe,* and *deep meditation,* are studied. Students put them in a vocabulary notebook with pronunciation guides and brief definitional information. As the words appear in the subtitles, Lee stops the movie and engages students in a discussion about how context shapes their meanings. Then, students include a brief description of the context and the actual sentence from the film in their vocabulary notebooks.

As they view the movie, Lee and her class pay particular attention to the roles of the lead male and female characters. The movie depicts women who do not want to take on the traditional roles their families have arranged for them. She uses this issue to explore gender stereotypes and the importance of honor and responsibility in her students' families and cultures. For example, students write short themes and conduct role plays to demonstrate how conflicts might occur based on traditional gender expectations in their cultures and societal norms in their new home in the United States.

While structuring learning experiences around the movie, Lee makes certain to stock the classroom with related fiction and nonfiction resources. These materials are sometimes read aloud or used by students during independent reading time. Favorites include *Beautiful Warrior: The Legend of the Nun's Kung Fu* (McCully, 1999), *Tofu Quilt* (Russell, 2009), *Saints* (Yang, 2013), *Chinese Cinderella: The True Story of an Unwanted Daughter* (Yen Mah, 2010), and *Eyewitness: Ancient China* (Cotterell, 2005).

Throughout the movie, Lee has her class focus on particular scenes for in-depth analysis. She models and has students conduct visual scans for different levels of meaning. For instance, a scene is frozen while students name all the immediately recognizable information, such as sword, Shu Lien (a female warrior), village, and so forth. This information is at the surface or literal level. Next, they scan the scene thinking about what the literal information means or suggest. Students during this phase of analysis will offer ideas and interpretations related to characters' motives or symbolic meanings of objects. Finally, Lee asks her students to consider broader themes related to the pivotal scenes under analysis. She prompts them to think of ways the meaning might relate to current events or ways people behave today.

Lee has seen the powerful influence that viewing and studying films has had on the language abilities and comprehension of her students, many of whom are ELs. Films are instantly motivating and provide a rich visual context for authentic communication. When combined with other meaning-making activities, films serve Lee and her students as an ideal source for expanding vocabularies and building comprehension abilities that transfer to print literacy.

Social Dimension Strategies

Virtually every comprehension strategy presented thus far has had a social learning element associated with it. As stated before, the reason is that comprehension comprises several dimensions, and teaching it effectively requires the orchestration of strategies and approaches that bring more than one or all of the dimensions into play. Skillful disciplinary teachers understand that the meaning-making and meaning-using process occurs more readily within supportive social contexts. Thus they create numerous opportunities for youth to learn from and with each other in the classroom.

Reciprocal Teaching

In secondary content classrooms in which reciprocal teaching takes place, the teacher and student take turns generating questions and summaries and leading a discussion about sections of a text. Initially, the teacher models questioning, summarizing, clarifying, and predicting activities while encouraging students to participate at whatever level they can manage. Gradually, students become more capable of contributing to such discussions and assume more responsibility for their own learning.

In the following exchange, Rob, a high school study skills teacher, and his students were reading and discussing paragraphs from their social studies textbooks. They took turns asking questions about the topic and summarizing. The first paragraph they discussed was about Commander Peary and his quest for the North Pole. On finishing reading of the short text segment, students immediately responded:

STUDENT 1: I have a question about this. What year did Peary write his diary?

ROB: Not a bad beginning, but I would consider that a question about details. Try to avoid the kind of question you can answer by looking word for word in the paragraph. See if next time you can ask a main idea question, and begin your question with a question word like *how, why, when.* Go ahead, try that.

STUDENT 2: What if I ask, Why is Peary's diary important?

ROB: A very good question. Notice how your question seems to be getting at the most important idea in the paragraph.

STUDENT 3: And you can't answer it by just looking at the words.

ROB: Right. Very good work! Now, can anyone give me a summary statement for the paragraph?

STUDENT 4: Well, the only way we really know if Peary got to the North Pole is from his diary.

ROB: And why is that?

STUDENT 4: Because there was no one else around who knew for sure where they were.

STUDENT 5: You can't bring back any proof you were there.

ROB: Okay, that explains why some think Peary may not have made it to the Pole first. Isn't that an important part of the summary? (*Several students agree.*) Let me try to make a summary for you. The most important thing we have learned is that we have to take Peary at his word when he said that he reached the North Pole because we don't have any other evidence to support that he did. Does that make sense? Have I left out anything important? Those are important questions to always ask yourself.

Rob's reciprocal teaching approach seems to be successful because it forces the students to respond, which allows him to evaluate their understanding and provide appropriate feedback. Also, by responding orally, the students are given the opportunity to self-diagnose their understanding and improve their ability to self-question, summarize, clarify, and predict—cognitive processes that active comprehenders use. Rob does not merely talk to his students about how to read and then tell them to open their texts and read that way. Instead, he demonstrates how he constructs meaning and, through interactions with students, gives them greater responsibility for learning from text.

Class Discussion

I draw the distinction throughout this book between the obvious difference in classrooms in which students are expected to be passive receivers of information and ideas and classrooms in which students are active participants in the learning process. Being a good lecturer in the middle and upper grades is not enough; students learn and remember best when they participate in the dialogue about class topics (Webb, 2009; Loh, 2015; Mohr & Mohr, 2007).

Samuel Johnson put it best more than 200 years ago when he said, "The seeds of knowledge may be planted in solitude, but must be cultivated in public" (Boswell, 1979, p. 121).

Providing young adults with plenty of opportunities to engage in public discourse is often a goal of middle and secondary school teachers, but it presents dilemmas that act to limit the extent to which discussion techniques are employed in content-area classrooms (Howe & Abedin, 2013). For example, in spite of our numerous demonstrations of ways to conduct class discussions, teachers often respond that it's never as easy for them as we make it appear. They are often hesitant to plan discussions because some of their students act immaturely. Yet they believe that immature discussants need to engage in discussions if they are ever to become skillful at it. And they are right. The reluctance is based on the fear that students will get out of control. One teacher told us flatly, "A Friday afternoon discussion? Forget it!"

Nonetheless, teachers can take measures to increase the likelihood of successful classroom discussions. For instance, Patty, a seventh-grade language arts teacher, spends a considerable amount of time at the beginning of each school year teaching her students about respect and about listening. She stresses that it is important to her that each student in her class has a voice, but of equal importance is that students allow others to have a voice as well. Building community at the front end of a new year pays rich dividends during the remainder of the year in the form of students who are more considerate of one another, who are more willing and comfortable risk takers, and who appreciate the importance of the social construction of knowledge (Webb, 2009).

Teachers who desire to exploit the learning potential of class discussion often tend to undermine it by doing most of the talking and asking most of the questions (Webb, 2009). These practices inhibit rather than foster the enrichment of understanding through the exchange of viewpoints. The goal is to encourage and orchestrate discussions that result in more student–student interaction patterns rather than student–teacher patterns (Nachowitz & Brumer, 2014). Figure 3.15 presents alternatives to questioning and teacher-dominated discussions that have been shown to increase student involvement in class talk and discussion.

Middle and secondary school teachers can use many other simple discussion techniques to energize the content-area classroom and heighten enthusiasm for learning (Zwiers & Crawford, 2011). Here are some of the best that we have witnessed:

TURN-TO-YOUR-NEIGHBOR-AND-DISCUSS

This is simple to implement. Before beginning an exploration of new content, ask students to consider a problem or question or make a prediction, then turn to the classmate sitting next to them and discuss a response. Limit the time for a response so students will start thinking quickly and stay on task. Thirty seconds to a minute may be best, though with weightier questions and problems, more time may be

1. Make a declarative or factual statement.

2. Make a reflective statement.

3. Describe the student's state of mind.

4. Invite the student to elaborate on a statement.

5. Encourage the student to ask a question.

6. Encourage students to ask questions of one another.

7. Maintain a deliberate silence.

8. Encourage other students to answer questions posed to you.

9. Help students link new information to their prior knowledge.

10. Model good listening strategies.

11. Allow for small-group brainstorming first before whole-group discussion.

FIGURE 3.15. Eleven strategies for increasing student engagement in class discussions.

needed. As students are discussing, move around the room to monitor their conversations and encourage equal participation. After the brief discussions, you can ask students to share their ideas without necessarily revealing the exact nature of the content to be presented. We have seen this strategy used successfully to overcome the problem of only the effusive students answering a whole-class discussion question. When all students are given even a brief opportunity to think and say something about a topic with one another, they seem to be better prepared to offer their comments afterward to the whole class.

THINK–PAIR–SQUARE–SHARE

This discussion strategy is very similar to the one just described. After being given an issue, problem, or question, ask students to think alone for a short period of time, then pair up with someone to share their thoughts. Then have pairs of students share with other pairs, forming, in effect, small groups of four students. Again, your role as teacher is to monitor the brief discussions and elicit responses afterward. Be sure to encourage student pairs not to automatically adopt the ideas and solutions of their partners. These short-term discussion strategies actually work best when a diversity of perspectives are expressed.

ROUND ROBIN

After placing students in or forming groups of three to five, pose a problem or question and have each group go around the circle quickly, sharing ideas or solutions. You can give students one opportunity to "pass" on a response, but eventually every student must respond. This technique is used most effectively when, after initial clockwise sharing, students are asked to write down on a single piece of paper each of their responses. This allows all opinions and ideas of the groups to be brought to the teacher's and the rest of their classmates' attention. It also provides a record of the group's thinking, which might be used in grading.

INSIDE–OUTSIDE CIRCLES

I have immensely enjoyed participating in this discussion strategy, so much so that I use it often in my own university classes. It offers a novel format and can bring about face-to-face dialoguing between students who might never have the opportunity otherwise.

Students stand and face each other in two concentric circles. The inside circle faces out and the outside circle faces in. After posing a readiness problem or question, ask students to discuss ideas and answers with the person standing most directly in front of them. The interesting aspect of this technique is that at any time you can ask the inner or outer circle to rotate until you say "stop." Then the discussion can begin anew. After a few rotations, we randomly ask individual students to share their own ideas or those of the person(s) with whom they have been discussing. The advantage of this strategy is the variety of inputs possible through simply rotating the circles of students. Be sure to make enough space in the room for this discussion activity, and move about the circle to listen in on students' brainstorming.

A variation on the Inside–Outside Circles technique is one called Line-Ups. When classroom space is too limited for two concentric circles, you can get essentially the same benefits of this approach by forming two lines of students close enough together so that they can face each other and discuss. Instead of rotating circles as in the previous technique, have one of the lines move down. When this happens, students on the ends will not have someone directly in front of them, so they can walk around to the end of the other line to begin a conversation with a new student.

VALUE LINES

This approach to readiness discussion is especially useful when preparing to present students with content that evokes strong responses and controversy or when you want students to take a stand on an issue. You can begin by creating an imaginary line or symbolic line in the classroom. We have seen teachers isolate a row of desks in the middle of the room to create a line. A long strip of colored paper or even a piece of yarn can work. Next, you read a statement or make an assertion and ask students to move to one side of the line reserved for those who agree with it and the other side for those who disagree. Then have the students turn to another person on their side of the line and discuss why they agree or disagree with the statement. After a short while, have students converse with someone across the line to share why they believe the way they do. At any time, you can ask pairs of opposing conversationalists to give their opinions and ideas. As you monitor discussion, encourage respectful disagreements and polite arguing.

FISHBOWL DISCUSSIONS

With this technique, a small group of students is asked to discuss an issue or problem while another group of students looks on. The idea of the fishbowl is that the outside group must listen but not contribute to the deliberations of the students "in the fishbowl." At some point during the discussion, those looking in should be given an opportunity to discuss among themselves their reactions to the conversation they observed. Then you can ask both groups to share with the entire class the nature of their discussions. This approach to discussion allows the outside group to assess and critique the ideas of the fishbowl discussants.

Strategies and practices for expanding comprehension are more effective when youth are able to interact with peers to explain and extend new understandings. Accounting for the social dimension of comprehension involves shifts in the physical arrangement of the classroom, as well as shifts in the patterns of interaction among class members. While we have spotlighted reciprocal teaching and discussion as representative strategies of teaching to the social dimension of comprehension, we have also demonstrated how the other strategies in this chapter can be extended to involve students in group and peer-to-peer activities.

Case Study Revisited

Charles, the biology teacher introduced at the beginning of this chapter, was searching for ways to engage his students in more meaningful interactions with his course content. Now that you have read this chapter, propose strategies that may help Charles move his students toward more elaborative and meaningful processing of text material related to the topic of genetic engineering.

Charles decided to use a variety of readiness strategies to introduce his students to the new content and gain their interest. He began by exposing them to alternative source material for exploration of the topic. He captured his students' interest by reading aloud daily from the graphic novel *Genome* (Glasgow & Schichtel, n.d.), about a futuristic world in which a megacorporation controls all human reproduction and holds patents on the entire human genetic code. This gripping novel helped motivate the class to dig deeper into the content.

Charles also presented examples of exciting experiments done by genetic researchers. For example, he read to students about researchers at the University of California, San Diego, who in 1986 took the gene that makes fireflies glow and inserted it into the DNA of tobacco. The researchers were then able to raise tobacco plants that glowed in the dark.

Charles asked his students to read articles on genetic engineering in news magazines and to summarize the key ideas on index cards. He reminded the students to include in their summaries the advantages and disadvantages of this technology. Using the discussion Web strategy, students met in pairs and groups of four to discuss and prepare what they would say to the whole class on the central question of whether genetic engineering was morally responsible.

When he assigned a section on genetics from the textbook for all the students to read, Charles took class time to carefully frontload the assignment. Then, on the next day, he gave the students a pop quiz with an index card to make sure they were reading and thinking about the key ideas. Finally, Charles helped his students write to the Food and Drug Administration explaining their views on the subject of genetically engineered food.

As a result of these efforts to prepare students for and introduce them to their new learning, Charles saw his students become active learners. They read and participated with enthusiasm and were motivated to work together in small groups and as a class to explore further the topic of genetic engineering.

LOOKING BACK, LOOKING FORWARD

In this chapter I address a ubiquitous concern among middle and secondary school teachers—how to increase youths' comprehension abilities while honoring their outside-of-school literacies, interests, and competencies. Four dimensions of comprehension were outlined, and strategies and practices associated with these dimensions were described. The comprehension strategies described and the teacher vignettes presented in this chapter demonstrate numerous ways to develop youths' meaning-making and meaning-using abilities. [Teachers executed practices that connected everyday literacies with academic literacy;] engaged and sustained students' efforts to think and read;] created opportunities for expression of critical perspectives and interpretations of text;]and employed print and nonprint sources, as well as information and communications technologies, to increase comprehension.\

Disciplinary and content-area teachers can use a variety of strategies consistent with the multidimensional nature of comprehension. To help students move toward a more sophisticated level of thinking about text, you, as an expert reader, can model processes of thinking, scaffold strategies for comprehension, and engage youth in interactive experiences that require them to go beyond mere memorization. Along with your apprenticing role, you should also be challenging students to accept more and more responsibility for their own critical and elaborative thinking. Although many different comprehension strategies were presented in this chapter,

I want to remind you that throughout this textbook you will find descriptions of numerous practices that challenge students to become active meaning makers and meaning users.

In the next chapter, you will see how assessment and instruction in the content areas and disciplines can be flip sides of the same coin. Assessment for learning involves practices that give the teacher greater insight into the reading and learning needs of students and give students greater insight into their own ways of knowing.

Assessment for Literacy Growth and Disciplinary Learning

As you read Chapter 4, reflect on the following questions:

- What are the differences between assessment *of* and assessment *for* literacy and learning?
- What makes assessment of literacy and learning *authentic*?
- In what ways can disciplinary teachers embed assessment into their regular instruction?
- What are the advantages and disadvantages of standardized tests?
- How can secondary teachers create a portfolio culture in their classroom?
- What critical questions need to be asked when planning and implementing portfolio assessment?
- How can actionable literacy be achieved through assessment?

More than 30 years of theory development and research has characterized literacy as an interactive, context-bound, purposeful process of meaning construction (Alvermann, Unrau, & Ruddell, 2013). During the same time, we have progressed in our understanding of how acts of literacy should be assessed, how that assessment should be represented, and which participants or stakeholders should be involved. At the middle and high school levels, these changes have translated into an emphasis on teachers defining what it means to be literate and knowledgeable in their classrooms and designing a variety of performance-based activities and authentic opportunities to assess their students as they interact with disciplinary concepts (Chang & Tseng, 2011; Kang, Thompson, & Windschitl, 2014).

In this chapter, issues and assessment practices are presented relative to one basic assumption: The goal of assessment is to provide teachers with knowledge about how best to improve and support learning and self-awareness for students so they will become more reflective, active, and purposeful learners. I demonstrate how your assessments can reveal to you and your students important information about students' thinking, language processes, and content knowledge. Because assessment guides and informs instruction and can be integrated into the daily flow of instructional events in the classroom, this chapter provides a foundation for assessment strategies that appear in later chapters.

Case Study

Selma is a seventh-grade general science teacher interested in discovering more about her students' ability to comprehend expository text. After attending inservice workshops on content-area assessment procedures, she began to recognize the need for alternative assessments to the chapter check tests in her science textbook. After 5 years of teaching, she discovered that she was relying more and more on the tests for grading purposes and less and less on other demonstrations of her students' abilities as learners and knowledge seekers. Moreover, the results of these tests were not providing Selma with information about why students performed the way they did. She had no way of discovering whether success or failure was tied in any way to students' study processes or their ability to understand the science text.

The inservice presenter emphasized the need to tie content material to the processes for learning it effectively. Suggestions were made concerning ways teachers could teach and assess at the same time using the class texts. Selma decided to use this information to develop teaching strategies for improving students' thinking about text structure.

To the reader: Think about Selma's concern as you read this chapter, and be prepared by the end of this chapter to suggest possible assessment/teaching solutions for her.

GUIDELINES FOR LITERACY ASSESSMENT

The following five guidelines are based on a synthesis of current research and theory about assessment of literacy and learning (Afflerbach, 2010). These guidelines should assist you as you plan your instructional units and determine the ways you hope to assess and evaluate your students.

Content-Area Assessment Is a Continuous Process of Becoming Informed about Students' Learning

For learning to occur, assessments should be rooted in activities that have genuine purposes (Wyatt-Smith & Cumming, 2009). In this way, acquiring information about student learning does not become an end in itself but is an evolving process of gathering feedback for the teacher and student so that instruction can become more engaging, more tied to real-world issues and concerns, and more personally meaningful.

What do we want to know about students that requires us to assess them? We want to know under what conditions they learn best, what instructional practices we can employ to facilitate their learning, and how to encourage independent, active reading and learning. In other words, as teachers, we need to know more about our students' prior knowledge, their beliefs, their interests or attitudes, and how they navigate through disciplinary text and why they choose to do so. We also want students to discover about themselves as learners so they can expand their abilities as literate knowledge seekers. Middle school and high school teachers want to know whether or not their students are likely to profit from instructional texts, reading and writing practices, research projects, collaborative learning, and so on.

The assessment tools we use for these purposes should, therefore, be designed to provide insights into students' reading, writing, and thinking strategies with the actual texts they must use daily and in the actual, authentic contexts of their use. In this way, the information gleaned from assessment can be immediately translated into more responsive instruction for the teacher and more refined literacy and learning approaches for the student.

Not only should assessment be authentic, but it also should occur over time (Afflerbach, 2007). This type of assessment is often referred to as *formative,* because it offers teachers and students views of learning at regular intervals throughout the instructional unit, instead of waiting until the end to determine whether content and processes were learned (Bennett, 2011). As I have noted previously, learning is a continuous and dynamic process that takes place over time and changes with each new instructional situation. Therefore, to obtain more useful and meaningful information about your students' literacy and learning abilities, I recommend that you base instructional decisions on long-term, formative, observations and assessments done on a frequent basis. Later in this chapter, I discuss specific assessment formats that use day-to-day information gained from observing students and gathering reflections on their progress. Only with such important assessment data can we expect to build a supportive learning environment in disciplinary classrooms.

Assessment of Literacy and Content Learning Should Use Multiple Data Sources across Multiple Contexts

A basketball coach who wants to find out how well new recruits can play the game does not give paper-and-pencil tests. The players are required to perform various tasks on the court, and their ability is assessed while being directly observed. By making multiple assessments of situated performances, a coach can learn the most about a player's true ability and potential. So it is with the assessment of literacy and learning in disciplinary classrooms. That is, no single standardized test, teacher-made quiz, or written task can provide teachers with the information they need to know to promote student learning (Gandy, 2013; Graham, 2014; Stiggins, 2005).

Rather than relying on one source of information about students, teachers need information from multiple and overlapping sources in order to plan appropriate instruction. Such a perspective, of course, requires careful planning on the part of teachers, because planning is an integral part of the assessment process (Harlacher, Sakelaris, & Kattelman, 2014). For example, a science teacher's assessment plan for the first semester could include three different data sources: (1) his or her students' ability to process and understand textual content, (2) his or her observations of the students' problem-solving abilities, and (3) his or her interpretation of their learning logs. The advantage of determining students' progress and understanding with the actual materials used in the science class is that the teacher would then have a much clearer idea about how to modify his or her instruction to improve students' learning.

This example reinforces the point that students' literacy skills are context-bound. No single test can adequately reflect the teaching and learning process. As a former student of mine said, the old "clump theory" of literacy no longer makes sense. Traditional views of literacy held that all of us possess a given, measurable quantity, or clump, of literacy ability and that reading tests could accurately weigh our clumps. As our conceptions of what it means to be literate have changed to include the social, dynamic, generative, and idiosyncratic nature of literacy, we have begun to realize that the process of assessment must be expanded to include multiple demonstrations of ability in situated contexts of authentic teaching and learning.

Effective Assessment Involves Students

Traditionally, assessment has been a professional activity that teachers "do to students." However, many who believe that assessment is an ongoing activity that involves both students and teachers in the improvement of instruction have challenged this traditional view (Andrade & Valtcheva, 2009; Hafen et al., 2015; Jacome, 2012). Stiggins (2005) eloquently explained the rationale for this differing perspective: "The instructional decisions that contribute the most to student success are, in fact, not made by the adults. Rather, the decisions that contribute the most to determining student success or failure in learning are made by students themselves" (p. 18).

This equal partnership means that students are involved in their own assessment in a variety of ways. For example, they can (1) recommend possible assessment activities, (2) assist in the creation of rubrics and checklists, (3) apply rubrics and checklists to their own work, and (4) participate in self-reflection and evaluation activities that encourage them to relate their performance to the strategies they have used.

When students participate in the assessment and evaluation of their own strengths and needs, over time you will notice differences in their behaviors (e.g., motivation, metacognitive awareness) and in their performances and products (Harris, Brown, & Harnett, 2015; Stiggins & Chappius, 2011). For example, in one long-term study, the students who wrote journal entries that encouraged them to self-reflect on and evaluate the strategies they used were the ones with the highest achievement in a history course (Hubbard & Simpson, 2003).

In addition to self-evaluation journal writing activities, rubrics are also a powerful way to involve students in assessment (Andrade, Huff, & Brooke, 2012). Simply defined, rubrics are scoring guides or rating systems that inform students in advance, through descriptions of different levels of achievement, what is expected of them in terms of demonstrations of knowledge. Rubrics generally include the quality features or characteristics that designate a targeted assignment, the criteria that students must meet, and a range of possible points. Although I discuss rubrics and all their variations in Chapter 7, the example in Figure 4.1 shows how one might be designed. This particular rubric was crafted by a vocal music teacher who asked her students to find a current article in a magazine or newspaper that critiqued some type of musical performance. Notice that she informed the students about how the total points for the assignment would be awarded. She also asks her students to use this rubric as a way of evaluating and monitoring their own work before they hand it in to her.

Directions: Use this checklist to evaluate your assignment before you hand it in to me. The criteria listed below should help you locate strengths and weaknesses in your work. I will also be using the checklist to evaluate your assignment.

☐ 1. The references were listed on the index card correctly and completely. (*worth 6 points*)

☐ 2. The two articles were appropriate to the assignment. (*worth 4 points*)

☐ 3. There was a complete and accurate summary of the key ideas of the two articles you read. (*worth 10 points*)

Total points:

Comments:

FIGURE 4.1. Library project rubric.

Effective Assessment Requires Planning, Interpreting, and Managing a Variety of Data

This fourth guideline reiterates the importance of viewing assessment in a comprehensive manner. As noted by Cronbach (1960) over 50 years ago, effective informal assessment involves teachers in careful observations, a variety of data collection methods, and the integration of the information. Over time, others (Cumming, 2013; Van der Kleij, Vermeulen, Schildkamp, & Eggen, 2015) have modified Cronbach's suggestions to include these elements of assessment: planning goals and purposes, collecting data using a variety of techniques, and interpreting the data (i.e., the products students create and processes students engage in during learning). These researchers have also stressed the importance of viewing assessment as a recursive process rather than a linear one. That is, once teachers reflect on and interpret their data, they should use this information to make needed modifications of their instructional practices and future assessment approaches.

Thus far, I have emphasized the importance of collecting data using a variety of methods. However, I must also address the importance of the other two assessment elements—planning and interpreting. Planning involves teachers in a reflection of their curricular goals and their views of literacy, especially what it means to be a successful reader, writer, and learner in their disciplines. The assessment methods and activities they choose should reflect these views and goals. Interpreting involves teachers during all phases of the instructional process, not just at the end of the lesson or assessment activity (Sarafini, 2010). This on-the-spot diagnosis involves teachers simultaneously explicating the nature of learning and teaching at the same time that they are collecting data and making decisions. The interpretation of data also implies that teachers have a variety of ways to record, manage, and summarize the assessment information they collect, whether that be in the form of field notes, memos, checklists, or charts that reveal class trends. Later in the chapter I examine how disciplinary teachers have managed these important assessment tasks.

Assessment Should Include Students' Interests, Attitudes, and Beliefs

Obtaining information about students' real-world needs and interests can be very useful in planning ways to teach and reach your students. Interest is one of the most potent motivators for students, and teachers can take full advantage of this fact in a number of ways (Paige, 2011). One obvious strategy is to introduce students to reading materials related to their interests. These materials may be tied to the topic of study or may simply be relevant to students on a personal level. In Chapter 5, numerous practices focusing on increasing student engagement in literacy and learning are described. And in Chapter 8, I explain how teachers can take full advantage of a range of alternative texts to capture students' interests in disciplinary topics.

In addition to assessing students' interests, teachers need to identify students' identities as readers and learners (Cantrell & Carter, 2009). Students with naïve conceptions about learning and about how knowledge is acquired and used tend to believe that reading and learning complex information and ideas in the disciplines does not involve much effort, even though, as we all know, these academic tasks are, in fact, often difficult undertakings (Salvatori & Donahue, 2005). As a result, they are less likely to use strategies that engage them in elaborative levels of thinking, choosing instead to use rote-level strategies emphasizing memorization of facts. For example, because many students believe that knowledge about science is simply the memorization of isolated facts, they tend to focus on those facts without thinking about the interrelationships between them and the concepts they represent. This type of learning is obviously something that students can do in a rather superficial fashion rather than investing much mental effort.

These implicit beliefs about learning have a subtle impact on how students comprehend what they read, the way they solve problems, and how they persist when confronting difficult assignments (Conderman, Hedin, & Bresnahan, 2013). In addition, Schommer (1994) found an association between students' grades and their naïve conceptions of learning. In her study of 1,000 high school students, a regression analysis that controlled for general intelligence indicated that the more students believed in quick learning, the more likely they were to have low overall academic achievement. Later in this chapter and in Chapter 9, I present assessment activities that will help you identify students' interests and beliefs about reading and learning and discuss how you can use that information to inform teaching.

Before I describe authentic assessment procedures that reflect the five guidelines just described, I address critical issues related to standardized tests.

OUR STANDARDIZED TESTING CULTURE

Over the many years of my career as a professor and consultant, I have traversed the globe working with ministries of education, school systems, universities, and nongovernmental organizations (NGOs). What I have learned from these experiences is that no other country is as test-obsessed as we are here in the United States. This is not to say that other countries fail to produce and administer standardized tests to their students, but to emphasize that the testing done in most other countries has nothing like the extent or frequency with which we subject our school-age youth to here. The No Child Left Behind Act instituted mandatory standardized testing starting in grade 3. Some states use forms of standardized measures as early as kindergarten. By the time these students reach middle and high school, they and their teachers are well familiar with the annual ritual of standardized high-stakes test taking.

In addition to district- and state-level tests, many of which have been around in one form or another for several decades, numerous elementary, middle, and high school students across the country participate in the NAEP, whereas many others sit for the two prominent international tests in which the United States participates, PIRLS (Progress in International Literacy Study) for 9-year-olds and PISA (Program for International Student Assessment), described in Chapter 1. Thus it is not out of the realm of possibility that certain students are tested on a state or national version of a standardized test every year of their public school lives.

If this seems like too much testing to you, you are not alone. Recently, movements have been afoot by parents, politicians, teacher organizations, and grassroots groups to stem the tide of standardized testing or at least give parents and students the choice to opt out (Chen, 2015; Strauss, 2014). Whether these movements will lead to major policy reforms to reduce the volume and frequency of standardized high-stakes testing in American schools remains unclear. What is clear, however, is the desire of many stakeholders to take a closer look at the purposes of such testing practices. Moreover, what has been characterized as overtesting may be particularly detrimental to ELs (Zacher Pandya, 2011).

The newest iteration of high-stakes standardized testing in the United States comes to us via the CCSS. Once the development and implementation of the standards occurred, tests were needed to ascertain the extent to which students had met these standards. Enter PARCC (Partnership for Assessment of Readiness for College and Careers) and Smarter Balanced, the names of the two tests being used in states that have aligned their curriculum to the CCSS (Batel & Sargrad, 2016). Like most of their predecessors, the English/language arts/literacy portions of these two tests have characteristics with which we have all become familiar, such as short readings and multiple-choice questions. Newer features of these assessments include questions and prompts that require test takers to infer themes across texts, organize summary statements in logical order, and write short essays with textual evidence to support assertions.

The Uses and Potential Limitations of Standardized Tests

While calls for limiting or even eliminating standardized testing continue, its place in most educational systems around the country is as firm as ever. It is important, therefore, to consider the ways standardized tests have been used to inform and improve programs and practices.

At the district level, superintendents and principals can use standardized test data to evaluate a special program or intervention in order to determine its effectiveness. For example, a school district in Louisiana where I was consulting was having difficulty getting "buy-in" from content-area and disciplinary teachers from the middle and high schools to expand their instructional repertoires to include literacy strategies and practices. To help make the case for content literacy professional development, administrators at the district and school levels compiled reading test scores from the state assessment (the Louisiana Educational Assessment Program [LEAP]) for individual students from content teachers' classes and correlated them with the students' grade point averages. In disciplinary- and grade-level meetings, these results were shared in order to make the point that the better readers, according to LEAP scores, were also the better students, according to the teachers' own grade reports. This approach provided teachers with a graphic documentation of what many had assumed—the better readers are the better students in most subjects. Afterward, the secondary teachers in the district were more motivated to learn about literacy practices, especially for their students with lower achievement scores on LEAP, in order to boost achievement in their content and disciplinary classes. The result was a more successful secondary literacy professional development program.

In addition, the data from a standardized test can often inform administrators and teachers about large-scale trends at the district level. These trends can reflect the skills being taught effectively and those that need more emphasis. For example, I know of one school district in which the middle school teachers and administrators examined the results of the Iowa Test of Basic Skills (ITBS) for the sixth graders' strengths and weaknesses. As a result of their analysis, they identified the need to improve vocabulary instruction and learning as a goal for the next school year because of a pattern of low achievement on this subtest.

Standardized test results can also be used by classroom teachers. Some teachers use these scores as a large-scale screening device to determine possible groupings or skills that need emphasis for the class and for individual students. For example, Maria examined her state's reading test results for Jose, an incoming sixth grader, who had the following scores:

Vocabulary: 5.1 grade equivalent
Comprehension: 3.8 grade equivalent

Jose's scores suggest that he needs work on reading comprehension but that his vocabulary background is not a contributing factor to his low score on comprehension. Maria hypothesized that Jose may need help with active reading for main ideas to improve his comprehension. Of course, Maria used that information as a preliminary hunch. She verified that hunch with her own assessment activities to learn more about the strengths and skill needs of Jose and the other students in her sixth-grade language arts classes.

These typical uses of standardized tests, as potentially useful as they are, have not diminished the considerable criticism many have leveled at these assessment practices. The majority of criticisms focus on how the test results will be used. Teachers and parents worry that students will be placed in classes and programs based on a single standardized test score. What needs to be remembered, however, is that standardized tests, like any other assessment instrument, are only one data source or sample of students' skills and strategies. As the assessment guidelines presented in this chapter suggest, any instructional decision about a student is best made using a variety of sources of information.

Other criticisms have focused on the fact that the passages, problems, and questions on standardized tests do not reflect the specific goals and curricula of a school or subject. For example, a 10th-grade health education teacher may wonder what the percentiles and grade equivalents she received about her students have to do with their reading and learning in her class. Perhaps very little, and for obvious reasons. First, the comprehension passages on a test such as the ITBS may not cover health issues such as nutrition or exercise. Second, the kind of reading demanded by comprehension questions and prompts on such an instrument may be significantly different from the ways students would read and study health education texts. It is typical on these tests to read one or two paragraphs under strict time limitations. In contrast, the reading assignment in the health education class may require students to spend an entire week reading and discussing a 20- to 30-page chapter, which allows enough time for students to learn the material and for the teacher to provide a variety of instructional activities to support understanding and application of the chapter. Finally, most standardized tests measure reading performance with multiple-choice questions. The health education teacher may require students to write short, constructed responses or longer essays as demonstrations of their understandings of the content.

In addition to these potential limitations, experts have suggested that standardized tests are only a gross estimation of a student's reading ability (McCuchen, Jones, Carbonneau, & Mueller, 2015). The reason is that these assessments cannot possibly measure all the needed abilities and processes of successful reading, such as students' background knowledge, their depth of engagement with the material, their metacognitive awareness, or the strategies they employ while they read (Cantrell & Carter, 2009).

Many of these limitations, of course, can apply to any teacher-designed assessment instrument or activity. Hence, sensitivity to the uses and limitations of standardized tests should help you in planning and crafting your own approaches to responsive student assessment.

AUTHENTIC ASSESSMENT OF STUDENTS

One of the key principles of assessment of literacy and content learning discussed earlier is to embed assessment within actual literacy and learning activities so that the results of assessment will have direct and immediate instructional implications. This approach of assessment *for* instruction contrasts sharply with the standardized testing just described (Brozo & Afflerbach, 2011; Flórez & Sammons, 2013).

Another important principle I presented earlier is concerned with assessing students' literacy and learning in multiple contexts. To achieve these goals, secondary teachers need to devise their own approaches to assessment to determine the extent to which their students can read and learn from the various materials used for instruction and the level of application students can achieve with their new knowledge.

It should be emphasized that the goal of formative assessment within the context of content-area classrooms is to gain knowledge about students' challenges and successes with the actual texts from which they are expected to read and learn. With this assessment information, teachers can adapt instruction in response to students' needs. It should be further emphasized that formative assessment occurs frequently, allowing content-area and disciplinary teachers to respond in an ongoing way to the literacy needs of their students (Webb & Jones, 2009).

When formative assessment information is available, content-area and disciplinary teachers are in the best position to help their adolescent students read successfully a textbook chapter, a newspaper or magazine article, a graphic novel, a website, or any other print or electronic text source.

Successful assessment always involves making accurate inferences from assessment information. Whether our assessment is focused on comprehension strategies, problem solving, analytical writing, or word learning, it is essential to craft appropriate assessments to uncover students' abilities and needs.

When planning assessments, teachers should keep in the forefront of their thinking that youth will need to acquire transferable, 21st-century literacy skills for work, life, and future learning. One critical 21st-century skill is adaptive and distributed expertise (in contrast to routine expertise). This means youth must possess more than the ability to employ routine literacy skills. They must also be able to: (1) use literacy to cross knowledge domains; (2) engage flexible, innovative literacy competencies to help them meet varied, changing, and unpredictable local and global challenges; and (3) participate in a community of learners. Furthermore, to thrive in the 21st century, youth must be able to communicate, share, and use information to solve complex problems; adapt and innovate in response to new and changing demands; marshal and expand the power of technology to create new knowledge; and expand human capacity and productivity (Ananiadou & Claro, 2009; Darling-Hammond, & Adamson, 2010; Seglem, Witte, & Beemer, 2012).

This means that secondary teachers will need to have learning and assessment opportunities that promote and scaffold youths' multiple literacy abilities to enable them (1) to be proactive in creating a viable niche in the global labor markets, (2) to navigate and help shape the mediasphere; and (3) to become engaged citizens.

Schooling that fails to do more than inculcate narrow units of information and procedures is now regarded as inadequate for the complex and ever-shifting demands of modern life and work (Darche, Nayar, & Bracco, 2009). Instead, to prepare youth adequately for changing real-world challenges, educators must develop their language tools, as well as their cognitive capacities, to improve problem solving, decision making, and interpersonal competence (Brozo, 2015).

Embedding Assessment in Classroom Activities

Astronomy

In order to assess his students' connected knowledge of astronomy, Jerome uses a fill-in concept map. This strategy entails creating a partially completed graphic that depicts networks of related concepts and requesting that students complete the graphic by supplying the appropriate missing terms in their correct places in the graphic. Jerome's students are asked to use the word list in Figure 4.2 at the top to complete the map. You will observe in this example 10 blank bubbles with only 7 terms, which means that some terms will be used more than once. Jerome scores the concept map based on the percentage of correct responses to the total number of blank bubbles.

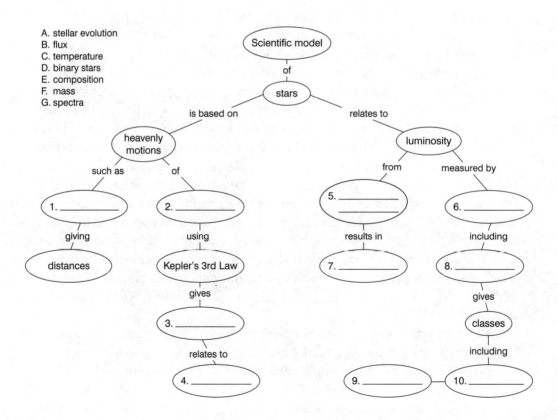

FIGURE 4.2. Science bubble map.

Because Jerome's approach to teaching astronomy and all his science subjects is to facilitate knowledge connections, his use of concept maps for assessing his students' abilities to demonstrate critical links in their new knowledge lends further authenticity to his efforts. An added benefit is that his students like completing the maps, especially students with lower levels of communication skills.

Assessments conducted as students interact with text and complete daily assignments, engage in class discussions, or work cooperatively to solve problems can provide a rich source of information about students' relative strengths and needs, as well as how instruction can be modified to facilitate learning. Throughout this book, you will encounter numerous practices and activities that can be used to assess your students while improving their learning.

Assessing through Observations

Suggesting to teachers that they assess through observation is like asking them to breathe or walk; it comes so naturally to most of them that its importance and power as an assessment strategy is often overlooked. Observational assessment provides teachers with a vast amount of information, especially when combined with other data sources, such as samples of student work (Spinelli, 2008).

Assessing through observation requires teachers to become more sensitive to the entire instructional situation: the student, the text, the tasks required of the reader, the processes needed to complete the tasks, the environment in which tasks occur. Observing students over time in a variety of classroom situations can provide teachers with a more complete view of students' strengths and needs. Earlier, I critiqued the limitations of making instructional decisions based on a single assessment at one point in time—specifically stating that single assessments can offer only a limited perspective of students' literacy and learning performance. In contrast, observational assessments are ongoing and occur within the context of normal classroom activities while students are engaged in learning disciplinary information and concepts.

In addition to capitalizing on teachable moments that observational assessment enables, teachers can structure targeted observations with the use of a checklist. These observation checklists can focus on a variety of literacy contexts, such as when students (1) read for enjoyment, (2) read from different text sources, (3) write responses and essays, and (4) discuss and present ideas.

English

Margot created an observation checklist in order to collect information on which students may be having difficulty with the readings she required in her English classes. The checklist is composed of a continually expanding list of statements of student behaviors that Margot has recorded (see Figure 4.3). These behaviors have been exhibited by those adolescents who struggle to keep up with the reading and comprehension of assigned texts. Interpreted as "symptoms" according to Margot, she records how often she sees these behaviors, especially early in the school year or when new students come into her classroom. Once her suspicions are aroused about a particular student, based on documentation on the checklist, she has a conference with the student to explore further the nature of her or his reading challenges. The ultimate goal is to use the observational tool as a screening device to identify which students may need special supports.

Social Studies

Audra created an observational checklist based on what she has come to learn are characteristics of effective readers in her eighth-grade social studies classroom (see Figure 4.4). The items in her checklist derive from knowledge gained about disciplinary and content literacy through university coursework, professional development experiences, consultations with the school reading specialist, and her own informed practices. Notice how she has designed the checklist in a way that allows summarizing patterns among students in order to identify priority areas.

Because Margot's and Audra's observations occur as a natural part of their content-area lessons, students can demonstrate their normal abilities. This allows the teachers to obtain highly relevant and useful information by focusing on what they regard as priorities for ensuring they understand the challenges and strengths of struggling students.

Student:

1. Avoids eye contact with me, especially when I'm asking questions of the class over the reading assignment.

2. May create the impression that he or she knows the answer to my question by looking intently and flagging his or her hand.

3. During oral reading of the textbook, tries to be the first one to read to get it over with.

4. During oral reading, tries to be the last one to read or tries to avoid being called on to read.

5. Frequently forgets to bring to class books and other materials that may be used for oral reading or needed to do in-class work.

6. Twists and turns restlessly in seat, often talking with another student.

7. Attempts to disrupt class.

8. Uses manipulative techniques within and outside of class to try to create a positive perception of his or her ability in spite of poor performance.

9. Uses another student for information about assignments and answers to questions.

FIGURE 4.3. Observational checklist to screen for struggling readers.

	Maria	Jade	Josh	Heather	Andres	Keidra
Comprehension Behaviors						
1. Establishes purposes for reading						
2. Identifies and understands key ideas						
3. Follows the chapter's organizational structure	.					
4. Summarizes important ideas, using own words						
5. Monitors understanding						
6. Adjusts reading rate to material being read						
7. Concentrates and begins tasks appropriately						
8. Has a variety of ways to determine the meaning of new words						
Study Behaviors						
1. Utilizes book parts						
2. Knows how to skim, preview, and scan						
3. Interprets visual aids correctly and appropriately						
4. Takes effective class notes						
5. Knows how to prepare for tests						
6. Organizes information						
7. Identifies useful sources for research						
8. Understands how to critique research sources						
Attitude and Interest						
1. Chooses material for personal reading						
2. Demonstrates enjoyment of reading						
3. Has varied reading interests						
Key: 1 = Excellent (consistently) **2 = Good (usually)** **3 = Average (sometimes)** **4 = Below average (seldom)** **5 = Poor (never)**						

FIGURE 4.4. Observational checklist of effective reading practices.

Assessment Activities Using Students' Writing

Writing is a powerful communication tool because it mirrors our understanding of information and ideas. Writing is also permanent, allowing us to reflect on the meanings that we attempted to construct, recorded on paper or in digital form. Hence, it is logical to use writing activities as one way to assess students' comprehension and application of text (Graham, Harris, & Hebert, 2011; Sedita, 2013).

Math

One approach that seventh-grade teacher Anna employs to help herself and her math students discover more about their interests, attitudes, and beliefs concerning learning math is with *autobiographical sketches* (Angelo & Cross, 2008). The idea is that students need opportunities to examine their personal histories as readers, writers, and learners both in and out of school. By exploring their past, students might better understand their current approaches and beliefs about learning, and teachers gain invaluable insight that can be translated into responsive instructional practices.

Anna asks her seventh graders to write in response to prompts that result in their math autobiographies. At the beginning of the school year, her students make their first entry in their math journal. She tells them to write about experiences they have had that relate to math, and guides them with the following questions:

- "How did you feel about math in elementary school?"
- "What are your experiences with math teachers?"
- "Is there one particular experience that stands out?"
- "Was there a time when you liked math? Hated it? Why did you feel that way?"
- "Did you have any special strategies for getting through math classes? Have these strategies worked for you? Why or why not?"

Anna quickly learns a great deal of useful information about her students' attitudes, anxieties, and math strategies from these autobiographies. She then uses classroom observations of her students, as well as their work and other assessments, to validate these self-reports. One of her students, Zena, is the author of the following entry that provided Anna with some useful clues to Zena's mindset about math:

"When I was in elementary school I had a little trouble with adding and subtracting. Now I have difficulties with my multiplication tables. Story problems really bother me so my mother tries to help me with these. I still am nervous about math, especially if the test is timed. In stores I always make sure they give me correct change, but I have trouble figuring out the prices when things are on sale. I wish teachers would show us how to use math in the things we do every day. If I have good teachers I do great, but when my teachers aren't so good I do bad. I had a teacher who didn't like me and tried her hardest to make me fail. My parents told me to just do the best I can and not to worry about how the teacher feels about me. My father and brothers are all good in math, so I am the only math dummy in our house. I like math when I understand it, but if I don't understand it, I don't like it. I usually am afraid to ask questions when I am lost—so please be patient with me."

This assessment practice can be modified for any discipline or content area. To have your students reflect on their past experiences as language users and learners, I recommend the following approach:

1. In small groups, ask students to brainstorm their past as readers, writers, and learners. They should try to remember something about a time, person, school year, class, event, assignment, text, teacher, friend, relative, or the like.
2. After brainstorming with group partners, students should write about that event, time, or person that had a positive or negative impact on their thinking and feeling about literacy and learning.
3. Be sure students focus on two critical questions: What happened that influenced the way you presently read, write, and learn? How do you feel about that influence now?
4. Students should be allowed to write as much as necessary to describe and reflect fully on their past influences and experiences related to how they currently think about themselves as readers, writers, and learners.
5. After thinking and writing, students could be allowed to exchange their drafts with members of their brainstorm group for comment, questions, and feedback.
6. Students could be asked to share their autobiographies, but only on a voluntary basis.
7. I recommend that you also take part in this activity by writing and sharing your autobiography with the class.

Chemistry

If you feel uncomfortable using this approach with the learner autobiography, you can ask students to write parts of the autobiography throughout the school year. For example, a chemistry teacher, Hector, asks his students to write in their e-journals what they think it means to read, study, and learn in a chemistry course. He makes this request at the beginning of the class period the first week of school. After students forward their entries to Hector and he reviews them, he talks to his class about what literacy practices he uses to learn chemistry content.

During the school year, Hector follows up this initial assignment by asking students to write on other topics, using a template such as the following:

> This week I really liked _____ because _____. What really confused me this week was _____; and I would like to know more about _____ because _____.

These brief written responses have at least two advantages. First, students react positively to them because the required amount of writing seems less intimidating. For Hector, the e-journal entries allow him to assess quickly what his students are thinking, learning, and feeling as they study chemistry.

The information gained from students' written autobiographies can help you make instructional decisions, deconstruct maladaptive attitudes and beliefs about literacy and learning, target certain activities and projects to particular students, and improve and support healthy attitudes about literacy and learning.

The Content Literacy Inventory

The content literacy inventory is extremely valuable because it asks students to demonstrate their reading, thinking, and study processes with the texts disciplinary teachers expect their students to read (Bean, Readence, & Baldwin, 2011). This inventory is an informal assessment to be completed silently by students. Thus it can be easily administered to the entire class within a single class period. Furthermore, since it is teacher-constructed using the students' actual disciplinary text, the information garnered can be translated directly into instructional modifications for individuals, groups, or the whole class. Teachers can easily assess which areas of the text or which skills and strategies may provide potential problems for students (Vacca, Vacca, & Mraz, 2014).

It is important to emphasize that content literacy inventories can take any form needed to acquire desired information about students, though when designed around a class textbook, it is common to structure them around sections (see Figure 4.5). For example, one section might assesses students' knowledge of and ability to utilize the various textual and reading aids, such as the table of contents, glossary, index, pictures, charts, maps, and graphs. Ability to use these aids is tantamount to successfully learning the content of the textbook. Another section could require students to read portions of the text and then respond to questions and prompts of the type the teacher might typically pose, for instance, explicit and implicit comprehension questions, as well as questions that reflect their ability to manipulate text structure. Another section might gather students' responses to questions that assess their knowledge and use of technical or specialized vocabulary pertinent to the content.

Section I: Study and Reading Aids (*answered using the entire text*)

1. On what page would you find a map of the solar system? (tests ability to find a map or table in a science textbook)

2. On what page does Chapter 7 begin? What is the title of the unit that contains this chapter? (tests ability to use table of contents)

3. How can the introduction on page 18 and the summary on page 49 help you to study the chapter? (tests understanding of unit introduction and chapter summary)

4. Why are the chapter questions and vocabulary exercises on pages 50–53 valuable? (tests understanding of specific study aids)

5. Look at the chart on page 32. From the information given, tell what the jobs of the specific cell parts are. (tests ability to understand charts)

Section II: Vocabulary (*answered using a section of text*)

6. Define **nucleus**.

7. Read the third paragraph on page 31. From the information given in that paragraph, what do you think a **nuclear membrane** is?

8. What is a **vacuole**?

9. Give an example of **diffusion**.

Section III: Text Explicit and Text Implicit Information (*answered using a section of text*)

10. What six elements make up most of the living matter of our earth? (text explicit)

11. What do chloroplasts contain? (text explicit)

12. Why are mitochondria often called the powerhouses of the cells? (text implicit)

13. How do mitochondria and chloroplasts differ? (text implicit)

14. What is found between the cell membrane and the nucleus? (text explicit)

15. Read the section entitled "Cells and Their Jobs." Create a mind map or an outline that clearly illustrates the cells and the specific jobs they do. (text implicit)

FIGURE 4.5. Example of a content literacy inventory for science.

The following are recommended steps for developing your own content literacy inventory.

1. Select a short passage or section from the course textbook or other core text. The section should provide enough context so as to allow students to be able to learn from the reading. Typically, these sections are about 4–6 pages in length.

2. Construct questions and prompts about using the study and reading aids found in the text, such as the table of contents, index, glossary, chapter

introductions, and summaries, and visual aids, such as charts, maps, graphs, and pictures. These will vary depending on the type of text used in the assessment. *Students are provided with the entire text for responding to these questions and prompts.*

3. Construct questions and prompts on content-specific vocabulary.
4. Construct questions and prompts assessing both explicit and implicit understanding of textual information, including those that assess students' abilities to make sense of the text's structure.
5. Analyze the results of the inventory by looking for patterns of responses for individual students and the whole class.
6. Use the results of the inventory to determine areas students have mastered and those in which they will need further instruction. Target specific instructional interventions for individuals and embed disciplinary literacy strategies within daily instruction for the whole group.

The content literacy inventory can help you see patterns in the skills for which students will need additional teaching and reinforcement. Rosa, a sixth-grade math teacher, developed a summary form to help her see these patterns. As illustrated in Figure 4.6, Rosa listed one class of student in the left column and, along the top of the form, listed the reading skills she expects her students to master in the math course. Notice how Rosa placed a checkmark in the appropriate column for the students who missed more than half of the questions on a specific skill. For example, any student who responded incorrectly to three inventory questions about understanding math symbols received a check on the summary form in that column. Rosa believes this additional analysis helps her identify the reading and problem-solving skills that most of her students will need to be taught to succeed in mathematics in general and in her course, specifically.

To help you better understand the value of a content literacy inventory approach to assessment, read through the cases and examples in Figure 4.7 and then follow the directions. I want you to notice the stark difference between the broad standardized reading test results that history teacher Kristien receives for his students and those science teacher Maria is able to obtain by employing a content literacy inventory.

Vocabulary Self-Awareness: Assessing Word Knowledge in the Secondary Classroom

Because students bring a range of word understandings to the reading of content area and disciplinary texts, it is important to assess their vocabulary knowledge before reading (Fisher, Brozo, Frey, & Ivey, 2015). This awareness is valuable for secondary teachers, as well as for students, because it provides a reflection of the critical academic language they know, as well as what they still need to learn

Classroom Summary Form: Content-Area Inventory

Names	Using parts of the book					Following directions				Understanding math symbols				Understanding vocabulary				Noting main ideas				Drawing conclusions				
	1	2	3	4	5	6	7	8	9	10	11	12	13	14	15	16	17	18	19	20	21	22	23	24	25	26
Jason	✓					✓	✓	✓		✓	✓	✓		✓		✓	✓	✓	✓		✓	✓	✓	✓	✓	✓
Tamika										✓	✓		✓	✓						✓		✓	✓	✓	✓	✓
Jorge										✓	✓		✓		✓	✓										
Michelle		✓	✓	✓	✓				✓						✓							✓	✓	✓	✓	✓
Tyrone	✓	✓	✓			✓	✓	✓		✓	✓	✓	✓	✓	✓	✓	✓		✓			✓	✓	✓	✓	✓
Gareth										✓	✓							✓				✓		✓	✓	
Avery	✓					✓				✓	✓			✓	✓	✓		✓	✓	✓		✓		✓		
Judd			✓			✓				✓	✓	✓		✓			✓	✓	✓	✓		✓	✓			
Chanda	✓	✓				✓	✓	✓	✓					✓	✓	✓		✓	✓	✓		✓	✓	✓	✓	✓
Jennifer		✓				✓	✓	✓	✓					✓				✓	✓			✓	✓	✓	✓	

Place a checkmark under the number of the question that was missed and alongside the name of the student who missed it.

FIGURE 4.6. Classroom summary form: Content literacy inventory.

Directions: Read this first case study carefully. After reading it, fill out the Assessment Reflection Sheet for one student in Kristien's class. Discuss the case study and your responses on the form with a colleague and then with the whole group.

Case Study 1

Kristien is a history teacher in a secondary school. His school director decided that all students should be tested at the beginning of the school year, so teachers would know how well they read. For the first week of school, students were required to complete a standardized reading test. The test was composed of questions about general vocabulary in the first section and short reading selections followed by comprehension questions in the second section. Neither the vocabulary nor the comprehension sections had words or passages related to the history content in his textbook. Once the results of the test were processed for each student, teachers received a spreadsheet that looked like this:

Student	Vocabulary (total correct/total possible)	Comprehension (total correct/total possible)
Erik	40/50	37/50
Beatriz	35/50	32/50
Josef	29/50	27/50
Ana	47/50	44/50

Assessment Reflection Sheet

Student:

Assessment tool:

Student work: Areas of strength

Student work: Areas of weakness

Teacher practice: What instructional approaches should be used?

Teacher practice: What interventions or unit modifications should be made?

Unanswered questions:

FIGURE 4.7. Assessment activity.

Directions: Read this second case study carefully. After reading it, fill out the Assessment Reflection Sheet for Maria's student, Katarina. Discuss the case study and your responses on the form with a colleague and then with the whole group. Compare and contrast your responses to the first and second case studies.

Case Study 2

Maria is an eighth-grade science teacher. After attending a professional development workshop on content-area assessment procedures, she became interested in discovering more about her students' ability to comprehend textbook information. She realized she needed alternative assessments to the tests at the end of the chapters in her science book. Maria was relying more and more on these tests for grading purposes and less and less on other assessments of her students as readers and learners. Moreover, she was not using the chapter test results to adjust the way she taught the textbook content.

The professional developer emphasized the need to tie content material to the processes for learning it effectively. The professional developer made suggestions for ways teachers could teach and assess at the same time. Maria decided to use this information to develop her own assessment tool using the class textbook. For an upcoming unit on geology, she designed an assessment that was composed of several short sections with a few questions in each section. The textbook assessment with sample questions looked like this:

Name:

Unit: Geology

Section I: Reading Engagement and Interest

1. **It is hard to pay attention to what I'm reading in the science textbook.**

   Not at all like me!   Not much like me   Can't decide   Kind of like me   A lot like me!

2. **I get nervous when I read on a new topic like geology.**

   Not at all like me!   Not much like me   Can't decide   Kind of like me   A lot like me!

3. **I like to read about rocks, volcanoes, and earthquakes.**

   Not at all like me!   Not much like me   Can't decide   Kind of like me   A lot like me!

4. **Reading will be easier for me because I like rocks, volcanoes, and earthquakes.**

   Not at all like me!   Not much like me   Can't decide   Kind of like me   A lot like me!

Section II: Prior Knowledge

1. **I know a lot about rocks, volcanoes, and earthquakes.**

   Not at all like me!   Not much like me   Can't decide   Kind of like me   A lot like me!

2. **I have read other books and magazines about geology.**

   Not at all like me!   Not much like me   Can't decide   Kind of like me   A lot like me!

3. **I have a rock collection and know the names of several rocks.**

   Not at all like me!   Not much like me   Can't decide   Kind of like me   A lot like me!

(continued)

FIGURE 4.7. *(continued)*

Section III: Vocabulary

1. _____ rocks form from **2.** _____. **3.** _____ is made up of pieces of rock, shell, sand, mud, or organic matter that have been transported from one place to another by a force such as wind, water, ice, or simply gravity. When the movement stops, these particles settle layer upon layer forming **4.** _____ rocks. When these layers **5.** _____, **6.** _____ rock forms.

igneous, metamorphic, sedimentary, magma, lithify, sediment

Section IV: Comprehension

1. According to the paragraphs you have just read, what are the three main types of rocks?

2. Name one characteristic of each type of rock.

3. How are these rocks different?

4. What words or phrases did the author use to cue you that the rocks were different in some ways?

Section V: Reading Strategies

1. Using the information from the paragraphs just read, construct a set of organized notes for studying.
2. Underline the key ideas in the paragraphs just read.
3. Write a summary of the paragraphs just read.

Student Profile: *Katarina*

Section I: Reading Engagement and Interest

Very little interest in the topic of geology

Section II: Prior Knowledge

Limited background knowledge on geology, including rock types, volcanoes, and earthquakes

Section III: Vocabulary

Supplied one out of six correct words in the blank spaces and may have guessed

Section IV: Comprehension

Answered two out of the four questions correctly

Section V: Reading Strategies

Her notes were disorganized and were taken verbatim from the paragraphs.

She underlined nearly the entire text, making it difficult to distinguish between important and less important information and ideas.

Her summary was too long and was not in her own words.

FIGURE 4.7. (*continued*)

Formative Assessment Reflection Sheet
Student:
Assessment tool:
Student work: Areas of strength
Student work: Areas of weakness
Teacher practice: What instructional approaches should be used?
Teacher practice: What interventions or unit modifications should be made?
Unanswered questions:

Directions: Now, reflect on assessments and a student in your own class and attempt to fill this Formative Assessment Reflection Sheet out again. Discuss your responses with a colleague and then the whole group.

Formative Assessment Reflection Sheet
Student:
Assessment tool:
Student work: Areas of strength
Student work: Areas of weakness
Teacher practice: What instructional approaches should be used?
Teacher practice: What interventions or unit modifications should be made?
Unanswered questions:

FIGURE 4.7. *(continued)*

in order to fully comprehend the reading (Goodman, 2001; Pearson, Hiebert, & Kamil, 2012).

The process involves providing students with a vocabulary self-awareness chart before they begin reading new material. The chart should list key terms from the passage that students should be expected to know and learn. Students are asked to rate each vocabulary word according to its level of familiarity and their understanding of it. A plus sign (+) indicates a high degree of comfort and knowledge; a checkmark (✓) indicates uncertainty; and a minus sign (–) indicates the word is brand new to them. Also, students should to try to supply a definition and example for each word. For words with checkmarks or minus signs, students may have to make guesses about definitions and examples. Students should not be given definitions or examples at this stage.

Over the course of the readings and exposure to other information sources throughout the unit, students should be told to return often to the chart so they can revise original entries and add new information about each vocabulary word. The goal is for students to replace all the checkmarks and minus signs with plus signs by the end of the reading or unit. Because students continually revisit their vocabulary charts to revise their entries, they have multiple opportunities to practice and extend their understanding of important content terminology.

The vocabulary self-awareness activity provides another formative assessment of students' content-area vocabulary knowledge and learning. Information about students from this assessment can be added to the other assessment information gathered from the content literacy inventory to guide instruction in content-area vocabulary building and reading. The vocabulary self-awareness activity, like the content literacy inventory, is evaluated informally.

Using Vocabulary Self-Awareness Results

Students can use vocabulary self-awareness to determine the extent of their prior knowledge of key content-area vocabulary and monitor their growth in word learning. By observing students' responses to the key terms on the vocabulary self-awareness chart, teachers can identify students who need vocabulary instruction before, during, and after reading.

A teacher's analysis of Nathan's performance with this vocabulary self-awareness activity could read:

- His prior knowledge of key vocabulary, as reflected, was sufficient to aid in comprehending the passages, and he enriched his understanding of key terminology through reading.
- Nathan does not appear to need any additional vocabulary instruction of these key terms.

Nathan's Vocabulary Self-Awareness Responses *before* Reading about Early Civilization

Word	+	✓	–	Definition	Example
Artifacts		X		Unsure, maybe like facts from art.	
archaeology			X	I'm not sure what this means.	
Specialized		X		I think it's anything that's real special to you.	Like, someone who's real special to you.
anthropology			X	It's some kind of scientist, but I'm not sure.	

Nathan's Vocabulary Self-Awareness Responses *after* Reading about Early Civilization

Word	+	✓	–	Definition	Example
Artifacts	X			Something made or given shape by man, such as a tool or a work of art.	A gold chain from ancient Egypt.
archaeology	X			Study of human activity in the past by analysis of the physical culture.	Learning about ancient Egyptian culture by analyzing the pyramids and tombs.
Specialized		X		I think it's having a special skill or being able to make something that does one thing.	Ancient Egyptians had a special tool for making jewelry.
anthropology	X			Study of humans in the past and today.	Margaret Mead was an anthropologist who studied Samoans.

A teacher's analysis of Jodi's performance with this vocabulary self-awareness activity could read:

- Jodi's low level of familiarity with key vocabulary from the passages before reading and her difficulty acquiring new vocabulary knowledge through reading appeared to contribute to her overall problems with comprehension.
- Jodi will require additional instruction related to these and other key science terms before reading: preteach key vocabulary and use vocabulary cards;

during reading: use concept of definition and student-friendly definition approaches; after reading: word study guides.

Jodi's Vocabulary Self-Awareness Responses *before* Reading an Introduction to Science

Word	+	✓	–	Definition	Example
subdividing		X		To divide something.	
application		X		Apply to a job.	Like at McDonalds.
interdependent			X	I don't know.	
antibiotics		X		It's some kind of medicine.	

Jodi's Vocabulary Self-Awareness Responses *after* Reading an Introduction to Science

Word	+	✓	–	Definition	Example
subdividing		X		Something to do with categories.	Animals
application		X		Using something.	Using science
interdependent		X		Living together.	Like birds and bees
antibiotics		X		Some kind of medicine.	For the flu

Self-Report Inventories and Questionnaires

Inventories and questionnaires are the simplest and most direct way of acquiring information about students' skills, interests, and attitudes. Some of these self-report assessments, such as the Interest Inventory (Figure 4.8) and the Survey of Study Strategies (Figure 4.9), require students merely to read and place a checkmark in the appropriate space. Other inventories, such as the Interest Inventory II (Figure 4.10), ask students to write more elaborate answers to questions regarding their interests. The Writing Strategies Questionnaire in Figure 4.11 has been used by middle and high school teachers to discover important past experiences their students have had with writing and how they think and feel about writing.

Although your students' attitudes about themselves as learners in your classroom may be difficult to uncover with one simple inventory or questionnaire, they are a starting point for acquiring more in-depth information about your students (Pitcher, Albright, DeLaney, Walker, & Seunarinesingh, 2007). The key is that opportunities are provided on a regular basis for students to explore and share their underlying attitudes toward literacy and learning. Remember, the examples of the

Directions: Check off each activity you like to do in your spare time.

Interests Outside of School

☐ Television	☐ Hobbies	☐ Traveling
☐ Outdoor games	☐ Playing sports	☐ Cooking
☐ Watching sports	☐ Fishing or hunting	☐ Music
☐ Hiking and camping	☐ Dancing	☐ Motorcycles
☐ Video games	☐ Socializing	☐ Cars
☐ Volunteer work	☐ Movies	☐ Other(s):
☐ Reading	☐ Computer and Internet	

FIGURE 4.8. Interest Inventory I.

inventories and questionnaires I have presented are merely suggestions of the kinds of issues and questions you may find relevant to your teaching situation. I urge you to use these suggestions to develop your own inventories that suit your particular need to know more about your students.

Authentic Assessment with e-Portfolios

Portfolios for instruction and assessment remain popular with teachers in nearly every field. I'm sure most of you are by now quite familiar with the term and have, perhaps, even used portfolios in your own teaching. Barrett (2007) offers a helpful description of this form of assessment:

> An educational portfolio contains work that a learner has collected, reflected upon, selected, and presented to show growth and change over time, work that represents an individual's or an organization's human capital. A critical component of an educational portfolio is the learner's reflection on the individual pieces of work (often called artifacts) as well as an overall reflection on the story that the portfolio tells about the learner. (p. 436)

With the omnipresence of computers and the Internet in secondary schools, as well as an array of versatile apps, today's portfolios are more often than not compiled, maintained, and presented in an electronic format. The biggest advantage of electronic portfolios over organized hard-copy collections of student work is that they create an efficient visual space for traditional print-based artifacts, as well as artifacts that go well beyond these traditional genres (Goodson, 2007). In addition to written texts, digital portfolios can include video, images, hyperlinks, and audio,

Your name: _____   Date: _____

Survey of Study Strategies

	Strongly Agree	Agree	Neutral	Disagree	Strongly Disagree
Time Management					
1. I put off my homework until the last minute.					
2. I plan regular times to study.					
3. I study less than an hour a day outside class.					
4. I cram for tests the night before the exam.					
5. I study with the radio, stereo, or TV on.					
6. I have a specified and quiet place for study.					
Remembering and Understanding					
1. I examine each of my textbooks for its overall organization.					
2. I look over a chapter before reading it in detail.					
3. I have to read a chapter several times before I understand it.					
4. I'm halfway through a chapter before I understand what it is about.					
5. I do not know which information in a chapter is important and which is not.					
6. My mind wanders to other things while I am reading an assignment.					
7. I have trouble remembering what I read.					
8. I try to set purposes and questions to be answered in my reading assignments.					
9. I find reading difficult because of the big words.					
Notetaking and Listening					
1. I take notes on my assigned readings.					
2. My notes on my textbooks are unorganized and messy.					
3. My notes don't make any sense to me.					
4. I don't know what to write down in my notes.					
7. I find myself doodling or writing letters during lectures.					
8. I can't pick out important ideas from a lecture.					

FIGURE 4.9. Survey of study strategies.

	Strongly Agree	Agree	Neutral	Disagree	Strongly Disagree
7. I find myself doodling or writing letters during lectures.					
8. I can't pick out important ideas from a lecture.					
9. I review my lecture notes as soon as possible after class.					
Test Taking and Test Preparation					
1. I study the wrong things for a test.					
2. I do not perform well on tests.					
3. I have mental blocks when I take a test.					
4. I know how to prepare for an essay exam.					
5. I have an effective strategy for approaching my upcoming exams.					
6. I know techniques for memorization.					
Reading Rate Strategies					
1. I hurry through all my assignments as quickly as I can.					
2. My reading speed is fast enough for my assignments.					
3. It takes me a long time to read any assignment.					
4. I can scan for specific information with little difficulty.					
5. I read most material at the same rate.					
6. I read as quickly as most people in my class.					

FIGURE 4.9. (*continued*)

which allows a much richer and varied representation of student accomplishments (Williams, 2007). Furthermore, digital portfolios offer teachers an excellent vehicle for meeting the calls by education experts and policy makers for performance-based measures of reading, writing, and learning (Gardner, Harlen, Hayward, & Stobart, 2011; National Governors Association Center for Best Practices and Council of Chief State School Officers [NGA & CCSSO], 2010).

Before saying more about the advantages of teaching and assessing with portfolios, and electronic portfolios in particular, I want to offer a word of caution. The mere inclusion of digital technology for presenting student work does not transform print and hard-copy versions of that work into an e-portfolio. As Hicks and his colleagues (2007) stress, without clear standards and objectives for the e-portfolio, it may become nothing more than a multimedia show, a digital anthology, or a flashy resume. Therefore, as you read further in this section, you will see ideas

Directions: Finish each sentence so that it tells something about you. You may write as much as you wish to finish each sentence.

1. After school I like to _____

2. On weekends I like to _____

3. _____ is my favorite TV show because _____

4. The kind of music I like is _____

5. When I graduate from high school, I want to _____

6. If I could go anywhere in the world, I'd go to _____ because _____

7. If I could take only one book with me on a trip to Mars, that book would be _____ because _____

8. I have seen the movie _____ and wish I could find a book similar to it because _____

9. I have reread the book _____ because _____

10. When I read the newspaper or a magazine, I like to read _____ because _____

FIGURE 4.10. Interest Inventory II.

and practical applications of e-portfolios framed around guidelines and offered to students with clear objectives. In this way, the full benefits of digital technology for "containing" and documenting students' efforts, achievements, and reflections can be exploited.

For any of us who have wondered why the allure of portfolio assessment has persisted for the past few decades in spite of the challenges it poses, I believe the answer, simply put, is that portfolios offer an assessment framework that reflects our

1. If you knew someone was having trouble writing, what would you do to help?
2. What would a teacher do to help that student?
3. If you were told you have to write an essay due in 1 week, what would you do to make sure it is done on time and is well written?
4. Think about someone you know who is a good writer. What makes that person a good writer?
5. What is the best advice you've ever been given about writing?
6. How did you learn to write? When? Who helped you?
7. What would help you improve your writing?
8. Do you think you're a good writer? Why or why not?
9. Why do people write? What are your reasons for writing?
10. Does the writing you do in school interest you? Why or why not?

FIGURE 4.11. Writing strategies questionnaire.

current understanding of the process of literacy and content learning. We know, for instance, that:

- Learning takes place over time—portfolios are collections of learning demonstrations at many points during the learning cycle.
- Learning occurs in multiple contexts—portfolios sample work from a variety of teaching/learning/performance situations.
- Effective learning occurs when learners are engaged in meaningful, purposeful learning activities—portfolio teaching and assessment provide teachers an ideal way to promote authentic learning.
- Effective learning requires reflection and self-evaluation—portfolios have self-reflection built into the process.

To take full advantage of the portfolio system, advocates suggest that the following five questions should be answered during the planning stage.

What Will the e-Portfolio Look Like?

All portfolios, including e-portfolios, should have a "physical" as well as a conceptual structure. Physically, a portfolio may be structured chronologically, by discipline, or by style of work. More and more secondary teachers are using free open-source bulletin board software technology, such as Vanilla Forums (*https://vanillaforums.org*), for creating the digital spaces to structure students' e-portfolios. The conceptual structure refers to your goals for student learning. After identifying goals, you should decide the best ways to document students' work relative to the goals.

What Goes in the Portfolio?

To determine what goes in the portfolio, several related questions must be answered first: Who will evaluate the portfolios (teachers, specialist, administrators, parents)? What will these individuals want to know about student learning? Will portfolio samples document student growth that test scores cannot capture? Or will they further support the results of test scores? What is the best evidence to be included in the portfolio to document student progress toward goals? Will students include their best work only, or will the portfolio contain a progressive record of student growth, or both? Will the portfolio include drafts, sketches, and ideas for unfinished work as well as work in finished form?

Because portfolio assessment is authentic in that it represents genuine meaningful learning activities inside and potentially outside the classroom, work samples should come from the variety of daily and weekly assignments and projects in which students are engaged. If you are documenting the literacy progress of a seventh grader, for example, then her e-portfolio would likely contain (1) samples of a writing folder, (2) excerpts from journals and literature logs, (3) early and final drafts of written reports and themes, (4) video and/or audio recordings of oral reading, (5) video recordings of book talks, (6) hyperlinks to various books and articles read, along with audio commentary, and (7) copies of assignments from various samples of reading and writing from other disciplines (e.g., science reports, math proofs, analysis of sources in history). Each of these entries would be accompanied by audio captioning and reflection, along with a written and audio/video overall reflection and self-assessment.

A 10th-grade biology student's e-portfolio might include lab reports documenting his ability to conduct an experiment and analyze and interpret the results, questions and hypotheses for further scientific inquiry, hyperlinks to scientific articles and reports used to inform research with audio commentary, and digital records of actual project hardware and field-based activities, as well as photos and logs.

An eighth-grade math student might include in her e-portfolio documentation of her improving ability to understand increasingly complex story problems or algebraic equations, audio and written explanations of problem-solving strategies, samples of computations, video/audio recordings of her describing mathematical properties, explanations of why certain mathematical processes work, and evidence of using math to solve everyday problems.

Jade, a high school physics teacher, requires her students to demonstrate mastery of each objective she reviews at the beginning of a new unit. Typical objectives might ask students to determine the average speed of an object in motion or explain changes in velocity and acceleration of a ball when it is thrown up and returns to the thrower. Students need to provide evidence in their e-portfolios of ways in which the critical physics concept under investigation reveals itself in the real world. Jade allows evidence such as:

- A written description and analysis of an experiment or demonstration conducted either in class or at home.
- A written description and analysis of an article with hyperlink or picture from a newspaper, magazine, or an online source that shows the concept in action.
- A video recording of the concept in action accompanied by audio narration explaining it.
- A written and audio-narrated description of the student's neighborhood or community in which the physics concept can be applied to solve a problem, accompanied by digital photos and video.
- Audio/video interviews of experts, such as mechanics, engineers, scientists, professors explaining the concept and its application in their work.

In addition to work samples, portfolios should contain reflective records. Vital to the process of learning through portfolio teaching/assessment, reflective records consist of documentation of students' personal reflections on and self-evaluations of the learning experiences related to portfolio development. Students should study their portfolios at various points throughout the year, focusing on a single work, a set of revisions, evidence of growth in a particular area, or portfolio materials as a whole. In reflecting on these samples, students should ask themselves the following types of questions:

- "Why did I select this piece of work?"
- "Is this a sample of my best work?"
- "What special strengths are reflected in this work?"
- "What was particularly important to me during the process of completing this work?"
- "What have I learned (about math, history, writing, etc.) from working on this piece or project?"
- "If I could continue working on this piece or project, what would I do?"
- "What particular skill or area of interest would I like to try out in future work?"

Self-evaluative questions concerned solely with writing might include the following:

- "How has my writing changed since I wrote this?"
- "If I revised this, what would I change?"
- "What have I learned since I wrote this report that I would include in a follow-up report?"
- "How did drafting and revising help me develop this essay?"
- "How have I used this process to create other essays and reports?"

Answers to these questions in the form of audio/video comments and reflections then become part of the student's digital portfolio. Students should also date their work and comment briefly on why it was included in the portfolio.

You should also include brief notes about why certain samples of students' work were chosen. At the same time, you should keep personal and anecdotal records of students' work and progress based on classroom observations, inspection of portfolio samples, and conferences on the portfolio with students, parents, and other teachers. These records can complement students' reflective records.

Given secondary school teachers' busy schedules, record keeping of this kind can often pose the biggest challenge in portfolio assessment. Teachers like Jenny, whose 11th-grade English students maintain digital portfolios, write brief comments directly on work samples, including why the activity was completed, why the sample was included, and what the sample shows about the student's progress toward achieving instructional and personal goals. During classroom activities, Jenny uses an iPad to record observations and take anecdotal notes, which she later uploads to students' portfolios.

When reviewing portfolios, I recommend you work through a set of critical questions intended to focus your attention to the most important aspects of student work. The series of questions below that Jenny asks herself when analyzing student portfolio work samples and other documents are adaptable to virtually any discipline or unit topic:

- "What did the student learn as a result of this unit?"
- "How does this relate to what the student has learned before?"
- "Of the learning in English the student has done lately, what areas of strength and confidence are exhibited in this work?"
- "What aspects of this work reflect a lack of or incomplete understanding?"

How and When Will Samples Be Selected?

It is important to establish a clear and efficient system for selecting materials to go into and come out of the electronic portfolio throughout the school year. Most teachers make these decisions at the end of a unit, grading period, semester, or school year. These are all good times to keep and add work samples that provide the clearest and most compelling evidence of student growth and achievement and, where appropriate, to remove other samples. Many teachers establish timelines so the entire class is aware of when portfolio checks, revisions, and new entries will occur. In this way, students are brought into the decision-making process about what to include in their portfolios and further develop the ability to monitor their own progress.

Jade, the physics teacher mentioned earlier, schedules at least 1 day per week for her students to use class time to work on their portfolios. The time is spent in conference, both formally and informally, with individual students about the best evidence to include, monitoring peer sharing and brainstorming, and assisting students in setting up and documenting experiments, as well as generating data for their objectives. Jade also provides technical support to students to ensure that they are properly uploading work samples, photos, video, and other relevant documents into the portfolio site.

How Will Portfolios Be Evaluated?

It is essential that evaluative criteria be established relative to the learning goals you and your students determine at the outset of the unit. I recommend that the greater part of a student's portfolio be evaluated on the basis of growth, in terms of both academic achievement and self-knowledge, as the goal of this authentic assessment process is to document change and improvement over time.

In middle and high school classrooms where portfolio teaching and assessment occurs, the evaluation process normally occurs like this:

1. The teacher discusses and negotiates goals for the portfolio with the students.
2. The teacher and the students develop guidelines and procedures for showcasing portfolios.
3. A showcase portfolio is developed by the students with assistance and feedback from peers and the teacher.
4. The students develop self-evaluation comments and present their portfolios.
5. The students evaluate their portfolios according to criteria they helped develop with the teacher (e.g., evidence of improvement, evidence of effort, quality of self-evaluation, range of projects, presentation, future goals).
6. The students submit a weblink to their portfolios to the teacher, who reviews them, along with students' self-evaluations and peer comments.
7. A grade is awarded.

Jade, the physics teacher, gives her students a timeline with due dates for uploading possible items to include in their portfolios and for the final showcase portfolio. She also gives her class three scoring rubrics: one for evaluating the overall portfolio, which counts toward 70% of students' final grades; another for self-evaluation, which counts for 20%; and one for peer evaluation, which counts for 10%.

About 2 weeks into the unit, Jade conducts a portfolio preview to check students' progress. She writes comments in the electronic space of the e-portfolios in progress. Her students use this feedback to make needed modifications and find that this deadline motivates them to get work done.

On the day final portfolios are due, Jade assigns students to groups of three to share their work. The students take turns presenting from their own laptops or with some available from the laptop cart in the school. Presenters explain how their portfolio documents meet the unit's objectives, while the peer reviewers, the other students in the group, listen, peruse, and evaluate. Jade continually rotates throughout the room to listen in on the presentations, occasionally asking a clarifying question or challenging a student's assertion, and to monitor group activity. When students finish with their presentations, Jade grades the portfolios according to a rubric that includes critical documentation criteria. Evaluating portfolio previews and using a rubric results in an efficient grading process.

How Can Portfolios Be Passed On?

Many teachers have recognized one of the special advantages of e-portfolios—that the electronic records of student progress can be passed on readily to succeeding teachers. In this way, the portfolio process promotes continuity in a student's education and collaboration among teachers of various grade levels and disciplines. I suggest that as the school year draws to a close, you get together with other teachers at the next grade level to discuss their expectations and to find out what kind of information from portfolios your students created would be most helpful to them in determining areas of strength and those that may need further development. This collaborative process allows you to make decisions about what to include or exclude before passing on portfolios. This is also a good time to have a kind of exit conference with students about their portfolios to make certain the work they believe would best reflect their growth and achievement for the following year's teachers is passed on.

A Study of Portfolio Assessment: What I Learned

I participated in a 6-month-long research project during which my co-researcher and I worked with and observed an experienced high school French teacher, Jayne, as she engaged in portfolio instruction and assessment (Moje, Brozo, & Haas, 1994). Our goal was to gain insights into the potential effectiveness of portfolio practices, as well as the teacher-change process itself, since this was Jayne's first ever foray into portfolio territory. In addition, we hoped to develop a better understanding of the realities of using portfolios in a secondary school classroom where an individual teacher was attempting to put ideas from the literature into practice.

Although Jayne taught using a traditional hard-copy portfolio structure, the important discoveries we made from this study that were related to how teachers should launch and sustain the portfolio process with students will be helpful to any initiates to portfolio assessment. Our discoveries based on data gathered throughout the 6-month research timeframe are captured in the following five principles.

Start with Simple Activities

I suggest you begin to use portfolios by asking students to complete simple, short writing activities. The activities can take any form. For example, in an advanced algebra class, students could make journal entries that allow them to reflect on their reasons for taking the advanced class, or they could prepare goal statements or biographies that link the class to their needs and interests. Starting with simple activities with foreseeable deadlines will allow students to work up slowly to more comprehensive projects.

Negotiate Firm Deadlines

When students are not used to the cognitive ambiguity and uncertainty of the portfolio process, it is essential that they set deadlines to keep them focused on their work. Despite the fact that the portfolio is designed to be an ongoing activity as opposed to a finite project, students who are accustomed to due dates may require your guidance in setting deadlines to get work completed and meet project goals.

Encourage Students to Set Concrete Goals

Rather than expecting all students to be able to generate their own projects and samples for the portfolios, I suggest you conduct conferences with students to create a plan of action. Such a plan would provide students with short-range goals that could be accomplished according to agreed-on deadlines, giving students a clearer view of their progress toward long-range goals. Plans of action can also provide students with a means of self-assessment because they would be able to evaluate both their progress toward meeting steps in the plan and the wisdom of steps they chose.

Provide Initial Resources

Providing initial resources is critical in classrooms where portfolios will be composed of project materials and samples. Students who are not used to conducting extended research that might require involved Internet searches, findings contacts, following up leads, composing appropriate emails, making phone calls, and the like will need an initial source of specific information to get started. These sources can help students sustain their research efforts while they learn valuable reference skills in the process.

Integrate Other Classroom Activities with the Portfolios

Many teachers feel the necessity of covering certain concepts that are integral to their discipline by means of direct instruction to ensure that students at least receive initial exposure to the content. Jayne, for example, felt it was necessary to continue using the French textbook and to provide direct instruction in grammar and vocabulary. She understood that students might be unprepared for complete immersion in the portfolio project and consequently moved back and forth between teacher-directed practices and independent student activities. The stark contrast, however, between the teacher-led instruction and student-led portfolios created tension and ambiguity among students.

Although Jayne wanted the portfolio writings to be applications of the textbook lessons, students did not readily make the connections on their own. On reflection, Jayne decided she could have tied together activities in a variety of ways. For example, she could have demonstrated the grammar rules the students read about in the textbook by pointing out the uses of grammatical structures in their portfolio writing samples. Integration helps students see the utility and value of portfolios as an integral part of the learning process in disciplinary classrooms.

Perhaps the most outstanding benefit of portfolio assessment is that it invites students and teachers to be allies in the assessment process. When a portfolio culture is established, there is a good chance that students will become more concerned, thoughtful, and energetic learners. At the same time, teachers will find renewed enthusiasm for providing guidance of students' learning while growing as learners themselves (Hicks et al., 2007).

Authentic Assessment of Literacy and Learning in the 21st Century

In the suburban sprawl ever expanding around the nation's capital, where I live, there are many new, modern school buildings and more being built every year as the school-age population grows. I was working as a literacy consultant for 3 years in one such newly built high school. I vividly recall my first visit. I drove around the massive structure a couple of times searching for parking and then had to walk almost the entire length of the school to reach the main entrance where the office was located. On my walk, I passed numerous classrooms and couldn't help looking in on the classes in session as I went. What I saw reminded me that we should never judge a book by its cover or, as the late Stephen J. Gould was fond of saying, a sausage by its casing. The reason is that, despite the modern, stylized architecture of this 21st-century edifice, what I was seeing inside was 19th-century instruction—a teacher standing in the front of the room talking/lecturing while students sat at desks in rows facing the teacher, pencils or pens in hand, taking notes on a worksheet or lined paper.

I bring this up because we cannot assume that 21st-century learning and assessment are occurring merely because students and teachers are going about business as usual in a modern, gleaming school building. I have made the point throughout this book that literacy learning should be meaningful and purposeful and not an end in itself. When students are rewarded for learning small units of language or reproducing narrow units of information from text, then they may be able to demonstrate "mastery" on assessments designed to detect these abilities. And, unfortunately, too often what we expect students to take from their literacy experiences is limited by our reductive assessment practices. But a progressive, 21st-century perspective on learning and assessment points to the need for students to possess what I refer to as actionable literacy, meaning the ability to do something meaningful and purposeful with their literacy.

In an age of increasingly complex home, community, and workplace tasks, today's youth require instruction that promotes cognitive skill development in authentic learning contexts (Brozo, 2007; Price, Pierson, & Light, 2011). To develop this type of expertise, we need to develop learning and assessment contexts that move youth from knowledge acquisition to meaningful use and authentic performance—in other words, an actionable literacy.

In Figure 4.12, the knowledge–performance assessment pyramid, based on Binkley et al. (2012), illustrates the idea that in a 21st-century learning context, teachers should be striving to move students from reproducing information, a vestige of 19th-century schooling, to demonstrations of meaningful use of knowledge and authentic performance in real-world settings. In the two vignettes that follow, you will learn how teachers employed assessments that prompted their students to move from demonstrations of what they know to actionable literacy that requires simulated and real-world performance.

Connecting School and Work with ICT Tools

Students in Mr. Aldape's health careers class are participating in an experimental general educational development (GED) program that allows them to attend school in the morning and gain valuable work experiences in the afternoon. Students are provided with integrated reading, writing, math, and GED test-preparation instruction within the study of various vocational areas. Each day, students are engaged in activities involving writing as meaningful communication; using information and communications technologies (ICTs) for research and production; reading for working; and developing test-taking strategies. Mr. Aldape's students are not required to sit in desks and rows but are instead given freedom of movement to pursue the completion of assignments tailored to their unique career interests and workplace experiences.

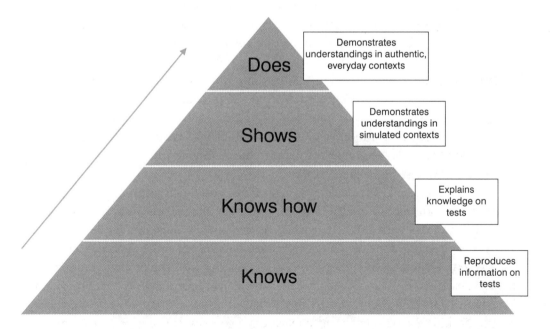

FIGURE 4.12. Knowledge-performance assessment pyramid.

Lettie is in Mr. Aldape's class because of her interest in seeking a career in the health field. Her assignments are applied to the content and texts of her work placement in a doctor's clinic. Thus she practices the split-page technique for taking notes by separating the major concepts from the significant details and recording them in a two-column format using content from brochures and manuals available to clinic employees. Various office brochures, such as "Countereffects of Aspirin with Other Drugs," "Life Expectancy Is Going Up," and "Preoperative Precautions," provide Lettie with the practice material for constructing appropriate prequestions as guides to reading.

With this same material, Mr. Aldape models reading strategies such as previewing, self-questioning, determining word meanings from context, "gisting," organizing information into graphic displays, and checking for understanding. As each of these literacy processes is modeled, he immediately elicits similar behaviors from Lettie and her classmates. For example, with a passage about deep-vein thrombophlebitis, they work side by side, moving through the text in a model–elicit process, thinking aloud about content and processes for organizing and understanding it. When they come upon the word *anticoagulant*, Mr. Aldape draws attention to the other words in the sentence that refer to treatments involving thinning the blood, which helps Lettie understand it. Later, when Lettie encounters the word *vascular*, she is able to use the words and sentences around it to determine that it is related to the veins.

The approach of tying literacy strategies to workplace content creates a highly engaged atmosphere of learning for Lettie and her classmates in the health careers course. She becomes a more interested and participatory learner than she had been as a student in the general high school curriculum. This is most apparent during the development of a work-based project as one of the major assignments of Mr. Aldape's class. The project's goal is to help students think critically about their work settings and how to better inform and serve the intended clientele or consumer. They have to create an actual "product" using ICT tools and make it available to employers as a demonstration of their meaningful and creative contributions to the business. Mr. Aldape employs a performance rubric to evaluate students' ICT project effectiveness (see Figure 4.13).

For her project, Lettie decides to help make the office waiting room a more consumer-friendly environment. In the month since she started work, she has been called upon to visit with and help relax unaccompanied seniors in the waiting room and patient rooms. With her fluent Spanish, she aids the nurse practitioners and the two office doctors when they are communicating with the growing number of Latino/a patients. It is in this capacity that the idea of creating an interactive video for Spanish-speaking clients occurs to her. It will answer basic questions for them about checking in, payments and copayments, government and privately funded medical insurance, preventative health, and more. Pulling information on these

KNOWS/KNOWS HOW

Mr. Aldape constructs assessments of students' knowledge of reading literacy processes composed of short constructed response items.

Sample Questions for an Article on Health and Disease

1. According to the chart on page 4, what is the second largest cause of death among children?

2. What does the graph on page 7 imply about the relationship between cancer and cigarette smoking?

3. What does the cartoon on page 10 suggest about ways obesity influences national health policy?

Sample Assessment for Determining Meanings of Words in Context

4. In the past, if you didn't have an illness, you were considered healthy. Today, the term *health* no longer means just the absence of illness. Instead, health refers to the overall (1) happiness, well-being, interests of your body, your mind, and your relationships with other people. Two factors that can be used to (2) price, evaluate, weigh health are life (3) expectancy, stability, anticipation and (4) quality, excellence, worth of life.

5. At the time when your great-grandparents (5) lived, resided, breathed, it was quite an accomplishment for a person to (6) perish, carry, survive until age 50. Today, most people (7) die, wander, live well beyond age 50. The number of (8) years, existence, time a person can expect to live is called (9) living, days, life expectancy. In the United States, life expectancy (10) enlarged, increased, bigger by 30 years between 1900 and 2000. Some reasons for this increase were better (11) education, healthcare, matrimony, nutrition, sanitation, and (12) working, operational, running conditions.

6. Two women are born in the same year. One woman is physically (13) vigorous, active, unstable and mentally (14) vigilant, alert, informed throughout her life. She has close (15) relationships, contact, dealings with family and friends. The other woman has a series of health (16) evils, problems, tribulations during her life that (17) shrink, reduce, ease her ability to enjoy life. Although the women have the same life expectancy, they have a (18) different, dissimilar, distinct quality of life. Quality of life is the (19) degree, grade, step of overall (20) liking, satisfaction, compensation that a person gets from life. For many people, a high quality of life is one of their goals. A goal is a result that a person aims for and works hard to reach.

Example of Short Constructed Response Question for Taking Two-Column Notes

7. Imagine that you will have a multiple-choice and short-answer test on the article titled "Dangers of Caffeine Powder." Organize the information and ideas in that article by taking notes over it in the two-column format that would help you prepare for the test.

Shows/Does				
Criteria	4	3	2	1
Project goals and technology	Technology selected for the project is strongly aligned with one or more of the project goals.	Technology selected for the project is aligned with one or more of the project goals.	Technology selected for the project is partially aligned with one or more of the project goals.	Technology selected for the project is not aligned with any project goals.
Workplace needs and technology	Technology use optimally supports workplace needs.	Technology use supports workplace needs.	Technology use minimally supports workplace needs.	Technology use does not support workplace needs.
Technology tools selected	Technology tools are exemplary given the project goals.	Technology tools are appropriate given the project goals.	Technology tools are minimally appropriate given the project goals.	Technology tools are not appropriate given the project goals.
Facility with technology	Solved all technology-related problems associated with the project.	Solved most technology-related problems associated with the project.	Solved some of the technology-related problems associated with the project.	Was unable to resolve most technological obstacles relating to the project.

FIGURE 4.13. Performance rubric for students' ITC project effectiveness.

topics from brochures and forms, along with FlashPlayer and IntuiFace technology and with Mr. Aldape's help, Lettie creates a colorful, interactive computer screen in Spanish accompanied by video, photos, and clip art. One can read or, for those with reading or vision problems, listen to directions and information by touching tabs on the screen. There is even a button for frequently asked questions and answers.

A special evening reception is held at the high school to showcase student work. The staffs of the workplace partners, high school teachers and administrators, and parents are invited. At the event, Lettie and her classmates unveil for the first time their various technology-mediated projects to a much appreciative audience. Lettie's coworkers in attendance are quick to try out the interactive program she and Mr. Aldape have developed. They are certain it will improve information dissemination for Spanish-speaking clients and help them feel more welcomed.

The office doctors allow Lettie to set up two computers in the waiting room, and bright flyers in Spanish invited users to give them a try. On the table next to the computers are response forms, also written in Spanish, in order to gather feedback from users on problems with the system and suggestions for improving it. When Latino/a patients arrive, Lettie guides them to the computers to make certain they feel comfortable using the program. She shows them which buttons to touch for information about the clinic's services, as well as insurance and methods of payment. Patients catch on quickly and seem to have little trouble maneuvering through the interactive program.

Creating an e-Zine in Culinary Arts

Mrs. Baker always stresses the need for effective communication skills in her culinary arts class, and so she incorporates into her lessons real-world reading and writing tasks. For example, during activities related to food sanitation and safety, she introduces Occupational Safety and Health Administration (OSHA) pamphlets and literature on procedures to follow in order to keep equipment and work surfaces properly sanitized and in good condition and to avoid cross-contamination of foods. She also requires students to use the newspaper for restaurant reviews and the Internet for reports from the health department on sanitation ratings of local eateries. Mrs. Baker assesses her students' knowledge of textual content using a grid like the one in Figure 4.14. Students receive a blank grid, and then as they read, they fill out the grid based on information from the text.

So when Mrs. Baker's students submit several outstanding original recipes in fulfillment of a culminating assignment on cooking main course dishes, she decides

Knows/Knows How							
Source of food-borne illness	Infection	Intoxication	Aerobic	Anaerobic	Time symptoms begin	Most likely food source	Prevention
Clostridium perfringens	X	X		X	4–22 hours	Foods served at large buffet-type gatherings	Keep hot foods hot; refrigerate uneaten foods promptly.
Staphylococcus aureus		X	X	X	1–7 hours	Moist meat dishes, starchy foods	Refrigerate uneaten foods immediately.
Clostridium botulinum		X		X	12–24 hours	Improperly processed home-canned foods (especially low-acid types)	Boil home-canned foods; do not give infants honey.

FIGURE 4.14. Example of a grid to assess knowledge of textual content.

that they should put their communication skills into action and make the recipes available to a wider audience. She and the class brainstorm possible outlets for distributing the recipes, such as a cookbook or website. Although these ideas generate some interest, it isn't until someone suggests creating a culinary e-zine that the students become really enthused.

Because theirs is a technology high school, endowed with state-of-the-art computer labs, high-speed Web connections, and plenty of innovative software, Mrs. Baker knows the technology infrastructure will support Internet publishing, so they all get to work on the project. e-Zines, or electronic magazines, have become a new and blossoming medium for student writing on the Internet. Already there are hundreds of these cyber-creations available on the Web, covering every imaginable area of interest, with a growing number designed, composed, and maintained by young adults. After talking with the technology support staff, Mrs. Baker decides to assign the class into teams to take on the different aspects of the project. One team focuses on the content; another, the technology involved; and a third, promotional and advertising concerns.

The content group works on tasks not unlike those involved in publishing a school newspaper. They organize and edit the recipes for uniformity, write a short piece introducing the class and the e-zine, and plan columns for future installments, such as food reviews, healthy eating tips, and information about careers in the food services industry. The technology team helps Mrs. Baker create and design the e-zine. Using Adobe PageMaker, they format the recipes and experiment with various onscreen palettes for logos and colors to make the presentation visually appealing. The advertising group generates a title for the e-zine and formulates a plan that will ensure that potential readers will be aware of its existence on the Web.

Mrs. Baker's culinary arts class is given special attention by the principal during morning announcements on the day the e-zine is launched. She and her students are broadcast from the school's TV studio on the closed-circuit television monitors in each classroom, where they explain the history of the project and their various assignments and then unveil the school's newest electronic publication, "Teen Eats Dog: A Guide to Food, Healthy Eating, and Careers in Culinary Arts."

With the launching of "Teen Eats Dog," Mrs. Baker's class has a new and richly deserved sense of pride about their learning that comes from the heightened sense of responsibility and accountability in producing an e-zine. Furthermore, the project improves students' skills in research, writing, spelling, and critical thinking.

To assess students' work on the e-zine project, Mrs. Baker used the observation checklist below, which made it possible for her to document the level of participation of the groups, the process of creating and editing content, and the technical production aspects.

SHOWS/DOES

1. Connect as a group. Share email addresses with each other and create a group folder where all e-zines' documents go, and include teacher on the sharing list.

   To a great extent ——————————————————————————— No evidence

2. Assign a moderator. Create first Google document called Magazine Brainstorming. Include all brainstormed ideas from each member.

   To a great extent ——————————————————————————— No evidence

3. Look at student and professional e-zines that are related to culinary arts for most interesting and inspiring content and format.

   To a great extent ——————————————————————————— No evidence

4. Generate list of coverage ideas and assign topics based on member interest.

   To a great extent ——————————————————————————— No evidence

5. Consult each other and technical staff to learn to use Photoshop, InDesign, Illustrator, and MagCloud for formatting and producing e-zine content.

   To a great extent ——————————————————————————— No evidence

Case Study Revisited

Selma, the seventh-grade science teacher introduced in the case study in the beginning of the chapter, was searching for classroom-based assessment practices to determine her students' ability to understand their science texts. Now that you have read about and explored a variety of assessment approaches in this chapter, reflect again on Selma's concerns and generate a few suggestions for meeting her assessment needs. Afterward, read about the actual assessment practices she employed with her students.

Mindful of the problems students have in thinking like writers, Selma decided to combine her own ideas with some of the suggestions she obtained from a professional development workshop. From the workshop she learned how to construct a content literacy inventory using the materials from her science course. The portion of text she selected was about rocks, a typical reading assignment that required students to identify types and characteristics, as well as similarities and differences. Because Selma wanted to assess how well students could read to determine these writing patterns, her content literacy inventory contained many items like the following:

- According to the reading, what are two types of igneous rocks?
- According to the reading, what are some characteristics of these types of rocks? Name one characteristic of each rock.
- According to the reading, how are these types of rocks different?
- What words or phrases did the author use to cue you that the rocks were different in some ways? One such phrase was *in contrast*. What were the others?

In addition to the information she gained about her students from the content literacy inventory, Selma carefully observes her students in a variety of settings. For example, she pays special attention to the following signals that her students understand text organization and structure:

- As students are summarizing or discussing an assignment, she determines whether they are using the author's organizational structures as their ideas or whether comments are shared.
- When students are writing responses to text reading, she looks for indications that they are using text structure knowledge as a framework for developing their writing.

Selma has also found useful a classroom activity that her students enjoy. She gives them articles that have been cut up at paragraph boundaries and tells them they will be reading a text that is mixed up. Working in pairs, students are asked to put the article back together in its original form. While doing so, they are asked to think out loud and explain their decisions to their partner during the text reconstruction process. Selma looks for evidence that her students grasp the problem–solution pattern employed by the author. Her evidence comes from students' comments and statements such as "Number five has to go near the end because it sounds like a summary of the problems with deforestation in developing countries."

By combining text reconstruction activities with the content literacy inventory and classroom observations, Selma has learned much more about her students and why they struggle or succeed with text. This information has helped her realize the importance of using a variety of strategies for reading and thinking about text to help her students understand important concepts in science.

LOOKING BACK, LOOKING FORWARD

Assessment of literacy and content learning is a process of becoming informed about teaching and learning to improve instruction for the teacher and increased self-knowledge for students. In this chapter, I emphasized the importance of authentic assessments that integrate process and content and help make the boundary between assessment and teaching nearly indistinguishable. Because disciplinary teachers need to develop a variety of responsive assessment practices, I described how teachers have created embedded and formative assessments, such as portfolios, observations, student writing, and the content literacy inventory.

The advantages and limitations of standardized testing were discussed in this chapter. Emphasized were ways these tests can be used most profitably by secondary teachers to further literacy and disciplinary learning for students. This is especially true for struggling readers and learners. When results from standardized reading and achievement tests heighten teachers' sensitivity to the needs of these students, then curricular and instructional changes might be made to improve learning progress for them.

In this chapter, I also made clear the importance of middle and secondary school teachers finding ways to catalyze and assess demonstrations of actionable literacy. Structuring learning and assessment challenges that moved students from acquiring information and knowledge to demonstrating what they can do with their newly acquired knowledge was epitomized in the vignettes of Mrs. Baker and Mr. Aldape. The creation of an e-zine by Mrs. Baker's culinary arts class transformed a cooking assignment into a communication medium for expanding trade knowledge and applying literacy skills. And Mr. Aldape seized on the opportunity for expanding technology, problem-solving, and communications skills within a school-to-work experience. These two teachers share the common attribute of employing instructional practices and assessments that hold great promise for preparing youth to be flexible, adaptive, and critical thinkers in their multifarious roles as adults.

Although I devote this entire chapter to issues and practices of assessment, throughout this book I present ways in which content-area and disciplinary teachers can use practices to assess particular literacy and learning processes. For example, in Chapter 6, I describe vocabulary instructional practices that have built-in assessments for teachers and self-assessment for students. And in Chapter 7, I demonstrate how students' writing can be used in assessment and development of comprehension abilities. Finally, you will discover in the next chapter, on creating motivating literacy and learning contexts, a variety of special assessment practices and those embedded in various learning activities.

CHAPTER 5 ▰▰▰▰▰▰▰▰▰▰▰▰▰▰

Creating Motivating Contexts
for Literacy and Learning

As you read Chapter 5, reflect on the following questions:

- What is the evidence for the benefits of engaged reading and learning?

- What important guidelines can be derived from motivational theory for teaching students to become more engaged readers and learners?

- How can the learning of disciplinary content be linked to students' own needs, issues, concerns, and interests inside and outside of school to increase engagement while helping them discover real-world purposes for learning?

- What are effective practices for engendering interest in new learning and generating local interest in classroom topics?

- How can a variety of interesting texts be integrated into the disciplinary classroom?

- How can secondary teachers employ instructional practices that expand student choices and options for reading and learning?

- What are the most effective practices for structuring collaboration for motivation?

What really motivates one to read and learn? This question has been challenging researchers, theorists, and practitioners for decades. When I reflect on the question for myself, I quickly realize that what motivates me to choose certain texts for pleasure reading, for self-improvement, to satisfy a curiosity, or to solve a problem is unique to me. It stands to reason, then, that each one of us is impelled by factors based on our experiences, needs, and goals. This, of course, applies to adolescent students as well.

When I was a boy growing up on the east side of Detroit, I had little time for reading. What really motivated me were sports and games. The day was not long enough to contain my boundless energy for baseball, football, and hockey. And many a summer night I recall begrudgingly heading back to my house wondering why a wonderful game of hide-and-seek or one-catch-all had to end, just because it was getting dark. And then one summer morning everything changed. None of my friends were around, and after walking aimlessly through my neighborhood for a time, I found myself directly in front of a branch of the Detroit public library. Although the library was literally just down a short block and across the street from my house, I had never really paid much attention to it. It had started to rain, so I stepped inside.

People often talk about pivotal events that shift their life's trajectory, and walking into the Montieth branch of the Detroit public library was such an event for me. Little did I know then that reading would become my life's project; but I remember a certain giddiness that struck me as I gazed at the rows of shelved books and magazines. I was attending a very modestly appointed parish school that had nothing like this. Within minutes a librarian, Mrs. Oshob, approached me and guided me to a section of children's books and magazines. She asked me what I was interested in and what I liked to do. Once she learned that I was a sports nut and that I wished I could spend time wandering the countryside (a place very unlike where I lived, in the middle of a large city), Mrs. Oshob pulled several selections for me to peruse. I settled on *Boys' Life* magazines and, quite literally, reading about surviving in the wilderness, making a fire with wooden tools and stones, eating wild berries and mushrooms, and making a compass with water and toothpicks was how I took my first tentative steps down the path of lifelong literacy.

From *Boys' Life* Mrs. Oshob encouraged me to read "juvenile" novels by authors like Stephen Meader, who wrote amazing tales of young boys about my age sailing on whaling ships, working in lumberjack camps, and wandering the countryside in one of my favorites, *Boy with a Pack* (Meader, 1939), a Newberry Honor book. In reflecting on my own literate journey, I now know these entry point texts had a profound influence on my reading skills and identity as a reader (Brozo, 2010a). For the first time I began to see myself as a reader, with no loss of enthusiasm for sports. And the journey was launched by a caring and sensitive librarian who understood that introducing a young person to texts that are engaging to her or him is the key.

Within the past couple of decades, volumes have been written about student motivation and engagement, and countless workshops and conference presentations have been devoted to the topic. Yet virtually all the teachers I meet, as well as teachers from across the nation, feel they need more information and strategies to motivate adolescents to read and learn (Andermann, Andrezejewski, & Allen,

2011; Yonezawa, Jones, & Joselowsky, 2009). And there is evidence that justifies this need. I spoke in Chapter 1 about the well-documented slump in achievement and motivation during the upper elementary and middle school years (Martin, 2009). Curiously, this phenomenon is not restricted to the United States. Youth from across the globe exhibit a similar decline in performance and interest as they move from primary to secondary school (Brozo et al., 2014). Some of our best thinkers and researchers in youth literacy have proposed that this decline in academic motivation results from a disjuncture between adolescents' need for content and learning experiences that are accessible and relevant on the one hand and traditional school-related reading, writing, and disciplinary practices on the other (Alvermann & Eakle, 2007; Fecho, 2011; Thomson & Hall, 2008).

The critical point here is that motivation cannot be detached from social contexts, such as classrooms, families, and communities. An individual youth's motivation to read and learn is linked closely to the social worlds that are part of that youth's daily life. And while teachers may have little influence on the social worlds youth navigate outside of school, they have a great deal of control over the arrangement of conditions within the classroom that can effect positive academic motivation for adolescents.

Not only should youth be engaged in interesting experiences related to *what* they learn but, more important, they should understand *why* the content is being discussed and studied. To tell students "You must learn this because it's in our curriculum guide" may be the truth but does little to motivate youth to become active knowledge seekers. Instead, by linking the learning of disciplinary content to students' own needs, issues, concerns, and interests inside and outside of school, we increase engagement while helping them discover real-world purposes for learning (Maloy & LaRoche, 2010; Taylor & Parsons, 2011). Greenleaf, Jimenez, and Roller (2002) put it this way: "Only when adolescents read material that is important to them will they understand why one uses . . . reading strategies and skills, [and] only if adolescents understand why they might want to use these skills will they master them and use them" (p. 490). Speaking about how reading, learning, and motivation are tied to functionality, purpose, and meaningfulness echoes an important theme in my definition of comprehension from Chapter 3. Simply put, teachers who work with youth must look to students' own reasons to learn as the source for motivational strategies.

Nobel Prize–winning economist James Heckman argues in favor of what he refers to as "soft skills"—those personality traits that may be even more essential than cognitive abilities to successful learning and achievement inside and outside the classroom (Heckman & Kautz, 2012). According to Heckman and his colleagues (Heckman et al., 2006), traits such as curiosity and perseverance are thought to have greater predictive power for success in life than cognitive skills. Engagement for learning, such as perseverance, is one of the soft skills that has been shown to be a potent predictor of academic success (Schunk, Meece, & Pintrich, 2013).

Evidence for the benefits of engaged learning is quite compelling. We know that correlational data from the NAEP continue to show that adolescents who identify themselves as being interested in reading not only achieve better scores on the NAEP but have better high school grade-point averages than their less inter-ested peers (Loveless, 2015). Even more convincing are data derived from PISA, the global study of reading literacy for 15-year-olds that I described in Chapter 1. Engagement is the variable above all others that has the strongest relationship to performance on PISA (OECD, 2013b). Higher reading engagement, as indicated by reading enjoyment, extensive daily and weekly reading time, and reading a wide variety of fiction and nonfiction texts, was correlated with higher achievement (Brozo, Sulkunen, et al., 2014). The students who were highly disengaged readers found themselves behind their highly engaged peers by nearly 2 years of schooling. Remarkably, that's like being absent from 2 years of instruction.

What is truly fascinating about the findings from PISA related to engage-ment is that youth from the lowest SES families who were highly engaged read-ers performed as well on the assessment as youth from the middle-SES group and cut in half the disparity between themselves and their high-SES peers (see Figure 5.1). In other words, highly motivated adolescents made up for low family income

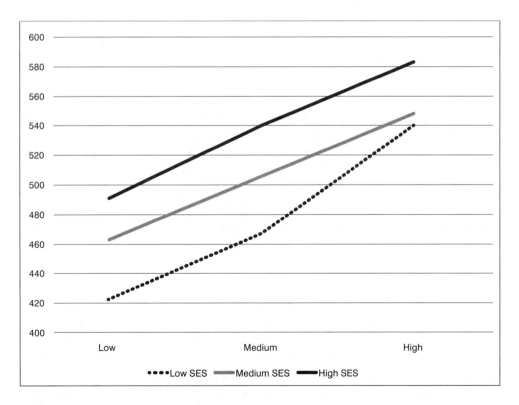

FIGURE 5.1. Reading performance and socioeconomic background by level of reading engage-ment for 15-year-olds on PISA.

and parents' limited educational attainment, two oft-considered risk factors in the school lives of students. This should be ground-shaking news, because it strongly suggests that if we can keep students engaged in reading and learning they may be able to overcome what might otherwise be insuperable barriers to academic success.

Before leaving the PISA study, one last important finding related to engagement has to do with gender. As might be expected, given their overall superior performance on most measures of verbal ability (Brozo, 2010a), girls from the United States had significantly higher indices of reading engagement as compared with boys. Girls enjoyed reading more, spent a greater amount of time reading, and had a wider range of reading preferences as compared with their male peers (Brozo, Sulkunen, et al., 2014). So it should not come as a surprise to learn that girls' higher levels of engagement contributed to their superior achievement to that of the boys.

Because capturing students' imaginations for reading and learning and sustaining engagement is so vital to all youths' academic futures, I put my entire focus in this chapter on strategies and activities secondary teachers can integrate into their instructional practices that increase student motivation. The practices I present of actual middle and secondary school teachers adapting existing strategies or engaging students in creative activities of their own design can all be supported by sound theories of interest and motivation (Christensen, Reschly, & Wylie, 2012; Guthrie et al., 2013; Schunk et al., 2013).

I begin by drawing from motivational theory several important guidelines for teaching. These are followed by descriptions of innovative motivational practices and ways teachers applied them in their particular classroom contexts. Because learning at the middle and secondary school levels must occur as a result of exposure to a variety of information sources, I describe strategies that can apply equally effectively to (1) chapters from textbooks, (2) newspapers and popular magazines, (3) novels, (4) a guest speaker, (5) a video, (6) an experiment, (7) a field trip, (8) a discussion or debate, (9) a computer-based learning activity; or (10) a lecture. I hope the guidelines for effective motivational instructional practices and the numerous classroom examples described in this chapter will stimulate the development of your own innovative approaches to increasing student engagement in reading and learning.

Case Study

Theresa is an eighth-grade social studies teacher. She has noticed that her students appear to have become increasingly uninterested and passive over the past 10 years. Although she has typically taught units from the textbook, her efforts to enlist students in learning social studies content have been moving further and further from the text—with encouraging results. For instance, early in the school year she employed some new strategies to help students develop a broader sense of community responsibility. To her delight, the class took off with the strategy, exhibiting a level of enthusiasm Theresa hadn't seen for some time.

Theresa is in the process of planning a unit on early Native Americans. Last year was the first year she deviated from the textbook approach to teaching about native peoples by having a member of a local Huron tribe talk to the class about history and customs. He also shared costumes and artifacts. This year she would like to do more to help students develop a better understanding of what is known about the early Native American cultures and how to learn about these cultures. She wants to devise active, hands-on approaches to engage her class in the study of this important topic.

To the reader: As you read and work through this chapter, think about possible strategies and teaching approaches Theresa might use to engage her students in learning about early American cultures. Be prepared to offer your suggestions when we revisit this case study at the conclusion of the chapter.

GUIDELINES FOR CREATING MOTIVATING CONTEXTS FOR LITERACY AND LEARNING

Elevate Self-Efficacy

The research literature makes evident that students with high, school-related self-efficacy—the belief and confidence that they have the capacity to accomplish meaningful tasks and produce a desired result in academic settings—are more engaged and motivated than students with low self-efficacy (Pajares & Urdan, 2006). Content-area teachers can create the conditions for youth that are associated with increased perceptions of competence and, consequently, a willingness to sustain effort to be successful (Schunk & Zimmerman, 2008). These conditions are created with such practices as introducing new content in engaging ways (Brozo, 2004), making a variety of accessible texts available to youth (Brozo & Hargis, 2003a; Ivey, 2011), giving youth choices (Ho & Guthrie, 2013), exploiting youths' everyday literacies (Moje et al., 2008), and creating multiple opportunities for collaborative learning (Guthrie, Wigfield, & You, 2012). These practices are described in more detail within the next few pages and embodied in the strategies presented throughout the chapter.

Engender Interest in New Learning

A self-evident and empirically grounded truth about learning is that students will expend the energy necessary to learn if they are interested in the material (Hulleman, Godes, Hendricks, & Harackiewicz, 2010; Guthrie & Klauda, 2014). This is certainly not a recent revelation. More than 300 years ago, the philosopher Rousseau (1979) made a compelling case for exploiting "present interest" as the single best way to motivate students to read and learn. John Dewey, in the early 20th century, promoted the idea that when students are interested in a topic or activity, they will learn "in a whole-hearted way" (1913, p. 65). Today, the desire among educational researchers and practitioners to know more about the influence of student interest on literacy and learning is as strong as ever (Gambrell, 2011). The realization that students must have both the skill and the will to learn has led to a variety of instructional practices designed to support the affective as well as the cognitive aspects of literacy development and school achievement.

Unfortunately, although we all pay lip service to this guideline, we often fail to follow it. Perhaps that is what is contributing to a nationwide, and perhaps even a worldwide, decline in youths' interest in traditional print literacy both for pleasure and for school purposes (Brozo, 2006; National Endowment for the Arts, 2007). Disciplinary teachers who understand the importance of interest in acquiring new knowledge do not automatically assume that each of their students eagerly desires to learn course content (Brozo, 2005a). Instead, they prepare students for learning by helping them become active participants in the learning process (Wigfield et al., 2008), demonstrating how the content can relate to youths' lives and concerns (Alvermann & Eakle, 2007), and providing opportunities for youth to enjoy reading and learning (Brozo & Flynt, 2008).

Generate Local Interest

Even if youth are generally interested in a topic, this does not diminish the need to employ practices that capture their attention and motivate them to read and learn for a particular day and lesson (Rotgans & Schmidt, 2014; Schraw & Lehman, 2001). For example, a 10th-grader who finds the topic of the American Civil War interesting may not stay focused in class nor be eager to read on the topic without specific strategies that gain and hold his attention. Even worse, the student's interest might fade if his teacher does little more than lecture or require oral reading from the textbook. Unlike our 10th-grader, many of his classmates are going into history, science, math, and other content classrooms without a general interest in any of the topics to be studied. For these students, local, daily strategies for helping them sustain effort are essential (Rotgans & Schmidt, 2011).

Thankfully, there are a variety of engaging strategies that disciplinary teachers can apply to any content and information source that will often entice even the most reluctant readers and learners to play more active roles in the classroom (Del Favero Boscolo, Vidotto, & Vicentini, 2007; Holstermann, Grube, & Bögeholz, 2010; Long, Monoi, Harper, Knoblauch, & Murphy, 2007; Palmer, 2009). If we can spark an interest in learning for just one day, the knowledge gained that day may make it easier to assimilate information and ideas covered the next day (Guthrie, Hoa, Wigfield, Tonks, & Perencevich, 2006). An 11th-grade math teacher explained it to me this way: "I have to get some of my students to learn in spite of themselves. So I have to do things to get them interested in every lesson. Even small things can work. But you have to do something to motivate them."

Connect Outside with Inside School Literacies and Learning

Columnist Patrick Clinton (2002) described youth who are disaffected with school in this way:

> They're in the last row, wearing a look that all teachers know, one that says, "I'm invisible. I have nothing to say. Don't call on me." They don't have their books. They didn't read the assignment: They forgot; they had to work; it was just boring. . . . There are kids like these in the back row of almost every high school classroom in America. In some poor schools, they're in all the rows. . . . High school teachers will tell you they can read the words but not the content. (pp. 4–5)

The same students who may be disconnected from academic life and who are aliterate within the domain of school-related reading may also be active readers and users of new media at home and in their communities (Alvermann, 2011;

MAKING SCHOOL-BASED TOPICS RELEVANT FOR YOUTH

Effective disciplinary teachers take an additional step in planning lessons and experiences for youth by making links to life outside the school walls. Virtually any topic can be connected to the real world, resulting in greater student participation, deeper understandings, and more permanent learning. Below is a list of typical content-area topics. After each one, suggest an activity for youth that connects the topic to familiar experiences and contemporary events. Then add some of your own topics and real-world connections. The first one is completed for you.

Content-Area Topic	Connections to Real-World Experiences/Events
1. Covalent bonding—chemistry	1. Role-play a marriage ceremony bringing families and property together.
2. The American Civil War—history	2.
3. The human brain—science	3.
4. *Romeo and Juliet*—literature	4.
5. Measuring area—math	5.
6.	6.
7.	7.
8.	8.

Skerrett & Bomer, 2011). Over 40 million strong, youth of the Net Generation and Generation Z (International Reading Association, 2012), many of whom may find little motivation for traditional print-based textbook and other academic reading, are nonetheless engaging in literate practices such as texting, networking through social media, and consulting online computer and video game magazines for strategies (Gee & Hayes, 2011). Motivating these students to learn material in content-area classrooms may be possible by tapping into their everyday multiliteracy practices (Agee & Altarriba, 2009; Hinchman et al., 2003–2004; Kajder, 2010).

Middle and secondary school teachers can create the space for youth to find and make connections between science, math, history, and literature topics and the media they use to know their worlds (Clarke & Besnoy, 2010; Williams, 2005). Through exploring innovative ways of motivating youth to become academically engaged by linking everyday literacies with traditional textbook reading and print media, teachers will also build youths' capacity and efficacy as learners (Dredger, Woods, Beach, & Sagstetter, 2010; Moje & Tysvaer, 2010).

Make an Abundance of Interesting Texts Available

When eighth graders across the United States were asked on the NAEP how often they read for enjoyment, only 19% reported doing so every day (National Center for Education Statistics, 2013). For 12th graders, the figure was about the same. Of even more concern were the sizable percentages of students who reported reading for fun on only a monthly or yearly basis, or not at all. Why are such large numbers of students turning off to traditional print media? One explanation, of course, is that they are turning to other media with which they engage in alternative literacy practices, no less enjoyable than traditional print, but not easily accounted for on surveys like the one used on the National Assessment.

Another possible explanation requires a closer look at the types of texts youth encounter in school and how this might influence attitudes toward reading. For example, books and texts that may have appealed to youth of previous generations are still all too common in secondary classrooms today (Fisher & Ivey, 2007). It has also been found that the books youth would prefer to read are often scarce to nonexistent in school (Baines & Fisher, 2013). When this is the case, students' only print encounters in school may be with the texts they are required to read. Students often find school-related texts difficult and uninspiring, leading to negative attitudes toward reading. These negative feelings may become generalizable to all types of text, including texts that might otherwise be enjoyable to youth. If reading is seen by many adolescents as not pleasurable, it becomes easier to understand why so many indicated on the NAEP survey that they read for enjoyment so infrequently.

A Gates Foundation–commissioned survey of some 40,000 teachers (*www. scholastic.com/primarysources/PrimarySources-2014update.pdf*) found that few believe traditional textbooks can engage today's digitally facile youth and prepare them for success in college and the workplace. Teachers in the survey said they prefer digital resources or alternatives to textbooks, such as magazines, newspapers, primary documents, information books, and even picture books. In fact, only 12% surveyed said textbooks help students achieve, while only 6% said textbooks engage their students in learning.

If you spend any time working with textbooks, you will soon notice that invariably the prose is abstract, formal, and lifeless (Hartley, 2003; Thomas Fordham Institute, 2004). These features of textbook prose are surely contributing to youths' disaffection with school-based reading. Many are hopeful that new textbooks being produced by the major publishers to accommodate the CCSS will be an improvement over older versions. Some states are not waiting, opting instead to create their own Common Core–inspired curricular materials and texts (Monahan, 2015). Regardless of whether school texts are created by publishers or independent curriculum designers, it is critical that disciplinary teachers make every effort to get students interested in the textbook topic through the use of alternative texts, such as fictional works, graphic novels, and new media (Baines & Fisher, 2013; Brozo, Moorman, & Meyer, 2014; Simon, 2012).

In my own experiences (Brozo & Hargis, 2003a), I have found that when secondary schools and classroom teachers make a total commitment to ensuring that every adolescent has readable print within easy access, then motivation for and attitudes toward reading improve (Brozo & Flynt, 2008). In order to become enthusiastic readers and learners, youth need to see firsthand the value their teachers and other school staff place on reading for personal pleasure and growth. Valuing this type of reading should take the form of strategies and programs that include stocking school and classroom libraries with a variety of interesting texts related to a host of disciplinary topics at a range of difficulty levels, creating opportunities for self-selection of texts, and structuring time for sustained print encounters (Brozo & Hargis, 2003b; Lapp & Fisher, 2009; Olness, 2007).

Expand Student Choices and Options

Choice may be one of the most critical elements of motivation (Guthrie & Davis, 2003; Patall, Cooper, & Wynn, 2010). As students enter preteen and teen years, their choices about many things outside of school increase significantly, yet options in school remain limited. For instance, teachers may require students to answer a question in only one way or read just the assigned texts.

In Chapter 1, I suggested that, from a developmental perspective, allowing students more input into curricular decision making could help increase their sense of autonomy and agency, while building academic competence and identities (Vieira & Grantham, 2011). We know from good evidence that students in middle school (Freeman, McPhail, & Berndt, 2002) and high school (Moley, Bandre, & George, 2011; Patall et al., 2010), when given the choice, are quite capable of identifying activities they believe are helpful to their learning. Adolescents from all ability levels can be informants to help bring about more motivating literacy and disciplinary practices (Brozo, 2011). Many have documented the benefits of acquiring students' input into classroom practices and materials and then giving them choices based on this input. Youth feel empowered and motivated to participate constructively in their education when invited to help choose how and what they learn (Aboudan, 2011; Cook-Sather, Bovill, & Felten, 2014), while teachers gather critical information that helps them better appreciate the lifeworlds of youth and make their teaching more responsive to youths' experiences and perspectives (Cook-Sather, 2003; Wasley, Hampel, & Clark, 1997).

Structure Collaboration for Motivation

I have asserted in previous chapters, and once again maintain, that learning is, above all, a social process. Thus when disciplinary teachers create opportunities for students to work together in the pursuit of new knowledge, they are taking advantage of the social nature of learning. An added benefit to youth is the sense of belonging that grows out of cooperative and collaborative engagement in the classroom (Juvonen, Espinoza, & Knifsend, 2009). This sense of belonging for adolescents has been associated with an increase in motivation for reading and learning (Ivey & Broaddus, 2007; Malloy, Marinak, & Gambrell, 2010).

Students can be unmotivated for many reasons, but it seems clear that disengagement is as much a social challenge as it is any other. Consequently, content-area teachers will be more successful in motivating youth if they employ practices consistent with those surveyed by Cambria and Guthrie (2011), who found that students are motivated when they are allowed to sit with someone who will help them learn, to work in cooperative learning groups, and to choose a project to do with another student.

Another important advantage of creating collaborative contexts for increasing motivation and engagement is that shared experiences become *experiential referents* to which future learning can be linked. Experiential referents as shared motivational experiences bind a community of learners and allow teachers to regularly remind students, as a topic is further explored, that "we have all done this together, we have all witnessed this phenomenon, we have all made this common discovery." Frequent references to shared experiences increase students' chances of making connections between what they learned as a result of the experience and the new information they're encountering.

A great variety of strategies based on these guidelines have been shown to be useful with adolescents. The balance of this chapter is devoted to describing successful motivational strategies that we have observed middle and high school teachers use with their students. The unexpected benefit of teachers' efforts to develop imaginative, motivational activities is that, as they witnessed an increase in engagement among their students, the teachers themselves became more interested in the content and excited about teaching it, as well. As you heighten engagement in your classroom, I fully expect this same benefit will accrue to you. And, as you know, the more enthusiastic you are about reading and learning, the greater the chance of awakening interest in your students (National Council of Teachers of English Commission on Reading, 2008; Powell-Brown, 2003–2004).

MOTIVATING LITERACY AND LEARNING IN THE CONTENT CLASSROOM

The strategies and practices described in this section have all proven to motivate youth to be more actively involved in reading and learning. For convenience, I have organized them according to the particular guideline for creating motivating contexts that is most prominent. However, it's important to recognize that each strategy, whether unique or familiar, can be linked to several of the guidelines. The reason is that the teachers' motivational practices that I describe may have been crafted without any particular guideline in mind. Outstanding strategies to engage youth in reading and learning are, more often than not, generated by disciplinary teachers with an intelligent and caring disposition and a global understanding of the need to motivate their students. So, although the guidelines remind us of different aspects of motivation and the range of possible approaches that can be employed to motivate reading and learning, no single guideline is more important than this simple injunction: *Incorporate motivational practices into every lesson.*

Practices That Elevate Self-Efficacy

Social Studies/English

In my personal experience with eighth-grade Mexican American students from the barrio, I have discovered the crucial role direct experiences can have on their motivation for learning and their sense of competency as learners (Brozo et al., 1996). Throughout a unit on Hispanic American culture, their teachers and I had students explore the cultural roots within their families with the help of community members.

Before the unit began, we took the students on a walking field trip just two blocks away from their school to visit Gracie's garden. Gracie possessed extensive Mexican folk knowledge of the healing powers of plants and herbs. As the eighth graders and we walked through her garden, she explained in a mix of English and Spanish how for generations the native peoples of South Texas, which was once part of Mexico, kept themselves healthy and cured ailments ranging from indigestion to urinary tract infections with "green medicines." Students also went to the local university to participate in Cinco de Mayo (the "Fifth of May," a Mexican

American holiday) festivities. There the eighth graders enjoyed a talk and demonstration from a local Mexican American scholar on the curative benefits of herbs and plants. These experiences helped provide the students with a common reference and relevant background information for the stories and books we read about Mexican American folk medicines and culture.

Another way we were able to integrate direct experiences into the unit while taking advantage of community and cultural resources was through Integrated Parent Involvement Packets (IPIPs; Prouty & Irby, 1995). The IPIPs we used were packaged in a three-ring binder. The IPIP was introduced to parents with a letter thanking them for taking the time to participate in the unit. On the flip side of the letter was a sign-out chart with a place for the parents' and students' signatures when they completed the IPIP. Next, there was an explanation of what was required to complete the IPIP successfully. This was followed by a story by a Hispanic author, along with a short biography of the author. The stories reflected authentic Hispanic cultural experiences and were meant to be read aloud by the parents and the students to one another (Hayden, 1995).

The final component of the IPIP was a hands-on activity for students and parents to share. The activities were typically suggested by the IPIP readings. For example, in one of the stories we included in the IPIPs, Sandra Cisneros's (1990) "Three Wise Guys: Un Cuento de Navidad," a Mexican American family celebrates Christmas with the smell of cinnamon in the holiday air. We then asked parents and students to make cinnamon sticks from the ingredients we provided in a zippered plastic pouch in the IPIP binder. After reading Rudolpho Anaya's (1990) "Salomon's Story," which contains information about brewing traditional teas from local herbs, parents and students were given directions and ingredients for making their own native tea, manzanilla.

Overall, our efforts to involve students directly in learning experiences based in community–school collaboration during the Hispanic culture unit resulted in the eighth graders' exhibiting greater enthusiasm for learning, improved literacy behavior, and heightened awareness of their positive cultural identity.

English

One of the most important roles a teacher leader can play in middle and secondary schools is to work in concert with disciplinary teachers to buoy youths' academic competence and build positive academic identities (Sturtevant et al., 2006). The right educational experiences can make the difference between motivated students who sustain commitment to reading and learning and those who fail to become or remain engaged. Teacher leaders are ideally postured to support their content-area colleagues in the development of creative, student-centered motivational practices.

In her position as McArthur High School's reading coach, Bianca spends a good part of each day keeping in touch with teachers who are trying to integrate literacy strategies into their content classrooms. She team teaches, provides lesson demonstrations, and arranges for teachers who are applying certain strategies to observe and debrief with one another. Last year was Inez's first year as a ninth-grade English teacher, so she was quick to take advantage of the support Bianca offered her. Inez thought her students were not focusing closely enough on their readings and wondered if Bianca might have some suggestions. After a couple of classroom observations, Bianca soon recognized that one of the reasons the freshmen were frequently off task or appeared uninterested was the lack of constructivist, interactive teaching strategies. Inez tended to remain near the lectern at the front of the room, from which she called on students to read aloud and interjected questions for the whole class. Bianca could see that Inez's repertoire of teaching strategies was limited and developed a plan for improving her class dynamics.

A simple strategy Bianca introduced was having Inez give students a minute or two to talk with a partner before responding to her whole-class questions. This immediately improved attention and participation. In another strategy to increase motivation, Inez, instead of calling on individual students to read aloud from the novel or story, asked small groups of students to take parts, including the narrator, and to read scenes together. After a few pages, a new group would take over. Students were encouraged to read with expression and use simple gestures.

Although these approaches created a more engaging learning atmosphere, some continued to resist participation and remained marginalized from the flow of instruction. Zoran, in particular, a recent immigrant from Eastern Europe, was uninvolved in spite of the new class dynamics; but because he was diffident by nature and nondisruptive, Inez tended to tolerate his behavior, though she was unsure how to get him more involved. Bianca urged Inez to have a conference with Zoran to find out if he had any ideas about how he might become a more active member of the classroom community. Inez did this and listened to Zoran talk about how he felt uncomfortable speaking English with his strong accent. She also learned about his carpentry and painting skills, which his father had taught him in his native country.

Inez and Bianca decided to find a way to showcase Zoran's talent as a carpenter by asking him to create a set for a classroom reading of Ambrose Bierce's (2000) "An Occurrence at Owl Creek Bridge." Bianca borrowed material from the drama teacher and got permission from the industrial arts teacher to allow Zoran to use the shop during his study period to construct the props for the scenes in the story. Zoran's skill and imagination resulted in sets for the two main scenes in the story, one of the bridge, and one of the antebellum mansion. Zoran was so pleased with this assignment and the compliments he received from his classmates that he also finally agreed to participate in the reading of the story. Bianca and Inez invited other teachers and parents to observe the delivery of the story. All were impressed with Zoran's sets, which helped increase the verisimilitude of the class's presentation.

Finding a way for Zoran to be involved based on his out-of-school expertise and identity turned out to be the critical experience for transforming his attitude toward English class. With his increased level of participation in Inez's classroom, he was also remaking his academic identity from one of limited confidence in his own ability to read and comprehend to a growing sense of competence and agency.

Practices That Engender Interest in New Learning

History

A class of sophomore history students was failing to comprehend the full significance of Julius Caesar's move to publish the activities of the Roman senate. When students came to class the next day they immediately noticed what Terrell, their teacher, had written on the board "Jay picks his ears," "Myra sniffs glue." Jay and Myra, students in the class who had secretly agreed to participate in the put-on, began protesting vehemently as the others roared. "How many of you would like to have your foolish acts made public?" asked Terrell. "The point is," he went on, "Jay and Myra do not want their private and foolish acts made public, nor do you. And nor did the Roman senators." Caesar felt that the senators were behaving without decorum, Terrell went on to explain, and believed that having their behavior posted for all to read would pressure them into changing their ways. Terrell then apologized to Myra and Jay for libeling them. By using information gained from what we might call on-the-spot assessment, Terrell modified his instruction to include a concrete example to make his point clearer. He was able to motivate his students to learn by linking new information from a historical study of 2,000 years ago—a disparate culture and time—with the experiences and attitudes of adolescents today.

Chemistry

Brian introduced the study of carbon bonding to his chemistry class through one of the most unique and clever activities I have ever witnessed. With the desks moved to the walls of the classroom, leaving a large open area in the middle, Brian asked his students to stand up and then distributed paper bag vests to each of them that were labeled with a large, colorful H, C, or O (for hydrogen, carbon, and oxygen). After students donned the vests, he gave a fellow teacher a printed square dance call. He then pulled out a fiddle from its case, and with everyone set, he started to play the "Carbon Bonding Hoedown," as the square dance caller called the moves. Meanwhile, students moved around the room searching for partners; by the conclusion of the square dance, all carbon atoms had bonded appropriately, as represented by the students and their vests. Everyone had fun with this activity, and it formed a meaningful and motivating introduction to the exploration of the topic. It also provided the class with a memorable experience to which Brian could refer as they progressed through the study of carbon atoms and carbon bonding.

Foreign Language

Engaging her French I students in a study of French history, Marie scoured her imagination and came up with a way of transforming the classroom into the Lascaux Cave of southwest France. In the 1940s a group of boys stumbled upon the caves, which were later found to have great caverns decorated with some of the oldest known cave drawings in the world. Because Marie knew she couldn't take her students to the actual caves, she created a virtual field trip to Lascaux right in the classroom.

The day before, Marie prepared the classroom to simulate the darkness of a cave. To block out as much light as possible, she drew the blinds and taped black paper over the windows. She also taped to the walls large sheets of white and brown butcher paper on which were drawn pictures of animals, hands, and people in the style of prehistoric cave dwellers, as well as some of the French terms associated with caves, the discovery of the Lascaux cave, and exploration. The desks were pushed snug against the walls of the classroom, making a large open area in the middle.

The next day Marie waited outside the room for her students to arrive. When everyone had gathered, she explained that they were going on a virtual field trip for class that day and that they would need to be equipped with the proper gear. Most of her students remembered to bring flashlights, though she had a few extras for students who had forgotten. With flashlights on, she opened the door and asked everyone to proceed to the center of the room and have a seat on the floor.

Once students were seated, Marie asked them to turn their flashlights off, leaving the classroom in complete darkness. She then asked them to take a moment to think about things that are permanent, things that last forever and don't go away. She instructed students to position their flashlights under their chins so as to be recognized when they responded. Answers included things like paint, permanent markers, graffiti, death, tattoos, and even school.

To form pairs of student explorers, Marie instructed one student at a time to find a partner by randomly shining her or his flashlight at a classmate. Once grouped, Marie handed out paper and pencils for taking field notes and invited students to shine their lights around the room to learn about their surroundings. Students were asked to record on paper any words or symbols they encountered on the walls. Later, student pairs analyzed these recordings and wrote a brief explanation of what they thought they meant.

Finally, Marie turned on the lights, and while students waited for their eyes to reacclimatize to the brightness of the room, Marie invited them to select markers and create their own "cave drawings" on the butcher paper. While drawing, the class listened to Marie as she described in French the Lascaux Cave and its archeological significance. She concluded the lesson by reminding her students that French history, as well as the history of Europe, really begins with the drawings and symbols left behind by the ancient peoples who inhabited caves such as Lascaux.

With this approach, Marie introduced the topic in such an engaging way that she had little difficulty keeping her students' attention for the remainder of the unit on French history. Often they would refer back to "Lascaux" as though they had actually been there. The cave experience helped bring about shared understandings of the new content and reinforced a sense of community the students were feeling about the class.

Special Education

Jamal's role as a special education teacher has changed over the past few years. At one time all students were pulled out of their regular classes and provided separate modified instruction in math, science, history, and English in a self-contained environment. Today, Jamal's caseload of special education students is attending all regular classes, where he provides instructional and classroom management assistance to teachers and direct help for his students. His overall goal is to sensitize the regular education teacher to the need to modify ways in which information is disseminated and to help create an engaging learning environment that will hold the attention of his special learners.

In a 10th-grade history class, for example, Jamal worked with the teacher on a readiness activity that had been successful in his self-contained setting. One of his principal objectives for a unit about how the American colonies gained their freedom was to develop a thorough understanding of the concept of taxation without representation. Jamal knew that in the past his students were reasonably excited about the topic, but he found in his assessments that they failed to grasp the significance of the essential concepts leading to a full understanding of the antecedents and consequences of the American Revolution. Jamal also knew that the more he transformed lifeless textual information into something tangible and personal, the greater the students' involvement was, and the more they seemed to learn.

As a motivator and as a way of personalizing the concept, Jamal and the history teacher had the class participate in a simulation activity. They called it a "government experiment" as they handed out written directions and guided the class through them. The students were divided into two groups: one was called the "Oros" and the other the "Bindus." Jamal appointed himself the king of the Oros, while the history teacher joined the side of the Bindus. Each group was given a set of directions for electing representatives to make laws or rules. The Bindus were told they could only make rules that applied to themselves, whereas the Oros could impose rules on the Bindus if they chose. Each group also was given a lump sum of 1,000 play dollars for its treasury.

Jamal, as king of the Oros, immediately began imposing laws on the Bindus that roughly paralleled the Stamp Act and the Tea Act. The "Paper and Pencil Rule" taxed every Bindu 5 dollars for every pencil, pen, and piece of paper used; the "Pop Rule" taxed the Bindus 10 dollars for having a soda or any other drink in class (the history teacher permitted his students to have soft drinks in the classroom). Interestingly, the turn of events in the history classroom resembled what had happened between the British and the American colonies. Complaining fell on deaf ears, so at first the Bindus gave in to the Oros' rules. Soon, however, the Bindus began to protest—first by not bringing paper or pencils to class and then by simply ignoring the rule and disdainfully using as many sheets of paper and pencils as they wished. The same thing happened with their soda drinking. Soon the Bindus were challenging the Oros' authority by drinking without paying taxes. By week's end, the Oros were debating among themselves as to whether they should drop the taxes or impose penalties and stiffer taxes, while the Bindus were prepared to resist at all costs.

Practices That Generate Local Interest

Journalism

A wonderful example of a *prediction* strategy that was used to gain and hold students' attention for a daily lesson was provided by Ty, a senior high journalism teacher. Ty was instructing students in editorial writing by sharing examples of editorials and analyzing them. He handed out a sheet of paper with the title "A No-Lose Proposition," by Stanley J. Lieberman (1984) and the first paragraph, which read:

> America is the most litigious society in the world. We are suing each other at an alarming and increasing rate, and we have more lawyers per capita than any other nation. Since 1950 the number of lawyers in America has increased 250 percent. We have well over half a million lawyers—one for every 450 people. In New York state the ratio is one lawyer per 18. By contrast, the ratio in West Germany is one lawyer per 2,000. (p. 14)

After reading this material, the students worked in small groups and discussed the possible directions the editorial might take. Each group was to make two predictions. Ty moved around the room, listening in on each group, assisting when asked. Next, each group's predictions were presented to the whole class while the teacher wrote them on the board. A lengthy and immensely beneficial discussion then ensued, which included a class-derived definition of *litigious* and an impassioned defense of lawyers by a student whose father and mother were attorneys. An impressive amount of background and related knowledge poured out, as did the exchange and exploration of biases, opinions, and beliefs. Ty played a facilitative role during the discussion. He prodded when necessary, refocused the conversation when it seemed to stray too far from the task of determining what the author was likely to say in the passage, and clarified points and details.

When the debate over which predictions were likely to be verified by the text wound down, the students were eager to finish reading the editorial. Three agreed-on predictions remained on the board, and the students were reminded to read and discover to what extent, if any, the text supported them. After reading, the class discussed the accuracy of their predictions. No one had foreseen that the author would make a pitch for mediation as a way to unblock a clogged court system, although one prediction anticipated some kind of workable solution to this problem based on the editorial's title.

Reflect for a moment on how the preceding scene differs from the way a typical reading assignment is given—with little or no preparation or direction. By the time these students were ready to read the editorial, they had developed an interest in the topic through small-group and whole-class discussions that challenged beliefs and biases and piqued curiosity. As a result, attention to the text and comprehension could not help but improve.

Geography

To motivate her eighth graders to focus on the day's lesson, Keitha used the KWL (Know–Want to know–Learned) strategy (Carr & Ogle, 1987; Ogle, 1992). A perennial favorite among teachers at all levels, KWL continues to be used to gain and sustain students' attention by activating their prior knowledge, stimulating questioning, and prompting close reading of and thinking about the information source (Alger, 2009; Al-Khateeb & Idrees, 2010; Buehl, 2009; Tok, 2013). Keitha's geography class was about to begin the study of how mountain ranges are formed. First, she had students form groups of three and gave them 3 minutes to brainstorm everything they knew about mountains. When time was up, one student from each group reported the brainstormed information to the whole class. This resulted in a liberal exchange of ideas, until it was decided that the class knew two to three facts about mountains for certain. Keitha wrote these on the board in the "K" column, which stands for *What I Know* (see Figure 5.2). Her students had individual blank KWL charts on which they wrote the same information.

Keitha then asked the groups to reconvene and take a couple of minutes to generate three questions they would like answered about the topic of mountains. As students talked among themselves, she moved around the room to listen in, clarify, and answer any questions. Once the time was up, Keitha invited group spokespersons to share their questions with the class. When an agreed-upon list was ultimately derived, these were written in the "W" column of the KWL chart. This column represents what learners *want* to know.

K	W	L
Volcanoes help form mountains. The Rocky Mountains are very tall.	Do mountains grow? How do they erode? Why are the Rockies taller than the Smokies?	Mountains form when heat within the earth pushes up bedrock. Lava forces its way up and hardens into rock, causing mountains to grow bigger. Rain and wind wear them down. Mountains are part of a cycle-ocean sediment to solid rock pushed up to form mountains, then worn down into the sea again. Mountains in the eastern U.S. are very old. Mountains in the West are not as old.

FIGURE 5.2. A KWL chart for the formation of mountains.

At this point, Keitha's students were poised to receive and seek the information sources to answer their questions. Completing the "K" and "W" processes of the KWL strategy hadn't exactly transformed the class into a group of mountain enthusiasts, but it did accomplish the goal of impelling students to attend more closely to the immediate task of finding answers to their own KWL-generated questions. While listening to Keitha read aloud and share the remarkable photographs from Bredeson's (2001) *Mount Saint Helens Volcano*, students were to stop her when information was provided to help answer a question from the KWL chart. Keitha could see that most were listening attentively and freely interrupted her throughout the read-aloud. At the conclusion of the book, at least two questions remained unanswered, so groups were asked to select another book on mountains and volcanoes from the collection Keitha had stacked on a table in the classroom. With the books, such as Winchester's (2015) *When the Earth Shakes*, O'Meara's (2007) *Into the Volcano*, and Claybourne's (2014) *100 Most Destructive Natural Disasters*, students worked in their groups until answers were found to the lingering questions.

Health

Dimitrius has found he can motivate his health students to engage more meaningfully with class topics by using *anticipation guides* (Fisher et al., 2015). You should be somewhat familiar with the anticipation guide strategy already since you have been asked to complete one for each chapter of this book.

First, Dimitrius looks over the information sources his students will receive for the day's topic, in this case on diet and nutrition. Based on his lecture notes, the related textbook chapter, and websites, he comes up with several statements. He makes sure his guide statements are: (1) related to the major ideas and information students would encounter; (2) representative of the content Dimitrius wanted students to be sure to learn; (3) alluring or challenging; and (4) an appropriate blend of text- and reader-based items. In addition, he goes over his statements another time to ensure that some are written to appear correct but are incompatible with the information students will encounter and that others seem incorrect yet are compatible with the information to follow.

Dimitrius formats his anticipation guides in a way that makes it simple for him to present them to his students without having to create a formal, typed, and photocopied guide (see Figure 5.3). Often, he simply writes the statements on the board, including a *before* and *after* column with *true* and *false* as response options. His students copy the statements into their notebooks with the date and title, so they can hand in their completed guides for a grade.

Dimitrius designs his anticipation guides in ways that do not require students to write extended answers to prompts that resemble discussion or essay questions. Instead, he has students respond with simple checkmarks. But, to guard against students making random responses without careful thinking as they encounter new content related to the guide, he adds a feature that requires them to verify the information used to corroborate or amend their initial responses (see Figure 5.3).

Dimitrius uses anticipation guides not only as a motivator to learn, but also as a vehicle for clearing up misconceptions about the topic. This function seems especially important given research evidence indicating that students' existing prior knowledge and biases will be superimposed on the information sources when the two are at odds (Diakidoy, Mouskounti, & Ionnides, 2011; Tippett, 2010).

Environmental Science

A more formal anticipation guide was given to students by Paula, their environmental science teacher, to motivate them to think critically about the topic of pollution (see Figure 5.4). Although this guide required a good deal more planning and time to complete than the health guide created by Dimitrius, it nonetheless possesses the same essential features as the simpler guide.

Common to both guides is the all-important accountability feature. As students encounter text, lecture, or multimedia on the topic, they must find information that either reinforces and verifies existing beliefs, forces them to be altered or modified, or requires completely rejecting them. This process motivates students to focus closely on new content. As relevant information is found, it can be written in the form of terse statements with page numbers, as URLs, or as lecture note entries.

Part I

Directions: Read each statement. If you believe that a statement is true, place a checkmark in the *Agree* column. If you believe the statement is false, place a checkmark in the *Disagree* column. Be ready to explain your choices.

Agree   **Disagree**

_____   _____   1. About 45% of the total food dollar is spent on food away from home.

_____   _____   2. More cookbooks are being purchased today than ever before.

_____   _____   3. Soft drinks are essentially sugar.

_____   _____   4. The average person's diet consists of between 60% and 70% fat and sugar.

_____   _____   5. People are eating fewer fruits today than in the 1940s.

_____   _____   6. Many so-called primitive cultures have more nutritious diets than many affluent Americans.

_____   _____   7. Vitamin C has been used effectively to treat mental diseases.

Part II

Directions: Now you will be reading and listening to information related to each of the statements in Part I of this guide. If the information supports your choices in Part I, place a checkmark in the *Support* column. If the information does not support your choices, place a checkmark in the *No support* column. Write in your own words the relevant text and/or lecture information for your answer.

Support   **No support**   **Text/Lecture information**

1.   _____   _____   _____

2.   _____   _____   _____

3.   _____   _____   _____

4.   _____   _____   _____

5.   _____   _____   _____

6.   _____   _____   _____

7.   _____   _____   _____

FIGURE 5.3. Anticipation guide for diet and nutrition.

Part I

Directions: Below are statements and situations related to the environment. If you agree with the statement, place a checkmark in the *Agree* column. If you disagree with the statement, place a checkmark in the *Disagree* column. Be prepared to explain your responses.

Agree   Disagree

_____   _____   1. A poor landowner wants to sell his land to a large chemical refinery. The environmentalists say there is an endangered species on the land. The court says he can't sell the land. Do you agree with the court ruling?

_____   _____   2. It doesn't matter if I recycle my aluminum cans or not. One person doesn't make a difference.

_____   _____   3. A small business garage owner goes to a vacant lot to empty motor oil into the ground. The police pick him up for suspicious behavior and find out what he has been doing. He is fined $50,000, which ruins his business and forces him into bankruptcy. Do you agree with the judgment? He says everybody else does it, so what difference does it make?

_____   _____   4. Your next-door neighbor has a beautiful yard. He sprays the plants almost every day. He never seems to be picking weeds; instead, he sprays his lawn with poison. Do you agree with his technique?

_____   _____   5. A man and his family saved for years to buy the home of their dreams. After they moved in, the younger child became very ill. He had headaches most of the time. The man eventually found out that he had bought a house on top of an old landfill. He sued the real estate agent and lost the case. Do you agree with the court ruling?

_____   _____   6. The richest and most diverse terrestrial ecosystems on earth are the tropical forests. Some people want to develop this land for cattle grazing. Do you think that would be a good idea?

Part II

Directions: Now that we have studied facts and issues related to environmental pollution, look back at your responses to the statements in Part I. If you found support for your response, check the *Support* column below; if you didn't find support for your response, check the *No support* column. Regardless of what column you check, write a sentence in your own words explaining your response.

Support   No support   Your explanation

1.   _____   _____   _____

2.   _____   _____   _____

3.   _____   _____   _____

4.   _____   _____   _____

5.   _____   _____   _____

6.   _____   _____   _____

FIGURE 5.4. Anticipation guide for the topic of environmental pollution.

This should include corroborative as well as amended statements that correct unanticipated information.

Another common feature of the two guides is how the teachers used them with students. In both classrooms, students were presented with the anticipation guide statements and asked to pair up to discuss them. Next, a discussion of the statements was opened up to the entire class, wherein students could debate and defend responses. Then the class was given the opportunity to revise initial responses to the guide statements. At this point, students were provided with the information sources. Periodically, as students explored these sources, they were stopped and asked to refer back to a particular guide statement about which information was supplied. This was followed by student pairs and then the whole class discussing the statement's veracity. The process continued until all guide statements had been considered and reconsidered in light of the information sources.

Working with anticipation guides helps create the urge in students to know more and sustains interest in topics, at least within the context of a single day's lesson. Guides motivate students to confront the topic ideas and information purposefully and enthusiastically (Fisher et al., 2015; Kozen, Murray, & Windell, 2006) and facilitate assimilation of new information into existing schemata (Fisher & Frey, 2015).

Reading/Language Arts

Renard, an eighth-grade reading/language arts teacher, employs the *lesson impression* strategy to motivate his students to focus more closely on the reading material for any given day. This strategy helps students develop an impression of what the forthcoming lesson will cover, which impels them to read, listen, and observe the lesson content with heightened attentiveness in order to discover whether their predictions are correct. It can be used before exposing students to content regardless of how information and ideas are delivered. In other words, it is equally effective for engendering an immediate and local interest in the variety of typical information sources in middle and secondary schools, such as reading material, lectures, guest speakers, videos, and field trips. Lesson impressions can increase motivation by heightening anticipation and providing a meaningful purpose for learning.

Renard conducted a lesson impression by first presenting students a list of words and phrases taken directly from the material to be covered. Renard put the following words and phrases on the overhead:

CDs	penny	music	club	hidden commitments	contract
	monthly selections		"return to sender"	rip-off	

He then asked students to write what they thought they were about to read by creating a short description or narrative in which all of the words were used. Renard asked his students to write the words in their notebooks and directed them to craft short compositions on what they thought the lesson would be about, making sure to use all the words.

When his students finished writing, they were given the opportunity to exchange their written impressions with a peer. In this way, they could compare and contrast one another's predictions about the content to be covered in the forthcoming lesson, which acts to heighten their anticipation. After students read one another's impression writing, Renard eventually invited several to share what they had written with the entire class. His goal was to gather a variety of impressions so that students were left with a sense that either theirs or that of any one of their classmates may be the most accurate.

In response to the lesson impression words Renard gave his students, Juwon created a kind of personal story about the topic. He read to the class:

> "I saw an ad in a magazine that said I could buy 10 **CDs** for a **penny** if I joined this **music club**. They had all this cool music so I decided to join. After getting my first 10 choices, I received a **contract** that had all these **hidden commitments**, like I had to pick out so many **monthly selections** or I'd have to pay for those CDs that were only a penny. By then I knew this was a **rip-off**, so I packed everything back up in the box and wrote **"return to sender."**

At this point in the strategy process, Renard's students were ready to receive the information. As Renard passed out copies of the article entitled "Ten CDs for a Penny? If It's Too Good to Be True, It Probably Isn't," he stressed that he now wanted the class to pay very close attention to determine whether the content jibed with their written impressions, though they were so eager to read that he hardly had to remind them. Renard also required his students to keep a record of the similarities and differences between their impressions and the actual content by creating a Venn diagram or a compare–contrast chart. I recommend such practices because they add an accountability feature that raises the level of assurance that students are remaining engaged throughout the lesson.

Students paired up and read sections of the short article aloud together, trading off reading paragraphs. Renard stopped them at regular intervals to ask questions and get responses based on their predictions in their lesson impressions.

Science

Tammy, an eighth-grade science teacher, presented her students with the following words by writing them on the board:

breathing	oxygen	inhale	exhale	mucus
nose	carbon dioxide	vocal cords	lungs	

Next, she asked her students to write for 5–7 minutes using as many of these words as possible in their short compositions. Tammy said they could write what they expected to hear during the upcoming presentation on the human respiratory system. She urged students to be creative, incorporating the words in a song, poem, or story.

Many of the students wrote what they knew about the respiratory system, which helped Tammy discover the extent of their prior knowledge. Others, who were more comfortable with the content, chose to be creative and were eager to share their work before her presentation began. Tammy found her students paying closer attention during the lesson. Since she had not picked up their compositions, several students corrected their stories with the information they gleaned from the presentation. It was clear that the lesson impression strategy had engendered focused listening and heightened motivation to learn due to students' desire to compare their impression texts with the content of Tammy's presentation.

When Tammy asked students after her presentation what they liked or disliked about the strategy, their responses were consistent. They liked the freedom to be creative and to have a default option in case the creative juices weren't flowing. The students further commented that they thought the lesson impression activity helped them focus on information about the respiratory system of which they were unsure. Two examples of the students' readiness compositions follow.

Student 1

My breathing takes in air that contains oxygen. It goes through my nose and the mucus cleans the air before it enters my lungs. But first it goes through the vocal cords. After it enters my lungs, I exhale the carbon dioxide that I don't need.

Student 2

My nose is very big although I'm very small. When I sneeze my mucus goes all over the wall. My lungs are breathing oxygen that's a proven fact. I exhale carbon dioxide and that's all I have to say about that. Please don't ask me to sing this hour, because with my vocal cords the notes will be awfully sour.

Biology

Tenth-grade biology teacher Roberta is able to get her students highly motivated to read and learn the daily content through a variety of creative strategies. One of those strategies is called Student Questions for Purposeful Learning, or SQPL. SQPL promotes engaged and purposeful exploration of the topic as students search for answers to their own questions.

As a critical first step in preparing to conduct an SQPL lesson, Roberta looked over the day's reading material and her notes on the topic she was introducing, human genetics, then crafted a short, thought-provoking statement to present to her class. She wrote it in big letters across the board:

IT IS NOW POSSIBLE TO CLONE HUMAN BEINGS.

She knew even though the statement wasn't necessarily factually true, it would instigate lively conversation among her students and stimulate plenty of good questions in preparation for reading an article on genetic engineering.

For the next phase of the lesson, Roberta allowed her students to pair up and brainstorm questions they would like to have answered based on the statement. After asking her students to turn to their neighbors, Roberta told them to come up with three questions they would like answered about the statement on the board. While students worked together on their questions, Roberta moved throughout the room to monitor their progress and help clarify the task.

When they were finished, Roberta went around the room and gathered questions from each of the student pairs, writing them on the board. The goal here was to gather a variety of questions by making sure each student pair contributed at least one of its questions.

After every student had an opportunity to add a question to the total, Roberta drew the class's attention to those questions that were essentially the same and added stars next to those questions. Some questions, such as "How do you clone someone?" had five stars, because at least five separate pairs of students came up with the same or a highly similar question. Another question, "Who will get cloned?" was repeated four times, and "How much does it cost?" had three stars. Like Roberta, I recommend that you highlight or star questions asked by more than one pair of students; these become class consensus questions. You can also consolidate questions by combining similar ones.

At this stage, Roberta's students were more than ready to get answers to their questions, and they immediately began reading just as soon as Roberta handed them the article titled "Can Humans Be Cloned Like Sheep?" Like all of the strategies discussed in this section and chapter, SQPL is adaptable to virtually any information source, such as reading material, lecture, discussion, video, and the Internet. Students should be directed to pay close attention to information that answers the questions the class generated, especially class consensus questions.

Roberta told the class that, as information was encountered that answered one of the readiness questions, the information should be written in their notebooks. Throughout the reading of the article, Roberta stopped students periodically to discuss the piece in general and answers to student questions in particular.

SQPL motivates Roberta's students to invest in the learning process, since they become gatherers of information based on their own inquiry and not on prompts given them by her or the textbook. Nonetheless, it is important to point out that student-generated questions do not necessarily have to constitute the only questions for a given reading or topic. This is especially true when students are first learning the strategy and may fail to derive questions that cover critical information. For instance, if Roberta noticed certain vital questions missing but necessary to direct attention to important aspects of the topic, she would contribute her own questions to the list in a tactful way.

Many highly effective classroom strategies can be employed to increase motivation for reading and learning for a particular day's lesson or topic. In this section, I demonstrated how five useful strategies—prediction, KWL, anticipation guides, lesson impressions, and SQPL—can be used to increase student engagement by generating local interest in various content-area topics. These strategies increase engagement by inducing students to establish purposes for reading and learning, which leads to active exploration of the content to answer their own questions and satisfy their own curiosities. When youth attend to topics more closely, interact with them in more meaningful ways, and combine their world knowledge with new information, higher level thinking and broader understandings are the result.

AN SQPL ACTIVITY

As you just learned, the key to an effective SQPL lesson is how well the thought-provoking statement given to students in advance of new information stimulates meaningful queries. Below are typical topics covered in content classrooms using print, visual texts, and lectures. For each of these topics, generate possible SQPL statements to prompt good questions before students in disciplinary classrooms are provided information sources on these topics. A suggestion for the first topic is provided as an example.

Content-Area Topics	SQPL Statements
1. The Aging Process	1. *Age is just a state of mind: Even you can live to be a hundred.*
2. The Atom Bomb	2.
3. Asteroids	3.
4. The Civil Rights Movement	4.
5. Symbolism in Poetry	5.

Practices That Connect Outside with Inside School Literacies and Learning

Science

Judy, a sixth-grade science teacher, borrowed her school's old home economics room with its four ovens for a class experiment. She arranged several food items, mixing bowls, and pizza tins on a table at the front of the room. She told her students that they were home alone and were hungry for pizza; however, without money to buy a pizza and no pizzas in the freezer, they would have to create one with the ingredients on the table. Judy divided the class into groups of three, gave each group a sheet for recording the steps involved in their pizza-making adventure, and told them to get started. Under her watchful eye, the groups discussed and gathered, mixed, poured, stirred, baked, and laughed their way through this discovery process.

After the fun, Judy asked each group to show off its "pizza," identify its ingredients, and describe the steps taken to create it. Brave volunteers stepped forward to taste-test the pizzas. After the class cleaned up and resettled, Judy gave the groups a handout with a detailed description of the five steps of the scientific method. On a poster board with the same five steps listed, she and the students wrote out how the steps they took to create their pizzas corresponded with the steps in the scientific method.

Judy's hands-on class experience satisfied several guidelines of motivational teaching. First, it immediately generated a great deal of enthusiasm on the part of the class. Second, students were allowed to work together as they searched for the best possible ingredients and steps to create pizzas from scratch. Third, situating learning within a familiar, home-like context helped Judy's students bridge everyday experiences with school subjects. Finally, the pizza-making activity provided students with an experiential referent for their ongoing study of the scientific method. In fact, throughout the next several days and weeks, Judy constantly referred back to the pizza-making adventure to remind students of a related aspect of the scientific method they were studying.

Chemistry

Angelina used students' everyday experiences as links to classroom topics to create a more engaging context for learning about covalent bonding. To help them better understand this concept and generate interest, Angelina exploited the class's knowledge of marriage, reasoning that just as the bonding of two people in matrimony has certain conditions, so too does the bonding of atoms.

Angelina split her class into two groups, telling one they represented the Doe family and the other, the Smith family. The Does were asked to select a groom for a marriage ceremony, and the Smiths were asked to select a bride. Angelina gave each family an index card with background information to establish a context for forging a successful marriage contract between the two families. As it happens, the two families have had a long-standing dispute, the resolution of which depends upon the terms of the marriage agreement being acceptable to both groups. The Does own land, whereas the Smiths own seeds. The groups appointed negotiators to meet and work out the contract. Once both families agreed to the terms, the happy couple was joined in matrimony amid a festive class atmosphere. Angelina even brought out a cake for the occasion.

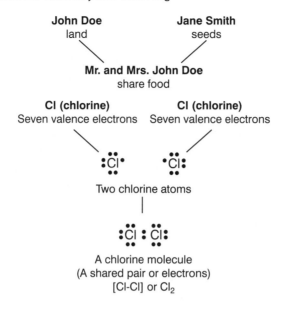

FIGURE 5.5. Marriage bonding as an analogy for covalent bonding.

While the class settled down to enjoy the confection, Angelina put the activity in chemical terms. Using the graphic display in Figure 5.5, she explained that all atoms strive to become noble gases by having eight valence electrons. Two atoms will come together and share a bond to reach this goal. She went on to ask the students to imagine the Doe and Smith families are atoms and the seeds and lands are electrons. As long as the couple stays married and share that bond, they will share the seeds and land between the families. Both families will have food and will prosper together. At the atomic level, when atoms share electrons and form a noble gas, the result is covalent bonding.

United States History

A group of Alamo battle reenactors tumbled into Hector's eighth-grade history classroom, including a Mexican soldier, a Tennessee volunteer, and a Texas frontiersman. Outfitted in authentic attire, carrying authentic weaponry, and remaining in character for the entire class period, these three performers talked about their lives and the events at the Alamo as though the battle had happened yesterday. Thus Hector's students began the study of the Alamo with the help of these memorable guests. Not only did the reenactors create an engaging atmosphere for learning in Hector's classroom, but they also helped breathe life into the ideas and information in the history textbook by helping students see a connection to real people and events.

Ecology

I watched the eyes of a group of seventh graders grow to saucer proportions as a local ornithologist walked into the classroom with a great horned owl on one arm and an osprey on the other—both nearly 2 feet tall! The guest speaker explained the life habits of these birds of prey and gave demonstrations. Students asked questions and were nearly able to touch the birds as they gathered around the speaker. It was a memorable day for Diane's science class, especially when the osprey unexpectedly let out a loud whistling call. Thus began Diane's unit on birds of prey.

In both of these cases, Diane, the science teacher, and Hector, the history teacher, were clever enough to recognize the power of bringing into class members of the community with expert knowledge. Students began their study of the topics with increased anticipation, excitement, and a store of useful, new knowledge to help them better negotiate the texts and ideas to follow. Furthermore, by inviting people and animals from outside the classroom into the classroom, she gave her students unique, real-world experiences to which they could link new learning.

I believe guest speakers and performers are perhaps the most underused resources teachers can employ to increase student motivation for reading and learning. Even in the remotest communities there is a wealth of knowledge to be tapped—individuals who lived through critical times in history, local authors and artists, and members of the political, industrial, and scientific worlds. Often local municipalities have information services about local experts. Colleges and universities have public information offices with names and addresses of professors and notes on their areas of expertise. I recently contacted a city office for information about local Native American groups and was put in touch with a couple of organizations that supplied guest speakers to a ninth-grade teacher's classroom.

I agree with those who advise that to get the most out of guest speakers and performers, students and guests should be prepared (Larson & Keiper, 2013; Kamoun, 2007). Students should be given time to generate questions, and guests should know in advance your expectations for their visit, how much time they will have, and any special requests. These preparation procedures can avoid potential problems such as embarrassing comments, rambling, or information unrelated to the topic.

Lindy Poling (2000), a high school social studies teacher, has found that guest speakers in her classroom motivate students to think more critically and provide them with a real-world perspective on the curriculum. Being prepared, however, is critical, and she recommends:

- Contacting local organizations that provide effective guest speakers (e.g., local universities, public information offices of local municipalities, veterans and civic organizations).
- Screening the guest beforehand to make certain his or her background truly matches the objectives of the classroom content.

- Preparing the guest by informing him or her about what students have been studying in relation to the topic of his or her expertise and what particular aspects of that expertise you would like emphasized in the presentation.
- Establishing a careful question-and-answer plan that requires students to generate questions in advance and submit them to the teacher for screening and possible forwarding to the guest speaker.

Chemistry

Toni, a high school chemistry teacher, invited to her class a friend who was an organic chemist in the research and development department of a large local company. She had her students spend a couple of class periods preparing for the guest speaker by first brainstorming their areas of interest about which the guest would likely have information. These included original discoveries and patents, new and future uses of polymers, employment opportunities for women in chemistry, and the day-to-day operation of a research and development department. Toni then asked her students to form small groups based on their interests and generate a set of 10 questions each that they would like answered by the guest chemist. Toni looked over the questions and helped each group refine its list to five good questions. Meanwhile, Toni contacted her friend and told her what the students were most interested in learning. This information made it possible for the chemist to prepare effectively for the classroom visit.

When the day arrived, the school newspaper and science club wanted to cover the presentation, so a video camera was set up to record the event. The chemist gave a brief overview and then asked for questions. Each group was given the opportunity to ask all five of its questions in a set to avoid forcing the guest speaker to jump from topic to topic in a disjointed way. She brought in examples of products developed by her center and diagrams, notes, and computer graphics on future developments. She talked from experience about her interest and schooling in chemistry and the process of gaining employment in the company. She described how patents are obtained and showed the class some of the patented products for which she was responsible. Finally, using a web-based presentation, she took the class through a video field trip of her research and development center.

Practices That Make an Abundance of Interesting Texts Available

Social Studies

One morning while I was walking down the hall of large suburban middle school where I was providing year-long consulting, Marcus, a second-year seventh-grade social studies teacher, approached me and invited me into his classroom for a chat.

He explained that he had been taught in his university methods classes to teach history using a textbook but came to realize that he was losing his students to boredom because topics were treated so lifelessly in the class text. He wondered how he could get his students more interested in reading and learning history. My reply was to create frequent opportunities for engaged reading using alternative texts and that, if he were willing to give this approach a try, I would support him in every way possible.

Marcus was excited to get started and began by building a classroom library of interesting trade books, graphic novels, and magazines with connections to many of the history topics he covered in his class. He visited secondhand bookstores, thrift shops, and garage sales, checked out discards from public libraries, sought donations of "irregulars" from bookstore chains, and made purchases from online discount sellers. He found a couple of old but solid metal bookcases and a magazine display case in the school district's furniture warehouse, covered them with a fresh coat of paint, and put them in the corner of his classroom. In the same corner, he added a couple of beanbag chairs and inexpensive outdoor folding chairs to create a reading space for his students.

At my urging, Marcus met with the school librarian to enlist her help in finding relevant books and magazine she had that he could add to his class collection. These were texts Marcus would keep in his room during the exploration of certain units and return to the school library when the unit concluded. The librarian was more than willing to assist him, so he gave her his syllabus with topics and dates to help her organize relevant collections ahead of time.

As Marcus gathered new books and reading material, he found a renewed interest in reading for his own personal pleasure and growth. Though many of the historical novels, biography, and information books Marcus found were written for adolescents, he was pleasantly surprised to discover that the quality of writing was often first rate. This discovery made him all the more eager to get these materials into the hands of his students. How to do that was the focus of my next conversation with him.

Informally, Marcus's students were already picking out books and magazines from his classroom collection to browse, and, although he was happy with this development, he was also interested in planned approaches to exposing students to these alternative texts. We brainstormed a variety of possible ways of creating opportunities for engaged reading in Marcus's classroom, including:

- Using information books to research history topics.
- Reading novels and graphic novels related to class topics.
- Making time for sustained silent reading of student self-selected material about any topic related to the class.
- Reading aloud from a novel or information book related to a class topic.

Next, I asked Marcus to think ahead and identify an upcoming unit that would lend itself to a multiple-text approach. With little hesitation, Marcus suggested the American Civil War, because he had been especially successful finding a range of books and other reading material on that topic. Among the outstanding sources Marcus had collected included:

• Butzer's (2008) *Gettysburg: The Graphic Novel* depicts the Battle of Gettysburg and the national movement to create a memorial there. Using only primary sources for the text and drawing from first-person letters and diaries, speeches, and Lincoln's own writing, Butzer explores this series of historical events. Eighteen pages are devoted to the address itself, with every phrase given a visual interpretation.

• Pinkney's (2001) *Abraham Lincoln: Letter from a Slave Girl*, a fictional correspondence between a 12-year-old slave and President Lincoln. Although the letters are fictional, the information contained in the letters is based on historical facts, giving the reader a sense of the times and emotions of the day.

• Murphy (2009), in *A Savage Thunder: Antietam and the Bloody Road to Freedom*, recounts how two great armies faced off across Antietam Creek, near Sharpsburg, Maryland, in September 1862. From behind-the-scenes conversations to the action on the front lines, Murphy's nonfiction book provides an in-depth look at the battle that prompted Abraham Lincoln to issue the Emancipation Proclamation and change America forever. The book contains numerous photographs, maps, and first-person accounts to heighten the sense of chaos and confusion of the bloodiest battle of the war.

• Avi's (2010) *Iron Thunder: The Battle between the Monitor and the Merrimac* is a historical novel about the Union army's iron ship, the Monitor, and the Confederate "sea monster," another ironclad called the Merrimac. The story follows Tom, an assistant to the ship's inventor, Captain John Ericsson, and describes the buildup, the fight of these two "iron coffins," and the aftermath for Tom.

• Durrant's (2006) *My Last Skirt: The Story of Jennie Hodgers, Union Soldier* tells the story of Jennie Hodgers, who dressed as a boy to help support her impoverished Irish family with a shepherd's wages. When she leaves Ireland and arrives in America, Jennie maintains her outward identity as a boy, which helps her find paying jobs. During the Civil War, Jennie becomes a recruit in the 95th Illinois Infantry and survives 3 years in combat with her true identity undiscovered.

• Hart (2008), in *Gabriel's Journey*, tells the story of ex-slave Gabriel, who leaves behind a successful horse racing career to join his parents at Camp Nelson, where his father is a sergeant in the Fifth U.S. Colored Cavalry of the Union Army. When the cavalry receives orders to join white regiments in an attack on the Confederate army in Virginia, Gabriel surreptitiously gets a hold of a horse and a uniform and joins the troops. Bad weather, rough riding, dwindling supplies, and blatant racism hound the 12-year-old.

- Hale's (2015) *Nathan Hale's Hazardous Tales: The Underground Abductor: An Abolitionist Tale about Harriet Tubman* tells Harriet Tubman's story in graphic novel format. The panels depict Tubman's early life growing up as a slave and her eventual journey to freedom. The novel shows how Tubman, once free, dedicated the rest of her life to helping slaves run away as she did and took her own life in her hands to do so.

- Bordewich's (2004) "Free at Last," an article in *Smithsonian* magazine, is about a museum that has opened in Ohio that celebrates the Underground Railroad. This article shows middle school students the efforts to preserve evidence from the historical period they are studying. The article provides very helpful background information on the Underground Railroad.

- The website *http://bensguide.gpo.gov* contains numerous passages for striving readers on American history topics, including a wide assortment focusing on the Civil War. The website is colorful, animated, and user friendly.

With these sources, Marcus decided to read aloud to his class *Abraham Lincoln: Letters from a Slave Girl*. At the same time, he formed several cooperative groups of students and allowed them to select a source from the other materials to research the topic of the American Civil War. As these topics were encountered in the class textbook, students responsible for gathering information from the other texts were asked to share with their classmates. Students were also given dedicated time each day throughout the unit to browse the bookshelves and magazine rack for self-selected reading of any material related to the topic. They could also lounge in the beanbag chairs or on the floor while reading. In this way, most students obtained multiple exposures to varying perspectives from the material Marcus had collected on the Civil War.

By using interesting alternative sources, Marcus was able to inspire his students to levels of engaged learning he had not seen before. Also, the feedback he received from his class was that the Civil War unit was the most interesting and fun up to that point in the school year. Furthermore, student test scores were among the highest Marcus received for any unit.

Biology

Loy, who taught tenth-grade biology in a high school in the same district as Marcus, used Farley Mowat's *Never Cry Wolf* (1979) in conjunction with a unit on "food chains." His students seemed to become increasingly unmotivated and listless as the school year progressed. He noticed, however, that when he read aloud from virtually any source, their attention improved. Out of desperation, he decided to incorporate a novel into his food chain unit and observed the kind of heightened involvement and sustained effort he had hoped to see.

During one class period, after employing a short PowerPoint presentation that defined and characterized causes and effects of population crashes in the natural world, Loy asked students to work in pairs to seek out as much evidence and as many examples as they could find of such population crashes using the print and nonprint resources available to them. Students were given a recording sheet to document their research. Many began by thumbing back through the novel, *Never Cry Wolf*, and writing down information related to Mowat's description of what happened to the vole population when too many wolves were killed or relocated.

Afterward, Loy organized a review of the last chapter read in the novel. The review was in a "popcorn" format whereby Loy gave the class the first critical event of the chapter, then waited for other students to stand up and supply a statement about what happened next. Using this approach, the class was able to cover most of the chapter plot within 5 minutes.

Loy then asked for volunteers to come to the front of the room and take parts reading the next chapter aloud. In this chapter, a bush pilot and a party of hunters make camp near to where Farley is conducting his research on a wolf pack. He and the hunters have a threatening encounter. Loy took the role of narrator while the others read the parts of Farley and members of the hunting party. Students participated eagerly, and after a couple of pages a new set of students went up to continue the read-aloud. Loy was patient with all students and waited until one asked for help with a word before he or a classmate provided it. At several points in the action, Loy invited class members who were not reading aloud to ask questions of the students who were. This seemed to keep everyone focused on the plot.

Earlier in the year, Loy had learned from me that his biology book was written at a level too difficult for several of his students. When he allowed his students to read from sources that were easier for them, such as young adult novels, he found that they tended to read the assigned pages and stay on task. (See Chapter 8 for a comprehensive discussion of strategies for using trade books in the content classroom.)

Practices That Expand Student Choices and Options

Math

Jaqui is the kind of teacher who proves the skeptics wrong. In spite of the odds, she always seems to bring her freshman general math students into the flow of instruction. She knows many enter her class with negative attitudes toward math, often the result of years of failure and struggle, but instead of viewing their dispositions as detractors from learning, she sees them as starting points for change.

Transforming dispirited youth into risk takers begins by discovering who they are and what they value. Using the My Bag strategy Jaqui is able to find something unique about each of her students. The My Bag strategy is a way of getting to know students. It allows them to showcase their strengths, loves, hobbies, and dreams. The strategy involves placing items in a bag or some other container, such as a backpack. The decision-making process used to select items for the bag forces students to think critically about themselves and about how certain items symbolize different aspects of their life. In one class of 32, for instance, Jaqui learned from the My Bag activity that all but 2 were living with their biological fathers and mothers, but each one possessed an interest or desire that defined them as special in her eyes. For instance, 12 were born outside of the United States. One was the daughter of refugees of the war in Kosovo. One played jazz trumpet. One worked with his uncle as a farmworker during the summers. And three were on the junior varsity football team.

With information gleaned from the My Bag activity, Jaqui was quick to demonstrate how much she valued her students' diversity and wanted to connect mathematics to their histories and experiences. She discussed with the class an upcoming unit on basic statistics—finding averages, compiling and organizing data, determining trends—and invited their suggestions for how they could learn it together. This act of using students as curricular informants helps Jaqui create learning environments and activities that are responsive to students' actual needs. In this way, she builds the math curriculum around students instead of imposing it on them. Examples of the kinds of suggestions her students offered to make learning statistics worthwhile are as follows:

- Jesús: "Keep it real."
- Benita: "Don't embarrass us."
- Corey: "Let us use our hands and stuff."
- Mondelique: "What can we do with it?"

From here, Jaqui pooled My Bag information and student suggestions, then conferred with small groups and individual students to discuss possible projects for using statistics that related to their lives. For example, in consultation with the three football players in class, she helped them decide to maintain a statistics scrapbook on the team's performance throughout the fall season. The student from Kosovo wanted to explore the numbers behind the war and ethnic cleansing her parents were fortunate enough to escape. The youth who played the trumpet thought it would be "cool" to study how many times he played certain notes while improvising by taping his improvisations, then tallying frequencies and percentages. Other groups of students agreed to work together to research statistics related to recent immigrants in their neighborhoods and apartment complexes.

Jaqui met with students on a regular basis to get progress reports, provide additional resources, clarify the assignment, and take advantage of the myriad teaching moments that arose during these face-to-face encounters. Jaqui also helped students put their project work into presentable form, such as PowerPoints, graphs and charts on poster paper, or videos. When projects were completed, she organized a celebration forum for sharing students' discoveries with statistics. Parents, relatives, neighbors, other teachers, community members, and administrators were invited to join the forum, which was well attended. Cake and punch were served, as students, some in lab coats, talked about why they chose to do their projects, their data-gathering techniques, the findings of their research, and what the projects meant to them.

The power of student choice and student input in learning is epitomized in the words of Mondelique, who was insistent that Jaqui teach statistics in a way that made it apparent to her why it was important. When wrapping up her presentation, she told the audience: "I was never good in math. And I didn't want to be in this class. But our teacher made it easy because she let us do something we wanted to do with math. I understand it better and feel more confident because she let us do it our way."

Practices That Structure Collaboration

History

As part of an excellent simulation experience designed to maximize student engagement in learning about westward expansion, Aurora had her sixth graders work together to set up a wagon master election. After asking four students to join her, she formed groups of three with the rest of the class. The groups were given a scenario describing that they were pioneers in the 1850s about to go on an adventure to the West. Before they took their trip, however, they needed to select the best possible wagon master for the job. Groups were given rating sheets with critical criteria for a good wagon master, such as being experienced in dealing with Indians, knowledgeable about the best water sources and smoothest trails, and so on.

Meanwhile, the four students Aurora had chosen were to be the individuals vying for the job of wagon master. Each was given a name, a brief biography, and a few minutes to prepare for his or her pitch to the pioneers. When ready, characters like "Calico Katie" and "Buck Duke" told the groups in impassioned tones why they were best suited for the job, given the many successful wagon trains they had led back and forth across Indian territories. After all the wagon master candidates had presented themselves, the pioneers checked their ratings and voted on their top choice.

This activity and the discussion that followed served as a highly motivating and instructive way to involve Aurora's students in the study of the topic.

Business

To motivate student-centered discussion on the topic of the effects of a recession on the economy, Kish, the business teacher, wrote the word *recession* in large letters on the board. Without saying anything, he waited for students to react, question, and elaborate. In no time, students began to make associations with the word. These initial associations with the concept provided students the opportunity to find connections to their prior knowledge and experiences. As students commented, Kish wrote their responses on the board while purposely avoiding reacting to every response. Responses such as "inflation" and "higher gas prices" were typical, but everyone was surprised to hear the word "grounded" shouted out by a student in the corner. Instead of asking a question himself, Kish looked around the room and asked if anyone had a question for this student. Students were eager to find out what "grounded" had to do with recession and pressed the student for an explanation. She explained that she had inflated her parents' already whopping cell phone bill during a financially tight period that she said was caused by a recession. Her parents punished her by taking away her mobile phone privileges and restricting her after-school activity for a couple of weeks.

By using discussion as a readiness-to-learn activity, Kish helped students develop an awareness of their network of associations and allowed them to listen to one another, weigh, reject, revise, and integrate ideas in their own minds. The grounded student's contribution turned out to be profitable because the textbook chapter they were assigned to read devoted a major section to the everyday, personal effects of a recessionary economy.

After the discussion, Kish restated students' initial associations with the concept. This allowed students to reflect on their own thinking and offer any new ideas about the concept of recession. They could verbalize associations that had been elaborated or changed through the discussion and probe their memories to expand on their prior knowledge. Interestingly, several other personal connections with the topic were discovered. One student talked about having to limit his "cruising" because he couldn't afford to waste gas. Another mentioned that his brother had to put off finding a bigger apartment because he felt his job as a salesman was not secure. By participating more actively in class discussion, students had a better idea when the class ended of how much they knew about the topic. Kish, who created the conditions for an effective student-centered discussion, knew his class was motivated to learn more about the topic as a result of the experience.

Literature

A much more elaborate debate strategy, as compared with the one just described in a business class, is conducting a mock trail (Beck, 1999; Maloy & LaRoche, 2010). Ya Pin's seventh-grade class was poised to read the breathtaking courtroom chapters in Harper Lee's (1960) English-curriculum stalwart, *To Kill a Mockingbird*. Instead of a teacher-led oral review to bring students to the point of this new episode in the novel, Ya Pin heightened motivation for reading by organizing a simulated court scene with parallels to themes from the novel. Here was the premise for the defense:

> "You are lawyers representing 18-year-old Michael Soo in a court case. Michael, a Korean American, along with his father and brother is being charged with theft of a motorcycle owned by 19-year-old John Adams.
>
> "Here are the facts presented to you by Michael Soo:
>
> "On the morning of Thursday, October 12, 2000, Michael met Mr. Adams in Mr. Adams's driveway to look at a Suzuki motorcycle John was selling. Michael test-rode the bike and then negotiated a purchase price with John of $2,000. Because his father was going to help pay for the motorcycle, Michael hoped he would return the following day, Friday, to buy the motorcycle.
>
> "Michael went home, and when his father returned from work at 6:00 P.M., he talked with him about buying the motorcycle. Michael's father said before he would help pay for the bike, he would need to see it first.
>
> "Michael, his father, and his younger brother drove to John Adams's house around 8:30 P.M. to look at the bike. There were no lights on in the house. Michael rang the doorbell, but no one answered. Michael's father aimed the truck so the headlights would shine on the motorcycle that was parked in the driveway. The three of them then inspected the bike.
>
> "Michael's father told Michael he wouldn't pay $2,000 for the motorcycle because he didn't think it was worth that much money. John Adams had not returned by the time Michael, his father, and brother drove home. It was 9:15 P.M. Michael decided he would keep looking for a better deal on a Suzuki motorcycle.
>
> "Two days later, Saturday, police officers came to Michael's house asking questions. They explained that John Adams's motorcycle had been stolen and that Michael, his father, and brother had been seen late Thursday evening at the scene of the crime. The Soos denied any involvement, explaining their purpose for being at John Adams's home Thursday evening.
>
> "Granting a police request to look around, the officers found in the Soo's garage hundreds of motorcycle parts and two or three partially built motorcycles. Many of the parts had the Suzuki name and logo on them. The Soos explained that motorcycles were their hobby and that they had owned several Suzuki motorcycles in the past. Unfortunately, they could not find receipts of purchase for any of the motorcycles or parts.
>
> "Michael, his father, and brother were then issued a warrant for their arrest for stealing John Adams's motorcycle.

"It is your job as a legal team to prove the Soos are being falsely accused because they are Korean American."

Ya Pin formed several groups and made certain each student had a role. For instance, there were teams of lawyers representing the Soos and John Adams, witnesses, and a jury. Other individuals played the part of a judge, a bailiff, and Michael and John. Her students performed their roles with flair and feeling, swept up in the moment by an imaginary setting and list of accusations that seemed all too real. When the jury found in favor of the plaintiff, John, the stage was set perfectly for reading about what was to happen to Atticus, Bob and Mayella Ewell, and Tom Robinson.

With this motivational debate activity, Ya Pin had created a context that brought the issue of racial prejudice into the present day, set the debate in a place similar to the one in the novel, and made the fictionalized characters ones the students might recognize from their own communities and neighborhoods. Ya Pin's students brought a heightened level of enthusiasm and interest to the reading of the court scene chapters in *To Kill a Mockingbird* motivated by their desire to find out if Tom Robinson's fate would be similar to Michael's.

Case Study Revisited

Remember Theresa, the eighth-grade social studies teacher? She was preparing for a unit on the early Americans. Take a moment to write your ideas for Theresa to help motivate her students to study this content and become engaged in learning.

Theresa introduced students to a motivational activity on the first day that I thought was exceptional. She began by involving the class in a discussion of the role of archaeologists in understanding the relationship of artifacts to past societies. She then explained that one way to understand the past is to relate it to the present, and one way they could do that was by making a time capsule. After defining a time capsule, she asked students to think of objects they felt would be important to include in one that would be buried today and excavated 1,000 years later. Theresa jotted down ideas on the board and asked students to explain why their particular object would help people living 1,000 years later to understand what life was like today. Clearly, the purpose of exploring the idea of a time capsule was to motivate students to learn about the past by making it relevant to their own lives. The students were genuinely enjoying this activity, as reflected in interchanges such as this:

STUDENT 1: Did you see that Coke commercial where this class sometime way in the future is walking through a 20th-century ruin and they find a Coke bottle?

CLASS: Yeah, I've seen that.

THERESA: What does a bottle of Coke say to these future people about ourselves and our culture?

STUDENT 1: That we like to drink Coke.

THERESA: Would it? How could you be sure? Let's say people aren't drinking Coke a thousand years from now, and let's say these people you're talking about also found a tattered T-shirt with "Selena Gomez" written on it and a broken television or computer or cell phone. How would they piece together the way we lived if this is all they found?

STUDENT 2: They might think Selena Gomez was our president or something.

STUDENT 3: They might not even know what a television or computer was. I read a science fiction story about these people who could put this machine on their heads, like a headset, and see images in their heads and feel what you would feel if you were there.

THERESA: That's interesting. So they might not even be able to recognize that it was a television or computer or exactly what it was used for, especially if it was really badly broken up. Do you see now how hard it would be for future people to describe who we were and how we behaved from the few things they might find?

STUDENT 4: Maybe if we put a Coke can in our time capsule, we should tape a piece of paper to it that tells what it is and all about it.

THERESA: If the paper didn't crumble and rot away, that would be very helpful for future people. Good idea. Unfortunately for archaeologists, the original inhabitants of North America didn't leave written directions and explanations with all of their artifacts.

STUDENT 5: Didn't they draw pictures in caves of hunting buffalo and stuff like that?

THERESA: That's right, and those wall paintings help us quite a bit, but they don't tell the whole story. For instance, the wall pictures don't tell whether men and women married like they do today, or whether one man could have several wives. They don't tell us if they were nomadic or whether they lived in one place for long periods of time. Did these people have music or play games, and so forth?

Eventually, the class formulated a list of things to put in their time capsule. It was fascinating to listen to the students rationalize why certain items would be appropriate to include. For instance, one young man wanted to contribute his tennis shoes; one was green, the other orange, and both were untied. He argued that they would reflect what young people are like today. The class concluded that his mismatched tennis shoes would give a misleading impression because only a small minority dresses that way. Instead, it was decided that pictures from magazines depicting many different fashions would be better. Another student said the time capsule should have an iPhone with hundreds of examples of contemporary music. This didn't seem feasible, the class agreed, because in 1,000 years, probably no means of charging the smartphone would exist.

The final list included a Coke can, accompanied by a picture of someone drinking from a can of Coke; a copy of *Time* magazine; several photographs of cars, fashions, TVs, computers and other high-tech electronics, and houses; lyrics and sheet music to a couple of popular songs; and a class portrait. The activity culminated at week's end with a ceremonial burial on a section of the school grounds of a time capsule (actually a large plastic canister) containing the items the class had decided on.

Theresa conducted a couple of other motivational activities during the week, including a word scavenger hunt, which involves students in a game for learning keywords from their readings (see Chapter 6 for details), and viewing a film that traced the journey of the first people to emigrate from Europe to the area we now call Iowa. Students were also provided with a structured overview of the migration patterns, names, and terms associated with the first Americans.

This case study makes clear how varied and yet how effective creative and meaningful activities for motivating reading and learning can be. It demonstrates how a talented teacher takes her students far beyond the traditional boundaries of a content-area lesson by generating interest in the topic and keeping youth engaged in learning from the moment the topic is introduced until consideration of the topic concludes.

LOOKING BACK, LOOKING FORWARD

Over 40 years ago, Illich (1970) advocated a curriculum that engendered "self-motivated learning instead of employing teachers to bribe or compel the student to find the time and the will to learn" (p. 104). Today, Illich's recommendation is as viable as ever (Guthrie, 2008; Schunk et al., 2013). What is more, attention to student engagement should be heightened given the powerful connection this "soft skill" has to other academic and career successes (Heckman & Kautz, 2012). Evidence shows that students become independent knowledge seekers when they perceive what they are learning to be personally meaningful and relevant to their lives and futures. On one level, then, I am suggesting that meaningful purposes for learning can be established only when the learning itself is meaningful.

Because I believe that the degree of success with a topic of study in the content areas depends on how motivated students are, I have focused this chapter on a range of classroom practices that teachers in middle and secondary schools have used to increase student engagement. The examples included here represent only a few of the potentially endless possibilities for making learning meaningful and getting students excited about the content to be read and studied. Some are content-based applications and adaptations of established literacy strategies, such as KWL and anticipation guides, and others are purely inventive and tied directly to the disciplinary content under consideration in the classroom, such as the carbon bonding hoedown and the election of a wagon master.

I hope these guidelines and examples help you become more sensitive to the importance of creating motivating learning conditions for virtually every disciplinary lesson and inspire you to expand your notions about the kinds of learning dynamics possible in your classroom.

In the next chapter, you will read about a variety of interesting vocabulary strategies that can motivate youth to expand their word knowledge. As you will see, the more students are engaged in word-learning activities, the better are their chances for deeper and more meaningful understanding of disciplinary concepts.

Developing Academic Vocabulary Knowledge

As you read Chapter 6, reflect on the following questions:

■ What does it mean for students to truly know a word?

■ How is conceptual knowledge different from definitional knowledge of words?

■ How do evidence-based guidelines inform effective vocabulary instruction?

■ Why is it important for students to know both types of academic language?

■ Which vocabulary strategies and practices are particularly effective for English learners?

■ How can students acquire new academic vocabulary independently?

For as long as I can remember I have always loved words. Word battles and word play were a part of my household growing up. My brothers and sisters and I took great delight in purposely creating outlandish malapropisms by using funny or inappropriate words in place of similar-sounding ones. For instance, once at a bakery across the street from our parish school on Detroit's east side, when I was asked my order, I answered with a straight face, "I'll have a Freudian twist, please" to which the baker's daughter, who knew me, replied "You must mean a *cinnamon* twist." Even today I still engage in this kind of witty exploitation of the meanings and ambiguities of words for amusing effect.

Surely this early interest in words and puns was a precursor to my fascination with language. I realize now just how far that interest has been able to take me.

Expansive word knowledge creates the possibility for expansive understandings. I'm reminded each time I articulate this truism about words and meaning of the great African American liberator and statesman, Frederick Douglass, who describes in his autobiography how, when he clandestinely learned to read as a boy, the blinders fell away, and he could see his circumstances of bondage more clearly than ever before. Words are the medium of ideas, expressed and received. Thus limited word knowledge circumscribes the range and depth of knowledge and imagination (Alexander, Singer, Jablansky, & Hattan, 2016).

So what does it mean to actually "know" a word? That question has been debated for decades. Is being able to produce a definition an adequate gauge of one's word knowledge? When asked what the word *light* meant, 4-year-old Ryan's reply was "It comes from the sun and helps us see things." A good answer for a young boy; however, he had no idea what "light as a feather" meant, nor did he know the meaning of *light* in the sentence "I saw the birds light on the tree." Does Ryan really know the word *light*?

One of the primary goals of vocabulary development at the middle and high school levels is not simply to increase the breadth of students' vocabularies (i.e., the number of words for which students have a definition), but also to increase the depth and precision of their word knowledge. In other words, the goal is to help students like Ryan develop a full and complete understanding of words. But the goal is much more than improving students' word knowledge. The Anchor Standards of the CCSS emphasize that students need to

> acquire and use accurately a range of general academic and domain-specific words and phrases sufficient for reading, writing, speaking, and listening at the college and career readiness level; demonstrate independence in gathering vocabulary knowledge when encountering an unknown term important to comprehension or expression. (*www. corestandards.org/ELA-Literacy/CCRA/L*)

Given that all secondary students are expected to read and navigate through content and disciplinary texts packed with concepts and technical vocabulary that they must understand fully if they are to learn from these sources, the relationship between word knowledge and comprehension becomes even more significant (Harmon, Hedrick, & Wood, 2005; Townsend, 2009). When the processing demands for reading complex content-area and disciplinary text become elevated because of the vocabulary load, many students will have little, if any, cognitive energy left for thinking about key concepts or monitoring their understanding. As a result, students can become frustrated outsiders to the learning process (Riccomini, Smith, Hughes, & Fries, 2015).

In this chapter, I describe and explain a range of instructional practices for expanding students' academic and disciplinary vocabularies. The result of this word learning will increase students' knowledge of concepts and ideas in academic contexts. Throughout this chapter, I also reiterate the importance of instructional routines involving demonstrations and modeling, small-group interactions, discussions and role plays, and writing activities in support of vocabulary-building strategies and practices.

Case Study

Miranda, curriculum director of a multicultural suburban school district, analyzed the results of the high-stakes state test that was given to 10th graders in the spring. Much to her dismay, the vocabulary scores were again low. She called the principals to highlight her concerns and to recommend that a district committee be formed to investigate the problem and offer a specific plan for addressing students' challenges with learning academic vocabulary. Consequently, a committee was formed of teachers who taught 10th graders across the district. They met regularly during the school year to discuss the problem in more depth, but they could not agree on what should be done. Several committee members thought the language arts teachers should be responsible for improving students' vocabulary scores. Other members complained that the additional burden of teaching vocabulary words would rob them of precious instructional time. And still others on the committee recommended that the district purchase computer-based programs designed specifically to teach vocabulary. Patience was wearing thin as the school year drew to a close and a clear plan had not yet been provided by the committee.

To the reader: As you read and work through this chapter on expanding academic and disciplinary word knowledge, consider ways in which the committee could solve this districtwide problem. Think about the characteristics of effective vocabulary instruction and potential strategies and practices this school district might infuse into teacher professional development programs and across the curriculum.

The relationship between reading and vocabulary acquisition is mutually supportive—the more one reads, the more exposure one gets to words, and the broader one's vocabulary becomes; the broader one's vocabulary is, the easier it is to comprehend texts and assimilate new information and ideas. Thus, for struggling readers and English learners, frequent and wide reading is critical to language development (Krashen, 2012; Stewart, 2013)

UNDERSTANDING THE NATURE OF WORD KNOWLEDGE

One of the underlying themes of this chapter is that word-learning strategies and practices should require students to combine new text information with their prior knowledge to yield conceptual understandings of words. The admonitions of vocabulary researchers are entirely consistent with this theme (e.g., Ajayi, 2015; Lesaux, Harris, & Sloane, 2012). Earlier in this chapter, I mentioned 4-year-old Ryan, who had a partial definitional understanding of the word *light*. But Ryan did not have a full understanding of *light* that would have allowed him to interpret its meaning in multiple contexts.

Scott and Nagy's (2009) work with vocabulary made the distinction between definitional and contextual word knowledge. Definitional knowledge is essentially knowing a dictionary-like definition for a word. It is important word knowledge, but it limits understanding because students often do not make the connection between the definition of a word and its meaning in a particular text. When students are not making those connections or inferences, their understanding of the text is usually compromised (Frishkoff, Collins-Thompson, Hodges, & Crossley, 2016). Contextual knowledge, on the other hand, is meaning gained from encountering and thinking about words in various textual and language settings (e.g., a novel, an article, a picture, in conversation, on the Internet). Sophisticated readers use a combination of definitional and contextual knowledge to determine word meanings.

To help you understand the important distinction between definitional and contextual word knowledge, read the following sentence, with two keywords defined, and in the space provided, write what the statement means in your own words

Surrogate: judge or magistrate

Testator: one making a claim on a will

The learned *surrogate* has held that an intent to have an apportionment will be imputed to the testator.

In your own words: _____

For the next sentence, the topic area is provided. Given the topic, write in your own words the special definition of the two italicized words in the sentence.

Topic: commodities futures

Live hogs *found* November *unchanged*.

Your definition of *found*: _____

Your definition of *unchanged*: _____

Now that you have finished this word challenge exercise, some explanation is in order. In the first sentence, you undoubtedly discovered that even with a couple of the key terms defined, you were still unable to make sense of it. Why? Because the meaning of the sentence is larger than the sum of the definitions of each of its individual words. To state it another way, to understand this sentence, you must connect individual definitions to a broad context of meaning. You must possess the schema or relevant prior knowledge for these words; otherwise, the sentence is an unintelligible collection of fragments and definitions. If, however, you were a lawyer of contracts, estates, and probate law, this sentence would be perfectly understandable.

What about the second sentence? Were you able to supply the appropriate definitions for the commonly understood words *found* and *unchanged?* If not, it is likely due to the fact that your schema for the language of commodities futures is not especially well developed. Once again, without the necessary relevant prior knowledge, the sentence is as oblique as a line from a surrealistic poem. Of course, if you are a member of the Chicago Board of Trade familiar with hog futures in the commodities market, the expression would make perfect sense to you.

As you know from your own experience, definitional word knowledge does not imply a deep level of understanding. Hence, the principles and practices discussed in this chapter are not meant to make students experts at reciting definitions. If a strategy or program focuses only on correctly matching a word to a definition, then this kind of learning is not likely to be transferred to actual reading, writing, listening, or speaking contexts (Freeman & Freeman, 2009; Shore, Ray, & Gooklasian, 2015). Before examining strategies and practices that content-area and disciplinary teachers can use to help their students understand academic and domain-specific vocabulary words and concepts, I present six guidelines that should be considered when planning instruction around word learning.

GUIDELINES FOR EFFECTIVE VOCABULARY INSTRUCTIONAL PRACTICES

Many would agree that no single method, material, or strategy will consistently guarantee that students will improve their word knowledge. Therefore, it seems advantageous for teachers to select a range of approaches to increasing students' academic and disciplinary vocabulary words (Flynt & Brozo, 2008; Zwiers, 2008), and this can be accomplished using the following evidence-based guidelines:

- Teach vocabulary in multiple language contexts.
- Reinforce word learning with repeated exposures over time.
- Emphasize students' active role in the word-learning process.
- Give students tools to expand word knowledge independently.
- Stimulate students' awareness and interest in words.
- Build a language-rich environment to support word learning.
- Encourage students to read widely.

Teach Vocabulary in Multiple Language Contexts

When my daughter, Hannah, was in elementary school, a major part of her language arts curriculum involved learning a list of 20 words every week. As a literacy professor, I was naturally dubious about this approach to word learning, but I discovered after inquiry with Hannah's school principal that the words were part of the state curriculum requiring children at the various grade levels to "learn" an established grade-appropriate corpus of vocabulary words. So I held my tongue and watched how this weekly routine of word learning evolved. On Monday, Hannah brought home her list of 20 words, each one unrelated to the others, and I would ask her on Monday evening if she wanted help studying the words. "No thanks, Dad," she would reply, "I've looked them over myself." On Tuesday, my same offer would be met with a similar response. This went on until Thursday evening, when Hannah eagerly accepted as much help as I would give her with learning the words, because Friday was quiz day. Invariably, she would return home after school on Friday with a perfect or near perfect score on her vocabulary quiz. "Thanks for the help with my words, Dad," she might say.

Before thinking that all is well with this approach to learning vocabulary, as Hannah's quiz grades might suggest, consider this important caveat. On the following Monday, I would often ask Hannah for the definition of a random collection of words from her previous Friday quiz. And, much to my chagrin, she could rarely supply the correct answer, commenting, "Those are last week's words, Dad. I have a new list to learn for this week." As sorry as I was about this outcome, it validated my reservations about expecting vocabulary learning to occur through an isolated, decontextualized word list approach. What Hannah was demonstrating is referred to by psychologists as target memory, or the ability to study and memorize specific information for one particular task at one point in time. Students who cram for final exams often take advantage of target memory. The problem with this approach is that the information memorized is quickly forgotten, as I discovered when Hannah forgot the meaning of words from her list within just a couple of days.

Today, we know from the research literature on vocabulary instruction that there is a preponderance of evidence pointing to the need to teach vocabulary in numerous authentic language contexts (Cervetti, Wright, & Hwang, 2016; Stahl & Nagy, 2006). Words taught in the context of a discipline such as biology will be learned more effectively than words taught in isolation, because context allows students to integrate words with previously acquired knowledge. The implication, of course, is that students will not improve their long-term vocabulary knowledge and understanding by memorizing definitions of a list of essential academic vocabulary words that secondary-level students should know (Snow & Lawrence, 2011).

Thus content-area and disciplinary teachers need to involve students in word-learning activities and experiences with authentic text and within authentic language contexts. Once targeted words have been selected for study from the various text sources from which students are expected to read and learn, students should be provided with multiple opportunities to converse with the words, write the words, read the words, and hear the words spoken. For example, if students are reading a speech by Martin Luther King, Jr., on the Newsela website (*https://newsela.com*), words such as *civil rights, boycott, sit-in, discrimination,* or *segregation* could be studied. To reinforce understanding of these important terms, the history teacher might engage his students in mock trials and debates, RAFT (Role of the writer, Audience, Format, Topic) writing, or additional reading from topically and thematically related graphic novels and comics, such *March* (Lewis, Aydin, & Powell, 2013), *Martin Luther King and the Montgomery Story* (2011), or *The Silence of Our Friends* (Long, Demonakos, & Powell, 2012). Regardless of the specific instructional techniques and activities, approaches to word learning that emphasize context and organizing schema will ensure that key terms and concepts introduced on Monday and tested on Friday will not be forgotten on Saturday.

Reinforce Word Learning with Repeated Exposures over Time

Students' word knowledge takes time to develop and increases in small, incremental steps (Nagy, 2010). Although it is impossible to identify a specific time frame for all students, an important evidence-based principle for vocabulary development is that word ownership is reinforced when students receive multiple exposures to targeted words over the course of days, weeks, and in some cases even months, particularly for struggling readers and for those students learning English (August, Artzi, & Barr, 2016; Kelley, Lesaux, Kieffer, & Faller, 2010). A math teacher puts this principle into practice by building vocabulary through (1) extensively discussing key terms and symbols and exploring what students already know about them, (2) previewing how the words and symbols are used in their math texts, (3) asking students to record the words and symbols in a vocabulary notebook, (4) practicing the words and symbols with a variety of activities and exercises that require students to think and write rather than identify a correct answer, and (5) reviewing and testing in a formative fashion. Vocabulary reinforcement approaches such as these ensure students' long-term understanding of academic and disciplinary-related words and concepts.

Emphasize Students' Active Role in the Word-Learning Process

The importance of students' active participation and elaborative processing in learning new words is a consistent theme that emerges from vocabulary research for the past 30 years (Carlo, August, & Snow, 2010; Stahl, 1986). When students take an active role in vocabulary development, they understand how to define new words and how to use these words in different contexts (Nagy & Scott, 2000; Diaz, 2015). Stahl (1999) described the benefits to learners of active involvement in the word-learning process, such as the ability to (1) sense and infer relationships between targeted vocabulary and their own background knowledge, (2) recognize and apply vocabulary words to a variety of contexts, (3) identify examples and nonexamples, and (4) generate novel contexts for the targeted words. In contrast, passive involvement in vocabulary learning is conditioned when students are given worksheet-type tasks that require selecting definitions in matching or multiple-choice formats or filling in blanks with words from a list.

Give Students Tools to Expand Word Knowledge Independently

Vocabulary development involves both the "what" and the "how." The "what" focuses on the processes involved in knowing a word. The "how" is equally important because it involves students in learning strategies for unlocking words on their own. Think about it this way: If you teach students some words, they will be able to recognize and add those particular words to their repertoire of known words; but if you teach students independent word-learning strategies, they will be able to leave your instructional contexts and independently expand their vocabularies continually, which will result in more successful reading experiences with increasingly complex text (Zhang & Lu, 2015).

Secondary teachers should be prepared to teach important academic and disciplinary vocabulary directly, as well as to endow their students with independent word-learning tools (Fisher & Frey, 2008a). Thus students should be exposed to and actively involved in learning key terms and concepts related to the topics under study in the content and disciplinary classroom but should also be shown how to become independent consumers and users of new words.

Stimulate Students' Awareness and Interest in Words

As teachers, we all know the role that interest plays in our daily instruction. As you have learned from Chapter 5, when students are interested in what they hear in class, read in an assignment, or discover through Internet research, there is an increase in attention, effort, and persistence and an improvement in their thinking processes and performance. Unfortunately, approaches such as asking students to look up dictionary definitions of 20 words and then write them in sentences, an approach not dissimilar to the one Hannah, my daughter, had to endure, does little to generate interest or motivate middle and high school students (Tseng & Schmitt, 2008). Instead, teachers should employ practices that increase students' awareness of words and create situations in which learning new words is an engaging knowledge-seeking activity (Hurley, 2010; Snow, Lawrence, & White, 2009).

The best starting point for building word enthusiasm is with you, the teacher. We can hardly expect our students to become sensitive to words and interested in expanding word knowledge if we cannot demonstrate an ardor for words ourselves.

Over four decades ago, Manzo and Sherk (1971) asserted that "the single most significant factor in improving vocabulary is the excitement about words which teachers can generate" (p. 78). This assertion is as valid today as it was then (Dalton & Grisham, 2011; Wells & Narkon, 2011).

As I emphasized in previous chapters, modeling is a powerful teaching tool. If you want students to learn particular words, then talk about words you heard or encountered recently. Show students that you use paper and online definitional resources to look up words you do not understand, for definitions you need to clarify, or for synonyms and antonyms to make your written and spoken texts richer and more accurate. In this way, students will come to appreciate that vocabulary acquisition is a lifelong goal. During class discussion, in conversation with students, or when responding to student writing, use words you want them to integrate into their written and spoken vocabularies. Above all, be playful with words and exhibit excitement about words (Huang & Huang, 2015).

Build a Language-Rich Environment to Support Word Learning

Research findings make clear that students with strong expressive and receptive vocabularies are the ones who are immersed in home and school environments characterized by "massive amounts of rich written and oral language" (Nagy & Scott, 2000, p. 280). Teachers can best promote vocabulary growth by working with students to create an environment in which new words are learned, celebrated, and used in authentic communication tasks. Students should be given opportunities to experiment with using words in low-risk situations, to discuss new ideas daily, to talk freely and openly about how text concepts relate to their real-world experiences, to read texts from a variety of genres related to the topics under study, and to write purposeful and meaningful texts that employ keywords and demonstrate understanding of important concepts (Nagy, 2009).

Once students become comfortable with a set of new words, teachers can then reinforce and extend their learning by providing regular writing experiences. For example, in order to enhance his students' understanding of the words *egocentric* and *altruistic,* Ricardo asked them to write two different email messages to another student in class—one from an egocentric person's perspective and one from an altruistic perspective. Of course, the revision and editing stages of the writing process became excellent opportunities to engage students in searches for "that one perfect word" that conveys the precise meaning they had in mind.

Encourage Students to Read Widely

Children's vocabularies grow exponentially through the first 4–6 years. Virtually all of this growth results from exposure to words in conversational language contexts. Eventually, however, new word learning in these everyday communicative settings begins to slow until at some point it plateaus. The reason is that there is a limit to the words children are exposed to in their homes and communities. For some who grow up in language-privileged environments, the level of exposure to new words in parental and familial contexts may be several years beyond children without the same privileges or for those challenged by learning a mother-tongue language and a second language, such as new immigrants to the United States (Cummins, 2008). Regardless of the level of privilege, eventually children must have exposures to a source of new words if their vocabulary knowledge is to grow. One of these critically important sources is text, in print or digital form.

Early vocabulary researchers discovered that growth in word knowledge could be accelerated through wide reading (see, e.g., Sachs, 1943). Since that time, we have also come to understand that reading comprehension and vocabulary learning are mutually supportive processes. As word knowledge increases, the ability to make meaning from text grows as well (Lervåg & Aukrust, 2010; Schmitt, Jiang, & Grabe, 2011). Researchers continue to verify that students who choose to read widely and frequently have the breadth and depth of word knowledge necessary to understand vocabulary and language in academic contexts (Nagy & Townsend, 2012).

Wide reading has also been associated with higher achievement on national and international assessments of reading literacy. Adolescents who report reading frequently and across genres were the ones with higher scores on NAEP (Kena et al., 2016) and PISA (OECD, 2010b). Although these findings are correlational in nature, the trend suggests that students who read frequently have more opportunities to learn new words than students who read less frequently or not at all.

The implication for content-area and disciplinary teachers is obvious: If we want our students to understand what they read in our courses, we must encourage them to read beyond what they are assigned to read (Bromley, 2007). Teachers, therefore, should stimulate reading by encouraging students to read newspapers, magazines, graphic novels, informational articles and books, and the like. Teachers can bring into the classroom intriguing supplementary materials or direct students to websites with interesting topic- and thematically related texts. For example, a health teacher begins each class period by reading aloud a brief selection from an online news magazine. He calls it the "reading minute" and uses the brief time to discuss the content (e.g., the closing of an upscale city restaurant because of multiple food poisoning cases) and to highlight important words that might be problematic or useful to students (e.g., *salmonella*).

SELECTING KEY TERMS AND CONCEPTS

Learning new words and concepts in a discipline or content area is obviously a complex task dependent upon students' prior knowledge and experience, their level of motivation, and the quality of instruction. Graves (2009a) has proposed three tasks involved in word learning. The first task is learning a new word for a concept when the student understands the concept but has not heard of the label for that concept. For example, most students understand the processes involved in defense mechanisms such as rationalization because they have all rationalized their behaviors in some way. The label, however, will probably be new to them. Words such as these are not as difficult to teach students because they have the experiences to draw upon to understand and learn them.

The second and third tasks involved in word learning are more difficult because students are not as familiar with the underlying concept. With the second task, students are learning a new concept for a known word. In psychology and mathematics, for example, the word *set* has a different meaning from what students understand the word to mean when they talk about having to "set the table for dinner." The third task involves students in learning a new concept for which they have no label and minimal, if any, understanding or background. These tasks challenge both students and teachers. For example, in an ecology unit, the concept of eutrophication (a gradual and natural process that turns lakes into marshes because of an excess amount of algae) is probably new to most 10th graders, as is the label. Hence, the science teacher would need to spend more time on this word than on others, such as *mercury, detergents,* or *biodegradable.* In addition to understanding the three tasks involved in learning a word, it is important to understand the types of vocabulary students encounter in content-area and disciplinary classrooms.

Types of Vocabulary

If you were to skim a chapter in this book, you would probably discover that the vocabulary words could be classified in two ways. The first type are general academic words that are not particularly associated with any single content area or discipline. Academic vocabulary are the words we use to describe complexity, higher-order thinking, and abstraction. Academic vocabulary is found in figurative expressions, and it is also used to support points for evidence and to convey nuances of meanings. Academic vocabulary crosses content domains and text genres. For example, a science teacher who asked his ninth-graders to read a brief excerpt from Rachel Carson's groundbreaking environmentalist book, *Silent Spring,* identified the following general words he thought should be taught: *maladies, blight, moribund, specter, stark,* and *droned.* A British novelist could have easily used some of these same words to describe a winter day in London, because they are common to many text genres and communication contexts.

The second type are the technical content-area and disciplinary words that are unique to a particular subject, such as physics, chemistry, civics, English literature, and culinary arts. Technical vocabulary words have restricted meanings within particular content domains and include both general words that are used in a specialized way and words that have only one distinct definition and application. These are the kinds of terms and concepts that require the second and third tasks of word learning described above. Examples of the former are words such as *table, matter, set,* or *drive,* which take on specialized meanings dependent on the content-area or disciplinary contexts. Examples of the latter include words such as *alveoli* in science, *sonority* in music, *parabola* in math, and *matte effect* in art. In addition, symbols that occur in domains such as mathematics, physics, and chemistry are part of the language of those disciplines, as well. Technical content-specific vocabulary has been described as the "brick," whereas the "mortar" includes general academic words often needed to explain the "bricks" (Marzano & Pickering, 2010). Knowledge of both types of academic language is critical within a Common Core framework (Marzano & Simms, 2013).

The Process of Selecting Words to Teach

Because it is impossible to teach all the general and domain-specific academic vocabulary words from any reading assignment in a particular content area or discipline, an important first step in teaching vocabulary is to decide which terms and concepts should be taught (Nagy & Hiebert, 2011). Traditionally, teachers have used a textbook or some other core text as a guide, focusing on highlighted words. Basing vocabulary instruction on these words alone, however, may not meet your overall goals for teaching the content or unit. Researchers have made clear that students will learn what is emphasized. If instruction focuses on important and meaningful details, concepts, and issues, those aspects of the content will be what students learn and remember. Vocabulary instruction, then, should focus on words related to those important ideas. Sometimes the words the core text author has chosen to highlight will match the concepts you choose to emphasize; sometimes they will not. It is important, therefore, that you have a system for selecting the appropriate vocabulary terms that help students better understand the key ideas of the unit.

Another issue related to selecting words to teach is that it is impossible to teach students every word they may not fully understand in their texts. Time constraints alone preclude our doing so. Any of you who have tried to identify and teach all the words in a text you think cause your students difficulty have discovered that your entire lesson can be taken up with vocabulary instruction. It is simply not feasible to attempt to teach every word that might potentially pose trouble for your students. A far more efficient and effective approach is to select the salient terms and concepts that carry and represent the most important ideas and to teach them well. A thorough and elaborative understanding of those vocabulary terms will, in turn, contribute to your students' enhanced understanding of the texts themselves, especially if the target words relate to other words or are generative in nature. The criteria listed in Figure 6.1 should help you determine which vocabulary words should be taught as a part of a unit of study.

INSTRUCTIONAL PRACTICES TO EXPAND STUDENTS' ACADEMIC VOCABULARIES

In this section I describe and exemplify multiple practices of secondary teachers for teaching new words and word-learning strategies to their middle and high school students. These practices demonstrate the range of effective instructional options available to content-area and disciplinary teachers for expanding word knowledge of general and specific academic vocabulary.

---

1. Determine what you want your students to learn as a result of reading and studying the content. This may be laid out clearly in established unit objectives or be determined by you and your goals for a particular unit. For instance, a music teacher may want students to develop a sense of musical interpretation after covering a unit on opera, or an art teacher may wish students to develop a sense of character as a result of reading biographies with well-developed characters for a unit on portrait painting.

2. Identify key terms that are related to the unit's objectives. For example, considering the theme of Sparta and its unique political structure, the history teacher would likely select technical terms such as *euphors*, *assembly*, *council of elders*, and *helots* because they are important words related to the overall unit objective.

3. Decide on appropriate activities or strategies to introduce and reinforce the words. For example, the words related to Sparta could be put into word maps, a strategy described in this chapter.

4. Identify the general words that are not necessarily central to the objectives of the unit but lend themselves to various word-learning practices. Nagy (2009) proposes that the following questions be asked by teachers to determine to which of these general academic vocabulary words to give instructional attention:

   - "Does this word occur often enough in written language to make it worth spending time on?"
   - "Do I want my students to be able to use this word?"
   - "Does this word occur in a variety of genres and subject areas?"
   - "Do students need to know this word to understand the main point of the text?"
   - "Does the word lend itself to a particular strategy students can learn to apply on their own?"

Note. You should not underestimate the importance of these steps in teaching key terms and concepts related to your units of study. The more discriminating you are in selecting vocabulary that potentially has the highest payoff regarding comprehension and strategic application, the greater is the likelihood that students will learn the content and the word-learning processes.

FIGURE 6.1. Criteria for selecting words to teach.

Contextual Analysis

Contextual analysis refers to our attempt to understand the meaning of a word by analyzing the meaning of the words that surround it. Put another way, contextual analysis is figuring out a word's meaning by how it is used in a particular text. For example, one way to figure out the meaning of words is by paying attention to extended descriptions or appositives, such as in these two examples:

1. There was a strange sound *emanating* from the hood of my car. When I opened the hood, I found a stray cat huddling to keep warm and meowing in fear.
2. The *decadent,* or overindulgent, society in which we live spoils children by buying them whatever they see on TV and the Internet.

On the surface, the idea of learning words from context makes a great deal of sense. As logical as it seems, however, the research on students' incidental learning from context seems to indicate that some learning will occur but that the effect is not very powerful, especially with a single encounter of the targeted word (Graves, 2009b; McKeown, Beck, & Sandora, 2012). One reason the utility of contextual analysis is challenged is that many previous studies have used contrived, unnatural texts as their materials of study and high-frequency words as their target of study. The following examples illustrate the oversimplified exercises that have been used in studies and in workbooks designed to teach students how to use context clues. Can you figure out the meaning of the highlighted nonsense words?

1. The boys bought their tickets for the brand new 3-D *Star Wars* movie and entered the theater with mystic expectations written all over their *whitors.*
2. Some even looked alive, though no *fome* flowed beneath the skin.

If you were able to determine that *whitors* means "faces" and *fome* means "blood," congratulations. But is your performance on these sentences indicative of your genuine ability to use contextual analysis? Imagine students who correctly complete 20 sentences similar to those you have just tried. The students may be left with the impression that they have mastered the use of context clues for determining word meanings. Then imagine their enthusiastic attempt to apply their new skills with a real passage in the case below—a sentence in an article about bitcoins from a high school accounting course (Nakamoto, n.d.).

For our timestamp network, we implement the proof-of-work by *incrementing a nonce* in the block until a value is found that gives the block's hash the required zero bits. Once the CPU effort has been expended to make it satisfy the proof-of-work, the block cannot be changed without redoing the work. As later blocks are chained after it, the work to change the block would include redoing all the blocks after it. (p. 3)

I highlighted the phrase *incrementing a nonce* to demonstrate that in authentic text—text not written purposefully to teach students to determine meanings of unknown words through context—it is often a bigger challenge to acquire knowledge of new vocabulary through context alone. Did you figure out what these words mean, even with the inclusion of the two sentences that follow it? If not, this is because the topic and terminology are too technical to be construed merely by reading the surrounding words. As noted by McKeown and colleagues (2012), students may learn a few new words in the disciplinary and content-area text using contextual analysis, but this vocabulary knowledge develops slowly and is not particularly effective for those who struggle with reading or for English learners (Çetinavcı, 2014; Hamada, 2009; Mokhtar & Rawian, 2012).

To sum up what we know about the role of context in vocabulary acquisition, context clues do support incidental word learning, but with limitations. It has been determined that the odds of accurately predicting a word's meaning from text for both native English speakers and students who are English learners range from 5 to 15% (Nagy, 2009, 2010).

If real text is not always so generous in providing clues to the meaning of unknown words, you might ask why we should teach our students contextual analysis strategies at all. Contextual analysis skills are important, but, as I have stressed, the instruction should (1) be explicit, (2) involve frequent teacher modeling, (3) include realistic practice and feedback with authentic text, and (4) emphasize the metacognitive nature of using context clues. Also, bear in mind that the probability of learning an unknown word from context increases significantly with multiple exposures to the word in many different contexts (Graves, 2009b).

Blachowicz and Fisher (2015) recommend that teachers use the following 4-step instructional routine to develop students' contextual analysis skills: (1) look before, at, and after the word; (2) reason by connecting what is known with what the author has written; (3) predict a possible meaning; and (4) resolve or redo by deciding whether enough is known about a word to proceed, to try again, or to seek another source. In addition to these suggestions, let's consider two specific approaches to using context clues that can be incorporated into content-area and disciplinary lessons: previewing in context and possible sentences (Beers & Probst, 2015).

Previewing in Context

Previewing in context is a teacher-directed activity that relies on modeling and demonstrating to students how word meanings can sometimes be inferred from context. Modeling how you go about finding clues to word meanings with actual texts of instruction allows students to see the practical application of this approach. Kiedra, an eighth-grade history teacher, provides a helpful example of how modeling can be used to help students understand key vocabulary, in this case taken from a primary document in the form of a Union prisoner's diary about life in the Andersonville Prison and the notorious Andersonville Raiders.

First, she read the text carefully and identified general and specific key vocabulary and all the words and terms likely to pose difficulty for her students. Her list included the following words:

debilitating	*predators*
strident	*inhumane*
depredations	*emaciated*
retributions	*notorious*
atrocities	*expired*

Next, Keidra carefully reviewed the list and pared it down to those words she felt were essential to the overall understanding of the material and consistent with her unit objectives. She included those words that could be used most instructively for teaching contextual analysis. The reasons for this step were to avoid spending too much valuable class time on teaching less essential vocabulary and to leave several unfamiliar words for students to analyze independently. Through this process, Keidra's list was reduced to the following:

debilitating	*emaciated*
predator	*expired*
inhumane	

When Keidra directed her students to each word and its surrounding context, she "thought out loud," modeling the use of context clues to determine word meanings. She also questioned students to help them discover a word's probable meaning in the existing contexts. Some of her specific practices included the following:

1. Keidra spent a considerable amount of time activating students' prior knowledge for the topic. She knew that most of her eighth graders had some information about prison conditions in general. Perhaps they had seen on TV or the Internet documentaries of World War II concentration camps or had read about what it is like to be in prison. Using what her students already knew about the topic, she made it easier for them to figure out many difficult words in this primary document, especially the word *emaciated.*

2. She reminded students of what they already knew about syntax and word order in sentences. This clue was helpful in narrowing the possible definition of *debilitating* because it appeared between a modifier (unhealthy) and a noun (conditions).

3. Keidra activated prior knowledge that the students had acquired in studying other topics and subjects. She thought it likely that they had encountered the word *predator* in science class as a technical vocabulary term related to animals that hunt and kill other animals for food. They were shown how to apply their understanding of the word in science to this context.

4. She impressed on the students the importance of taking advantage of any obvious clues provided. For instance, in the last sentence, the students were given an obvious clue to the meaning of *expired,* as the author of the diary had used the word *died* earlier in the sentence.

5. She alerted students to clues within words—for example, the prefix *in-* in the word *inhumane.*

6. Keidra made students aware of the idea that context is more than just the few words surrounding an unknown word or even the sentence in which the unknown word appears. She helped expand their notion of context to include information and ideas within, before, and after the text.

7. Finally, she demonstrated how to check a definitional resource on the Web to validate her hunches about the meaning of a word in the primary document.

Previewing in context is an honest way of demonstrating how challenging it is for readers to employ contextual analysis for determining word meanings in text. Although students' attempts to use context clues may not always produce precise meanings, the use of contextual analysis in conjunction with other sources and approaches should increase their understanding of important academic vocabulary and their overall comprehension of the material.

Possible Sentences

Possible sentences is another teacher-directed prereading activity that prepares students for the technical and general academic vocabulary they will encounter in a text (Beers & Probst, 2015). During this activity, students make predictions about content, establish connections between words and concepts, write, discuss, and read their texts carefully to verify their predictions. Notice that the activities involved in possible sentences actively engage students in their word learning, an important vocabulary guideline.

The possible sentence activity requires minimal advance material preparation but a considerable amount of teacher time in thinking and planning. First, the teacher identifies the general or technical vocabulary that is key to the objective of the unit and that is adequately defined by the context. For this activity to succeed, at least five to eight words should be taken from a text. For example, in the primary document diary passage about the Andersonville Prison, Keidra used the following words in a possible sentences activity with her students:

debilitating   *predators*   *inhumane*   *expired*

Teachers need to select the targeted words carefully because students must be able to verify their predicted meanings by reading the text during the third step of this approach.

During the second step, the teacher asks students to select at least two words from the list and generate one sentence they think might possibly be in the text. Students can either write their sentence before sharing or dictate their sentences to the teacher spontaneously. As students share their predicted sentences, the teacher writes or projects them on the board. It is important for the teacher to write the sentences just as they are dictated, even if students provide inaccurate information or use words incorrectly. With the Andersonville Raiders diary excerpt, Keidra allowed students to work with a partner, and a couple of pairs of students generated the following sentences with the targeted words:

> In the Andersonville Prison the predators expired.
> During the Civil War the inhumane generals were debilitating.

Note that the second example uses the word *debilitating* in a syntactically incorrect manner, but Keidra recorded it as dictated. This sharing of predicted sentences should continue until all the words on the list have been included in at least one sentence.

In step 3, the teacher asks the students to read their text to verify the accuracy of the sentences they created. Once students have finished their reading, during step 4 they evaluated the predicted sentences. It is recommended (Moore, Moore, Cunningham, & Cunningham, 2010) that students ask these questions to evaluate the sentences:

1. Which sentences are accurate?
2. Which need further elaboration?
3. Which cannot be validated because the passage did not deal specifically with them?

For example, with the first possible sentence Keidra received, she helped students realize that the predators did die, but not a natural death. The possible sentence merely needed more elaboration (i.e., "The predators were caught, tried, and expired as a result of hanging."). With the second possible sentence, Keidra engaged the class in a discussion of the meaning of the word *debilitating*, and then led them to recognize that the text provided adequate information for evaluating and revising that possible sentence.

In the fifth and final step of the possible sentences approach, students are asked to create new sentences using the target words. As students share their revised sentences, everyone should be involved in checking the text and the agreed-upon definitions generated during class discussion. Although the possible sentences approach involves students in elaborative thinking processes, it may not be feasible for all units of study. This is especially true for units containing a large number of domain-specific vocabulary for which students may have little if any prior knowledge.

Previewing in context and possible sentences are two teacher-directed practices for helping students become more comfortable in using textual analysis to unlock the meaning of difficult words. If students can learn how to use context clues in conjunction with other vocabulary acquisition approaches, they will increase their chances of expanding critical academic language (Blachowicz & Fisher, 2015).

Morphological Analysis

In Chapter 2, you first encountered ideas and strategies related to word morphology, discussed with diverse learners in mind. Thus you should already be familiar with the basis of morphemic analysis or the process of unlocking the meaning of unknown words using familiar word parts or morphemes, such as prefixes, suffixes, and roots. For example, students who know the meaning of the prefix *in* and the Latin root *cred* should be able to conclude that the meaning of *incredible* is "not to be believed." Because of this logic, morphemic analysis has been a traditional part of vocabulary instruction and has routinely appeared in commercial materials and district-level curriculum guides.

Recent research has reinforced the value of teaching students to pay attention to word parts when attempting to unlock the meaning of new terms and concepts (Templeton, 2012). This process may be particularly helpful to secondary-level English learners, who must learn not only conversational English but also complex general and technical academic language (August et al., 2016; Graves, August, & Mancilla-Martinez, 2012; Kieffer & Lesaux, 2007). The renewed emphasis on word morphology, when combined with other techniques such as contextual analysis, emerges from the need to meet the ever-increasing language development needs of recent immigrants to our middle and high schools (Calderon & Minaya-Rowe, 2011; Haneda, 2014; Kieffer & Lesaux, 2010).

Several authorities in vocabulary research and instruction have outlined guidelines for teaching morphemic analysis, most of which circumvent the possible disadvantages of using this vocabulary acquisition approach in isolation (Blachowicz & Fisher, 2015; Graves, Ruda, Sales, & Baumann, 2012; Templeton, 2011/2012). In general, these guidelines emphasize the following:

1. Make sure students understand how morphemic analysis works so they can disassemble words into their parts. For example, they should realize that a word such as *subordinate* consists of the prefix *sub* and the base word, *ordinate*. Adolescents, unless prompted, often do not break longer words into their meaningful parts.

2. Provide explicit instruction and modeling, using words from the students' reading assignments. Content-area and disciplinary teachers should find it relatively easy to locate key terms that possess prefixes, suffixes, and roots. Indeed, over 82% of the words in Coxhead's (2000) academic word list, the most definitive list of its kind, have Greek or Latin origins. Thus, in the content domain of math, many words with Latin and Greek roots, such as *pent* and *oct*, can be found; similarly in science (e.g., *bio, aqua, photo*), social studies (e.g., *demo, dict, ethno*), psychology (e.g., *ego, mania, idio*), and all other disciplines.

3. When possible, group the instruction by word families. For example, an English teacher helping her students learn the word *pseudonym* also taught additional words with the prefix *pseudo,* including *pseudointellectual* and *pseudoscience.* By doing this, her students were better able to grasp the power of morphemic analysis as an independent word-learning strategy.

4. Select prefixes and roots that have high utility and consistent meanings (e.g., the prefix *trans* or the root *graph*).

5. Model situations for students in which morphemic analysis does not work, and then demonstrate alternative approaches for deriving meaning (e.g., consulting definitional resources, such as dictionaries or glossaries, focusing on context, or asking someone).

6. Prompt students to use morphemic analysis as an independent word-learning strategy. Encourage students to exploit this strategy by making lists of the most common or domain-specific affixes and roots readily available to them or by displaying charts with these word parts in the classroom.

Ideally, students can employ a combination of contextual and morphemic analysis, along with definitional resources, as tools for independently acquiring new vocabulary. As noted previously, if students are to use these tools effectively, content-area and disciplinary teachers will need to introduce the targeted words, model the appropriate word-learning practices frequently and whenever a teachable moment presents itself, and prompt students to engage in these practices when reading and studying.

The instructional strategies and practices I describe next offer options for introducing challenging academic vocabulary, as well building students' awareness and interest in their own word knowledge. Guided by the principle that students will understand and remember more when they experience concepts in a direct and meaningful fashion, I begin by explaining and exemplifying the power of demonstrations.

Firsthand Concept Development

Because the terminology in academic texts is often sterile, abstract, and lifeless, students not particularly motivated to read them find it difficult to retain the information in these texts. Standing before the class and stating glossary-type definitions of key vocabulary words merely reinforces students' passivity. One of the guidelines for effective vocabulary instruction is to make important terms and concepts come alive for students so they are motivated to read and learn. This can be done by giving students opportunities to have direct contact with critical vocabulary from a unit or lesson.

Bernardo, a high school psychology teacher, frequently capitalizes on this guideline by providing his students with firsthand demonstrations of essential terminology. In one of his lessons on human memory, he began the class by asking students to write 10 things they did the first day of second grade. Over the initial moans and groans, Bernardo insisted that each student produce a list of 10 items within a few minutes to "play the game" properly. Eventually, all students were busy working on their lists. When they were finished, Bernardo asked to read the items on their lists and to talk about how they produced the items even though they could not recall with certainty. Students read off such things as "met the teacher," "talked with my friends from first grade," "took my seat," "received my books," and so on. Most said they could not remember all the details about what they did the first day of second grade, but listed the things they assumed they had done. Afterward, Bernardo explained that the students had been "confabulating" by creating their lists on the basis of related experience rather than definite memory.

Defined in the traditional way, with a glossary or dictionary definition, *confabulation* is a sterile term. When students were allowed to experience confabulation firsthand, however, they had an experience to which they could affix the meaning of the concept in memory. In turn, the texts on human memory they then had to read were easier for them to understand. Using similar simulated and direct experience approaches to vocabulary instruction, Bernardo found that his students remembered the meaning of important terms and concepts long after his lessons and units were completed. For instance, 2 weeks after his short unit on human memory, Bernardo asked his students to turn to a partner and discuss the definition of *confabulation*. His students were quick to recall the activity the word prompted—writing down 10 things they did the first day of second grade—and the memory of the experience then triggered the memory of the word. The same would be true for any content area or discipline because demonstrations are a form of firsthand concept development that will encourage students' deeper understanding and long-term memory of the academic vocabulary.

Word Maps

Students will become more independent in their vocabulary learning if they are provided with instruction that gradually shifts responsibility for generating meanings for new words from the teacher to them (Fisher & Frey, 2008b; Frey & Fisher, 2009). One effective way of encouraging this transition is with word maps. Schwartz and Raphael developed this strategy back in the mid-1980s for helping students establish a concept of definition for academic vocabulary, and the approach continues to be advocated by vocabulary researchers and practitioners today (Templeton et al., 2015).

To build a word map, students write the concept being studied, or the word they would like to define, in the center box of a map. Using charts and shapes from any word processing program facilitates the design of a map, such as the one for the word *quark* in Figure 6.2. In the top box students put a brief answer to the question "What is it?" This question seeks a name for the class or category that includes the concept. In defining *quark,* the category is "subatomic particle." In responding to the question to the right, "What is it like?" Students write critical attributes, characteristics, or properties of the concept or word. In the example, three critical properties of quarks are listed. The question along the bottom, "What are some examples?" can be answered by supplying examples of different kinds of quarks, such as *top* and *charmed.*

Teaching students how to create word maps gives them a strategy for generating word meanings independently. Because of the checking process they go through

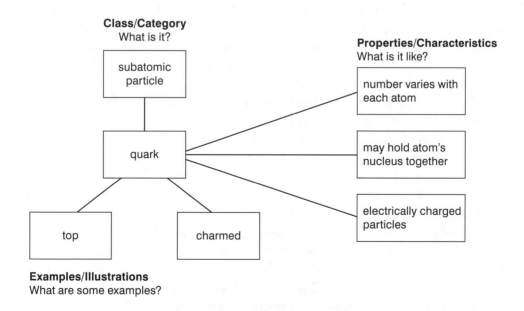

FIGURE 6.2. Word map for *quark.*

in asking questions about the concept, this strategy also fosters self-monitoring and metacognitive abilities (Swartz, Costa, Kallick, Beyer, & Reagan, 2007). The goal, therefore, is to help students internalize this questioning process for all of the important words they must learn. All of us ask similar questions when we encounter unfamiliar words in context, though we rarely, if ever, create a word map with the information we are learning about the word. Think of a word map as a visual representation of students' thought processes while trying to determine word meanings in context. Eventually, after they have demonstrated an understanding of the process by creating appropriate word maps, students should be shown that they do not have to generate a visual for every word they do not know. Instead, they should go through the questioning process in their heads, as mature readers do, and develop a word map for studying particularly complex terms they need to know for tests or other demonstrations of understanding.

Tonya, an eighth-grade science teacher, began her vocabulary lesson by displaying the structure of a word map on the interactive whiteboard and introducing it as a visual guide to remind her students of what they need to know to understand a new and important word or concept. As the components of the map were discussed, she supplied a concept and filled in answers to the questions on the map with information from a recently read article on biomes.

Tonya then directed students to the article they were about to read about boreal ecosystems and identified a key concept, *conifer*, on the first page. She asked the students to work in cooperative groups to find information in the article, as well as to use any relevant prior knowledge to answer the questions on the word map. As they read about conifers, they discussed the related information that helped define the concept and inserted it into the appropriate spaces on the map they were creating. When they completed their maps, Tonya modeled how information about class/ category, properties/characteristics, and examples related to *conifer* could be pulled from the text. Drawing on the input from the groups, the whole class then worked together to create a word map for *conifer* (see Figure 6.3).

At this point, Tonya asked her students to write a definition for *conifer* based on the word map activity. Afterward, she asked them to work in their cooperative groups and evaluate each other's definitions to determine whether they were complete and, if not, to include any essential additional information. Definitions were then returned to their owners, who responded to the group's feedback. With their maps and definitions completed, students were shown that their work could serve as excellent study aids for rehearsal and long-term retention of the concept.

Tonya ended the day's lesson by assigning the students to create word maps for three other concepts in the article. Before leaving, students began their assignment by identifying the possible concepts. This procedure of modeling and assigning continued throughout the school year until Tonya was sure her students knew how to apply the word map strategy independently to important science vocabulary. She

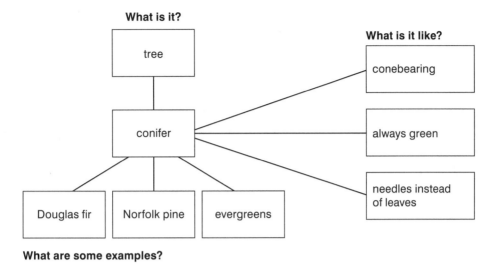

FIGURE 6.3. Word map for *conifer.*

has found that word maps help her students organize and see connections between ideas, monitor their understanding, and improve their comprehension of what they have read and studied.

Word Grids/Semantic Feature Analysis

To read successfully in the content areas and the disciplines, students need to have a deep-level understanding of key concepts and terms and the relationships among these important vocabulary terms. Word grids, known also by the initial label for this strategy, *semantic feature analysis* (Johnson & Pearson, 1978; Pittelman, Berglund, & Heimlich, 1991), is a highly effective visual strategy for accomplishing this goal with academic vocabulary (Blachowicz & Fisher, 2015). This approach to concept development involves building a grid in which essential related vocabulary is listed on one axis of the grid and major features, characteristics, or important ideas are listed on the other axis. Students fill in the grid, indicating the extent to which the keywords possess the listed feature, characteristic, or idea. Once the grid is completed, students are led to discover both the shared and unique characteristics of the vocabulary words.

Figure 6.4 is word grid created by a geometry teacher for the study of polygons. Notice that the vertical axis contains the names of geometric figures, whereas the horizontal axis contains important features or characteristics of these figures.

Sulaiman, a 10th-grade history teacher, introduces the word grid strategy to his U.S. history students with a simple version that all his students will understand (see Figure 6.5). He begins by asking his class for the names of fruit, writing

	opposite sides parallel	equilateral	equiangular	4-sided	3-sided	
square						
rectangle						
triangle						
rhombus						
trapezoid						

FIGURE 6.4. Word grid for polygons.

	edible skin	tree grown	bunches	citrus	fleshy	
banana	0	2	2	0	2	
peach	2	2	0	0	2	
orange	1	2	0	2	0	
apple	2	2	0	0	2	
grapes	2	0	2	0	2	
grapefruit	0	2	0	2	0	

FIGURE 6.5. Word grid for fruit.

them as a vertical list into a grid template that's projected on the whiteboard from the doc camera. After students call out several types of fruit and they are listed, he writes a couple of general features of fruit along the top horizontal axis of the grid, such as "tree grown" and "edible skin"; then he asks for additional features. Finally, he asks the class to consider each type of fruit and whether it possesses any of the listed features. As they go down the list of fruit, they discuss each one relative to the characteristics listed across the top, and Sulaiman puts a 0, 1, or 2 in the box where the fruit and feature meet on the grid. A 0 indicates the fruit possesses none of the feature, a 1 indicates it possesses some of that feature, and a 2 means it possesses all of the feature. When the grid is entirely filled in, Sulaiman explains to the students how they can, at a glance, determine the key characteristics of a particular type of fruit, as well as the similarities and differences between fruits.

By involving students in the construction of a simple word grid, Sulaiman has introduced them to the semantic feature analysis process. He then follows up this demonstration by introducing a word grid appropriate for his mini-unit on political parties of the late 19th century. Sulaiman distributes a partially filled-in grid to his students with the names of the first two political parties (populist and republican) described in the chapter of their history e-textbook. The grid also included the first two features, which in this case are actually issues, acts, and events (no subsidies for private corporations and the McKinley Tariff Act). As he and his students work through the chapter, they encounter description and explanation of additional political parties and decide together what to add to the vertical and horizontal dimensions of the grid. Meanwhile, Sulaiman and his students fill in the grid by placing a 0 (none), 1 (some), or 2 (all) in the appropriate box. Once the chapter is completed, they review the grid and decide whether to amend it by adding new terms and/or features. Figure 6.6 is the final grid Sulaiman and his 10th-grade U.S. history students crafted from the textbook chapter.

Sulaiman further demonstrates the value of learning the key concepts through the grid approach by showing the students how to use the word grid to study for quizzes and short constructed responses. He asks students to compare and contrast the different political parties with such questions as "What are two ways in which the populist and republican parties are alike?" "What is one important difference between the Greenback labor party and the progressives?" His students consult the grid for their responses. Finally, he forms pairs of students and provides them the opportunity to quiz each other over the content represented in the grid before being asked to write out short responses to compare–contrast quiz questions.

The word grid strategy requires minimal preparation on the part of the teacher while providing students with an excellent review of critical terms and concepts

	No subsidies for private corporations	McKinley Tariff Act	Gold Standard	Pendleton Act	Increase money supply	Lower tariffs	Australian ballot
Populist							
Republican							
Democrat							
Greenback labor							
Progressive							

FIGURE 6.6. Word grid for political parties of the late 19th century.

related to content-area and disciplinary topics. For those teachers who assign narrative or descriptive text, the word grid gives students a visual format for comparing and contrasting themes or characters across several different stories, plays, poems, or novels (see Figure 6.7). Whether the text is narrative or expository, secondary teachers embrace the word grid strategy because it encourages their students to think critically and divergently as they determine the relationships between and among key vocabulary and concepts.

	Rhyme	Hyperbole	Metaphor	Allusion			Author
"Ivy Crown"							Williams
"A Bird Came Down"							Dickinson
"The Road Not Taken"							Frost
"Barbie Doll"							Piercy
"After Tonight"							Soto
"Theme for English B"							Hughes

FIGURE 6.7. Word grid for elements of style.

Vocabulary Cards

It's probably apocryphal, but I heard a story about how the best speller in the school prepared for the upcoming spelling bee with his best friend's help. The two made scores of flash cards with difficult words, their definitions, and sentences containing the words. For days they could be found rehearsing—the friend reading the word, the other either offering a spelling or asking for a definition and/or the word in context first, and the prompter checking and correcting. The spelling bee finally arrived, and both participated in it. And though everyone expected the best speller to win again, the spelling bee trophy actually went to the prompter.

Whether true or not, this story offers an important lesson about the potential learning power of using cards for learning. The approach embodies many of the significant principles of vocabulary learning, such as repeated exposure and multiple textual (definitions, sentence) and linguistic (the word is spoken, read, heard) contexts. Indeed, it may be that because the prompter brought more of these linguistic and contextual systems to the processes of learning to spell the words, he was victorious over his friend.

Vocabulary cards for learning important academic terms and concepts take advantage of the same critical word-learning principles (Fisher et al., 2015). You may have used these or something similar, such as a flash card, in your own studying. Based on the time-honored Frayer model (Frayer, Frederick, & Klausmeier, 1969), a correctly completed vocabulary card includes important aspects of what is involved in knowing a word or a concept in a deep and full manner. Vocabulary cards can be used in all content areas and disciplines to help students acquire knowledge of specific words necessary to understand the ideas and information (Fisher et al., 2015; Stephens, 2011)

The research evidence for vocabulary cards and the word-learning principles inherent in the use of cards is very encouraging (Butler et al., 2010; Dodigovic, 2013; Kornell, 2009; Nakata, 2008; Nation, 2013). By creating and rehearsing with cards, students learn to see relationships among key terms, differentiate between relevant and irrelevant examples of words, and connect critical attributes with words. This word-learning routine also helps students link what they are already familiar with to academic language and concepts.

On the front of the vocabulary card, students write the targeted word. On the back of the card, the desired information about the word or concept is provided. This can vary depending on the goal for word learning and the overall learning goals of the unit or lesson. It is most common to include at least a definition and an example. Added to this might be a picture or illustration, a synonym or an antonym, or a personal sentence (see Figure 6.8). Students can either make vocabulary cards using index cards and handwriting the information on the card or design them using interactive online tools, such as Cram, Quizlet, or Flashcard Machine. These online card-making apps have save and retrieval features, so words can be

Sometimes the drama in my relationship with Jacob reminds me of Romeo and Juliet.	A piece of writing that tells a serious or comedic story and is performed by actors
 CONJECTURAL RECONSTRUCTION *by G. Topham Forrest*	Ancient Greek tragedies—*Antigone, Oedipus Rex* Middle ages—Miracle plays Elizabethan theater—Shakespeare, Marlowe, Jonson

FIGURE 6.8. Example of a vocabulary card from English literature for the word *drama*.

studied over time and amended and revised if necessary. Additionally, these apps are available to iPhones and iPads, so students can review their words just about anywhere.

Sara has her students create vocabulary cards in her 9th-grade history classes. Many of her students are English learners, who need visual support for acquiring new academic concepts (August, 2012). Students were shown how to use shapes from Microsoft Word to make the e-vocabulary cards and save them in their own document files. Figure 6.9 is an example of the kind of card her students made during the study of World War II. One advantage of making cards using MS Word features is that Sara's students are able to grab interesting and accurate images from the Internet that depict the targeted words and paste them into the card, for example, the photograph of the Hitler look-alike character issuing an ultimatum.

Sara is a strong believer in taking time to discuss words so that students, especially her English learners, can hear the words repeated as often as possible with the definitional and contextual information from the vocabulary cards. Working in pairs and small groups, she prompts her students to quiz each other with the e-cards, which further emphasizes repetition, contextualization, and accuracy of word knowledge. Sara has noticed that the use of vocabulary cards, along with other vocabulary strategies and practices, has produced substantial improvement in her students' retention of word meanings and application of new general and content-specific vocabulary in their class discussions and written work.

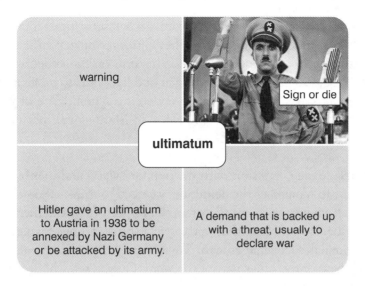

FIGURE 6.9. Example of a vocabulary card from history for the word *ultimatum.*

Imagery and Keywords

Have you ever created a mental picture to help you remember a difficult word or procedure? Many of us do this routinely because we know that images can be powerful reminders. For example, if the targeted word you need to learn is *acrophobia,* what mental picture could you invoke to remember that the word means "fear of high places"? One option would be to focus on the first part of the word, *acro,* and develop the image of an acrobat who is afraid of heights walking on a tightrope high in the sky. You could follow up with a sentence such as this: "The acrobat, who has always been afraid of high places, suffered from acrophobia." When we make pictures in our minds to help us remember what a word means or how it relates to another word or superordinate concept, we are using the imagery strategy (Sarcoban & Basibek, 2012). Research suggests that imagery can be a powerful tool for reinforcing vocabulary knowledge because students are actively involved in their learning (Gryder & Vesely, 2007; Mastropieri & Scruggs, 2013; Zahedi & Abdi, 2012).

The keyword strategy differs slightly from imagery approaches in that catchy phrases or sentences related to the word are created and remembered. For example, if you were having trouble remembering the word *amorous,* you might think about a phrase such as "more love for us," which sounds like amorous but has a synonym for the word in it. Although the research findings on keyword and imagery strategies are generally positive, they will not work for every vocabulary word or for every student. In addition, it is important to remember that students' personal images and clever phrases will always be more powerful than the images or phrases provided by their teachers.

Marquis, a 10th-grade biology teacher, uses a combination of imagery and keywords to help his students with learning disabilities remember difficult definitions and relationships between concepts. During his unit on the endocrine system, he modeled the process he used to create images and keywords to remember the functions of the glands and hormones in the endocrine system. One of his students, Araceli, had difficulty applying the strategies, so Marquis met her during homeroom to help her.

MARQUIS: Araceli, let's start with the pituitary gland and the thyrotropic hormone. To remember the definition, we need to think of something memorable from part of the word *thyrotropic*. I'll start first, and then I'll have you help me. When I hear the word *tropic*, I think of jungles where rain causes or stimulates extreme growth. Thyrotropic hormones stimulate growth in the thyroid, the other part of the word. Do you see what I did, Araceli? I took parts of the word that I could remember because they were already familiar to me. Then I made up a sentence to help me remember the definition. Which word would you like to try next?

ARACELI: I missed *prolactin* on the quiz. Can we try this one?

MARQUIS: Okay, Araceli. Let's look at the word carefully—each letter and the parts. Can you divide the word into familiar parts?

ARACELI: Well, there is the word *pro*, which makes me think of a professional. There is also the word *tin*.

MARQUIS: Okay, Araceli. Will either of them help you remember the definition of prolactin, a hormone that stimulates milk production?

ARACELI: No, I don't see how.

MARQUIS: Okay. Let's see if we can play with the middle part of the word, *lac*. This part of the word sounds like what word in our language, Araceli?

ARACELI: *Lack?*

MARQUIS: That's right! Has your mother ever told you that you lack milk— that you should drink more milk to have healthy bones and teeth?

ARACELI: Yes! And I hate the stuff.

MARQUIS: Could we use the letters *l–a–c* to remind us of milk? Many people do not drink the proper amount of milk.

ARACELI: Yes but what about the *pro* part of the word?

MARQUIS: Good question. Could we use *pro* to remind us in some way that prolactin is a hormone that stimulates milk? Think about this for a moment, Araceli.

ARACELI: Yes! Professional athletes should not drink more milk. Will that work?

MARQUIS: Will it work for you? That's what makes the difference.

ARACELI: Hmm. Yes, I can use that—it makes sense. Professional athletes should not suffer from a lack of milk. Prolactin stimulates milk production.

MARQUIS: Let's review before we go to the next word. Give me the definitions of *thyrotropic* and *prolactin*.

ARACELI: Prolactin stimulates the production of milk, and the thyrotropic hormone stimulates the thyroid. This was easy. I wish I had thought of this before the quiz.

MARQUIS: The next hormone you missed on the quiz is *thyroxine*. Okay, Araceli, what are the steps in remembering a definition of a difficult word?

Notice how Marquis encourages Araceli to state the steps of this vocabulary strategy before she applies it independently to another word. Had Araceli not been able to use the strategy after this individualized lesson, Marquis would have shown her another strategy to help her learn the definitions and functions of the various content-specific vocabulary in the unit. Marquis tries to offer a variety of word-learning options for his students, especially those with learning disabilities, because he knows each student learns in different ways. With Araceli, however, imagery and keywords worked once she realized the processes involved.

Case Study Revisited

Let us now return to Miranda's school district, where a districtwide committee of teachers has been meeting throughout the school year to solve the problem of extremely low vocabulary scores in the 10th grade. After reading this chapter, you probably have some thoughts about what the committee could propose to solve this problem. Take a moment now to write or talk with a colleague about your suggestions.

By the end of the school year, Miranda, the curriculum director, and the 10th-grade biology teachers on the committee had reached only one decision. One of the biology teachers had brought to the committee's attention an article he had read on the characteristics of effective vocabulary instruction, prompting critical discussion among the committee members, who decided there were no "quick fixes" and that no single commercial program or material would fully address the problem. Perhaps that decision was the most important because it removed as an option the computer-based vocabulary program that several members were urging the school to adopt. The committee members realized the computer program expected students to learn the targeted words in lists with no context and that only rote-level definitional tasks were emphasized. Hence, they were concerned about whether students would learn the words well enough to be able to apply them to new situations.

Although the committee did reach agreement to look to alternatives to published vocabulary programs for their students, they still disagreed about the English teachers' role in improving students' vocabularies. Some teachers saw the teaching of vocabulary as a time-consuming intrusion into an already hectic teaching schedule. Moreover, they viewed vocabulary instruction as a natural and logical part of the English curriculum. Consequently, Miranda, the curriculum director, suggested that the issue be tabled for a while, at least until they had finished their intensive study of evidence-based vocabulary teaching and learning practices.

During the summer the committee members were provided with a stipend to continue to read and plan. Miranda had the money for further study because expensive commercial materials had not been purchased from the school budget. At their first meeting, she suggested the committee begin with some general goals that could serve to guide each school's specific goals for vocabulary instruction. Meanwhile, the teachers on the committee continued to read intensively about vocabulary development and kept personal learning logs. They chose articles from journals in their own content areas, articles from the *Journal of Adolescent and Adult Literacy*, and recent books on the topic from respected educational publishers. A major breakthrough occurred when one of the more vocal teachers, who had been dubious about the committee's reaching consensus on a solution, read a review of the literature explaining how vocabulary knowledge was closely related to students' ability to make meaning of content-area and disciplinary texts. She shared that information with her colleagues on the committee and made a compelling case for the importance of vocabulary knowledge to learning across the curriculum. From that point on, the committee embraced the idea that all teachers should assume responsibility for their students' vocabulary development.

After considerable reading and discussion, Miranda facilitated the committee's development of the following goals for the school district:

1. The students should develop a long-term interest and enjoyment in developing and refining their vocabularies.
2. The students should learn independent strategies for learning general academic and content-specific vocabulary words.
3. The students should become skilled in strategies that promote both definitional, contextual, and conceptual understanding of words.

Pleased with their goals, the committee members decided their next step was to outline how each goal could be incorporated into their own curricula and how the departments could reinforce each other. They also decided that these goals should not be limited to the 10th-grade teachers but should involve all grade levels. Their reasoning was that an effective program of vocabulary improvement needed to be comprehensive and cumulative if real growth and change were to occur.

Because the school year was about to begin, the committee decided to implement the first two goals and to evaluate the impact of their unified effort at the end of the school year. They concluded, however, that students' scores on the competency-based reading test would probably not increase suddenly as a result of these small steps toward their overall plan to improve students' word knowledge and text comprehension abilities. From their readings and discussions, they realized that their overarching goal of improving students' vocabulary knowledge would involve a long-term commitment by all teachers.

LOOKING BACK, LOOKING FORWARD

In this chapter, I have stressed the importance of students' possessing deep and full understanding of general and content-specific academic vocabulary in order to improve their learning across the curriculum. Because simple definitional knowledge of a word is not sufficient for text comprehension, teachers need to stress contextual and conceptual understandings, as well. As I demonstrated in this chapter, there are many practices available to both teachers and students that promote this level of word knowledge. These vocabulary practices, along with word-learning practices described in other chapters of this book (e.g., Chapters 2 and 4), will go a long way toward meeting the CCSS goals for students to be successful learners and independent knowledge builders of academic language.

In order to meet Common Core standards and ensure successful word learning for our diverse adolescents, teachers need to emphasize the vocabulary of their content areas and disciplines, so that everyone contributes to students' abilities to acquire new vocabulary both through instruction and independently (Scott, Nagy, & Flinspach, 2008). I therefore described and exemplified strategies such as word maps and vocabulary cards that students can create based on their readings and use as a source of review as they study the content. Whether they are teacher directed or student initiated, these vocabulary strategies become even more powerful and useful when anchored in instructional practices that emphasize demonstrations, modeling, small-group interactions, class discussions, and reciprocal teaching. None of the strategies I shared in this chapter is mutually exclusive; they can and should be used in logical and responsive combinations. For instance, helping students focus on context and word morphology will likely have greater impact and a longer-lasting effect than focusing on either of these strategies alone.

As with nearly all the approaches to teaching and learning presented in this book, the vocabulary strategies presented here will not always engender immediate enthusiasm for learning words or produce an automatic effect on text comprehension. As Nagy (2010) reminds us, word learning, especially of academic language, takes time to develop, so teachers should engage in practices that foster students' expertise over the long term.

Finally, remember that any approach, regardless of its novelty, will eventually become ineffective if overused. Therefore, it is wise to vary the vocabulary strategies often, based on the motivational and learning needs of students, in order to sustain their energy and engagement in learning academic vocabulary. In the end, however, any vocabulary development strategies that require students to process terms and concepts in elaborative, meaningful, and unique ways will help them understand words and text more fully and retain important concepts and information much longer.

In the next chapter, I take up the topic of writing to learn. The same principles that guide effective vocabulary practices apply equally to the strategies and practices of effective writing at the secondary level. As I point out, new research and social practices suggest that content-area and disciplinary teachers should approach the inclusion of writing in their daily and weekly lessons with renewed vigor.

CHAPTER 7

Writing to Learn in the Disciplines

As you read Chapter 7, reflect on the following questions:

- How are reading process and the writing process similar?
- What differentiates "high-stakes" and "low-stakes" writing assignments?
- How can evidence-based elements of effective writing guide the development of writing-to-learn activities for adolescents?
- What kinds of writing strategies or activities encourage students to construct meaning and monitor their understanding?
- How can writing be used to encourage students to think critically about content-area concepts?
- What writing practices in youths' everyday lives can be linked to content-area and disciplinary writing activities?
- In what ways do RAFT and SPAWN writing increase engagement in writing and learning?
- What is the relationship between disciplinary writing and the expected outcomes of the Common Core State Standards?
- How can digital media facilitate writing to learn?

My father was a writer. Well, not exactly a published author, but a writer nonetheless. His essays and two novels for young adults were read and enjoyed within the immediate family. And he was an inveterate writer of letters. Some of my earliest memories of dad are of him sitting in his makeshift office upstairs in our small Detroit bungalow tapping away on a sturdy cast iron 1920s vintage Underwood typewriter. He wrote almost every day, and as I came to learn, he produced a memoir of his time on ship in the South Pacific during World War II; two interesting though rather crude full-length novels for teens, *Buxton's Cowards* and *I Swear on My Ma'*, as well as essays and commentaries on current politics and countless letters to family and friends.

Once all seven of us children had left the house and were in far-flung regions of the United States, from New York to Florida to California, my father told me before he passed away that there was a time when he was writing at least one letter per day to his kids. These were either handwritten or from a manual typewriter. And they were always welcome finds in the mailbox or door slot, as they conveyed news about home and updates on my brothers and sisters, along with random interesting tidbits and now and again even photographs. Remember, these were the days before computers, the Internet, and iPhones.

In no small way, my father's interest in writing contributed to my own interest. As a young boy, when that old Underwood was free, I began to try my hand at composing something. I remember feeling like an author when I sat before the daunting black metal machine. It was the sense that anything I typed would be original, would be mine. I still can recall one of my earliest efforts about a man attempting to cross the ocean in a bathtub. Of course, I hardly knew then where those tentative first acts of playing with words on paper would lead me. Reflecting now after these many decades on a body of work consisting of well over 100 published journal articles, numerous book chapters, and ten books, I realize that writing is nearly as essential to me as eating and breathing.

Writing for most adolescents is also essential to them, though they may not always recognize it as writing. Their thumbs and fingers are pressing out missives, notes, abbreviated responses to friends, family, and even strangers in virtual social spaces all day, every day, so reflexively as if not to be noticed (Boyd, 2014). But this chapter is concerned with more than teens' and preteens' personal writing; it focuses on writing in academic contexts as well and on how the skills and abilities developed there can position youth for an efficacious life beyond the school walls. Writing to learn in school and beyond, to demonstrate and share one's knowledge, and to teach and guide others are the purposes and goals foregrounded in this chapter. Thus the admonishment that every secondary teacher should not only assign but teach discipline- and content-specific writing in order to prepare youth for college, careers, and life is made all the more compelling by the eloquent rationale from the National Writing Project (*www.nwp.org/cs/public/print/doc/about.csp*):

> Writing is essential to communication, learning, and citizenship. It is the currency of the new workplace and global economy. Writing helps us convey ideas, solve problems, and understand our changing world. Writing is a bridge to the future. . . . [We] envision(s) a future where every person is an accomplished writer, engaged learner, and active participant in a digital, interconnected world (2013).

When writing guided by this perspective is integrated into middle and high school classrooms, it is especially advantageous to students (Gillespie, Graham, Kiuhara, & Hebert, 2014). Writing has been shown not only to facilitate the learning of content but also to engage students in higher-level thinking and reasoning (Klein, Arcon, & Baker, 2016). Furthermore, disciplinary teachers, once brought to see the benefits of writing for their students, have embraced practices that integrate writing into daily instruction (Adu-Gyamfi, Bosse, & Faulconer, 2010; McNaught, 2010).

Case Study

Dave, a first-year teacher, is a member of the biology department at an urban high school. His students were bored with his first unit; most failed to read the assigned chapters or complete the homework. And many students did not make a passing grade on the first unit exam. Dave's department chair urged him to be stricter with the students. Another teacher in the English department, with whom he shared lunch duty, suggested that he incorporate more interesting texts and assignments into his next unit. The English teacher suggested that Dave incorporate writing assignments with the alternative texts so that students could appreciate the relevance of biology in their lifeworlds.

To the reader: As you read this chapter, think about how Dave might introduce writing experiences for his students to make his next unit on the environment more meaningful and engaging to them.

READING AND WRITING IN THE 21ST CENTURY

Reflect for a moment on all of the reading and writing you do in the course of your daily routine. You might start with rolling over in bed and finding your iPhone to check emails and texts. After these have been screened, you might respond to one or two quickly, saving the more important ones for longer considered responses using a larger keyboard device. From there you might find yourself sitting at the breakfast table with the newspaper or your iPad reviewing the major events of the day. After breakfast, you might compose responses to the more involved email correspondence. On the commute to work, you might make oral recordings on your smartphone of ideas for a report you need to finish. At work, you screen and read regular mail and monitor the constant flow of incoming messages, compose replies and informative missives throughout the day, and read additional documentation to finish writing the report. On the way home after work, you text your spouse reminders about dinner and weekend plans. After dinner, you read a novel, and then in bed before calling it a day, you check messages one last time, dashing off a few quick replies. Lights out.

If this scenario resembles your life, then upon reflection you can appreciate that, like millions of others in the United States and around the world in the 21st century, we routinely spend a large portion of our day with our hands on keyboards and our minds on audiences. In fact, according to Brandt (2015), we are writing so often that our time and desire for reading may be decreasing. Brandt suggests that writing has overtaken reading as the primary daily literate experience. In such a world, she argues, literacy research and teaching should focus on more than just skills of reading. For most teachers and scholars, reading is considered the fundamental skill, the prior skill, the formative skill, the gateway to writing. How many would readily agree that you can only read as well as you can write? Or that the best way to learn how to read is to write, write, and write some more? Brandt sees this bias against writing in favor of reading as a vestige of 20th-century American experiences and perceptions:

> Whereas people tend to remember reading for the sensual and emotional pleasure that it gave, they tended to remember writing for the pain or isolation it was meant to assuage. People's descriptions of the settings of childhood and adolescent writing—a hospital bed, the front steps of a house, and . . . a highway overpass—were scenes of exile, hiding, or at least degraded versions of domesticity, in marked contrast to the memories of pillowed, well-lit family reading circles. . . . (p. 156)

But in the wider society and over the last 50 years or more, writing has ascended as the main basis of many people's daily literacy experiences and the main platform for their literacy development. This has profound implications for the way students learn literacy in school and how their literacy learning is situated. If, indeed, most adults today are spending 4 or more hours with fingers on keyboards, this suggests that secondary schools should be giving much greater emphasis to developing adolescents' writing abilities to better prepare them for the literate challenges of this evolving century.

If writing truly is the neglected literacy skill, as Brandt and others have characterized it, then data from the National Assessment of Educational Progress would seem to confirm this perception. Results show that for both eighth and 12th graders as many as 20% scored at the below basic level and another 53% at the basic level, while only 27% had scores in the proficient range and a mere 3% reached the highest achievement category of advanced. When the results are explored further, we find that girls outperform boys at both age groups to a significant degree. Furthermore, Black and Hispanic students and students from city schools have the lowest achievement levels of all groups. Finally, for English learners, a full 80% were at the below basic level, with another 20% at the basic level and a mere 1% at the proficient level (*www.nationsreportcard.gov/writing_2011/writing_tools.aspx*). These NAEP findings surely point to the need for schools to prioritize high-quality writing instruction for all youth, particularly for those who struggle and for multiethnic, multilinguistic, and multicultural learners, by implementing a sociocultural approach to writing (Diaz-Rico, 2014; Graham & Perin, 2007).

Writing and Reading

For the past few decades, literacy researchers have attempted to demonstrate how reading and writing represent similar thinking processes. For instance, in the 1990s it was common to hear and read about the so-called "reading and writing connection." Reading and writing were thought to be overlapping processes that offer students alternative ways of constructing meaning (Shanahan, 1997; Tierney & Shanahan, 1991). Today, it is generally understood that reading and writing are interrelated processes and that purposeful instruction designed to develop these processes in tandem will benefit both (Gogan, 2013; Lockhart & Soliday, 2016).

According to a variety of authorities (Bazerman & Prior, 2008; Graham & Perin, 2007; MacArthur, Graham, & Fitzgerald, 2006), the writing process, like the reading process, has these overlapping and recursive elements:

1. *Planning.* Just as active learners use what they already know and set purposes before they begin to read, they also spend extended periods of time before actual writing to plan, to discover ways of approaching the compositional task, to self-question, and to identify purposes or problems. This phase of the writing process is often ignored because of an inordinate concern for generating a finished product to be evaluated. If students could be provided more time to brainstorm ideas and discuss writing plans with peers and their teachers, the quality of their writing would significantly increase (Applebee & Langer, 2011; Kellogg & Whiteford, 2009).

2. *Drafting.* The second phase of the writing process focuses on the initial draft. At this point, the writer is attempting to get words onto screen or paper, into sentences, paragraphs, and sections. Similar to the challenge for readers, writers work to make things cohere and fit between the whole and parts and among the parts. Most writers, however, do not follow an orderly process in this initial drafting. Often students aren't allowed enough in-class time for this initial drafting. Instead, writing may occur mostly outside of class, where peers and the teacher are not available for support and coaching.

3. *Revising.* The third phase of the writing process involves students in revising and reformulating. Just as active readers pause to reflect and monitor and then reread to verify and evaluate, effective writers take the time to read, reflect, and evaluate writing as another individual would. By taking the role of reader during this phase, students begin to see their "writing" as a piece of "reading."

When students are involved in the revising process, they think about their main assertions, modifying them when they are not clear for their anticipated readers.

They may also reorganize their papers, adding support and deleting information elsewhere, especially if they have not made their case for their audience. Hence, the recursive nature of the revising process often leads writers back to previous phases and processes (e.g., planning).

4. *Editing and polishing.* At this phase writers move from macro- to micro-level text concerns. They do so by examining their sentence structure, searching for correct word choices, and proofreading for basic errors in spelling, punctuation, or grammar.

5. *Postwriting and sharing.* Just as readers use and share the information they have read in some meaningful way, so should writers by sharing and making public their texts. In most situations, this sharing typically occurs in a private and limited way, because teachers are the sole readers of students' compositions. Ideally, the audience for students' writing should be more public, whether that means other students, administrators, parents, community members, or individuals outside the community (e.g., politicians, business leaders, a virtual public).

The intensity and willingness that students devote to any of these phases depends on the two conditions that we, as teachers, can control. When teachers share with their students the processes of their own writing tasks, students are often surprised to discover that professional and competent writers must evaluate and revise extensively before they concern themselves with the surface features of spelling and grammar, aspects novice and challenged writers tend to focus on. Furthermore, students who have never written for anyone but the teacher often feel that their ideas are not worthy of extended writing and revision or that the teacher already understands the ideas, so there is no need to be explicit and clear. They may also have difficulty believing in a real audience, because the writing task to them is no more than an occasion for a grade. We can change this misconception by providing our students with real and intriguing audiences for their writing so the urgency of communicating ideas becomes a passion and a drive. Evidence shows that students who know that their writing will have an audience other than the teacher are more likely to participate in the revising and editing phase of the writing process (Elbow, 2012; Guo, Zhang, & Zhai, 2012; Patchan, Schunn, & Correnti, 2016).

In sum, teachers can help their students understand these recursive and overlapping stages by reserving time in class for brainstorming, planning, drafting, revising, editing/polishing, and sharing. However, it is important to bear in mind that not all students' writing in content and disciplinary classrooms requires revision, editing, and publishing. For example, students in biology who maintain a journal to document experiments, pose questions, and add comments that connect the learning that occurs in biology with their own lives and aspirations will likely only need to keep their journal entries in draft form, since this repository of questions, ideas, and descriptions is intended as a reflective tool and study aid for students.

How Writing Benefits Content-Area and Disciplinary Teachers

A common concern I hear from secondary teachers is that learning doesn't stick, especially ideas and information from required reading. Students might be able to pass quizzes and tests, but afterward, all is forgotten. One cause for this phenomenon is the tendency for students to be sentence surfers, as a colleague of mine labels it. In other words, their reading is superficial, resulting at best in memorized bits and pieces, but without depth, or fails to infer overall patterns.

The following example from a high school government class demonstrates the proclivity for shallow reading and its fallout. Ernesto assigns his 11th graders to read the first part of Chapter 2, which describes the characteristics of public opinion, and to come to class prepared for discussion. In their reading, the students come across one of the characteristics of public opinion, latency, and its corresponding definition: "an opinion not yet crystallized or formed."

Martrez, an especially diligent student, repeats that definition several times before going to class, confident that he is prepared for discussion or an unannounced quiz (for which Ernesto is infamous). Ernesto lives up to his reputation. He asks the students to list and define the five characteristics of public opinion and to give an example of each. Martrez, confident of the definition of latency, writes the words "not yet crystallized" but gives no example. In fact, none of the students give examples, and they complain loudly about this aspect of the quiz. "There were no examples in the textbook! You are not being fair. We really read the assignment."

Was Ernesto unfair? Did Martrez really understand the concept of latency or the words "not yet crystallized"? Should Ernesto's students be expected to create examples of concepts? Although I believe Ernesto was justified in not accepting rote memorization by his students, I also believe he could have prevented this minor student revolt by integrating processes of reading and writing into his instruction. The combined use of reading and writing in this government class would have provided students and Ernesto with several advantages. A synthesis of the literature makes clear that, when students write, the following are true:

- At the most simple level they are paraphrasing, summarizing, organizing, and linking new understandings with familiar ones (Chuy, Scardamalia, & Bereiter, 2012; Monte-Sano & De La Paz, 2012).
- They are monitoring their comprehension, making it easier for them to identity what they know and what is confusing to them (Hebert, Gillespie, & Graham, 2013).
- They are provided affordances in higher-level thinking, such as elaborating,

synthesizing information across texts, and expressing critical perspectives and interpretations (Schwartz, 2015).
- Teachers have an additional tool to motivate students and engage them in learning activities (Bernacki, Nokes-Malach, Richey, & Belenky, 2016).
- Teachers can readily identify students' lack of conceptual understandings (Manzo & Manzo, 2013).

Let us reconsider Ernesto's classroom in order to examine each of these advantages in more detail.

Ernesto could have capitalized on writing if he had assigned his students to read the textbook section and then summarize the key ideas, using their own words. In giving the assignment, Ernesto could have modeled how he summarizes and explained how he uses brief summary notes and annotations to monitor his comprehension. In the following class students could have compared their summaries while Ernesto circulated around the room to eavesdrop on conversations. By doing this, he could have gained valuable insights into the students' depth of knowledge and the problems they were having with the text. Moreover, he could have used this input as a way to open a whole-class question-and-answer session.

Alternatively, Ernesto could have capitalized on the power of writing by front-loading the assignment he gave his students. That is, he could have introduced the chapter and unit by asking the students to take 5 minutes to describe in their journals their opinions about a controversial policy or law. After several students had shared their journal entries, he could have asked them to brainstorm reasons why there were so many differences of opinion across the classroom. Ernesto's students would have been better prepared and more motivated to read about the five characteristics that influence political opinion, having brainstormed many of them already.

Finally, Ernesto could have used writing as a way to encourage his students to think critically and creatively. For example, if Ernesto wanted his students to apply the concepts in the textbook chapter to situations in the community, he could have asked his students to work in small groups and poll a representative sample of 25 individuals about a variety of important issues (e.g., bike lanes, marijuana law, homeless shelters). Once they completed their interviews, the groups could have then prepared a written report that summarized their findings and explained the results in light of the characteristics of public opinion presented in the chapter. Ernesto could have also encouraged the students to formulate additional characteristics of public opinion or challenge the authors' assertions about these characteristics.

The writing options for Ernesto and his students were many and varied, as they are for all content-area and disciplinary teachers. Regardless of the option, students' reading cannot remain superficial if they are asked to write out their ideas about what they read. Writing demands participation by every student, not just the ones who volunteer. More important, when students share their writing, teachers can quickly discover which students do and do not understand and where understanding breaks down so that reteaching can occur as needed.

GUIDELINES AND PRACTICES FOR CONTENT-AREA AND DISCIPLINARY WRITING

In this section, I describe four overarching guidelines for making writing integral to learning across the content areas and disciplines and for ensuring that students come to see writing as a natural way to explore and extend understandings.

Integrate Low-Stakes Writing into Daily Lessons

You can maximize the potential of writing in your classroom if you remember that writing is a process that may or may not end in a written product that will be handed in for a grade. Of course, there are occasions when students should produce a final written product to be evaluated, such as responses to essay questions in history or a summary of findings in a lab report for chemistry. These are "high-stakes" assignments that may be evaluated formally and thoroughly. However, a considerable amount of writing should be informal or "low-stakes" (Bean, 2011). The benefits of low-stakes writing are many, including the following:

- Low-stakes writing promotes active engagement in the ideas and subject matter of a course, as compared with listening to lectures or even class discussion.
- Low-stakes writing helps students find and develop their own language for the issues and content in a disciplinary classroom. As I have noted, learning a discipline means learning its "discourse," but students don't really know a field unless they can write and talk about the concepts in their own informal and personal language. Successful parroting of the textbook language can mask a lack of understanding.
- Frequent low-stakes writing improves high-stakes writing. Students will already be warmed up and fluent before they write something we have to respond to. And when they turn in an impenetrable high-stakes essay (and who hasn't tangled up one's prose through extensive revising?), we don't have to panic. We can just say, "Come on. You can revise this some more into the clear lively voice I've already seen you using."
- Low-stakes writing helps us understand how students' minds are working: how they are understanding the course material, feeling about it, and reacting to our teaching.
- There's a special application of low-stakes writing to math and science courses—and to problem solving in general: Ask students to write the story

of the paths their minds followed as they tried to solve a problem. These paths are interestingly idiosyncratic but instructive, and it's useful to have students share these metacognitive stories.

- Regular low-stakes assignments make students keep up with the assigned reading every week. This means that they contribute more and get more from discussions and lectures. Quizzes can do this job, but they invite an adversarial climate and don't bring the other benefits described here—including pleasure.

- And don't forget: low-stakes writing takes little of our time and expertise. We can require it but not grade it. We can read it but not comment on it. In many cases, we don't even need to read it. Yet we can get students to read each other's informal pieces—and (if we want) discuss them.

Low-stakes writing can take a multitude of forms depending on the content, the level of engagement of students, and the creative imagination of teachers. When learning is deconstructed, it quickly becomes apparent how readily writing of an informal nature can be infused into daily lessons. As the benefits just enumerated make clear, since this type of writing does not require formal grading or even comment, it can occur in planned or spontaneous ways.

A pristine example of situationally driven low-stakes writing comes from Lawrence, who was surprised but pleased with how charged his computer programming students became when reading about the FBI's purchase of an expensive decryption program to unlock messages on mobile phones of alleged criminals, since phone companies were not legally obliged to so. They wondered seriously about the advantages to law enforcement and for careers in customized programming, as well as the dangers to citizens' privacy rights by big government. On the spot, Lawrence asked the students to take out their notebooks and write a one-paragraph position statement and rationale. Once completed, he arranged the class into two rows of 10 standing students facing one another at a normal conversational distance. He set his computer timer for 1 minute, then asked students to exchange their points of view based on their written assertions. When the alarm sounded, he had them shift like an elongated rubber band, so that students faced someone new and commenced their dialogue again. This process continued for about 10–12 minutes. Afterward, Lawrence asked his students to return to their notebooks and write about any new insights gleaned from the conversations with various classmates.

RAFT and SPAWN Writing

Two engaging approaches to low-stakes writing that can be easily incorporated into the flow of daily content-area and disciplinary instruction are known by the acronyms RAFT (Santa & Havens, 2012) and SPAWN (Brozo & Simpson, 2007; Martin, Martin, & O'Brien, 1984). *RAFT* stands for:

- *Role* of the writer—Is the author a person, a thing, a concept, an animal?
- *Audience*—To whom is the author writing?
- *Form*—What format or discourse mode is the author going to use?
- *Topic*—What topic is the author writing about?

RAFT writing is typically done after particular content is learned, or text sections, chapters, poems, or articles are read. Although this approach allows for creativity, whatever students write must be grounded in the content, that is, the information and ideas of the text or other sources. Thus, even though RAFT writing allows novel formatting, it must be text- or information-source-based, and not purely imaginary. RAFTs should provide teachers and students a reflection of important information and ideas just learned.

Each letter of the SPAWN acronym represents a category of writing prompts that move students beyond restating textual details to demonstrations of higher-level thinking.

- *Special powers*—Students are given the power to change an aspect of the text or topic.
- *Problem solving*—Students are asked to write solutions to problems posed or suggested by the texts being read or material being studied.
- *Alternative viewpoints*—Students write about a topic or story from a unique perspective.
- *What if?*—Similar to *special powers,* the teacher introduces the aspect of the topic or text that has changed, then asks students to write based on that change.
- *Next*—Students are asked to write in anticipation of what the author will discuss next.

These prompts can be crafted in a limitless variety of ways to stimulate students' meaningful thinking about content-area topics (Fisher, Brozo, Frey, & Frey, 2011). The goal is to require students to write thoughtfully and verifiably about a text or topic. Prompts should be designed in such a way that requires students to use textual evidence in their responses but that also instigates critical thinking about aspects of content and ideas under study. The writing prompted by SPAWN is typically short in length and can be kept in students' class notebooks or logs.

English Literature

Ivy's 10th graders use their English journals frequently to document and reflect on new learning and anticipate content. For example, by the end of Act I of *Romeo and Juliet,* the young couple have already expressed their love for one another even while discovering that one is a Capulet and the other a Montague, the two deadly rival families of Verona. Before moving on to Act II, Ivy asks her students to write a RAFT either from Romeo's or Juliet's perspective, importuning the other's parent to accept their betrothal of love. Once students completed their RAFTed compositions, Ivy invited volunteers to read theirs aloud to the class. Andrew first described what each letter of his RAFT represented before reading his with feigned emotion:

R—Romeo
A—Lady Capulet
F—Letter
T—persuade her to let him marry Juliet

Dearest Lady Capulet,

Please do not throw this letter away! I am pouring out of my heart to ask you to see beyond a name and recognize my love for your amazing daughter, Juliet.

I know you think I am just a dirty Montague, but there's more to me than my name. Isn't it time the ancient feud between our families be put to rest? The love Juliet and I have can heal the wounds our families have caused each other.

I just want to love and cherish Juliet and take care of her the rest of our lives. She is more beautiful than a rose in May. Please let me love her . . . or I shall die.

Your humble servant,
Romeo Montague

After calling on several other volunteers to read their RAFTs, Ivy's students were anxious to get back to the play to discover what happened to the star-crossed lovers. This was precisely the goal of the particular RAFT assignment Ivy had given her class; by allowing students to creatively anticipate in a short, focused written composition possible directions the play's plot might take, she was able to heighten engagement and sustain attention.

History

The study of World War I is not the most popular topic for many students in Ricardo's history classes. Yet he has learned to use low-stakes writing on a near daily basis to keep his students from losing focus and to reflect on important content in their reading in preparation for quizzes, tests, and class discussions.

After his students read about possible reasons for the United States' involvement in the war, Ricardo invited them to construct a RAFT from the perspective of an individual who did or could have experienced the actual historical events leading up to President Wilson's decision to join the effort against the Germans and their allies. Ricardo instructed his class that they could use the history text and other sources from class as they composed their RAFTs. Their RAFTs could be creative, he instructed, but must be historically accurate.

Jaramillo took full advantage of this assignment. His father was in the Navy on a ship that had cruised the waters around the British Isles and in the Mediterranean, so he enjoyed designing and composing the following RAFT:

R—Ship's commander
A—Himself
F—Log/diary
T—Sinking of the *Lusitania*

7 May, 1915—14:12 GMT—Kinsale Head, Ireland

Attacked today. German U-boat #20. Torpedoed amidship between the boilers and coal room. Panic everywhere and sinking fast. My orders are to prepare lifeboats and rafts for the women and children first, but these are ignored. I watch helplessly while everyone, including cowardly men, fight their way into whatever will float. Within minutes, a second explosion, maybe another torpedo or perhaps the coal dust ignited. At this point it hardly mattered. We were listing hard to starboard. Within the hour she was lost and so were the souls of 1,198 of my passengers and crew, including 138 Americans.

Something must be done to stop the submarine threat and the wanton destruction of unarmed non-military vessels. Maybe Mr. Wilson and his countrymen will now join the fray. I pray they must.

—WT Turner

Ricardo formed groups of three students to read their RAFTs and told students to provide feedback, focusing on the verifiable details in their peers' compositions. Jaramillo's group partners were able to find evidence from the history textbook for the details and facts in his RAFT. For instance, they confirmed the total number who died in the *Lusitania* sinking, the number of Americans reported to have been killed, the location of the torpedoing, the speculation about the second explosion, and the name of the surviving ship's commander.

Biology

Sahir has found that requiring her students to complete regular short focused writing in their learning logs has made a big difference in how well they ultimately perform on her biology tests. This writing has served as a reflection for her of what students have learned and as a metacognitive tool for students to determine firm understandings as well as gaps in their knowledge.

RAFTing is one form of regular writing in Sahir's biology courses. After viewing an interactive video from the Internet projected on the whiteboard about the role of certain proteins in metabolic processes of digestion and absorption, Sahir asked her class to write to a specific RAFT, which she labeled "A Biomolecule's Tale":

R—Protein
A—Heterotroph
F—Letter
T—Biochemistry/biomolecules

She emphasized the inclusion of accurate details of the processes involved and the related terminology in their RAFTs. Ahsad's letter was lauded by Sahir and his classmates for its cleverness and adherence to the actual facts.

Dear Heterotroph,

I hope you appreciate the processes I had to endure to help fuel your metabolism. First, I was ripped from the muscle of a ribeye by the gnawing of white incisors. I was then mixed with a transfusion of saliva and forced down a long tube to finally land in a dark, highly acidic environment. I was at once attacked by the enzyme pepsin and was forced to undergo hydrolysis. With the aid of water, I was ripped into smaller parts known as amino acids.

Approximately two hours later, the agitations of this organ forced me into a narrow tube. Whatever parts of me that remained intact could not escape the actions of more enzymes in this ever moving pipe. Little fingers called villi sucked me into a rich, warm blood supply. In my amino acid form, I crossed the cell membrane by diffusion. I was then picked up by the RNA and transported to the ribosome to be used in the making of human protein. So there it is heterotroph. I was once cow protein and now I am your protein. You are what you eat!

Sincerely,
Mr. Polypeptide Protein

Civics

Sixth-grade teacher Maricia knows her English learners need as many opportunities as possible to use their multiple language systems to learn academic language and social studies information and concepts (Cummins & Man, 2007). Data from the NAEP Writing assessment show that English learners have the lowest achievement levels of all subgroups (NCES, 2011, 2015b). Ensuring that her students write regularly, Maricia assigns various composition tasks that can be completed during class time, as they read and study civics content. She favors the SPAWN framework because it allows for continuous variation and novelty, which motivates her English learners. Furthermore, the prompts can be given as a bell ringer, in the middle of a lesson, or to close out a class period.

Maricia's students write the prompt and their responses in their social studies journal. Once finished, they always read their responses to a partner and talk about them to bring their other language systems into the learning process and stimulate oral language production (Hu & Lam, 2010; Leki, Cumming, & Silva, 2008). Maricia has learned to structure prompts in ways that tap various levels of text processing required by the writing standards of the CCSS. For a unit on the U.S. Constitution and the rights it guarantees its citizens, Maricia presented her class with the following prompt:

Special Powers Example

"A group of students who are not in favor of war wear black armbands to school. The principal tries to force students to take the armbands off. He says there is a school rule against it. The students refuse and are expelled from school. The students' parents take the case before a judge.

"You are the judge in the case. How would you rule and why? What effect would your ruling have on freedom of speech rights of students?"

In response, Beatriz wrote:

If I were the judge in this case I would allow the students to wear the armbands. Even though students aren't adults they have rights too. Wearing armbands is the way the students are saying they do not like the war. That means it's like speech. The Constitution says all of us have freedom of speech. So the students should be free to say they're against the war by wearing the armbands. If the students were allowed back to school with the armbands other students would feel free to express their feelings about the war. Some might want to say they are in favor of the war. That would be okay too.

Beatriz and the rest of her classmates were then divided into two groups— those who took positions in favor of the students and those who sided with the judge. The groups reviewed their responses and rationales and then faced each other for a debate. Maricia knows from experience and from the research literature that this kind of oral language context is especially supportive of student dialoguing. This in turn reinforces the learning of academic vocabulary while forcing students to link their oral assertions and arguments to their SPAWN texts and other source evidence.

Science

After a series of lessons on stem cells within a broader unit on genes and genetic engineering, Cordell's students had created charts and diagrams using Inspiration software on their iPads. Using these records of learning, Cordell refocused his class on the topic they had been covering from various print and electronic sources. He formed pairs of students and had them respond to one of the five SPAWN writing prompts meant to force his students to use textual evidence in their responses but also to instigate critical thinking about differing perspectives on stem cell research, its medical value and ethics, and the role of government.

- *Special powers*—"The President of the United States has assigned you to be chairman of the committee on funding stem cell research. He has given you full authority to make decisions regarding the funding of stem cell research. How will you use your power?"
- *Problem solving*—"You are the lead researcher in a lab that specializes in stem cell research. Your lab is located in a conservative state. You are offered private funding from a major corporation. What do you do?"
- *Alternative viewpoints*—"You are a journalist who has been assigned to report on a university debate on stem cell research. What do you hear?"
- *What if?*—"What if the federal government decided to provide unlimited funding for stem cell research?"
- *Next*—"Your child has just been in an accident. The doctors say he is paralyzed and will never walk again. However, you have been offered an opportunity to have your child participate in an experimental therapy involving embryonic stem cells. What do you do next?"

A student pair writing to the problem-solving prompt responded in this way:

We will accept private funding; however, we will only conduct experimentation with adult stem cells. We refuse to experiment with embryonic stem cells not only because we are located in a conservative state but because of our own personal beliefs. We believe there is no harm done in extracting adult stem cells from already mature living tissues; there's no harm done to the donor of the stem cells; the recipients who receive the products of their own stem cells will not experience immune rejection. Adult stem cells are proven to be highly beneficial and effective in curing disease. We oppose embryonic stem cell research because we do not agree it is ethical to sacrifice a life to help continue another.

A pair of students writing to the Alternative Viewpoints prompt composes the following:

At this debate we heard opinions from people with different views concerning stem cell research. One group, Group A, supported embryonic stem cell research, and the other group, Group B, supported adult stem cell research.

Group A backed up its opinions by stating how versatile embryonic stem cells can be. They have the ability to form all cell types, such as insulin-secreting cells, nerves and heart cells. Also, embryonic stem cells have the ability to repair cells damaged by a heart attack by forming heart cells, as stated above. They also mentioned that although embryonic stem cell research involves the destruction of human life, it has the potential to cure diseases that could continue the life of another.

Group B defended their stance by saying adult stem research involved no ethical issues because no lives are destroyed. There is low risk to tumor growth and these cells will not be rejected by the immune system. Also, they stated that adult stem cells can be used to treat several major diseases, including leukemia, lymphoma, and some inherited blood disorders.

Each group clearly had interesting and valid information to back up their viewpoints in this debate.

These prompts sampled students' ability to read texts closely, to use their graphic notes on stem cells, and to make logical inferences from them, as well as to cite specific evidence when writing to support conclusions drawn from the texts and notes. This is a critical Common Core literacy standard, and Cordell's students' responses provided evidence of these important reading skills. SPAWN writing challenged his students to combine big, provocative ideas with the specific information on stem cells gleaned from the readings on the topic and their notes.

Biology

Rena uses SPAWN writing because the prompts can be tailored to fit the goals of learning and studying for virtually any topic in her biology curriculum. Exploring articles and reports on recent infectious diseases and epidemic-causing viruses, such as Influenza A, Ebola, and Zika, for a unit labeled Pandemic Alert, Rena's students entered each class session to find a different SPAWN prompt on the board (see Figure 7.1). They were instructed to write to the prompt at different points in the daily lesson depending on the timing of content delivery and other class activities.

S—Special powers	The CDC and the WHO have issued a pandemic alert. The influenza virus has now infected an alarming number of people. The state governments have been given unlimited power in order to contain outbreaks. How will they use this power?
P—Problem solving	A vaccine must be created to halt this deadly viral infection. What stages of viral infection will the vaccine target in order to prevent infection or to stop its transmission? How will this vaccine work?
A—Alternative viewpoints	The government has decided to limit access of the vaccine to children and the elderly. Write a letter from the government to those denied access to the vaccine explaining why they will not receive the vaccine.
W—What if?	What if the influenza virus mutated and the available vaccines are no longer effective? How will state governments prevent transmission of this deadly virus?
N—Next	There is news of a tribe genetically resistant to influenza infections in a remote Alaskan village. What do you think the CDC and the WHO will do next?

FIGURE 7.1. SPAWN prompts for Rena's unit, *Pandemic Alert.*

Varying the writing prompts on a daily basis kept Rena's students attentive and engaged in the readings, class discussions, and other related learning activities.

English Literature

Myung's senior high English literature students were required to write in response to SPAWN prompts while reading and analyzing Shakespeare's *Hamlet, Prince of Denmark*. Myung knew from experience that this intensely complex drama needs her students' full participation if they are to appreciate the depth of meaning, the intricate twist and turns of the plot, and the evocative language. By requiring low-stakes writing at different intervals as they progress through the play, Myung helps make obvious what her students are gleaning from the drama and provides the students themselves with a reflection of their burgeoning understanding of *Hamlet*.

Myung set up a class blog where students could post their responses for comment and write reactions to the responses of their peers. In this way, the network of connections, interpretations, and meaning making were expanded, leading to new perspectives on Hamlet's behavior and insights into his and the other main characters' motivations.

- *Special powers*—"You have given Hamlet special powers to read the mind of the devious Polonius. What would he know and how would that change his actions? What would happen as a result of your change?"
- *Problem solving*—"Hamlet is confronted by a central problem: How does he keep from committing murder himself even while he knows his father has been murdered by Claudius? What could he do to reconcile his feelings?"
- *Alternative viewpoints*—"Retell the events of Hamlet's father's death from King Claudius's point of view. What does he see and do? How does he rationalize his behavior?
- *What if?*—"What if Hamlet followed through with his intent to kill King Claudius? What do you think would happen to Hamlet and for the remainder of the play?"
- *Next*—"Ophelia has just drowned herself. What do you think Hamlet will do next?"

Learning Logs

RAFTed assignments, responses to SPAWN prompts, and virtually all the low-stakes writing students produce should be kept in a central repository or log. The generic name "learning log" can become a science log, math log, or even a civics journal depending on the content area, discipline, and preference of teachers and students. Regardless of the exact name given to the log, the purpose is to use it to record all low-stakes and exploratory writing. This includes "on the spot" reflections, connections, summaries, explanations, critiques, and more that content-area and disciplinary teachers might request any time during a lesson.

Research evidence has shown that students have much to gain from maintaining a learning log (Englert et al., 2009; Koedinger, Corbett, & Perfetti, 2012). For example, students who write in logs have demonstrated higher test performance, the ability to use higher-level reading and thinking strategies, and greater capacity to monitor their understandings.

Clarese, an eighth-grade math teacher, asks her students to write a learning log entry for each unit of study. Her students respond to a variety of open-ended probes designed to stimulate their reflection and provide her with valuable assessment information about their knowledge and possible misconceptions concerning a mathematical concept. For a unit on averages, Clarese begins the lesson by asking the students to answer the following questions:

1. "Where have you heard about averages?"
2. "Who uses averages and for what?"
3. "What is the purpose of averaging?"
4. "What do you know about forming an average?"

As a follow-up to these open-ended probes, Clarese asks her students to share their log entries with their study partners before sharing them with the entire class. Clarese believes that writing activities such as these help her teach more effectively because she learns so much about her students in a short amount of time.

Rosa, a biology teacher, also likes to have her students write in their learning logs before she begins a new unit or lesson. Sometimes she initiates her students' thinking and writing by asking them to preview the next assignment. When students preview a piece of text or selection, they examine the title, headings, subheadings, charts, and summaries. Based on this preview, the biology students then write in the learning logs what they already know or think they know about the topic. After the students read their assignment, Rosa has them write another entry focusing on what they learned, noting any misconceptions in their original log entries, as in the example below related to an article on common diseases such as strokes and heart attacks.

Learning Log Entry before Reading

In this article I'm going to learn about the human brain. I know the brain is split into a right and left half. I think the halves control different things, but I'm not sure what. I also know that when someone has a stroke, blood vessels break in the brain.

Learning Log Entry after Reading

This article mentioned the brain, but it was not the main focus. I learned that the two halves of the brain are called the right and left cerebral hemispheres. But, really, there are four main parts of the brain: the medulla oblongata, the pons, the cerebellum, and the cerebrum. The most important point I learned concerned strokes; they are caused by a blockage in the arteries in the brain. This keeps the brain from getting enough oxygen, and it becomes damaged.

In a similar way to Rosa's students' use of their learning logs, Isaac has his ninth-graders write frequent entries in their logs for nearly everything they read. Using a split-column format, his students write first in the left column what they anticipate the text will be about based on the title and any other available information (e.g., photos, illustrations). As they read and after reading they make an entry in the right column that summarizes what was learned and clarifying anything that was left unclear in the before-reading entry (see Figure 7.2).

As these entries demonstrate, the students were able to use writing as an aid in the process of constructing meaning from text. The first entry served as a reflection of prior knowledge, whereas the second entry allowed the students to reconsider their initial understandings (e.g., the nature of strokes, the details of the process of a presidential impeachment) and derive new understandings based on their reading of the text.

Foster Discipline-Based Writing

I have talked in previous chapters about current theorizing and instructional practices related to reading in the disciplines (Moje, 2008; Shanahan & Shanahan,

Learning Log Entry Before Reading	Learning Log Entry After Reading
This section is "The Impeachment of a President"—I know this has to do with trying to get rid of a president before an election. I think President Clinton was impeached.	I learned that an impeachment of a president is rare. There have only been a four attempts in the history of our nation. Only one actually happened with President Tyler. No president was ever kicked out, though. The process is that a president has done something illegal and the Judiciary Committee will recommend impeachment to the House of Representatives. If they vote for impeachment then the Senate holds a kind of trial of the president. A 2/3rds vote by the Senate means guilty. Then the Senate still has to vote whether to kick the president out.

FIGURE 7.2. Learning log with entries before and after reading.

2008). Just as reading discipline- and domain-specific texts requires specialized approaches and purposes, so too does writing. This is not to say that generic writing strategies cannot be applied across content areas. Indeed, in the previous section, I have described and presented creative and relevant applications of RAFT and SPAWN to various content areas. Later in this chapter you will find additional ways to effectively apply general writing routines to the learning of specific content. Nonetheless, secondary teachers should also be mindful of and plan ways of demonstrating and involving students in writing activities that fit the specific content under study. This type of writing will move students closer to the kind of thinking, problem solving, and communicating engaged in by scientists, historians, mathematicians, engineers, language specialists, and other disciplinary insiders.

Wissinger and De La Paz (2015) point out that virtually every discipline demands the ability to form and defend arguments in writing, though how this looks in the study of the U.S. bicameral system of government may be different than it looks in an exploration of DNA extraction processes from ancient carcasses and bones. To be sure, the Common Core State Standards (CCSSI, 2010), which integrate writing, like reading, into the four major content domains as well as technical subjects, expects students in middle and high school to demonstrate proficiency at composing logical arguments linked to major claims and supported by valid reasoning and pertinent evidence (see the complete list of the anchor CCSS for writing in Figure 7.3).

Moje (2010) describes how a persuasive essay, which might typically be taught to students as a single form applicable across disciplines, actually takes on unique features and purposes depending on the content area. Notice in Figure 7.4 that a persuasive essay in the form of a letter to the editor in social studies differs in significant ways from one students might write in English class or science. To get to the core of disciplinary writing, Moje encourages teachers and their students to ask the following questions:

- "How do members of the discipline use language on a daily basis?"
- "What kinds of texts do they turn to or produce as part of their work?"
- "How are interactions with members of the discipline shaped (or governed by) texts?"
- "Who are the primary audiences for written work in your discipline?"
- "What are the standards demanded by those audiences?"
- "Are there words or phrases that are demanded by or taboo in your discipline?"
- "Are there writing styles that are demanded by or taboo in your discipline?"
- "What is unique about your discipline in terms of reading, writing, speaking, and listening?"

Writing Standards: Grades 6–12 All Subjects

Text Types and Purposes

1. Write arguments to support claims in an analysis of substantive topics or texts using valid reasoning and relevant and sufficient evidence.
2. Write informative/explanatory texts to examine and convey complex ideas and information clearly and accurately through the effective selection, organization, and analysis of content.
3. Write narratives to develop real or imagined experiences or events using effective technique, well-chosen details and well-structured event sequences. (Note: for Grades 6–12 ELA Only)

Production and Distribution of Writing

4. Produce clear and coherent writing in which the development, organization, and style are appropriate to task, purpose, and audience.
5. Develop and strengthen writing as needed by planning, revising, editing, rewriting, or trying a new approach.
6. Use technology, including the Internet, to produce and publish writing and to interact and collaborate with others.

Research to Build and Present Knowledge

7. Conduct short as well as more sustained research projects based on focused questions, demonstrating understanding of the subject under investigation.
8. Gather relevant information from multiple print and digital sources, assess the credibility and accuracy of each source, and integrate the information while avoiding plagiarism.
9. Draw evidence from literary or informational texts to support analysis, reflection, and research.

Range of Writing

10. Write routinely over extended time frames (time for research, reflection, and revision) and shorter time frames (a single sitting or a day or two) for a range of tasks, purposes, and audiences.

FIGURE 7.3. Common Core Anchor Standards related to writing. From the Common Core State Standards Initiative. Copyright © 2010 by the National Governors Association Center for Best Practices and Council of Chief State School Officers. All rights reserved.

Letter to the editor in civics	Essay about a poem for English	Essay for science
Personal opinion or experience; may include argumentation; clear stance; language used to indicate personal opinion	Personal opinion or experiences *and* logical reasoning or illustrative imagery; language used to argue a point or to convey images and experiences	Distanced stance; evidence to support stance; logical reasoning to tie evidence to claim; language used to convey distance and objectivity

FIGURE 7.4. Differences in features of persuasive essay across content areas.

Math

National and most state mathematics standards now emphasize critical thinking in addition to rote calculation; thus instructional practices will need to change to reflect this new degree of rigor. According to the National Council of Teachers of Mathematics' (NCTM) Principles and Standards (2000), wrestling with complex problems, reflecting on thinking, and communicating that mathematical thinking to others is an integral part of learning and studying mathematics. Indeed, the NCTM's communication standards stress the need to develop students' abilities to: (1) organize and consolidate mathematical thinking through communication, (2) communicate mathematical thinking coherently and clearly to peers, teachers and others, (3) analyze and evaluate the mathematical thinking and strategies of others, and (4) use the language of mathematics to express mathematical ideas precisely.

Antwuan gives his math students writing tasks that are tied directly to the content under study. In addition, he emphasizes how writing can relate directly to math-related issues in the real world. For Antwuan, whose inner-city students need, above all, to see the relevance of their learning in order to remain engaged, mathematical thinking is not solely a cognitive activity but also an important life skill. He helps his students come to appreciate this by constantly making connections between mathematical concepts and processes and solving genuine everyday problems with those particular concepts and processing tools. This is a typical type of math writing prompt Antwuan gives his students:

Help Ms. Hicks Save Money on Her Gas Bill

"Ms. Hicks installs new insulation to save money on heating costs, but then learns that her bills have not declined by much from the previous year. Her contractor points out that heating costs have risen and weather has been colder. Ms. Hicks wants to find out how much she has actually saved due to the insulation she installed."

On the basis of the situation described above, Antwuan gives his students additional details about Ms. Hicks's heating bills (rates, units of heat used), temperature changes, and some initial information to help them begin to research "heating degree days" on the Internet. With this information, students are given two tasks:

1. Assess the cost-effectiveness of Ms. Hicks's new insulation and window sealing. In their assessment, they must do the following:
   - Compare Ms. Hicks's gas bills from January 2014 and January 2015.
   - Explain Ms. Hicks's savings after the insulation and sealing.

- Identify circumstances under which Ms. Hicks's January 2015 gas bill would have been at least 10% less than her January 2014 bill.
- Decide if the insulation and sealing work on Ms. Hicks's house was cost-effective and provide evidence for this decision.

2. Create a short e-brochure for gas company customers to guide them in making decisions about increasing the energy efficiency of their homes. The e-brochure must do the following:

- List the quantities that customers need to consider in assessing the cost-effectiveness of energy efficiency measures.
- Generalize the method of comparison used for Ms. Hicks's gas bills with a set of formulas and provide an explanation of the formulas.
- Explain to gas customers how to weigh the cost of energy efficiency measures with savings on their gas bills.

The e-brochures Antwuan's students create using a PDF app called InDesign are made available through links on the class Blackboard site. In this way, he and his students can see all of the brochures, offer comments and suggestions, and check for accuracy in the formulas and explanations. Another benefit of this approach is that it provides students with an audience made up of all their peers in addition to the teacher, who is typically the only reader and evaluator of writing assignments.

English/Language Arts

To stimulate her third-year high school students' abilities to think critically and analytically, Alisha crafts writing assignments with the role of a literary critic firmly in mind. She knows, for example, that insiders to the community of literary criticism write reviews of fiction and nonfiction, compare and contrast multiple texts related to a central theme, and raise questions about and derived from the texts. Alisha also knows that these higher-level thinking processes are called for in the CCSS's reading and writing standards.

After exploring a unit on the immigrant experience in the United States in which Alisha and her class read and analyzed short stories, poems, novels, and essays from authors and literary critics representing Asian American, Hispanic American, African American, Jewish American, and Arab American perspectives, Alisha challenged her students with a culminating assignment based on the following prompt:

"Imagine that you are editing an online digital anthology for 11th graders entitled, 'Multiculturalism in 21st-Century America.' Your job is to prepare the introduction to this anthology. In your introduction, please do the following things:

1. Decide which texts you want to include and in which order (you must include at least six texts). Texts can include books, poems, songs, short stories, essays, photographs, articles, films, television shows, or Internet media. The six texts must represent at least two different perspectives and must include at least two different types of text (e.g., print text, visual media, audio media, multimedia, digital media).
2. Identify and discuss different perspectives on the multiculturalism in America represented in the six texts you selected.
3. Write a short paragraph about each text, in which you make clear why you have included it and how it relates to the other texts in your anthology.
4. Propose a set of questions to focus readers as they consider the perspectives represented in these texts."

As with all of her "graded" writing assignments, Alisha created space for her students to collaborate during drafting stages of their compositions. Groups of students worked together to brainstorm potential texts, plan, draft, revise, and edit their pieces comparing and contrasting different perspectives on multiculturalism, their paragraphs relating the texts selected for the anthology, and the critical questions for readers. This process resulted in more thoughtful and carefully crafted compositions that adhered to expectations of the prompt.

Science

Ivana lived the life of a scientist before becoming a high school teacher, so she understands the actual responsibilities of that profession and the kinds of communication skills required to be successful in the field. She knows, for instance, that with respect to writing, scientists need to be able to explain and describe technical terminology, document experiments and results, and advocate certain positions and theories based on available evidence. Armed with this insider knowledge, she makes sure that her biology students' iPads are always at hand for low-stakes writing and notetaking as they navigate through labs, observe documentaries and video of national and international experts, and conduct Internet searches. Ivana has found that, when her students faithfully document, react, pose questions, and propose explanations through writing, their bigger end-of-unit written assignments are of higher quality.

Performance on one such assignment at the conclusion of a unit on understanding causes of and treating infections depended on how faithfully Ivana's students kept written records of their evolving understanding of the topic over the previous 3 weeks. During that time the class read, analyzed, and discussed several related articles and technical reports; had a Skype interview with a Centers for Disease Control (CDC) researcher studying the new and growing strain of bacteria resistant to last-resort antibiotics; conducted lab experiments with bacteria; and explored numerous websites for up-to-date information and video on scientists' infection-fighting tools. Ivana's culminating activity was designed to tap the knowledge and skills her students acquired from the unit study. To do so, she gave them the following prompt:

> "When scientists attempt to find medications to fight against infectious agents, the term *drug design* is often used.
>
> 1. Explain what is meant by this term.
>
> "Scientists aim to develop a drug against a particular virus that infects humans. The virus has a protein coat, and different parts of the coat play different roles in the infective cycle. Some sites assist in the attachment of the virus to a host cell; others are important in the release from a host cell. The structure is represented in the following diagram:

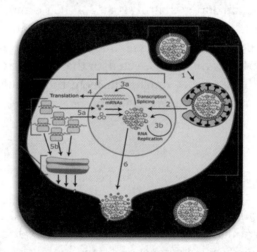

> "The virus reproduces by attaching itself to the surface of a host cell and injecting its DNA into the host cell. The viral DNA then uses the components of the host cell to reproduce its parts, and hundreds of new viruses bud off from the host cell. Ultimately the host cell dies.
>
> 2. Design a drug that will be effective against this virus. In your answer, outline the important aspects you would need to consider. Outline how your drug would prevent continuation of the cycle of reproduction of the virus particle. Use diagrams in your answer. Space for diagrams is provided on the next page.
> 3. Before a drug is used on humans, it is usually tested on animals. In this case, the virus under investigation also infects mice. Design an experiment, using mice, to test the effectiveness of the drug you have designed."

As was typical for large assignments at the end of a unit, Ivana allowed her students to work in teams, in this case in groups of three, to complete this assignment. She awards a group grade and individual grades based on an honest description of each member's level of participation.

Evaluating disciplinary writing necessitates rubrics that match the form and purposes of writing within particular content areas. For example, ninth-grade science teacher Connie assesses final drafts of her students' written explanations of scientific phenomena or problems using the rubric in Figure 7.5. She emphasizes instruction through modeling explanation writing, sharing quality examples, and engaging her classes in process writing with peer support. Through these approaches,

	Level 1	Level 2	Level 3
Makes a claim about the problem.	Does not make a claim or makes an inaccurate claim.	Makes a claim that reveals partial understanding. The claim may include accurate and inaccurate details, or it may omit important details.	Makes an accurate claim.
Provides evidence for the claim.	Does not provide evidence or provides inaccurate evidence for the claim.	Provides some accurate evidence for the claim but not sufficient. (May include some inaccurate evidence for the claim.)	Provide accurate and sufficient evidence for the claim.
Provides reasoning that links evidence to the claim.	Does not provide reasoning or provides rationale that does not link evidence to the claim.	Provides some reasoning that links evidence to the claim, but the rationale is not sufficient. (May include rationale that does not link evidence to the claim.)	Provides sufficient reasoning that links the evidence to the claim. (May use linking words like *because, so,* and *therefore* to make the connection.)
Uses precise and accurate scientific language.	Does not use scientific language or uses scientific language inaccurately.	Uses some scientific language correctly, but some may be incorrect or imprecise.	Uses precise and accurate scientific language.
Is written clearly (anyone interested in science almost anywhere can understand it).	Is not written clearly; does not provide contextual details.	Is written relatively clearly. (May include only some of the necessary contextual details, or may include both necessary and unnecessary details.)	Is written clearly; focuses on a particular phenomenon; includes all necessary contextual details (and no unnecessary details).

FIGURE 7.5. Rubric for evaluating scientific explanation writing.

her students learn how to (1) make claims about a scientific phenomenon or problem, such as global warming or plate tectonics; (2) provide evidence for the claim; (3) provide reasoning that links evidence to the claim; (4) use precise and accurate scientific language; and (5) write clearly.

Promote Real Writing with Real Audiences

I have stressed repeatedly in this chapter that the writing we ask students to do in school should help them learn to write to a variety of specific genuine audiences, instead of for insular academic purposes. A writing task, such as crafting a five-paragraph essay, that satisfies a curriculum standard but that only the teacher will read and evaluate does little to foster the perception of students that writing can be used for authentic and meaningful communication. In the school-based literacy practicum I teach for graduate students, we often ask the children and adolescents being tutored what they perceive as real reading and real writing. Not surprisingly, many do not think of magazine, comic book, or graphic novel reading as "real" reading. Nor do they consider texting, emailing, tweeting, or writing comics as "real" writing. This perception is due in large measure to how school defines reading and writing for youth as exclusively academically based. From this perspective, academic writing and reading are meant to prepare students for more academic reading and writing. In light of this curriculum-entrenched view, consider Yancey's (2009) assertions that

> 21st century writing marks the beginning of a new era in literacy, a period we might call the Age of Composition, a period where composers become composers not through direct and formal instruction alone (if at all), but rather through what we might call an extracurricular social co-apprenticeship. (p. 5)

Clearly, we must do a better job of preparing youth for writing in the real world. One way to do this is to target student writing to public audiences (Yancey, 2009).

Science

A medium for students' public-based writing on the Internet is the electronic magazine—e-zine, or just zine (pronounced *zeen*). Zines are electronic publications created by individuals and classes as alternatives to commercial magazines (Koh, 2008). As independent media, they represent the ideas and vision of their creators, called *zinesters* (Guzzetti, Campbell, Duke, & Irving, 2003; Poletti, 2008). Already there are hundreds of these cyber-creations available on the Web covering every imaginable area of interest, with a growing number designed and composed by young adults (Knobel & Lankshear, 2002; Lang, 2012).

Irene's third-block general science class comprised 22 freshmen, 12 of whom were receiving special education services and all of whom resided in the inner-city neighborhood around the school. To maximize motivation and engagement, she worked tirelessly to make the learning personally meaningful and relevant to the students' lives and futures. In fact, the inspiration for a science class zine grew out of a project tied to one of the class topics, viral diseases. Working collaboratively with her students, Irene helped them explore the extent of diseases such as AIDS and hepatitis in their own community. The class began their investigation by doing Internet-based searches of local newspapers and conducting phone interviews. With Irene's support, students organized a panel of community volunteers, patients, social workers, and experts to dialogue with class and guests on the relationships between viral diseases and conditions of poverty, malnutrition, poor health care, race, gang violence, teen pregnancy, and other factors. Her students videotaped the panel discussion and later, when they were replaying it, realized they had something quite special and worthy of sharing with a much wider audience. Since theirs was a technology high school, endowed with state-of-the-art computer labs, high-speed Internet connections, and plenty of innovative software, Irene knew the technology infrastructure would support sophisticated Internet publishing. Her students loved the idea, so they all went to work.

Irene began by assigning the class into teams to tackle different parts of the project. One team focused on the technology; another, the content; and a third, promotional and advertising concerns. The content group operated in much the same way students do when they publish a school newspaper. They wrote informational stories, editorials, events summaries, and public information announcements all based on their work during the study of viral diseases, including, of course, the wealth of information gathered from the panelists. The technology group helped Irene create and design the class zine. Using Adobe PageMaker, they first formatted the zine for regular content, including columns for articles. Next, they experimented with onscreen palettes to find the right logos to drag onto the documents and colors to make the product visually appealing. The advertising group spent time brainstorming a title for the zine and ways of ensuring that an audience of potential readers would be aware that it was available. Among all of the interesting titles this group pitched to the rest of the class, "Science in the City" was the one that clicked. The class decided to publish three more editions during the balance of the school year focusing on major units: environmental pollution, human reproduction, and fueling and maintaining the human machine.

With the launching of "Science in the City," Irene's class had a new and entirely deserved sense of pride about their learning. More important, they developed a heightened sense of responsibility and accountability that comes with producing a zine, improved research skills, writing and spelling skills, and critical thinking skills.

Civics

Becka's seventh-grade social studies curriculum emphasizes civics. Therefore, her goal has been to raise consciousness among her students about the challenges and responsibilities of active citizenship. An ideal opportunity for this kind of con-sciousness raising came along when Becka learned of an upcoming Washington, DC, continental congress concerning becoming an official state of the union. She decided to turn this into an authentic writing experience for her students. The proposed District of Columbia's state constitution was made available online for public input. As Becka and her students were residents of the District of Columbia, they approached reading and analyzing the details of the constitution and the new responsibilities outlined for its citizens with an added level of engagement. Becka guided them in brainstorming, formulating, refining, and eventually uploading sug-gested amendments available on the website through texting, Skyping, email, Ins-tagram, tweets, and other e-communication platforms. In this way, she exploited the students' interest in and competencies with digital media while ensuring that they produced clear, polished compositions before putting them before the public (Andrews & Smith, 2011; Wolsey & Grisham, 2012).

Reading

Hermalinda is another teacher who strives to keep her struggling readers engaged in the texts they read and write by connecting these to issues and events relevant to adolescents. For example, while reading Walter Dean Myers's (2004) Monster, she prompted her students to research why young people turn to delinquency. Herma-linda structured a WebQuest (Barnes, Marateo, & Ferris, 2007; Halat, 2008; Salso-vic, 2009) as a guide to online sites, reports, and articles on the topic. These served as a valuable resource for current facts, trends, analysis of causes, and successful prevention and treatment programs. When a question came up in their conversa-tion or reading that seemed to require an immediate answer, they consulted sites and links in the WebQuest. Through this process, for instance, they discovered that youth crime has actually been on the decline since the mid-1990s, in contrast to a widespread public perception that it is ever increasing. They also found statisti-cal documentation that youth of color are processed in the juvenile justice system in numbers far out of proportion relative to their white peers. This issue came up when they were reading a newspaper article about a 14-year-old African American boy convicted of murdering his teacher in Florida.

Shortly into Monster, Hermalinda and her students realized that virtually all the issues of juvenile crime and justice were embodied in the experiences of the main character and narrator, Steve Harmon. Steve, a teenager and aspiring scriptwriter who is accused of complicity in a murder, tells the story of his experience from arrest through trial verdict in the form of a film score. This unique perspective draws the reader into the details of his life in a way that evokes empathy, disgust, suspicion, and finally vindication. Hermalinda's students were drawn in from the very first page.

As they read Monster together, Hermalinda and her class kept an e-journal of their reactions to critical questions that arose during conversation and discussion.

For example, she asked them to compare and contrast how the American legal system is portrayed in the novel with what they were learning about it from the WebQuest sources. To do this, Hermalinda taught her students how to employ a split-page approach, putting direct quotes and brief descriptions in one column and what they learned about youths' treatment in juvenile court and detention in the other. At one point in the book, Steve says "The best time to cry is at night, when the lights are out and someone is being beaten up and screaming for help." The students put this in their journal, then recorded a description from one of their WebQuest readings of a juvenile offender remembering his own crying at night once he realized for the first time he was behind bars and would be for the next 2 years.

Another interesting writing activity Hermalinda employed with her students while reading *Monster* was to have them assume the identities of different figures in the courtroom and compose arguments based on the scenes of the trial and details of the case from those points of view. One group of students chose to look at the events in one chapter from the perspective of Mr. Petrocelli, a witness for the prosecution, while the group pretended to represent O'Brien, Steve's attorney. They presented their written arguments orally, asserting that most of the jurors saw a teenage Black kid and assumed he was guilty, even if they didn't tell the lawyers that upfront. One of the students in the group, responding as if he were Petrocelli, said that all the kids involved in the fatal shooting were equally guilty; that included the one who took the cigarettes, the one who wrestled the gun from the convenience store owner, and Steve, the one who made sure the coast was clear.

At the conclusion of *Monster* and related readings on juvenile crime, Hermalinda's students felt so strongly about what they believed was the unfair treatment of minors in the criminal justice system that she urged them to express their feelings in some way that might influence lawmakers. This led to further research, taking them online to find information on their district's state representatives' policy positions related to youth crime. Their search uncovered some interesting facts. While both representatives had cosponsored a youth advocacy task force, they also voted in favor of trying minors as adults, and one even supported legislation to make the death penalty an option for minors found guilty of capital murder. Hermalinda formed several small teams of writers to compose an email letter to make their case to these legislators. The composition process itself necessitated discussion and work on form, punctuation, and grammar, as well as finding statistics and quotes from the various articles and books they had accumulated during their exploration of the topic. Hermalinda observed a level of enthusiasm for this effort unlike any she had seen from her class before. Even though their sense of empowerment was diluted once the students received a perfunctory reply from their state representatives, stating that they appreciated the students' input and asking them to continue to remain engaged in the political process, Hermalinda's students remained proud of themselves for doing it.

Use Evidence-Based Principles to Guide Writing Activities

In compiling the major report *Writing Next*, Graham and Perin (2007) scoured the research literature on writing for adolescents and found substantial evidence to support 11 elements (see Figure 7.6). The researchers make clear that these elements are broad enough to account for a variety of specific instructional practices. For example, the different studies that were found to have significant positive effects related to the 11th element, *writing for content learning*, approached writing to learn in the content areas in several different ways. In fact, virtually all of the strategies and practices described in this chapter can be identified as expressions of one or more of the 11 evidence-based elements in this important report.

Social Studies

In the *Writing Next* report, summarization was the element ranked second among all 11 elements based on the overall level of significance among all the studies reviewed in this category. Summarizing was found to be a highly effective approach to improving student writing and reading. (In Chapter 9, I present summarizing strategies for improving text reading.) As stated above, summarization, like all the elements, represents a category of different specific instructional approaches. One

---

1. *Writing strategies*—teaching students strategies for planning, revising, and editing their compositions
2. *Summarization*—explicitly and systematically teaching students how to summarize texts
3. *Collaborative writing*—using instructional arrangements in which adolescents work together to plan, draft, revise, and edit their compositions
4. *Specific product goals*—assigning students specific, reachable goals for the writing they are to complete
5. *Word processing*—using computers and word processors as instructional supports for writing assignments
6. *Sentence combining*—teaching students to construct more complex, sophisticated sentences
7. *Prewriting*—engaging students in activities designed to help them generate or organize ideas for their compositions
8. *Inquiry activities*—engaging students in analyzing immediate, concrete data to help them develop ideas and content for a particular writing task
9. *Process writing approach*—interweaving a number of writing instructional activities in a workshop environment that stresses extended writing opportunities, writing for authentic audiences, personalized instruction, and cycles of writing
10. *Study of models*—providing students with opportunities to read, analyze, and emulate models of good writing
11. *Writing for content learning*—using writing as a tool for learning content material

---

FIGURE 7.6. Eleven elements of effective writing instruction. Based on Graham and Perin (2007).

such approach that matches the goals of this element by explicitly and systematically teaching students how to summarize texts is the GIST strategy.

GIST as an acronym stands for Generating Interaction between Schemata and Text (Frey, Fisher, & Hernandez, 2003); as a general term, *gist* means the essence of a text or speech. As a text summarization strategy, it involves systematically reducing the ideas and significant details of text to a preset number of words, such as 15, 20, or 25, depending on the length of the text being summarized. For example, with a paragraph composed of four sentences, the first sentence is summarized within the predetermined word limit, and then, after the second sentence is read, the initial summary is revised to incorporate new information and to delete less important information, all the while keeping the GIST within the predetermined word limit. This process continues for the remaining sentences until one final GIST for the entire paragraph using the set number of words is completed.

Benita decided to teach her seventh-grade social studies students the GISTing strategy because they tended to either produce too little, as in one sentence for an entire article, or too much, as in trying to copy nearly all the words of a paragraph. Her goal was to help her students use their inferencing and paraphrasing skills to condense paragraphs and texts so the summary contained essential information at an appropriate length. She began instruction of the GIST strategy by going through the following sequence of steps:

1. She distributed copies of a short text, *Julius Caesar: The Roman Ruler You Never Knew,* composed of four paragraphs of one page total.

2. She explained the GIST strategy, telling her students they would read a passage about Julius Caesar and write a sentence that summarized the "gist" of the passage. At the end of the text, students would have written one GIST sentence for each of the four paragraphs, or a concise summary of the text.

3. She introduced the *Julius Caesar* text by building prior knowledge and discussing key vocabulary.

4. She projected on the whiteboard 15 blank lines to represent 15 words spaced out in a sequence like a sentence, explaining the significance of the lines and how the goal was to reduce each paragraph of the *Julius Caesar* passage to a 15-word sentence.

5. She read aloud the first sentence of the first paragraph while students read along silently and then led the class in a discussion about important ideas and details from the sentence, writing a sentence to capture their ideas on the board in the 15 spaces.

6. She moved to the next sentence and repeated this process of reading aloud and inviting students to identify the important information. She then invited the class to review the first sentence of 15 words and decide what could remain and what could be deleted in order to include the new important information from the second sentence. Eventually, she wrote a second sentence on the whiteboard in the 15 spaces that included ideas and facts from both the first and second sentences.

7. She continued the process for the third and for the fourth and final sentence of the first paragraph about Julius Caesar. The result was a single sentence of 15 words that included something important from each of the four sentences. This, she told her class, was a GIST.

8. She then asked her students to work with a partner and attempt to make a GIST statement for the next paragraph in the passage by using the same process of GISTing one sentence at a time of no more than 15 words for each of the sentences until a final GIST statement of no more than 15 words was derived. (See Figure 7.7 for all the GIST statements and the final GIST.)

Benita continued to model and elicit the GISTing process throughout the following weeks to reinforce the newly learned skill with the ultimate goal of preparing

---

Julius Caesar: The Roman Ruler You Never Knew

Julius Caesar was famous as a statesman, a general, and an author, but he was also renowned in other ways, including for being a traffic engineer. Ancient traffic jams were so acute in the marketplace of Imperial Rome and around the Circus Maximus that he imposed a ban on all chariots and ox carts for ten hours after sunrise. Only pedestrians were allowed into the streets and markets. Caesar also found it necessary to abolish downtown parking and establish one-way streets.

Gist after sentence 1:

   Julius   Caesar   was   famous   for   many   things   including   traffic   engineer.
   _____   _____   _____   _____   _____

Gist after sentences 1 and 2:

   As   traffic   engineer   Julius   Caesar   banned   chariots   and   ox carts   from
   Rome   during   the   daytime.

Gist after sentences 1, 2, and 3:

   As   traffic   engineer   Julius   Caesar   banned   all   but   pedestrians   from
   Rome   during   the   daytime. _____

Gist after sentences 1, 2, 3, and 4 (final paragraph gist statement):

   As   Rome's   traffic   engineer   Julius   Caesar   allowed   only   pedestrians,
   created   one-way   streets,   and   banned   parking.

FIGURE 7.7. Example of a GIST strategy using a paragraph about Julius Caesar.

her students to create GISTs automatically when they read. Eventually, she guided students in constructing summaries without having to GIST each sentence of a paragraph; instead, Benita gathered overall GISTs for sections of text by having her students combine essential information from summary statements made from several paragraphs. Through a gradual release approach over the course of a few months, Benita was able to effect a level of transfer of summarization thinking by her students for most texts they encountered throughout the year (Ambrose et al., 2010). Furthermore, they came to realize that writing GISTs provided them a reflection of their increasingly accurate summary thinking.

Sociology

Threaded discussions create a digital space for students to communicate in writing to a broader audience than solely the teacher, though teachers can and often do participate in these discussions. This type of writing also capitalizes on another important evidence-based element from *Writing Next*—collaborative writing. As a form of electronic communication, threaded discussions, along with classroom blogging, promote collaboration and interaction among students by providing an environment for recording responses and engaging in critical dialogue over relevant issues in disciplinary texts and content (Arend, 2009; Ellison & Wu, 2008; English, 2007; Sawmiller, 2010).

Using the Google Classroom app (*www.google.com/edu*), Holli and her eighth-grade students carried out a threaded discussion based on opinionnaire statements (Fisher, Brozo, Frey, & Ivey, 2015; Zoghi, Mustapha, & Maasum, 2010) related to an article on teen alcohol abuse. (To refresh your memory of opinionnaires, see Chapter 3.) Figure 7.8 presents excerpts from the online threaded discussion about that statement that took place in the Google Classroom space among the students and between Holli and her students. The discussion is based on the opening entry by Holli, which is the first opinionnaire statement among several Holli posted as prompts for the discussion.

What is immediately recognizable in this threaded discussion are the rich and considered responses made by students. This was possible because, instead of controlling the lesson, Holli granted her students the freedom to take advantage of the discussion platform to write ideas and reactions and build knowledge about the topic of teen alcohol abuse through communication and collaboration with their peers.

English

Another instructional approach that fosters collaborate writing, an important Writing Next evidence-based element, is blogging. Blogging began as a self-publishing movement for those who wanted to express opinions in an open online forum. Blogs

This is an online opinionnaire to be used for an article we will be reading on teen alcohol abuse. All sixth-grade students should post their responses to and explanation for each statement from the opinionnaire. If someone posts a response different from yours, please respond to the sender. Be sure to post any comments, personal opinions, and guesses related to the upcoming article. Once you have read the article, post new responses.

The content frame shows the title of all articles posted to the discussion. When you select a title it will load the corresponding article into this frame.

You should also feel free to:

- Post a new article and start a new thread
- Search the articles for a particular word or phrase

Remember also that each article has links to let you continue the thread and navigate the article list.

Please post your reactions to the following opinion statements and tell why.

From: Holli   **Date:** 10/14/05   **Time:** 10:15:11 A.M.

Alcohol must not be really bad for teens otherwise kids in Europe wouldn't be allowed to drink beer and wine just like the adults.

From: Dez   **Date:** 10/14/05   **Time:** 10:47:03 A.M.

I've heard of that. Don't real young kids get to drink with their parents, like in Italy and France? So maybe if we grew up drinking with our families we wouldn't want to get drunk as teenagers.

From: Truann   **Date:** 10/14/05   **Time:** 1:04:32 P.M.

I disagree with the statement and with Dez. I think kids who drink probably grow up to be even worse drinkers. Alcohol is a drug that's in your body all the time if you drink *every* day.

From: Truann   **Date:** 10/15/05   **Time:** 3:01:55 P.M.

The article agrees with my opinion and not the statement. Teenagers in Europe abuse alcohol just as much as teens do in America. It says that in some countries like Finland and Russia teenagers are the worst drinkers of all.

From: Holli   **Date:** 10/15/05   **Time:** 3:22:41 P.M.

I remember on a trip I took to Scandinavia a few years ago how surprised I was to see so many young people overdrinking in public. During the summer it stays light well into the evening, as late as 10:00 or 11 PM, so teenagers stay out *very* late. Do you think teens around the world abuse alcohol because they're trying to act like adults and because of peer pressure?

From: Fareed   **Date:** 10/15/05   **Time:** 3:27:13 P.M.

Adults abuse alcohol so kids do too. That's what we see so why do adults expect us to be any different?

From: Corinne   **Date:** 10/16/05   **Time:** 8:42:38 P.M.

I agree with Fareed. How can parents' and teachers say don't drink when they drink? I'll bet *everyone* in this class has beer or wine at home. It's like smoking, too. Parents always tell their kids, "Don't smoke" but then smoke. I think kids won't drink if they have parents who don't drink.

FIGURE 7.8. Excerpts from a threaded discussion based on opinionnaire statements.

are frequent, chronological publications of thoughts and Web links that often mix what is happening in a person's life and what is happening on the Web. In this way, blogs are kinds of hybrid diary/guide sites, with as many unique types of blogs as there are people (Williams & Merten, 2008). With new automated publishing systems tailored to school-based blogging, such as Edublog.com, Kidblog.com, and WordPress.org, it is now easier than ever for teachers and students to set up their own sites, and, consequently, blogging has now become a powerful communications tool in all the disciplines.

Blogging is the process of writing and publishing to a blog. Blogs have been variously described as public records of private thoughts that can be updated (Williams & Merten, 2008) and as journal-type entries published on public hosting websites (Mazur & Kozarian, 2010). Their uniqueness as a communication tool is best captured in this description by Kennedy (2003): "Unlike most Web sites, which generally combine static and dynamic features, a blog is produced with an active writer in mind, one who creates in an online writing space designed to communicate an identity, a personality, and most importantly, a point of view" (p. 11).

Because blogs emphasize publishing and are theoretically accessible to anyone online, especially when they are linked to social media sites such as Facebook, Twitter, and Pinterest, they encourage ownership of and responsibility for content, heighten youths' sense of audience, and build agency in writing (Alvermann, 2010).

Richard is among the growing number of educators exploring the literacy and learning potential of blogs in his high school English classroom. Using the Web-based blogging tool Livejournal.com, he has developed a class blog to which all student work is exclusively posted. In fact, it has evolved into a totally paperless course, with writing and critiques on the blog. For instance, in journalism, his students work collaboratively to select possible stories from online newspapers to include in the appropriate blog department. These are further vetted by Richard and the department editors until the best stories of the day are selected. Along with posting daily stories, students also write about them, expressing their reactions, opinions, and related experiences. This discussion feature of the journalism class blog has been found to be one of the most helpful tools for building writing confidence and editing skills.

In his American literature class, students blog in response to the books and stories they read. These include commentary, criticism, and artistic interpretations of important fictional events and images. Since the blog is accessible to the vast audience of the Internet, parents and local writers and poets are invited to join the discussion, forming a book club of cyber proportions. When the class read Sue Monk Kidd's (2002) *The Secret Life of Bees*, Richard was able to entice Kidd to make a virtual appearance at their site, where students asked her questions about the novel and other aspects of being a writer.

Richard is always on the lookout for ways of collaborating with virtual and professional communities. By forging links with one of the local universities, he now has college journalism and English majors serving as volunteer editors and mentors for the class blogs. This arrangement is mutually beneficial in that the university students learn more about digital tools for promoting writing while providing general encouragement of these adolescent writers and considered critique of their blogged text.

Since Richard has been using blogging in his classes, he has seen important ways in which the process is contributing to students' understanding of writing. Not only are they developing more thoughtful and critical understandings of the news stories and fictional pieces they read, but they are also approaching their own compositions from the stance of a reader. This new positioning in the writing process keeps them ever mindful of the need to express themselves clearly and communicate meaningfully to a broad audience.

Case Study Revisited

At the beginning of this chapter, I described the problems that Dave was experiencing in his first year of teaching biology to his students, many of whom were struggling and disengaged. You probably have some suggestions on how he could use writing to motivate his students to become more active participants in the learning of biology. Write your suggestions now.

After talking to the English teacher and doing some of his own research and planning, Dave decided to spark his students' interest in the environment unit in several ways. He began the unit with an activity designed to assess his students' present attitudes toward the environment. The students were expecting another lecture and textbook assignment when they entered class on the second day of the unit. Instead, they were greeted with rapper Prince Ea's YouTube video "Man vs Earth," with its powerful message about environmental degradation, climate change, and animal extinctions. When the video concluded, Dave projected the following on the whiteboard:

> Respond as completely as possible. There are no right or wrong answers, so express yourself freely.
>
> 1. How did the video make you feel?
> 2. What message did you take away from the video?
> 3. Is there a place outdoors that you especially like to go? Where? Why?
> 4. Have you ever thought or read or heard about the ideas in the video? If so, explain.

Dave read his students' responses and during class the next day initiated a discussion before he revealed the overall objective of the unit. That is, he wanted his students to localize and personalize the issue of the environment and reinforce for his students the personal impact they can have on reversing environmental degradation. To do so, he first engaged the class in brainstorming what they could do to help improve problems with environmental pollution, global warming, and endangered species. Among the many interesting suggestions was to write letters to legislators. This idea quickly took hold, and Dave helped students write a letter to one of their senators or representatives.

He allowed each student to work with a partner for this activity, which involved Internet research of legislators' email addresses. Local environmental and wildlife writing teams were given time to begin their rough drafts. He asked students to post these drafts on the class Blackboard site and encouraged everyone to read and respond to the drafts. This input, along with Dave's own revisionary assistance to each writing pair, improved all of the letters. Dave attached his students' letters to his own emails to either a senator or representative, explaining the intent of the assignment and urging replies to the specific issues raised in the letters. Within a week, responses arrived, which Dave posted to the Blackboard site. Many students were unsatisfied with the lack of specifics in the emails from the legislators, so they continued to research each of their particular positions and voting records on environmental issues. This led to follow-up letters with questions, which eventually resulted in more detailed responses from the legislators' offices.

LOOKING BACK, LOOKING FORWARD

In this chapter I made the case that the writing process can be a powerful tool for students' content-area and disciplinary learning. Writing, like reading, is a constructive process that can stimulate passive learners to become active learners as they negotiate meanings and reflect on burgeoning understandings.

I emphasized the known benefits of writing as a process of literacy growth and knowledge development. I demonstrated that writing helps students (1) prepare for reading assignments and class activities, (2) summarize and organize information and concepts and monitor comprehension, and (3) think critically and creatively. Based on these important evidence-based outcomes, I described and exemplified a variety of writing strategies and practices that promote the writing-to-learn habit, that create contexts for meaningful communication with authentic audiences through writing, and that capitalize on aspects of writing inherent in the digital media that youth today navigate and contribute to daily.

CHAPTER 8 ▰▰▰▰▰▰▰▰▰▰

Reading and Learning from Multiple Sources

As you read Chapter 8, reflect on the following questions:

- What print and digital sources in addition to the course textbook can be integrated into disciplinary content lessons?

- What is the theoretical rationale for integrating multiple text sources into the content-area classroom?

- How can multiple sources be used as effective schema and interest builders?

- How can secondary teachers organize classrooms and topics to take full advantage of multiple sources?

- What role can graphic novels play in enriching disciplinary teaching and learning?

- In what ways can disciplinary teachers blend instruction of multiple sources with textbooks to help ensure that students are more actively involved in reading and learning?

In my first year out of the University of North Carolina's teacher education program, I took a job as an English/language arts teacher in rural South Carolina. The student body of this first- through 12th-grade school was all African American, a product of de facto segregation and "white flight" common in the period right after school integration. I recall vividly, 40 years later, how I embarked on this challenge with enthusiasm, ready to put into place the creative and student-centered instructional practices I had learned in my previous 2 years in Chapel Hill.

My zeal quickly faded, however, when I discovered that a new literature anthology and grammar book were the required texts in my 10th- and 11th-grade classes.

I remember walking around the room placing the massive literature textbooks on each students' desk, trying to be upbeat about the plays, stories, poems, and essays inside. Just as I passed William's desk, however, I heard a loud slam and turned around to see his book on the floor. While the rest of the class laughed and snickered, I picked the book up and placed it back on William's desk, when he leaned in close to my ear to say "I can't read." Here was this 6-foot-7-inch hulking 17-year-old 11th grader, star of the school's basketball team, admitting to me that it was futile to expect him to read and learn from the shiny new textbook. Within the next couple of weeks I learned that several other students were reading at levels far too low to use the literature anthology profitably.

This situation turned out to be fortuitous for me, because I was able to convince my principal and lead English teacher to allow me to bring in alternative sources to ensure that my most struggling readers had accessible and engaging texts. We had the most fun reading Alice Childress's (1973) *A Hero Ain't Nothin' but a Sandwich*, about Benjie, a 13-year-old junkie. I read the book aloud and embedded impromptu readers' theater, reading strategies for main ideas and details, and asked my students to explore linkages between their worlds and Benjie's through reader response writing, role plays, and debates.

I can't claim to have transformed William into an excited, competent reader, but he did pick up *Hero* after we had covered it as a class and made his way through it on his own. He told me it was the only book he had ever read cover to cover. Unfortunately, the last I saw of William was his looming frame hanging out downtown with other known potheads and druggies after he dropped out of school. I'm happy to report that several others of my students went on to college, though; three of them surprised me in my office at the University of South Carolina a couple of years later when they knocked on my door and told me they were now students there. We reminisced about 10th- and 11th-grade English class and the memories of reading young adult books, magazine and newspaper articles, and other texts I had to incorporate into the classes to make them more enticing and meaningful to my students.

My commitment to expanding the range of text options for middle and high school teachers and students has never waned. In this chapter I ask disciplinary teachers to take a new look at the possibilities for teaching using a variety of texts. I do so because in typical upper-grade classrooms today there remain two ever-present, authoritative information sources—the teacher and the textbook (Shanahan et al., 2011; Walker & Bean, 2002). Yet youth of the digital age have access to and facility with a wide array of richly informative print and multimedia sources. Furthermore, it has been asserted that providing content in a variety of forms of representation increases students' abilities to think and communicate using different symbol systems (Daisey, 2012; Goldman, 2012; Melinee, 2014).

I know from my own experiences and those of my innovative middle and high school colleagues that when alternative sources are given legitimacy in history, science, math, literature, and the other content classrooms, youth benefit from their unique perspectives on topics. I further maintain that these sources, although they are going largely untapped in traditional school settings, may hold the key to engaging adolescents in meaningful reading and learning, as well as elevating their achievement.

The guiding principle that informs this chapter is that secondary students should receive their first serious look at different cultures, historical eras and events, politics, and scientific advances of the human race through a variety of interesting media in addition to content-area textbooks. Because of the demands of limited space, adoption committees, and readability constraints, textbook publishers often present a distilled version of content-area information. Emphasis is placed on important facts, broad views, pivotal characters, and general effects on whole populations, resulting inevitably in a detached tone and dry material.

At the same time, however, I recognize that for many American middle school and high classes a core textbook remains the designated information source. In this chapter I do not advocate suppression of textbooks but the inclusion of alternative sources to enrich teaching and learning in the content classroom. Such sources as (1) young adult literature, (2) graphic novels, (3) primary documents, (4) newspapers, magazines, and real-world reading material, and (5) a variety of multimedia have the potential to transform bland, textbook-centered learning environments into exciting venues for authentic exploration of disciplinary topics.

Case Study

Linda is a high school teacher who has two junior-level American history classes. In planning a unit on immigration to the United States, she established three primary goals. First, she wanted her students to recognize and appreciate that the United States is made up of immigrants from virtually every country of the world who have played a role in the creation of our country and our culture. Second, she wanted her students to recognize, explain, and describe the concept of cultural diversity and determine the advantages and challenges that cultural diversity has brought to this country. Finally, she wanted her students to recognize that immigration is an ongoing part of America's history that contributes to an ever-evolving American identity. During the year, the class discussed immigration several times as it related to various eras of our country's history, from colonial times through global migrations to the United States in the 20th century and continuing today.

To the reader: As you read and work through this chapter on the use of multiple sources to improve content learning, consider ways in which Linda could incorporate a variety of print and nonprint texts into her unit in order to meet her goals. Think about how the strategies described and those from your own experience and imagination could be applied to the teaching of a unit on immigration.

COMMON TYPES OF MULTIPLE SOURCES TO ENRICH THE CONTENT CLASSROOM

In this section I describe several common alternative text and media sources that disciplinary teachers have made use of in their instruction.

Young Adult Literature

Within textbook treatments of cultures, social movements, historical eras, and scientific advances lie richly detailed stories about the people who made them or who watched them being made and were affected by them. The narrative element—the stories that lie within all human interactions—is often left out of many content-area lessons (Conner, 2003). Thirty years ago my colleague Carl Tomlinson and I (Brozo & Tomlinson, 1986) recognized this impoverished state of textbook-based instruction and worked with teachers to use stories and novels to make content more exciting and memorable to youth. Our call then is just as valid today, as teachers and researchers continue to discover the value of narrative for bringing disciplinary content to life (Arya & Maul, 2012; Bean, 2003; Cox, 2012; Koellner, Wallace, & Swackhamer, 2009; Maples & Groenke, 2009; Olness, 2007; Roberts, 2012). One rich source of narrative is young adult literature.

Any literature read by young adults can be considered young adult literature (Bean, Dunkerly-Bean, & Harper, 2013). This would include a large variety of texts, such as classics, popular adult fare, and bestsellers. For our purposes, young adult literature refers to books written or marketed primarily for teens and preteens. It is literature that deals specifically with issues and themes relevant to their interests and needs. Another distinguishing feature of these books is that the protagonists and other main characters are typically of the same age as the readers for whom the books were written.

There are several major genres or types of young adult books. Indeed, the world of young adult literature is wonderfully rich, with countless high-quality books of fiction and nonfiction that cover a wide range of topics (Short, Tomlinson, Lynch-Brown, & Johnson, 2014). Three genres more amenable to disciplinary teaching include historical fiction, science fiction, and nonfiction.

Historical Fiction

Historical fiction allows adolescents to appreciate important historical events in human terms through the eyes of adolescents who lived through them (Jewett, 2007). Because these books deal with events of the near and distant past, they often have a timeless quality that permits their use for many years (Allbery, 2010; Philpott, 2015).

Science Fiction

Youth who are interested in science are often great fans of science fiction (Vrasida, Avraamidou, Theodoridou, Themistokleous, & Panaou, 2015). By the same token, quality science fiction books can play an important role in developing students' interest in science (Avraamidou & Osborne, 2009).

Nonfiction

An important genre of adolescent literature, nonfiction books written for youth draw them into the reading and learning process the way no textbook ever could (Coombs, 2013; Dorfman & Cappelli, 2009). Nonfiction books, often referred to as informational books, are typically written by authorities who cover topics from dinosaurs to dating using engaging and informative writing styles and writing from the perspectives of their intended readers. According to Sullivan (2014), nonfiction is the most frequently read literature among adolescents.

Using young adult literature in the content classroom has been widely recommended for a variety of topics and virtually every content area (Chenelle & Fisch, 2016; Fresch & Harkins, 2009; Groenke, Maples, & Henderson, 2010; Lattimer, 2010).

Graphic Novels and Comic Books

It wasn't that long ago when comic books were not to be dignified in libraries, schools, and classrooms. Perhaps it was because they were regarded as the bottom of the literary food chain by librarians, teachers, and parents that many youth spent their outside-of-school leisure time reading exclusively comics. But then in 1992, Art Spiegelman's *Maus* was awarded a Pulitzer Prize, and the term *graphic novel*, which had been in use among devotees as far back as the 1960s, came into vogue. Since then, the comic book format has changed dramatically. Graphic novels are now being recognized for their literary and artistic merit, and their authors and illustrators are taking on everything from the Palestinian–Israeli conflict to growing up with an epileptic sibling (Cromer & Clark, 2007; Griffith, 2010).

Although I use the terms interchangeably in this chapter, *graphic novel* is commonly used to distinguish works from comic books, which for many have juvenile and humorous connotations. It implies a more serious, mature, and literary work than traditional comics. Another distinguishing feature is that the graphic novel generally refers to any long-form comic book or the comic's analogue to a prose novel, novella, or play.

Graphic novels come in numerous genres, including fiction, historical fiction, biography, science fiction, and nonfiction. This variety, along with their enormous popularity with youth, make graphic novels and comic books an engaging and useful additional resource for teaching and learning in any content classroom (Brozo, Moorman, & Meyer, 2014; Carter, 2009; Gavigan & Tomasevich, 2011).

Finally, graphic novels and comic books have been shown to be an invaluable tool for motivating reluctant readers (Chun, 2009; Gavigan, 2010). The illustrations can provide the needed contextual clues to the meaning of the written narrative, especially for struggling and visual learners. And though these materials have been shunned in the past by librarians, many are observing how graphic novels are generating a whole new energy among youth. Stephen Krashen (1993), in asserting the legitimacy of reading material such as comic books in school settings, says:

> Perhaps the most powerful way of encouraging children to read is by exposing them to light reading, a kind of reading that schools pretend does not exist and a kind of reading that many children, for economic or ideological reasons, are deprived of. I suspect that light reading is the way that nearly all of us learned to read. (pp. 47–48)

Primary Documents

A textbook is a distillation of a variety of source material. By their very nature, textbooks are at least one and more commonly several times removed from the original sources. Textbooks that students encounter in schools rarely include primary documents, those texts written by and about individuals and groups who experienced the events of history, who made or were affected by the discoveries of science, or who logged the development of their own ideas, leading to new geometrical principles in math and engineering.

Primary documents are the authentic pieces of evidence historians use to interpret and describe the past. Vivid and personal documents, such as a letter or a photograph, when made available to youth, will intrigue them and provoke thoughtful and engaged responses (Barton, 2005; Mandell & Malone, 2008; Sandwell, 2008). This is the case because historical artifacts used by scholars faithfully depict the language, thinking, and behavior of the past without the sanitizing and glossing characteristic of textbook treatments.

Though these texts rarely find their way into most classrooms, it is worth noting that those students who read primary documents on a fairly frequent basis, as often as at least once per week, have higher achievement scores than their peers who see these sources rarely (U.S. Department of Education, 2002). So there's something about primary sources that make them more attractive and engaging to students than traditional textbook treatments of topics and that promotes meaningful and long-lasting learning (Brown & Dotson, 2007; Colby, 2009).

Newspapers, Magazines, and Other Real-World Texts

It almost seems too commonsensical to remind disciplinary teachers of the value of using newspaper and magazine articles and other documents in the everyday lives of youth and adults as teaching resources. And yet my own informal observations of hundreds of secondary school classrooms reveal that these alternative, commonsense texts are not being utilized nearly as often as they could be or to the best extent possible.

Teachers who have discovered the benefits of incorporating these types of texts into their instructional practices find students are more engaged and thoughtful learners because the content is more relevant to their lives and experiences (Al Azri & Al-Rashdi, 2014; Berardo, 2006; Gilmore, 2007). Science teachers can increase involvement by structuring activities that allow students to read and consult popular science magazines, such as *Scientific American* or *Popular Science,* during class time. Government teachers can focus students' attention on the role of government in establishing rules and regulations for the protection of citizens' health by reading and analyzing food preparation and food handling brochures published by the Food and Drug Administration. Economics teachers can elevate student interest by bringing into class credit card forms, bank statements, and other personal finance documents as accompaniments to textbook coverage of the topic.

Virtually every issue that emerges from the study of science, math, history, and literature can be enriched and made more relevant with newspaper and magazine articles and a great variety of other real-world documents (Jarman & McClune, 2003). Furthermore, to help youth see the importance and utility of learning disciplinary content, we recommend that teachers bring into the classroom and provide electronic access to familiar, everyday texts and documents that students encounter outside school that link directly to school-based topics (Krajcik & Sutherland, 2010; Tafani, 2009). Every imaginable form, from loan applications to drug and health brochures, are readily available online, and countless newspapers and magazines can be viewed online, as well.

There are many examples of teachers who routinely integrate real-life reading materials into their content instruction to help students see connections between disciplinary content inside the classroom and real-world issues and events outside the classroom boundaries.

- A health teacher has students bring in menus from restaurants and cookbooks from home when working on food preparation and nutrition.
- A business education teacher, for his unit on career explorations, brings in several examples of employment applications. He also urges students who may be applying for part-time jobs to bring in their applications.
- A chemistry teacher asks students to bring in labels from household cleaning products and foods indicating that certain chemicals are being used.
- A government teacher uses popular news magazines to relate text topics to current events.
- An accounting teacher asks students to bring in actual bills and account statements to teach accounting terms and budgeting.
- A math teacher asks students to write/create math problems using tables, maps, and graphs from the local newspaper.

The list could go on and on because the possibilities for integrating everyday reading materials into the content classroom are virtually limitless.

Popular Media and Music

An obvious source for enlivening disciplinary learning is popular media and music (Hagood, 2009; Knabb, 2003; Pailliotet, 2003; Silberman-Keller, Bekerman, Giroux, & Burbules, 2008). Because today's youth live in the "mediasphere," as I explained in Chapter 1, it makes good sense to find as many linkages as possible between the images and music with which they are familiar and topics under study in the classroom. One of the more interesting youth media/literacy phenomena is "fanfiction"—a text of any genre created about a cartoon or video game character. This new form has been described as coming from fans of mass culture who base their writing on media texts and images (Black, 2008; Bok, 2013; Chandler-Olcott & Mahar, 2003; Mathew & Adams, 2009). Later in this chapter we describe an English teacher who took full advantage of fanfiction in her classroom.

Frequently in this book I have asserted and exemplified the importance of honoring youths' outside-of-school media and literacies while bridging them to academic concepts and information. Music, as a medium of identity construction for many youth, is also a very viable alternative text form underexploited by most content-area teachers (Bitz, 2009; Mangram & Weber, 2012). Scaffolding for new understandings means working with what adolescents bring to the classroom, including their interest and knowledge of popular music (Duncan-Andrade & Morrell, 2007).

Of course, the most pervasive popular entertainment and learning tool in youths' lives is the computer. Throughout this book I have described how computers, whether smartphones, iPads, laptops, or desktops, can be utilized to increase various aspects of content learning (Diamond & Gaier Knapik, 2014; Guzzetti, Elliott, & Welsch, 2010). This chapter, too, will have frequent references to computers and the alternative texts they offer disciplinary teachers.

GUIDELINES AND PRACTICES FOR INTEGRATING MULTIPLE SOURCES INTO CONTENT CLASSROOMS

The contributions that multiple sources can make to the teaching of disciplinary content are limited only by your own sensibilities. But regardless of whether you tend to plan conservative or more flamboyant lessons, what is of overarching importance is that you strive to take greater advantage of the numerous print and other resources available to you and your students. As I stated in the introduction to this chapter, while advocating for the use of multiple texts, I am not suggesting that the traditional textbook has become passé for today's classroom. In fact, you will see, in most of the teaching examples described, that the textbook serves a helpful role as a reference resource among several resources at students' disposal as they expand their understandings of information and ideas and become more engaged and thoughtful learners.

I urge the use of these alternative texts because we know that youth will quickly turn off to reading if they find texts difficult or boring (Guthrie et al., 2013; Guthrie et al., 2012; Ranck-Buhr, 2012). On the other hand, Guthrie and Wigfield (2000), in reviewing research on the influence of affect in the reading process, observed that when students find reading pleasurable and interesting, their positive attitudes toward reading rapidly become generalized to most other subjects, which leads to a deeper love of reading as a primary source of information and enjoyment. Furthermore, students' reading comprehension has been shown to be greater with high-interest materials because interesting material maintains their attention more effectively (Flowerday & Shell, 2015; Fulmer, D'Mello, Strain, & Graesser, 2015).

Each of the multiple sources I have described can be a powerful motivator for reading, writing, and learning, as well as an important schema builder. In earlier chapters you learned that schema theorists posit that the more developed are the knowledge structures readers possess about a particular topic, the greater is the likelihood that they will be successful in dealing with new information related to that topic. The most important instructional implication of schema theory is that teachers should build bridges between new information to be learned and students' prior knowledge (Ambrose, 2010). Texts and media familiar and interesting to youth can provide the background information and call to mind related ideas, building the foundation for easier assimilation of new textual information (Arends & Kilcher, 2010; Fisher, Frey, & Lapp, 2012).

The duration and scope of any lesson or series of lessons that integrates multiple sources will depend on the topic and on your judgments and preferences. Throughout this book, we have noted the benefits of planning and teaching in units, whereby students experience a series of lessons often lasting up to several weeks that revolve around a unifying theme with related subtopics. The primary benefit of this approach to both you and your students is time—sufficient time to investigate a topic thoroughly through reading, discussion, writing, and research and, therefore, time to get interested in and excited about learning while producing considered responses. The following guidelines and methods are most applicable to unit-based teaching.

Identify Salient Themes and Concepts

The process of identifying important themes and concepts for a unit of study is essential for integrating appropriate sources. Multiple sources should be bridged by overarching themes and concepts related to the most important information and ideas of the unit. The process involves, first, deciding what you want your students to know as a result of the unit and then using this theme as a guide, identifying the related concepts and subtopics.

Here is where textbooks can most helpful, because they are usually organized by units, which makes it easier to identify broad themes for unit plans. As I have recommended before, however, you should develop unit themes that are meaningful to you and your students, regardless of the extent to which the topics are dealt with in the textbook or main source.

Unfortunately, although textbooks are excellent dispensers of facts, they often lack explicit development of important themes. Therefore, you must infer essential ideas from them in order to develop unit themes that are meaningful to you and your students, regardless of the extent to which the topics are dealt with in the textbook. In this way, you can take advantage of your own and your students' special skills or interests. Try asking yourself the following questions as you look over a textbook unit:

- What are the driving human forces behind the events?
- What phenomena described in the textbook have affected ordinary people (including me and my students) or may do so in the future?
- What universal patterns of behavior related to this reading should be explained?

Answers to these questions will go a long way toward helping you decide what students should know as a result of the unit and thereby will provide direction for selecting appropriate sources to tie in with the theme (see Figure 8.1 for an exercise in determining a unit's theme). For example, when Hahnan, a seventh-grade social studies teacher, applied these questions to the textbook's unit on Australia, she inferred that the geography of a place affects the lives of its inhabitants. This theme seemed particularly apparent in the case of Australia, with its curiously evolved wildlife and bush country lifestyles, so Hahnan believed that this would be an advantageous context in which to teach it.

After establishing a theme for a unit of study, I recommend you explore the content further to identify important concepts and subtopics related to the unit's theme. To accomplish this, I suggest you create a visual display or a web (Pappas, Kiefer, & Levstik, 2005). Beginning with the unit topic or theme written in the center of a large piece of paper, you, with help from your students, generate related subtopics and write them around the main topic. These ideas may come directly from the text or from prior knowledge. Figure 8.2 is an example of a web co-constructed by Dora and her ninth-grade science class for their unit on astronomy.

Another important benefit of unit teaching is that the scope is broad enough to reveal relationships between different aspects of a topic, thereby helping students knit information together, expand schemata, and improve their overall understanding of the topic. With the completed web, Dora then decided which subtopics were

To further illustrate the process of establishing important themes related to textbook topics, consider the following excerpt about the Nazis, the Jews, and the Holocaust taken from an 11th-grade American history book. Indeed, the quoted section is nearly the extent of text related to the Holocaust in this history book. As you read the excerpt, ask yourself the three questions posed in the text. Then write down a theme you believe would be important to teach in relation to this content.

> When news of the Holocaust—the term later given to the Nazis' extermination of European Jewry—first leaked out in early 1942, many Americans discounted the reports. . . . How much could have been done remains uncertain. . . . The War Refugee Board managed to save the lives of just two hundred thousand Jews and twenty thousand non-Jews. Six million other Jews, about 75 percent of the European Jewish population, were gassed, shot, and incinerated, as were several million gypsies, communists, homosexuals, Polish Catholics, and others deemed unfit to live in the Third Reich. (Boyer, Clark, Kett, Salisbury, Sitkoff, & Woloch, 2004, pp. 807, 810)

Theme: _____

_____

You probably found that this preceding text is like most textbook prose. It covers the facts but offers few ways of identifying the underlying critical themes and concepts. By asking our three recommended questions, however, we believe you can identify one of the most important themes of this content—*the dangers of racial prejudice*—only hinted at in the sweeping, factual account of Nazism and the Holocaust.

FIGURE 8.1. Exercise for determining a textbook unit's theme.

most relevant to the theme of the unit. Rarely is there time to cover every aspect of a topic generated in the webbing process, and some subtopics must be deemphasized or omitted entirely—even though the information may be covered in the textbook. Finally, under the subtopic headings to be included in the unit, Dora listed related sources (Figure 8.2). I talk more about how Dora organized instruction with multiple sources later in this chapter.

Identify Appropriate Sources to Help Teach Concepts

Once an important theme for the unit is established and related subtopics and concepts have been identified, the next step is to find multiple sources that are directly and/or thematically related.

Becoming more knowledgeable about the multitude of sources available to teach disciplinary unit themes will seem like a daunting task at first. It can be made easier by the many bibliographies, reference guides, lists, and reviews of current comics, graphic novels, and young adult literature available to all of us on the Internet. Other invaluable resources for identifying alternative texts are your school and local librarians. Librarians can do Internet searches to find accessible articles

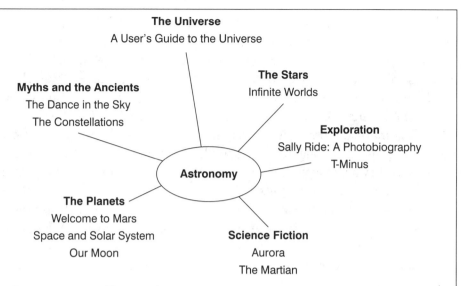

Alternative Texts for Astronomy Unit

Aldrin, B., with Dyson, M. J. (2015). *Welcome to Mars: Making a home on the red planet.* Washington, DC: National Geographic Children's Books.

Coder, E. J. (2012). *The constellations: Myths of the stars.* CreateSpace Independent Publishing Platform.

Goldberg, D. (2010). *A user's guide to the universe: Surviving the perils of black holes, time paradoxes, and quantum uncertainty.* Hoboken, NJ: Wiley.

Hand, E. (2016, January 20). Astronomers say a Neptune-sized planet lurks beyond Pluto. Retrieved from *www.sciencemag.org/news/2016/01/feature-astronomers-say-neptune-sized-planet-lurks-unseen-solar-system.*

Hoffmann, K. (2014). *Space and solar system: An eBook for children about the universe, our planets and space exploration.* Amazon Digital Services.

Lowe, S., & North, C. (2015). *Cosmos: The infographic book of space.* London: Aurum Press.

Munroe, R. (2014). *What if?: Serious scientific answers to absurd hypothetical questions.* Boston: Houghton Mifflin Harcourt.

Munroe, R. (2015). *Thing explainer: Complicated stuff in simple words.* Boston: Houghton Mifflin Harcourt.

O'Shaughnessy. T. (2015). *Sally Ride: A photobiography of America's pioneering woman in space.* London: Roaring Brook Press.

Ottavani, J., Cannon, Z., & Cannon, K. (2009). *T-Minus: The race to the moon.* New York: Aladdin.

Robinson, K. S. (2015). *Aurora.* New York: Orbit.

Scott, E. (2016). *Our moon: New discoveries about earth's closest companion.* New York: Clarion Books.

Soluri, M. (2014). *Infinite worlds.* New York: Simon & Schuster. (space photography)

Weir, A. (2014). *The Martian.* New York: Random House.

Williamson, R. A., & Monroe, J. G. (2007). *They dance in the sky: Native American star myths.* Boston: HMH Books for Young Readers.

FIGURE 8.2. Web for an astronomy unit, including appropriate sources.

and scour holdings for relevant graphic novels, young adult books, magazine and newspaper articles, and government documents.

Regarding the topic of Jews in Europe during World War II, Keshawn, an eighth-grade history teacher, located a wealth of related sources using electronic references. He also found ideal young adult books right within his neighborhood and school libraries. These included one of my timeless favorites, *Friedrich* (Richter, 1970), and many other fine selections. (For a list and description of each of Keshawn's sources, see Figure 8.3.) Boundless rewards awaited Keshawn and his students as they approached the unit on the Holocaust, which would include this marvelous range of interesting texts.

Once relevant multiple sources are located, the most enjoyable aspect of this process begins—you get to read them before using them in class. We have found that as teachers become acquainted with multiple sources, they rediscover the joy of reading, they develop fresh perspectives on the topic, and their enthusiasm for teaching grows.

On reading these various texts that Keshawn introduced to his students, you will note that they and others like them are, first of all, human. You will understand that the effects of distant, large-scale events such as war will become real to students only when translated into terms of what they mean to fictional and factual characters who witnessed it and were victimized by it. After hearing Keshawn read *Friedrich* aloud to the class, one of his eighth-grade students commented, "This book describes the life of these people so well you'd think that Friedrich and his mother and father were a part of your own family." Were it not for alternative texts like those Keshawn found and brought into his classroom, most historical events of national and international scope and most notable human achievements and tragedies would remain for many young adults distant or even mythical notions with no emotional connection to their own lives and experiences.

A second notable characteristic of quality alternative sources, such as those Keshawn had his students read, is that unlike a typical "bloodless" textbook they describe the effects of large-scale events on ordinary people (Brozo & Tomlinson, 1986). Within the narration of realistic human interaction, concepts can be made understandable and real to youth. Earlier, we referred to prejudice as an important concept to be explored in the study of Nazism and World War II. Excellent passages and activities for exploring the nature of this concept can be found in the multiple sources Keshawn gathered for his students. Consider, for example, the following passage from Richter's (1970) *Friedrich*. In it, the 13-year-old Jewish boy is trying to retrieve his clothes from a swimming pool attendant in Germany in 1938.

> "Just take a look at this!" the attendant said. "You won't get to see many more of them." Everyone could hear his explanation: "This is one of the Jewish identification cards. The scoundrel lied to me. He claims his name's Friedrich Schneider—it's Friedrich Israel Schneider, that's what it is—a Jew that's what he is! A Jew in our swimming pool!" He looked disgusted.

Young Adult Novels

Bartoletti, S. C. (2008). *The boy who dared*. New York: Scholastic.—In October 1942, 17-year-old Helmuth Hubener, imprisoned for distributing anti-Nazi leaflets, recalls his past life and how he came to dedicate himself to bring the truth about Hitler and the war to the German people.

Chapman, F. S. (2010). *Is it night or day?* New York: Farrar Straus and Giroux.—In 1938, Edith Westerfeld, a young German Jew, is sent by her parents to Chicago, Illinois, where she lives with an aunt and uncle and tries to assimilate into American culture while worrying about her parents and mourning the loss of everything she has ever known.

Gleitzman, M. (2010). *Once*. New York: Henry Holt.—After living in a Catholic orphanage for nearly 4 years, a naïve Jewish boy runs away and embarks on a journey across Nazi-occupied Poland to find his parents.

Gleitzman, M. (2010). *Then*. New York: Henry Holt.—In early 1940s Poland, 10-year-old Felix and his friend Zelda escape from a cattle car headed to the Nazi death camps and struggle to survive, first on their own and then with Genia, a farmer with her own reasons for hating Germans. This is the follow-up to *Once*.

Polak, M. (2008). *What world is left?* Victoria, British Columbia, Canada: Orca Publishers.—Anneke, a Dutch Jewish teenager, is sent with her family to Theresienstadt, a "model" concentration camp, where she confronts great evil and learns to do what it takes to survive.

Richter, H. P. (1987). *Friedrich*. New York: Puffin Books—In this young adult novel, the reader meets a German boy and his Jewish playmate and learns how both are gradually victimized by Nazi propaganda and pogrom during the years 1925 to 1942.

Sharenow, R. (2011). *The Berlin boxing club*. New York: HarperTeen.—In 1936 Berlin, 14-year-old Karl Stern, considered Jewish despite a nonreligious upbringing, learns to box from the legendary Max Schmeling while struggling with the realities of the Holocaust.

Nonfiction

Ruelle, K. G. (2008). *The Grand Mosque of Paris: A story of how Muslims saved Jews during the Holocaust*. New York: Holiday House.—During the Nazi occupations of Paris, many Jews found refuge in an unlikely place: the sprawling complex of the Grand Mosque of Paris.

Taylor, P. L. (2007). *The secret of Priest's Grotto: A Holocaust survival story*. Minneapolis, MN: Kar-Ben. Two explorers survey caves in the Western Ukraine and relate the story of how an extended Jewish family, fleeing persecution by the Nazis, lived for 2 years in a large cave, Popowa Yama, and survived the war.

Thompson, R. (2011). *Terezin: Voices from the Holocaust*. Somerville, MA: Candlewick.—Through inmates' own voices—from secret diary entries and artwork to excerpts from memories and recordings narrated after the war—*Terezin* explores the lives of Jewish people in one of the most infamous of the Nazi transit camps.

Wood, A. G. (2007). *Holocaust: The events and their impact on real people*. London: DK Publishing.—An encyclopedic overview of the Jewish Holocaust.

(continued)

FIGURE 8.3. Multiple sources for teaching a unit on the Holocaust in eighth-grade social studies.

Biography

Koestler-Grack, R. (2009). *Elie Wiesel: Witness for humanity.* New York: Gareth Stevens Publishing.—In this true story of Holocaust survivor Elie Wiesel, readers learn about Wiesel's shocking experiences during imprisonment in Auschwitz, his survival, and his determination to speak out against all forms of genocide.

Kor, E. M. (2009). *Surviving the angel of death: The story of a Mengele twin in Auschwitz.* Terre Haute, IN: Tanglewood Press.—The story of 10-year-old Evakor, who, along with her twin sister, faced extreme evil and cruelty at the hands of Dr. Josef Mengele.

Levy, D. (2010). *The year of goodbyes: A true story of friendship, family and farewells.* New York: Disney-Hyperion.—Narrative poems that detail life in Nazi Germany, based on the 1938 autograph book belonging to the author's mother.

Rubin, S. G. (2011). *Irena Sendler and the children of the Warsaw Ghetto.* New York: Holiday House.—Using ingenious methods, Irena Sendler saved and hid Jewish children and kept a secret list of their identities.

Graphic Novels

Heuvel, E. (2009). *A family secret.* New York: Farrar Straus & Giroux.—While searching his Dutch grandmother's attic for yard sale items, Jeroen finds a scrapbook which leads Gran to tell of her experiences as a girl living in Amsterdam during the Holocaust, when her father was a Nazi sympathizer and Esther, her Jewish best friend, disappeared.

Jacobson, S., & Colon, E. (2010). *Anne Frank: The Anne Frank House authorized graphic biography.* New York: Hill & Wang.—These authors draw on the unique historical sites, archives, expertise, and unquestioned authority of the Anne Frank House in Amsterdam.

Websites

United States Holocaust Memorial Museum.

www.ushmm.org/learn/students/the-holocaust-a-learning-site-for-students

This is an interactive website that allows visitors to explore such items as photographs and personal diary excerpts from victims that leave youth with a deep appreciation for the human dimension of the Nazis' ethnic extermination campaign. At this site they also learn how to be vigilant to racial prejudice in their communities and even within themselves.

Websites for Holocaust Education

www.cumbavac.org/holocaust.htm

Simon Wiesenthal Center

www.wiesenthal.com/site/pp.asp?c=lsKWLbPJLnF&b=6212365

New York Times

learning.blogs.nytimes.com/2010/04/09/the-holocaust/?_r=0

FIGURE 8.3. *(continued)*

All those still waiting for their clothes stared at Friedrich. As if he could no longer bear to touch it, the attendant threw Friedrich's identification card and its case across the counter. "Think of it! Jewish things among the clothes of respectable human beings!" he screamed, flinging the coat hanger holding Friedrich's clothes on the ground so they scattered in all directions. (pp. 76–77)

When reading passages such as this, students cannot help but be affected by the injustice and humiliation suffered by this character they come to know as decent, likable, and intelligent. Furthermore, the theme of the dangers of prejudice—its meaning, its effect on people, and its often terrible results—is made startlingly clear. After hearing *Friedrich*, another of Keshawn's eighth-grade students wrote:

The book made you feel how you would have felt if you were Jewish or German at the time. I learned how brave the Jewish family was in the book. I also learned how cruel and unthinking people can be and not caring and thinking that these people are the same as we are—human. Another thing I learned is that war is horrible. I hope, even though I doubt it, that there will be no more wars and discrimination in this world. The book really touched me.

Organize the Content and the Classroom for Multiple Sources

Clearly, alternative sources to the textbook have the potential of affecting young adults deeply; even so, teachers who have never used anything other than the textbook often ask us questions such as "How can I find the time to work multiple sources into my daily plans when I barely have enough time to cover the chapters?" or "I have 20 to 25 students per class. How can I manage my classroom if I use the textbook and other sources?"

Making Time for Multiple Sources

The first concern is easy enough to understand when you consider the fragmented, fact-laden curricula within which so many content-area teachers try to operate. Not only is each content area taught as a separate entity, but each subject is broken down into bits of information that students are required to memorize (Benassi, Overson, & Hakala, 2014; Kohn, 2010; Moje, Stockdill, Kim, & Kim, 2011; Wiggins & McTighe, 2011). Almost invariably, so much time is spent learning the small details that no time is left to experience holistic treatments of the topic and to understand the big picture. As a result, many students rarely enjoy or see the point in studying history or science facts, forget them, and often have to relearn them the next year.

In contrast, time spent exploring various other texts and media can be both efficient and effective because it gets students interested in learning the content and, when the sources are chosen appropriately, can serve as the material for content instruction (Brozo, Moorman, & Meyer, 2014; Considine, Horton, & Moorman, 2009). Furthermore, Common Core proponents recognize that curricula that are a "mile wide and an inch deep" foster disconnected knowledge. Superficial presentations of information fail to help students develop conceptual understandings or help them retain the significant ideas and details—hardly the kind of teaching that prepares youth for future learning and work (McTighe & Seif, 2014). Finally, data from the most recent PISA study, which included more than 13 million adolescents worldwide, show that memorization of information is the least successful strategy for learning (OECD, 2014).

For example, one of the sources used in Dora's unit on astronomy was Buzz Aldrin and Marianne Dyson's (2015) *Welcome to Mars: Making a Home on the Red Planet*. From this book, students learned accurate and current information about Mars, as well as intriguing though plausible explanations about how humans might one day colonize the planet. Students benefitted from the experience of reading a whole, well-written work of nonfiction by a former astronaut and a NASA physicist with years of space program experience and a real passion for their subject matter. At the same time, the authors reinforced a message Dora sent her students about the importance of continuing space exploration.

I believe the best way to approach the problem of finding time to make use of multiple sources is to choose the most important themes and overarching concepts to be taught and then place instructional emphasis on them. Naturally, some of the textbook content is not as pertinent to the important themes as other content and, consequently, should be given less attention; deciding on a focus thus frees up time that can be spent on relevant, important information. For example, in his unit on the American Revolution, Frank decided to emphasize three important themes: (1) that freedom, both for countries and for people, has a price (the heavy toll of war, even on the victor; the responsibilities that accompany self-government and personal independence); (2) that war affects all citizens of a country; and (3) that alternatives to war exist.

Frank then selected several possible sources that would help to reinforce these themes, finally deciding to use one primary young adult historical novel, *Johnny Tremain*, (Forbes, 1945) and to suggest other sources for students' independent reading. *Johnny Tremain* is a classic of accurate and compelling historical fiction. By its copyright, this may seem to be a dated work for today's adolescents, but because its subject matter centers on events in our nation's past more than 200 years ago, it has a timeless quality that makes it as relevant now as ever.

Next, Frank went through the 12 chapters in the text unit and, keeping his salient themes in mind, made decisions about how to teach each chapter (Figure 8.4) and listed potential writing activities for many of the chapters (Figure 8.5).

Chapter	Suggested Activity
1	Life in New England—Students read; compare with trade book; write (see Figure 8.5)
2	Work, Church, and School—same as Chapter 1
3	Life in Southern Colonies—Teacher lecture-brief
4	Life in Middle Colonies—Teacher lecture-brief
5	Life in Wilderness—Teacher lecture; book talk: *Woods Runner* (Paulsen, 2011)
6	Government in the English Colonies—Teacher lecture; debates (see Figure 8.5)
7	Furs and Farming in New France—Teacher lecture-brief
8	French and English Fight—Students read; map study; develop timeline; write (see Figure 8.5); book talk and sharing: *Look to the Hills: The Diary of Lozette Moreau, a French Slave Girl* (McKissack, 2004)
9	England Tightens Its Grip—Students read
10	Colonists Become Angry—Students read; prioritize value of ways to cause change; compare text and trade book; write (see Figure 8.5); book talk and sharing: *Just Jane: A Daughter of England Caught in the Struggle of the American Revolution* (Lavender, 2014)
11	Liberty or Death—Students read; list causes of war; rank order and defend rankings
12	New Nation is Born—Students read; discuss Johnny Tremain's change of mind

FIGURE 8.4. Teaching activities for a unit on the American Revolution.

Managing the Classroom with Multiple Sources

I can address the second concern—how to manage the content classroom with multiple sources—by describing the experiences of three different teachers whose approaches represent three management systems.

READING ALOUD

Marques uses the simplest of systems. He reads to his eighth graders books and other sources that are thematically linked to the science topics under consideration. When studying the topic of genetics and genetic engineering, for instance, Marques read Glasgow and Schichtel's (n.d.) graphic novel *Genome*. In this Kindle edition,

Chapters 1 and 2

- Let Johnny Tremain have a dialogue with a person of today about living conditions in the 1700s. Make comparisons.
- Write a position paper for living in the 18th century or today.
- Compare and contrast women's roles in the 18th century and today based on reading in *Johnny Tremain.*

Chapter 6

- Debate: Develop arguments explaining the points of view of British and colonists; placards and posters can support either side.

Chapter 8

- Create thumbnail sketches of important Revolutionary War personalities.
- Write newspaper articles for *Colonial Times.*
- Write an editorial about British taxation.
- Create a dialogue between a colonist and King George III.
- List personal freedoms you have and value today. Which of these can be traced to the events of the 1770s? Which were actually fought for in the Revolutionary War?

Chapter 10

- Prioritize the relative value of various means of gaining one's ends and producing change:
    Voting
    Physical force
    Vigilante (scare) tactics
    Terrorism
    Diplomacy

Chapter 12

- You have just read Johnny Tremain. What part of this story did you react to most strongly? Do you see any connection between this part of the story and your own life?

FIGURE 8.5. Suggested composition assignments for unit on American Revolution.

Marques's students were asked to imagine a menacing future world in which the entire human genetic code or genome is patented by a single megacorporation and all human reproduction is strictly controlled. Parents must apply for licenses to have children and must make mortgage payments to keep them. This is the dark premise for the graphic novel. Marques made other sources available to students that were related to the topic of genetics and DNA, including *The Declaration* (Malley, 2008), which features a dystopian 22nd-century world in which humanity has cured all illness and aspires to eternal life; *Inhuman* (Falls, 2015), about the Feral Zone, the forbidden wilderness east of the Mississippi River where few have dared set foot since a devastating biological disaster that killed millions and left the survivors mutated; and *Wake Up Missing* (Messner, 2013), which tells the dramatic and chilling story of young people implanted with the DNA of dead scientific paragons such as Oppenheimer and Edison as part of a modern-day Manhattan Project.

Combining fiction with current information books, Marques has been able to include young adult literature in nearly all of his units. For example, he used *Buried in Ice: The Mystery of a Lost Arctic Expedition* (Beattie & Geiger, 1992), with its vivid, gripping photographs of mummified explorers found in the Arctic permafrost, to grab his students' interest in the topic. In conjunction with a unit on the systems of the body, he read to a captivated class Isaac Asimov's (1966) classic work of science fiction *Fantastic Voyage,* in which four men and a woman are reduced to a microscopic fraction of their original size and sent in a miniaturized atomic sub through a dying man's carotid artery to destroy a blood clot in his brain. His students also listened to and observed the often comical though accurate illustrations in the informative graphic novel *Human Body Theater* (Wicks, 2015) during this unit.

As Marques reads, he asks his students to be active listeners, paying attention not only to plot developments but also to how the ideas in the story relate to those in the text. With this approach, only a single young adult book is needed. Marques reads 15 to 20 minutes daily and is able to complete a book of average length in 2½ weeks. During the school year, he often reads as many as 15 books to his classes. Over the same period, he exposes his students to countless other magazine and newspaper articles, picture books and informational books, graphic novels, primary documents, and websites.

Like Marques, Courtney reads aloud from a young adult book nearly every day in her social studies classes. For example, to help put a human face on issues relating to citizenship addressed in sweeping fashion in the textbook, Courtney read Julia Alvarez's (2009) novel *Return to Sender,* which presents two points of view on citizenship: from Tyler, a Vermont farm boy, and Mari, a Mexican laborer working on the farm. Throughout the course of the novel, Courtney asked her students to consider various points of view, such as the farmers who need less expensive immigrant laborers in order to stay in business, and various policy issues, such as the deportation of children who are American citizens. As a prelude to reading aloud to students, she identifies good prediction points in the novel where students can speculate on the events described and future scenes they will encounter. By reading aloud for about 10 minutes at the end of a period, Courtney enriches content learning. Moreover, as an added benefit, she has seen how this practice has a soothing effect on her students.

WHOLE-CLASS TEXT

As an alternative to the teacher's reading aloud, the whole class can read or explore common sources together. Bernadette's seventh-grade social studies classes read four primary documents from the U.S. presidential election of 1860, which pitted

Stephen Douglas against Abraham Lincoln. Working from a website (*http://jefferson. village.virginia.edu/vshadow2/newspapers.html*), Bernadette made copies of articles and editorials from two newspapers with opposing perspectives on the election. Her students read the original texts from the *New York Tribune* and the *Richmond Enquirer* dated October 29 and November 6, 1860, a few days before and a few days after Lincoln defeated Douglas. They learned from these original sources that it was actually a four-way race for the presidency, with Douglas, a Democratic candidate from the North, and a separate Democratic candidate from the South, Lincoln as the Republican nominee, and an individual running for a third party. They compared and contrasted the positions and attitudes of the papers and debated each other over the issues. These original documents helped Bernadette's students get a feel for how people really felt at that time toward the issue at stake in the election. In particular, they learned the depth of secessionist feelings among Southerners expressed after Lincoln was elected in the editorial in the *Richmond Enquirer* entitled "The Day of Battle Has Arrived."

MULTIPLE GROUPS AND MULTIPLE TEXTS

A more complex but exciting and powerful management system involves student-directed cooperative learning groups and literature circles, both virtual and face-to-face, sharing multiple sources (Barone, 2014; Klages, Pate, & Conforti, 2007; Peterson & Eeds, 2007). Earlier, I described how Dora, a ninth-grade science teacher, builds webs for her units to identify salient concepts and subtopics and appropriate print and media for teaching these topics. For her astronomy unit, she decided to focus on two of the subtopics, *planets* and *the universe*. She gave groups of four students the following URLs and had them work in teams in the computer lab to learn the material:

- "Historic Gravitational Waves Rippled, but Left No Fireworks" (2016, February 18) (*www.space.com/31970-gravitational-wave-detection-no-fireworks.html*)
- "Super-Earth Exoplanet's Atmosphere Characterized for 1st Time" (2016, February 16) (*www.space.com/31946-exoplanet-super-earth-atmosphere-hubble-video.html*)
- "WFIRST: Next Decade's Space Telescope" (2016, February 22) (*www.skyandtelescope.com/astronomy-news/nasa-unveils-wfirst-next-decade-space-telescope-02222016*)
- "Astronomers Say a Neptune-Sized Planet Lurks Beyond Pluto" (2016, January 20) (*www.sciencemag.org/news/2016/01/feature-astronomers-say-neptune-sized-planet-lurks-unseen-solar-system*)

For another group of students she secured four copies of the graphic novel *Dan Dare Pilot of the Future: Marooned on Mercury* (Hampson, 2005).

Dora assigned students in each group particular roles to play in order to ensure everyone's participation. The "idea summarizer" was responsible for putting on paper the key information gleaned from the source; the "vocabulary enricher" looked up and helped define unfamiliar words encountered in the source; the "fact checker" had to find an independent corroborative source for any facts used in the presentation; and the "presenter" was responsible for sharing the key ideas and information learned from studying the source.

In the beginning, Dora carefully modeled each cooperative group assignment and helped clarify confusion through questions and discussions. She devised these cooperative learning group roles because they contribute to students' learning in the manner she desires and with the sources from which she wanted her students to learn. It is important to note that you can create your own cooperative learning group roles, depending on what kinds of learning you want to take place within the groups. (See Figure 8.6 for an exercise in assigning cooperative learning roles.)

Such a system as Dora's is admirably suited to teaching units because a variety of sources, each emphasizing a different aspect of the unit theme, will contribute much to the scope and depth of understanding for students of varying abilities (Harvey & Daniels, 2009; Richardson, 2010; Whittaker, 2012).

Using Multiple Sources as Schema and Interest Builders

Science

A sixth-grade science teacher had her students read Saci Lloyd's (2010) *The Carbon Diaries 2015* as a prelude to a unit on ecology. The story is about the United Kingdom, which in 2015 makes a drastic bid to combat climate change by becoming the first nation on Earth to institute mandatory carbon rationing, a 60% decrease in all energy use. Sixteen-year-old Laura documents the first year of rationing as her family spirals out of control trying to adjust to these new severe restrictions. The lessons the students learn about how global warming is rapidly changing the world set the stage for the theme of the ecology unit and class discussion by establishing an overall picture of how a human can choose either to live and thrive in harmony with nature or pay the consequences. In addition, the story gave students a store of unusual, dramatic examples of the consequences of poor environmental stewardship, a topic they then read about in expository form in their science textbooks. Other excellent selections for this topic include Mike Mullin's (2012) *Ashen Winter*, Sarah Crossan's (2012) *Breathe*, and Susan Beth Pfeffer's (2010) *This World We Live In*.

Mathematics

Tenth-grade students were introduced to the study of fractals in geometry by reading and exploring Lesmoir-Gordon, Rood, and Edney's (2009). *Introducing Fractals:*

For cooperative groups to function effectively, it is very important to assign roles to students that are unambiguous and that contribute positively to the whole group. Debbie created roles for her students that achieved these goals; however, equally effective groups can be formed with alternative roles and assignments. The key is that each individual member makes a contribution that relates to the purpose of the group work and improves the performance of the group overall.

Think about possible roles for individual students in cooperative groups with the following purpose, then list and briefly describe them:

Purpose: Students in math are to find a website that explains how to construct a sturdy, weight-bearing house of cards; follow the directions to build one; document the results; and explain the geometrical principles involved.

Role 1: _____

Role 2: _____

Role 3: _____

Role 4: _____

Role 5: _____

Now identify a typical purpose of cooperative learning in your own classroom and list possible roles:

Purpose: _____

_____

_____

_____

_____

Role 1: _____

Role 2: _____

Role 3: _____

Role 4: _____

Role 5: _____

FIGURE 8.6. Exercise in assigning cooperative learning roles.

A Graphic Guide. Fractals, like tessellations, are defined by their self-similarity or repetitive regular and irregular patterns found in nature. Fractal geometry allows mathematicians to describe such shapes as coastlines and mountain chains with geometrical precision. Students read about fractals in the graphic novel, and then they were given the opportunity to find examples of fractal patterns in their everyday worlds. Students enjoyed finding these complex patterns in tree leaves, veins in their hands, a puffy cumulus cloud, mold growing in the showers of the boys' locker room, and wrinkles on an unpressed school uniform shirt. With these experiences, the 10th graders were much more enthusiastic about continuing their study of geometry.

Students in Miriam's senior math class were introduced to probabilities and inferential statistics with the book *The Manga Guide to Statistics* (Takahashi, 2008). The book draws readers into an intriguing story in which the heroine, Rui, wants to learn statistics to impress Mr. Igarashi. After begging her father for a tutor, she begins her journey into the world of statistics. Her tutor, geeky Mr. Yamamoto, teaches her basics of statistics, including averages, graphing, and standard deviations, and then delves into the more difficult topics of probability, correlation coefficients, probability distributions, and testing hypotheses. Miriam recognized that the step-by-step calculations offered her students an opportunity to understand more deeply the real meaning of such concepts as variance and standard deviations.

Other good books to use with middle- and upper-grade students in conjunction with math content include Keith Devlin and Gary Lorden's (2007) *The Numbers Behind NUMB3RS: Solving Crime with Mathematics*, and Wendy Lichtman's (2008) *Do the Math: Secrets, Lies, and Algebra*.

Physical Education

Before starting the softball season, a physical education teacher read aloud to his students the interesting sports novel *The Big Field*, by the best of the baseball genre, Mike Lupica (2009). The story centers on Hutch, a shortstop playing in a summer league. Hutch has to give up his favorite place on the diamond to a hotshot newcomer, while living with a father who is a former professional player who doesn't have the time to watch his son play. With the summer league championship on the line, Hutch has to decide whether he wants to be a good teammate and do whatever it takes to help his squad win. The teacher used this particular book because of its realistic descriptions of the actual game and for the way Lupica deals with issues of sportsmanship and improving skill through hard work.

Over the past decade or so, numerous quality fiction and nonfiction trade books for young adults with sports themes and sports characters have become available. For the middle grades and less able high school reader, there is *LeBron James: King of Shots* (Hill, 2012), *Ichiro Suzuki* (Levin, 2008), *Jim Thorpe, Original All-American*

(Bruchac, 2008), *Real Justice: Jailed for Life for Being Black: The Story of Rubin "Hurricane" Carter* (Swan, 2015), and *Soccer Star Lionel Messi* (Torres, 2014).

Sports books with female protagonists and about women athletes continue to expand, as well. Some of the best biographies are *Breakaway: Beyond the Goal* (Morgan, 2015) and *Lindsey Vonn* (Gitlin, 2012). Good fictional narratives include *Shut Out* (Keplinger, 2011), *Playing with the Boys* (Tigelaar, 2008), and *Stealing Parker* (Kenneally, 2012). Information picture books in this same genre include *She's a Knockout!: A History of Women in Fighting Sports* (Jennings, 2014), *Mad Seasons: The Story of the First Women's Professional Basketball League, 1978–1981* (Porter, 2014), and *You Let Some Girl Beat You?: The Story of Ann Meyers Drysdale* (Drysdale & Ravenna, 2012).

A group of senior high students who had volunteered to be counselors for summer camp were asked to read Will Hobbs's (1991) enduring favorite, *Downriver*, in their training class. In the book, four 15-year-old Outward Bound trainees, better known among themselves as "hoods in the woods," steal their guide's equipment and raft and attempt to take on the mighty Colorado River on their own. They learn about responsibility the hard way, with disastrous consequences. The seniors read and discussed the book each evening. Although they enjoyed the gripping adventure and the adolescent mischief, the book forced them to look seriously at their role as counselors and served as a focal point for discussions about behavioral problems and health emergencies.

Science

Reading coaches, reading specialists, and curriculum directors can play instrumental roles in supporting disciplinary teachers' efforts to expand text options for students. Given their knowledge of print and nonprint resources, they can point their teaching colleagues in profitable directions for locating books, websites, media, and music. They can offer professional development sessions to describe the teaching and learning potential of multiple sources and to deal with practical considerations. They can meet with faculty units to discuss feasible ways of implementing practices with multiple texts. They can team up with content teachers to plan and teach lessons and units that infuse multiple sources. They can conduct demonstrations in the classroom of how particular sources might be used most advantageously. Finally, they can encourage and create opportunities for teachers to read and view materials to enrich disciplinary practices.

At the high school where Marco worked as a reading coach, he brought the science faculty together to form an after-school club to read, view, and discuss materials that could be used in addition to the textbook. At each meeting, club members brought books, URLs, DVDs, music, or some other source for the others to consider. Depending on length, a film might be viewed in part or in its totality followed by critical dialogue about the best ways to incorporate it into classroom instruction, as well as the potential obstacles to doing so. Club members gave book talks about young adult fiction and nonfiction, then brainstormed how they might be utilized and with which science topics.

Marco made certain he had something to share at each meeting. For instance, in response to one of the teacher's complaints that many of the print sources discussed in the club were too difficult for her low-achieving students, Marco researched a number of websites and found several with simplified and graphic presentations of complex science topics. The club met in the library/media center for that session to access the sites, explore them, and talk about their feasibility. After maneuvering around one site, *chem4kids*, the teacher was pleasantly surprised by the variety of topics covered and the easy reading level of the texts. With the help of the others, the teacher generated several options for using *chem4kids* texts with her low-ability readers, including creating booklets with appealing covers, and making these available during independent work time. Later, Marco was invited into the teacher's classroom to observe firsthand the success of this approach. He watched as three of the students who would formerly put their heads on the desk or engage in disruptive behavior during individual work time actually read the relevant booklets on the day's topic.

As a teacher leader, Marco was able to convince his colleagues of the value of forming the club and was the force that sustained the group throughout the year. The teachers agreed that what contributed most to their regular participation was the practical and supportive nature of the club. Marco made no demands, but enthusiastically encouraged his peers to give new sources a try and to talk openly about both triumphs and struggles.

English

In preparation for reading, studying, and doing dramatic interpretations of *Hamlet*, Vera had her 12th-grade students read *Shakespeare's Hamlet: The Manga Edition* (Shakespeare, Sexton, & Pantoja, 2008). With lively illustrations, this fast-paced graphic manga edition remains faithful to the story and retains much of the original dialogue and narration. Although Vera knew there is no substitute for the actual work, she nonetheless recognized the value of this illustrated comic book for introducing her students to the exciting world and remarkable ideas of *Hamlet*. In this way, the book served as a bridge to the original, offering students a story with rich artwork and skillful expressions of Hamlet's anguish and torment.

To create an atmosphere of the late Renaissance as a context for the plays and poems of Shakespeare, Vera provided layered experiences (Abrams & Gerber, 2015; Nicholson, 2000) using multiple forms of representation, such as music, art, and dance. Students listened to compositions both formal and bawdy by Elizabethan-era composers. A couple of members of a troupe of reenactors she had met at the state Renaissance Fair visited the class and got students involved in music, dance, and impromptu drama activities. From various websites, Vera projected late-Renaissance visual art on the screen and engaged the class in discussion about what these pieces could tell them as to the attitudes and values of the time period.

Because you know which concepts and information students will eventually encounter, when choosing to read orally from multiple texts, you can easily highlight key passages by reading them with particular emphasis or by reading them again after cuing the students. When multiple sources are read independently or in small groups, you can alert students to these passages before reading. You can also use discussion and demonstrate context strategies for learning terminology that appears in the sources and that will show up later in the textbook and as the content is studied more fully.

The principal benefit of using a variety of sources in disciplinary classes is that they elevate student interest (Brozo, 2013; Brozo & Mayville, 2012). Texts such as primary documents, young adult literature, graphic novels, and the like—often because they are simply an alternative to textbooks—engender immediate curiosity. Curiosity can be channeled to motivate youth to read with greater purpose and listen with greater attention. Combining multiple sources with strategies to encourage active participation, including discussion and written responses after daily reading, will build important schemas for more in-depth study of the topic.

Use Multiple Sources to Extend Textbook Ideas

During reading, students can work in small groups to discuss particular issues raised in the textbook and elaborated on in other sources. Students can share what they have found to be particularly informative sections of these sources that support and extend what textbook authors say and what the teacher says. For instance, the teacher and class could read a section of the textbook and then search alternative materials for additional and supporting information, as occurred in the following classroom examples.

History

Eleventh-grade students studying 20th-century history used a graphic novel, Marjane Satrapi's *Persepolis: The Story of a Childhood* (2004), in conjunction with the textbook to learn more about the rise of Islamic fundamentalism. In this autobiographical story, Satrapi recounts her childhood in Iran during the Islamic Revolution. Tracing the dethroning of the shah, the rise of fundamentalism, and the war with Iraq through a child's eyes, *Persepolis* gave students an informative overview of Iranian history and culture while serving as a nice point of comparison and contrast for America's own revolutionary roots. As the teacher read the graphic novel, students were asked to listen for passages describing the revolution from the indigenous Iranian people's point of view, a perspective omitted in their textbook treatment.

Science

Kim's seventh-grade science textbook, though of fairly recent vintage, fails to keep pace with the dizzying speed of new developments in space exploration. To keep her students engaged, she supplements the textbook with graphic novels such as *Orbiter* (Ellis & Doran, 2004). In this novel, a space shuttle named Orbiter had disappeared 10 years earlier. Then, suddenly, it mysteriously returns. The pilot, who hasn't aged a day, is speaking in a tongue no one understands. The authors' science fiction gives Kim's students plenty to ponder as they explore the scientific and cultural merit of manned spaceflight as well as the breathtaking look at the possibilities of the universe. Kim obtained multiple copies of *Orbiter* through a small science teacher grant and has her students work in small groups to read and document similarities and differences between the novel and information about space exploration in the science textbook.

Social Studies

Eighth graders learning about the Age of Exploration in the New World in their social studies textbooks also read in small groups Scott O'Dell's timeless trilogy, *The Captive* (1979), *The Feathered Serpent* (1981), and *The Amethyst Ring* (1983), which chronicle the 16th-century world of the Maya, Aztec, and Inca empires, respectively. Information in the textbook was embellished with input from students about the events taking place in their novels. For example, students found passages that helped to explain how and why a mere handful of Spaniards were able to overtake three enormous empires. As I noted earlier, too often the driving human forces behind important historical events are not made clear in textbook accounts. In O'Dell's trilogy, however, the reader is brought face-to-face with the greed and religious zeal that drove many explorers and their followers to fanatical behavior.

Biology

Gary, an experienced teacher of 14 years, teaches general biology in a high school set in an economically depressed area of an inner city. African Americans and Latinos/Latinas make up nearly 90% of the student body. Because of the special concerns his students bring to his classroom, Gary has become a resourceful teacher who is constantly searching for new ways to make his instruction more responsive to the needs of his students.

His classroom is an inviting setting for a young researcher and scientist. Next to his door in the hall is a large glassed-in display case that he and his students redo with each new 9-week grading period. During a unit on food chains, for example, the display included the book *Never Cry Wolf* by Farley Mowat (1979), a collage in the shape of a wolf's head composed of pictures of animals that wolves prey upon, a pair of binoculars, and a field book with pencil. The walls of his room are laden with posters, charts, student work, and photographs of field trips Gary and his students have taken over the past few years to such interesting places as the Elk Repopulation Center in Great Smoky Mountains National Park, the Florida Everglades, and the North Carolina Outer Banks. Three large lab tables hold animal specimens in jars, petri dishes, various artifacts from the natural world (e.g., rocks, grasses, mosses, snake skins, owl pellets), a large aquarium, and microscopes. Against one wall is a row of eight computers; against another are two large bookshelves—one filled with science-related paperbacks and magazines, the other with reference and informational books.

Gary's C-Block class had 24 students. The topic for the day's lesson was "Population Crashes," which Gary had projected on a large screen in the front of the room from his computer. After employing a 10-minute PowerPoint presentation that defined and characterized causes and effects of population crashes in the natural world, Gary asked students to work in pairs to seek out as much evidence and as many examples as they could find of such population crashes using the print and nonprint resources available to them. Students were given a recording sheet to document their research.

Tremayne and Elton used a total of four different information sources. They began by thumbing back through the novel *Never Cry Wolf,* which the class had been reading, and wrote down information related to Mowat's description of what happens to the vole population when too many wolves are killed or relocated. They moved from the novel to the Internet and found a site devoted to problems related to overpopulation of humans. Elton remembered something he had seen in a magazine related to human overpopulation and went to the bookshelf, returning with a copy of the *Smithsonian.* He and Tremayne looked through the article together and took notes. Finally, the two boys used one of the scientific reference books to look up information on Thomas Malthus—a person Gary mentioned in his presentation—for more leads about population crashes. There was a general biology textbook, but only a couple of students were consulting it for information.

Gary then passed out copies of *Never Cry Wolf* and organized a review of the last chapter read. The review was in a "popcorn" format, whereby Gary gave the class the first critical event of the chapter, then waited for other students to stand up and supply a statement about what happened next. Using this approach, the class was able to cover most of the chapter plot within 5 minutes.

Gary then invited volunteers to come to the front of the class and take parts reading the next chapter aloud. In this chapter, a bush pilot and a party of hunters make camp near to where Mowat is conducting his research on the wolf pack. He and the hunters have a threatening encounter. Gary took the role of narrator, while the others read the parts of Mowat and members of the hunting party. Students seemed eager to participate, and after a couple of pages a new set of students came to the front of the class to continue the read-aloud. Gary was patient with all students and waited until one asked for help with a word before he or a classmate provided it.

At several points in the action, Gary invited class members who were not reading aloud to ask questions of the students who were. This seemed to keep everyone focused on the plot. Student questions were mostly verbatim level. Gary welcomed all of them, however, while modeling higher-level-thinking questions.

Gary has a strong desire to help his students develop independent learning skills, so he always includes opportunities for them to explore topics on their own. Gary allows his students to use other resources than the textbook, because as he says, "That's what researchers do." When information is needed in his classroom, students are used to going to whatever sources are available. Gary knows the textbook is written at a level that's too difficult for many of his students, so he doesn't rely on it. When he allows his class to read about class topics from sources that may be easier for them, they tend to stay on task.

Gary uses novels because he wants his students to be interested in science. He recognizes that if the only way they received science is through a textbook, they would never want to explore science further or become scientists themselves. He is also sensitive to the fact that his kids are generally poor readers and that the only way they'll get any better is if they get time to read in school. In addition to Farley Mowat's book, Gary read aloud to his class *Mountains Beyond Mountains: The Quest of Dr. Paul Farmer, A Man Who Would Cure the World* (Kidder & French, 2014) when studying the role of cells in infectious disease and *The Radioactive Boy Scout: The Frightening True Story of a Whiz Kid and His Homemade Nuclear Reactor* (Silverstein, 2005) when covering a unit on nuclear waste and the environment.

English

Earlier in this chapter, I alluded to a middle school teacher who exploited students' interest in fanfiction (Chandler-Olcott, 2007) to elevate motivation for writing and increase understanding of story structure. Importing adolescents' personal literacies into classrooms requires a deft hand so that these preferred texts are not stripped of their enjoyment for youth. We need to bear in mind that youth pursue certain literate practices for the simple reason that they are not sanctioned inside of school. Nevertheless, in the hands of caring and knowledgeable teachers, personal and academic literacies can be successfully conjoined.

Kim's seventh-grade English classes had several students who were reading, viewing, and engaging in electronic discussions about anime, or the Japanese animated comics and video. Kim learned of their interest in anime early in the school year after students shared "My Bags" (see Chapter 5). Always on the lookout for ways of tying students' personal interests to school-based activities, Kim decided to establish a lunchtime club for devotees of anime-related fanfiction. As some who were interested in anime were in need of improvement in academic literacy, Kim hoped the club would serve as vehicle for critical reading and creative writing.

One of the anime series the club members wanted to read and write about was *Ranma ½* created by Rumiko Takahashi Ranma, when on a training excursion in China, falls into a spring where a girl had drowned and was transformed himself into a girl. Now every time Ranma splashes cold water on his face, he turns into a red-haired girl. Hot water reverses the transformation. So, within the various adventures Ranma experiences, Ranma is sometimes a girl and sometimes a boy. Ranma lives in "Tendo Dojo" with his father and two sisters. Other characters include Akane, handpicked by her father and Ranma's father to be Ranma's wife, and Dr. Tofu.

Club members read from a *Ranma ½* series comic, talked about the action, and wrote and exchanged episodes related to Ranma. Kim was careful not to turn the club into a substitute for English class but subtly encouraged students to consider such things as how the *Ranma ½* anime compared and contrasted with stories from their literature anthology and ways their writing might resemble narrative forms they discussed in class.

Gayle and Toni, two club members who were struggling in Kim's English class, liked to work together to write and illustrate their own *Ranma ½*-inspired comic that featured Nabiki, Ranma's eldest sister. Her character is presented as extremely smart and cunning. She has also turned her interest in taking pictures into a cottage industry, though Nabiki shows her greedy side when bargaining with customers. Gayle did all the artistic work while Toni wrote the text for their episodes of Nabiki. In one, they had her capture Ranma and force him to pose for her camera while cold and hot water are applied to either side of his face, creating a half-boy–half-girl image. Nabiki then sold these unique prints for many thousand yen.

With this particular fanfiction, Kim was able to draw club members into discussion about important narrative elements, such as protagonist, antagonist, conflict, resolution, and theme. And as students like Gayle and Toni felt more confident in their ability to compose a story with essential features, they showed improvement in understanding stories in the literature anthology.

In senior English, Jamal made space in his class for the music his urban students loved, hip-hop. In a unique unit designed to promote an appreciation for the currency of canonical texts in literature, Jamal asked his students to make linkages between the poems and stories they were required to read and hip-hop lyrics they listened to every day.

Several pairs of students were formed and given two texts to interpret and analyze. Critical in the analysis were the ways in which the texts shared common themes. Students were given a week to work on the assignment and then make a presentation to the class. Carla and Jarrod were assigned the T. S. Eliot poem "The Waste Land" and Grandmaster Flash's "The Message." As they read and reread these texts, important themes began to emerge for them. For instance, they realized that the authors were looking out on their worlds and seeing signs all around of decay and decline; both pieces were apocalyptic visions of death and disease; and both positioned the poet as a messenger or prophet. Jamal knew these kinds of critical and deep connections were made possible for youth by their affinity with the lived experience of the hip-hop artist and who then used this empathy to appreciate other voices with similar messages, though from disparate cultures and times.

Environmental Science

Every year during Mahmood's unit on hurricanes, he connects his ninth graders to primary sources for information and data on the most recent storms to make landfall along our U.S. coasts. Some years yield few significant storms of that type, whereas others have been so cataclysmic they demand extensive study to understand fully their impact on the environment. Such was the case with Hurricane Katrina, which transformed the city of New Orleans and surrounding coastal communities into uninhabitable disaster areas.

Mahmood first identifies key topics in the unit using the textbook and science standards, then guides his students to helpful websites to learn more about these topics. The National Hurricane Center (NHC; *www.nhc.noaa.gov*) is one site he often directs students to, with its invaluable maps, datasets, and extensive records of tropical storm activity. For learning more about Katrina, he included URLs with multimedia news clips of on-the-scene reporters and meteorologists; blog sites by those who experienced the hurricane from inside the Louisiana Superdome and the evacuation ordeal and weather reports from New Orleans and Biloxi, Mississippi, newspapers leading up to the storm's arrival.

Mahmood had his students consult the alternative sources for specific information on Hurricane Katrina after encountering important general information about hurricanes in the textbook. For example, students read in their textbooks about the storm tracking system of the National Oceanic and Atmospheric Administration (NOAA), then went to the NHC site for actual tracking charts of Hurricane Katrina. After studying a chart presented in their textbook with hurricane storm categories from 1 to 5 and the potential damage each one can cause, Mahmood's students looked at video clips and read news reports of the actual destruction by Katrina and read descriptions from blogs of witnesses to the storm to better appreciate its effects on human lives.

A particularly engaging source Mahmood added to the mix was the stunning graphic novel A.D.: *New Orleans after the Deluge* (Neufeld, 2009). In addition to the meteorological facts about Katrina, this human perspective documents the true stories of six New Orleanians who survived the hurricane and gave life to the data and images. Virtually all of Mahmood's students made time to go through the graphic novel and felt it was one of the more memorable texts of the unit.

Algebra

During Kim's unit on functions in her advanced algebra class, she directed students to some real estate websites to apply their new understandings. The sites list a variety of homes for sale in the community, with information about the house, a floor plan with room dimensions, and sales price. Students were to determine a functional relationship between a house's floor plan area and its cost. Kim puts students into groups of three and assigns them various questions and problems, such as:

- What function best describes this relationship?
- What other factors affect the sales price of a house?
- What comparisons and conclusions can you make about the additional data that describe the houses?
- Based on your analysis, what should be the current sales price of the house of someone in your group?

Throughout the unit, Kim provides time for groups to meet, access the websites, and discuss data gathering and analysis. She asks groups to present what they're learning to the class. They are expected to explain the reasoning, criteria, procedures, and data analyses when presenting their results. Kim points out differences in the groups' functions and encourages questions and challenges over which function best models the relationship.

Music

Twelfth-grade music teacher Nina asked her orchestral class to read *Lohengrin* as they prepared for a performance of the overtures that accompany Wagner's enchanting opera. Much more than a libretto, *Lohengrin*, written by the composer, resembles a novella. Because of its length, the story of *Lohengrin* is well developed, and character descriptions are rich. These features make the book ideally suited to instruction in musical interpretation. As the young musicians read the book, they also worked on the music. Cooperative groups were formed on the basis of orchestral sections (strings, woodwinds, percussion instruments, etc.). During each class session, groups were responsible for reflecting on the story, discussing plot and character, and then, based on story interpretations, presenting possible musical interpretations. After whole-class discussions and teacher input, the student musicians attempted to operationalize their interpretations in rehearsals.

Terrence used reading and writing in his music composition class. Every week his inner-city students gathered newspapers and used the headlines for inspiration in their composing. In another example, he read sections of the book *World of Medieval and Renaissance Musical Instruments* (Montagu, 1976). The book was filled with illustrations of instruments, some rather exotic, that have long since vanished and others that have evolved into modern instruments being played in orchestras today. The author explained how some contemporary craftspersons were attempting to re-create these extinct instruments. This book inspired the class to create their own instruments. Using junk from garages, closets, attics, and alleys piled in the classroom, students fashioned horns, drums, and stringed instruments. With this motley assemblage, they wrote and performed an original composition.

The female students were complaining that they were reading about and hearing compositions only by male composers. Terrence acquired information on and addresses of several contemporary female classical music composers, and his students found their addresses and websites in order to write emails to them. A couple of them wrote back, sending links to their work on the Internet, as well as sample scores. The class performed a composition given them by one of the composers and allowed her to listen and watch via Skype.

Terrence keeps many additional books for adolescents with music themes in his class library. Among them are such picture books as *The Voice That Challenged a Nation: Marian Anderson and the Struggle for Equal Rights* (Freedman, 2005) and *Leontyne Price: Voice of a Century* (Weatherford, 2014).

English

Jasmina takes every opportunity to bring real-world reading materials into the classroom so that, through interesting and meaningful activities, her students come to understand how reading needs to be a part of their adult lives. Newspapers, magazines, and various other print sources found in the adult world are used in her daily classroom instruction and made available in the classroom library or reading corner.

A prime example of integrating everyday reading materials into classroom instruction occurred when Jasmina was helping her students understand metaphor. The class grammar book, although a useful reference source, fails to demonstrate authentic applications of rules and forms that youth encounter daily. She knew that metaphors are found everywhere in newspapers, in headlines, advertisements, editorials, and even weather forecasts. Because newspapers are inexpensive, easy to obtain, and contain articles that are generally short and concise, they are an excellent source for figurative language instruction.

Jasmina began by distributing to small groups of students headlines that used metaphorical language, such as "Still Limping, Oil Patch Exits Intensive Care" and "Experts Zero in on Magic Bullet to Kill Cancer Cells." Using a reciprocal teaching strategy (explained in Chapter 3), she modeled a question-asking and -answering process out loud to demonstrate for students how she interpreted the metaphors in the headlines. For instance, with the first headline, she began by asking "What is an oil patch?" Then she dug into the article until she found information that helped her answer the question. The oil patch is a group of four states whose net worth and economic stability depend heavily on the production and sale of oil—namely, Louisiana, Oklahoma, Colorado, and Texas.

The next question Jasmina asked was, "In what way could four oil-producing states exit intensive care?" She pointed out that the statement clearly made no sense if interpreted literally, which, by default, made it a metaphor. This question led immediately to her next question, "Who would normally exit, 'limping,' from the intensive care ward?" Students were quick to respond by identifying a sick or injured person who is getting better but is basically still ill or injured. In this way students began to see the similarities between the oil patch and a patient just released from intensive care.

At this point, Jasmina asked students, working in their groups, to come up with an explanation of the metaphor. Most were able to explain that the oil-producing states were in trouble but were in far better financial shape than they were a few years ago, just as the hospitalized person who limps out of intensive care is still in trouble but in better physical condition than not long before.

Jasmina went on to engage students in a discussion of why the author chose to use a metaphorical headline in the first place. To make the article more attractive and "catchy" was one explanation. Another was that the author was "teasing" readers to entice them to read the article. The teacher pointed out that by linking the troubled economies of distant states with something familiar—hospitals, illness—the author was trying to make his subject accessible to more readers.

History

For the study of the Civil Rights movement, Angela selected the following teaching goals for her students: (1) to broaden their awareness of what everyday life was like in the decades before and during the Civil Rights era in America from different perspectives, (2) to help them appreciate the efforts of those who brought about positive change during this era, and (3) to sensitize them to the tragic consequences racial discrimination brings its victims. To accomplish these goals, Angela introduced her students to several sources, in addition to the textbook, that she found with the help of her school librarian. These sources and descriptions are in Figure 8.7.

While students had access to these wonderful sources for study and research, Angela chose to read aloud the young adult book, *Sources of Light* (McMullan, 2012) as students followed along in their own copies. As students read chapters in their textbook and the various other texts and listened to the trade book, they responded to study guides (discussed in Chapter 3) that were designed to help students see connections across sources, apply their new learning beyond the parameters of the unit, and involve them in dynamic class discussions. In the guide shown in Figure 8.8, students were asked to make inferences about the attitudes of story characters. In this way, students were helped to understand the various points of view on the Civil Rights movement.

Chumley, C. K. (2013, April 13). U.S. Civil Rights Commission warns that amnesty hurts blacks. *The Washington Times*. Retrieved from *www.washingtontimes. com/news/2013/apr/12/us-civil-rights-commission-members-warn-amnesty-hu.*—This article from the *Washington Times* addresses the possible ramifications of immigration reform policy that permits millions of illegal immigrants to legally remain and work in the United States. This article would permit Angela to see a side of the immigration debate which she may not have considered before, but which is germane to the issues of the Civil Rights movement: a limited number of low-skilled jobs must be shared among the large number of unskilled workers in the United States, whether they are native-born or immigrants. Specifically, the article warns that African Americans might be displaced by immigrant workers, thus dividing two minorities who historically have shared goals and action plans. It brings to light yet another aspect of the Civil Rights movement for students—the tension between shared causes and disparate origins.

Civil Liberties and Civil Rights. (n.d.). Civil liberties and civil rights. Retrieved from *www. ushistory.org/gov/10.asp*; Others Demand Equality. (n.d.).—Others demand equality. Retrieved from *www.ushistory.org/us/57f.asp.*—Both of these websites offer a variety of articles concerning civil rights in America. These sites serve as a useful research tool for helping students explore various topics, as the sites are well organized and easy to navigate.

Civil Rights Voices. (n.d.). Display voices. Retrieved from *www.digitalhistory.uh.edu/ voices/voices_content.cfm?vid=13.*—This particular website provides personal perspectives from various people who lived during the Civil Rights movement.

Jeffrey, G. (2012). *Rosa Parks and the Montgomery bus boycott: A graphic history of the civil rights movement*. New York: Gareth Stevens Publishing.—This graphic novel's 24 pages of iconic imagery helps students see in their minds the pivotal events of the Civil Rights movement. The perspectives and varying points of view in the drawings lend unique meaning; for example, one sees Dr. Martin Luther King, Jr. from over the giant marble shoulder of President Lincoln, thus connecting Dr. King's efforts in the Civil Rights movement with those of Lincoln in the Civil War. The text is limited to speech bubbles and captions, both of which are easy to read and understand, especially for Angela's struggling readers.

Kenworthy, E. W. (1964, June 20). Action by Senate. *New York Times*, p. 2; Robinson, L. (1964, January 3). Puerto Rican bid on civil rights is made. *New York Times*, p. 1.—These original articles both discuss political actions taking place in the 1960s concerning to civil rights. They give a realistic perspective of the struggle of these particular groups and what the public outcry actually did or did not accomplish.

Laird, R. O., Laird, T. N., & Bey, E. (2009). *Still I rise: A graphic history of African Americans*. New York: Sterling.—*Still I Rise* is a nonfiction visual representation of the history of African Americans from slavery to the present. Told from the African American perspective, this book chronicles the dense history of events and the struggles that contributed to what our country is today. From slavery to Black Power and racial issues today, this book visually informs the reader of important elements that are not always included in average textbooks. Angela chose this book based on the detail and poignancy with which the story of African Americans is told. The language is accessible, and the lives of many influential people are included, along with arguments from both sides.

(continued)

FIGURE 8.7. Alternative texts for a unit on Civil Rights in America.

Long, M., Venable, C. A., Tobey, E., Demonakos, J., & Powell, N. (2012). *The silence of our friends*. New York: First Second.—This semiautobiographical graphic novel takes place in Texas during the era of the Civil Rights movement. The story is about a White family from a racist neighborhood and a Black family from the most impoverished area of Houston. These families meet when five Black youths are unjustly accused of killing a police officer. The story is told from the point of view of a teenage boy whose father is a journalist documenting the events.

Manzano, S., & Parsi, E. B. (2012). *The revolution of Evelyn Serrano*. New York: Scholastic.— Angela chose this book because it tells a civil rights story from an uncommon perspective, a Puerto Rican girl in Spanish Harlem. The Civil Rights movement in America is often depicted as an African American experience. However, Latinos were very much a part of the struggle for fair treatment and were affected during the 1950s into the late 1960s as well. The revolution of Evelyn Serrano tells the story of the rise of the Young Lords, a Puerto Rican activist group in the late 1960s. Based on the author's childhood experience, the story exposes important truths about what Latino heritage means and the advocates who shaped this cultural identity.

McMullan, M. (2010). *Sources of light*. Boston: Houghton Mifflin Harcourt.—Set in Jackson, Mississippi, in 1962, Margaret McMullan's young adult novel spins an engaging tale of a girl and her family at a time of great racial tension. McMullan's writing weaves historical facts of racism with the fictional tale of the protagonist's family and friends. Many of the key conflicts of the Civil Rights movement are illustrated in this story as the characters connect and uncover the truth behind the death of a key character. The young woman learns photography from a Civil Rights activist, and her camera becomes a metaphor for the clear eye needed to view the racism and inequality of the era.

Tougas, S. (2011). *Birmingham 1963: How a photograph rallied civil rights support*. Mankato, MN: Capstone Books/Capstone Publishing.—A powerful cover photograph of children being slammed against a window by a police firehose irresistibly draws readers into this book about the children's march in Birmingham in 1963. The book focuses on the iconic photograph and how it mobilized more nonviolent demonstrations in the Civil Rights movement. It also contains information about the segregated community and local government structures. This relatively short book is filled with important facts about how the Civil Rights movement grew in size and scope, thus providing a springboard into the more complex textbook treatment of the topic.

FIGURE 8.7. (*continued*)

Directions: Listed across the page are forms of protest and other forms of political action related to events from *Sources of Light*. Listed down the left side are names of the main characters involved in the story. In each box indicate whether that character would agree or disagree with the action. Defend your response by including evidence from the novel, including page and paragraph numbers.

Agree = A Disagree = D	Sit-ins	Boycotts	Cross burning	Registering voters	Marches
Samantha	_____ Evidence:	_____ Evidence:	_____ Evidence:	_____ Evidence:	_____ Evidence:
Mrs. Thomas	_____ Evidence:	_____ Evidence:	_____ Evidence:	_____ Evidence:	_____ Evidence:
Perry	_____ Evidence:	_____ Evidence:	_____ Evidence:	_____ Evidence:	_____ Evidence:
Stone	_____ Evidence:	_____ Evidence:	_____ Evidence:	_____ Evidence:	_____ Evidence:
Willa Mae	_____ Evidence:	_____ Evidence:	_____ Evidence:	_____ Evidence:	_____ Evidence:

FIGURE 8.8. Process guide for *Sources of Light*.

In a study of immigrants to the United States in the early 20th century, Tom read aloud to his juniors from the award-winning book *Brooklyn Bridge* (Hesse, 2008). Steeped in the Jewish immigrant experience in early-20th-century New York City, this story centers on 14-year-old Joe and his personal narrative within his family's and community's struggles.

While studying the details and facts of immigration in their textbooks, students in Tom's class were discovering the human drama of immigration through the stories of Joe's parents, who escaped the pogroms of the Russian shtetl. Tom had his students trace Joe's family journey on a map of Europe and the United States. Students compared the joys and heartaches of the Russian Jewish immigrants with their own families' experiences. With so many of his students being recent immigrants themselves, Tom had them re-create their own experiences in the form of a diary or personal travelogue accompanied by graphic panels created at the Comic Master website (*http://comicmaster.org.uk*). Students were given regular opportunities to read entries to the class and share their illustrations.

Mathematics

Lori had been struggling to help her geometry students expand their perceptions of geometry and look for real-life parallels to geometric terms, postulates, and theorems. Her efforts accomplished little until she boldly decided to have her class read and discuss novels. She began her search for appropriate literature with some incredulity, but with the help of a local reference librarian, she soon discovered several books that appeared ideally suited to teaching geometry, including Abbot's (1927) *Flatland*, Hinton's (1907) *An Episode in Flatland*, and Dewdney's (1984) *The Planiverse*. She finally chose *Flatland*, a 19th-century British novel of science fiction, as an important tool in trying to humanize students' understanding of geometry.

In Flatland, all of the characters are two-dimensional geometric figures that represent different social classes. The first part is essentially a social satire. In the second part, the main character travels to other dimensions to describe the relative merits of different points of view. *Flatland* can be read for its straight geometric descriptions as well as for its social commentary and satire.

Lori found that *Flatland* could be incorporated into her geometry course without ignoring any of the basic material. She tied the book to a unit in the textbook dealing with geometric models of the universe. Class discussion centered on the basic plot: its purpose and social context; details of Flatland, other lands, and their inhabitants; and the symbolism. In small groups, students were asked to brainstorm solutions to problems in Flatland (not explained by the author) such as rain and snow patterns, locomotion, food, and writing. Then the whole class compared their solutions. As a writing activity, students were asked to select a known person and tell which Flatland class (geometric figure) he or she would be in and why.

Lori's geometry unit was very well received. Many students asked that more novels be used in the class. Lori found her efforts worthwhile because she was able to get to know her students better, how they thought and felt, as a result of the many opportunities to interact during the unit. She also accomplished her goal of humanizing the learning of geometry.

During the first grading period in Latife's physics class, she read aloud 3:59 (McNeil, 2014). The central character in the story, Josie, is a physics geek whose mother is known for her work in creating micro black holes. Josie begins seeing her twin, Jo, through an antique mirror in the house. Josie convinces Jo, who resides in a parallel universe, to trade places with her, and the adventure begins in earnest. Jo's universe is filled with menacing creatures that make meals out of humans. Not long after the swap, Josie wants to return to her universe, only to find that her double, Jo, is not too eager to change back, given the comfortable and safe world she has found herself in. Latife used this book for its humorous take on problems of physics and its thrills. She also uses the novel as a prod, especially for the girls in class, to keep up the work and effort and to accept problems in physics as challenges to be met and overcome.

Other good reads Latife has made available to her physics students include Kumar's (2011) *Quantum: Einstein, Bohr, and The Great Debate about the Nature of Reality*, Orzel's (2010) *How to Teach (Quantum) Physics to Your Dog*, and Zhang's (2015) *Falling into Place*.

French

To help a group of first-year students develop an appreciation for the similarities and differences in French and American cultures, Faith had her students read *My Secret Guide to Paris* (Schroeder, 2015). In this story, Nora, an American teen, finally gets her wish to travel to Paris. The mystery involves Nora's mother discovering an envelope with three plane tickets in a trunk of her recently deceased grandmother's house. The envelope also contains odd clues that send Nora and her mother on an interesting scavenger hunt through the City of Light. The story's tinge of mystery makes it even more engaging. As Faith's students read the book, she had them compare the French styles of eating, transportation, and other customs with the American way of life. Students were also required to research a particular aspect of French culture that presented the main character in the book with challenges and report back to the class.

Current Events

Glen's senior class was focusing on the former system of apartheid in South Africa. Resources for the unit included government and United Nations reports, essays by

Nelson Mandela, music lyrics by Black South African folk-song writers, and young adult books. These included two evocatively illustrated books, *Nelson Mandela: The Authorized Comic Book* (Nelson Mandela Foundation, 2009) and *Nelson Mandela: The Unconquerable Soul* (Helfand, 2012). In both graphic novels, the panels are accompanied by a text that contains an extraordinary amount of detail about Mandela's personal life and the history and politics of anti-apartheid.

The other books were two masterful novels written by Norman Silver. *No Tigers in Africa* (Silver, 1990) tells the story of Selwyn Lewis and his white racist upbringing in Cape Town, South Africa. When his family moves to England, however, Selwyn's new experiences force him to confront his racism and look within himself to find moral solutions to prejudice. In *An Eye for Color* (Silver, 1991), Basil Kushenovitz narrates interconnecting stories about growing up white and Jewish in Cape Town. About his ambivalent position in a racist culture, Basil says that, like a lizard, "My one eye sees one thing, and my other eye sees something quite different." Basil must try to reconcile his split vision—between his comforts and others' deprivation, between what is expected of a white man and what he himself is willing to become. Glen's goal in having his students read both of Silver's honest and painful novels was to rivet them to the compelling human stories of apartheid, making it possible for them to understand that racist systems leave victims on both sides of the color/culture fence.

Science

Gordy found the ideal novel to use in conjunction with his 10th-grade general biology students' study of molecular processes of life. *The Chromosome Game* (Hodder-Williams, 2016) features a future world, planned by 20th-century scientists, that has gone horrifyingly wrong. The aftermath of genetic experimentation has resulted in a ruined and barren world. Nonetheless, carefully selected DNA has been conserved in gene banks, holding the possibility of salvaging humankind, if only a chosen group can retrieve it in time. Gordy read the novel aloud to his class and exploited it both for its interesting and scientifically sound information about genetics and for its more challenging theme of the dangers of uncontrolled and unregulated manipulation of the genetic code. His students were required to keep a notebook of information gleaned from the novel that related to the biology textbook's treatment of the same topic. Gordy also had his class confront ethical issues of genetic engineering through debates and role plays.

Eighth-grade teacher Alicia captured her students' attention and enthusiasm for learning by using the illustrated informational book *Sports Science for Young People* (Barr, 2011). Filled with outstanding illustrations, this colorful, enjoyable book deals with scientific principles underlying major sports activities. By combining sports and science, Alicia found that students learned the facts of aerodynamics and understood the principles more thoroughly than when the textbook was the sole resource.

In another classroom, Gail taught a unit on the consequences of science and technology through the use of science fiction. Her goal was to promote problem-solving skills and help students clarify values regarding scientific technology. Knowing that science fiction can motivate students to take a greater interest in science (Fowler, 2010; Kilby-Goodwin, 2010), Gail used *Star Trek: The Next Generation* (Bornholt, 1989) to instigate discussion on controversial issues associated with cloning. In the story, members of the *Enterprise* spaceship, while on a planet populated by original clone settlers, are asked to allow their own tissues to be used to spawn a new generation of clones to replace a line that is malfunctioning. The crew members refuse but find that their tissues have been stolen while they were rendered unconscious. They return to the planet and destroy their clone look-alikes. The colony claimed that without the new clones they would die out in a few generations.

Given these story events, Gail posed the following question to her students and asked them to take a stand on a values continuum: Did the *Enterprise* crew members have the right to destroy the clones?

Pro-choice	*Right-to-life*
Do not provide tissue for cloning	Provide tissue for cloning

First, students were asked to write their positions on their own. Then they went to the board and plotted their positions on the values continuum by writing their names along it. This was followed by small-group interaction to crystallize their positions and respond to those of others. The activity concluded with class discussion. Gail has found science fiction to be a rich resource for teaching science because it motivates students to become more active learners and thinkers.

Art

Many students who are not blessed with artists' hands can learn something of how the artist sees the world through related young adult books (Andrelchik, 2015; Berk, 2015; Williams, 2008). Cal, a high school art teacher, began to recognize the connection between good books and art appreciation after reading sleuth books by Jonathan Gash and John Malcolm relating to crimes in the art world. This led him to investigate books for adolescents that would help students who struggle with drawing and painting assignments gain some insights into the way artists see the world and approach compositions. In his search he found several good books and began using them in his art classes. Among students' favorites are *Wake Up Our Souls: A Celebration of African American Artists* (Bolden, 2005); *Frida and Diego: Art, Love, Life* (Reef, 2014); *Graffiti Moon* (Crowley, 2012); and *Happyface* (Emond, 2011).

Cal has read these books aloud to his students, drawing their attention to their central theme: the artist's struggle to capture a vision. In addition, he has found that his students come to care deeply for the engaging characters, both fictional and real, who populate these books, thus learning things from them about artistic expression that Cal himself cannot teach.

Because art is visual, it makes sense to enrich the art class with young adult books that have painting and drawing themes. Cal has added to his school studio collection wonderfully illustrated books for his art classes, such as *Extreme Worlds: The Complete Guide to Drawing and Painting Sci-Fi Art* (Tsai, 2009), a practical guide for budding artists who want to create their own extreme sci-fi worlds; *Manga for the Beginner: Everything You Need to Know to Get Started Right Away!* (Hart, 2008), a comprehensive tutorial for the aspiring manga artist; *Renaissance Art* (Kallen, 2008); *The Fashion Sketchpad: 420 Figure Templates for Designing Looks and Building Your Portfolio* (Daniel, 2011); *Picture This* (Barry, 2010), a series of portraits featuring a myopic monkey protagonist and the author's most beloved character, Marlys; and *Andy Warhol, Prince of Pop* (Greenberg & Jordan, 2004), which covers his childhood and art school years in Pittsburgh, his successful career in commercial art, and his rise in the Pop Art movement.

Case Study Revisited

Remember Linda, the history teacher? She was preparing a unit on immigration to the United States, and I asked you to think of trade book strategies that might be helpful to her as she developed activities for her students. Write your suggestions now.

Linda taught the unit by including a variety of print and visual sources to enliven and personalize the history textbook version. She chose texts and media for their quality representation of the immigrant experience. After an extensive search with the help of her school librarian, she decided to make use in her unit of the following sources: (1) a film about the experiences of immigrant teens today; (2) a nonfiction anthology of writers telling about their immigrant experiences as youth; (3) websites with a wealth of information on immigration; and (4) a variety of nonfiction books about American immigrants.

Linda launched the unit with a film entitled *Teens in Between: The Story of Five Immigrant Teens in America* (Brodsky, 2002). Three female and two male teen immigrants attending Annandale High School in Virginia are featured in this film. The recent immigrant youth have similar adjustment issues, such as learning a new language, adopting a U.S. teen culture, and balancing between their homes and their new culture. Yet their adjustment priorities, strategies, and success levels vary depending on their language skills, family situations, preimmigration experiences, and individual characteristics. They came from Somalia, Egypt, Vietnam, and Honduras for various reasons—political freedom, educational benefits, or economic advancement. Instead of presenting a cookie-cutter portrayal of immigrant teenage struggles, Linda presented this film to her students so they could get an in-depth and realistic look of various immigration experiences for teenagers in high school.

Based on the depictions of these four teens, Linda's students were to work from a list of websites to conduct WebQuests. *WebQuests* (Halat, 2008) are focused searches designed to avoid endless Internet surfing and ensure that students find quickly and efficiently Web-based source material for answering questions and conducting research. Once directed to the sites, students, in teams of three, were to find specific information about the recent history of the countries of origin for the teens in the film and use this to help explain immigration patterns from these countries. Periodically, student teams were asked to report to the class on their information and analysis. Linda found the following four sites to be especially helpful for this activity:

1. Latino Issues Forum: *www.learningtogive.org/resources/latinos-issues-forum*
2. Migration Policy Institute: *www.migrationinformation.org*
3. Center for Immigration Studies: *www.cis.org*
4. Asia Society: *www.askasia.org*

Throughout the unit, Linda read aloud from an outstanding anthology borrowed from the librarian called *First Crossing: Stories about Teen Immigrants* (Gallo & Gallo, 2004). This nonfiction source features 11 well-known authors, who describe the experiences of coming to America as youth. These heartfelt and authentic stories reveal the wide variety of circumstances surrounding individual immigrant experiences. For example, Pam Muñoz Ryan recounts in the book's title story, "First Crossing," the perils of a teen boy being smuggled across the Mexican border. Marie G. Lee's "The Rose of Sharon" tells of a spoiled girl's animosity toward her adoptive parents and her desire to return to Korea to find her birth family. In Jean Davies Okimoto's "My Favorite Chaperone," an immigrant from Kazakhstan shares her relationship with her conservative parents, who rely on her to translate for them but still limit her freedom. Collectively, the underlying theme of these stories is the tension the young people feel caused by the eagerness to cut off ties to the homeland while feeling the need to respect the traditions their parents cannot abandon. The stories from this collection that Linda read aloud helped put a very real face on the broad-stroke treatment of immigration found in the history textbook.

To ensure active listening to these stories, Linda engaged students in prereading discussions designed to heighten anticipation and encourage predictions. Afterward, students were asked to write down in a learning log their reactions to what they heard each day: what they liked and did not like, the degree to which the authors' experiences were similar to their own or those of members of their families, and what overall impressions they had after listening.

As resources for independent research into students' own cultural backgrounds, Linda made available several nonfiction books on topics related to immigration. For example, Muslim students in her class had access to *Coming to America: A Muslim Family's Story* (Wolf, 2003). This big, brightly photographed book profiles a family of Egyptian immigrants living in New York City. The father, Hassan, works nights and worries about not having enough time for his family. His wife, Soad, is a shut-in because of her lack of English. Their three children, however, have adapted to their new country well. Linda's students said the book seemed to be an accurate portrayal of life for new Muslim immigrants while showing a personal and realistic side and not the stereotypes.

Another excellent source, *Growing Up Filipino: Stories for Young Adults* (Brainard, 2003), was read by Linda's Filipino students for the life histories of émigrés to the United States. There are more Filipinos living in the United States than most people realize, but finding literature reflective of their experiences is difficult, so Linda was pleased to uncover this source. And Asian American youth in her class had access to Susan Sinnott's (2003) *Extraordinary Asian Americans and Pacific Islanders*. This is a chronicling of the outstanding contributions to the arts, music, business, and government by newly immigrated and older-generation Asian and Pacific Islanders. The book also provides an overview of immigration to the United States and furnishes background information within which to measure the extraordinary accomplishments of these individuals. This resource is accompanied by black-and-white photographs.

Each group was responsible for making a daily oral report summarizing what had been read and learned from the information books. In this way, all students could gain essential content about the immigration experience for different major ethnic groups. As a whole class, students charted the problems each major group of immigrants has faced in American society and the ways in which society has sought to address and solve those problems. Linda's students did not affix blame to any one racial or ethnic group; rather, they recognized that they were all responsible for finding solutions.

LOOKING BACK, LOOKING FORWARD

This chapter has been devoted to explaining and describing ideas and practices for teaching disciplinary content with sources in addition to a course textbook or other single source. First, I presented a theoretical rationale, specific recommendations, and practical considerations for integrating multiple text sources into the content-area classroom. I have shown that the practical use of a variety of alternative texts can be supported by important theories of learning. These theories give credence to practices with these texts that help students build on past literacy successes, create interest and motivation, and develop schemas.

In this chapter, I provided specific instructional recommendations for (1) developing a unit overview and identifying key themes and concepts within the unit topic, (2) choosing multiple sources to help teach concepts, and (3) teaching with textbooks and other texts. And consistent with the overarching theme of this book, I have presented numerous visions of practice in middle and high schools in which teachers incorporate a variety of engaging texts to teach disciplinary content.

Inclusion of multiple sources in disciplinary instruction has been made all the more compelling in the era of the CCSS. The standards stress reading of authentic text in multiple genres in order to develop students' ability to navigate complex narrative and expository discourse forms, representing the various types of text found in academic, work, and leisure settings. It is also important to note that in the PISA reading literacy study, the highest achieving 15-year-olds were those who read a variety of genres. Creating a learning environment in which multiple texts are accessible and integral to disciplinary instruction will provide youth the opportunities they need to encounter and learn to appreciate the value of these multiple-genre texts.

Effective instruction with these texts has produced elaborate processing of information and greater enthusiasm for learning. The probability of success with this approach is enhanced when teachers responsible for content-area subjects look for opportunities to integrate other sources with their textbooks and when teachers and teacher leaders work together to bring about such an integration. Moreover, using alternative texts in content classrooms should not be perceived as a device or gimmick to create interest in a topic on Monday that is forgotten by Friday. To use multiple texts alongside a core source effectively, you need to make long-range plans, carefully considering how each unit's themes and salient concepts will be developed and how the alternative sources can be used to expand upon textbook concepts and information.

Quality texts, once made available to youth, will often sell themselves. The key is knowing the sources available for teaching unit themes and concepts. I recommend that you establish and maintain an independent reading and viewing program of young adult literature, graphic novels, informational nonfiction, primary documents, digital media, and other related sources geared to the students and the disciplines you teach. I also strongly urge you to form close alliances with your school and local librarians. Their knowledge of and skills in uncovering print texts and representational media that coincide with the topics you teach will prove invaluable.

The disciplines deal with interesting, vital information, but if you rely on textbooks as your sole teaching resource, you may render this information dry and lifeless. Use multiple text sources in conjunction with and in addition to textbooks or other core sources to help ensure that students are more actively involved in learning and that the vitality and spirit inherent in the content-area material are kept alive.

In the next chapter, you will discover several sound practices for supporting students in gathering and organizing information and ideas. These study strategies will make it possible for youth to become effective independent readers and learners. This is especially critical in disciplinary classrooms, where students are expected to read and learn from multiple sources, like the classrooms described in this chapter.

CHAPTER 9 ▰▰▰▰▰▰▰▰▰▰▰▰▰▰▰▰▰▰▰▰▰

Strategic Literacy and Learning Processes

As you read Chapter 9, reflect on the following questions:

- What are the five guidelines for teaching strategic literacy and learning processes?

- What are some basic processes that content-area and disciplinary teachers can emphasize to improve their students' metacognitive awareness?

- Why is student self-regulated learning important?

- How can content-area and disciplinary teachers reinforce the connection for students between strategic literacy and learning processes and task demands?

- How can students be taught to take effective notes from lectures and texts?

- What strategies and practices are effective for helping students synthesize ideas from multiple sources?

- How can students be taught to ask their own meaningful questions as they read and study text?

- How can content-area and disciplinary teachers provide formative feedback on their students' strategy attempts?

Like most of my friends in high school, I did not know how to study. I had never been taught to take notes in any particular style, nor was I shown how to highlight, underline, or summarize my required reading. Other than the occasional hint from a teacher, anything I learned back then about notetaking from a lecture or studying from a text I discovered through trial and error on my own. Fortunately for me and several of my friends, we were all fairly high achievers in spite of our lack of strategic reading and study knowledge and skills. This sliding by without strategic-learning knowledge, however, was destined to end once I entered a university.

Graduating with high honors from my small northern Michigan high school did not, unfortunately, accurately reflect how well prepared I really was to take on the reading volume and study requirements that confronted me my first year at the University of North Carolina. Out of desperation, I soon found myself in the student assistance office seeking help. The study skills center counselors gave me a few basic tools to survive those first couple of years while I continued to develop coping strategies for the crushing amount of reading, writing, and studying required to write papers and pass tests.

As a new secondary English teacher, I recall trying to emphasize to my own high school students the value of acquiring strategies for reading and studying. With varying degrees of success, I attempted to teach them how to take notes, how to underline, highlight, comment in the margins, and how to study for tests.

Indeed, it truly wasn't until I myself was in a graduate program at the University of South Carolina, working as a reading and study skills counselor in a center very much like the one I had sought help from in my undergraduate days, that I developed expertise with study reading and learning strategies. I felt an obligation then to have personal insider knowledge of the approaches I was advocating for floundering undergraduates, so I determined to turn strategies such as split-page notetaking, highlighting, marginal glossing, and self-questioning into successful ones for me.

Today's adolescents are in need of systematic instruction in study reading and learning processes as never before. The volume and range of reading required by the Common Core standards in order to prepare youth for postsecondary educational opportunities and future careers are substantial. Furthermore, students today need strategies for critically processing, generating, and reflecting understandings of electronic and digital texts and contexts.

The research literature consistently demonstrates that successful independent readers and learners are those who can gather and organize texts in task-appropriate and strategic ways (cf., Schunk & Zimmerman, 2008). In this chapter, I share foundational ideas and evidence-based practices intended to enhance students' cognitive and metacognitive processes while they read, solve problems, and study.

Wilbert McKeachie, renowned expert in strategic learning for over 70 years, asserts that the major goal of education should be the development of students' strategies for lifelong learning and problem solving (McKeachie, Pintrich, & Lin, 1985; McKeachie & Svinicki, 2014). I wholeheartedly concur with McKeachie that students should be taught how to become strategic, independent learners so they can thrive in our classrooms, in their careers, and in their personal and social worlds. In order to become successful independent learners, students need a wide repertoire of strategies (Alvermann et al., 2013; Guthrie et al., 2013). At the basic level, strategies are the behaviors or actions that students use during learning to make sense out of their texts, to monitor their understanding, and to clarify what they do not understand. Students typically employ learning strategies when they need to retain material for the purpose of taking a test, writing a paper, participating in class discussion, or any other demonstration of their learning. In addition, students need more elaborative strategies that will help them cope with content-area and disciplinary tasks requiring higher levels of thinking, such as when they are asked to organize, synthesize, and critique information from multiple sources.

Studies have shown us that students who use strategies that demand their critical thinking are more likely to do better on their assignments, exams, and papers (OECD, 2009; Lodewyk, Winne, & Jamieson-Noel, 2009). We also know from numerous studies that many students enter high school and many high school graduates enter college lacking more sophisticated learning strategies that will assist in their transition from high school–level tasks to college-level tasks (Berkeley & Riccomini, 2013; Lynch, 2010; Yeager et al., 2016). If these students, supposedly our best and brightest, are not equipped to be successful independent learners, then we can assume that most secondary-level students need our guidance and strategic instruction.

What, then, should be included in our strategic instruction? Although there is no one answer to that question, the research findings suggest that the strategies we teach students should embed a variety of cognitive and metacognitive processes (Bensley & Spero, 2014; Marin & Halpern, 2011). These processes include students' ability to:

- Select and summarize important ideas
- Reorganize and elaborate on these ideas
- Ask questions concerning the significance of targeted information
- Monitor understanding and "fix up" situations in which understanding is lacking
- Establish goals and define academic tasks
- Evaluate plans and reflect on the strategies selected

Such a list implies that no one technique or strategy will work for students in all situations (Schunk & Zimmerman, 2008). Rather than teaching our students a generic formulaic approach such as SQ3R, we need to provide instruction that ensures that they have the strategies to match the academic tasks and texts they will encounter now and in the future (Magno, 2010).

In this chapter, I address these cognitive and metacognitive processes by examining a variety of strategies and practices, both student initiated and teacher initiated, that will build strategic, independent learners across the content areas and within the disciplines.

Case Study

Ian is an English teacher who teaches several different classes of gifted students who all plan on attending college. Although most of them are receiving good grades in advanced courses such as chemistry and advanced placement (AP) history, Ian knows that these students have mediocre study habits. He has discovered in conversations with his students that they do not read their textbooks, choosing instead to listen carefully in class as the teachers discuss the material. The district coordinator for gifted education has provided Ian with a workbook that contains study tips and memory enhancement exercises, but his students have complained bitterly about the exercises. Ian also feels a certain amount of pressure from the parents, who have told him on various occasions that they expect the high school to prepare their children for the rigors of college.

To the reader: As you read and work through this chapter on learning strategies, decide what Ian might do to improve his approach with these gifted students. Consider the guidelines and strategies we examine and how Ian might use this information to help his students become more active learners.

GUIDELINES FOR INSTRUCTIONAL PRACTICES TO DEVELOP STRATEGIC LITERACY AND LEARNING

In order to develop successful independent learners who have a variety of strategies at their command, we need to acknowledge some basic guidelines drawn from current research and theory. A discussion of these five guidelines follows.

Understand the Importance of Students' Self-Knowledge

The research literature suggests that successful students are those who understand themselves as learners and are aware of their own motivations, beliefs, strengths, and weaknesses (Reeve, Ryan, Deci, & Jang, 2008). When students hold strong, positive views of themselves as learners, they have what Pajares (2008) and others have described as strong *self-efficacy*. Rather than attributing academic success to chance or the whims of a teacher, active learners with high self-efficacy ratings attribute what they learn to their own efforts and strategy use (Dweck & Master, 2008). Moreover, students with strong self-efficacy are more likely to choose learning strategies and approaches that require them to think critically and elaboratively (Ku & Ho, 2010; Schunk & Zimmerman, 2008).

In contrast, students with low self-efficacy are more likely to attribute their failures to external factors (e.g., the test was not fair) or to a fixed ability that they cannot change. For example, it is not atypical to hear adolescents say something like this: "I am not good at math and will never be." As a result, these students decide to give up before they even enter a classroom or at the first setback or challenge. Interestingly, you will find that students' self-efficacy varies across the content areas. For example, a student may have a strong sense of self-efficacy in a history course but feel totally overwhelmed or frustrated in an English course that requires her to write critical or creative responses to what she reads (Hofer, 2004; Job, Walton, Bernecker, & Dweck, 2015).

Another important aspect of students' self-knowledge consists of the beliefs or epistemologies that they have about what constitutes knowledge and learning. These personal beliefs or theories include students' beliefs about the certainty of knowledge, the organization of knowledge, and the control of knowledge acquisition (Forsyth & Beck, 2015; Heigl & Thomas, 2013). For example, some students perceive knowledge to be absolute, something handed down by authority that can be acquired quickly with little effort. In contrast, other students view knowledge acquisition as a tentative, gradual process derived from reason and thought after considerable effort on their parts.

How students define knowledge has a significant impact on how they proceed with their reading and learning in a content area (Bromme, Pieschl, & Stahl, 2010; Hubbard & Simpson, 2003). That is, if students believe that reading in biology requires them to focus only on definitions, more than likely they will memorize definitions to words such as *glucose* rather than employing elaborative strategies that involve them in searching for relationships between key concepts (e.g., glucose, insulin, glycogen). Hence, as teachers, it is important for us to know what students believe and to scaffold for them ways to expand their beliefs from simple to more complex.

Emphasize Task Awareness

Imagine that you are training to run an expensive new multipurpose office machine at work, and you prepare for your job by reading the manual about how to operate it. You read the manual a couple of times, skimming over it before you begin working. Then you are asked to use the machine for a job your supervisor needs completed quickly. Every few minutes you need to consult the manual; eventually, the machine breaks down, and your supervisor is not happy. The reason for your failure? A clear mismatch between the way you trained and the task's demands.

Now imagine that a student is studying for a biology test by using cards with the names of the hormones secreted by the endocrine system on one side and their definitions on the other. On the test, students are asked to interpret several diagrams, explaining the relationship between the hormones and their impact on other human behavior. What grade would you predict for this student? Would she pass the test? Was there a match between the way she studied and what she needed to know for the tests?

Like the office worker, this student experienced a mismatch between the strategy and the demands of the task. That is, the biology test required the student to integrate the information about the hormones in the endocrine system. The students, however, focused on rote memorization of definitions rather than the relationships between concepts.

These two examples point out the importance of the principle of *transfer of appropriateness*. This principle states that the more appropriate the match between a study process and an academic task, the more easily information can be transferred to long-term memory (Pressley, 2000). When students select strategies that match the tasks they have been assigned, their academic performances will be enhanced (Leopold, Sumfleth, & Leutner, 2013; Tseng, Chang, Lou, Tan, & Chiu, 2012). Conversely, many failures or mediocre performances by students can be explained by a mismatch between their perceptions of the task and their teachers' perceptions (Thomas & McDaniel, 2007).

The implication of this principle is that students must be taught how to analyze the tasks they will encounter in their content-area courses. Tasks, according to Doyle (1983, 2006) and Shkedi (2009), can be characterized in terms of their products and thinking processes. The products are the papers, projects, lab reports, or tests that students must complete for a course. More important than the product are the thinking processes that students must employ in order to complete the product. For example, if students are assigned a paper for a government class, that paper is the product. If the teacher asks the students to read an editorial by George Will and critique it, the thinking processes for that paper are far more involved than those required for a paper summarizing Will's key ideas. Students must be able to determine and understand the levels of thinking demanded in their academic tasks. More important, they need to be shown that it is acceptable for them to see information about the nature of their tasks and about other ways in which they will be held accountable for employing their learning strategy.

Not only should we teach students how to analyze an academic task such as the one required by the government class teacher, but we, as teachers, should provide clear and explicit information about what we want students to do and how we want them to do it (Joseph, 2009). By sharing product and process information with our students, we ensure that they will have the task knowledge to make informed strategy decisions.

Stress the What, How, When, and Why of Strategy Use

Students need to develop a repertoire of effective strategies and an ability to use the most appropriate ones to match the task demands of the content areas in which they are reading and studying. In order to do this, students must have three different kinds of strategic knowledge (Zpeda, Richey, Ronevich, & Nokes-Malach, 2015). The first is declarative knowledge, or the "what" of a strategy. For example, a student with declarative knowledge of previewing knows that previewing is done before reading and that it involves such steps as reading the introduction and summary. The second kind of strategic knowledge is procedural, or the "how" of a strategy. Strategic learners with declarative and procedural knowledge of the preview strategy could describe the steps for previewing and know how to modify those steps when they encounter different types of text (e.g., "If the text has no boldface headings, I could read the first sentence for each paragraph.").

In addition to these two types of knowledge, active learners possess conditional knowledge, perhaps the most critical form of strategic knowledge (Bugg & McDaniel, 2012; Schunk & Zimmerman, 2008). When active learners have conditional knowledge, they know the "when" and "why" to using various strategies. Thus, with the previewing strategy, they know that it may be appropriate to preview only certain texts. They also understand that the time involved in previewing a chapter before they read it is time well spent because it allows them to check the author's organization, set purposes for reading, and divide the reading into meaningful chunks. Students must develop all three kinds of strategic knowledge if they are to transfer the strategies we teach in the classroom to their own reading and learning tasks outside the classroom (Dunlosky & Metcalfe, 2009; Thiede, Griffin, Wiley, & Redford, 2009).

Take the Time to Develop Students' Strategic Expertise

Researchers remind us that students may not quickly transfer or use a new strategy they have just been taught (Griffin, Jee, & Wiley, 2009; Pressley & Gaskins, 2006). Most study strategies involve complex processes that cannot be mastered in brief teaching lessons or artificial exercises packaged in workbooks. Admittedly, students may learn the steps of a strategy from such instructional approaches, but they will not gain the conditional and procedural knowledge necessary for them to transfer the strategy to their own tasks. I believe it is critical for any teacher interested in training students to use study strategies to accept this principle; otherwise, the teacher and the class may give up on a strategy, in spite of its potential.

Validated training approaches and models are numerous, but they all agree that instruction should be direct, informed, and explanatory (e.g., Benjamin & Tullis, 2010; Dunlosky & Lipko, 2007; Dunlosky, Rawson, Marsh, Nathan, & Willingham, 2013). In other words, students can be taught to employ a strategy if they receive intensive instruction over a reasonable period of time that is characterized by (1) a description of the strategy and its characteristics; (2) an explanation of why the strategy is important; (3) modeling or demonstrations on how the strategy is used, including the process involved; (4) explanations as to when and where it is appropriate to apply the strategy; and (5) guidelines for evaluating whether the strategy is working and what to do if it is not. Content-area and disciplinary teachers should also provide strategy examples from the texts and materials students are expected to read and study. Strategy examples, especially ones that teachers develop, are important because many students believe teachers never need to study or make an effort to remember an idea. As one way of illustrating the strategy of split-page notetaking, one of my graduate students shared with her middle graders the notes she had created to document and learn the different theories of reading. That example was an excellent introduction to her lesson on how to use two-column notes as a means of capturing major ideas and critical supporting information.

The findings from research studies have suggested that it takes at least a few weeks before students begin to feel comfortable with a particular strategy (Benjamin & Tullis, 2010; Weinstein, McDermott, & Roediger, 2010). One way teachers have found to facilitate this process is to allow students to practice the strategy with material that is easy to understand, such as an informational text from an online magazine for students. In this way, students avoid overcrowding the cognitive workbench and can focus most of their attention on learning the strategy. Gradually, teachers can increase the difficulty of the material until students demonstrate that they can apply the strategy to their own textbooks. This may take several weeks, but the time is well spent, because the ultimate goal is to develop students' strategic expertise and ultimate independence in learning.

Use Content-Area Assignments as an Opportunity to Reinforce Learning Strategies

Classroom teachers need to make clear for students the connection between how they read and study their texts and the course expectations and requirements. To reinforce this effort–outcome connection, teachers should structure assignments that ask students to integrate particular strategies with the learning of the course content (Dweck, Walton, & Cohen, 2014). For example, a biology teacher who wants her students to learn the different glands and hormones in the endocrine system could require them to create a chart to summarize those concepts. Students could first brainstorm what information might be contained in the charts (e.g., locations, functions) and examine possible formats. Once the charts are created, students could meet in groups to compare and discuss their charts and identify any ambiguous information. The teacher could also give the students a low-stakes assessment task about the endocrine system, allowing them to use their newly created charts. In this way, the teacher receives feedback on how students are progressing in their mastery of the learning strategy simultaneously with information about how well they are learning the course content. Furthermore, as the teacher continues to reinforce the connection between particular study processes and positive course outcomes for her students, she is more likely to find them applying strategies to their course content while becoming more competent readers and independent learners (Blachowicz & Ogle, 2008; Schunk & Zimmerman, 2008).

Based on these five guidelines of effective study strategy instruction, I describe and exemplify in the remainder of this chapter a range of processes important to developing students' expertise as independent readers and learners.

STRATEGIC LITERACY AND LEARNING PROCESSES

Students who are strategic learners understand how their textbooks are organized, how to interpret and record an assignment, how to begin reading their assignments, how to take notes from texts and class activities, and how to "fix up" learning when they become lost or do not understand. As content-area and disciplinary teachers, we cannot assume that students have mastered these important processes of strategic literacy and learning in the earlier grades.

Knowing the Format and Organization of a Textbook

Students often fail to take full advantage of the features of either print or e-textbooks. One of my recent doctoral students, who is responsible for technology support to his high school colleagues, tells me how the teachers and their students alike are unaware and consequently do not avail themselves of the multitude of features of their e-textbooks. Once he provides training for his colleagues in how to capitalize on what electronic texts have to offer, this information is then normally shared with students. And once students learn how their e-textbook is organized and the features available to them, they increase their concentration, understanding, and remembering (Miranda, Williams-Rossi, Johnson, & McKenzie, 2011; Schugar, Schugar, & Penny, 2012).

Louisa, a high school culinary arts teacher, had attended a district workshop at which the speaker had stressed the importance of introducing the format and organization of e-textbooks to students. Before the workshop, like many other teachers, she had merely made textbook reading assignments, assuming most students take the time to explore their e-textbooks once they access them. Taking part of a class period to explain the "obvious characteristics" of a textbook seemed a bit unnecessary, especially as most of her students gave the impression of being tech-savvy, but she decided to give it a try.

Louisa began her discussion by explaining that textbooks contain only the theories, perspectives, and conclusions of certain scholars under contract from a publisher. She then asked the students to read the title page and preface of their textbook to gain information about their authors. The students discovered that three individuals had written their texts. After a discussion about the authors, Louisa stressed that the content of all their readings would be filtered through the biases and personal opinions of the authors.

After that brief orientation, which many students found intriguing, Louisa distributed a textbook introduction activity designed to orient her students further to their e-textbook (see Figure 9.1). In the workshop, Louisa had learned that many students knew neither where important textbook parts were located nor how they functioned. She therefore paired her students and gave them 15 minutes to familiarize themselves with the parts of the e-textbook through the questions on the

Title of textbook _____

Author(s) _____

Copyright date _____ Has the book been revised? _____

1. Read the **preface** carefully and completely. Summarize briefly what it says.
2. Find the **table of contents.** Answer these questions after studying it:
   a. Are the chapters broken down into many or few subheadings?
   b. Can you list five or six major topics included in the table of contents?
3. Find the **index.** On what page does it begin? Name two or three types of information you find there.
4. Find the **glossary.** How can it help you?
5. Find the **appendix.** What type of information can you find in it?
6. Find one **bibliography.** List two authors or titles that interest you.
7. Examine Chapter 1. Check the organizational features available in this textbook:
   a. Introduction

   b. Marginal notes _____

   c. Italicized or underlined words _____

   d. Boldfaced headings _____

   e. Pictures _____ Graphs _____ Maps _____ Charts _____

   f. Internal summaries _____ Summary _____

   g. Questions at the end _____

FIGURE 9.1. Getting acquainted with your textbook.

activity sheet. Each chapter, as the students soon discovered, had a general introduction, a summary that listed key ideas, and boldfaced headings, subheadings, and italicized words.

Louisa then made sure her students were familiar with the unique options available to them with e-texts, such as hyperlinking from individual words and phrases, names, and places to definitions, visuals, video, and other readings. She also showed them how they could exploit the electronic texts' other interactive features, such as typing notes in the margin, underlining, highlighting, and more. Louisa closed the period with a discussion of how these aids could help them as they read and studied their first assignment.

Louisa received positive feedback from her students on this lesson and decided to incorporate it into her beginning-of-the-year routine. I know some school districts insist that all teachers take the time during the first week of school to introduce their textbooks with an activity like the one in Figure 9.1. The form can obviously be modified to fit any content-area or disciplinary textbook. What Louisa and many other teachers hope is that students will become critical and savvy consumers of text, particularly electronic textbooks.

Understanding Assignments

As I explained in the guidelines for effective strategy instruction, if students are to select the most appropriate strategies, they must understand all the nuances of their academic tasks. Content-area and disciplinary teachers can help students in two fundamental ways. First, they must constantly strive to provide students with tasks that are explicit and descriptive. One way to do this is by making sure reading assignments contain enough information to make them effective, as described in Figure 9.2.

Implicit in all the suggestions in Figure 9.2 is the belief that giving an assignment is more than announcing what pages need to be read. If you want students to read, you must prepare them by making the task as explicit and specific as possible. That same advice applies to other academic tasks as well, such as a writing assignment or a lab experiment.

The second way to assist students to become independent learners is to provide them with questions they should ask themselves about an assignment or task they must complete. For example, the following are general questions students could ask themselves for almost any course:

- "What is the assignment? What am I to produce? What is the purpose of the assignment?"
- "What resources should I use: course texts, class discussion notes, electronic databases, outside reading, videos, class demonstrations, or laboratory experiments?"

The next time you assign your students to read a text or a selection, make the task more explicit for them by including this information:

1. How should your students read? Should they skim the assignment? Should they read slowly, pausing to study all charts, graphs, or example problems?

2. What should your students focus on when they read? Definitions? Examples? Theories? Functions? Trends? Descriptions? Causes and effects? Comparisons and contrasts? Significant events?

3. How should your students approach a difficult section? Should they use a diagram that explains the concept? Should they refer to their notes from the lab experiment or from the class discussion? Or should they read the chapter summary before they begin reading?

4. How should they break up their reading into smaller chunks?

5. How long should it take them to read the assignment?

6. What will be expected of them once they have read the material? Should they be prepared to write? Participate in a lab experiment? Solve some problems? Discuss?

FIGURE 9.2. Questions before making reading assignments.

- "What are the requirements for format, length, or size? Must the assignment be typed?"
- "When is the assignment due? Are there any penalties for late work?"
- "How will this assignment be evaluated? How much does it count in the total evaluation process?"
- "Do I understand all the words that the teacher used to explain the assignment?"

The last question is particularly critical, because we often use words such as *critique* or *respond creatively* when we give students assignments, assuming that they know what we mean. More often than we would like, students do not understand these words and the processes they embody (Simpson & Nist, 2003).

I know a team of ninth-grade teachers who have these six questions listed on a poster in their classroom in order to encourage students to "get all the information" when they write their assignments in their notebooks. In addition, they encourage students to ask questions about assignments and reinforce them when they do.

Previewing

Dominique and Andrea were preparing to go to a performance of the local symphony. As they were dressing, Andrea suggested that they read about the composer, Edvard Grieg, to learn about his life and musical philosophy. Using his iPad, Dominique went online and found numerous websites with biographies of Grieg and critiques of his music. He read aloud about Grieg as they finished dressing and continued reading to Andrea as she drove downtown. They arrived at Symphony Hall early and read further from the program about the compositions to be performed that evening. By the time the first note sounded, they had established a context for the music that greatly aided their interpretation and appreciation of what they heard.

This kind of context setting is at the heart of the previewing process. Students often seem to begin a reading assignment much like those people who entered Symphony Hall and scurried to find their seats just before the conductor's entrance on the stage. The music rushed over them, but because they did not plan for listening, they may not have known what the composer intended to communicate with his music. Likewise, when students are expected to gain a complete understanding of their text but approach their reading by opening their books at the beginning of the assignment and simply plowing forward, they fail to prepare for the flood of words they encounter and may find themselves in the middle of the chapter unsure about what the author is trying to convey.

To prepare for the reading assignments, students should be taught how to preview. The previewing strategy is a logical follow-up to learning the format and organization of any text, including print and e-textbooks, because it requires students to know and use those features. As students preview, they read the introductory paragraphs, summaries, topic markers or boldfaced headings, visual aids, summaries, and questions or problems provided by the author. Once students have previewed these text features, they need to take a moment to reflect on this information, allowing the ideas to sink in. By previewing, students should be able to answer questions such as these: (1) "What is the text about?" (2) "What are some key terms I will learn?" (3) "How should I read this text and divide up this task?"

I know of many teachers who demonstrate the steps of the preview strategy during the first month of school. Gradually, they shift the responsibility to preview their assignments to their students by assigning them to complete a worksheet similar to the one in Figure 9.3. This particular example from a driver's education

---

Directions: We previewed most of the chapter in class. In order to understand how the chapter is organized, complete the following skeletal outline. You can do this by identifying the author's major headings and subheadings. As you do this activity, be thinking of possible test questions.

Chapter 12: Adverse Conditions

I. Reduced Visibility (1st main topic)

   A. Car windows

   B. Sun glare

   C.

   D. Night

      1. Headlights

      2.

      3.

II. Reduced Traction (2nd main topic)

   A. Wet roads

      1.

      2.

   B. Snow

      1.

      2.

   C.

   D.

Finish the chapter's outline or structure. There are a total of four main topics in this chapter.

FIGURE 9.3. Previewing a driver's education chapter.

teacher guides students through the process of identifying key ideas and seeing the relationships between these ideas, an important step in the preview strategy. Content-area teachers can easily modify the example in Figure 9.3 to fit their particular needs and the unique characteristics of their texts. For instance, a chemistry or physics teacher might wish to emphasize the importance of graphics and example problems.

Why should students preview? As was noted in the guidelines, it is important to discuss with your students the advantages of any strategy so you can counter their initial concerns or doubts. In these discussions, you could stress the fact that previewing provides a meaningful organization of the material to be learned, an important aspect of reading comprehension and fluency (Bean et al., 2011). As students read introductory paragraphs and look over headings and subheadings, they will form a mental outline of the major topics and subtopics. This information will provide students with the data they need to make judgments about their readiness to learn the material, the difficulty of the material, and the actions they may need to take to learn the material (Ukrainetz, 2015).

As a strategy, previewing is neither relevant nor appropriate for all texts. Some texts are not considerately organized, and many literature anthologies do not contain textbook markers or summaries. Hence, students will need to modify the preview strategy (i.e., read the first sentence of each paragraph when there are no textbook markers) or select a more appropriate strategy. Occasionally, some teachers may not want their students to read and study an entire chapter or text but instead request that they memorize specific processes, steps, or formulas. For example, if a chemistry teacher told her class that all they would be required to know from a particular reading were the symbols and atomic weights for five specific elements, extensive previewing would not be appropriate. This example points again to the importance of students' knowing what they will be responsible for as a result of reading and studying so that they can employ the most relevant learning strategy (Dunlosky et al., 2013).

Previewing, although not a panacea, certainly will engage students in more active reading and learning. Moreover, previewing is one of the strategies that can be initially introduced by teachers, modeled and reinforced, and then gradually shifted to students for their own responsibility and control.

Fixing Up Difficult Situations

Fix-up strategies are the observable, or "in the head," practices that active learners use when they are trying to increase their understanding of particular content, especially when the content is challenging to comprehend (Dignath & Buttner, 2008; Huff & Nietfeld, 2009). To illustrate the importance of fix-up strategies, read the passage in Figure 9.4.

After reading the following passage, list all the techniques you used or would use to understand what you had read:

> Recent developments in the self-worth theory of achievement motivation attest to the potential heuristic value of maintaining Atkinson's original quadripolar model. In essence, self-worth theory argues that the need for self-acceptance is the highest human priority and that, in reality, the dynamics of school achievement largely reflect attempts to aggrandize and protect self-perceptions of ability. (Covington & Roberts, 1994, p. 161)

Your techniques: _____

_____

What techniques did you include in your list? Some of the more common fix-up strategies include:

1. Rereading the confusing sentence or paragraph

2. Adjusting your reading rate by slowing down or speeding up

3. Reading ahead to see if the information becomes clearer

4. Looking back at previous paragraphs, headings, or introductions to see if the author explains the concept in another way

5. Referring to visual aids provided by the author, such as maps, charts, pictures, or graphs

6. Making a picture in your mind of the concept being discussed

7. Noticing patterns in text structure (macrostructure)

8. Looking for text examples that clarify difficult abstractions

9. Making a connection between the text and your life and your knowledge of the world

10. Checking alternative sources such as textbooks, references, or the Internet

FIGURE 9.4. Fix-up strategies.

Most middle school and high school students have limited fix-up strategies (Baker & Beall, 2008), and the ones they do employ usually involve rereading for the rote memorization of information (Cantrell, Almasi, Carter, Rintamaa, & Madden, 2010). When grappling with difficult text, the struggling readers in your classroom will just give up and quickly close the textbook, perhaps forever (Berkeley, Mastropieri, & Scruggs, 2011). Teachers, however, can assist students by modeling and demonstrating effective fix-up strategies appropriate to their content area (Amzil, 2014; Baker, DeWyngaert, & Zeliger-Kandasamy, 2015). As explained in Chapter 3, an effective process-modeling session permits students to see that it is normal to experience comprehension difficulties and that even experts must solve these problems with some techniques or strategies (Mevarech & Amrany, 2008; Schraw, Crippen, & Hartley, 2006).

In addition, throughout the school year teachers can use a variety of other methods to highlight the various fix-up strategies they want their students to use. Angelica, a ninth-grade math teacher, begins the year by modeling the fix-up strategies she wants her students to adopt and then places those strategies on poster board in several parts of the room. She also posts the information on her website for students and parents to peruse. One of those Web-based strategies emphasizes the importance of reading word problems with a pencil and paper in hand. A general science teacher at the same school gives his students a bookmark that lists the appropriate fix-up strategies for making sense of the assigned material in his classroom. The options are limitless.

These important processes of strategic literacy and learning are essential to your students' abilities to become successful independent readers and learners, whether within the classroom or outside the classroom. The next section discusses an extremely important and powerful process that provides the foundation for almost every learning strategy or technique: summarization.

Summarization and Taking Notes from Texts

All of us summarize many times during the course of the day. When you ask your colleague in the hall, "How are you?" and she says, "Fine," she is summarizing—categorizing her collective experiences and feelings and labeling them with a single word. When you ask a fellow student about the weather and he says "Gloomy," this also is a summary, the selection of a single word that embraces a variety of weather characteristics.

As was stressed in Chapter 3, the ability to summarize text is a significant meaning-making process because it provides the foundation for a wide array of other thinking processes such as organizing and synthesizing (Yang, 2015). When students create written summaries, they also are monitoring or checking their level of understanding, an extremely important aspect of becoming strategic, independent learners (Y.-F. Yang, 2014). Unfortunately, many middle and high school students are not adept in summarizing what they have read (Spirgel & Delaney, 2016). Rather than summarize a concept using their own words, many students resort to memorizing irrelevant details, missing the big picture of what they have read or heard during a class discussion.

Fortunately, summarizing has been investigated over a period of time, and researchers have discovered that skilled, fluent readers use certain rules in summarizing (e.g., Brown & Day, 1983; Kintsch & van Dijk, 1978; H.-C. Yang, 2014). These rules include:

- Deleting irrelevant or unimportant information
- Selecting key idea statements when the author explicitly provides them

- Collapsing lists and forming categories for those lists of items (e.g., the cause of diabetes rather than glucose, glycogen, and insulin)
- Integrating the information into a written statement by using invented topic sentences and the first three rules as a guide

When students, especially struggling students, receive direct, explanatory instruction in the steps, their ability to summarize and comprehend text significantly improves (Brown & Day, 1983; Phillips & Wolcott, 2014). As noted in the guidelines at the beginning of the chapter, this instruction should be explicit and occur over time because summarization is a complex process (Marin & Halpern, 2011; Yu, 2008). For example, students may learn to master the first rule of deletion rather quickly, but the other three steps often necessitate extensive modeling and considerable guided practice with easier materials, at first.

Teaching Activities for Summarization

In addition to modeling the steps involved in summarizing, middle and high school teachers can help their students master the steps with a variety of activities. First, you can provide students with examples of summaries that you or former students have composed for a targeted piece of text. Projecting the sample summaries or making them available in a Google document for comment and editing allows students see how others might have paraphrased a challenging paragraph or how they link ideas together. Even more effective is an activity that involves presenting students three differing summaries for a piece of text—one that is exemplary, one that is satisfactory but lacks some important characteristics (e.g., generalizations), and one that is totally unsatisfactory because it lacks all the characteristics of effective summaries. Without labeling the summaries, you then ask the students to rate the summaries on a scale of 1–5, 1 being the best, and be prepared to discuss their evaluations. These discussions are usually quite animated.

A third way you can assist your students with any complex thinking processes such as summarization is to involve them in debriefing sessions with their classmates. During debriefing sessions, students work in small groups to compare and analyze their summaries and the content they used for practice. Each group is given three questions to answer and prepare for whole-class discussion: (1) What problems did you have in understanding the content? (2) What problems did you have in using the summarization strategy? and (3) What do you see as the advantages of summarizing? Both the small-group and large-class discussions provide teachers timely, specific feedback on students' growth in progress and excellent opportunities for emphasizing students' procedural and conditional knowledge of summarization.

A fourth practical way you can enhance your students' summarization skills is to provide them with concrete, specific feedback on their written products

(Duijnhouwer, Prins, & Stokking, 2012; Parr & Timperley, 2010; Shute, 2008). Of course, providing feedback takes considerable time, especially when you see more than 100 students in one day. In order to provide their students with quality feedback in an expedient manner, some teachers like to use a checklist. The checklist in Figure 9.5 is similar to one used by Joseph, a consumer economics teacher. He says he can review a class set of summaries in about 15 minutes when he uses a checklist. Gradually and over time, students can be encouraged to use this checklist to evaluate their own summaries. You, too, can try your hand in evaluating summaries by completing the activity in Figure 9.6.

As you probably determined, Susan's summary was more effective than Derek's for several reasons. What reasons did you list? Did you note that Susan focused on the overall structure of the section, the four types of pollution, and the solutions to water pollution? In contrast, Derrick focused on details with no sense of organization. Did you recognize that Susan used personal examples and offered a conclusion in her summary? Derrick's summary, in contrast, used only the information provided by the textbook and frequently bordered on plagiarism.

Although Derrick's summary was not as effective as Susan's, he certainly was making strides toward understanding the steps and processes involved in summarizing. To help him improve his summary, a teacher could work with him on paraphrasing, noting macrostructures of text (e.g., *problem–solution*) and using important microstructure features such as connectives (e.g., *on the other hand, however*).

In sum, if your students are to be able to summarize what they read or hear in your classroom, they will need specific instruction from you, the content-area and disciplinary expert. Asking students to summarize without giving them instruction is just not sufficient. Moreover, it is important to note that summarization is not just a skill that students practice for their teachers. Rather, when students summarize

---

To the student: I have checked the areas you need to work on in order to improve your summaries. Please read the checklist carefully and incorporate these suggestions when you revise your summary.

☐ 1. Your summary represents the author's key ideas. Good work!

☐ 2. You need to use your own words when summarizing the text.

☐ 3. Your summary focuses too much on unimportant details.

☐ 4. Your summary needs to focus more on key ideas and less on details.

☐ 5. You need to be briefer in your summary.

☐ 6. You need to be more specific and not so vague with your summary.

☐ 7. Your summary needs to show the relationships between ideas.

FIGURE 9.5. Summary checklist.

Read Susan's and Derrick's summaries, which they wrote for a selection on water pollution. Decide which is better and why.

Susan's Summary

According to this section of our textbook, there are four sources of water pollution: agriculture, industry, domestic, and other sources such as oil spills. Perhaps the most dangerous source of pollution comes from industry, though oil spills, such as the one in Alaska, have certainly had a large impact on our wildlife and on our economy. Pesticides, fertilizer, and animal waste, the three types of agricultural pollution, are usually not direct but indirect. A notorious example of a pesticide is DDT. There are three kinds of industrial pollution: chemical, thermal, and radiation. But problems associated with radiation seem to be the most severe in that skin cancer and leukemia are possible results of exposure. Organic waste and detergent builders are the main sources of domestic pollution. Both seem to have an adverse effect on our lakes and rivers so that the balance of nature is upset. This section of the chapter ended by discussing some solutions to the problem of water pollution—all of which are costly but very important.

Derrick's Summary

This section of the chapter discussed two different kinds of water pollution. Pesticides such as DDT are dangerous to use because they are not biodegradable. Some nitrates are toxic to animals and humans. Nitrates can be reduced to nitrites, which interfere with the transport of oxygen by hemoglobin in the blood. Mercury vapor is highly toxic and can be absorbed through the lungs. There are two types of radiation cell damage, direct and indirect. Detergents and organic waste can also harm our water sources. Oil spills hurt our aquatic life.

FIGURE 9.6. Evaluating two different summaries.

and organize what they have read, they have created important records they can use to study. Therefore, in the next section I discuss formats that students can use for their summaries that will allow them to rehearse and study content-area and disciplinary concepts.

Text Notetaking Approaches That Facilitate Students' Studying

Think back to your college experiences and how you dealt with all the textbooks, novels, primary sources, and articles that you were assigned to read. Like most undergraduate and graduate students, you were probably not taught either in secondary school or college how to cope with this volume of text and were forced to develop your own practices for interacting with the material so you could review and study it later. Perhaps they included underlining key ideas and making brief notations in the margin. Unlike our own inefficient trial-and-error approach, it is important to identify formats that allow students to interact efficiently with their texts and to help them learn effective practices for notetaking in systematic ways,

I examine three such approaches teachers have found useful that take advantage of sticky notes, foldables, and index cards. All three provide students an artifact for study and encourage them to monitor their understanding. Most teachers have found it useful to demonstrate all three approaches and allow students to choose the one they prefer.

Sticky Notes

When students create sticky notes for a content-area reading test, they typically summarize the ideas from a page and place the sticky note on that page. Some teachers encourage students to use sticky notes as a way of highlighting a confusing topic or concept that they want to clarify during class. The example in Figure 9.7 illustrates a students' sticky note for a genetics unit on inheritance.

If students receive sufficient instruction, they could also place the following on their sticky notes:

- Examples of important concepts or solutions to problems
- Steps, important characteristics, functions, trends, and significant events or individuals
- Motives, things, character descriptions, conflicts
- Critiques or critical notes in response to what has been read (e.g., does the author defend his position about global warming?)

Once students have finished a chapter or an assignment, they can place their sticky notes on a separate piece of paper. You might ask, why not just let the students

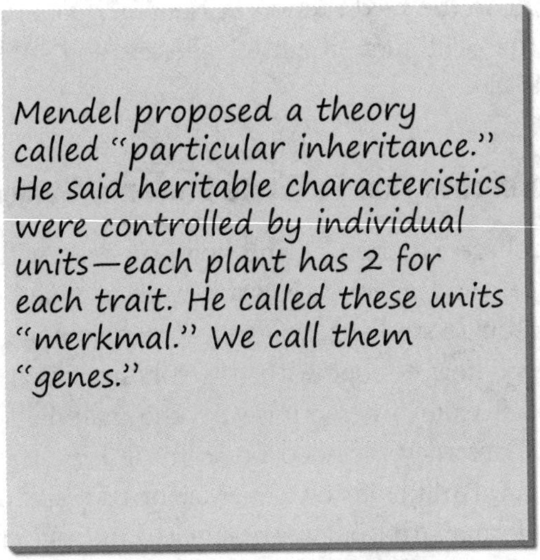

Mendel proposed a theory called "particular inheritance." He said heritable characteristics were controlled by individual units—each plant has 2 for each trait. He called these units "merkmal." We call them "genes."

FIGURE 9.7. Sticky note for genetics.

write those notes on the paper instead of using the sticky notes in the first place? Researchers and practitioners have found that students who take notes on a piece of notebook paper tend to become medieval monks who feel compelled to fill up a page. The use of sticky notes or any such abbreviated format encourages students to think about ideas and reduce them, using their own words (Brown, 2007; Fisher et al., 2015).

Students using e-textbooks should be able to take advantage of a digital sticky note feature that allows them to record the same type of information advocated here that they would write with pen or pencil on paper sticky notes.

Foldables

Foldables (Fisher, Zike, & Frey, 2007) are similar to sticky notes in that they are small in size and flexible in their use. An added advantage of foldables is that they provide students a ready-made tool to self-assess their learning of textual and course content, an important process of knowledge building and test preparation (Andrade & Valtcheva, 2009). As illustrated in Figure 9.8, students fold a piece of construction paper and label a concept or *key* idea (e.g., *memory processes*) on the front of the paper. Then the foldable is cut into parts or flaps and these are also labeled (e.g., *encoding, storage,* and *retrieval*). To study the foldable, students read the

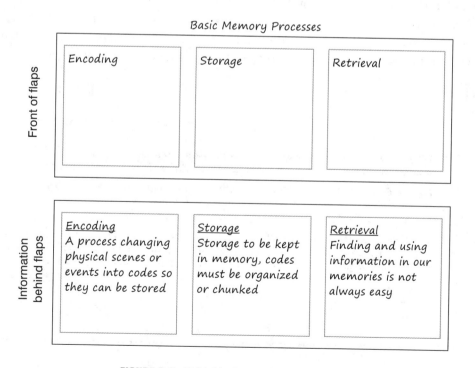

FIGURE 9.8. Foldable for psychology unit.

concept (e.g., *basic memory processes*) and then, before lifting the flaps, say aloud the information on the back of each flap. Foldables, like sticky notes, can be adopted to any content area or discipline.

Index Cards

I demonstrated in Chapter 6, in connection with vocabulary cards, the value of index cards as an effective way for students to study content-area and disciplinary concepts. Because they are more portable and durable than notebook paper or slips of paper and because they facilitate self-testing, they are particularly advantageous. Furthermore, they can be created and saved digitally, making for easy access and review. As illustrated in Figure 9.9, some students like to place questions on the front of their cards (i.e., What are the three essential parts of a workout?) and answers on the back, whereas other students use the more traditional flash card format.

Secondary teachers can help their students construct task-specific index cards in order to ensure that their students read and summarize the assigned material. A health and fitness teacher has his students read their assignments and complete the cards, which they are allowed to bring to class and consult when engaged in class discussions and while taking quizzes and tests.

Whatever format your students choose to use to summarize what they have read, it is always useful to provide them with models or examples of effective strategies (Marin & Halpern, 2011). For example, you might collect the students' foldables or index cards and search for ones that belong to students who are doing well in the course. Then, on the next day, share on document camera the effective

1. WARM-UP—to prevent injuries, stimulate heart and lungs, increase blood flow, prepare mentally; varies with the individual; can be done in a variety of ways

2. MAIN CONDITIONING—continuous and rhythmic activities such as running, biking, swimming, walking, aerobic dance; should work at your target heart rate; should modify and vary activities

3. COOL-DOWN—tapering off period where you continue working out but at a lower intensity; walking is good; if you skip this part blood may pool in the muscles or you could become dizzy; 5 minutes is recommended

FIGURE 9.9. Index card for health and fitness unit.

examples so students can modify their strategies accordingly. In sum, if you want your students to be able to summarize what they read in your class, they need specific steps, a format, and feedback. In the next section I address strategies pertaining to class notes.

Strategies for Taking Class Notes

If you have ever wondered why it is so difficult for your students to take notes during class discussions or during one of your demonstrations of a concept, consider all the prerequisite skills involved in notetaking. Students must be able to:

- Paraphrase and summarize
- Select key ideas and discard irrelevant details
- Establish purposes for listening or observing
- Identify organizational patterns such as problem–solution or cause–effect
- Record information quickly using abbreviations and symbols

In addition to these skill prerequisites, students need some prior experiences or background information to make sense of the concepts being discussed or presented during class. As you can see, taking class notes is a difficult skill for most middle school and high school students. In fact, many first-year college students have not mastered the skills involved in taking notes from lectures, demonstrations, and discussions (Bohay, Blakely, Tamplin, & Radvansky, 2011). Fortunately, this skill can be taught and reinforced across the content areas and disciplines (Bui, Myerson, & Hale, 2013; Lin & Bigenho, 2011; Mueller & Oppenheimer, 2014).

I have collected a variety of suggestions from secondary teachers about how they teach notetaking. The following are some of the activities they use:

- Begin the year with a discussion of your classroom notetaking expectations. Include the "why" of taking notes, whether you will check notes, how notes will be used, and in what format you would like the notes to be kept (e.g., in a spiral or three-ring notebook).

- Discuss the qualities of good notes in your course. Include general physical formats, organization, and content. Show examples of your own class notes or previous students' notes via handouts, the document camera, or a Web page.

- Model notetaking behaviors by using a framed outline during class. At the beginning of class, distribute a handout with the major points to be covered that day but with ample room for the development of your ideas. Specific cue words could be added for students with learning disabilities (e.g., "The second step of the tennis serve"). Then deliver your presentation and fill in the major points and details on the framed outline using the overhead projector. Require students to add your notes to their framed outline. Repeat this procedure at least once a week and gradually reduce the cues until you no longer present the notes on the overhead or on the framed outline.

• Teach the patterns of organization that are common to your content area or discipline (e.g., comparison–contrast, sequence). For example, after discussing the problem–solution organizational format, a teacher could deliver a brief lecture and assign students to note the nature of a problem, the courses of action proposed, and the advantages and disadvantages of these solutions.

• Teach and model physical and verbal cues that teachers commonly use during class presentations. Include physical cues such as tongue, facial expressions, pace, and gestures. Include verbal cues such as "Now we will consider the second point" or "In summary." Reserve time in class to discuss the students' notes to check whether they recorded the important points that were cued.

• Teach the common symbols and abbreviations and those unique to your specific content area or discipline. For example, students should be taught to use abbreviations such as *ex* to represent examples and = to represent the words *equals* or *equivalent*. Government teachers should teach students to use abbreviations such as *jud* and *leg* to represent the word *judiciary* and *legislation*.

In addition to these activities, it is important for secondary teachers to reinforce continually the usefulness and advantages of taking class notes. As I stressed earlier in this chapter, students are more likely to use a strategy if they see it as effective and worthy of their efforts (Schunk & Zimmerman, 2008). You can reinforce and reward your students in a variety of ways for taking class notes. I particularly like the following four ideas and have found them to be successful with middle school and high school students:

• Give unannounced quizzes in which students can use their class notes. Make sure that the questions asked pertain to the information and concepts you discussed during the class. Students will quickly learn that it is important to listen and take detailed, organized notes.
• After some instruction on how to take class notes, collect students' notes without warning, either at the end of the class period or the next day. Evaluate the notes and then discuss them the next day with the students.
• Have a weekly review of class notes. Ask questions that could be answered by using the notes. Points could be awarded for correct answers. This procedure could also be used at the beginning of each class period.
• Provide students with class time to review their notes with a partner, especially after an important lesson or before a test or quiz.

In the next section I explain two different formats that students can use to organize their class notes: the split-page notetaking format and the synthesis journal.

The Split-Page Notetaking Format

Some content-area and disciplinary teachers like their students to take notes in a predictable format, such as the split-page format (Fisher et al., 2014; Palmatier, 1973). With this format, during class students record their notes on the right-hand side of a piece of paper. During or afterward they write on the left-hand side of the paper key idea statements in order to reduce the information and to see the big picture (Ramsay & Sperline, 2011). The notes in Figure 9.10 illustrate how one student used the split-page format in his math class. In addition to writing key idea statements in the left-hand margin, students could be assigned to incorporate key

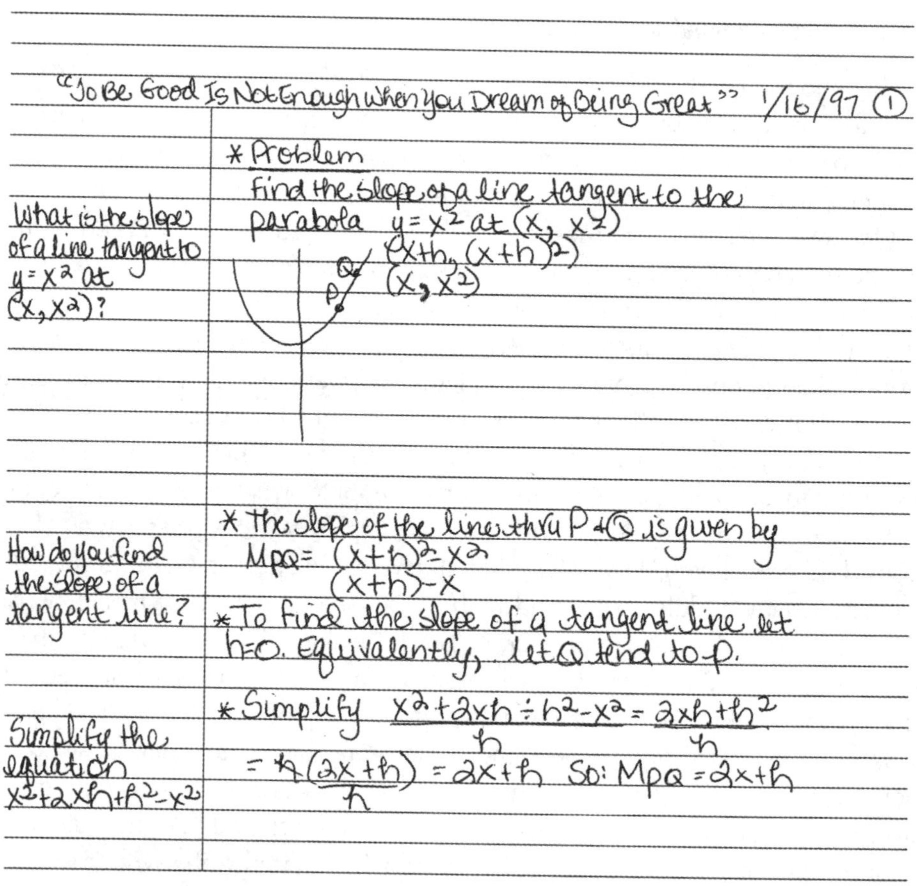
"To Be Good Is Not Enough When You Dream of Being Great" 1/16/97 ①

What is the slope of a line tangent to $y = x^2$ at (x, x^2)?	* Problem Find the slope of a line tangent to the parabola $y = x^2$ at (x, x^2) Q $(x+h, (x+h)^2)$ P (x, x^2)
How do you find the slope of a tangent line?	* The slope of the line thru P + Q is given by $M_{PQ} = \frac{(x+h)^2 - x^2}{(x+h) - x}$ * To find the slope of a tangent line, let $h \to 0$. Equivalently, let Q tend to P.
Simplify the equation $x^2 + 2xh + h^2 - x^2$	* Simplify $x^2 + 2xh \div h^2 - x^2 = \frac{2xh + h^2}{h}$ $= \frac{h(2x+h)}{h} = 2x + h$ So: $M_{PQ} = 2x + h$

FIGURE 9.10. Sample of split-page notes from a math course.

ideas from their assigned texts or other sources. In that way, they can collect and synthesize all the information on a particular topic (Reed, Rimel, & Hallett, 2016).

Anthony, a 12th-grade economics teacher, provides his students with considerable practice with the split-page format. He begins by asking them to take notes during class in their usual fashion. This assignment provides him and his students with some self-assessment data. Samples of actual notes produced by students are put on the whiteboard using the document camera and analyzed. Anthony asks the students to consider the note samples relative to the goals of studying, which stimulates discussion of the relevance and transfer appropriateness of notetaking strategies. When he introduces split-page notes, he first describes the format; then, unrehearsed, he creates a set of notes. This gives students a view of Anthony's thoughts and decisions during the notetaking process. In addition, Anthony demonstrates how he would study the notes by covering the right column and using the left-column entries as recall prompts, and vice versa.

The Synthesis Journal as a Notetaking Format

Synthesis journals (Burrell & McAlexander, 1998) are not really journals per se but a format that encourages students to identify, organize, and then synthesize various perspectives on an issue. They are particularly useful for content-area and disciplinary classrooms in which discussion predominates. As illustrated in Figure 9.11, when completing a synthesis journal, students determine and then write in the appropriate place the viewpoints and statements of authors they have read, of their teacher, of their classmates, and finally their personal viewpoints. The center is reserved for the students to synthesize the viewpoints and then write a generalization. The synthesis journal entry in Figure 9.11 was created by a seventh grader during a unit in his health course about drug use in adolescence.

Synthesis journals obviously have many advantages. They encourage students to think critically about an issue and synthesize multiple sources (Mateos & Sole, 2009). They stimulate students to identify and explain various perspectives (Lundstrom, Diekema, Leary, Haderlie, & Holliday, 2015; Stadtler & Bromme, 2013), a problem many middle school and high school students have with their writing (Goldman, Braasch, Wiley, Graesser, & Brodowinska, 2012; Mateos, Martin, Villalon, & Luna, 2008). Moreover, synthesis journals give students a strategy that assists them in taking notes during discussions. Far too often, what the teacher says in class during a discussion becomes more important than what other classmates say about the issue being discussed. In fact, I have observed students rarely taking notes during discussions or only including what the teacher said. The synthesis journal validates students' viewpoints as well as the teacher's. Finally, the synthesis journal provides content-area and disciplinary teachers who may use only a few written sources in their classrooms with a strategy for students to use in summarizing and thinking about ideas that have been presented orally during a unit. For example, under the "Author Says" section in Figure 9.11, students could write the ideas and viewpoints presented in a video, film, or class presentation by a guest speaker.

In sum, we should remember that when we ask students to take class notes, they are involved in several critical thinking processes. These processes cannot be mastered in a week or two. I would stress that if you believe a strategy is worth teaching, students should be given the opportunity to learn it well. More important, students need to develop facility with the notetaking strategy so that they can personalize it and tailor it to the task and the course in a controlled, comfortable manner. In the next section I discuss several additional strategies that will help students become more critical in their thinking and more metacognitively aware.

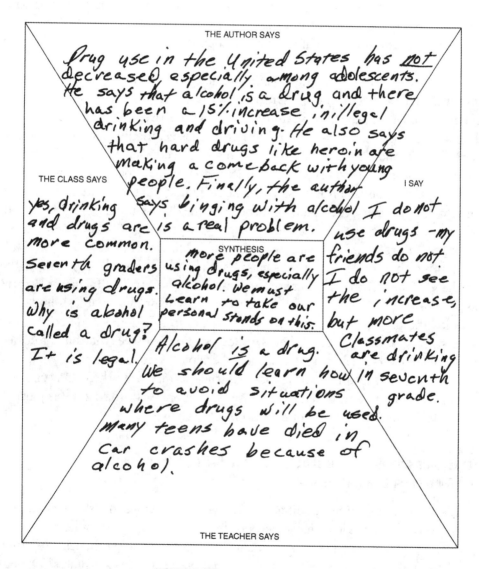

FIGURE 9.11. A synthesis journal.

The Synthesis Journal in Adaptive Physical and Health Education

Adrian teaches adaptive physical and health education to students in an inner-city school. She introduces the synthesis journal by explaining the purpose of the format, stressing that every perspective on a controversial issue deserves consideration, and that the synthesis journal recognizes and supports these viewpoints. For a unit on drug abuse in teenagers, Adrian begins by asking the students to read an article from a local newspaper about two well-known high school students, a football player and a cheerleader, who died in a car accident while under the influence of alcohol. She tells them to summarize the article briefly and write it in the "Author Says" section. For students who tend to write too much or have difficulty summarizing key ideas, she suggests that they think about these questions before they start writing: (1) What is the topic of this assignment? (2) What does the author say about the topic? (3) How does the author explain, support, and defend his or her position on this topic?

The next day in class, Adrian begins the discussion by asking students to share what they have written in their synthesis journals about the author's viewpoint. Before she invites students to share their own perspectives and a class discussion, she asks them to complete the "I Say" corner. Because Adrian reserves the synthesis journal for the more controversial issues in her health course, it does not take much prompting for students to voice their opinions after reading them. Perhaps the most difficult part of the lesson is to stop the discussion so that students will take the time to record what other students believe in the "Class Members Say" section. Adrian leads the discussion but also offers her viewpoints, giving her seventh graders opportunities to fill in the last section—"The Teacher Says."

During the last 15 minutes of class, Adrian asks the students to fill in the middle section, "Synthesis." Because this synthesis was initially difficult for her students, Adrian previously had explained what was meant by a synthesis and then modeled the process for them on an easier topic. In addition, she described how other students have completed their synthesis section on issues they had discussed in her health course. The next day in class, Adrian asks students to share what they have written. For this unit on drugs, she has students meet with their study partners to read each other's entries. Adrian's unit does not end with the synthesis journal, but it clearly starts it in the right direction.

Strategies and Activities That Encourage Critical Thinking and Metacognitive Awareness

In this section, I examine five different strategies or activities that share a common purpose of helping students move beyond the memorization level of learning. The first three learning strategies assist students in organizing and synthesizing information from multiple sources and in building their metacognitive awareness. The last two activities encourage students to think critically about information and reflect upon their performance.

Study Sheets

As was previously noted, students have great difficulty organizing and synthesizing ideas from multiple sources (e.g., Goldman et al., 2012). Thus, when you assign students to write a paper or present a speech using several outside sources, or when you ask them to combine their class notes with the information presented in their readings, what they produce will often not meet your expectations. Moreover, students may inadvertently resort to copying or cutting and pasting what they have read online or in print texts and listing these "borrowed ideas" without thinking about overall patterns or generalizations (Howard, Serviss, & Rodrigue, 2010; Maybee, Bruce, Lupton, & Rebmann, 2013). Study sheets can help address these difficulties.

Study sheets are similar to maps and charts in that they help students summarize and organize ideas from a variety of sources. Akeem, a 10th-grade American history instructor, teaches his students how to create study sheets, because he found the strategy extremely helpful when he was a student. He introduces the study sheet strategy during his Civil Rights unit in which students read several different newspaper articles published during the 1950s and 1960s and an excerpt from a recent book by John Louis. In addition, all his students watch a video documentary about the Civil Rights movement. Akeem selected these sources carefully so that they illustrated perspectives similar to and different from the ones contained in his students' history textbook.

Darrell, one of Akeem's students, created the study sheet illustrated in Figure 9.12. Notice how Darrell organized the information into smaller categories (e.g., events, groups, and their leaders) and combined ideas from a variety of sources (e.g., documentary, textbook, newspaper articles). Darrell and the other students learned a considerable amount of information merely from the decisions they had to make about the categories and subcategories and their arrangement. Fortunately, Akeem frontloaded the assignment by reminding his students of something he had stressed throughout the year: that history was not so much about dates and wars as it was a story about people, groups, and significant events. Akeem also made sure his students understood that their history textbook was just one version of the "story" written by several different authors.

Akeem tells us that his students use their study sheets in a variety of ways during the Civil Rights unit—as a resource for class discussions and small-group projects and as a test-preparation strategy for the essay exam that formally closes the unit. Although Akeem personally prefers the study sheet strategy, he also knows that it is important to teach his students a variety of organizing strategies and then orchestrate situations in which they can choose the ones they prefer.

Topic: Civil rights movement during the early 1960s	
Leaders	**Groups**
James Farmer: member of CORE, planned Freedom Rides James Meredith: integrated University of Mississippi, March Against Fear Martin Luther King, Jr.: campaign in Alabama, March on Washington, wins Nobel Peace Prize S. Carmichael: registers voters in Mississippi; suggests the need for Black Power Malcolm X: spokesperson for Black Muslims	CORE SCLC SNCC (changes direction under Carmichael) Black Panthers
Significant Events	**Legislation**
Sit-ins (Greensboro, SC, in 1960) Freedom Riders to Alabama, Mississippi Attempts to integrate universities (Alabama, Mississippi, and James Meredith, Georgia) MLK's campaign in Birmingham, AL (1963) MLK's March on Washington (1963) Explosion in Alabama church that kills four girls (1963) Violence in Selma, Alabama (MLK, Carmichael, and Malcolm X work to register voters in 1965) SNCC launches voter registration in Mississippi (1966) March Against Fear (1966)	*Boynton v. Virginia* Public Order Laws Civil Rights Act of 1964 24th Amendment Voting Rights Act of 1965

FIGURE 9.12. Study sheet on the Civil Rights movement.

Self-Questioning and the Questions–Answers Strategy

We could ask students to answer the questions provided by the authors of our textbooks and other published resources. Such a task, however, probably does not mesh with the goals and activities of our units of study. Moreover, these text-provided questions do not teach students how to ask their own questions or interrogate the texts they read. Yet the ability to generate and then answer appropriate questions is essential to becoming metacognitively aware (Bowker, 2010; Rothstein & Santana, 2011; Wilson & Smetana, 2011).

Students can learn how to ask thought-provoking questions by using high-utility stem question starters (King, 2008). The following question stems are useful for increasing engagement and learning of virtually any content material:

- "In my own words, what does this term mean?"
- "What are the author's key ideas?"
- "What is an example of . . . ?"

- "How would you use . . . to . . . ?"
- "What is a new or different example of . . . ?"
- "In my own words, explain why . . ."
- "How does . . . affect . . . ?"
- "What are the results or consequences of . . . ?"
- "What are the likenesses between . . . and . . . ?"
- "How is . . . different from . . . ?"
- "What are the advantages of . . . ?"
- "What are the disadvantages/limitations of . . . ?"
- "What are the functions of . . . ?"
- "What are the characteristics of . . . ?"
- "Do I agree or disagree with this statement . . . ?"
- "What were the contributions/influences of . . . ?"
- "How would you evaluate . . . ?"

King found in her research studies that students working in pairs who generated elaborate answers to question stems like those in the preceding list performed better on content-area objective tests than those who did not.

Students have options in organizing and answering their questions about expository text. They could, as did the participants in King's studies, meet in pairs and quiz each other. They could also write their questions and answers in a format that encourages organizing, synthesizing, and self-testing. One such format is the questions–answers strategy.

The Questions–Answers Strategy

Figure 9.13 illustrates how one student used the questions–answers strategy to prepare for a test in an ecology course. His predicted questions focused on information from the assigned readings and from the class discussions. When the questions and answers are written and organized this way, students can test themselves by folding the paper in half and reading the questions aloud. I have also encouraged students to create PowerPoint slides with questions on one side of a two-column slide, with the answer column blank until it is brought up with a keystroke or mouse click. Students can also test each other using either the paper or electronic versions of the questions and answers. The written or digital versions can be handed in or sent to teachers for feedback. By looking at the student self-generated questions, teachers can determine what misconceptions or difficulties students are encountering with a particular concept.

Questions like the ones in Figure 9.13 do not spring from students' mouths at the first try. In my experience, modeling, coaching, and specific feedback are necessary in teaching students how to ask and answer meaningful questions. Although it may take time to teach this strategy, the results are worth the effort because students learn how to control and monitor their own learning.

Questions	Answers
1. What is the major source of solid waste? 2. What is the effect of silting on our environment? 3. What causes acid mine drainage? 4. What is the danger of acid mine waste? 5. Why was DDT banned? 6. What chemical compound affects the central nervous system of humans and animals? 7. What is the specific problem associated with thermal pollution? 8. Give an example of a material that is *not* biodegradable.	Agriculture Silting reduces oxygen production and the food supply for fish; also fouls spawning beds of fish.

FIGURE 9.13. Questions–answers strategy in preparing for a test.

The Talk-Through

If you have ever verbally rehearsed what you wanted to tell the life insurance agent who kept pestering you with phone calls, you have conducted a talk-through. A talk-through is a study strategy that involves oral rehearsal of content-area concepts (Simpson, 1994). Many of the learning strategies previously discussed (e.g., synthesis journals) rely on written products. The talk-through, by contrast, involves students in expressing and explaining themselves orally. In fact, the talk-through is very much like teaching, except that the audience may be imaginary or another student. Students are told that when they conduct talk-throughs, they should imagine themselves giving a lecture on a topic to an uninformed audience. Students are urged to pace the room, gesture, and talk, if that helps create a stronger impression of actually delivering a talk. A teacher friend told me one of her students stood on the top of her desk and delivered her talk-throughs as a way of preparing for her essay exams in history.

Because most of us have used informal talk-throughs to practice delivering important information, it is not surprising to learn that talk-throughs as a learning strategy can improve understanding and remembering of academic concepts. Research has demonstrated that students who orally rehearse and explain their understanding of concepts, processes, and developments in science, math, and history exhibit improved learning (Broekkamp et al., 2007; Deslauriers, Schelew, & Wieman, 2011; Fang & Wei, 2010). This outcome is clearly related to the metacognitive and self-regulated nature of the talk-through process (Zimmerman, 2008).

Talk-throughs can be used in any content area or discipline, but they must be tailored to the demands of the texts and content. An effective talk-through in an American history class would necessarily differ from an effective talk-through in a geometry or physical education course. Depending on the content, a talk-through could contain any of the following information:

- The key ideas, using the student's own words
- Example, characteristics, processes, steps, causes, effects, and so on
- Personal or creative reactions
- Summary statements or generalizations
- Personal applications or examples

As with virtually all of the strategies and processes presented in this chapter, students will need teacher scaffolding to learn how to execute an effective talk-through. Middle-grade civics teacher Damien explains to his students the steps in developing an effective talk-through. He emphasizes that the process involves considerable cognitive and metacognitive effort and planning. His guidelines, which can be modified according to the unique demands of content-area and disciplinary content and the expectations of teachers, are as follows:

1. Think about the key ideas, trends, issues, and problems. Make sure you are using your own words when you explain them.
2. Organize the key ideas in some way. This can be done on an index card, but be brief because these notes are meant only to prompt your memory.
3. Find a quiet place, close your textbook or class notes, and use your cards to deliver your talk-through out loud.
4. After practicing your first talk-through, check your card to make sure you were precise and complete. Ask yourself if you made sense.
5. Find someone to listen to your talk-through. Ask your audience if you made sense.

Because science teacher Sara knows that her students will not use the talk-through strategy unless they find it has more benefits than costs, she asks them to generate a list of advantages to the strategy after they have used it several times. The following comments typify what Sara's science students and other students have seen as the advantages of the talk-through strategy:

- Talk-throughs help me determine what information I know and what information is still unclear.
- Talk-throughs improve my understanding of key terms because I am using my own words.
- Talk-throughs help store information in my long-term memory.
- Talk-throughs make me more actively involved in my learning.

Making these advantages explicit is a necessary part of strategy instruction because students need to know the "why" as well as the "what" and the "how" if they are to adopt new study routines or strategies.

THE TALK-THROUGH STRATEGY IN AN INCLUSION ALGEBRA CLASS

Anna, an algebra teacher, has found that her learning-disabled students benefit from using the talk-through strategy in her classes, especially when it comes to internalizing the steps for solving word problems. She begins the school year by teaching the following steps to her students:

1. Read the problem carefully, underlining keywords or phrases.
2. Reword the problem using the necessary facts.
3. Ask yourself, "What problem do I have to solve? What is unknown?"
4. Translate the reworded problem into an equation.
5. Solve the equation.
6. Check the answer by substituting the answer in the equation. Ask yourself, "Does this answer makes sense?"
7. State the answer to the problem clearly.

Anna posts these seven steps on her website. Throughout the first 9 weeks, she provides her own talk-throughs on how to implement the seven steps with sample problems taken from the textbook. However, Anna has added an extra dimension to the talk-through; she uses the interactive whiteboard as a support to her talk-through, sketching situations and setting up equations from the word problems. She has found that the verbal and visual involvement of the talk-through has greatly increased the attention and subsequent learning of her students with learning disabilities.

The following is an example of a talk-through that one of Anna's students, Emilio, did at the whiteboard for his classmates:

The problem: As a chef's assistant in a fancy restaurant, Kendra earns in 1 year a salary of $19,000. This is two-fifths of the head chef's salary. What is the head chef's salary?"

Emilio's talk-through: "First, I will reword the problem. Two-fifths of the head chef's salary is Kendra's salary. I was able to reword the problem because I knew that the word *this* in the second sentence referred to Kendra's salary. I also took out the extra words and reduced the problem to just the necessary facts and words. Second, I will translate these ten words into symbols and numbers to create an equation. My goal for this problem is to find the chef's salary, which I do not know. Thus, I will represent this unknown with an X (*Emilio uses the whiteboard to do this and to reinforce the rest of his talk-through*). I do know Kendra's salary: It is $19,000. I also know that two-fifths of the chef's salary, or 2/5 of X, is $19,000. Or, stated in another way, 2/5 times X = $19,000 or 2/5 (X) = $19,000. I use the parentheses to stand for 'multiplied by.' Now I am ready to solve the problem, which is step 5 of the process."

Although many of the math problems in Anna's class could probably be answered without using the seven steps or the talk-through, she believes that verbal rehearsal of the simple problems will help students later on in the school year with the more demanding problems.

Helping Students Think Critically about Texts

Students do not typically question or challenge what they read, especially their assigned texts. Researchers, for example, have found that many students believe that the ideas, details, and assertions in their school-based texts are true and nondebatable (Bråten, Strømsø, & Britt, 2009; Macedo-Rouet, Braasch, Britt, & Rouet, 2013). In order to feel comfortable challenging texts, students, like disciplinary experts, need to interact with a variety of sources on a topic, not just one source (Pressley & Lundeberg, 2008). When students encounter multiple texts on an issue or concept, they are more likely to discern differences across the authors, note omissions, and detect the voices of various authors (Cerdan & Vidal-Abarca, 2008; Stadtler & Bromme, 2007). However, I should stress that providing students with multiple sources on a topic, such as evolution or the Vietnam conflict, will not guarantee that students will immediately begin to think critically about authors' perspectives and textual topics. Secondary teachers will need to model and guide their students through these critical thinking processes while they are reading.

Marisol, a high school teacher of anatomy and kinesiology, decided to do just that. She began by locating several articles on the Internet concerning dieting and nutrition. One particular article intrigued her because it was written by an individual with a medical degree who was touting a particular diet program and book that could be purchased on the Internet for a considerable sum of money. Moreover, the author offered several statements in the article that contradicted what her students had learned from their other readings and class discussions. The second article Marisol selected for her students focused on less glamorous but more research-based methods of dieting, such as exercising and using common sense with food choices. The author, however, was not a doctor or researcher.

With a third article she located on the Internet, Marisol began the mini-unit by introducing the critical thinking guidelines she wanted to stress: (1) the authority and intent of the author and (2) the accuracy and objectivity of his or her ideas. After modeling and discussing these guidelines in conjunction with the third article, Marisol then informed the students that they, too, would have the opportunity to challenge and question the authors. She placed the students in pairs, giving them the link to their own article to read on school-issued tablets. Their assignment was to read the article and be prepared to teach their partners about the article when the class met again in a couple of days.

At the next class session, Marisol gave the partners 10 minutes to meet and teach each other. After 10 minutes, she placed the students into groups of four and distributed the handout titled "Questioning and Challenging the Author" (see

Figure 9.14). The groups of four were given 20 minutes to discuss the nine questions. Marisol circulated around the room listening to the discussions and guiding their participation, when necessary. When the bell rang on her computer timer, she gave the group the task of reaching an agreement on how they would "rate the author" (see Part Two in Figure 9.14). The students were also instructed to fill out Part One and to select a spokesperson who would report back to the class. Marisol was pleased to see that the students were all actively engaged in the discussion of the articles and in the rating of the authors. And, as she suspected, two of the groups rated the Internet article by the medical doctor as superior solely on the basis of his "authority." At the end of the class period Marisol helped the students debrief the experience and discuss how they might use these guidelines in their own reading, whether it be on the Internet or in print texts.

You need not teach anatomy to use these guidelines that encourage students to think critically about what they read. Any content-area or disciplinary teacher can design a similar lesson using multiple sources that provide students with alternative viewpoints or an alternative development of an idea.

Encouraging Students to Evaluate and Reflect

Successful independent learners reflect upon the strategies they have employed and evaluate whether these strategies were appropriate for the task and content area (Baker et al., 2015; Dignath & Buttner, 2008). In addition, successful students determine whether their self-selected strategies are appropriate for themselves as learners and make adjustments, when necessary, to remedy the situation and improve their academic performance (Thiede et al., 2009). Reflecting and evaluating in this manner are highly sophisticated thinking processes that encourage students to be even more metacognitively aware and successful in their independent learning across the disciplines and content areas (Schunk & Zimmerman, 2008; Zimmerman, 2008). Moreover, when students are engaged in activities that require them to reflect and evaluate, they are less likely to attribute their performance to luck, inherent skill, or "tricky" test questions that the teacher created (Dweck et al., 2014).

Content-area disciplinary teachers can employ a variety of practices to encourage their students to reflect on and evaluate their performance. Two effective approaches include the learning log and the self-reflection activity.

Learning Logs and Blogs

I introduced learning logs in Chapter 7 on writing. I demonstrated in that chapter how learning logs can serve as a repository for most low-stakes writing students do for content-area and disciplinary courses. I would like to give learning logs and their

Part One Directions: Think about the following questions as you read all the articles you were assigned. These questions force you to think critically about an author's authority, intent, accuracy, and objectivity. If you think of additional questions that would be useful to you and your group members, write them in the blank lines.

Authority

1. Who is the author or producer of this information?
2. What are the author's qualifications? Are these credentials credible? Are these qualifications sufficient to discuss the content presented in the article?

Intent

3. What is the author trying to say here? What is the message?
4. Did the author explain and support the ideas in a clear fashion? Explain.

Accuracy

5. When was this article written? What do you know about this time period.
6. Can this information be verified by another source? Explain.
7. Is this information consistent with what you already know about the topic? Why or why not?

Objectivity

8. Is there any sort of bias evident in this article? Explain.
9. Is the author's motivation for writing clear to you? What do you think that motivation was?
10. **Other questions:**

    _____

    _____

Part Two Directions: After answering the questions listed above and listening to your peers during the discussion. RATE the author of this article/essay. Complete the grid below so it represents what your group decides. You must reach a consensus and be prepared to defend your rating. Select a spokesperson for your group.

Rate the Author

	1	2	3	4	5
	Low		Average		High

Authority

Intent

Accuracy

Objectivity

Total score: _____

FIGURE 9.14. Questioning and challenging the author.

electronic permutation, blogs, more attention in this chapter, since these tools can be used by students to reinforce their new learning and provide a metacognitive reflection on the effectiveness of their reading and learning strategies relative to test and other task performance.

It is helpful to remember that since nearly the invention of print, literate people have maintained journals or logs. Scientists, explorers, naturalists, novelists, astronauts, ship captains, presidents, and professionals from every discipline have kept and continue to keep journals, diaries, and logs. I have enjoyed reading biography from childhood right up to the present day and am particularly fascinated by the journal and log entries of famous inventors and discoverers such as Thomas Edison, Alexander Graham Bell, and Marie Curie. In them, they describe what they know from past investigations, predict potential outcomes of their trials and tests, and describe the process and document the results of experimentation. Furthermore, these logs typically contain reflections on and speculations about what could be improved or done differently to bring a more desirable result. Creating a record of learning and discovery, including the steps involved, and how to improve the process and outcome are elements of the kind of strategic learning log or blog I am advocating.

Learning logs and journals as tools for learning in the content areas have enjoyed a good deal of positive attention in the literature for at least the past few decades (Audet, Hickman, & Dobrynina, 1996; Calkins, 1986; Halbach, 2000; McIntosh & Draper, 2001). With the advent and continuous development of school-based ICT tools, however, a transition has been occurring from traditional paper and pencil to digitally based journals and logs (Lankshear & Knobel, 2007). An increasing number of teachers from a range of content areas and disciplines are exploiting the affordances of classroom blogs to expand learning of course concepts and increase achievement (Bouldin, Holmes, & Fortenberry, 2006; Churchill, 2009; Du & Wagner, 2007; Leuhmann & Frink, 2009; Robertson, 2011; Sawmiller, 2010).

A traditional learning log is a notebook, binder, or some other repository that students maintain in order to record explanations, ideas, questions, reactions, and reflections and to summarize newly learned content. Blogs offer the same opportunities but include additional advantages, such as the possibility to interact and collaborate with peers and the teacher in this digital space.

Documenting ideas in a log about content being read and how it is studied forces students to "put into words" what they know or do not know, both in terms of declarative and strategic knowledge. Connie regularly requests that her middle graders write in their blog space before taking a math quiz or test. These entries not only allow students to consider what they know and can do relative to the task at hand but also allow Connie to review them in light of actual student test performance. She then offers formative feedback on the blogs to clarify any specific misconceptions and encourage certain study processes.

Connie's blog entry prompt: Before taking today's quiz, in your own words tell what you have learned about how to divide fractions from today's reading and activities.

Mario's blog entry—October 20, 2016, fifth period, Math
First you write down the problem (like 3/8 ÷ 5/2). Next I know that something like 8 ÷ 3 means the same as 8 × 1/3, so I have to multiply the first number by the reciprocal of the second fraction (5/2 would become 2/5, so 3/8 × 2/5). Then, if the answer is a number that can be reduced (6/40 = 3/20), reduce it. We learned how to do that today, but I remember learning this a long time ago. Then you write your answer.

Connie's feedback: Your explanation is accurate, Mario, but you had trouble using this information to answer the quiz questions correctly. Try putting different problems on flash cards and quizzing yourself for the correct answer. You can also team up with Gilbert to study together and check each other's problem-solving steps and answers; I'll give you time in class for that.

Kim, a 10th-grade biology teacher, asked her students to write a learning log entry immediately after they had finished their exam. Then, 2 days later, after discussing the exam during class and going over the answers, Kim asked them to reread their entries. She then assigned her students to write a second entry describing what they had learned about themselves and what they would do differently if they had the opportunity to retake the exam. One student, Jason, wrote the following log entries. As you read them, think about his strengths and challenges as an active learner and what he learned about himself.

Jason's learning log entry—immediately after the exam: Well, I predict that I will get an A on this test, I have always been smart in science the test was about what I expected—not too hard, not too easy. I didn't think we would have to diagram the female reproductive cycle—that was a surprise. I studied by scanning the chapters and looking at my notes during homeroom. I probably studied about 10 minutes—science is my thing so I really did not need to study much. By the way, did we talk in class about the regulation of glucose?

Jason's learning log entry—2 days later: Well, I guess I did not do as well as I predicted—I got a D on the test. I missed all the questions on the diagrams. My other science teachers never asked me to label and explain diagrams. I probably should have read the chapters rather than skimming them. I also should have looked at my class notes longer. If I could take the test again, I would certainly study longer, and I would memorize those diagrams you discussed with us in class. Otherwise, if I could take this test over, I probably would not change my strategies that much. I learned from this first test that biology may be different from general science.

What did you learn about Jason? What did you decide his strengths were? His areas that need further development? After reading Jason's evaluation paragraphs in his learning log, Kim hypothesized that Jason was not using active strategies for studying. He was merely skimming or looking at material—very passive strategies. Because Kim requires her students to integrate concepts, Jason's strategies were definitely not appropriate for the thinking processes she emphasizes in her course. Moreover, Jason probably was not listening intently in class, because Kim had stressed the importance of studying the diagrams and being able to explain how hormones interact with each other. Kim decided to watch Jason carefully and to work on his reading and study practices in the biology course. Kim, however, was not the only individual who gained important information from the learning log entries; Jason and Kim's other students were also gathering important information about themselves as learners in biology.

Learning logs and blogs can be very helpful metacognitive study tools, especially when students are honest in writing their entries. Students' entries will also provide you with some useful assessment information about them. More important, by thinking about what they know, their strategies for learning, and whether the strategies were appropriate to the task, your students will realize that they are the ones in control of their academic performance. Finally, your formative responses to their log and blog entries will reinforce students' independent strategic reading and learning.

Self-Reflection Activity

In addition to the learning log and blogs, middle and high school teachers can encourage students to evaluate their own strategies and techniques by asking them to participate in a self-reflection activity similar to the one in Figure 9.15. This particular checklist was developed by Nicole, a chemistry teacher, who was concerned about her students and their reactions to the first chemistry exam. Many of her students were dismayed by their mediocre performance and were making comments in class similar to these: "I am just not good at chemistry." "I studied for 8 hours last night and still received a C on the exam." "I am not going to try anymore, because when I study I still fail." Nicole knew these students were not reading and studying appropriately but wanted them to draw that conclusion themselves. Hence, she listed on the checklist all the strategies and techniques that she knew were task appropriate and productive for learning chemistry.

The following day Nicole distributed the checklist and asked her students to complete it. She stressed that the checklist, if done honestly, would help them determine what they needed to do to improve their exam performance. That evening Nicole divided the checklist into categories: students who received an A or a B on the exam and students who received a D or an F. She then read each checklist and coded the strategies that the students checked so that she could identify the strategies used by the high-performing students and the low-performing students. Although she knew what trends would emerge from this data analysis (e.g., the

Directions: In order to help improve your exam performance, I must know more about the techniques you are using to read and study. Please note that I am interested in how you really studied, not in how you wished you had studied. Be honest as there is no penalty for telling me that you did not read your assignments or did not do any chemistry problems. **Fill in the blanks and check the statements that pertain to you.**

Your name: _____

Estimate the amount of time you spent studying for this exam: _____ (hours/minutes)

When did you begin your serious studying? _____ (the night before, etc.)

I did these things to study for the chemistry exam:

☐   1. I read my assignments on a daily basis.

☐   2. After I read a chemistry assignment, I summarized the key ideas on a piece of paper, sticky note, or index card.

☐   3. I identified the material that I did not understand so I could ask questions in class.

☐   4. I reviewed my class notes on a daily basis.

☐   5. I read the lab manual and took the self-check quiz before I did the experiments in lab.

☐   6. I solved the assigned chemistry problems without looking at the solutions at the back of the book.

☐   7. I did extra chemistry problems at the end of each chapter.

☐   8. I did talk-throughs of the key concepts in the chapters.

☐   9. I quizzed myself or asked someone to quiz me over the key concepts.

☐ 10. Describe any other methods you used to study. _____

_____

FIGURE 9.15. Self-reflection activity for chemistry.

students who solved all the problems in the workbook were the ones who did well on the exam), she also knew her students would perceive the data from the checklists as extremely credible and useful.

Armed with the data and the trends, Nicole went to class the next day and presented the information to her students on PowerPoint slides. In Figure 9.16 you will note the trends that Nicole discussed with her students. As you can see, the students who received an A or a B on the first exam were the ones who were reading and studying on a daily basis, solving all the assigned problems, and asking questions during class to clarify concepts. Nicole also found no differences between the high-performing and low-performing students in terms of the amount of time spent studying. As expected, this information about time really surprised her students.

The students who received an A or B on the exam

Studied an average of 2 hours for the exam

Began their studying at least 2 days before the exam

Reported an average of 4.8 different strategies

Used these techniques:
(a) They all did extra chemistry problems
(b) They all summarized what they read
(c) They all reviewed their class notes on a daily basis
(d) They all asked questions during class

The students who received a D or F on the exam

Studied an average of 2.8 hours for the exam

Began their studying the night before the exam

Reported an average of 1.7 different strategies

Used these techniques:
(a) They all read their assignments
(b) They did most of the assigned problems

FIGURE 9.16. Data on successful students in chemistry.

After a discussion of the trends, Nicole asked her students to return to the checklist and circle the strategies and techniques they would be willing to try out for the next exam. This particular step was important because it placed the responsibility on the students to reflect on the techniques they had been using and to consider the possibility of changing to some more productive ones. Nicole has found that the time spent on the checklist and the debriefing of the trends from the checklist is time well spent. During the semester, she has observed numerous students making significant changes in their reading and studying behaviors. Because of the success of this lesson, Nicole decided to place the checklist on her website as a link for parents so they, too, would have a sense of how their children should be reading, studying, and thinking about chemistry.

I began this chapter with a comment from Wilbert McKeachie about the goals of education and the importance of emphasizing thinking processes, as well as content-area knowledge. I end this chapter by returning to what McKeachie and others have been saying for quite some time: When we build strategic, independent learners, we are building learners for the future.

Case Study Revisited

Return to the beginning of the chapter, where I described Ian, the English teacher concerned about his gifted students' learning strategies. After reading this chapter, you probably have some ideas about how he could be more creative and effective in his teaching. Take time now to write your suggestions.

As Ian was searching for instructional answers for his gifted students, a situation serendipitously occurred in their AP history class that stimulated considerable discussion and complaining. Most of the students felt that their most recent essay exam in AP history had been unfair and far too demanding. Ian therefore decided to talk to his colleague and running partner, Theo, who taught the history class. Theo was more than happy to discuss the questions and share some insights with Ian. It seems that the essay questions required students to read and synthesize several written sources about isolationism. Some of the questions asked students to form generalizations and another question asked them to compare and contrast some of the theories.

Armed with this information, Ian went to class the next day and asked his students to evaluate their exam performance by writing a paragraph that addressed several questions (e.g., How long did you study?; Describe how you read and studied; What techniques did you use?). That night as he read the students' paragraphs Ian discovered that several of them did not read all the assigned material and that a significant number of them waited until the night before the exam to finish their reading. He also learned that most of the students reported no special techniques or strategies to organize the multiple sources. Ian found his first "hook" for teaching his students more powerful learning strategies—their success in AP history.

The next day he decided to teach his students how to corroborate, an essential higher-level thinking process, by using the charting strategy. Corroboration involves students in comparing and contrasting text with another source, a process that his students had skipped in their study procedures. Rather than using the history curriculum, Ian decided to introduce the usefulness of charts with the short stories they had been reading in his class. The students selected several characters from the stories and then worked in pairs to compare and contrast them on several different features. Once all the students had completed their charts, Ian then debriefed the experience, stressing the advantages of the chart as a visual organizer in the preparation steps for writing.

Two days later Ian followed up the initial charting lesson by explaining to his students that they would be creating another chart in order to compare and contrast historical figures such as Churchill and Wilson. After brainstorming all the possible characteristics that could be used on the vertical axis of their charts (e.g., individual's background, belief), Ian placed the students in pairs to work. In order to emphasize the benefits of the charting strategy, the next day Ian gave the students a quick pop quiz over the content and their charts. The students were thrilled to discover that they "aced" the quiz because they had remembered all the information in their charts. This situation provided a perfect opportunity to discuss other ways in which to organize and synthesize ideas.

During the school year, Ian also read a few articles about the teaching of learning strategies in professional publications such as the *Journal of Adolescent and Adult Learning*. From his reading, he realized that he needed to demonstrate for his students how they should modify their reading methods for the different courses they were taking. His students were particularly impressed with his modeling because they had always thought they should read their chemistry assignments in the same way they should read their literature or history assignments.

The first semester has taught Ian many things. Most importantly, he has realized that students will not be able to transfer study strategies to their own tasks if they do nothing but complete workbook activities.

LOOKING BACK, LOOKING FORWARD

Strategic literacy and learning should be taught as processes instead of as a series of steps that, when followed, will automatically produce greater comprehension and retention. I have emphasized the learner's role in strategy instruction. If we do not give students opportunities to help shape the learning strategies they are being taught, we run the risk of offering them a series of meaningless formulas that have little relevance to their genuine study needs. This fact has important implications for content-area and disciplinary teachers who want their students to be active rather than passive learners. Your role should be to inform students of each study process and its best possible applications, and then guide them in developing personally meaningful adaptations that transfer to actual study tasks.

Although I shared several effective research-based strategies and activities in this chapter, I want to reiterate that it takes a great deal of time to develop expertise in using them. I also made it clear that no single strategic reading and learning process will be appropriate for every study need. Consequently, students should be encouraged to develop facility with a few flexible, meaningful literacy and strategic processes so that they can select the most appropriate ones to increase learning and achievement on specific academic tasks.

References

Aaronson, D., Barrow, L., & Sander, W. (2007). Teachers and student achievement in the Chicago public high schools. *Journal of Labor Economics, 25*(1), 95–135.

Aboudan, R. (2011). Engage them, don't enrage them: Student voices and what it takes to participate. *English Language Teaching, 4*(1), 128–134.

Abrams, S. S., & Gerber, H. R. (2015, Fall). Layering meaning across literate practices. *The ALAN Review*, pp. 101–105.

Adu-Gyamfi, K., Bosse, M., & Faulconer, J. (2010). Assessing understanding through reading and writing in mathematics. *International Journal for Mathematics Teaching and Learning, 11*(5), 1–22.

Afflerbach, P. (1986). The influence of prior knowledge on expert readers' importance assignment processes. In J. A. Niles & R. V. Lalik (Eds.), *National Reading Conference yearbook: Vol. 35. Solving problems in literacy: Learners, teachers and researchers* (pp. 30–40). Rochester, NY: National Reading Conference.

Afflerbach, P. (2007). *Understanding and using reading assessment, K–12.* Newark, DE: International Reading Association.

Afflerbach, P. (2010). *Essential readings on assessment.* Newark, DE: International Reading Association.

Afflerbach, P. (Ed.). (2015). *Handbook of individual differences in reading: Reader, text, and context.* New York: Routledge.

Agee, J., & Altarriba, J. (2009). Changing conceptions and uses of computer technologies in the everyday literacy practices of sixth and seventh graders. *Research in the Teaching of English, 43*(4), 363–396.

Agha, A. (2007). *Language and social relations.* New York: Cambridge University Press.

Aikens, N. L., & Barbarin, O. (2008). Socioeconomic differences in reading trajectories: The contribution of family, neighborhood, and school contexts. *Journal of Educational Psychology, 100*(2), 235–251.

Ainley, M., Hidi, S., & Berndorff, D. (2002). Interest, learning, and the psychological processes that mediate their relationship. *Journal of Educational Psychology, 94*, 545–561.

Ajayi, L. (2015). Vocabulary instruction and Mexican-American bilingual students: How two high school teachers integrate multiple strategies to build word consciousness in English language arts classrooms. *International Journal of Bilingual Education and Bilingualism, 18*(4), 463–484.

Akhondi, M., Malayeri, F. A., & Samad, A. A. (2011), How to teach expository text structure to facilitate reading comprehension. *The Reading Teacher, 64*(5), 368–372.

Al Azri, R. H., & Al-Rashdi, M. H. (2014). The effect of using authentic materials in teaching. *International Journal of Scientific and Technology Research, 3*(10), 249–254.

Alexander, P., & Jetton, T. (2000). Learning from text: A multidimensional and developmental perspective. In M. Kamil, P. Mosenthal, P. D. Pearson, & R. Barr (Eds.), *Handbook of reading research* (Vol. 3, pp. 285–310). Mahwah, NJ: Erlbaum.

Alexander, P. A., Singer, L. M., Jablansky, S., & Hattan, C. (2016). Relational reasoning in word and in figure. *Journal of Educational Psychology, 106,* 1021–1035.

Alfassi, M. (2004). Reading to learn: Effects of combined strategy instruction on high school students. *Journal of Educational Research, 97,* 171–184.

Alger, C. (2009). Content area reading strategy knowledge transfer from preservice to first-year teaching. *Journal of Adolescent and Adult Literacy, 53*(1), 60–69.

Al-Khateeb, O. S. M., & Idrees, M. W. K. (2010). The impact of using KWL strategy on grade ten female students' reading comprehension of religious concepts in Ma'an City. *European Journal of Social Sciences, 12*(3), 471–489.

Allbery, D. (2010). Bridging fact and story: Using historical fiction in middle school social studies. In S. Szabo, T. Morrison, L. Martin, M. Boggs, & R. LaVerne (Eds.), *Building literacy communities* (Vol. 32, pp. 63–82). St. Cloud, MN: Association of Literacy Educators and Researchers.

Allington, R. (2012). *What really matters for struggling readers: Designing research-based programs.* Boston: Pearson.

Allison, H., & Harklau, L. (2010). Teaching academic literacies in secondary school. In G. Li & P. A. Edwards (Eds.), *Best practices in ELL instruction* (pp. 835–851). New York: Guilford Press.

Alvermann, D. (2002). *Adolescents and literacies in a digital world.* New York: Peter Lang.

Alvermann, D. E. (2009). Sociocultural constructions of adolescence and young people's literacies. In L. Christenbury, R. Bomer, & P. Smagorinsky (Eds.), *Handbook of adolescent literacy research* (pp. 14–28). New York: Guilford Press.

Alvermann, D. E. (2010). *Adolescents' online literacies: Connecting classrooms, digital media, and popular culture.* New York: Peter Lang.

Alvermann, D. E. (2011). Popular culture and literacy practices. In M. L. Kamil, P. D. Pearson, E. B. Moje, & P. P. Afflerbach (Eds.), *Handbook of reading research* (Vol. 4, pp. 541–560). New York: Routledge/Taylor & Francis Group.

Alvermann, D. E., & Eakle, A. J. (2007). Dissolving learning boundaries: The doing, re-doing, and undoing of school. In D. Thiessen & A. Cook-Sather (Eds.), *International handbook of student experience in elementary and secondary school* (pp. 143–166). Dordrecht, The Netherlands: Springer.

Alvermann, D. E., Marshall, J. D., McLean, C. A., Huddleston, A. P., Joaquin, J., & Bishop, J. (2012). Adolescents' web-based literacies, identity construction, and skill development. *Literacy Research and Instruction, 51*(3), 179–195.

Alvermann, D. E., & Moje, E. B. (2013). Adolescent literacy instruction and the discourse of "every teacher a teacher of reading." In D. Alvermann, N. J. Unrau, & R. B. Ruddell (Eds.), *Theoretical models and processes of reading* (pp. 1072–1103). Newark, DE: International Reading Association.

Alvermann, D. E., Unrau, N., & Ruddell, R. (2013). *Theoretical models and processes of reading* (6th ed.). Newark, DE: International Reading Association.

Ambrose, S. A., Bridges, M. W., DiPietro, M., Lovett, M. C., & Norman, M. K. (2010). *How learning works: Seven research-based principles for smart teaching.* San Francisco: Jossey-Bass.

American Press Institute. (2014). How Americans get their news. Retrieved from *www.american pressinstitute.org/publications/reports/survey-research/how-americans-get-news.*

Amzil, A. (2014). The effect of a metacognitive intervention on college students' reading performance and metacognitive skills. *Journal of Educational and Developmental Psychology, 4*(1), 27–45.

Ananiadou, K., & Claro, M. (2009). *21st-century skills and competences for new millennium learners in OECD countries* [OECD Education Working Papers, No. 41]. Paris: OECD.

Anderman, E. M. (2010). Reflections on Wittrock's generative model of learning: A motivation perspective. *Educational Psychologist, 45*(1), 55–60.

Anderman, E. M., & Wolters, C. (2006). Goals, values, and affect. In P. Alexander & P. Winne (Eds.), *Handbook of educational psychology* (2nd ed., pp. 369–390). Mahwah, NJ: Erlbaum.

Anderman, L. H., Andrezejewski, C., & Allen, J. (2011). How do teachers support students' motivation and learning in their classrooms? *Teachers College Record, 113*(5), 969–1003.

Andrade, H., Huff, K., & Brooke, G. (2012). *Assessing learning.* Boston: Jobs for the Future. Available from *http://studentsatthecenter.org/topics/assessing-learning.*

Andrade, H., & Valtcheva, A. (2009). Promoting learning and achievement through self-assessment. *Theory into Practice, 48,* 12–19.

Andrews, R., & Smith, A. (2011). *Developing writers: Teaching and learning in the digital age.* New York: McGraw Hill.

Angelo, T. A., & Cross, K. P. (2008). *Classroom assessment techniques: A handbook for college teachers.* San Francisco: Jossey-Bass.

Annie E. Casey Foundation. (2014, November). Kids Count data center: Children whose parents lack secure employment. Retrieved from *datacenter.kidscount.org/data/tables/5043-children-whose-parents-lack-secure-employment#detailed/1/any/false/36,868,867,133,38/any/11452,11453.*

Anrelchik, H. (2015). Reconsidering literacy in the art classroom. *Art Education, 68*(1), 6–11.

Applebee, A., & Langer, J. (2011). *The National Study of Writing Instruction: Methods and procedures.* Albany, NY: Center on English Learning and Achievement. Retrieved from *www.albany.edu/cela/reports/NSWI_2011_ methods_procedures.pdf.*

Arend, B. (2009). Encouraging critical thinking in online threaded discussions. *Journal of Educators Online, 6*(1), 1–23.

Arends, R. I., & Kilcher, A. (2010). *Teaching for student learning: Becoming an accomplished teacher.* New York: Routledge.

Arias, M. B., & Morillo-Campbell, M. (2008). *Promoting ELL parental involvement: Challenges in contested times.* East Lansing, MI: Great Lakes Center for Education Research and Practice. Retrieved from *http://greatlakescenter.org/docs/Policy_Briefs/Arias_ELL.pdf.*

Arya, D. J., & Maul, A. (2012). The role of the scientific discovery narrative in middle school science education: An experimental study. *Journal of Educational Psychology, 104*(4), 1022–1032.

Atay, D., & Ozbulgan, C. (2007). Memory strategy instruction, contextual learning and ESP vocabulary recall. *English for Specific Purposes, 25*(1), 39–51.

Audet, R. H., Hickman, P., & Dobrynina, G. (1996). Learning logs: A classroom practice for enhancing scientific sense making. *Journal of Research in Science Teaching, 33*(2), 205–222.

August, D. (2012). *Developing literacy in Spanish-speaking children: Acquisition of vocabulary in English* (Technical Report 4). Washington, DC: Center for Applied Linguistics.

August, D., Artzi, L., & Barr, C. (2016). Helping ELLs meet standards in English language arts and science: An intervention focused on academic vocabulary. *Reading and Writing Quarterly: Overcoming Learning Difficulties, 32*(4), 373–396.

August, D., & Shanahan, T. (2008). *Developing reading and writing in second-language learners: Lessons from the report of the National Literacy Panel on language-minority children and youth.* New York: Routledge.

Avraamidou, L., & Osborne, J. (2009). The role of narrative in communicating science. *International Journal of Science Education, 31,* 1683–1707.

Baines, L., & Fisher, J. (2013). *Teaching challenging texts: Fiction, non-fiction, and multimedia.* New York: Rowman & Littlefield.

Baker, L., & Beall, L. C. (2008). Metacognitive processes in reading comprehension. In S. Israel & G. Duffy (Eds.), *Handbook of reading comprehension research* (pp. 373–388). Mahwah, NJ: Erlbaum.

Baker, L., DeWyngaert, L., & Zeliger-Kandasamy, A. (2015). Metacognition in comprehension instruction. In S. R. Parris & K. Headley (Eds.), *Comprehension instruction: Research-based best practices* (3rd ed., pp. 72–87). New York: Guilford Press.

Barnes, K., Marateo, R. C., & Ferris, S. P. (2007). Teaching and learning with the Net Generation. *Innovate: Journal of Online Education, 3*(4), 1–8.

Barone, D. (2014). Reading, learning and even arguing across multiple texts. *Voices in the Middle, 21*(4), 54–57.

Barrett, H. C. (2007). Researching electronic portfolios and learner engagement: The REFLECT initiative. *Journal of Adolescent and Adult Literacy, 50*(6), 436–449.

Barth, A. E., Tolar, T. D., Fletcher, J. M., & Francis, D. (2014). The effects of student and text characteristics on the oral reading fluency of middle-grade students. *Journal of Educational Psychology, 106*(1), 162–180.

Barton, P. E. (2004). Why does the gap persist? *Educational Leadership, 62*(3), 9–13.

Bass, H. (2006). Developing scholars and professionals: The case of mathematics. In C. M. Golde & G. E. Walker (Eds.), *Envisioning the future of doctoral education: Preparing stewards of the discipline: Carnegie essays on the doctorate* (pp. 101–119). San Francisco: Jossey-Bass.

Batel, S., & Sargrad, S. (2016). *Better tests, fewer barriers: Advances in accessibility through PARCC and Smarter Balanced.* Washington, DC: Center for American Progress.

Bazerman, C., & Prior, P. (2004). *What writing does and how it does it: An introduction to analyzing texts and textual practices.* Mahwah, NJ: Erlbaum.

Bean, J. (2011). *Engaging ideas: The professor's guide to integrating writing, critical thinking, and active learning in the classroom* (2nd ed.). San Francisco: Jossey-Bass.

Bean, T. (2003). *Using young-adult literature to enhance comprehension in the content areas.* Naperville, IL: Learning Point Associates.

Bean, T. W., Dunkerly-Bean, J., & Harper, H. (2013). *Teaching young adult literature: Developing students as world citizens.* Thousand Oaks, CA: Sage.

Bean, T. W., Readence, J. E., & Baldwin, R. S. (2011). *Content area literacy: An integrated approach* (10th ed.). Dubuque, IA: Kendall/Hunt.

Bean, T. W., & Valerio, P. C. (1997). Constructing school success in literacy: The pathway to college entrance for minority students. *Reading Research Quarterly, 32,* 320–327.

Beck, C. (1999). Francine, Kerplunk, and the Golden Nugget: Conducting mock trials and debates in the classroom. *Social Studies, 90,* 78–84.

Beers, K., & Probst, R. E. (2015). *Reading nonfiction: Notice and note stances, signposts, and strategies.* Portsmouth, NH: Heinemann.

Behrman, E. (2003). Reconciling content literacy with adolescent literacy: Expanding literacy opportunities in a community-focused biology class. *Reading Research and Instruction, 43,* 1–30.

Benassi, V. A., Overson, C. E., & Hakala, C. M. (2014). Applying science of learning in education: Infusing psychological science into the curriculum. Retrieved from *http://teachpsych.org/ebooks/asle2014/index.php.*

Benjamin, A. S., & Tullis, J. (2010). What makes distributed practice effective? *Cognitive Psychology, 61*(3), 228–247.

Bennett, R. E. (2011). Formative assessment: A critical review. *Assessment in Education: Principles, Policy and Practice, 18*(1), 5–25.

Bensley, D. A., & Spero, R. A. (2014). Improving critical thinking skills and metacognitive monitoring through direct infusion. *Thinking Skills and Creativity, 12*(1), 55–68.

Benson, J., & Borman, G. (2010). Family, neighborhood, and school settings across seasons: When do socioeconomic context and racial composition matter for the reading achievement growth of young children? *Teachers College Record, 112*(5), 1338–1390.

Berardo, S. A. (2006). The use of authentic materials in the teaching of reading. *Reading Matrix, 6*(2), 60–69.

Berk, S. (2015). Using literature to activate critical intention in secondary student art. *Art Education, 68*(5), 6–12.

Berkeley, S., Mastropieri, M. A., & Scruggs, T. E. (2011). Reading comprehension strategy instruction and attribute retraining for secondary students with learning and other mild disabilities. *Journal of Learning Disabilities, 44*(1), 18–32.

Berkeley, S., & Riccomini, P. J. (2013). QRAC-the-code: A comprehension monitoring strategy for middle school social studies textbooks. *Journal of Learning Disabilities, 46*(2), 154–165.

Berliner, D. (2009). *Poverty and potential: Out of school factors and school success.* Boulder, CO: National Education Policy Center.

Bernacki, M., Nokes-Malach, T., Richey, J. E., & Belenky, D. M. (2016). Science diaries: A brief writing intervention to improve motivation to learn science. *Educational Psychology, 36*(1), 26–46.

Best, R., Rowe, M., Ozuru, Y., & McNamara, D. (2005). Deep-level comprehension of science texts: The role of the reader and the text. *Topics in Language Disorders, 5*(1), 65–83.

Binkley, M., Erstad, O., Hermna, J., Raizen, S., Ripley, M., Miller-Ricci, M., et al. (2012). Defining twenty-first-century skills. In P. Griffin, E. Care, & B. McGaw (Eds.), *Assessment and teaching of 21st-century skills* (pp. 17–66). Dordrecht, The Netherlands: Springer.

Birkerts, S. (2006). *The Gutenberg elegies: The fate of reading in an electronic age.* New York: Faber & Faber.

Bitz, M. (2009). The Tupac effect: A case for socially relevant education. In M. Hagood (Ed.), *New literacies practices: Designing literacy learning* (pp. 7–24). New York: Peter Lang.

Blachowicz, C., & Fisher, P. J. (2015). *Teaching vocabulary in all classrooms* (5th ed.). Boston: Pearson.

Blachowicz, C., & Ogle, D. (2008). *Reading comprehension: Strategies for independent learners* (2nd ed.). New York: Guilford Press.

Black, R. (2008). *Adolescents and online fan fiction.* New York: Peter Lang.

Bohay, M., Blakely, D. P., Tamplin, A. K., & Radvansky, G. A. (2011). Note taking, review, memory, and comprehension. *American Journal of Psychology, 124*(1), 63–73.

Bok, E. (2013). Multiliteracies and participatory learning in English language learner's fanfiction writing. *Foreign Language Education, 20*(4), 1–28.

Bordewich, F. (2004). Free at last. *Smithsonian, 35,* 64–71.

Boswell, J. (1979). *The life of Samuel Johnson.* New York: Viking Press.

Bouldin, A. S., Holmes, E. R., & Fortenberry, M. L. (2006). "Blogging" about course concepts: Using technology for reflective journaling in a communications class. *American Journal of Pharmaceutical Education, 70*(4), 1–8.

Bowers, A. J. (2010). Grades and graduation: A longitudinal risk perspective to identify student dropouts. *Journal of Educational Research, 103*(3), 191–207.

Bowker, M. H. (2010). Teaching students to ask questions instead of answering them. *Thought and Action, 26*(1), 127–134.

Boyd, D. (2014). *It's complicated: The social lives of networked teens.* New Haven, CT: Yale University Press.

Boyer, P. S., Clark, C. E., Kett, J. F., Salisbury, N., Sitkoff, H., & Woloch, N. (2004). *The enduring vision: A history of the American people* (5th ed.). Belmont, CA: Wadsworth.

Brandt, D. (2015). *The rise of writing: Redefining mass literacy.* Cambridge, UK: Cambridge University Press.

Bråten, I., Strømsø, H. I., & Britt, M. A. (2009). Trust matters: Examining the role of source evaluation in students' construction of meaning within and across multiple texts. *Reading Research Quarterly, 44*(1), 6–28.

Braunger, J., Donahue, D., Evans, K., & Galguera, T. (2005). *Rethinking preparation for content area teaching: The reading apprenticeship approach.* San Francisco: Jossey-Bass.

Britt, M. A., & Rouet, J.-F. (2012). Learning with multiple documents: Component skills and their acquisition. In M. J. Lawson & J. R. Kirby (Eds.), *The quality of learning: Dispositions, instruction, and mental structures* (pp. 276–314). New York: Cambridge University Press.

Brock, C. H., Goatley, V. J., Raphael, T. E., Trost-Shahata, E., & Weber, C. M. (2014). *Engaging students in disciplinary literacy, K–6: Reading, writing, and teaching tools for the classroom.* New York: Teachers College Press.

Brodsky, D. (Producer/Director). (2002). *Teens in between: The story of five immigrant teens in America* [Motion picture]. Distributed MHz Networks.

Broekkamp, H., Bernadette, H., & Van Hout-Wolters, A. M. (2007). Students' adaptation of study strategies when preparing for classroom tests. *Educational Psychological Review, 19*(4), 401–428.

Bromley, K. (2007). Nine things every teacher should know about words and vocabulary instruction. *Journal of Adolescent and Adult Literacy, 50*(7), 528–535.

Bromme, R., Pieschl, S., & Stahl, E. (2010). Epistemological beliefs are standards for adaptive learning: A functional theory about epistemological beliefs and metacognition. *Metacognition and Learning, 5*(1), 7–26.

Brown, A., & Day, J. (1983). Macrorules for summarizing text: The development of expertise. *Journal of Verbal Learning and Verbal Behavior, 22,* 1–14.

Brown, C. A., & Dotson, K. (2007). Writing your own history: A case study using digital primary source documents. *TechTrends, 51*(3), 30–37.

Brown, K. M., Anfara, V. A., & Roney, K. (2004). Student achievement in high performing, suburban middle schools and low performing, urban middle schools: Plausible explanations for the differences. *Education and Urban Society, 36*(4), 428–456.

Brown, M. D. (2007). I'll have mine annotated, please: Helping students make connections with text. *English Journal, 96*(4), 73–78.

Brozo, W. G. (1995). Literacy without "risk": Reconsidering cultural and curricular differentiation in literacy. *The State of Reading, 2,* 5–11.

Brozo, W. G. (2003). *"It's like personalities going everywhere": Listening to youths' stories of life and literacy in a suburban high school.* Unpublished manuscript.

Brozo, W. G. (2004). Gaining and keeping students' attention. *Thinking Classroom/Peremena, 5,* 38–39.

Brozo, W. G. (2005a). Book review: Adolescents and literacies in a digital world. *Journal of Literacy Research, 36,* 533–538.

Brozo, W. G. (2005b). Avoiding the "fourth-grade slump." *Thinking Classroom/Peremena, 6,* 48–49.

Brozo, W. G. (2006). Tales out of school: Accounting for adolescents in a literacy reform community. *Journal of Adolescent and Adult Literacy, 49*(5), 410–418.

Brozo, W. G. (2007). Authentic contexts for developing language tools in vocational education (pp. 349–361). In J. Flood, D. Lapp, & N. Farnan (Eds.), *Content area reading and learning: Instructional strategies* (3rd ed.). Mahwah, NJ: Erlbaum.

Brozo, W. G. (2009). Response to intervention or responsive instruction? Challenges and possibilities of response to intervention for adolescent literacy. *Journal of Adolescent and Adult Literacy, 53,* 277–281.

Brozo, W. G. (2010a). *To be a boy, to be a reader: Engaging teen and preteen boys in active literacy* (2nd ed.). Newark, DE: International Reading Association.

Brozo, W. G. (2010b). The role of content literacy in an effective RTI program. *The Reading Teacher, 64*(2), 147–150.

Brozo, W. G. (2011). *RTI and the adolescent reader: Responsive literacy instruction in secondary schools.* New York: Teachers College Press.

Brozo, W. G. (2013). From Manga to math. *Educational Leadership, 71*(3), 58–61.

Brozo, W. G. (2015, December). *Global learning outcomes: Designs and metrics for the 21st century.* Paper presented at the International Conference on Assessment, Riyadh, Saudi Arabia.

Brozo, W. G., & Afflerbach, P. (2011). *Adolescent literacy inventory: Grades 6–12.* New York: Pearson.

Brozo, W. G., & Brozo, C. L. (1994). Literacy assessment in standardized and zero-failure contexts. *Reading and Writing Quarterly, 10,* 189–208.

Brozo, W. G., & Flynt, E. S. (2008). Motivating students to read in the content classroom: Six evidence-based principles. *The Reading Teacher, 62*(2), 172–174.

Brozo, W. G., & Hargis, C. (2003a). Taking seriously the idea of reform: One school's efforts to make reading more responsive to all students. *Journal of Adolescent and Adult Literacy, 43,* 14–23.

Brozo, W. G., & Hargis, C. (2003b). Use it or lose it: Three strategies to increase time spent reading. *Principal Leadership, 4,* 36–40.

Brozo, W. G., & Mayville, M. (2012). Reforming secondary disciplinary instruction with graphic novels. *New England Reading Association Journal, 48*(1), 11–21.

Brozo, W. G., Moorman, G., & Meyer, C. (2014). *Wham!: Teaching with graphic novels across the curriculum.* New York: Teachers College Press.

Brozo, W. G., Moorman, G., Meyer, C., & Stewart, T. (2013). Content area reading and disciplinary literacy: A case for the radical center. *Journal of Adolescent and Adult Literacy, 56*(5), 353–357.

Brozo, W. G., & Simpson, M. L. (2007). *Content literacy for today's adolescents: Honoring diversity and building competence.* New York: Pearson.

Brozo, W. G., Sulkunen, S., Shiel, G., Garbe, C., Pandian, A., & Valtin, R. (2014). Reading, gender, and engagement: Lessons from five PISA countries. *Journal of Adolescent and Adult Literacy, 57*(7), 584–593.

Brozo, W. G., & Tomlinson, C. M. (1986). Literature: The key to lively content courses. *The Reading Teacher, 40*(3), 288–293.

Brozo, W. G., Valerio, P., & Salazar, M. (1996). A walk through Gracie's garden: Literacy and cultural explorations in a Mexican-American junior high school. *Journal of Adolescent and Adult Literacy, 40,* 164–171.

Buehl, D. (2009). *Classroom strategies for interactive learning* (3rd ed.). Newark, DE: International Reading Association.

Bugg, J. M., & McDaniel, M. A. (2012). Selective benefits of question self-generation and answering for remembering expository text. *Journal of Educational Psychology, 104*(4), 922–931.

Bui, D. C., Myerson, J., & Hale, S. (2013). Note-taking with computers: Exploring alternative strategies for improved recall. *Journal of Educational Psychology, 105*(2), 299–309.

Bureau of Labor Statistics. (2013a). *Employment projections: Fastest growing occupations.* Washington, DC: U.S. Department of Labor.

Bureau of Labor Statistics. (2013b). International comparisons of annual labor force statistics, 1970–2012. Retrieved from *www.bls.gov/fls/flscomparelf/lfcompendium.pdf*.

Bureau of Labor Statistics. (2015). Occupational employment and wages—May 2014. Retrieved from *www.bls.gov/news.release/pdf/ocwage.pdf*.

Burke, A., & Hammett, R. R. (2009). *Assessing new literacies: Perspectives from the classroom*. New York: Peter Lang.

Burrell, K. I., & McAlexander, P. J. (1998). Ideas in practice: The synthesis journal. *Journal of Developmental Education, 22*, 20–22, 24, 26, 28, 30.

Butler, S., Urrutia, K., Buenger, A., Gonzalez, N., Hunt, M., & Eisenhart, C. (2010). *A review of the current research on vocabulary instruction*. Washington, DC: National Reading Technical Assistance Center. Retrieved from *www2.ed.gov/programs/readingfirst/support/rmcfinal1.pdf*

Caccamise, D., & Snyder, L. (2005). Theory and pedagogical practices of text comprehension. *Topics in Language Disorders, 25*(1), 5–20.

Calderon, M., & Minaya-Rowe, L. (2011). *Preventing long-term ELs: Transforming schools to meet core standards*. Thousand Oaks, CA: Corwin.

Calderon, M., Slavin, R., & Sanchez, M. (2011). Effective instruction for English learners. *Future of Children, 21*(1), 103–127.

Calkins, L., Ehrenworth, M., & Lehman, C. (2012). *Pathways to the common core: Accelerating achievement*. Portsmouth, NH: Heinemann.

Calkins, L. M. (1986). *The art of teaching writing*. Portsmouth, NH: Heinemann.

Cambria, J., & Guthrie, J. T. (2011). Motivating and engaging students in reading. *NERA Journal, 46*(1), 16–29.

Cantrell, S. C., Almasi, J. F., Carter, J. C., Rintamaa, M., & Madden, A. (2010). The impact of a strategy-based intervention on the comprehension and strategy use of struggling adolescent readers. *Journal of Educational Psychology, 102*(2), 257–280.

Cantrell, S. C., & Carter, J. C. (2009) Relationships among learner characteristics and adolescents' perceptions about reading strategy use. *Reading Psychology, 30*(3), 195–224.

Capps, R., Fix, M., Murray, J., Ost, J., Passel, J. S., & Herwantoro, S. (2005). *The new demography of America's schools: Immigration and the No Child Left Behind Act*. Washington, DC: Urban Institute.

Carden, A. (1983). Biblical texts and themes in American Puritan preaching, 1630–1700. *Andrews University Seminary Studies, 21*(2), 113–128.

Carlo, M., August, D., & Snow, C. (2010). Sustained vocabulary-learning strategy instruction for English-language learners. In E. Hiebert & M. Kamil (Eds.), *Teaching and learning vocabulary: Bringing research to practice* (pp. 137–153). New York: Routledge.

Carnoy, M., & Rothstein, R. (2013). *What do international tests really show about U.S. student performance?* Washington, DC: Economics Policy Institute.

Carr, E., & Ogle, D. (1987). K-W-L Plus: A strategy for comprehension and summarization. *Journal of Reading, 30*, 626–631.

Carter, J. B. (2009). Going graphic. *Educational Leadership, 66*(6), 68–72.

Cavallo, G., & Chartier, R. (1999). *A history of reading in the West*. Cambridge, UK: Polity Press.

Cerdan, R., & Vidal-Abarca, E. (2008). The effects of tasks on integrating information from multiple documents. *Journal of Educational Psychology, 100*(1), 209–222.

Cerra, R., Mancini, M., & Antonietti, A. (2013). Relationships between metacognition, self-efficacy and self-regulation in learning. *Educational, Cultural and Psychological Journal, 7*, 115–141.

Cervetti, G., Bravo, M., Hiebert, E., Pearson, P. D., & Jaynes, C. (2009). Text genre and science content: Ease of reading, comprehension, and reader preference. *Reading Psychology, 30*, 487–511.

Cervetti, G., & Pearson, P. D. (2012). Reading, writing, and thinking like a scientist. *Journal of Adolescent and Adult Literacy, 55*(7), 580–586.

Cervetti, G. N., Wright, T. S., & Hwang, H. (2016). Conceptual coherence, comprehension, and vocabulary acquisition: A knowledge effect? *Reading and Writing: An Interdisciplinary Journal, 29*(4), 761–779.

Çetinavcı, B. M. (2014). Contextual factors in guessing word meaning from context in a foreign language. *Procedia—Social and Behavioral Sciences, 116,* 2670–2674.

Chambliss, M. (1995). Text cues and strategies successful readers use to construct the gist of lengthy written arguments. *Reading Research Quarterly, 30,* 778–807.

Chandler-Olcott, K. (2007). Anime and manga fandom: Young people's multiliteracies made visible. In J. Flood, S. B. Heath, & D. Lapp (Eds.), *Handbook of research on teaching literacy through communicative and visual arts* (Vol. 2, pp. 247–258). New York: Routledge.

Chandler-Olcott, K., & Mahar, D. (2003). Adolescents' anime-inspired fanfactions: An exploration of multiliteracies. *Journal of Adolescent and Adult Literacy, 46,* 556–566.

Chang, C.-C., & Tseng, K.-H. (2011). Using a web-based portfolio assessment system to elevate project-based learning performances. *Interactive Learning Environments, 19*(3), 211–230.

Chang, H. J. (2011). *23 things they don't tell you about capitalism.* New York: Bloomsbury.

Chen, M. (2015, September 2). The rebellion against standardized tests is exploding. Retrieved from *www.thenation.com/article/the-rebellion-against-standardized-tests-is-exploding/.*

Chenelle, S., & Fisch, A. (2016). *Connecting across disciplines: Collaborating with informational text.* Lanham, MD: Rowman & Littlefield.

Chiesi, H. L., Spilich, G. J., & Voss, J. F. (1979). Acquisition of domain related information in relation to high and low domain knowledge. *Journal of Verbal Learning and Verbal Behavior, 18,* 257–273.

Christensen, S., Reschly, A., & Wylie, C. (2012). *Handbook of research on student engagement.* New York: Springer.

Chun, C. W. (2009). Critical literacies and graphic novels for English language learners: Teaching *Maus. Journal of Adolescent and Adult Literacy, 53*(2), 144–153.

Churchill, D. (2009). Educational applications of Web 2.0: Using blogs to support teaching and learning. *British Journal of Educational Technology, 40*(1), 179–183.

Chuy, M., Scardamalia, M., & Bereiter, C. (2012). Development of ideational writing through knowledge building: Theoretical and empirical bases. In E. L. Grigorenko, E. Mambrino, & D. D. Preiss (Eds.), *Writing: A mosaic of new perspectives* (pp. 175–190). New York: Psychology Press.

Clark, C. (2014). *Children's and young people's reading in 2013: Findings from the 2013 National Literacy Trust's annual survey.* London: National Literacy Trust.

Clarke, L. W., & Besnoy, K. (2010). Connecting the old to the new: What "technology-crazed" adolescents tell us about teaching content area literacy. *Journal of Media Literacy Education, 2*(2), 47–56.

Clinton, P. (2002, September/October). Literacy in America: The crisis you don't know about and what we can do about it. *Book, 24,* 4–9.

Clotfelter, C., Ladd, H. F., & Vigdor, J. (2005). Who teaches whom?: Race and the distribution of novice teachers. *Economics of Education Review, 24,* 377–392.

Coiro, J. (2011). Talking about reading as thinking: Modeling the hidden complexities of online reading comprehension. *Theory into Practice, 50,* 107–115.

Coiro, J. (2015). Purposeful, critical, and flexible: Key dimensions of online reading and learning. In R. Spiro, M. DeSchrvyer, M. Schira-Hagerman, P. Morsink, & P. Thompson (Eds.), *Reading at a crossroads?: Disjunctures and continuities in current conceptions and practices* (pp. 53–64). New York: Routledge Press.

Coiro, J., Knobel, M., Lankshear, C., & Leu, D. (2008). Central issues in new literacies and new literacies research. In J. Coiro, M. Knobel, C. Lankshear, & D. Leu (Eds.), *The handbook of research on new literacies* (pp. 25–32). Mahwah, NJ: Erlbaum.

Colby, S. L., & Ortman, J. M. (2015, March). Projections of the size and composition of the U.S. population: 2014 to 2060. Retrieved from *www.census.gov/content/dam/Census/library/publications/2015/demo/p25–1143.pdf.*

Colby, S. R. (2009). Contextualization and historical empathy: Seventh-graders' interpretations of primary documents. *Curriculum and Teaching Dialogue, 12*(1–2), 69–83.

Coleman, D., & Pimentel, S. (2012). Revised publishers' criteria for the Common Core State Standards in English Language Arts and Literacy, grades 3–12. Retrieved from *www.achievethecore.org/stealthesetools.*

Common Core State Standards Initiative. (2010). *Common Core State Standards for English language arts and literacy in history/social studies, science, and technical subjects.* Washington, DC: Authors. Retrieved from *www.corestandards.org/assets/CCSSI_ELA%20Standards.pdf.*

Common Sense Media. (2015). The common sense census: Media use by tweens and teens. Retrieved from *www.commonsensemedia.org/research/the-common-sense-census-media-use-by-tweens-and-teens.*

Conderman, G., Hedin, L., & Bresnahan. V. (2013). *Strategy instruction for middle and secondary students with mild disabilities: Creating independent learners.* Thousand Oaks, CA: Corwin Press.

Conley, M. W., Freidhoff, J. R., Gritter, K., & Vriend Van Duinen, D. (2008). Strategies that improve adolescents' performance with content-area texts. In M. W. Conley, J. R. Freidhoff, M. B. Sherry, & S. F. Tuckey (Eds.), *Meeting the challenge of adolescent literacy: Research we have, the research we need* (pp. 88–103). New York: Guilford Press.

Connell, J. M. (2008). The emergence of pragmatic philosophy's influence on literary theory: Making meaning with texts from a transactional perspective. *Educational Theory, 58*(1), 102–122.

Conner, J. J. (2003). "The textbooks never said anything about . . ." Adolescents respond to *The Middle Passage: White Ships/Black Cargo. Journal of Adolescent and Adult Literacy, 47*(3), 240–246.

Considine, D., Horton, J., & Moorman, G. (2009). Teaching and reaching the millennial generation through media literacy. *Journal of Adolescent and Adult Literacy, 52*(6), 471–481.

Cook-Sather, A. (2003). Listening to students about learning differences. *Teaching Exceptional Children, 35,* 22–26.

Cook-Sather, A. (2010). Students as learners and teachers: Taking responsibility, transforming education, and redefining accountability. *Curriculum Inquiry, 40*(4), 555–575.

Cook-Sather, A., Bovill, C., & Felten, P. (2014). *Engaging students as partners in learning and teaching: A guide for faculty.* San Francisco: Jossey-Bass.

Coombs, D. (2013). Fiction and nonfiction: A symbiotic relationship. *The ALAN Review, 41*(1), 7–15.

Cox, C. (2012). *Literature based teaching in the content areas.* Thousand Oaks, CA: Sage.

Coxhead, A. (2000). A new academic word list. *TESOL Quarterly, 34*(2), 213–238.

Craig, H. K., Zhang, L., Hensel, S. L., & Quinn, E. J. (2009). African American English-speaking students: An examination of the relationship between dialect shifting and reading outcomes. *Journal of Speech, Language, and Hearing Research, 52,* 839–855.

Cramer, L. (2015). Inequities of intervention among culturally and linguistically diverse students. *Perspectives on Urban Education, 12*(1). Retrieved from *www.urbanedjournal.org/archive/volume-12-issue-1-spring-2015.*

Crawford, J. (2004). *Educating English learners: Language diversity in the classroom* (5th ed.). Los Angeles: Bilingual Educational Services.

Crawford, J., & Krashen, S. (2007). *English learners in American classrooms: 101 questions, 101 answers.* New York: Scholastic.

Cromer, M., & Clark, P. (2007). Getting graphic with the past: Graphic novels and the teaching of history. *Theory and Research in Social Education, 35*(4), 574–591.

Cronbach, L. J. (1960). *Essentials of psychological testing* (3rd ed.). New York: Harper & Row.

Crossley, S., McCarthy, P., Louwerse, M., & McNamara, D. (2007). A linguistic analysis of simplified and authentic texts. *Modern Language Journal, 91*(2), 15–30.

Cumming, A. (2013). Multiple dimensions of academic language and literacy development. *Language Learning, 63*(1), 130–152.

Cummins, J. (2008). BICS and CALP: Empirical and theoretical status of the distinction. In B. Street & N. H. Hornberger (Eds.), *Encyclopedia of language and education: Vol. 2. Literacy* (2nd ed., pp. 71–83). New York: Springer Science.

Cummins, J., & Man, E. Y. (2007). Academic language: What is it and how do we acquire it? In J. Cummins & C. Davidson (Eds.), *International handbook of English language teaching* (pp. 797–810). New York: Springer.

Daisey, P. (2012). The promise of secondary content area literacy field experiences. *Literacy Research and Instruction, 51*(3), 214–232.

Dalton, B., & Grisham, D. L. (2011). eVoc strategies: 10 ways to use technology to build vocabulary. *The Reading Teacher, 64*(5), 306–317.

Dalton, B., & Proctor, P. (2008). The changing landscape of text and comprehension in the age of new literacies. In J. Coiro, M. Knobel, C. Lankshear, & D. J. Leu (Eds.), *Handbook of research on new literacies* (pp. 297–324). Mahwah, NJ: Erlbaum.

Darche, S., Nayar, N., & Bracco, K. R. (2009). *Work-based learning in California: Opportunities and models for expansion.* San Francisco: WestEd. Retrieved from *www.wested.org/online_pubs/workbasedlearning.pdf*.

Darling-Hammond, L., & Adamson, F. (2010). *Beyond basic skills: The role of performance assessment in achieving 21st century standards of learning.* Stanford, CA: Stanford University, Stanford Center for Opportunity Policy in Education.

David, J. L., & Cuban, L. (2010). *Cutting through the hype: The essential guide to school reform.* Cambridge, MA: Harvard Education Press.

DeCapua, A., & Marshall, H. (2010). Serving ELLs with limited or interrupted education: Intervention that works. *TESOL Journal, 1*(1), 49–70.

Del Favero, L., Boscolo, P., Vidotto, G., & Vicentini, M. (2007). Classroom discussion and individual problem-solving in the teaching of history: Do different instructional approaches affect interest in different ways? *Learning and Instruction, 17,* 635–657.

Desimone, L., & Long, D. A. (2010). Teacher effects and the achievement gap: Do teacher and teaching quality influence the achievement gap between Black and White and high- and low-SES students in the early grades? *Teachers College Record, 112*(12), 3024–3073.

Deslauriers, L., Schelew, E., & Wieman, C. (2011). Improved learning in a large-enrollment physics class. *Science, 332*(6031), 862–864.

Dewey, J. (1913). *Interest and effort in education.* Boston: Houghton Mifflin.

Diakidoy, I.-A., Mouskounti, T., & Ioannides, C. (2011). Comprehension and learning from refutation and expository texts. *Reading Research Quarterly, 46*(1), 22–38.

Diamond, J. E., & Gaier Knapik, M. C. (2014). *Literacy lessons for a digital world: Using blogs, wikis, podcasts, and more to meet the demands of the Common Core.* New York: Scholastic.

Diaz, I. (2015). Training in metacognitive strategies for students' vocabulary improvement by using learning journals. *Profile: Issues in Teachers' Professional Development, 17*(1), 87–102.

Diaz-Rico, L. (2014). *The crosscultural, language, and academic development handbook: A complete K–12 reference guide* (5th ed.). New York: Pearson.

Dignath, C., & Buttner, G. (2008). Components of fostering self-regulated learning among students: A meta-analysis on intervention studies at primary and secondary school level. *Metacognition and Learning, 3,* 231–264.

Dixon, L. Q., Zhao, J., Shin, J.-Y., Wu, S., Su, J.-H., Burgess-Brigham, R., et al. (2012). What we know about second language acquisition: A synthesis from four perspectives. *Review of Educational Research, 82,* 5–60.

Dodigovic, M. (2013). Vocabulary learning with electronic flashcards: Teacher design vs. student design. *Voices in Asia Journal, 1*(1), 15–33.

Dong, Y. R. (2002). Integrating language and content: How three biology teachers work with non-English-speaking students. *International Journal of Bilingual Education and Bilingualism, 5,* 40–57.

Dorfman, L. R., & Cappelli, R. (2009). *Nonfiction mentor texts: Teaching informational writing through children's literature, K–8.* Portland, ME: Stenhouse.

Doyle, W. (1983). Academic work. *Review of Educational Research, 53*(2), 159–199.

Doyle, W. (2006). Ecological approaches to classroom management. In C. Evertson & C. Weinstein (Eds.), *Handbook of classroom management: Research, practice, and contemporary issues* (pp. 97–125). New York: Erlbaum.

Draper, R. J. (2008). Redefining content-area literacy teacher education: Finding my voice through collaboration. *Harvard Educational Review, 78*(1), 60–83.

Dredger, K., Woods, D., Beach, C., & Sagstetter, V. (2010). Engage me: Using new literacies to create third space classrooms that engage student writers. *Journal of Media Literacy, 2*(2), 85–101.

Du, H. S., & Wagner, C. (2007). Learning with weblogs: Enhancing cognitive and social knowledge construction. *IEEE Transactions on Professional Communication, 50*(1), 1–16.

Dufrene, B. A., Reisener, C. D., Olmi, D. J., Zoder-Martell, K., McNutt, M. R., & Horn, D. R. (2010). Peer tutoring for reading fluency as a feasible and effective alternative in response to intervention systems. *Journal of Behavioral Education, 19*(3), 239–256.

Duijnhouwer, H., Prins, F. J., & Stokking, K. M. (2012). Feedback providing improvement strategies and reflection on feedback use: Effects on students' writing motivation, process, and performance. *Learning and Instruction, 22,* 171–184.

Duke, N. K., & Carlisle, J. (2011). The development of comprehension. In P. D. Pearson, M. L. Kamil, P. Afflerbach, & E. Moje (Eds.), *Handbook of reading research* (Vol. 4, pp. 199–228). Mahwah, NJ: Erlbaum.

Duke, N. K., Caughlan, S., Juzwik, M. M., & Martin, N. M. (2012). *Reading and writing genre with purpose in K–8 classrooms.* Portsmouth, NH: Heinemann.

Duke, N. K., & Pearson, P. D. (2008–2009). Effective practices for developing reading comprehension. *Journal of Education, 189*(1/2), 107–122.

Duke, N. K., Pearson, P. D., Strachan, S. L., & Billman, A. K. (2011). Essential elements of fostering and teaching reading comprehension. In S. J. Samuels & A. Farstrup (Eds.), *What research has to say about reading instruction* (4th ed., pp. 51–93). Newark, DE: International Reading Association.

Duncan-Andrade, J., & Morrell, E. (2007). Critical pedagogy and popular culture in an urban secondary English classroom. In P. McLaren & J. L. Kincheloe (Eds.), *Critical pedagogy: Where are we now?* (pp. 184–199). New York: Peter Lang.

Dunlosky, J., & Lipko, A. R. (2007). Metacomprehension: A brief history and how to improve its accuracy. *Current Directions in Psychological Science, 16,* 228–232.

Dunlosky, J., & Metcalfe, J. (2009). *Metacognition.* Thousand Oaks, CA: Sage.

Dunlosky, J., Rawson, K. A., Marsh, E. J., Nathan, M. J., & Willingham, D. T. (2013). Improving students' learning with effective learning techniques: Promising directions from cognitive and educational psychology. *Psychological Science in the Public Interest, 14*(1), 4–58.

Dweck, C., Walton, G. M., & Cohen, G. L. (2014). *Academic tenacity: Mindsets and skills that promote long-term learning.* Retrieved from *https://ed.stanford.edu/sites/default/files/manual/dweck-walton-cohen-2014.pdf.*

Dweck, C. S., & Master, A. (2008). Self-theories motivate self-regulated learning. In D. H. Schunk

& B. J. Zimmerman (Eds.), *Motivation and self-regulated learning: Theory, research and applications* (pp. 31–53). New York: Erlbaum.

Dymock, S. (2007). Comprehension strategy instruction: Teaching narrative text structure awareness. *The Reading Teacher, 61*(2), 161–167.

Echevarría, J., Vogt, M., & Short, D. J. (2010). *Making content comprehensible for secondary English language learners.* Boston: Allyn & Bacon.

Elbow, P. (2012). *Vernacular eloquence: What speech can bring to writing.* Cambridge, UK: Cambridge University Press.

Elley, W. B. (1991). Acquiring literacy in a second language: The effect of book-based programs. *Language Learning, 41*(3), 375–411.

Ellison, N. B., & Wu, Y. (2008). Blogging in the classroom: A preliminary exploration of student attitudes and impact on comprehension. *Journal of Educational Multimedia and Hypermedia, 17*(1), 99–122.

Englert, C. S., Mariage, T. V., Okolo, C. M., Shankland, R. K., Moxley, K. D., Courtad, C., et al. (2009). The learning-to-learn strategies of adolescent students with disabilities: Highlighting note taking, planning, and writing expository texts. *Assessment for Effective Intervention, 34*(3), 147–161.

English, C. (2007). Finding a voice in a threaded discussion group: Talking about literature online. *English Journal, 97*(1), 56–61.

Erikson, E. (1980). *Identity and the life cycle.* New York: Norton.

Fang, Z. (2008). Going beyond the Fab Five: Helping students cope with the unique linguistic challenges of expository reading in intermediate grades. *Journal of Adolescent and Adult Literacy, 51*(6), 476–487.

Fang, Z. (2012). Language correlates of disciplinary literacy. *Topics in Language Disorders, 32*(1), 19–34.

Fang, Z., & Pace, B. G. (2013). Teaching with challenging texts in the disciplines. *Journal of Adolescent and Adult Literacy, 57*(2), 104–108.

Fang, Z., & Wei, Y. (2010). Improving middle school students' science literacy through reading infusion. *Journal of Educational Research, 103*, 262–273.

Farrant, B., & Zubrick, S. (2012). Early vocabulary development: The importance of joint attention and parent–child book reading. *First Language, 32*(3), 343–364.

Fecho, B. (2011). *Teaching for the students: Habits of heart, mind, and practice in the engaged classroom.* New York: Teachers College Press.

Federal Interagency Forum on Child and Family Statistics. (2015). *America's children: Key national indicators of well-being, 2015.* Retrieved from *childstats.gov/americaschildren.*

Fisher, D. (2001). Cross age tutoring: Alternatives to the reading resource room for struggling adolescent readers. *Journal of Instructional Psychology, 28*, 234–240.

Fisher, D., Brozo, W. G., Frey, N., & Frey, G. (2011). *50 instructional routines to develop content literacy* (2nd ed.). New York: Pearson.

Fisher, D., Brozo, W. G., Frey, N., & Ivey, G. (2015). *50 instructional routines to develop content literacy* (3rd ed.). New York: Pearson.

Fisher, D., & Frey, N. (2008a). *Word wise and content rich: Five essential steps to teaching academic vocabulary.* Portsmouth, NH: Heinemann.

Fisher, D., & Frey, N. (2008b). *Better learning through structured teaching: A framework for the gradual release of responsibility.* Alexandria, VA: Association for Supervision and Curriculum Development.

Fisher, D., & Frey, N. (2015). Best practices in adolescent literacy instruction. In L. B. Gambrell & L. Mandel Morrow (Eds.), *Best practices in literacy instruction* (5th ed., pp. 149–168). New York: Guilford Press.

Fisher, D., Frey, N., & Lapp, D. (2012). Building and activating students' background knowledge: It's what they already know that counts. *Middle School Journal*, *43*(3), 22–31.

Fisher, D., & Ivey, G. (2007). Farewell to *A Farewell to Arms*: Deemphasizing the whole-class novel. *Phi Delta Kappan*, *88*(7), 494–497.

Fisher, D., Zike, D., & Frey, N. (2007, August). Foldables: Improving learning with 3-D interactive graphic organizers. *Classroom Notes Plus: A Quarterly of Teaching Ideas*, 1–12.

Flanigan, K., Templeton, S., & Hayes, L. (2010). What's in a word?: Using content vocabulary to generate growth in general academic vocabulary knowledge. *Journal of Adolescent and Adult Literacy*, *56*(2), 132–140.

Flórez, M. T., & Sammons, P. (2013). *Assessment for learning: Effects and impacts*. Reading, UK: CfBT Education Trust. Retrieved from *http://cdn.cfbt.com/~/media/cfbtcorporate/files/research/2013/r-- assessment-for-learning-2013.pdf*.

Flowerday, T., & Shell, D. F. (2015) Disentangling the effects of interest and choice on learning, engagement, and attitude. *Learning and Individual Differences*, *40*(5), 134–140.

Flynt, E. S., & Brozo, W. G. (2008). Developing academic language: Got words? *The Reading Teacher*, *61*(6), 500–502.

Folse, K. (2004). *Vocabulary myths: Applying second language research to classroom teaching*. Ann Arbor: University of Michigan Press.

Forsyth, B., & Beck, B. (2015). Epistemological world view preference predicts recall patterns from a history text. *Journal of Cognitive Education and Psychology*, *14*(1), 143–160.

Fowler, D. (2010) Mathematics in science fiction: Mathematics as science fiction. *World Literature Today*, *84*(3), 48–52.

Frayer, D. A., Frederick, W. C., & Klausmeier, H. J. (1969). *A schema for testing the level of concept knowledge* (Working Paper No. 16). Madison: University of Wisconsin.

Freeman, D., & Freeman, Y. (2011). *Between words: Access to second language acquisition*. Portsmouth, NH: Heinemann.

Freeman, J. G., McPhail, J. C., & Berndt, J. A. (2002). Sixth graders' views of activities that do and do not help them to learn. *Elementary School Journal*, *102*, 335–347.

Freeman, Y., & Freeman, D. (2009). *Academic language for English language learners and struggling readers: How to help students succeed across content areas*. Portsmouth, NH: Heinemann.

Fresch, M. J., & Harkins, P. (2009). *The power of picture books: Using content area literature in middle school*. Urbana, IL: National Council of Teachers of English.

Frey, N., & Fisher, D. (2009). *Learning words inside and out: Vocabulary instruction that boosts achievement in all subject areas*. Portsmouth, NH: Heinemann.

Frey, N., Fisher, D., & Hernandez, T. (2003). "What's the gist?": Summary writing for struggling adolescent writers. *Voices from the Middle*, *11*(2), 43–49.

Friere, P. (1987). *Literacy: Reading the word and the world*. South Hadley, MA: Bergin & Garvey.

Frishkoff, G. A., Collins-Thompson, K., Hodges, L., & Crossley, S. (2016). Accuracy feedback improves word learning from context: Evidence from a meaning-generation task. *Reading and Writing: An Interdisciplinary Journal*, *29*(4), 609–632.

Fulmer, S. M., D'Mello, S. K., Strain, A., & Graesser, A. C. (2015). Interest-based text preference moderates the effect of text difficulty on engagement and learning. *Contemporary Educational Psychology*, *41*(1), 98–110.

Gallo, D., & Gallo, D. (2004). *First crossings: Stories about teen immigration*. Cambridge, MA: Candlewick Press.

Gambrell, L. (2011). Seven rules of engagement: What's most important to know about motivation to read. *The Reading Teacher*, *65*(3), 172–178.

Gandara, P., & Contreras, F. (2010). *The Latino education crisis: The consequences of failed school policies*. Cambridge, MA: Harvard University Press.

Gandy, S. E. (2013). Informal reading inventories and ELL students. *Reading and Writing Quarterly: Overcoming Learning Difficulties, 29*(3), 271–287.

García, O., & Kleifgen, J. (2010). *Educating emerging bilinguals: Policies, programs, and practices for English language learners.* New York: Teachers College Press.

García, S. B., & Guerra, P. L. (2004). Deconstructing deficit thinking: Working with educators to create more equitable learning environments. *Education and Urban Society, 36*(2), 150–168.

Gardner, J., Harlen, W., Hayward, L., & Stobart, G. (2011). Engaging and empowering teachers in innovative assessment practice. In R. Berry & B. Adamson (Eds.), *Assessment reform in education: Policy and practice* (pp. 105–119). London: Springer.

Gates, B. (2009, July 21). Address to the National Conference of State Legislatures. Retrieved from *www.gatesfoundation.org/media-center/speeches/2009/07/bill-gates-national-conference-of-state-legislatures-ncsl.*

Gavigan, K. W. (2010). *Examining struggling male adolescent readers' responses to graphic novels: A multiple case study of four, eighth-grade males in a graphic novel book club.* Retrieved from ProQuest Dissertations and Theses database (No. AAT3418818).

Gavigan, K. W., & Tomasevich, M. (2011). *Connecting comics to curriculum: Strategies for grades 6–12.* Santa Barbara, CA: Libraries Unlimited.

Gee, J. P. (1996) *Social linguistics and literacies: Ideology in discourses* (2nd ed.). London: Taylor & Francis.

Gee, J. P. (2001). Teenagers in new times: A new literacy studies perspective. *Journal of Adolescent and Adult Literacy, 43,* 412–420.

Gee, J. P. (2008). *Social linguistics and literacies: Ideology in discourses* (3rd ed.). New York: Routledge.

Gee, J. P. (2012). *Social linguistics and literacies: Ideology in discourses* (4th ed.). Abingdon, Oxon, UK: Routledge.

Gee, J. P., & Hayes, E. R. (2011). *Language and learning in the digital age.* New York: Routledge.

Gillespie, A., Graham, S., Kiuhara, S., & Hebert, M. (2014). High school teachers' use of writing to support students' learning: A national survey. *Reading and Writing, 27*(6), 1043–1072.

Gillet, J. W., & Temple, C. (1986). *Understanding reading problems* (2nd ed.). Boston: Little, Brown.

Gillis, V. (2014). Disciplinary literacy: Adapt not adopt. *Journal of Adolescent and Adult Literacy, 57*(8), 614–623.

Gilmore, A. (2007). Authentic materials and authenticity in foreign language learning. *Language Teaching, 40,* 97–118.

Glennie, E., Bonneau, K., Vandellen, M., & Dodge, K. A. (2012). Addition by subtraction: The relation between dropout rates and school-level academic achievement. *Teachers College Record, 114*(8), 1–26.

Gogan, B. (2013). Reading at the threshold. *Across the Disciplines, 10*(4). Retrieved from *http://wac.colostate.edu/atd/reading/gogan.cfm.*

Goldenberg, C. (2008). Teaching English language learners: What the research does—and does not—say. *American Educator, 32*(2). Retrieved from *www.aft.org/pdfs/americaneducator/summer2008/ae_summer08.pdf.*

Goldenberg, C., & Coleman, R. (2010). *Promoting academic achievement among English learners: A guide to the research.* Thousand Oaks, CA: Corwin Press.

Goldhaber, D., Lavery, L., & Theobald, R. (2015). Uneven playing field?: Assessing the teacher quality gap between advantaged and disadvantaged students. *Educational Researcher, 44*(5), 293–307.

Goldman, S. R. (2012). Adolescent literacy: Learning and understanding content. *Future of Children, 22,* 89–116.

Goldman, S. R., Braasch, J. L. G., Wiley, J., Graesser, A. C., & Brodowinska, K. (2012). Comprehending and learning from Internet sources: Processing patterns of better and poorer learners. *Reading Research Quarterly, 47*(4), 356–381.

Goldman, S. R., & Rakestraw, J. A. (2000). Structural aspects of constructing meaning from text. In M. L. Kamil, P. B. Mosenthal, P. D. Pearson, & R. Barr (Eds.), *Handbook of reading research* (Vol. 3, pp. 311–335). Mahwah, NJ: Erlbaum.

Goodman, L. (2001). A tool for learning: Vocabulary self-awareness. In C. Blanchfield (Ed.), *Creative vocabulary: Strategies for teaching vocabulary in grades K–12*. Fresno, CA: San Joaquin Valley Writing Project.

Goodson, F. T. (2007). The electronic portfolio: Shaping an emerging genre. *Journal of Adolescent and Adult Literacy, 50*(6), 432–434.

Graesser, A. C., McNamara, D. S., & Kulikowich, J. M. (2011). Coh-Metrix: Providing multilevel analysis of text characteristics. *Educational Researcher, 40*(5), 223–234.

Graesser, A. C., McNamara, D., Louwerse, M., & Cai, Z. (2004). Coh-Metrix: Analysis of text on cohesion and language. *Behavioral Research Methods, Instruments, and Computers, 36*, 193–202.

Graham, S. (2014). The use of multiple forms of assessment in the service of writing. *Literacy Research and Instruction, 53*(2), 96–100.

Graham, S., Harris, K., & Hebert, M. A. (2011). *Informing writing: The benefits of formative assessment*. Washington, DC: Alliance for Excellent Education.

Graham, S., & Perin, D. (2007). *Writing next: Effective strategies to improve writing of adolescents in middle and high schools*. Washington, DC: Alliance for Excellent Education.

Graves, M. F. (2009a). *Teaching individual words: One size does not fit all*. New York: Teachers College Press.

Graves, M. F. (2009b). *Essential reading on vocabulary instruction*. Newark, DE: International Reading Association.

Graves, M. F., August, D., & Mancilla-Martinez, J. (2012). *Teaching vocabulary to English learners*. New York: Teachers College Press.

Graves, M. F., Ruda, M., Sales, G. C., & Baumann, J. F. (2012). Teaching prefixes: Making strong instruction even stronger. In E. J. Kame'enui & J. F. Baumann (Eds.), *Vocabulary instruction: Research to practice* (2nd ed., pp. 95–115). New York: Guilford Press.

Greenleaf, C., Cribb, G., Howlett, H., & Moore, D. W. (2010). Inviting outsiders inside disciplinary literacies: An interview with Cynthia Greenleaf, Gayle Cribb, and Heather Howlett. *Journal of Adolescent and Adult Literacy, 54*(4), 291–293.

Greenleaf, C. L., & Hinchman, K. (2009). Reimagining our inexperienced adolescent readers: From struggling, striving, marginalized and reluctant to thriving. *Journal of Adolescent and Adult Literacy, 53*, 4–13.

Greenleaf, C. L., Jimenez, R. T., & Roller, C. M. (2002). Reclaiming secondary reading interventions: From limited to rich conceptions, from narrow to broad conversations. *Reading Research Quarterly, 37*, 484–496.

Griffin, T. D., Jee, B. D., & Wiley, J. (2009). The effects of domain knowledge on meta-comprehension accuracy. *Memory and Cognition, 37*, 1001–1013.

Griffith, P. E. (2010). Graphic novels in the secondary classroom and school libraries. *Journal of Adolescent and Adult Literacy, 54*(3), 181–189.

Groenke, S., Maples, J., & Henderson, J. (2010). Raising hot topics through young adult literature. *Voices from the Middle, 17*(4), 29–36.

Gryder, N., & Vesely, P. (2007). Teaching visual imagery for vocabulary learning. *Academic Exchange Quarterly, 11*(2), 51–55.

Guo, S., Zhang, G., & Zhai, R. (2012) An alternative way of organizing groups for peer writing evaluation. *British Journal of Educational Technology, 43*(2), 64–66.

Guthrie, J. T. (2008). *Engaging adolescents in reading*. Thousand Oaks, CA: Corwin.

Guthrie, J. T., & Davis, M. (2003). Motivating struggling readers in middle school through an engagement model of classroom practice. *Reading and Writing Quarterly, 19*, 59–85.

Guthrie, J. T., Hoa, L. W., Wigfield, A., Tonks, S. M., & Perencevich, K. C. (2006). From spark to fire: Can situational reading interest lead to long-term reading motivation? *Reading Research and Instruction, 45*(2), 91–117.

Guthrie, J. T., & Klauda, S. L. (2014). Effects of classroom practices on reading comprehension, engagement, and motivations for adolescents. *Reading Research Quarterly, 49*(4), 387–416.

Guthrie, J. T., Klauda, S. L., & Ho, A. N. (2013). Modeling the relationships among reading instruction, motivation, engagement, and achievement for adolescents. *Reading Research Quarterly, 48*(1), 9–26.

Guthrie, J. T., & Wigfield, A. (2000). Engagement and motivation in reading. In M. Kamil, P. Mosenthal, R. Barr, & P. D. Pearson (Eds.), *Handbook of reading research* (Vol. 3). Mahwah, NJ: Erlbaum.

Guthrie, J. T., Wigfield, A., & You, W. (2012). Instructional contexts for engagement and achievement in reading. In S. L. Christenson, A. L. Reschly, & C. Wylie (Eds.), *Handbook of research on student engagement* (pp. 601–634). New York: Springer.

Guzzetti, B., Campbell, S., Duke, C., & Irving, J. (2003, July/August). Understanding adolescent literacies: A conversation with three zinesters. *Reading Online, 7*(1). Available at *www.reading online.org/newliteracies/lit_index.asp?HREF=guzzetti3.*

Guzzetti, B., Elliott, K., & Welsch, D. (2010). *DIY media in the classroom: New literacies across content areas.* New York: Teachers College Press.

Hafen, C. A., Hamre, B. K., Allen, J. P., Bell, C. A., Gitomer, D. H., & Pianta, R. C. (2015). Teaching through interactions in secondary school classrooms: Revisiting the factor structure and practical application of the Classroom Assessment Scoring System–Secondary. *Journal of Early Adolescence, 35*(5–6), 651–680.

Hagood, M. C. (2009). *New literacy practices: Designing literacy learning.* New York: Peter Lang.

Halat, E. (2008). A good teaching technique: WebQuests. *Clearing House: A Journal of Educational Strategies, Issues and Ideas, 81*(3), 109–112.

Halbach, A. (2000). Finding out about students' learning strategies by looking at their diaries: A case study. *System, 28*(1), 85–96.

Hamada, M. (2009). Development of L2 word-meaning inferences while reading. *System, 37*(3), 447–460.

Haneda, M. (2006). Becoming literate in a second language: Connecting home, community, and school literacy practices. *Theory into Practice, 45*(4), 337–345.

Haneda, M. (2014). From academic language to academic communication: Building on English learners' resources. *Linguistics and Education, 22*(1), 126–135.

Harlacher, J. E., Sakelaris, T. L., & Kattelman, N. M. (2014). *Practitioner's guide to curriculum-based evaluation in reading.* New York: Springer.

Harmon, J. M., Hedrick, W. G., & Wood, K. D. (2005). Research on vocabulary instruction in the content areas: Implications for struggling readers. *Reading and Writing Quarterly, 21*, 261–280.

Harper, C. A., & de Jong, E. J. (2009). English language teacher expertise: The elephant in the room. *Language and Education, 23*(2), 127–151.

Harris, L. R., Brown, G. T. L., & Harnett, J. A. (2015). Analysis of New Zealand primary and secondary student peer- and self-assessment comments: Applying Hattie and Timperley's feedback model. *Assessment in Education: Principles, Policy and Practice, 22*(2), 265–281.

Hartley, J. (2003). Designing instructional and informational text. Retrieved from *www.aect.org/edtech/ed1/34.pdf.*

Hartman, D. K., Morsink, P. M., & Zheng, J. (2010). From print to pixels: The evolution of cognitive conceptions of reading comprehension. In E. A. Baker (Ed.), *The new literacies: Multiple perspectives on research and practice* (pp. 131–164). New York: Guilford Press.

Harvey, S., & Daniels, H. (2009). *Comprehension and collaboration: Inquiry circles in action.* Portsmouth, NH: Heinemann.

Haycock, K., & Crawford, C. (2008). Closing teacher quality gap. *Educational Leadership, 65*(7), 14–19.

Hayden, R. (1995). Training parents as reading facilitators. *The Reading Teacher, 49,* 334–336.

Hebert, M., Gillespie, A., & Graham, S. (2013). Comparing effects of different writing activities on reading comprehension: A meta-analysis. *Reading and Writing, 26*(1), 111–138.

Heckman, J. J., & Kautz, T. (2012). *Hard evidence on soft skills.* Bonn, Germany: Institute for the Study of Labor.

Heckman, J. J., Stixrud, J., & Urzua, S. (2006). The effects of cognitive and noncognitive abilities on labor market outcomes and social behavior. *Journal of Labor Economics, 24*(3), 411–482.

Heigl, N. R., & Thomas, J. (2013). The effectiveness of epistemic beliefs and the role of self-efficacy in the solving of cross-curricular problems. *Psychology Learning and Teaching, 12*(2), 126–135.

Heller, R., & Greenleaf, C. L. (2007). *Literacy instruction in the content areas: Getting to the core of middle and high school improvement.* Washington, DC: Alliance for Excellent Education. Retrieved from *http://all4ed.org/reports-factsheets/literacy-instruction-in-the-content-areas-getting-to-the-core-of-middle-and-high-school-improvement.*

Hermann, A., & Lucas, G. (2008). Individual differences in perceived esteem across cultures. *Self and Identity, 7*(2), 151–167.

Hernandez, D. J. (2004). Demographic change and the life circumstances of immigrant families. *Future of Children, 14*(2), 17–47.

Heron, A. H. (2003). A study of agency: Multiple constructions of choice and decision making in an inquiry-based summer school program for struggling readers. *Journal of Adolescent and Adult Literacy, 46,* 568–579.

Heuboeck, A. (2009). Some aspects of coherence, genre and rhetorical structure—and their integration in a generic model of text. *Language Studies Working Papers, 1,* 35–45.

Hicks, T., Russo, A., Autrey, T., Gardner, R., Kabodian, A., & Edington, C. (2007). Rethinking the purpose and processes for designing digital portfolios. *Journal of Adolescent and Adult Literacy, 50*(6), 450–458.

Hill, N. E., & Torres, K. (2010). Negotiating the American dream: The paradox of aspirations and achievement among Latino students and engagement between their families and schools. *Journal of Social Issues, 66*(1), 95–112.

Hinchman, K., Alvermann, D., Boyd, F., Brozo, W., & Vacca, R. (2003–2004). Supporting older students' in- and out-of-school literacies. *Journal of Adolescent and Adult Literacy, 47,* 304–310.

Ho, A. N., & Guthrie, J. T. (2013). Patterns of association among multiple motivations and aspects of achievement in reading. *Reading Psychology, 34*(2), 101–147.

Hofer, B. K. (2004). Epistemological understanding as a metacognitive process: Thinking aloud during online searching. *Educational Psychologist, 39,* 43–55.

Holmes, K. P. (2005). *Engaging reluctant readers through foreign films.* Lanham, MD: Scarecrow Education.

Holstermann, N., Grube, D., & Bögeholz, S. (2010). Hands-on activities and their influence on students' interest. *Research in Science Education, 40*(5), 743–757.

Hones, D. F. (2002). In quest of freedom: Towards critical pedagogy in the education of bilingual youth. *Teachers College Record, 104,* 1163–1186.

Howard, R. M., Serviss, T., & Rodrigue, T. K. (2010). Writing from sources, writing from sentences. *Writing and Pedagogy, 2*(2), 177–192.

Howe, C., & Abedin, M. (2013). Classroom dialogue: A systematic review across four decades of research. *Cambridge Journal of Education, 43*(3), 325–356.

Hu, G., & Lam, S. (2010). Issues of cultural appropriateness and pedagogical efficacy: Exploring peer review in a second language writing class. *Instructional Science, 38,* 371–394.

Huang, F. L., & Moon, T. R. (2009). Is experience the best teacher?: A multi-level analysis of teacher characteristics and student achievement in low performing schools. *Educational Assessment: Evaluation and Accountability, 21*(3), 209–234.

Huang, Y. M., & Huang, Y. M. (2015). A scaffolding strategy to develop handheld sensor-based vocabulary games for improving students' learning motivation and performance. *Educational Technology Research and Development, 63*(5), 691–708.

Hubbard, B. P., & Simpson, M. L. (2003). Developing self-regulated learners: Putting theory into practice. *Reading Research and Instruction, 42,* 62–89.

Huff, J. D., & Nietfeld, J. L. (2009). Using strategy instruction and confidence judgments to improve metacognitive monitoring. *Metacognition Learning, 4*(2), 161–176.

Hulleman, C. S., Godes, O., Hendricks, B. L., & Harackiewicz, J. M. (2010). Enhancing interest and performance with a utility value intervention. *Journal of Educational Psychology, 102*(4), 880–895.

Hurley, P. (2010, Winter). Academic language: Equipping English learners to speak and write confidently in secondary classrooms. *Gifted Education Communicator,* pp. 21–25.

Hutchins, D. J., Greenfeld, M. G., Epstein, J. L., Sanders, M. G., & Galindo, C. (2012). *Multicultural partnerships: Involve all families.* New York: Eye on Education, Taylor & Frances/Routledge.

Illich, I. (1970). *Deschooling society.* New York: Harper & Row.

International Literacy Association. (2015). Preliminary report on teacher preparation for literacy instruction. Newark, DE: ILA. Retrieved from *www.literacyworldwide.org/docs/default-source/where-we-stand/teacher-preparation-report.pdf?sfvrsn=4.*

International Reading Association. (2009). *New literacies and 21st century technologies* (Position statement). Newark, DE: Author. Available from *www.reading.org/General/AboutIRA/PositionStatements/21stCenturyLiteracies.aspx.*

International Reading Association. (2012). Adolescent literacy: A position statement of the International Reading Association. Retrieved from *www.reading.org/Libraries/resources/ps1079_adolescentliteracy_rev2012.pdf.*

Ivey, G. (2011). What not to read: A book intervention. *Voices from the Middle, 19*(2), 22–26.

Ivey, G., & Broaddus, K. (2007). A formative experiment investigating literacy engagement among adolescent Latina/o students just beginning to read, write, and speak English. *Reading Research Quarterly, 42,* 512–545.

Jacobson, J., Thrope, L., Fisher, D., Lapp, D., Frey, N., & Flood, J. (2001). Cross-age tutoring: A literacy improvement approach for struggling adolescent readers. *Journal of Adolescent and Adult Literacy, 44,* 528–537.

Jacome, E. P. (2012). Promoting learner autonomy through teacher–student partnership assessment in an American high school: A cycle of action research. *Profile: Issues in Teachers' Professional Development, 14*(2), 145–162.

Janzen, J. (2008). Teaching English language learners in the content areas. *Review of Educational Research, 78*(4), 1010–1038.

Jarman, R., & McClune, B. (2003). Bringing newspaper reports into the classroom: Citizenship and science education. *School Science Review, 84,* 121–129.

Jewett, S. (2007). The stories of people's lives: Thematic investigations and the development of a critical social studies. *Social Studies, 98*(4), 165–171.

Jeynes, W. H. (2007). The relationship between parental involvement and urban secondary school student academic achievement: A meta-analysis. *Urban Education, 42*(1), 82–110.

Jeynes, W. H. (2012). A meta-analysis of the efficacy of different types of parental involvement programs for urban students. *Urban Education, 47,* 706–742.

Jiang, Y., Ekono, M., & Skinner, C. (2015, January). *Basic facts about low-income children: Children aged 12 through 17 years, 2012*. Retrieved from the National Center for Children in Poverty at *nccp.org/publications/pub_1099.html*.

Jiménez, R. (2014). *Teaching English language learners*. Los Angeles, CA: Annenberg Learner. Retrieved from *http://learner.org/workshops/teachreading35/session6/resources.html*.

Jiménez, R. T., Eley, C., Leander, K., & Smith, P. H. (2015). Transnational immigrant youth literacies: A selective review of the literature. In P. Smith & A. Kumi-Yeboah (Eds.), *Handbook of research on cross-cultural approaches to language and literacy development* (pp. 345–366). Hershey, PA: IGI Global.

Jimerson, S. R., & Ferguson, P. (2007). A longitudinal study of grade retention: Academic and behavioral outcomes of retained students through adolescence. *School Psychology Quarterly, 22*(3), 314–339.

Job, V., Walton, G. M., Bernecker, K., & Dweck, C. S. (2015). Implicit theories about willpower predict self-regulation and grades in everyday life. *Journal of Personality and Social Psychology, 108*(4), 637–647.

Johnson, D. D., & Pearson, P. D. (1978). *Teaching reading vocabulary*. New York: Holt, Rinehart, & Winston.

Johnston, P. H. (2004). *Choice words: How our language affects children's learning*. Portland, ME: Stenhouse.

Joseph, N. (2009). Metacognition needed: Teaching middle and high school students to develop strategic learning skills. *Preventing School Failure: Alternative Education for Children and Youth, 54*(2), 99–103.

Jun, S. W., Ramirez, G., & Cumming, A. (2010). Tutoring adolescents in literacy: A meta-analysis. *McGill Journal of Education, 45*(2), 219–238.

Juvonen, J., Espinoza, G., & Knifsend, C. (2009). The role of peer relationships in student academic and extracurricular engagement. In K. R. Wenzel, & A. Wigfield (Eds.), *Handbook of motivation at school* (pp. 387–403). New York: Routledge.

Kajder, S. B. (2010). *Adolescents and digital literacies: Learning alongside our students*. Urbana, IL: National Council of Teachers of English.

Kalogrides, D., Loeb, S., & Beteille, T. (2013). Systematic sorting: Teacher characteristics and class assignments. *Sociology of Education, 86*,103–123.

Kamenetz, A. (2015). *The test: Why our schools are obsessed with standardized testing—but you don't have to be*. New York: PublicAffairs.

Kamil, M. L., Borman, G. D., Dole, J., Kral, C. C., Salinger, T., & Torgesen, J. (2008). *Improving adolescent literacy: Effective classroom and intervention practices: A practice guide*. Washington, DC: U.S. Department of Education, Institute of Education Sciences.

Kamoun, F. S. S. (2007). A framework towards assessing the merits of inviting IT professionals to the classroom. *Journal of Information Technology Education, 6,* 81–103.

Kang, H., Thompson, J., & Windschitl, M. (2014). Creating opportunities for students to show what they know: The role of scaffolding in assessment tasks. *Science Education, 98*(4), 674–704.

Kelley, J. G., Lesaux, N. K., Kieffer, M. J., & Faller, S. E. (2010). Effective academic vocabulary instruction in the urban middle school. *The Reading Teacher, 64*(1), 5–14.

Kellogg, R. T., & Whiteford, A. P. (2009). Training advanced writing skills: The case for deliberate practice. *Educational Psychologist, 44,* 250–266.

Kena, G., McFarland, J., de Brey, C., Musu-Gillette, L., Wang, X., Zhang, J., et al. (2016). *The condition of education 2016*. Washington, DC: National Center for Education Statistics.

Kena, G., Musu-Gillette, L., Robinson, J., Wang, X., Rathbun, A., Zhang, J., et al. (2015). *The condition of education 2015* (NCES 2015-144). Washington, DC: U.S. Department of Education, National Center for Education Statistics.

Kendeou, P., & van den Broek, P. (2007). The effects of prior knowledge and text structure on comprehension processes during reading of scientific texts. *Memory and Cognition, 35*(7), 1567–1577.

Kennedy, K. (2003). Writing with Web logs. *Technology and Learning, 23,* 11–12.

Kieffer, M. J., & Lesaux, N. K. (2007). Breaking down words to build meaning: Morphology, vocabulary, and reading comprehension in the urban classroom. *The Reading Teacher, 61,* 134–144.

Kieffer, M. J., & Lesaux, N. K. (2010). Morphing into adolescents: Active word learning for English-language learners and their classmates in middle school. *Journal of Adolescent and Adult Literacy, 54,* 47–56.

Kilby-Goodwin, K. (2010). Putting the science in science fiction. *Science Teacher, 77*(5), 60–63.

King, A. (2008). Structuring peer interaction to promote higher-order thinking and complex learning in cooperating groups. In R. M. Gillies, A. F. Ashman, & J. Terwel (Eds.), *The teacher's role in implementing cooperative learning in the classroom* (pp. 73–91). New York: Springer.

Kintsch, W. (1998). *Comprehension: A paradigm for cognition.* New York: Cambridge University Press.

Kintsch, W., & Kintsch, E. (2005). Comprehension. In S. Paris & S. Stahl (Eds.), *Current issues on reading comprehension and assessment* (pp. 71–92). Mahwah, NJ: Erlbaum.

Kintsch, W., & van Dijk, T. A. (1978). Toward a model of text comprehension and production. *Psychological Review, 85,* 363–394.

Klages, C., Pate, S., & Conforti, P. A., Jr. (2007). Virtual literature circles: A study of learning, collaboration, and synthesis in using collaborative classrooms in cyberspace. *Curriculum and Teaching Dialogue, 9*(1–2), 293–309.

Klein, P. D., Arcon, N., & Baker, S. (2016). Writing to learn. In C. A. MacArthur, S. Graham, & J. Fitzgerald (Eds.), *Handbook of writing research* (2nd ed., pp. 243–256). New York: Guilford Press.

Klingner, J. K., Boardman, A. G., Eppolito, A. M., & Schonewise, E. A. (2012). Supporting adolescent English language learners' reading in the content areas. *Learning Disabilities: A Contemporary Journal, 10*(1), 35–64.

Klingner, J. K., Morrison, A., & Eppolito, A. (2011). Metacognition to improve reading comprehension. In R. E. O'Connor & P. F. Vadasy (Eds.), *Handbook of reading interventions* (pp. 220–253). New York: Guilford Press.

Knabb, M. (2003). Rapping to review: A novel strategy to engage students and summarize course material. *Advances in Physiological Education, 27,* 157–159.

Knobel, M.,& Lankshear, C. (2002). Cut, paste, publish: The production and consumption of zines. In D. Alvermann (Ed.), *Adolescents and literacies in a digital world* (pp. 164–185). New York: Peter Lang.

Knoester, M. (2010). Independent reading and the "social turn": How adolescent reading habits and motivation relate to cultivating social relationships. *Networks, 12*(1), 1–13.

Koedinger, K. R., Corbett, A. T., & Perfetti, C. (2012). The knowledge–learning instruction framework: Bridging the science–practice chasm to enhance robust student learning. *Cognitive Science, 36*(5), 757–798.

Koellner, K., Wallace, F. H., & Swackhamer, L. (2009). Integrating literature to support mathematics learning in middle school. *Middle School Journal, 41*(2), 30–39.

Koh, R. (2008). Alternative literature in libraries: The unseen zine. *Collection Building, 27*(2), 48–51.

Kohn, A. (2010). How to create nonreaders: Reflections on motivation, learning, and sharing power. *English Journal, 100*(1), 16–22.

Kornell, N. (2009). Optimising learning using flashcards: Spacing is more effective than cramming. *Applied Cognitive Psychology, 23,* 1297–1317.

Kozen, A. A., Murray, R. K., & Windell, I. (2006). Increasing all students' chance to achieve: Using and adapting anticipation guides with middle school learners. *Intervention in School and Clinic,* *41*(4), 195–200.

Krajcik, J. S., & Sutherland, L. M. (2010). Supporting students in developing literacy in science. *Science, 328,* 456–459.

Krashen, S. (2012). Developing academic language: Some hypotheses. *Journal of Foreign Language Teaching, 7*(2), 8–15.

Ku, K. Y. L., & Ho, I. T. (2010). Metacognitive strategies that enhance critical thinking. *Metacognition and Learning, 5*(3), 251–267.

Kumpf, E. (2000). Visual metadiscourse: Designing the considerate text. *Technical Communication Quarterly, 9*(4), 401–424.

Kymes, A. (2004). Teaching online comprehension strategies using think-alouds. *Journal of Adolescent and Adult Literacy, 48*(8), 492–500.

Labov, W. (2003). When ordinary children fail to read. *Reading Research Quarterly, 38,* 128–131.

Ladd, H. F. (2012). Education and poverty: Confronting the evidence. *Journal of Policy Analysis and Management, 31*(2), 203–227.

Ladson-Billings, G. (2005). Is the team all right?: Diversity and teacher education. *Journal of Teacher Education, 56*(3), 229–234.

Ladson-Billings, G. (2009). *The dream keepers: Successful teachers of African-American children* (2nd ed.). San Francisco: Jossey-Bass.

LaGue, K. M., & Wilson, K. (2010). Using peer tutors to improve reading comprehension. *Kappa Delta Pi Record, 46*(4), 182–186.

Lang, A. (2012). *From codex to hypertext: Reading at the turn of the twenty-first century.* Amherst: University of Massachusetts Press.

Langer, J. (2011). *Envisioning knowledge: Building literacy in the academic disciplines.* New York: Teachers College Press.

Lankshear, C., & Knobel, M. (2007). Researching new literacies: Web 2.0 practices and insider perspectives. *e-Learning, 4*(3), 224–240.

Lankshear, C., & Knobel, M. (2011). *Literacies: Social, cultural and historical perspectives.* New York: Peter Lang.

Lankshear, C., & Knobel, M. (2013). Introduction: Social and cultural studies of new literacies from an educational perspective. In C. Lankshear & M. Knobel (Eds.), *A new literacies reader: Educational perspectives* (pp. 1–19). New York: Peter Lang.

Lapp, D., & Fisher, D. (2009). It's all about the book: Motivating teens to read. *Journal of Adolescent and Adult Literacy, 52*(7), 556–561.

Lapp, D., Fisher, D., & Grant, G. (2008). "You can read this text—I'll show you how": Interactive comprehension instruction. *Journal of Adolescent and Adult Literacy, 51*(5), 372–383.

Lapp, D., Fisher, D., & Jacobson, J. (2008). Useful instructional routines for adolescent English language learners' vocabulary development. *California Reader, 42*(1), 10–22.

Larson, B. E., & Keiper, T. A. (2013). *Instructional strategies for middle and high school* (2nd ed.). New York: Routledge.

Larson, L. C. (2011). E-reading and e-responding: New tools for the next generation of readers. *Journal of Adolescent and Adult Literacy, 53*(3), 255–258.

Lattimer, H. (2010). *Reading for learning: Using discipline-based texts to build content knowledge.* Urbana, IL: National Council of Teachers of English.

Lawrence, J., Capotosto, L., Branum-Martin, L., White, C., & Snow, C. (2012). Language proficiency, home-language status, and English vocabulary development: A longitudinal follow-up of the Word Generation program. *Bilingualism: Language and Cognition, 15,* 437–451.

Lawrence, J., White, C., & Snow, C. (2010). The words students need. *Educational Leadership, 68*(2), 22–26.

Learning Metrics Task Force. (2013). *Toward universal learning: What every child should learn*. Montreal, Ontario, Canada and Washington, DC: UNESCO Institute for Statistics and Brookings Institution.

Lee, C. (2006). *Denver public schools: Resegregation, Latino style*. Cambridge, MA: Harvard University Civil Rights Project.

Lee, C. D. (2007). *Culture, literacy, and learning: Taking bloom in the midst of the whirlwind*. New York: Teachers College Press.

Lee, C. D., & Spratley, A. (2010). *Reading in the disciplines: The challenges of adolescent literacy*. New York: Carnegie Corporation.

Legault, L., Green-Demers, I., & Pelletier, L. (2006). Why do high school students lack motivation in the classroom?: Toward an understanding of academic motivation and the role of social support. *Journal of Educational Psychology, 98*, 567–582.

Lehman, B., Freeman, E., & Scharer, P. (2010). *Reading globally, K–8: Connecting students to the world through literature*. Thousand Oaks, CA: Corwin.

Lei, S. A., Rhinehart, P. J., Howard, H. A., & Cho, J. K. (2010). Strategies for improving reading comprehension among college students. *Reading Improvement, 47*(1), 30–42.

Leki, I., Cumming, A., & Silva, T. (2008). *A synthesis of research on second language writing in English*. New York: Routledge.

LeMoine, N., & Hollie, S. (2007). Developing academic English for standard English learners. In H. S. Alim & J. Baugh (Eds.), *Talkin Black talk: Language, education, and social change* (pp. 43–55). New York: Teachers College Press.

Leopold, C., Sumfleth, E., & Leutner, D. (2013). Learning with summaries: Effects of representation mode and type of learning activity on comprehension and transfer. *Learning and Instruction, 27*, 40–49.

Lervåg, A., & Aukrust, V. G. (2010). Vocabulary knowledge is a critical determinant of the difference in reading comprehension growth between first and second language learners. *Journal of Child Psychology and Psychiatry, 51*(5), 612–620.

Lesaux, N. K., Harris, J. R., & Sloane, P. (2012). Adolescents' motivation in the context of an academic vocabulary intervention in urban middle school classrooms. *Journal of Adolescent and Adult Literacy, 56*(3), 231–240.

Lesko, N. (2012). *Act your age!: A cultural construction of adolescence* (2nd ed.). New York: Routledge.

Leu, D. J., Forzani, E., Rhoads, C., Maykel, C., Kennedy, C., & Timbrell, N. (2015). The new literacies of online reading and comprehension: Rethinking the reading achievement gap. *Reading Research Quarterly, 50*(1), 37–59.

Leu, D. J., Kinzer, C. K., Coiro, J., Castek, J., & Henry, L. A. (2013). New literacies: A dual-level theory of the changing nature of literacy, instruction, and assessment. In D. Alvermann, N. Unrau, & R. Ruddell (Eds.), *Theoretical models and processes of reading* (6th ed., pp. 1150–1181). Newark, DE: International Reading Association.

Leuhmann, A. L., & Frink, J. (2009). How can blogging help teachers realize the goals of reform-based science instruction?: A study of nine classroom blogs. *Journal of Science Education and Technology, 18*(3), 275–290.

Lewis, C., Enciso, P., & Moje, E. B. (2007). *Reframing sociocultural research on literacy: Identity, agency, and power*. Mahwah, NJ: Erlbaum.

Li, G., & Protacio, M. S. (2010). Best practices in professional development for teachers of ELLs. In G. Li & P. A. Edwards (Eds.), *Best practices in ELL instruction* (pp. 353–380). New York: Guilford Press.

Lieberman, S. J. (1984, February 21). A no-lose proposition. *Newsweek*.

Lightbrown, P., & Spada, N. (2006). *How languages are learned*. Oxford, UK: Oxford University Press.

Lin, L., & Bigenho, C. (2011). Note-taking and memory in different media environments. *Computers in the Schools, 28*(3), 200–216.

Lockhart, T., & Soliday, M. (2016). The critical place of reading in writing transfer (and beyond): A report of student experiences. *Pedagogy, 16*(1), 23–37.

Lodewyk, K. R., Winne, P. H., & Jamieson-Noel, D. L. (2009). Implications of task structure on self-regulated learning and achievement. *Educational Psychology, 29*(1), 1–25.

Loh, V. (2015, September). The power of collaborative dialog. *Art Education*, 14–19.

Long, J. F., Monoi, S., Harper, B., Knoblauch, D., & Murphy, P. K. (2007). Academic motivation and achievement among urban adolescents. *Urban Education, 42*(3), 196–222.

Louwerse, M. M., & Graesser, A. C. (2006). Macrostructure. In E. K. Brown & A. Anderson (Eds.), *Encyclopedia of language and linguistics* (pp. 426–429). Boston: Elsevier.

Loveless, T. (2015). The 2015 Brown Center Report on American Education: How well are American students learning?Retrieved from *www.brookings.edu/~/media/research/files/reports/2015/03/bcr/2015-brown-center-report_final.pdf*.

Lucas, T. (2011). *Teacher preparation for linguistically diverse classrooms: A resource for teacher educators*. New York: Taylor & Francis.

Lundstrom, K., Diekema, A. R., Leary, H., Haderlie, S., & Holliday, W. (2015). Teaching and learning information synthesis: An intervention and rubric based assessment. *Communications in Information Literacy, 9*(1), 60–82.

Lynch, D. J. (2010). Motivational beliefs and learning strategies as predictors of academic performance in college physics. *College Student Journal, 44*(4), 920–927.

Lynch, R. G., & Oakford, P. (2014). *The economic benefits of closing educational achievement gaps: Promoting growth and strengthening the nation by improving the educational outcomes of children of color*. Washington, DC: Center for American Progress. Retrieved from *https://cdn.americanprogress.org/wpcontent/uploads/2014/11/WinningEconomyReport2.pdf*.

MacArthur, C., Graham, S., & Fitzgerald, J. (2006). *Handbook of writing research*. New York: Guilford Press.

Macedo-Rouet, M., Braasch, J. L. G., Britt, M. A., & Rouet, J.-F. (2013). Teaching fourth and fifth graders to evaluate information sources during text comprehension. *Cognition and Instruction, 31*(2), 204–226.

Magno, C. (2010). The role of metacognitive skills in developing critical thinking. *Metacognition and Learning, 5*(2), 137–156.

Males, M. (2002). *Framing youth: 10 myths about the next generation*. Monroe, ME: Common Courage Press.

Males, M. (2010). *Teenage sex and pregnancy: Modern myths, unsexy realities*. Santa Barbara, CA: Praeger.

Malloy, J., Marinak, B., & Gambrell, L. B. (Eds.). (2010). *Essential readings on motivation*. Newark, DE: International Reading Association.

Maloy, R. W., & LaRoche, I. (2010). Student-centered teaching methods in the history classroom: Ideas, issues, and insights for new teachers. *Social Studies Research and Practice, 5*(2), 46–61.

Mandell, N., & Malone, B. (2008). *Thinking like a historian: Rethinking history instruction*. Madison: Wisconsin Historical Society Press.

Mandler, J. (1987). On the psychological reality of story structure. *Discourse Processing, 10*, 1–29.

Mangram, J. A., & Weber, R. L. (2012). Incorporating music into the social studies classroom: A qualitative study of secondary social studies teachers. *Journal of Social Studies Research, 36*(1), 3–21.

Manzo, A. V., & Sherk, J. (1971). Some generalizations and strategies to guide vocabulary acquisition. *Journal of Reading Behavior, 4*, 78–89.

Manzo, U., & Manzo, A. V. (2013). The Informal Reading–Thinking Inventory: Twenty-first-century assessment formats for discovering reading and writing needs—and strengths. *Reading and Writing Quarterly: Overcoming Learning Difficulties, 29*(3), 231–251.

Maples, J., & Groenke, S. (2009). Who is an American?: Challenging middle school students' assumptions through critical literacy. *Voices from the Middle, 17*(2), 28–35.

Mariage, T. V., & Englert, C. S. (2010). Constructing access and understanding in inclusive middle-grade content classrooms: A sociocognitive apprenticeship in literacy with bilingual students and those with language/learning disabilities. In G. Li & P. A. Edwards (Eds.), *Best practices in ELL instruction* (pp. 151–188). New York: Guilford Press.

Marin, L. M., & Halpern, D. F. (2011). Pedagogy for developing critical thinking in adolescents: Explicit instruction produces greatest gains. *Thinking Skills and Creativity, 6*(1), 1–13.

Marmot, M. (2004). *The status syndrome: How social standing affects our health and longevity.* New York: Owl Books.

Martin, A. J. (2009). Motivation and engagement across the academic life span: A developmental construct validity study of elementary school, high school, and university/college students. *Educational and Psychological Measurement, 69,* 794–824.

Martin, C., Martin, M., & O'Brien, D. (1984). Spawning ideas for writing in the content areas. *Reading World, 11,* 11–15.

Martínez-Roldán, C. M., & Fránquiz, M. E. (2009). Latina/o youth literacies: Hidden funds of knowledge. In L. Christenbury, R. Bomer, & P. Smagorinsky (Eds.), *Handbook of adolescent literacy research* (pp. 323–342). New York: Guilford Press.

Marzano, R. J., & Pickering, D. J. (2010). *Building academic vocabulary.* Alexandria, VA: Association for Supervision and Curriculum Development.

Marzano, R. J., & Simms, J. A. (2013). *Vocabulary for the Common Core.* Bloomington, IN: Marzano Research.

Mastropieri, M. A., & Scruggs, T. E. (2013). *The inclusive classroom: Strategies for effective differentiated instruction* (5th ed.). Boston: Pearson.

Mateos, M., Martin, E., Villalon, R., & Luna, M. (2008). Reading and writing to learn in secondary education: Online processing activity and written products in summarizing and synthesizing tasks. *Reading and Writing: An Interdisciplinary Journal, 21*(7), 675–697.

Mateos, M., & Sole, I. (2009). Synthesising information from various texts: A study of procedures and products at different educational levels. *European Journal of Psychology of Education, 24*(4), 435–451.

Mathew, K. L., & Adams, D. C. (2009). I love your book, but I love my version more: Fanfiction in the English language arts classroom. *The ALAN Review, 36*(3), 35–41.

Maybee, C., Bruce, C. S., Lupton, M., & Rebmann, K. (2013). Learning to use information: Informed learning in the undergraduate classroom. *Library and Information Science Research, 35*(3), 200–206.

Mazur, E., & Kozarian, L. (2010). Self-presentation and interaction in blogs of adolescents and young emerging adults. *Journal of Adolescent Research, 25*(1), 124–144.

McCrudden, M. T., & Schraw, G. (2007). Relevance and goal-focusing in text processing. *Educational Psychology Review, 19*(2), 113–139.

McCuchen, K. L., Jones, M. H., Carbonneau, K. J., & Mueller, C. E. (2015, January). Mindset and standardized testing over time. *Learning and Individual Differences, 45,* 208–213.

McIntosh, M. E., & Draper, R. J. (2001). Using learning logs in mathematics: Writing to learn. *Mathematics Teacher, 94,* 554–555.

McKeachie, W. J., Pintrich, P. R., & Lin, Y.-G. (1985). Teaching learning strategies. *Educational Psychologist, 20,* 153–160.

McKeachie, W. J., & Svinicki, M. (2014). *McKeachie's teaching tips* (14th ed.). Boston: Cengage Learning.

McKeown, M. G., Beck, I. L., & Sandora, C. (2012). Direct and rich vocabulary instruction needs to start early. In E. J. Kame'enui & J. F. Baumann (Eds.), *Vocabulary instruction: Research to practice* (2nd ed., pp. 17–33). New York: Guilford Press.

McNamara, D. (2004). SERT: Self-Explanation Reading Training. *Discourse Processes, 38,* 1–30.

McNamara, D. S., & Magliano, J. (2009). Toward a comprehensive model of comprehension. *Psychology of Learning and Motivation, 51,* 297–384.

McNaught, K. (2010). Reflective writing in mathematics education programmes. *Reflective Practice, 11*(3), 369–379.

McTighe, J., & Seif, E. (2014). Teaching for understanding: A meaningful education for 21st century learners. *Teachers Matter, 24,* 15–17.

Melinee, L. K. (2014). Policy, pedagogy, and research: Three issues affecting content area literacy courses for secondary-level teacher candidates. *Literacy Research and Instruction, 53*(1), 50–71.

Mevarech, Z. R., & Amrany, C. (2008). Immediate and delayed effects of metacognitive instruction on regulation of cognition and mathematics achievement. *Metacognition Learning, 3*(2), 147–157.

Migration Policy Institute. (2015). Limited English proficient individuals in the United States: Number, share, growth, and linguistic diversity. Retrieved from *www.migrationpolicy.org/research/ limited-english-proficient-individuals-united-states-number-share-growth-and-linguistic.*

Miller, D., Topping, K., & Thurston, A. (2010). Peer tutoring in reading: The effects of role and organization on two dimensions of self-esteem. *British Journal of Educational Psychology, 80,* 417–433.

Miranda, T., Williams-Rossi, D., Johnson, K., & McKenzie, N. (2011). Reluctant readers in middle school: Successful engagement with text using the e-reader. *International Journal of Applied Science and Technology, 1*(6), 81–91.

Mistry, R. S., Biesanz, J. C., Chien, N., Howes, C., & Benner, A. D. (2008). Socioeconomic status, parental investments, and the cognitive and behavioral outcomes of low-income children from immigrant and native households. *Early Childhood Research Quarterly, 23*(2), 193–212.

Mlodinov, L. (2015). *The upright thinkers.* New York: Pantheon.

Mohr, K. J., & Mohr, E. S. (2007, February). Extending English-language learners' classroom interactions using the response protocol. *The Reading Teacher, 60*(5), 440–450.

Moje, E. (2007). Youth cultures, literacies and identities in and out of school. In J. Flood, S. B. Heath, & D. Lapp (Eds.), *Handbook of research on teaching literacy through the communicative and visual arts* (Vol. 2, pp. 207–219). Mahway, NJ: Erlbaum.

Moje, E. (2008). Foregrounding the disciplines in secondary literacy teaching and learning: A call for change. *Journal of Adolescent and Adult Literacy, 52,* 96–107.

Moje, E. B. (2010). *Disciplinary literacy: Why it matters and what we should do about it.* Orlando, FL: National Writing Project Annual Meeting.

Moje, E. B. (2011). The role of text in disciplinary learning. In M. L. Kamil, P. D. Pearson, E. B. Moje, & P. P. Afflerbach (Eds.), *Handbook of reading research* (Vol. 4, pp. 453–486). New York: Routledge.

Moje, E. B., Brozo, W. G., & Haas, J. (1994). Portfolios in a high school classroom: Challenges to change. *Reading Research and Instruction, 33*(4), 275–292.

Moje, E. B., Ciechanowski, K. M., Kramer, K., Ellis, L., Carrillo, R., & Collazo, T. (2004). Working toward third space in content area literacy: An examination of everyday funds of knowledge and discourse. *Reading Research Quarterly, 39,* 38–70.

Moje, E. B., & Luke, A. (2009). Literacy and identity: Examining the metaphors in history and contemporary research. *Reading Research Quarterly, 44*(4), 415–437.

Moje, E. B., Overby, M., Tysvaer, N., & Morris, K. (2008). The complex world of adolescent literacy: Myths, motivations, and mysteries. *Harvard Educational Review, 78*(1), 107–154.

Moje, E. B., & Speyer, J. (2008). The reality of challenging texts in high school science and social studies: How teacher can mediate comprehension. In K. Hinchman & H. Thomas (Eds.), *Best practices in adolescent literacy instruction* (pp. 185–211). New York: Guilford Press.

Moje, E. B., Stockdill, D., Kim, K., & Kim, H.-J. (2011). The role of text in disciplinary learning. In M. L. Kamil, P. D. Pearson, E. B. Moje, & P. P. Afflerbach (Eds.), *Handbook of reading research* (Vol. 4, pp. 453–486). New York: Routledge.

Moje, E. B., & Tysvaer, N. (2010). *Adolescent literacy development in out-of-school time: A practitioner's guide.* New York: Carnegie Corporation.

Mokhtar, A. A., & Rawian, R. M. (2012). Guessing word meaning from context has its limit: Why? *International Journal of Linguistics, 4*(2), 288–305.

Mol, S., & Bus, A. G. (2011). To read or not to read: A meta-analysis of print exposure from infancy to early adulthood. *Psychological Bulletin, 137,* 267–296.

Moley, P. F., Bandre, P. E., & George, J. E. (2011). Moving beyond readability: Considering choice, motivation, and learner engagement. *Theory into Practice, 50*(3), 247–253.

Monahan, R. (2015, March 31). How Common Core is killing the textbook. Retrieved from *http://hechingerreport.org/how-common-core-is-killing-the-textbook.*

Montagu, J. (1976). *World of medieval and renaissance musical instruments.* New York: Overlook Press.

Monte-Sano, C., & De La Paz, S. (2012). Using writing tasks to elicit adolescents' historical reasoning. *Journal of Literacy Research, 44*(3), 273–299.

Moore, D. W., Moore, S. A., Cunningham, P. M., & Cunningham, J. W. (2010). *Developing readers and writers in the content areas K–12* (6th ed.). Boston: Pearson.

Morrell, E. (2008). *Critical literacy and urban youth: Pedagogies of access, dissent, and liberation.* New York: Routledge.

Mueller, P. A., & Oppenheimer, D. M. (2014). The pen is mightier than the keyboard: Advantages of longhand over laptop note taking. *Psychological Science, 25*(6), 1–10.

Nachowitz, M., & Brumer, N. (2014). Teaching the talk, not the text. *Voices from the Middle, 22*(1), 15–21.

Nagy, W. (2009). Understanding words and word learning: Putting research on vocabulary into classroom practice. In S. Rosenfield & V. Berninger (Eds.), *Implementing evidence-based academic interventions in school settings* (pp. 479–500). New York: Oxford University Press.

Nagy, W. (2010). Why vocabulary instruction needs to be long-term and comprehensive. In E. Hiebert & M. Kamil (Eds.), *Teaching and learning vocabulary: Bringing research to practice* (pp. 27–44). New York: Routledge.

Nagy, W., & Scott, J. (2000). Vocabulary processes. In M. Kamil, P. Mosenthal, P. D. Pearson, & R. Barr (Eds.), *Handbook of reading research* (Vol. 3, pp. 269–284). Mahwah, NJ: Erlbaum.

Nagy, W., & Townsend, D. (2012). Words as tools: Learning academic vocabulary as language acquisition. *Reading Research Quarterly, 47*(1), 91–108.

Nagy, W. E., & Hiebert, E. H. (2011). Toward a theory of word selection. In M. Kamil, P. D. Pearson, E. Moje, & P. Afflerbach (Eds.), *Handbook of reading research* (Vol. 4, pp. 388–404). New York: Routledge.

Nakamoto, S. (n.d.). Bitcoin: A peer-to-peer electronic cash system. Retrieved from *https://bitcoin.org/bitcoin.pdf.*

Nakata, T. (2008). English vocabulary learning with word lists, word cards and computers: Implications for cognitive psychology research for optimal spaced learning. *ReCALL, 2*(1), 3–20.

Nation, I. S. P. (2013). *Learning vocabulary in another language* (2nd ed.). Cambridge, UK: Cambridge University Press.

National Center for Education Statistics. (2011). Writing 2011 National Assessment of Educational Progress at grades 8 and 12. Retrieved from *https://nces.ed.gov/nationsreportcard/pdf/main2011/2012470.pdf.*

National Center for Education Statistics. (2013). *The nation's report card: Trends in academic progress 2012* (NCES 2013 456). Washington, DC: U.S. Department of Education Institute of Education Sciences.

National Center for Education Statistics. (2015a). *The condition of education 2015 (NCES 2015–144): Status dropout rates.* Retrieved from *https://nces.ed.gov/fastfacts/display.asp?id=16.*

National Center for Education Statistics. (2015b). *The condition of education 2015 (NCES 2015–144): English language learners.* Retrieved from *https://nces.ed.gov/fastfacts/display.asp?id=96.*

National Clearinghouse for English Language Acquisition. (2010). *The growing numbers of English learner students: 1997/98–2007/08.* Retrieved from *www.ncela.gwu.edu/files/uploads/9/growing LEP_0708.pdf.*

National Council of Teachers of English Commission on Reading. (2008). *On reading, learning to read, and effective reading instruction: An overview of what we know and how we know it.* Urbana, IL: Author. Retrieved from *www.ncte.org/positions/statements/onreading.*

National Council of Teachers of Mathematics. (2000). *Executive summary: Principles and standards for school mathematics.* Retrieved from *www.nctm.org/uploadedFiles/Standards_and_Positions/ PSSM_ExecutiveSummary.pdf.*

National Endowment for the Arts. (2007). *To read or not to read: A question of national consequence.* Washington, DC: Author. Retrieved from *www.arts.gov/file/2667.*

National Governors Association Center for Best Practices and Council of Chief State School Officers. (2010). *Common Core State Standards for English language arts and literacy in history/social studies, science, and technical subjects.* Washington, DC: Authors.

National Institute of Child Health and Human Development. (2000). *Report of the National Reading Panel: Teaching children to read: An evidence-based assessment of the scientific research literature on reading and its implications for reading instruction* (NIH Publication No. 00-4769). Washington, DC: U.S. Government Printing Office.

National Writing Project. (2013). *Writing is essential.* Retrieved from *www.nwp.org/cs/public/print/ doc/about.csp.*

Nicholson, D. W. (2000). Layers of experience: Forms of representation in a Waldorf school classroom. *Journal of Curriculum Studies, 32,* 575–587.

Nist, S., & Simpson, M. (2000). College studying. In M. Kamil, P. Mosenthal, P. D. Pearson, & R. Barr (Eds.), *Handbook of reading research* (Vol. 3, pp. 645–666). Mahwah, NJ: Erlbaum.

Nokes, J. D. (2010). Observing literacy practices in history classrooms. *Theory and Research in Social Education, 38*(4), 515–544.

Obama, B. (2010, February 22). *Address to the National Governors Association,* Washington, DC.

O'Brien, D. (2001, June). "At-risk" adolescents: Redefining competence through the multiliteracies of intermediality, visual arts, and representation. *Reading Online, 4*(11). Retrieved from *www. readingonline.org/newliteracies/lit_index.asp?HREF=/newliteracies/obrien/index.html.*

O'Brien, D., & Scharber, C. (2008). Digital literacies go to school: Potholes and possibilities. *Journal of Adolescent and Adult Literacy, 52*(1), 66–68.

Ogle, D. (1992). KWL in action: Secondary teachers find applications that work. In E. Dishner, T. Bean, J. Readence, & D. Moore (Eds.), *Reading in the content areas: Improving classroom instruction* (pp. 270–281). Dubuque, IA: Kendall/Hunt.

Olness, R. (2007). *Using literature to enhance content area instruction: A guide for K–5 teachers.* Newark, DE: International Reading Association.

Olsen, L. (2010). *Reparable harm: Fulfilling the unkept promise of educational opportunity for California's long term English learners.* Long Beach: Californians Together. Retrieved from *www. californianstogether.org/docs/download.aspx?fileId=12.*

Olsen, L. (2012). *Secondary school courses designed to address the language needs and academic gaps of long term English learners.* Long Beach: Californians Together.

O'Reilly, T., & McNamara, D. S. (2007). Reversing the reverse cohesion effect: Good texts can be better for strategic, high-knowledge readers. *Discourse Processes, 43*(2), 121–152.

Orellana, M. F. (2007). Moving words and worlds: Reflections from "the Middle." In C. Lewis, P. Enciso, & E. B. Moje (Eds.), *Reframing sociocultural research on literacy: Identity, agency, and power* (pp. 123–136). Mahwah, NJ: Erlbaum.

Organization for Economic Cooperation and Development. (2009). *PISA 2009 assessment framework: Key competencies in reading, mathematics and science.* Paris: Author.

Organization for Economic Cooperation and Development. (2010a). *The high cost of low educational performance: The long-run economic impact of improving PISA outcomes.* Paris: Author.

Organization for Economic Cooperation and Development. (2010b). *PISA 2009 results: What students know and can do—Student performance in reading, mathematics and science* (Vol. 1). Paris: Author.

Organization for Economic Cooperation and Development. (2013a). *OECD skills outlook 2013: First results from the survey of adult skills.* Paris: Author.

Organization for Economic Cooperation and Development. (2013b). *PISA 2012 results: Ready to learn: Students' engagement, drive and self-beliefs* (Vol. 3). Paris: Author.

Organization for Economic Cooperation and Development. (2014). *PISA 2012 results: What students know and can do—Student performance in mathematics, reading and science* (Vol. 1). Paris: Author.

Organization for Economic Cooperation and Development. (2015a). *Students, computers and learning: Making the connection.* Paris: Author.

Organization for Economic Cooperation and Development. (2015b). *The ABC of gender equality in education: Aptitude, behaviour, confidence.* Paris: Author.

Ortman, J. (2013, February 7). *U.S. population projections: 2012 to 2060* [Slide 33]. Retrieved from *www.gwu.edu/~forcpgm/Ortman.pdf.*

Ozuru, Y., Dempsey, K., & McNamara, D. S. (2009). Prior knowledge, reading skill, and text cohesion in the comprehension of science texts. *Learning and Instruction, 19*(3), 228–242.

Paige, D. D. (2011). Engaging struggling adolescent readers through situational interest: A model proposing the relationships among extrinsic motivation, oral reading proficiency, comprehension, and academic achievement. *Reading Psychology, 32*(5), 395–425.

Pailliotet, A. W. (2003). Integrating media and popular-culture literacy with content reading. In R. C. Richards & M. C. McKenna (Eds.), *Integrating multiple literacies in K–8 classrooms: Case commentaries and practical applications* (pp. 172–189). Mahwah, NJ: Erlbaum.

Pajares, F. (2008). Motivational role of self-efficacy beliefs in self-regulated learning. In D. H. Schunk & B. J. Zimmerman (Eds.), *Motivation and self-regulated learning: Theory, research and applications* (pp. 111–140). New York: Erlbaum.

Pajares, F., & Urdan, T. (Eds.). (2006). *Self-efficacy beliefs of adolescence.* Greenwich, CT: Information Age.

Palamatier, R. A. (1973). A notetaking system for learning. *Journal of Reading, 17*(1), 36–39.

Palincsar, A. M., & Brown, A. (1984). Reciprocal teaching of comprehension fostering and monitoring activities. *Cognition and Instruction, 12,* 117–175.

Palmer, D. H. (2009). Student interest generated during an inquiry skills lesson. *Journal of Research in Science Teaching, 46*(2), 147–165.

Pappas, C., Kiefer, B., & Levstik, L. (2005). *An integrated language perspective in the elementary school* (4th ed.). New York: Pearson.

Paris, S. R., & Block, C. C. (2007). The expertise of adolescent literacy teachers. *Journal of Adolescent and Adult Literacy, 50*(7), 582–596.

Parr, J. M., & Timperley, H. S. (2010). Feedback to writing, assessment for teaching and learning and student progress. *Assessing Writing, 15*(2), 68–85.

Patall, E. A., Cooper, H., & Wynn, S. R. (2010). The effectiveness and relative importance of providing choices in the classroom. *Journal of Educational Psychology, 102*(4), 896–915.

Patchan, M. M., Schunn, C. D., & Correnti, R. J. (2016, April 7). The nature of feedback: How peer feedback features affect students' implementation rate and quality of revisions. *Journal of Educational Psychology.* Available at *www.researchgate.net/publication/299998625_The_Nature_of_Feedback_How_Peer_Feedback_Features_Affect_Students'_Implementation_Rate_and_Quality_of_Revisions.*

Paterson, P. O., & Elliot, L. N. (2006). Struggling reader to struggling reader: High school students' responses to a cross-age tutoring program. *Journal of Adolescent and Adult Literacy, 49*(5), 378–389.

Pearson, P. D., Hiebert, E. H., & Kamil, M. (2012). Vocabulary assessment: Making do with what we have while we create the tools we need. In E. Kame'enui & J. Baumann (Eds.), *Vocabulary instruction: Research to practice* (2nd ed., pp. 231–255). New York: Guilford Press.

Pearson, P. D., Moje, E. B., & Greenleaf, C. (2010). Literacy and science: Each in the service of the other. *Science, 328*(5977), 459–463.

Perry, K. H. (2012). What is literacy?: A critical overview of sociocultural perspectives. *Journal of Language and Literacy Education, 8*(1), 50–71.

Peterson, R., & Eeds, M. (2007). *Grand conversations: Literature groups in action* (2nd ed.). New York: Scholastic.

Petscher, Y. (2010). A meta-analysis of the relationship between student attitudes towards reading and achievement in reading. *Journal of Research in Reading, 33*(4), 335–355.

Pew Internet and American Life Project. (2012). *Teens, smartphones and texting.* Retrieved from *www.pewinternet.org/files/old-media/Files/Reports/2012/PIP_Teens_Smartphones_and_Texting.pdf.*

Pfost, M., Dörfler, T., & Artelt, C. (2013). Students' extracurricular reading behavior and the development of vocabulary and reading comprehension. *Learning and Individual Differences, 26,* 89–102.

Phillips, F., & Wolcott, S. (2014). Effects of interspersed versus summary feedback on the quality of students' case report revisions. *Accounting Education, 23*(2), 174–190.

Philpott, S. (2015). Historical fiction: Reality meets imagination. In T. N. Turner, J. Clabough, & W. Cole (Eds.), *Getting at the core of the Common Core with social studies: Teaching and learning social studies* (pp. 139–151). Charlotte, NC: IAP Information Age.

Pichette, F. (2005). Time spent on reading and reading comprehension in second language learning. *Canadian Modern Language Review, 60*(2), 243–262.

Pilgreen, J. (2007). Teaching the language of school to secondary English learners. In J. Lewis & G. Moorman (Eds.), *Adolescent literacy instruction: Policies and promising practices* (pp. 238–262). Newark, DE: International Reading Association.

Pintrich, P. R., & Schunk, D. H. (2002). *Motivation in education: Theory, research, and applications* (2nd ed.). Englewood Cliffs, NJ: Merrill.

Pitcher, S., Albright, L., DeLaney, C., Walker, N., & Seunarinesingh, K. (2007). Assessing adolescents' motivation to read. *Journal of Adolescent and Adult Literacy, 50*(5), 376–396.

Pittelman, S. D., Berglund, R. L., & Heimlich, J. E. (1991). *Semantic feature analysis: Classroom applications.* Newark, DE: International Reading Association.

Plato. (2007). *Phaedrus.* Minneapolis, MN: Filiquarian.

Plester, B., Wood, C., & Bell, V. (2008). Txt msg n school literacy: Does texting and knowledge of text abbreviations adversely affect children's literacy attainment? *Literacy, 42*(3), 137–144.

Pol, J., Volman, M., & Beishuizen, J. (2010). Scaffolding in teacher–student interaction: A decade of research. *Educational Psychology Review, 22*(3), 271–296.

Polakow, V., & Brozo, W. G. (1994). Deconstructing the at-risk discourse: Power, pedagogy, and the politics of inequity. *Review of Education, 15,* 217–221.

Poletti, A. (2008). Zines making zinesters. In A. Poletti (Ed.), *Intimate ephemera: Reading young lives in Australian zine culture* (pp. 59–103). Carlton, Victoria, Australia: Melbourne University Press.

Poling, L. (2000). The real world: Community speakers in the classroom. *Social Education, 64,* 8–10.

Powell-Brown, A. (2003–2004). Can you be a teacher of literacy if you don't love to read? *Journal of Adolescent and Adult Literacy, 47,* 284–288.

Prensky, M. (2009). *H. sapiens* digital: From digital immigrants and digital natives to digital wisdom. *Innovate: Journal of Online Education, 5*(3). Retrieved from *http://nsuworks.nova.edu/cgi/viewcontent.cgi?article=1020&context=innovate.*

Pressley, M. (2000). What should comprehension instruction be the instruction of? In M. Kamil, P. Mosenthal, P. D. Pearson, & R. Barr (Eds.), *Handbook of reading research* (Vol. 3, pp. 545–562). Mahwah, NJ: Erlbaum.

Pressley, M., & Gaskins, I. W. (2006). Metacognitively competent reading comprehension is constructively responsive reading: How can such reading be developed in students? *Metacognition Learning, 1,* 99–113.

Pressley, M., & Hilden, K. (2004). Toward more ambitious comprehension instruction. In E. Silliman & L. Wilkinson (Eds.), *Language and literacy learning in schools* (pp. 151–174). New York: Guilford Press.

Pressley, M., & Lundeberg, M. (2008). An invitation to study professionals reading professional-level texts: A window on exceptionally complex, flexible reading. In K. B. Cartwright (Ed.), *Literacy processes: Cognitive flexibility in learning and teaching* (pp. 165–187). New York: Guilford Press.

Price, J. K., Pierson, E., & Light, D. (2011, January). *Using classroom assessment to promote 21st century learning in emerging market countries.* Paper presented at Global Learn Asia Pacific 2011, Melbourne, Australia.

Prouty, J. L., & Irby, M. (1995, February). *Parent involvement: Integrated packets.* Paper presented at the Student/Beginning Teacher Conference, Nacogdoches, TX.

Puranik, C., Lombardino, L. J., & Altmann, L. J. (2008). Assessing the microstructure of written language using a retelling paradigm. *American Journal of Speech Language Pathology, 17,* 107–120.

Quezada, R., Alexandrowicz, V., & Molina, S. (2013). Family, school, community engagement and partnerships: An imperative for K–12 and colleges of education in the development of 21st century educators. *Teaching Education, 24,* 119–122.

Ramsay, C. M., & Sperline, R. A. (2011). Exploring main idea generation via electronic note-taking. *Journal of Literacy and Technology, 12*(1), 26–64.

Ranck-Buhr, W. (2012). Motivating readers through voice and choice. *Voices from the Middle, 20*(2), 58–59.

Raphael, T. E., & Pearson, P. D. (1985). Increasing students' awareness of sources of information for answering questions. *American Educational Research Journal, 22,* 217–236.

Ravitch, D. (2010). *The death and life of the great American school system: How testing and choice are undermining education.* New York: Basic Books.

Reardon, S. F., Valentino, R. A., & Shores, K. A. (2012). Patterns of literacy among U.S. students. *Future of Children, 22*(2), 17–38.

Reed, D. K., Rimel, H., & Hallett, A. (2016). Note-taking interventions for college students: A synthesis and meta-analysis of the literature. *Journal of Research on Educational Effectiveness, 9*(3), 307–333.

Reeve, J., Ryan, R., Deci, E. L., & Jang, H. (2008). Understanding and promoting autonomous self-regulation: A self-determination theory perspective. In D. H. Schunk & B. J. Zimmerman (Eds.), *Motivation and self-regulated learning: Theory, research and applications* (pp. 223–244). New York: Erlbaum.

Reich, R. (2011). *Aftershock: The next economy and America's future.* New York: Vintage.

Reisman, A. (2012). The document-based lesson: Bringing disciplinary inquiry into high school history classrooms with adolescent struggling readers. *Journal of Curriculum Studies, 44*(2), 233–264.

Resmovits, J. (2013, October 8). OECD skills test: U.S. adults lag in practical workplace skills. Retrieved from *www.huffingtonpost.com/2013/10/08/oecd-skills-test_n_4061097.html.*

Rhodes, L., & Dudley-Marling, C. (1996). *Readers and writers with a difference: A holistic approach to teaching struggling readers and writers.* Portsmouth, NH: Heinemann.

Riccomini, P. J., Smith, G. W., Hughes, E. M., & Fries, K. M. (2015). The language of mathematics: The importance of teaching and learning mathematical vocabulary. *Reading and Writing Quarterly: Overcoming Learning Difficulties, 31*(3), 235–252.

Richards, J. C., & Lassonde, C. (2009). *Literacy tutoring that works: A look at successful in-school, after-school, and summer programs.* Newark, DE: International Reading Association.

Richardson, A. E. (2010). Exploring text through student discussions: Accountable talk in the middle school classroom. *English Journal, 100*(1), 83–88.

Rideout, V. (2014). *Children, teens and reading.* Retrieved from *www.commonsensemedia.org/research/children-teens-and-reading.*

Rideout, V. J., Foehr, U. G., & Roberts, D. F. (2010). *Generation M2: Media in the lives of 8- to 18-year-olds.* Menlo Park, CA: Henry J. Kaiser Family Foundation.

Rivers, C., & Barnett, R. C. (2011). *The truth about girls and boys: Challenging toxic stereotypes about our children.* New York: Columbia University Press.

Roberts, M. (2012). Why should we have all the fun?: Encouraging colleagues to read YA novels across the curriculum. *English Teacher, 102*(1), 92–95.

Robertson, J. (2011). The educational affordances of blogs for self-directed learning. *Computers and Education, 57*(2), 1628–1644.

Rotgans, J. I., & Schmidt, H. G. (2011). The role of teachers in facilitating situational interest in an active-learning classroom. *Teaching and Teacher Education, 27*(1), 37–42.

Rotgans, J. I., & Schmidt, H. G. (2014). Situational interest and learning: Thirst for knowledge. *Learning and Instruction, 32*, 37–50.

Rothman, R. (2011). *Something in common: The Common Core standards and the next chapter in American education.* Cambridge, MA: Harvard Education Press.

Rothstein, D., & Santana, L. (2011). *Make just one change: Teach students to ask their own questions.* Cambridge, MA: Harvard Education Press.

Rouet, J.-F., & Britt, M. A. (2011). Relevance processes in multiple document comprehension. In M. T. McCrudden, J. P. Magliano, & G. Schraw (Eds.), *Text relevance and learning from text* (pp. 19–52). Greenwich, CT: Information Age.

Rousseau, J. J. (1979). *Emile: Or, on education.* New York: Basic Books.

Roy-Campbell, Z. (2012). Meeting the needs of English learners. *Journal of Adolescent and Adult Literacy, 56*(3), 186–188.

Rubinstein-Ávila, E., & Leckie, A. G. (2014). Meaningful discipline-specific language instruction for middle school students for whom English is an additional language. In K. A. Hinchman & H. K. Sheridan-Thomas (Eds.), *Best practices in adolescent literacy instruction* (2nd ed., pp. 20–35). New York: Guilford Press.

Ruddell, R., & Unrau, N. (2004). Reading as a meaning-construction process: The reader, the text, and the teacher. In R. Ruddell & N. Unrau (Eds.), *Theoretical models and processes of reading* (Vol. 3, pp. 954–976). Newark, DE: International Reading Association.

Rueben, K., & Murray, S. (2008). *Racial disparities in education finance: Going beyond equal revenues.* Washington, DC: Urban Institute. Retrieved from *www.urban.org/UploadedPDF/411785_equal_revenues.pdf.*

Ryan, C. (2013, August). *Language use in the United States: 2011.* Retrieved from *www.census.gov/prod/2013pubs/acs-22.pdf.*

Sachs, H. J. (1943). The reading method of acquiring vocabulary. *Journal of Educational Research, 36*(6), 457–464.

Salsovic, A. R. (2009). Designing a WebQuest. *Mathematics Teacher, 102*(9), 666–671.

Salvatori, M. R., & Donahue, P. (2005). *The elements (and pleasures) of difficulty.* New York: Longman.

Samson, J. F., & Collins, B. A. (2012). *Preparing all teachers to meet the needs of English language learners: Applying research to policy and practice for teacher effectiveness.* Washington, DC: Center for American Progress.

Sandwell, R. W. (2008). Using primary documents in social studies and history. In R. Case & P. Clark (Eds.), *The Canadian anthology of social studies: Issues and strategies for secondary teachers* (pp. 295–307). Vancouver, BC: Pacific Educational Press.

Santa, C. M., & Havens, L. T. (2012). *Project CRISS: Creating independence through student-owned strategies: Helping teachers teach and learners learn* (4th ed.). Dubuque, IA: Kendall-Hunt.

Sarafini, F. (2010). *Classroom reading assessments: More efficient ways to view and evaluate your readers.* Portsmouth, NH: Heinemann.

Sarcoban, A., & Basibek, N. (2012). Mnemonics technique versus context method in teaching vocabulary at upper-intermediate level. *Education and Science, 37,* 251–266.

Sawmiller, A. (2010). Classroom blogging: What is the role in science learning? *The Clearing House, 83*(2), 44–48.

Schiff, R., & Lotem, E. (2011). Effects of phonological and morphological awareness on children's word reading development from two socioeconomic backgrounds. *First Language, 31*(2), 139–163.

Schleppegrell, M. J. (2004). *The language of schooling: A functional linguistics perspective.* Mahwah, NJ: Erlbaum.

Schleppegrell, M. J., Greer, S., & Taylor, S. (2008). Literacy in history: Language and meaning. *Australian Journal of Language and Literacy, 31*(2), 174–187.

Schmitt, N., Jiang, X., & Grabe, W. (2011). The percentage of words known in a text and reading comprehension. *Modern Language Journal, 95,* 26–43.

Schommer, M. (1994). An emerging conceptualization of epistemological beliefs and their role in learning. In R. Garner & P. A. Alexander (Eds.), *Beliefs about text and instruction with text* (pp. 25–40). Hillsdale, NJ: Erlbaum.

Schraw, G., Crippen, K. J., & Hartley, K. (2006). Promoting self-regulation in science education: Metacognition as part of a broader perspective on learning. *Research in Science Education, 36,* 111–139.

Schraw, G., & Lehman, S. (2001). Situational interest: A review of the literature and discussions for future research. *Educational Psychology Review, 13,* 23–52.

Schugar, J., Schugar, H., & Penny, C. (2012). A Nook or a book?: Comparing college students' reading comprehension levels, critical reading, and study skills. *International Journal of Technology in Teaching and Learning, 7*(2), 174–192.

Schunk, D. H., Meece, J. L., & Pintrich, P. R. (2013). *Motivation in education: Theory, research, and applications* (4th ed.). Englewood Cliffs, NJ: Prentice Hall.

Schunk, D. H., & Zimmerman, B. J. (2007). *Motivation and self-regulated learning: Theory, research, and applications.* New York: Routledge.

Schwartz, L. H. (2015). A funds of knowledge approach to the appropriation of new media in a high school writing classroom. *Interactive Learning Environments, 23*(5), 595–612.

Schwartz, R. M., & Raphael, T. E. (1985). Concept of definition: A key to improving students' vocabulary. *The Reading Teacher, 39*, 198–205.

Scott, J., & Nagy, W. (2009). Developing word consciousness. In M. Graves (Ed.), *Essential readings on vocabulary instruction* (pp. 106–117). Newark, DE: International Reading Association.

Scott, J. A., Nagy, W. E., & Flinspach, S. L. (2008). More than merely words: Redefining vocabulary learning in a culturally and linguistically diverse society. In A. E. Farstrup & S. J. Samuels (Eds.), *What research has to say about vocabulary instruction* (pp. 182–210). Newark, DE: International Reading Association.

Sedita, J. (2013). Learning to write and writing to learn. In M. D. Hougen (Ed.), *Fundamentals of literacy instruction and assessment 6–12*. Baltimore: Brookes.

Seglem, R., Witte, S., & Beemer, J. (2012). 21st century literacies in the classroom: Creating windows of interest and webs of learning. *Journal of Language and Literacy Education, 8*(2), 47–65.

Serafini, F., Bean, T. W., & Readence, J. E. (2004). Reconceptualizing adolescent identities. *Reading Research Quarterly, 39*, 482–489.

Shanahan, C., Shanahan, T., & Misischia, C. (2011). Analysis of expert readers in three disciplines: History, mathematics, and chemistry. *Journal of Literacy Research, 43*(4), 393–429.

Shanahan, T. (1997). Reading–writing relationships, thematic units, inquiry learning: In pursuit of effective integrated literacy instruction. *The Reading Teacher, 51*, 12–20.

Shanahan, T., & Beck, I. L. (2006). Effective literacy teaching for English-language learners. In D. August & T. Shanahan (Eds.), *Developing literacy in second-language learners: Report of the National Literacy Panel on Language-Minority Children and Youth* (pp. 415–488). Mahwah, NJ: Erlbaum.

Shanahan, T., & Shanahan, C. (2008). Teaching disciplinary literacy to adolescents: Rethinking content-area literacy. *Harvard Educational Review, 78*, 40–59.

Shanahan, T., & Shanahan, C. (2012). What is disciplinary literacy and why does it matter? *Topics in Language Disorders, 32*(1), 7–18.

Shkedi, A. (2009). From curriculum guide to classroom practice: Teachers' narratives of curriculum application. *Journal of Curriculum Studies, 41*, 833–854.

Short, D., & Fitzsimmons, S. (2007). *Double the work: Challenges and solutions to acquiring language and academic literacy for English language learners: A report to the Carnegie Corporation of New York*. Washington, DC: Alliance for Excellent Education.

Short, K. G., Tomlinson, C. M., Lynch-Brown, C. M., & Johnson, H. M. (2014). *Essentials of young adult literature* (3rd ed.). New York: Pearson.

Shute, V. J. (2008). Focus on formative feedback. *Review of Educational Research, 78*(1), 153–189.

Siebert, D., & Draper, R. J. (2008). Why content-area literacy messages do not speak to mathematics teachers: A critical review of the literature. *Literacy Research and Instruction, 47*, 229–245.

Silberman-Keller, D., Bekerman, Z., Giroux, H. A., & Burbules, N. C. (2008). *Mirror images: Popular culture and education*. New York: Peter Lang.

Silverman, J., & Thompson, P. W. (2008). Toward a framework for the development of mathematical knowledge for teaching. *Journal of Mathematics Teacher Education, 11*, 499–511.

Simon, R. (2012). "Without comic books, there would be no me": Teachers as connoisseurs of adolescents' literate lives. *Journal of Adolescent and Adult Literacy, 55*(6), 516–526.

Simpson, M. L. (1994). Talk throughs: A strategy encouraging active learning across the content areas. *Journal of Reading, 38*, 296–304.

Simpson, M. L., & Nist, S. L. (2003). An update on strategic learning: It's more than textbook reading strategies. In N. Stahl & H. Boylan (Eds.), *Teaching developmental reading* (pp. 157–178). Boston: Bedford/St. Martins.

Skerrett, A. (2012). "We hatched this in class": Repositioning of identity in and beyond a reading classroom. *High School Journal, 95*(3), 62–75.

Skerrett, A., & Bomer, R. (2011). Border zones in adolescents' literacy practices: Connecting out-of-school literacies to the reading curriculum. *Urban Education, 46*(6), 1256–1279.

Smagorinsky, P. (2001). If meaning is constructed, what is it made from?: Toward a cultural theory of reading. *Review of Educational Research, 71,* 133–169.

Smith, P., & Kumi-Yeboah, A. (2015). *Handbook of research on cross-cultural approaches to language and literacy development.* Hershey, PA: IGI Global.

Snow, C. E., & Lawrence, J. F. (2011). *Word generation in Boston public schools: Natural history of a literacy intervention.* Washington, DC: Council of Great City Schools.

Snow, C. E., Lawrence, J., & White, C. (2009). Generating knowledge of academic language among urban middle school students. *Journal of Research on Educational Effectiveness, 2*(4), 325–344.

Snow, C. E., & Uccelli, P. (2009). The challenge of academic language. In D. R. Olson & N. Torrance (Eds.), *The Cambridge handbook of literacy* (pp. 112–133). New York: Cambridge University Press.

Sparrow, B., Liu, J., & Wegner, D. M. (2011). Google effects on memory: Cognitive consequences of having information at our fingertips. *Science, 333*(6043), 776–778.

Spinelli, C. G. (2008). Introduction: The benefits, uses, and practical application of informal assessment procedures. *Reading and Writing Quarterly: Overcoming Learning Difficulties, 24*(1), 1–6.

Spirgel, A. S., & Delaney, P. F. (2016). Does writing summaries improve memory for text? *Educational Psychology Review, 28*(1), 171–196.

Springhall, J. (1999). *Youth, popular culture and moral panics: Penny gaffs to gangsta rap, 1830–1996.* New York: Palgrave.

Squire, K. (2011). *Video games and learning: Teaching and participatory culture in the digital age.* New York: Teachers College Press.

Stadtler, M., & Bromme, R. (2007). Dealing with multiple documents on the WWW: The role of metacognition in the formation of documents models. *International Journal of Computer-Supported Collaborative Learning, 2*(2–1), 191–210.

Stadtler, M., & Bromme, R. (2013). Multiple document comprehension: An approach to public understanding of science. *Cognition and Instruction, 31*(2), 122–129.

Stahl, S. (1986). Three principles of effective vocabulary instruction. *Journal of Reading, 29,* 662–668.

Stahl, S., & Nagy, W. (2006). *Teaching word meanings.* Mahwah, NJ: Erlbaum.

Stearns, E., Moller, S., Blau, J., & Potochnick, S. (2007). Staying back and dropping out: The relationship between grade retention and school dropout. *Sociology of Education, 80*(3), 210–240.

Steinberg, L. (2008). *Adolescence.* New York: McGraw-Hill.

Stephens, P. (2011). Art vocabulary cards. *School Arts, 111*(2), 64.

Stewart, M. A. (2013). Giving voice to Valeria's story: Support, value, and agency for immigrant adolescents. *Journal of Adolescent and Adult Literacy, 57*(1), 42–50.

Stiggins, R. J. (2005). From formative assessment to assessment for learning: A path to success in standards-based schools. *Phi Delta Kappan, 87*(4), 324–328.

Stiggins, R. J., & Chappius, J. (2011). *An introduction to student-involved assessment for learning* (6th ed.). Boston: Pearson.

Strauss, V. (2014, October 30). The rise of the anti–standardized testing movement. Retrieved from *www.washingtonpost.com/news/answer-sheet/wp/2014/10/30/the-rise-of-the-anti-standardized-testing-movement.*

Street, B. (2009). The future of "social literacies." In M. Raynham & M. Prinsloo (Eds.), *The future of literacy studies* (pp. 21–37). Basingstoke, UK: Palgrave Macmillan.

Stronge, J. H. (2010). *Effective teachers = student achievement: What the research says.* New York: Routledge.

Stronge, J. H., Ward, T. J., Tucker, P. D., & Hindman, J. L. (2008). What is the relationship between teacher quality and student achievement?: An exploratory study. *Journal of Personnel Evaluation in Education, 20*(3–4), 165–184.

Sturtevant, E., Boyd, F., Brozo, W. G., Hinchman, K., Alvermann, D., & Moore, D. (2006). *Principled practices for adolescent literacy. A framework for instruction and policy.* Mahwah, NJ: Erlbaum.

Suárez-Orozco, C., Onaga, M., & de Lardemelle, C. (2010). Promoting academic engagement among immigrant adolescents through school–family–community collaboration. *Professional School Counseling, 14*(1), 15–26.

Suárez-Orozco, C, Suárez-Orozco, M. M., & Todorova, I. (2008). *Learning a new land: Immigrant students in American society.* Cambridge, MA: Belknap Press of Harvard University Press.

Sullivan, A. S., & Brown, M. (2013). *Social inequalities in cognitive scores at age 16: The role of reading.* London: Institute of Education, Center for Longitudinal Studies.

Sullivan, E. (2014). The truth about nonfiction. In J. Flood, S. B. Heath, & D. Lapp (Eds.), *Handbook of research on teaching literacy through the communicative and visual arts* (Vol. 2, pp. 555–556). New York: Routledge.

Swartz, R. J., Costa, A., Kallick, B., Beyer, B., & Reagan, R. (2007). *Thinking-based learning: Activating students' potential.* Norwood, MA: Christopher-Gordon.

Sylvan, C. (2013, Summer). Newcomer high school students as an asset: The internationals approach. *Voices in Urban Education,* 19–30.

Taboada, A., Tonks, S. M., Wigfield, A., & Guthrie, J. T. (2009). Effects of motivational and cognitive variables on reading comprehension. *Reading and Writing: An Interdisciplinary Journal, 22*(1), 85–106.

Tafani, V. (2009). Teaching English through mass media. *Acta Didactica Napocencia, 2,* 81–96.

Tarchi, C. (2010). Reading comprehension of informative texts in secondary school: A focus on direct and indirect effects of reader's prior knowledge. *Learning and Individual Differences, 20*(5), 415–420.

Tatum, A. (2006) Adolescents' multiple identities and teacher professional development. In D. Alvermann, K. Hinchman, D. Moore, S. Phelps, & D. Waff (Eds.), *Reconceptualizing the literacies in adolescents' lives* (2nd ed., pp. 65–70). Mahwah, NJ: Erlbaum.

Tatum, A. (2009). *Reading for their life: (Re)Building the textual lineages of African American adolescent males.* Portsmouth, NH: Heinemann.

Tatum, A. W., & Muhammad, G. E. (2012). African American males and literacy development in contexts that are characteristically urban. *Urban Education, 47*(2), 434–463.

Taylor, L., & Parsons, J. (2011). Improving student engagement. *Current Issues in Education, 14*(1). Retrieved from *http://cie.asu.edu/ojs/index.php/cieatasu/article/view/745.*

Templeton, S. (2011/2012). Teaching and learning morphology: A reflection on generative vocabulary instruction. *Journal of Education, 192*(2/3), 101–107.

Templeton, S. (2012). The vocabulary–spelling connection and generative instruction: Orthographic development and morphological knowledge at the intermediate grades and beyond. In E. J. Kame'enui & J. F. Baumann (Eds.), *Vocabulary instruction: Research to practice* (2nd ed., pp. 116–138). New York: Guilford Press.

Templeton, S. R., Bear, D. R., Invernizzi, M., Johnston, F., Flanigan, K., Townsend, D. R., et al. (2015). *Vocabulary their way: Word study with middle and secondary students.* Boston: Pearson.

Thiede, K. W., Griffin, T. D., Wiley, J., & Redford, J. (2009). Metacognitive monitoring during and after reading. In D. J. Hacker, J. Dunlosky, & A. C. Graesser (Eds.), *Handbook of metacognition in education* (pp. 85–106). New York: Routledge.

Thomas, A. (2007). *Youth online: Identity and literacy in the digital age.* New York: Peter Lang.

Thomas, A. K., & McDaniel, M. A. (2007). The negative cascade of incongruent generative study-test processing in memory and meta-comprehension. *Memory and Cognition, 35,* 668–678.

Thomas Fordham Institute. (2004). *The mad, mad world of textbook adoption*. Washington, DC: Author.

Thomson, P., & Hall, C. (2008). Opportunities missed and/or thwarted?: "Funds of knowledge" meet the English national curriculum. *Curriculum Journal, 19*(2), 87–103.

Tierney, R. J., & Shanahan, T. (1991). Research on the reading–writing relationship: Interactions, transactions, and outcomes. In R. Barr, M. L. Kamil, P. Mosenthal, & P. D. Pearson (Eds.). *Handbook of reading research* (Vol. 2, pp. 246–280). New York: Longman.

Tippett, C. D. (2010). Refutation text in science education: A review of two decades of research. *International Journal of Science and Mathematics Education, 8*(6), 951–970.

Tok, S. (2013). Effects of the know–want–learn strategy on students' mathematics achievement, anxiety and metacognitive skills. *Metacognition and Learning, 8*(2), 193–212.

Tong, H. K., & Cheung, L. H. (2011). Cultural identity and language: A proposed framework for cultural globalisation and glocalisation. *Journal of Multilingual and Multicultural Development, 32*(1), 55–69.

Topping, K., & Ferguson, N. (2005). Effective literacy teaching behaviours. *Journal of Research in Reading, 28*(2), 125–143.

Townsend, D. (2009). Building academic vocabulary in after-school settings: Games for growth with middle school English-language learners. *Journal of Adolescent and Adult Literacy, 53*(3), 242–251.

Trumbull, E., & Pacheco, M. (2005). *Leading with diversity: Cultural competencies for teacher preparation and professional development*. Providence, RI: Brown University, The Education Alliance.

Tseng, K.-H., Chang, C.-C., Lou, S.-J., Tan, Y., & Chiu, C.-J. (2012). How concept-mapping perception navigates student knowledge transfer performance. *Journal of Educational Technology and Society, 15*(1), 102–115.

Tseng, W.-T., & Schmitt, N. (2008). Toward a model of motivated vocabulary learning: A structural equation modeling approach. *Language Learning, 58*(2), 357–400.

Ukrainetz, T. A. (2015). Improving text comprehension: Scaffolding adolescents into strategic reading. *Seminars in Speech and Language, 36*(1), 17–30.

Underwood, J. S., & Tregidgo, A. P. (2006). Improving student writing through effective feedback: Best practices and recommendations. *Journal of Teaching Writing, 22*(2), 73–97.

United Nations Educational, Scientific, and Cultural Organization. (2014). *Reading in the mobile era: A study of mobile reading in developing countries*. Paris: Author.

Uro, G., & Barrio, A. (2013). *English language learners in America's great city schools: Demographics, achievement, and staffing*. Washington, DC: Council of the Great City Schools.

U.S. Census Bureau. (n.d.). Annual estimates of the resident population for selected age groups by sex for the United States, states, counties, and Puerto Rico commonwealth and municipios: April 1, 2010 to July 1, 2013 [New York]. Retrieved March 20, 2015, from *factfinder.census.gov/bkmk/table/1.0/en/PEP/2013/PEPAGESEX/0400000US36*.

U.S. Census Bureau. (2013). Age and sex composition in the United States: 2012: Table 1. Retrieved from *census.gov/population/age/data/2012comp.html*.

U.S. Department of Education. (2002). *National Assessment of Educational Progress (NAEP), 2001 U.S. history assessment*. Washington, DC: National Center for Education Statistics.

U.S. Department of Education National Center for Education Statistics. (2014). *Report on regulatory adjusted cohort graduation rates limited English proficient 2010*. Retrieved from *http://eddataexpress.ed.gov/data-element-explorer.cfm*.

Vacca, R. T., Vacca, J., & Mraz, M. E. (2014). *Content area reading: Literacy and learning across the curriculum* (11th ed.). Boston: Pearson.

Vadeboncoeur, J. A., & Stevens, L. P. (Eds.). (2005). *Re/constructing "the adolescent."* New York: Peter Lang.

Van der Kleij, F. M., Vermeulen, J. A., Schildkamp, K., & Eggen, T. J. H. M. (2015). Integrating data-based decision making, Assessment for Learning and diagnostic testing in formative assessment. *Assessment in Education: Principles, Policy and Practice, 22*(3), 324–343.

van Dijk, T. A. (2007). The study of discourse: An introduction. In T. A. van Dijk (Ed.), *Discourse studies* (pp. xix–xlii). London: Sage.

Van Ryzin, M. J., Gravely, A. A., & Roseth, C. J. (2009). Autonomy, belongingness, and engagement in school as contributors to adolescent psychological well-being. *Journal of Youth Adolescence, 38*, 1–12.

Vaughn, S., Swanson, E. A., Roberts, G., Wanzek, J., Stillman-Spisak, S. J., Solis, M., et al. (2013). Improving reading comprehension and social studies knowledge in middle school. *Reading Research Quarterly, 48*(1), 77–93.

Vieira, E. T., Jr., & Grantham, S. (2011). Perceptions of control facilitate reading engagement. *Reading Psychology, 32*(4), 322–348.

Vrasidas, C., Avraamidou, L., Theodoridou, K., Themistokleous, S., & Panaou, P. (2015). Science fiction in education: Case studies from classroom implementations. *Educational Media International, 52*(3), 201–215.

Walker, C. L., & Stone, K. (2011). Preparing teachers to reach English language learners: Preservice and in-service initiatives. In T. Lucas (Ed.), *Teacher preparation for linguistically diverse classrooms* (pp. 127–142). New York: Taylor & Francis.

Walker, T. (2013). Testing changes course: A new era is here. Are schools and teachers ready? *NEA Today, 31*(3), 38–39.

Walker, N., & Bean, T. W. (2002, December). *Sociocultural influences in content area teachers' selection and use of multiple texts.* Paper presented at the 52nd annual National Reading Conference, Miami, FL.

Wallace, F. H., & Clark, K. K. (2005). Reading stances in mathematics: Positioning students and texts. *Action in Teacher Education, 27*(2), 68–79.

Walsh, M. (2010). Multimodal literacy: What does it mean for classroom practice? *Australian Journal of Language and Literacy, 33*(3), 211–239.

Wasley, P. A., Hampel, R. L., & Clark, R. W. (1997). *Kids and school reform.* San Francisco: Jossey-Bass.

Webb, M., & Jones, J. (2009). Exploring tensions in developing assessment for learning. *Assessment in Education, 16*(2), 165–184.

Webb, N. M. (2009). The teacher's role in promoting collaborative dialogue in the classroom. *British Journal of Educational Psychology, 79*(1), 1–28.

Weinstein, H. (Producer), & Yuen, W.-P. (Director). (2016). *Crouching tiger, hidden dragon II: The green legend* [Motion Picture]. China & United States: Pegasus Media, China Film Group Corporation, & The Weinstein Company.

Weinstein, Y., McDermott, K. B., & Roediger, H. L. (2010). A comparison of study strategies for passages: Re-reading, answering questions, and generating questions. *Journal of Experimental Psychology: Applied, 16*, 308–316.

Wells, J. C., & Narkon, D. E. (2011). Motivate students to engage in word study using vocabulary games. *Intervention in School and Clinic, 47*(1), 45–49.

White, B., & Johnson, T. S. (2001). We really do mean it: Implementing language arts standard #3 with opinionnaires. *The Clearing House, 74*, 119–123.

White, S., Chen, J., & Forsyth, B. (2010). Reading-related literacy activities of American adults: Time spent, task types, and cognitive skills used. *Journal of Literacy Research, 42*(3), 276–307.

Whittaker, C. R. (2012). Integrating literature circles into a co-taught inclusive classroom. *Intervention in School and Clinic, 47*(4), 214–223.

Wigfield, A., Guthrie, J. T., Perencevich, K. C., Taboada, A., Klauda, S. L., McRae, A., et al. (2008). The role of reading engagement in mediating effects of reading comprehension instruction on reading outcomes. *Psychology in the Schools, 45*(5), 432–445.

Wiggins, G., & McTighe, J. (2011). *The understanding by design guide to creating high-quality units* (2nd ed.). Alexandria, VA: Association for Supervision and Curriculum Development.

Wilhelm, J. (2001). *Improving comprehension with think-aloud strategies.* New York: Scholastic.

Williams, A. L., & Merten, M. J. (2008). A review of online social networking profiles by adolescents: Implications for future research and intervention. *Adolescence, 43*(170), 253–274.

Williams, B. T. (2005). Leading double lives: Literacy and technology in and out of school. *Journal of Adolescent and Adult Literacy, 48,* 702–706.

Williams, B. T. (2007). I'm ready for my close-up now: Electronic portfolios and how we read identity. *Journal of Adolescent and Adult Literacy, 50*(6), 500–504.

Williams, R. M.-C. (2008). Image, text, and story: Comics and graphic novels in the classroom. *Art Education, 61*(6), 13–19.

Willis, A. I., Garcia, G. E., Barrera, R., & Harris, V. (2003). *Multicultural issues in literacy research and practice.* Mahwah, NJ: Erlbaum.

Wilson, N. S., & Smetana, L. (2011). Questioning as thinking: A metacognitive framework to improve comprehension of expository text. *Literacy, 45*(2), 84–90.

Wissinger, D. R., & De La Paz, S. (2015). Effects of critical discussions on middle school students' written historical arguments. *Journal of Educational Psychology, 108*(1), 43–59.

Wittrock, M. (1990). Generative processes of comprehension. *Educational Pscyhologist, 24,* 345–376.

Wolsey, T. D., & Grisham, D. L. (2012). *Transforming writing instruction in the digital age: Techniques for grades 5–12.* New York: Guilford Press.

Worthy, J., & Roser, N. (2010). Productive sustained reading in a bilingual class. In E. Hiebert & R. Reutzel (Eds.), *Revisiting silent reading: New directions for teachers and researchers* (pp. 241–257). Newark, DE: International Reading Association.

Wyatt-Smith, C., & Cumming, J. (2009). *Educational assessment in the 21st century: Connecting theory and practice.* New York: Springer.

Wyatt-Smith, C., & Elkins, J. (2008). Multimodal reading and comprehension in online environments. In J. Coiro, M. Knobel, C. Lankshear, & D. J. Leu (Eds.), *Handbook of research on new literacies* (pp. 899–942). Mahwah, NJ: Erlbaum.

Yancey, K. B. (2009). *Writing in the 21st century.* Urbana, IL: National Council of Teachers of English.

Yang, H.-C. (2014). Toward a model of strategies and summary writing performance. *Language Assessment Quarterly, 11*(4), 403–431.

Yang, Y.-F. (2014). Preparing language teachers for blended teaching of summary writing. *Computer Assisted Language Learning, 27*(3), 185–206.

Yang, Y.-F. (2015). Automatic scaffolding and measurement of concept mapping for EFL students to write summaries. *Journal of Educational Technology and Society, 18*(4), 273–286.

Yatvin, J. (2009, October 23). Rediscovering the "Pygmalion effect." *Education Week, 29*(9), 24–25.

Yeager, D. S., Romero, C., Paunesku, D., Hulleman, C. S., Schneider, B., Hinojosa, C., et al. (2016). Using design thinking to improve psychological interventions: The case of the growth mindset during the transition to high school. *Journal of Educational Psychology, 108*(3), 374–391.

Yonezawa, S., Jones, M., & Joselowsky, F. (2009). Youth engagement in high schools: Developing a multidimensional, critical approach to improving engagement for all students. *Journal of Educational Change, 10,* 191–209.

Yu, G. (2008). Reading to summarize in English and Chinese: A tale of two languages? *Language Testing, 25*(4), 521–551.

Zacher Pandya, J. (2011). *Overtested: How high-stakes accountability fails English language learners.* New York: Teachers College Press.

Zahedi, Y., & Abdi, M. (2012). The impact of imagery strategy on EFL learners' vocabulary learning. *Procedia–Social and Behavioral Sciences, 69,* 2264–2272.

Zhang, X., & Lu, X. (2015). The relationship between vocabulary learning strategies and breadth and depth of vocabulary knowledge. *Modern Language Journal, 99*(4), 740–753.

Zimmerman, B. J. (2008). Investigating self-regulation and motivation: Historical background, methodological developments, and future prospects. *American Educational Research Journal, 45*(1), 166–183.

Zoghi, M., Mustapha, R., & Maasum, T. N. R. M. (2010). Collaborative strategic reading with university EFL learners. *Journal of College Reading and Learning, 41*(1), 67–94.

Zpeda, C. D., Richey, J. E., Ronevich, P., & Nokes-Malach, T. J. (2015). Direct instruction of metacognition benefits adolescent science learning, transfer, and motivation: An in vivo study. *Journal of Educational Psychology, 107*(4), 954–970.

Zwiers, J. (2008). *Building academic language.* San Francisco: Jossey-Bass.

Zwiers, J., & Crawford, M. (2011). *Academic conversations: Classroom talk that fosters critical thinking and content understandings.* Portland, ME: Stenhouse.

YOUNG ADULT LITERATURE

Abbot, E. A. (1927). *Flatland.* Boston: Little, Brown.

Aldrin, B., & Dyson, M. (2015). *Welcome to Mars: Making a home on the red planet.* Washington, DC: National Geographic Children's Books.

Alvarez, J. (2009). *Return to sender.* New York: Knopf.

Anaya, R. (1990). Salomon's story. In C. Tatum (Ed.), *Mexican American literature* (pp. 179–185). Orlando, FL: Harcourt Brace Jovanovich.

Asimov, I. (1966). *Fantastic voyage.* Boston: Houghton Mifflin.

Avi. (2010). *Iron thunder: The battle between the Monitor and the Merrimac.* Logan, IA: Perfect Learning.

Barr, G. (2011). *Sports science for young people.* Mineola, NY: Dover.

Barry, L. (2010). *Picture this.* Montreal, Quebec, Canada: Drawn & Quarterly.

Beattie, O., & Geiger, J. (1992). *Buried in ice: The mystery of a lost Arctic expedition.* Toronto: Madison Press Books.

Bierce, A. (2000). *Tales of soldiers and civilians: and other stories.* New York: Penguin.

Bolden, T. (2005). *Wake up our souls: A celebration of African American artists.* New York: Abrams.

Bornholt, J. (1989). *Star Trek: The next generation.* New York: Dell.

Brainard, C. M. (2003). *Growing up Filipino: Stories for young adults.* Minneapolis: Rebound by Sagebrush.

Bredeson, C. (2001). *Mount Saint Helens volcano.* New York: Enslow.

Bruchac, J. (2008). *Jim Thorpe, original all-American.* New York: Speak—Penguin Books.

Butzer, C. M. (2008) *Gettysburg: The graphic novel.* New York: HarperCollins.

Childress, A. (1973). *A hero ain't nothin' but a sandwich.* New York: Puffin Books.

Cisneros, S. (1990). Three wiseguys: Un cuento de Navidad. In C. Tatum (Ed.), *Mexican American literature* (pp. 236–242). Orlando, FL: Harcourt Brace Jovanovich.

Claybourne, A. (2014). *100 most destructive natural disasters.* New York: Scholastic.

Colato Lainez, R., & Vanden Broeck, F. (2010). *My shoes and I.* Honesdale, PA: Boyds Mills Press.

Cotterell, A. (2005). *Eyewitness: Ancient China.* New York: DK.

Crossan, S. (2012). *Breathe*. New York: Greenwillow Books.

Crowley, C. (2012). *Graffiti moon*. New York: Ember.

Daniel, T. (2011). *The fashion sketchpad: 420 figure templates for designing looks and building your portfolio*. San Francisco: Chronicle Books.

Davis, J. (2014). *Spare parts: Four undocumented teenagers, one ugly robot, and the battle for the American dream*. New York: FSG Originals.

Devlin, K. J., & Lorden, G. (2007). *The numbers behind NUMB3RS: Solving crime with mathematics*. New York: Plume.

Dewdney, A. K. (1984). *The planiverse*. New York: Poseidon Press.

Drysdale, A. M., & Ravenna, J. (2012). *You let some girl beat you?: The story of Ann Meyers Drysdale*. Lake Forest, CA: Behler.

Durrant, L. (2006). *My last skirt: The story of Jennie Hodgers, Union soldier*. New York: Clarion Books.

Ellis, E., & Doran, C. (2004). *Orbiter*. New York: DC Comics.

Emond, S. (2011). *Happyface*. New York: Little, Brown Books for Young Readers.

Falls, K. (2015). *Inhuman*. New York: Scholastic.

Forbes, E. (1945). *Johnny Tremain*. Boston: Houghton Mifflin.

Freedman, K. (2005). *The voice that challenged a nation: Marian Anderson and the struggle for equal rights*. New York: Scholastic.

Gitlin, M. (2012). *Lindsey Vonn: People in the news*. San Diego, CA: Lucent Books.

Glasgow, A. D., & Schichtel, J. M. (n.d.). *Genome: The graphic novel*. Seattle, WA: Amazon.

Greenberg, J., & Jordan, S. (2004). *Andy Warhol, prince of pop*. New York: Random House Children's Books.

Hale, N. (2015). *Nathan Hale's hazardous tales: The underground abductor: An abolitionist tale about Harriet Tubman*. New York: Abrams.

Hampson, F. (2005). *Dan Dare pilot of the future: Marooned on Mercury*. Santa Monica, CA: Titan Books.

Hart, A. (2008). *Gabriel's journey*. Atlanta, GA: Peachtree.

Hart, C. (2008). *Manga for the beginner: Everything you need to know to get started right away!* New York: Watson-Guptill.

Helfand, L. (2012). *Nelson Mandela: The unconquerable soul*. New Delhi, India: Campfire.

Hesse, K. (2008). *Brooklyn Bridge*. New York: Macmillan.

Hijuelos, O. (2009). *Dark dude*. New York: Atheneum Books for Young Readers.

Hill, A. (2012). *LeBron James: King of shots*. Minneapolis, MN: Twenty First Century Books.

Hinton, C. H. (1907). *An episode in Flatland*. London: Swan Sonnenschein.

Hobbs, W. (1991). *Downriver*. New York: Macmillan.

Hodder-Williams, C. (2016). *The chromosome game*. Venture Press.

Jennings, L. A. (2014). *She's a knockout!: A history of women in fighting sports*. Lanham, MD: Rowman & Littlefield.

Kallen, S. A. (2008). *Renaissance art*. Farmington Hills, MI: Lucent Books.

Kenneally, M. (2012). *Stealing Parker*. Naperville, IL: Sourcebooks Fire.

Keplinger, K. (2011). *Shut out*. New York: Poppy.

Kidder, T., & French, M. (2014). *Mountains beyond mountains: The quest of Dr. Paul Farmer, a man who would cure the world*. New York: Ember.

Kumar, M. (2011). *Quantum: Einstein, Bohr, and the great debate about the nature of reality*. New York: Norton.

Lavender, W. (2014). *Just Jane: A daughter of England caught in the struggle of the American Revolution*. Boston: Houghton Mifflin Harcourt.

Lee, H. (1960). *To kill a mockingbird.* New York: Warner Books.

Lesmoir-Gordon, N., Rood, W., & Edney, R. (2009). *Introducing fractals: A graphic guide.* Thriplow, Cambridge, UK: Icon Books.

Levin, J. (2008). *Ichiro Suzuki.* New York: Checkmark Books.

Lewis, J., Aydin, A., & Powell, N. (2013). *March: Book one.* Marietta, GA: Top Shelf Productions.

Lichtman, W. (2008). *Do the math: Secrets, lies, and algebra.* New York: Greenwillow Books.

Lloyd, S. (2010). *The carbon diaries 2015.* New York: Holiday House.

Long, M., Demonakos, J., & Powell, N. (2012). *The silence of our friends.* New York: First Second.

Luen Yang, G., & Pien, L. (2006). *American born Chinese.* New York: First Second.

Lupica, M. (2009). *The big field.* New York: Puffin Books.

Malley, G. (2008). *The declaration.* London: Bloomsbury.

Manguel, A. (1996). *A history of reading.* New York: Viking.

Martin Luther King and the Montgomery story. (2011). Nyack, NY: Fellowship of Reconciliation. (Original work published 1958)

McCully, E. A. (1999). *Beautiful warrior: The legend of the nun's kung fu.* New York: Scholastic.

McKissack, P. (2004). *Look to the hills: The diary of Lozette Moreau, a French slave girl.* New York: Scholastic.

McMullan, M. (2012). *Sources of light.* Boston: HMH Books for Young Readers.

McNeil, G. (2014). *3:59.* New York: Balzer & Bray.

Meader, S. W. (1939). *Boy with a pack.* San Diego, CA: Harcourt Brace.

Messner, K. (2013). *Wake up missing.* London: Walker Childrens.

Morgan, A. (2015). *Breakaway: Beyond the goal.* New York: Simon & Schuster Books for Young Readers.

Mowat, F. (1979). *Never cry wolf.* New York: Bantam.

Mullin, M. (2012). *Ashen winter.* Terre Haute, IN: Tanglewood.

Murphy, J. (2009). *A savage thunder: Antietam and the bloody road to freedom.* New York: Margaret K. McElderry Books.

Myers, W. D. (2004). *Monster.* New York: Amistad.

Nazario, S. (2007). *Enrique's journey.* New York: Random House.

Nelson Mandela Foundation. (2009). *Nelson Mandela: The authorized comic book.* New York: Norton.

Neufeld, J. (2009). *A.D.: New Orleans after the deluge.* New York. Pantheon Books.

O'Dell, S. (1979). *The captive.* Boston: Houghton Mifflin.

O'Dell, S. (1981). *The feathered serpent.* Boston: Houghton Mifflin.

O'Dell, S. (1983). *The amethyst ring.* Boston: Houghton Mifflin.

O'Meara, D. (2007). *Into the volcano: A volcano researcher at work.* Toronto, Ontario, Canada: Kids Can Press.

Orzel, C. (2010). *How to teach (quantum) physics to your dog.* New York: Scribner.

Paulsen, G. (2011). *Woods runner.* New York: Random House Children's Books.

Pfeffer, S. B. (2010). *This world we live in.* Boston: Harcourt.

Pinkney, A. (2001). *Abraham Lincoln: Letters from a slave girl.* New York: Winslow Press.

Porter, K. (2014). *Mad seasons: The story of the first women's professional basketball league, 1978–1981.* Lincoln, NE: Bison Books.

Pratt, G. (1992). *Enemy ace: War idyll.* New York: Warner Books.

Rae, I. (2015). *The misadventures of awkward Black girl.* New York: Atria.

Reef, C. (2014). *Frida and Diego: Art, love, life.* Boston: Clarion Books.

Richter, H. P. (1970). *Friedrich.* New York: Holt, Rinehart & Winston.

Russell, C. Y. (2009) *Tofu quilt.* New York: Lee & Low Books.

Saeed, A. (2015). *Written in the stars*. New York: Nancy Paulsen Books.

Satrapi, M. (2004). *Persepolis: The story of a childhood*. New York: Random House.

Schroeder, L. (2014). *My secret guide to Paris*. New York: Scholastic Press.

Shakespeare, W., Sexton, A., & Pantoja, T. (2008). *Shakespeare's* Hamlet: *The manga edition*. Boston: Houghton Mifflin Harcourt.

Silver, N. (1990). *No tigers in Africa*. New York: E .P. Dutton.

Silver, N. (1991). *An eye for color*. New York: E. P. Dutton.

Silverstein, K. (2005). *The radioactive boy scout: The frightening true story of a whiz kid and his homemade nuclear reactor*. New York: HarperCollins.

Sinnott, S. (2003). *Extraordinary Asian Americans and Pacific Islanders*. New York: Scholastic Library.

Speigelman, A. (1992). *Maus: A survivor's tale*. New York: Pantheon Books.

Swan, B. (2015). *Real justice: Jailed for life for being black: The story of Rubin "Hurricane" Carter*. Toronto, Ontario, Canada: Lorimer.

Takahashi, S. (2008). *The manga guide to statistics*. San Francisco: No Starch Press.

Tan, S. (2006). *The arrival*. Melbourne, Australia: Arthur A. Levine Books.

Tigelaar, L. (2008). *Playing with the boys*. New York: Razorbill.

Torres, J. A. (2014). *Soccer star Lionel Messi (Goal!: Latin stars of soccer)*. New York: Speeding Star.

Tsai, F. (2009). *Extreme worlds: The complete guide to drawing and painting sci-fi art*. Cincinnati, OH: Impact.

Vansant, W. (2014). *The Red Baron: The graphic history of Richthofen's flying circus and the air war in WWI*. London: Zenith Press.

Weatherford, C. B. (2014). *Leontyne Price: Voice of a century*. New York: Knopf Books for Young Readers.

Wicks, M. (2015). *Human body theater*. New York: First Second.

Winchester, S. (2015). *When the earth shakes: Earthquakes, volcanoes, and tsunamis*. Washington, DC: Smithsonian.

Wolf, B. (2002). *Coming to America: A Muslim family's story*. New York: Lee & Low.

Yang, G. L. (2013). *Saints*. New York: First Second.

Yen Mah, A. (2010). *Chinese Cinderella: The true story of an unwanted daughter*. New York: Ember.

Zhang, A. (2015). *Falling into place*. New York: Greenwillow Books.

Index